AF837248

Communitarianism in Law and Society

Rights and Responsibilities:
Communitarian Perspectives
Series Editor: Amitai Etzioni

Marriage in America: A Communitarian Perspective
edited by Martin King Whyte
Autonomy and Order: A Communitarian Anthology
edited by Edward W. Lehman
Between Consent and Dissent: Democracy and Peace in the Israeli Mind
by Ephraim Yuchtman-Ya'ar and Yochanan Peres
Civic Repentance
edited by Amitai Etzioni
Community Justice: An Emerging Field
edited by David R. Karp
National Parks: Rights and the Common Good
by Francis N. Lovett
The Essential Communitarian Reader
edited by Amitai Etzioni
Repentance: A Comparative Perspective
edited by Amitai Etzioni and David E. Carney
Rights vs. Public Safety after 9/11: America in the Age of Terrorism
edited by Amitai Etzioni and Jason H. Marsh
Voluntary Simplicity: Responding to Consumer Culture
edited by Daniel Doherty and Amitai Etzioni
Law and Community: The Case of Torts
by Robert F. Cochran Jr. and Robert M. Ackerman
The Communitarian Reader: Beyond the Essentials
edited by Amitai Etzioni, Andrew Volmert, and Elanit Rothschild
Public Intellectuals: An Endangered Species?
edited by Amitai Etzioni and Alyssa Bowditch
Communitarianism in Law and Society
edited by Paul van Seters

Communitarianism in Law and Society

Edited by
Paul van Seters

ROWMAN & LITTLEFIELD PUBLISHERS, INC.
Lanham • Boulder • New York • Toronto • Oxford

ROWMAN & LITTLEFIELD PUBLISHERS, INC.

Published in the United States of America
by Rowman & Littlefield Publishers, Inc.
A wholly owned subsidiary of The Rowman & Littlefield Publishing Group, Inc.
4501 Forbes Boulevard, Suite 200, Lanham, Maryland 20706
www.rowmanlittlefield.com

PO Box 317
Oxford
OX2 9RU, UK

Copyright © 2006 by Rowman & Littlefield Publishers, Inc.

All rights reserved. No part of this publication may be reproduced, stored in a retrieval system, or transmitted in any form or by any means, electronic, mechanical, photocopying, recording, or otherwise, without the prior permission of the publisher.

British Library Cataloguing in Publication Information Available

Library of Congress Cataloging-in-Publication Data

Communitarianism in law and society / edited by Paul van Seters.
p. cm. — (Rights and responsibilities)
Includes bibliographical references and index.
ISBN-13: 978-0-7425-2270-1 (cloth : alk. paper)
ISBN-10: 0-7425-2270-9 (cloth : alk. paper)
ISBN-13: 978-0-7425-2271-8 (pbk. : alk.paper)
ISBN-10: 0-7425-2271-7 (pbk. : alk. paper)
1. Sociological jurisprudence. 2. Communitarianism. 3. Pluralism (Social sciences)
I. Seters, Paul van. II. Series: Rights and responsibilities (Lanham, Md.)

K370.C66 2006
340'.115—dc22 2005031258

Printed in the United States of America

∞™ The paper used in this publication meets the minimum requirements of American National Standard for Information Sciences—Permanence of Paper for Printed Library Materials, ANSI/NISO Z39.48-1992.

Contents

Part III: The Social Values of Law

Preface

Law and Communitarianism: Constraints and Opportunities

Paul van Seters

This book had its beginning in a conference on "Law and Communitarianism" held at the Faculty of Law, Tilburg University, the Netherlands, in June 1993. The conference brought together people from a variety of academic disciplines, especially from law, sociology, economics, and political science. Early versions of some of the chapters were presented as papers there (by Philip Selznick, Jos de Beus, Anton Hemerijck, and Paul de Beer), though all of these have been substantially revised and updated at later stages. Some of the other chapters are revised versions of papers presented or published more recently elsewhere (by Paul van Seters, Roger Cotterrell, Toon Peters, Winfried Brugger, and Dorien Pessers). Two chapters were originally written for this book (by Sanne Taekema and Willem Witteveen). But what all these chapters have in common is that they reflect on the remarkable rise of communitarianism in contemporary studies of law and society. To provide a first introduction to this book, I shall briefly comment on the significance of communitarianism in this context and give an outline of the main topics that are addressed in these chapters.

For some time now, we have been witnessing the emergence of a perspective in legal, moral, and political philosophy that has acquired currency under the name of communitarianism. Not tied to a particular school of thought or specific group of people, this communitarian perspective is more loosely associated with the writings of a variety of philosophers, legal scholars, and social scientists, including Benjamin Barber, Robert Bellah, Amitai Etzioni, Christopher Lasch, Alasdair MacIntyre, Michael Sandel, William M. Sullivan, Charles Taylor, Michael Walzer, Robert Paul Wolff, and Roberto Unger. The common thread running through the work of these otherwise rather diverse authors is a trenchant, principled criticism of the premises of contemporary liberalism. The distinctive target of the communitarians is not just neoclassical or laissez-faire liberalism (as represented by people like Friedrich A. Hayek, Michael Oakeshott, or Robert Nozick) but also, even more importantly, so-called welfare-state liberalism (as exemplified in the writings of, e.g., John Rawls, Ronald Dworkin, or Bruce Ackerman). Rejecting the liberal conception of individual autonomy and self-sufficiency, these critics of liberalism stress the moral worth and significance of community.

The debate between liberals and communitarians has been largely an American affair. Yet some of the most prominent work in social and political theory in Europe today too can be read as a highly critical reflection on the reigning paradigm of liberalism. One may think in this context of the commanding positions of Jürgen Habermas or Michel Foucault. What then is the relation between critical thought of this nature and that conveyed by the new critics in the United States? And what can be learned, from a European perspective, from these cross-Atlantic communitarian writings? These questions constitute the common background for all of the chapters in this book.

While it is true that communitarianism has been defined primarily in terms of its antithesis to liberalism, this strategy of excluded opposites can mislead in several ways. First, despite the impressive volume of communitarian writings published over the past twenty-five years, the core idea of community remains problematic. Within the communitarian tradition, no clear and precise elaboration of the concept of community has been put forward as yet. Worse, among the communitarians themselves on this point considerable confusion prevails. Notice this statement by Alasdair MacIntyre (1991, 91): "In spite of rumors to the contrary, I am not and never have been a communitarian. For my judgment is that the political, economic, and moral structures of advanced modernity in this country, as elsewhere, exclude the possibility of realizing any of the worthwhile types of political community which at various times in the past have been achieved, even if always in imperfect forms. And I also believe that attempts to remake modern societies in systematically communitarian ways will always be either ineffective or disastrous." So much for the advocates of civic virtue and political community! MacIntyre does believe, however, in the possibility and importance of building *particular* communities, informed by an adequately shared conception of human good, in *local* environments. He refers to schools, farms, other workplaces, clinics, parishes, and the like (ibid.).

Second, contemporary liberalism may not be as blind to the realities of community, and to the values implicit therein, as the critics charge. Particularly Rawls's principle of social justice, the "difference principle," has been recognized to alter the tenor of classical utilitarian liberalism and to provide it with a more communitarian sensibility (Rawls 1971). The difference principle, after all, is devised to guarantee the welfare of the least advantaged. It thus expresses a genuine, though elementary, form of human solidarity. More recently, Dworkin (1989) has turned the tables on his communitarian critics by making a case for the idea of "liberal community": liberalism as the best interpretation of the idea of political community, and liberal theory as the best account of its importance.

The ambiguities that inhere both in communitarianism as such and in its criticism of liberalism suggest it may be important not to focus on the opposition between communitarianism and liberalism, as has become habit in academic and political circles over the years, but instead to explore the fundamental *continuities* between the two. The quest would be for some kind of middle ground, acknowledging and retaining the achievements of the liberal tradition while testing these against the realities and values that are central in communitarian thought. Perhaps the guiding theme here could be the notion of "communitarian liberalism."

The chapters in this book draw their inspiration in part from this idea of communitarian liberalism. The principal objective of the book is to critically assess the communitarian perspective as this has been molded by diverse intellectual, social, and political forces. That is to say, this communitarian perspective is closely examined in order to gain more systematic insight into what its distinctive constraints are and into the special opportunities it provides. In this context, legal thought and legal experience are of particular relevance. Much of contemporary jurisprudence and social policy, at least in the Western world, is rooted in the soil of liberalism. To the extent that communitarianism can be understood as an effort to reconstruct liberalism, and not just debunk it, what good is to come of this for legal theory and legal practice? At the same time, the legal tradition may be read as the historical reflection of community, of its diverse manifestations, its evolving values and aspirations, its recurring vicissitudes and pitfalls. Law necessarily presupposes community, but also essentially extends it. This is because, in the words of James Boyd White (1985, 42), "the law should take as its most central question what kind of community we should be."

Elaborating on these considerations, the following themes are explored in more detail in the separate chapters of this book.

LAW AND COMMUNITY: HISTORICAL AND THEORETICAL PERSPECTIVES

This theme is devoted to the concept of community, with special reference to major issues of law and jurisprudence, for example the interpretation of constitutions, the sources of obligation and of fundamental rights, custom and tradition, and, autonomy and responsiveness of legal institutions. Any assessment of the contemporary—and legal—relevance of communitarianism for law and society must first consider what "community" means and what baggage it carries. This requires a conceptual analysis that pays attention to intellectual antecedents as well as to historical and comparative experience. We need a theory of community that speaks to problems of modernity while taking account of a broad range of community-fostering policies and community-oriented cultures. Such a theory must be both normative and descriptive, based on the actual experience of living in communities and, at the same time, capable of guiding the fulfillment of communitarian ideals. A key issue is the relation between diversity and integration. Community is not the same as *Gemeinschaft*; for their survival, if not their vitality, communities depend on individual distinction and commitment.

THE PUBLIC HOUSEHOLD

In the classical tradition of economics, two realms of economic activity are typically distinguished: the domestic household and the market economy. Daniel Bell (1976, 220–82) has suggested how in recent times a third sector, the public household, has come to overshadow these two. Broadly defined, the public household is "the agency for the satisfaction of public needs, as against private wants." The nature of a household, according to Bell, "consists of sharing things in common—the domestic goods, the village green, the defense of the city—and necessarily has to come to some common understanding of the common good" (ibid., 221–22). Thus the value of community is highly pertinent to the public household. Health, education, transportation, environmental protection, welfare—these and other staples of the public household derive their significance from the contribution they can make to a shared destiny. Yet the core of the public household too resides in the sphere of labor, or work. Apart from the family, work today remains the most important vehicle of social integration. How is this reflected in the design of our major economic institutions? In the management of the welfare state? In the organization of the political process?

STATES, PEOPLES, AND COMMUNITIES

Here the focus is on the nation state as a vehicle of community and as an obstacle to community. The contemporary nation state experiences pressure from within and from without. Internally, where ethnic diversity is strong, the quest for self-determination threatens national coherence. Externally, the integration of multinational markets, and the more widespread acceptance of universal ideals, places national sovereignty in doubt. The dynamic of the European Union clearly represents a movement "beyond the nation state." Can we still speak here of a genuine and effective form of community? How do we assess, in this respect, the spectacular rise of European law? What form should this law take if the ideals and urgencies of autonomy and federalism are to be achieved and sustained? The challenge to the nation state has given new life to the doctrine of legal pluralism. In the pluralist perspective, notions such as "indigenous law," "nonofficial law," "private regulation," and "community law" express a sentiment that seriously questions the supposed legal monopoly of the state. While the antithesis between state and community seems too rigid, legal pluralism may well be an important source of information and guidance for the emergence of regional, multistate unities.

The background and context of this book will be further introduced in the next chapter (by Paul van Seters). In part one, on Law and Community in Socio-Legal Studies, there are separate chapters by Philip Selznick, Roger Cotterrell, and Toon Peters. In part two, on Communitarianism in the European Arena, there are chapters by Jos de Beus, Anton Hemerijck, and Paul de Beer. In part three, on Social Values of Law, there are chapters by Winfried Brugger, Dorien Pessers, and Sanne Taekema. All of these separate chapters are briefly introduced and commented upon in the concluding chapter of this book, by Willem Witteveen. For this reason, I abstain here from any further introduction to these chapters.

REFERENCES

Bell, Daniel. 1976. *The Cultural Contradictions of Capitalism*. New York: Basic Books.

Dworkin, Ronald. 1989. Liberal Community. *California Law Review* 77:479–504.

MacIntyre, Alasdair. 1991. I'm Not a Communitarian. But . . . *The Responsive Community* 1 (3): 91–92.

Rawls, John. 1971. *A Theory of Justice*. Cambridge, MA: Harvard University Press.

White, James Boyd. 1985. *Heracles' Bow*. Madison: University of Wisconsin Press.

Introduction

Communitarianism in Law and Society[1]

Paul van Seters

THE LIBERAL-COMMUNITARIAN DEBATE, ONCE MORE

A few years into the new millennium, the debate between liberals and communitarians that has animated political, moral, and legal philosophy since the early 1980s, has lost little of its initial zeal and sense of urgency. Throughout this period, books dealing with the liberal–communitarian debate kept appearing, journals continued to devote their pages to the subject, and academic conferences were being organized to sort out unresolved, or newly discovered questions (Avineri and de-Shalit 1992; Bell 1993; Honneth 1993; Frazer and Lacey 1993; Mullhall and Swift 1996; Tam 1998; Frazer 1999; Tam 2001; Forst 2002). For students of law and society, the undiminished attention for this debate contains a special message. On the one hand liberalism, the reigning paradigm in contemporary jurisprudence, on the other communitarianism, one of the prominent critical responses to liberal jurisprudence: this pair of presumed opposites constitutes the intellectual context of a movement in modern law that, borrowing from the title of a book by Joel Handler (1990), may be labeled the "search for community."

The word "communitarianism" obviously derives from "community." The ascent of communitarianism in law and society indeed suggests community is something law may, or even should search for. But *who* is searching *for what kind* of community? In order to deal with this question, I propose to distinguish between three kinds of communitarianism: philosophical, political, and socio-legal communitarianism. These three may be seen as historical stages in the development of the liberal–communitarian debate, especially as it regards jurisprudential matters. That debate started around 1980 as an intellectual exercise strictly among philosophers. Subsequently communitarianism grew into some sort of political movement. Then in the 1990s a number of distinctly sociological studies dealing with law and community were published. My main interest here is with these latter. But to get a good view of socio-legal communitarianism, I think it is instructive first to look more systematically at philosophical and political communitarianism. As we will see, there is considerable overlap among the three types of communitarianism. Yet by distinguishing them this way, I can bring out some of the major crosscurrents that run through the liberal–communitarian debate and that have caused—continue to cause—much misunderstanding.

PHILOSOPHICAL COMMUNITARIANISM

In 1971 John Rawls published his enormously influential study, *A Theory of Justice*. Many people consider this book to be the single most important work in political philosophy of recent decades. The normative position Rawls elaborated in *Theory of Justice* is commonly referred to as "left," "social," or "welfare liberalism"—to be distinguished from "right," "laissez-faire," or "neoclassical liberalism" commonly associated with the names of Friedrich Hayek, Michael Oakeshott, and Robert Nozick. Apart from Rawls, welfare liberalism in the course of time became prominently associated, particularly in legal circles, with the names of Bruce Ackerman and, most notably, Ronald Dworkin.

The natural focus of liberalism—neoclassical as well as welfare liberalism—is the autonomy and freedom of the individual. Liberal principles of justice, that is, the principles that liberals claim ought to govern society, vary on one single theme: the priority to be given, always and under all circumstances, to individual rights of freedom. That is the reason liberals draw a sharp line between the idea of justice on the one hand, and the idea of the good life or the good society on the other. The former is held to be independent from and antecedent to the latter. In Rawls's own famous maxim (1971, 560): "The right is prior to the good." Therefore the state ought to restrict its activities to the realization of principles of justice and to refrain from propagating, let alone imposing, the good. In the liberal universe, the state is categorically neutral.

These central tenets of modern liberalism—the focus on moral autonomy; the separation of principles of justice from conceptions of the good life; the defense of a neutral state—became the target of massive criticism by a number of otherwise diverse political philosophers, mainly American, who in the course of the 1980s were being labeled as communitarians. The four philosophers unfailingly referred to as communitarian in this sense are Alasdair MacIntyre, Michael Sandel, Charles Taylor, and Michael Walzer (Mulhall and Swift 1996, 35–164). And though predated by some of the key writings of Taylor and Mac-

Intyre, it is the publication of Sandel's *Liberalism and the Limits of Justice* in 1982 that is generally considered to be the start of the liberal–communitarian debate.

Sandel's book was fairly restricted in scope: it amounted to a close, though highly critical reading of Rawls's *Theory of Justice.* Sandel directed his criticism of Rawls first and foremost at the axiomatic starting point of liberalism: the autonomous, free-floating individual. Liberals such as Rawls ground their theory in a concept of the person that Sandel claimed was untenable: the person thought of as a unit or identity existing prior to and independent from his or her choice for certain values and ends. This liberal conception of the person Sandel described as the "antecedently individuated" or "unencumbered" self. In contrast to this Sandel saw a person as someone who is defined or constituted by the very values and ends he or she chooses. Normally that choice is being made in the larger context of a community, of whatever nature, and thus the idea of community was a necessary element in Sandel's concept of the person (1982, 172):

> [W]e cannot be wholly unencumbered subjects of possession, individuated in advance and given prior to our ends, but must be subjects constituted in part by our central aspirations and attachments, always open, indeed vulnerable, to growth and transformation in the light of revised self-understandings. And in so far as our constitutive self-understandings comprehend a wider subject than the individual alone, whether a family or tribe or city or class or nation or people, to this extent they define a community in the constitutive sense.

Was liberalism blind then for the role or value of community? Certainly not, but the premise of absolute individual autonomy restricts the liberal idea of community, Sandel argued, to forms of voluntary cooperation, whether for instrumental or for sentimental reasons. (I will return to this point.) The opposition between Sandel's communitarianism and Rawls's liberalism turns on this criticism of a too-restricted view of community:

> [T]o say that members of a society are bound by a sense of community is not simply to say that a great many of them profess communitarian sentiments and pursue communitarian aims, but rather that they conceive their identity—the subject and not just the object of their feelings and aspirations—as defined to some extent by the community of which they are a part. For them, community describes not just what they *have* as fellow citizens but also what they *are*, not a relationship they choose (as in a voluntary association) but an attachment they discover, not merely an attribute but a constituent of their identity (Sandel 1982, 150).

Here we have the hard core of the debate between liberals and communitarians: with these notions of the person and the community, attributed to Rawls, and with Sandel's criticism of them.

The other protagonists of philosophical communitarianism—MacIntyre, Taylor, and Walzer—in the 1980s voiced similar objections against the emotivist, isolated, atomistic individualism that they identified as a central deficiency in modern liberal thought and practice. MacIntyre's best-known work, *After Virtue*, was published in 1981. Walzer's most important contribution, *Spheres of Justice*, appeared in 1983. And Taylor's magnum opus, *Sources of the Self*, came out in 1989 (though Taylor's article on "Atomism," a major source of reference in the liberal–communitarian debate, originally appeared in 1979). Obviously these communitarian writings, including those of Sandel, differed from each other in many and important ways. Yet it is possible to distill from them a common denominator. According to Mulhall and Swift (1996, 162), in their well-known study of the liberalism–communitarianism debate, the four major communitarian philosophers "are alike in basing their work upon a particular, communally oriented conception of the person":

> Taylor's fundamental view of human beings as self-interpreting animals in linguistic communities is very similar to MacIntyre's neo-Aristotelian view that human beings can only make sense of themselves as persons and moral agents through the concepts and standards bequeathed to them by practices and traditions. [Much of Walzer's work] depends in a very similar way upon his view that human beings are essentially culture-producing and culture-inhabiting creatures. And Sandel's concern to rescue and reemphasize the possibility of constitutive attachments to the community can easily be reinterpreted as a way of highlighting the degree to which the identity of human beings is bound up with their inhabitation of and identification with the smaller and larger communities of which they are members.

All four communitarians, Mulhall and Swift conclude, "are united around a conception of human beings as integrally related to the communities of culture and language that they create, maintain and inhabit."

Philip Selznick (1987, 450–53; 1992, 201–6) has described this communitarian concept of the person as the "implicated self." According to Selznick (1987, 447), the idea of an implicated self follows from an elementary sociological truth:

> Society is not made up of preformed, wholly competent individuals endowed by nature with reason and self-consciousness. In the beginning is society, not the individual. To say that humans are social animals is to say that they depend on others for psychological sustenance, including the formation of their personalities.

As biological and social constructs, human beings are decisively shaped by circumstances not of their own choosing, among which at least are their own family and community. This unavoidable relationship creates obligations and responsibilities for the individual that, unlike what is presupposed in the liberal tradition, do not depend on free choice and explicit approval:

> A morality of the implicated self builds on the understanding that our deepest and most important obligations flow from identity and relatedness, rather than from consent. Consent suggests agreement, bargaining, reciprocity, specificity. The obligations I have in mind are characteristically open-ended and unspecific; they are often unilateral; and they are largely involuntary, at least in detail (Selznick 1987, 451).

In this way in philosophical communitarianism the idea of personhood or human agency is conceived of as inseparable from the wider circles—the communities—in which the life of individuals is always and inevitably lived.

POLITICAL COMMUNITARIANISM

Instigated by the communitarian impulse in moral, political, and legal philosophy, but clearly moving on a different, more practical plane, in the late 1980s in the United States a new political movement was founded that named itself "communitarian." From its inception, this movement has been uniquely associated with the vision and energies of Amitai Etzioni, professor of sociology at The George Washington University. In 1990 Etzioni started a new quarterly journal, *The Responsive Community*, which for some fifteen years functioned as figurehead and forum of the movement. In the summer of 2004, the final issue was published and the journal closed.

In the editorial preface to the very first issue of *The Responsive Community*, the editors emphasized the need for a new balance between individual rights and social responsibilities (Etzioni 1990/1991). ("Rights and Responsibilities" also was the official subtitle of the journal.) A year later the journal published a much broader statement of the main principles and goals of the movement, entitled "The Responsive Communitarian Platform" (Communitarian Platform 1991/1992). This Platform more comprehensively stressed the importance of finding balances between individuals and groups; between rights and responsibilities; between institutions of state, market, and civil society. This "basic communitarian quest for balances" underlay many of the substantive policy ideas in the Communitarian Platform, for example with respect to the family (parental leave, protection of the interest of the children in divorces), schools (moral education, integration between work and schooling), workplace (flextime, child care), communities (national and local service, jury duty), and political reform (campaign contributions, social movements).

The Communitarian Platform was signed by more than fifty people—most of them prestigious university professors—including Benjamin Barber, Robert

Bellah, Jean Bethke Elshtain, Albert O. Hirschman, and Philip Selznick. The Platform suggested a "major social movement" was required, "akin to the progressive movement of the beginning of the century." But that rather grandiose goal has remained elusive, if not wishful thinking. Etzioni clearly did succeed in placing communitarianism on the political agenda, hence "political communitarianism." Since 1990, he has written a number of books explicating his ideas about communitarianism (especially relevant are Etzioni 1993, 1996, and 2004). Important politicians such as Bill Bradley, the Democratic senator from New Jersey, and Vice President Al Gore became involved. Some high-profile conferences were organized. William Galston (coeditor of *The Responsive Community*) for a number of years served in the White House as special assistant to President Bill Clinton. But it would be unrealistic to believe that activating a group of prominent academic intellectuals is the same as creating a social movement, as is sometimes claimed by the protagonists of political communitarianism. Etzioni himself (2003, 200–1) was probably not far off the mark when, in his recent memoirs, he compared the actual impact of communitarians on American public life with that of the neoconservatives.

The perhaps typically American invention of political communitarianism was even made into a successful export-article, again primarily by the singular talents of Etzioni. Etzioni (2003, 319–63) tirelessly travels around the world to address meetings and advise political leaders. This explains the appearance of communitarianism in a political magazine in the United Kingdom halfway through the 1990s, in an essay by Paul Anderson on the intellectuals New Labour wanted to bring aboard. Anderson reported on the lukewarm response of the center-left intelligentsia toward New Labour, but also on the paucity of new political ideas in Britain generally. In that context, though, he referred to communitarianism as "the most important exception":

> [T]he only significant import of recent years in the field of political ideas [is] the communitarianism of the American polemicist and activist Amitai Etzioni. Etzioni's emphasis on responsibilities as well as rights chimes with the austere Christian socialism of [Tony] Blair and shadow home secretary Jack Straw, and the Labour leader has declared himself a communitarian (Anderson 1996).

So Etzioni managed to generate worldwide interest in the idea of political communitarianism. This explains, at least to some extent, why communitarianism was involved in what subsequently grew out of New Labour, namely, the Third Way.

In the second half of the 1990s in Europe and in the United States, a public debate arose on so-called Third Way politics. In Europe this theme was prominently associated with Tony Blair's New Labour, but also with Gerhard Schröder 's *Neue Mitte*; counterpart and close allies in the United States were the new Democrats Bill Clinton was thought to represent. The English sociologist Anthony Giddens (1998) may be taken as the most representative source on this subject. The Third Way stands for the idea of a political alternative to the "old left" and the "new right." As conceived of by Giddens, the Third Way aims for the renewal of social democracy in a world where the views of the old left have become obsolete, while those of the new right are inadequate and contradictory. Obviously the Third Way and political communitarianism share the quest for a middle ground, but Giddens (1998, 65) is particularly concerned about the relationship between the individual and the community: "Having abandoned collectivism, third way politics looks for a new relationship between the individual and the community, a redefinition of rights and obligations." He even suggests an ethical principle or prime motto for the new politics: "no rights without responsibilities." While this may sound very much like communitarianism, Etzioni (2000, 29) has argued that "no rights without responsibilities" violates a central principle of communitarianism, wich recognizes rights even in cases where people utterly disregard their social obligations. Yet it is somewhat curious that Giddens, by political commentators frequently referred to as Tony Blair's guru, nowhere in his original explication of the Third Way mentioned communitarianism, neither as a theoretical nor as a practical source of inspiration. It was only in a more recent book that Giddens (2000, 62–65) paid attention to the communitarian roots of the Third Way, though his reading there of political communitarianism is surprisingly narrow, if not parochial. On the other hand, the Third Way shares with political communitarianism its rather lukewarm, if not outright hostile, reception in some academic circles (Philips 1993; Dahrendorf 1999).

SOCIO-LEGAL COMMUNITARIANISM

Over the past ten to fifteen years, a remarkably strong interest in community, or communitarianism, has surfaced also in the field of socio-legal studies. Clearly, both philosophical and political communitarianism have contributed to and in many ways are implied in this new socio-legal communitarianism. But socio-legal communitarianism is much broader: it has deep roots in the disciplinary tradition of sociology. Of course, the sociological tradition has always been centrally concerned with "community." The new communitarian perspective in socio-legal studies encompasses both the arcane questions of philosophical communitarianism and the down-to-earth policy problems of political communitarianism, but adds to these a strongly historical, sociological dimension.

This type of sociological communitarianism is particularly manifest in three books, published in the first half of the 1990s, by scholars who otherwise represent rather different positions on the spectrum of socio-legal studies: *Law and the Search for Community*, by Joel F. Handler (1990); *The Moral Commonwealth: Social Theory and the Promise of Community*, by Philip Selznick (1992); and *Law's Community: Legal Theory in Sociological Perspective*, by Roger Cotterrell (1995). More recently, Selznick summarized his views on communitarianism in *The Communitarian Persuasion* (2002). In a way, these titles conjunctly embody the perspective of socio-legal communitarianism. The underlying aim is to employ the rich intellectual resources of the sociological tradition in order to explore and assess the contribution law can or may make to community.

Handler (1990, 94) is interested in the idea of "strong" community, which he distinguishes from "instrumental" community and "sentimental" community. The distinction between these three types of community Handler has straight from what we have seen before forms the historical centerpiece of philosophical communitarianism, namely the Rawls–Sandel debate. Rawls (1971, 520–29), in his discussion of the "idea of social union," had distinguished two senses of the "good of community." When individuals cooperate merely to achieve their own private ends, and regard cooperation only as a necessary burden, then community is to be conceived in purely instrumental terms. From this instrumental conception of community Rawls had distinguished the situation in which individuals have certain "shared final ends"; cooperation under these conditions has to be regarded as a good in itself. This Sandel called the sentimental conception of community. As we have seen, Sandel (1982, 150) stressed the need to distinguish a third conception of community, the strong sense of community, as a constitutive conception:

> A theory of community whose province extended to the subject as well as the object of motivation would be individualistic in neither the conventional [read: instrumental] sense nor in Rawls' [read: sentimental]. It would resemble Rawls' conception in that the sense of community would be manifest in the aims and values of the participants—as fraternal sentiments and fellow-feeling, for example—but would differ from Rawls' conception in that community would describe not just a *feeling* but a mode of self-understanding partly constitutive of the agent's identity.

In his book Handler (1990, 141–61) explores the material and social conditions conducive to this third type of constitutive or strong community. He claims moral, rather than merely instrumental or sentimental community is dependent especially on trust—"morally decent trust"—and on dialogue or conversation—"dialogism." Trust and dialogue or conversation are necessary to transform unequal participants into equal moral agents. The special task of law is to "create the arenas for [such] conversation." Handler is well aware that the dialogic community "requires an extensive reconceptualization of the way we conduct our public business," but this nonetheless is the kind of community he thinks the law ought to search for.

Cotterrell too is strongly interested in the prospects of a communitarian jurisprudence. He approaches the subject not by way of philosophical communitarianism, like Handler, but from a distinctly sociological perspective. More particularly, Cotterrell employs the Durkheimian tradition focusing on the essential continuities between law, morality, and solidarity. Key problems for legal development that are identified in *Law's Community* are the restoration of moral authority to law and the elaboration of a concept of community that can guide legal regulation. Now admittedly law cannot in any direct way create solidarity or community. But, according to Cotterrell (1995, 269), "it can aim to create conditions for human existence that *symbolize* a moral commitment of the community in its care for its members as individuals." The main task of communitarian jurisprudence, then, is "to explore sociologically the conditions under which law can become a principled component of social life, a direct expression of community interests, structures and concerns" (ibid., 301).

For Cotterrell the content of the concept of community is by no means self-evident. On the contrary, he calls it the ultimate aim of his study "to clarify the almost terminally vague idea of community" (ibid., 18). How does he go about this clarification? The introductory chapter contains the following programmatic statement:

> The main challenge that faces the legal imagination at the present time is to envisage what "law's community" might be; to draw on the vast accumulated experience of modern legal regulation to imagine and to work towards regulatory structures that are responsive to local moral milieux and that clearly reflect the diversity of social experience of citizens. This is a task of making law morally meaningful as an aspect of everyday existence, rather than an alien intrusion, an inaccessible resource, or a special component only of particular professional or commercial settings (ibid., 21).

The third and last part of *Law's Community* ("Law, Power, and Community") is devoted to a specification of this "vague idea." The last two sections of the last chapter ("The Concept of Community" and "The Regulation of Communities") give concrete answers to the questions, first, "What is a community?" and, second, "What is the role of law in communities so conceived?" (ibid., 221–337).

The more orthodox approaches available in the sociological literature derive the idea of community from the concept of *Gemeinschaft*. Cotterrell takes a very different approach. He prefers to conceptualize the idea of community from the interplay of certain general orientations of social interaction. In this interactionist concept of community, a key role is played by the notion of "trust." Trust, or rather "mutual interpersonal trust," according to Cotterrell is "the basic building block of community—the fundamental orientation that makes it possible." Mutual interpersonal trust he calls "the essence of community." Therefore Cotterrell defines communities as "patterns of interaction that involve a high degree of mutual interpersonal trust" (ibid., 325–32).

This theory of community largely determines, in Cotterrell's eyes, the role of contemporary law, or "law-government." Regulatory forms and institutions should be designed to foster and support relations of mutual trust within communities. But under modern conditions—that is conditions that make for a highly varied, complex, fragmented world—this kind of mutual interpersonal trust can be achieved only "on a relatively 'local' level" or "in relatively specific social fields." This fundamentally affects law-government. Its focus must become, increasingly, these local levels or specific fields, "rather than the purportedly all-embracing unitary jurisdiction of the contemporary centralized state" (ibid., 332–37).

Cotterrell builds his communitarian jurisprudence on a fairly strong notion of social, political, and legal pluralism. He writes: "[E]ven judicial rhetoric from relatively unified legal systems of contemporary states suggests that a concern for relationships between law and community is a concern with legal and moral *pluralism*." And: "To postulate, with some sociological sensitivity, the utility of a concept of community is necessarily to recognize diversity in social arrangements and radical pluralism in moral life as the essential conditions of existence of those areas of moral agreement that can underpin social solidarity today" (ibid., 322). That is the reason Cotterrell advocates regulatory pluralism or "devolution," that is, "devolution of substantial regulatory powers from the state to communities." Law-government at the state level will then become rather different from that at the community level: "The primary regulatory role of the centralized state may be that of coordinating communities within the political society as a whole, guaranteeing peace and security for all citizens, and promoting the welfare of the whole political society within a larger international environment" (ibid., 334).

Selznick deals with these matters of communitarian jurisprudence employing both the perspective of philosophical communitarianism, like Handler, and that of the sociological tradition, like Cotterrell. Indeed, these three studies of socio-legal communitarianism show a strong affinity. Yet there are also considerable differences. While Handler embraces the concept of dialogic community, and Cotterrell prefers an interactionist conceptualization of community, Selznick stresses the importance of treating "community" as a *variable* aspect of group experience: "Groups can be more or less full-blown communities, and they can approximate community in different ways." That is why Selznick (1992, 358) wants to define "community" much more *comprehensively* than either Handler or Cotterrell: "A group is a community to the extent that it encompasses a broad range of activities and interests, and to the extent that participation implicates whole persons rather than segmental interests or activities."

But on the basis of this inclusive, or weak, *definition* of community, Selznick develops a *theory* of community that is much more discriminating, much stronger than those of Handler or Cotterrell. Selznick's theory builds on the following recurrent elements of community: historicity, identity, mutuality, plurality, autonomy, participation, and integration. These seven elements represent the prime values of human life lived in communities. This presumes anything but homogeneity. On the contrary, "[d]ifferent types of community—religious, political, occupational, institutional, international—will have different mixes of the main elements" (ibid., 364). Furthermore, the interplay of these elements itself creates variety and diversity.

Discussion of community habitually centers on the organic unity of *Gemeinschaft*. But living communities, Selznick argues, are plural as well as solidary: "communities are characterized by structural differentiation as well as by shared consciousness" (ibid., 367). Thus Selznick (ibid., 369) advances a theory of community that is as pluralistic as that of Cotterrell:

> What we prize in community is not unity of any sort, at any cost, but unity that preserves the integrity of persons, groups, and institutions. Thus understood, community is profoundly *federalist* in spirit and structure. It is a unity of unities.

Here too there are important differences between the various modes of communitarian jurisprudence. While Handler and Cotterrell rely on trust to hold a community together, Selznick has a broader view. He sees not *one*, but *two* sources of moral integration competing for preeminence as "foundations of community": civility and piety. To these two sources of morality he devotes an entire chapter (ibid., 387–427). *Civility* "governs diversity, protects autonomy, and upholds toleration"; *piety* "expresses devotion and demands integration." "The norms of civility are impersonal, rational, and inclusive, whereas piety is personal, passionate, and particularistic." While these two sets of norms or aspirations are not antagonistic, they represent rather heterogeneous modes of thinking and feeling. "Civility is a characteristically liberal ideal . . . it looks to a universalistic ethic, whereas piety builds on primordial ties of origin and kinship. The distinctive virtue of piety is loyalty, whereas in civility respect is the salient value, not love, not commitment." The conflict between these very different principles forms the heart of Selznick's communitarian jurisprudence. Their reconciliation he sees as "a prime object of theory and policy" (ibid., 387).

THE FUTURE OF COMMUNITARIAN JURISPRUDENCE

What have we learned from the review of communitarianism in socio-legal studies so far? Three points stand out. One, the importance of legal pluralism, that is, the deeply plural character of modern law, is recognized and accounted for in the perspective of socio-legal communitarianism. Second, the communitarian perspective emphasizes the moral dimension, the moral underpinnings of law, and directs our attention to the interdependence of law, solidarity, and community. Third, these new socio-legal communitarians acknowledge the primacy of community without diminishing the worth of values central to the liberal tradition: freedom, equality, and rationality. Indeed, communitarianism and liberalism are joined in a point of view that has been called, most explicitly so by Selznick himself (1992, xi), "communitarian liberalism." Perhaps the most lasting contribution of socio-legal communitarianism may be seen in the way it helps transcend—dialectically resolve—the polarities that were popularized by philosophical liberals and communitarians some twenty-five years ago. Let us return, by way of conclusion, to that original liberal–communitarian debate.

In the years since the appearance of *A Theory of Justice*, in 1971, Rawls wrote a large number of articles in which he refined and reformulated his original position. The most important of these articles were included as chapters in the book he published in 1993, entitled *Political Liberalism*. Many commentators have argued that these more recent writings of Rawls have to be understood as a response to his communitarian critics. In the introduction to the new book Rawls himself denied this explicitly: "The changes in the later essays are sometimes said to be replies to criticisms raised by communitarians and others. I don't believe there is a basis for saying this" (1993, xviin6). Whether Rawls is right here or not, the contents of his work show that the debate between liberals and communitarians had moved forward considerably from the sharp antithesis with which it once began.

This view is confirmed in the commentary on Rawls's later work that can be found in the new edition of Sandel's *Liberalism and the Limits of Justice*, which was published in 1998. In much of the liberal–communitarian debate, Sandel (1998, 186) there pointed out, the term communitarianism was rather "misleading . . . insofar as it implies that rights should rest on values or preferences that prevail in any given community at any given time." For that was not at all the view of the so-called communitarian critics of Rawlsian liberalism. "The question is not whether rights should be respected but whether rights can be identified and justified in a way that does not presuppose any particular conception of the good." Accordingly, Sandel emphasized, the central issue in the liberal–communitarian debate was not the weight of individual claims versus that of communal claims, but the terms of relation between these two, that is between the right and the good. In other words, the main project of communitarianism was to expand the horizon of liberalism, to highlight issues of substantive good that were neglected, or even rejected on principle, by proponents of neutralist liberalism such as Rawls, Dworkin, and Ackerman. Thus communitarianism was seen not as an alternative to liberalism, but as its supplement.

The idea implicitly suggested here by both Rawls and Sandel is to focus not on the *opposition* between liberalism and communitarianism, as had become habit in academic and political circles over the years, but instead to explore the fundamental *continuities* between the two. The call for a more integrative approach to liberalism and communitarianism is not new, of course. It was heard already way back in 1985 in an influential article written by Amy Gutmann, who pointed out some of the shortcomings and blind spots of communitarianism, but nonetheless argued that the latter "has the potential for helping us discover a politics that combines community with a commitment to basic liberal values." Therefore, Gutmann (1985, 322) concluded, "the worthy challenge posed by the communitarian critics . . . is not to replace liberal justice, but to improve it."

This more enlightened liberalism, that is, a liberalism committed to a strong notion of community as a substantive good, is also to be found in the twenty-three socio-legal contributions to a recent volume that was inspired by the work of Philip Selznick (Kagan, Krygier, and Winston 2002), and in two recent books expressly devoted to the elaboration of a communitarian jurisprudence, *To Promote the General Welfare: A Communitarian Legal Reader*, edited by David E. Carney (1999), and *Law and Community: The Case of Torts*, by Robert F. Cochran Jr. and Robert M. Ackerman (2004). These writings can be read as variations on the theme of communitarian liberalism. For anyone interested in the future of communitarian jurisprudence, or in what communitarianism may contribute to the study of law and society, this may be the direction to look.

NOTE

1. This chapter is a substantially revised and updated version of my essay "Law, Society, and the Search for Community," which was previously published in Kagan, Krygier, and Winston 2002, 373–87.

REFERENCES

Anderson, Paul. 1996. Where Are the Brains behind Blair? *New Statesman and Society,* March 15, 14–15.

Avineri, Shlomo, and Avner de-Shalit, eds. 1992. *Communitarianism and Individualism*. Oxford: Oxford University Press.

Bell, Daniel. 1993. *Communitarianism and Its Critics*. Oxford: Clarendon Press.

Carney, David E., ed. 1999. *To Promote the General Welfare: A Communitarian Legal Reader*. Lanham, MD: Lexington Books.

Cochran Jr., Robert F., and Robert M. Ackerman, eds. 2004. *Law and Community: The Case of Torts*. Lanham, MD: Rowman and Littlefield.

Communitarian Platform. 1991/1992. The Responsive Communitarian Platform: Rights and Responsibilities. *The Responsive Community* 2 (1): 4–20.

Cotterrell, Roger. 1995. *Law's Community: Legal Theory in Sociological Perspective*. Oxford: Clarendon Press.

Dahrendorf, Ralf. 1999. Whatever Happened to Liberty. *New Statesman*, September 6, 25–27.

Etzioni, Amitai. 1993. *The Spirit of Community: Rights, Responsibilities, and the Communitarian Agenda*. New York: Crown.

———. 1996. *The New Golden Rule: Community and Morality in a Democratic Society*. New York: Basic Books.

———. 2000. *The Third Way to a Good Society*. London: Demos.

———. 2003. *My Brother's Keeper: A Memoir and a Message*. Lanham, MD: Rowman and Littlefield.

———. 2004. *From Empire to Community: A New Approach to International Relations*. New York: Palgrave Macmillan.

Etzioni, Amitai, Jim Fishkin, William Galston, and Mary Ann Glandon. 1990/1991. Editorial Statement: The Responsive Community, Rights and Responsibilities. *The Responsive Community* 1 (1): 2–5.

Forst, Rainer. 2002. *Contexts of Justice: Political Philosophy beyond Liberalism and Communitarianism*. Trans. John M.M. Farrell. Berkeley: University of California Press.

Frazer, Elizabeth. 1999. *The Problems of Communitarian Politics: Unity and Conflict*. Oxford: Oxford University Press.

Frazer, Elizabeth, and Nicola Lacey. 1993. *The Politics of Community: A Feminist Critique of the Liberal–Communitarian Debate*. Hemel Hempstead: Harvester Wheatsheaf.

Giddens, Anthony. 1998. *The Third Way: The Renewal of Social Democracy*. Cambridge: Polity Press.

———. 2000. *The Third Way and Its Critics*. Cambridge: Polity Press.

Gutmann, Amy. 1985. Communitarian Critics of Liberalism. *Philosophy and Public Affairs* 14:308–22.

Handler, Joel F. 1990. *Law and the Search for Community*. Philadelphia: University of Pennsylvania Press.

Honneth, Axel, ed. 1993. *Kommunitarismus: Eine Debatte über die moralischen Grundlagen moderner Gesellschaften*. Frankfurt am Main: Campus Verlag.

Kagan, Robert A., Martin Krygier, and Kenneth Winston, eds. 2002. *Legality and Community: On the Intellectual Legacy of Philip Selznick*. Lanham, MD: Rowman and Littlefield; Berkeley, CA: Berkeley Public Policy Press.

MacIntyre, Alasdair. 1981. *After Virtue: A Study in Moral Theory*. London: Duckworth.

Mulhall, Stephen, and Adam Swift. 1996. *Liberals and Communitarians*. 2nd ed. Oxford: Blackwell.

Phillips, Derek 1993. *Looking Backward: A Critical Appraisal of Communitarian Thought*. Princeton, NJ: Princeton University Press.

Rawls, John. 1971. *A Theory of Justice*. Cambridge, MA: Harvard University Press.

———. 1993. *Political Liberalism*. New York: Columbia University Press.
Sandel, Michael. 1982. *Liberalism and the Limits of Justice*. Cambridge: Cambridge University Press.
———. 1998. *Liberalism and the Limits of Justice*. 2nd ed. Cambridge: Cambridge University Press.
Selznick, Philip. 1987. The Idea of a Communitarian Morality. *California Law Review* 75:445–63.
———. 1992. *The Moral Commonwealth: Social Theory and the Promise of Community*. Berkeley: University of California Press.
———. 2002. *The Communitarian Persuasion*. Washington, DC: Woodrow Wilson Center Press; Baltimore, MD: Johns Hopkins University Press.
Tam, Henry. 1998. *Communitarianism: A New Agenda for Politics and Citizenship*. New York: New York University Press.
———, ed. 2001. *Progressive Politics in the Global Age*. Cambridge: Polity Press.
Taylor, Charles. 1985. Atomism [1979]. In *Philosophy and the Human Sciences: Philosophical Papers*, vol. 2, 187–210. Cambridge: Cambridge University Press.
———. 1989. *Sources of the Self: The Making of Modern Identity*. Cambridge: Cambridge University Press.
Walzer, Michael. 1983. *Spheres of Justice: A Defense of Pluralism and Equality*. New York: Basic Books.

Part I

LAW AND COMMUNITY IN SOCIO-LEGAL STUDIES

1

The Jurisprudence of Communitarian Liberalism[1]

Philip Selznick

What is communitarian liberalism? What difference can it make for how we think about law and justice? I shall try to answer these questions but must do so, of course, with broad strokes.

It should come as no surprise that much of what I have to say amounts to pouring old wine into new bottles. Moreover, I am aware that the American interest in communitarian thought may seem naive and irrelevant to some Europeans. For the union of communitarian and liberal perspectives is not news to European social democrats and Christian democrats. Such a union is strongly evident in the German *Grundgesetz*, which combines the liberal conception of a *Rechtsstaat* with the more communitarian ideal of a *Sozialstaat* or social welfare state. Nevertheless, the intellectual foundations of communitarian liberalism remain elusive and insecure; and its implications for other realms of thought, such as jurisprudence and the theory of democracy, have not been seriously considered.

The quest for a communitarian morality, to counter the excesses of individualism and rationalism, has been a perennial theme of post-Enlightenment thought. The response has taken conservative, liberal, and radical forms. For Americans, a prominent example is the social philosophy of John Dewey. Dewey was a great spokesman for communitarian liberalism. He combined a spirit of liberation and social reconstruction with a strong commitment to responsible participation in effective communities.

On the other hand, some more stringently communitarian doctrines, especially communism and fascism, have given solidarity a very bad name. As we try to think afresh—as we try to identify what is desirable and necessary in a communitarian perspective—we can never let ourselves forget these dreadful ways of justifying evil in the name of the good.

What *is* that good? Seen in its best light, the communitarian ideal is an affirmation of basic morality. It is a way of upholding ideals of fellowship, that is, of mutual concern and respect. The concept of fellowship has rich connotations, which resist reduction to subservience or duty or wholly other-regarding conduct. Properly understood, fellowship does not contemplate extinction of self-regard or the dissolution of self into collective life. There is a dual concern for one's own integrity as well as for the interests of others.

The fear of excessive solidarity—of a stifling *Gemeinschaft* or authoritarian government—is soundly based, but this should not deter us from appreciating and fulfilling the promise of community. Every important human commitment carries a threat of enslavement. For some, this threat justifies renouncing responsibility, and may even create an incapacity for commitment. But most of us understand the good sense of negotiating a healthy balance between what is required to maintain our integrity as unique individuals and what it takes to maintain relationships based on commitment, care, and nurture. A similar balance is needed in political and institutional life.

A communitarian morality looks to the enhancement of personal and social responsibility; exhibits a preference for cooperation and reconciliation in all spheres of life; affirms the interdependence of belonging and freedom; and respects the particularity and diversity of human existence. This doctrine presumes that selfhood can be *enlarged* as a result of social experience; and also that selfhood requires *rootedness*. The tension between this enlargement and this rootedness creates the central problems of communitarian thought. It is an inescapable source of both promise and peril; and it is the reason we should think of communitarian ideas as *amendments* to the liberal project rather than as a rejection of it.

Communitarian liberalism deepens our understanding of liberalism itself. This it does by bringing to light how much the great pillars of liberalism—freedom, equality, rationality—depend on social support, including social discipline and social integration. Freedom, equality, and rationality become weak and vulnerable if they are not sustained by shared values, by personal commitment, and by appropriate institutions. This infrastructure is incompatible with radical individualism. Therefore if liberal ideals are to be made good—even in limited, formal ways—something more than autonomy is required. Responsible liberalism requires *ordered* liberty; and ordered liberty presumes a viable community.

Furthermore, communitarian liberalism extends and enriches liberal ideas in that it seeks *effective* freedom, *substantive* rationality, and *social* justice. This move from form to substance distinguishes classical or laissez-faire liberalism from social democracy or what we in the United States call welfare liberalism. Thus one strand of communitarian liberalism speaks to the foundations of liberalism, that is, to its social preconditions; another demands a fuller realization of liberal ideals.

This interplay of idealism and realism is a key to understanding what we are about. Liberalism appeals to moral realism when it insists, as Thomas Jefferson said, that "free government is founded in jealousy, and not in confidence; it is jealousy, not confidence which prescribes limited constitutions, to bind down those whom we are obliged to trust with power . . . in questions of power, then, let no more be heard of confidence in man, but bind him down from mischief by the chains of the Constitution." This reliance on definite constitutional safeguards, including recognition of unalienable rights, and on other safeguards, such as the separation of powers and of institutional spheres, is a form of moral realism. It asks what we must guard against and what we can *rely upon*, and has less concern for what we can *aspire to*. At the same time, liberalism upholds a lofty ideal of universalism, brushing aside the insistent claims of local, particularistic, parochial perspectives.

The communitarian ethos is more idealistic than liberalism insofar as it looks to the *flourishing* of personality and community rather than only to baseline standards of equality and justice. This is not without danger to political and institutional morality, for example when we endorse more open-ended forms of constitutional interpretation and thus enlarge judicial discretion; when we limit rights by taking account of attendant responsibilities and trade-offs; when we blur the boundaries between different agencies of government and different spheres of life; and when we adopt a more inclusive approach to democracy and equality. These risks are offset, however, by a more realistic focus on diversity and particularity, and by a deeper understanding of the limits of universalism and the many ways abstract ideals can be misused and misunderstood.

THEORY OF COMMUNITY

To understand the communitarian perspective, as it modifies liberalism, we must look first to the theory of community. An adequate theory will be careful to avoid the common fallacy of identifying community as a generic phenomenon or universal ideal with particular *kinds* of community, such as the *Gemeinschaft* model, the Greek *polis*, or the liberal political community variously envisioned by Locke, Rousseau, and Rawls. Rather, we should take our departure from a sociological theory which builds on recurrent features of community, and which brings to light characteristic problems, tensions, and affinities. As historical and comparative studies reveal, the elements of community are found in different mixes, with very different consequences for human well-being. To find the proper mix, we must know what values are at stake in the experience of community, and what contingencies must be taken account of in the design of communities. The beginning of wisdom is to recognize that community is a multifaceted phenomenon and a multivalued ideal.[2]

Discussion of community tends to center upon the ties that bind. That is fair enough. Indeed, a communitarian morality must surely emphasize the virtues of belonging and the costs of liberation. We learn from the experience of living in communities that normal communities are plural as well as solidary. Too much unity, as Aristotle recognized, can create a parody of community rather than fulfillment of the communitarian ideal. A flourishing community requires integration, but the point of the integration is to regulate a *variety* of groups and practices, which are independent as well as interdependent, self-regarding as well as other-regarding. What we prize in community is not unity of any sort, at any cost, but unity that preserves the integrity of persons, practices, groups, and institutions. Thus understood, community is inherently a "federal" unity, a unity of unities. It is undermined by too much solidarity, too much management, too much coordination, just as surely as it is weakened by an excess of individualism or by cultural incoherence.

An important corollary, often overlooked, is the preservation of personal rationality within the experience of community. We do not normally think of participation in communities as irrational or self-destructive. On the contrary, communities are distorted—they become at best pseudocommunities—if they demand ecstatic forms of mass participation, undisciplined by the requirements of everyday interests, relationships, and pursuits. This follows from the idea that communities are settings within which ordinary life goes forward. And ordinary life is based on mediated, self-preserving participation. We belong to more comprehensive communities by way of participation in more immediate, more person-centered unities of family, friendship, locality, church, and occupation. As these elements of plurality weaken, so do the texture and quality of community.

Even when we focus on integration rather than plurality, we must ask what *kinds* of integration prevail and how they are reconciled. Two forms of moral integration are especially important as foundations of community: *civility* and *piety*. Civility is a characteristically liberal ideal, one that presumes diversity, protects autonomy, and upholds toleration. Piety—here I quote George Santayana ([1933] 1954, 285)—"may be said to mean man's reverent attachment to the sources of his being, and the steadying of his life by that attachment." The norms of civility are impersonal, rational, and inclusive; whereas piety is personal, passionate, and particularist. Civility looks to a universalist ethic, whereas piety builds on primordial ties of origin and kinship. The distinctive virtue of piety is loyalty, whereas in civility respect is the salient value, not love, not commitment. The conflict between these very different principles generates major issues of morality and community. Their reconciliation is a prime object of theory and policy. A distinctive feature of *communitarian* liberalism is that it takes this tension seriously.

The most important lesson to be drawn from the sociology of community is the significance of variation. Rightly understood, a group (small or large, informal or institutionalized) is a community *insofar* as it embraces a wide range of activities and interests; *insofar* as it takes account of whole persons, not just specialized contributions or roles; and *insofar* as bonds of commitment and culture are shared. This focus on variability shifts attention from the question, "is this a community?" to the question, "how far and in what ways does this group experience the bonds, benefits, and deficits of community?" This way of thinking permits us to focus on the uneven and difficult task of building or strengthening communities; especially important is the implication that the values we associate with community can be sought, with different strategies and uneven success, wherever sustained human interaction takes place: in family life, work, education, health care, urban design, and much else. In each sphere we can find ways of enlarging responsible conduct; we can identify opportunities for mutual caring and concern. We can find the right recipe, taking account of the context, for achieving a union of solidarity and respect.[3]

Keeping these ideas in mind, I turn to some major themes in jurisprudence as seen through the lens of communitarian liberalism. I shall touch, very briefly, on four topics: First, the communitarian alternative to legal positivism; second, the critique of rights-centeredness; third, the integration of law and society; and finally, the irrepressible tension between universalism and particularism.

LIBERALISM, COMMUNITARIANISM, AND LEGAL POSITIVISM

A communitarian jurisprudence resists any deep or ontological separation of law and morality, law and history, law and politics. Instead of treating law as an autonomous system, with its own premises, its own code, and its own integrity, we think of law as "in society," fatefully conditioned by social contexts, enmeshed in networks of activities and institutions, sharing as well as defining a comprehensive moral order. This perspective finds much support in sociological jurisprudence. *It is driven, however, by moral concerns*, especially the quest for enhanced responsibility, competence, and authenticity. An important outcome is the blurring of boundaries that separate institutions, practices, and modes of thought.[4]

Therefore communitarian jurisprudence is necessarily in tension with the doctrines of legal positivism. Positivism celebrates and protects the autonomy of legal ideas and institutions; insists on the difference between legal outcomes and just or moral outcomes; and identifies law with norms that are posited and determinate rather than inchoate, emergent, and problematic.

In modern Western thought there has been a marked affinity between political liberalism and legal positivism. That is so because positivism is more concerned with procedure than substance, including procedural values of clarity, certainty, and legitimacy; with external compliance rather than character and motivation; with a moral minimum rather than what Lon Fuller called a "morality of aspiration"; with definite rules rather than less determinate principles or standards.

This positivist outlook has shaped liberalism's conception of the rule of law, which seeks to limit the reach of government by binding it to definite rules and procedures; and by providing a neutral framework within which equal liberty and fair adjudication is guaranteed to all. Positivism has been attractive to the liberal mind in part because drawing a bright line between law and justice demystifies law and makes it more readily subject to external criticism. On this view, if we are careful to distinguish legal validity from moral justification, we can avoid treating law as presumptively just.

The affinity of liberalism and legal positivism is sustained by the idea that a moral order—the place where high ideals are fulfilled, and where fundamental obligations are acknowledged—should be distinguished from law as a practical foundation for protecting liberty and facilitating cooperation. The more exacting demands of moral duty belong to another, more personal, more spiritual, realm. Kantian *morality* transcends inclination and limits individuality; but Kantian *law* allows for maximum freedom of private choice, including choice of self-defining ends, so long as that freedom does not interfere with the equal freedom of others.

Like many such entrenched dichotomies, a strong separation of law and morality tends to impoverish the very values it seeks to uphold. While it properly denies their *necessary* connection, liberal-legal positivism neglects the *affinities* of law, justice, and morality. The moral order of a community must suffer if the mission of law is too narrowly conceived and if, as a corollary, justice is taken to be no more than a baseline morality or a negative virtue.[5]

The alternative is to recognize that justice has a vital part to play, not only as a guarantor of basic liberty and rudimentary fairness, but in reaching for a greater human flourishing as well. In doing justice we draw insight and justification from a larger context of moral experience and reflection. For justice cannot be even modestly realized if there is no appreciation of personal dignity, trust, fidelity, caring, and rationality. In other words, the quest for justice has its own dynamic, which includes the elaboration and refinement of values. Although justice *emerges* as a response to practical urgencies, under appropriate conditions it *eventuates* in ideas and practices that are more subtle and more value-laden.

If we reduce justice to a negative virtue or to a way of achieving minimal cooperation, we lose a great deal of its resonance and promise. We fail to garner the psychological and intellectual benefits that come from receiving justice and doing justice. Most important, we miss the full contribution justice can make to the enrichment and enlargement of community.

In making the connection between law and justice, communitarian liberalism shifts attention from rules to principles. Among contemporary writers this move is most clearly seen in the work of Ronald Dworkin, although others have had similar ideas. Dworkin came upon the scene as a powerful critic of the legal positivism of H. L. A. Hart, especially what Dworkin called "the model of rules." He stressed the importance of legal principles as authoritative resources for criticizing and reconstructing specific rules. These principles include the historically determined premises of the legal order, and more universal precepts as well. In either case, whether we think of principles as timeless or timebound, the rule-centered ethos of legal positivism needs criticism and reform.

This alternative calls for something more than the discovery and clarification of a community's moral and legal commitments. A communitarian ethos cannot be content with *any* set of principles, or even with the idea of a "community of principle." Rather, the true objective is a jurisprudence that would enrich the abstract principles of justice by infusing them with ideals of mutual trust, respect, reconciliation, and interdependence; and by testing them in the light of substantive outcomes.

The limits of positivism are also revealed when we examine the connection between law and history. In its quest for determinacy, and therefore for a clear line between law and not-law, positivism resists recognizing as law norms that are incipient, implicit, emergent, or otherwise imperfectly formed. Yet the historical study of law must necessarily look beneath and beyond explicit expressions of positive law, whether enunciated by courts, legislatures, or executive agencies. The historicity of community is reflected in the historicity of law, which can only be understood if latent values, reciprocal influences, and unconscious adaptations are taken into account. As these work themselves out they extend the realm of what is legally meaningful or relevant.

A corollary is the understanding that formal or positive law—including a written constitution and its judicial gloss—can only be an abridgment, an elliptical rendering, of the community's legal and constitutional experience. The legal system cannot spell out all the expectations, rights, and responsibilities that are implicit in the history of the community's institutions. Nor can it specify all the powers of government. To be sure, the positive law can be made *formally* complete by incorporating suitably abstract principles. But this only recognizes, it cannot deny, the open-ended character of the legal system and the necessary interaction between law and life.

These remarks about positive law strongly echo the well-known criticisms made by earlier "historical" and "sociological" schools of jurisprudence.

There has long been some difficulty in characterizing this perspective, because it includes conservative admirers of tradition as well as other scholars who simply respect the historicity of law, and still others who assert the significance of social practice for judicial interpretation and the integrity of legislation. The last of these ideas is by no means necessarily conservative; it often leads to liberal attacks on legal rigidity and insularity.

The perspective I have outlined has sometimes been called the "democratic" theory of law, thereby emphasizing the dependence of law on changes in popular awareness, expectation, and belief (Walker 1988, chap. 14). The "democratic" label is unsatisfactory, however, because much more is involved than consciousness and because democracy presumes specific institutions of self-government, which may or may not be present. I suggest that the perspective is better understood as a *communitarian* theory of law. The starting point, and the main thrust of the argument, is the recognition that law draws form and substance from the experience of community. In that experience historicity and social practice are vital elements; and those elements are informed by ideals, implicit as well as explicit, as well as by the urgencies of everyday life.[6]

RIGHTS AND AUTONOMY

A major theme in communitarian liberalism is the moral primacy of the community—of civil society—over the state. Here is the most profound connection between communitarian liberalism and classical liberal doctrine, as expressed by John Locke and Thomas Paine. The primacy of the community over the state can only be insured by an array of rights, institutional as well as personal. Some of these are "fundamental," "human," or "generic" rights, grounded in the human condition or guaranteed to all citizens or persons within a political community. Such rights do not stem from specific projects, relationships, or entitlements. Rather, they derive from the fact that some vital human interests are routinely threatened by the community's own organization, especially where power is exercised and authority is asserted. Therefore we recognize, as applicable to every human situation, generic rights of life, liberty, and justice.

The experience of community is the crucible within which generic rights become specific and contextual. Here competing interests and relevant conditions are considered. The will of the community with respect to rights is discerned by examining its traditions, practices, and institutions, not necessarily or exclusively by counting votes. Furthermore, in deciding what interests merit protection as rights, the courts look to the needs of historically situated persons and groups. They translate abstractly stated rights into principles that take account of multiple values, constraining contexts, and historical opportunities.

A corollary is the communitarian critique of rights-*centered* liberalism. From the standpoint of communitarian jurisprudence, a preoccupation with rights has two main drawbacks. First is a perceptible retreat from discipline and duty. At least those virtues tend to be moved from the foreground to the background of consciousness. The idea that rights should be exercised *responsibly* tends to be forgotten. Rights-centered politics fails to take account of multiple interests and values; and it is insufficiently sensitive to the difference between rights that are truly fundamental and those that are contingent or defeasible.

This divorce of rights from responsibilities is largely due to the liberal dedication to autonomy and self-assertion. The brave proclamations of human rights, and the long struggle to redeem those rights—a struggle very much unfinished—have encouraged thoughtways that were always troublesome to critics of the Enlightenment. Those criticisms are more poignant today as we watch the steady erosion of taken-for-granted assumptions regarding civic and personal responsibility.

Second, rights-centered liberalism tends to impoverish and confuse public debate regarding the common good. For understandable reasons, but with negative consequences, rights have come to be perceived as inherent in individuals rather than socially useful devices for achieving collective purposes and shared ideals. To be sure, rights are not meaningful if they do not trump or restrain what the community can do in the name of the common good. But that only tells us what rights are; it does not say what rights should be recognized or how far they should be indefeasible. That requires a collective decision as to what interests should be protected, in what ways, and for what ends.

Consider, for example, the continuing debate in the United States regarding the moral foundations of freedom of speech, including academic freedom. The strictly liberal voice seeks to make freedom of speech an absolute, bound firmly to a premise of personal autonomy, unresponsive to the claims of special-purpose institutions or the community as a whole. The communitarian alternative is to take seriously what speech is for, thus inviting inquiry into what kinds of speech require what kinds of nurture and protection. The governance of speech will take one form if its objective is to serve and enhance deliberative democracy, or education, or science, or the arts; it will be quite different if its starting point is an individual claim to autonomous self-expression. Thus the content of academic freedom depends on whether such freedom is tied to institutional purposes or to the rights of individuals. When rights derive mainly from social goals, such as education, science, democracy, or economic prosperity, they must ultimately yield to the sovereignty of purpose. Such rights are necessarily contingent; there are always boundaries; but they are not necessarily insecure. Their security may require constitutional safeguards, but the nature of that protection—how the constitution is interpreted—must depend on how we perceive the values at stake or at risk.

A much-discussed example of the evil that may come from a preoccupation with rights is the debate over abortion in the United States. The opposing sides have counterposed the rights of the mother and the rights of the fetus. In championing the idea that even the fertilized ovum is a constitutionally protected person, the anti-abortion advocates have espoused a rigid and uncompassionate doctrine. Driven by a hardened ideology, they have embraced a highly unrealistic conception of maternal responsibility and have greatly exaggerated the claims of emergent life. They have failed to take account of their own reservations regarding the moral status of the fetus, as evidenced in the exceptions allowed for aborting a fetus produced by rape, sometimes including statutory rape.

For their part, the pro-choice advocates have offered only a limited vision of *responsible* choice, and their slogans do not make sense of the limits they themselves accept on the exercise of choice during the last months of pregnancy. Pro-choice extremism limits the meaning of motherhood and denies respect for the emergent human being. It offers no basis for safeguarding the vulnerable continuities of biology and morality, procreation and commitment.

Although the sanctity of human life is a bedrock value, it is subtle in its claims, uncertain in its boundaries, forever troubled by conflicting interests. Thus the biological fact of conception—abstracted from other biological facts, including the precarious and extremely rudimentary nature of the fertilized ovum, and from the whole experience of procreation and nurture—does not settle any moral issue. Conception is indeed an important event, but birth is far more important. The biological changes between conception and birth are accompanied by progressive transformations of meaning, attachment, and obligation. To overlook these differences is to impoverish moral judgment.

The alternative to rights-centeredness, in this context, is to treat the sanctity of human life, and the special respect for procreation, as values to be upheld by the community as a whole. To uphold these values we need not rely mainly on the allocation and balancing of individual rights. The maintenance of respect for developing life is a social policy whose implementation should be considered in the light of competing values, such as education and opportunity for women, population control, and resistance to conception by rape or incest. It should consider all the relevant realities, including the urgencies of sexuality, the various hardships entailed, and the resources available for a policy of unlimited concern for every stage of life. This perspective takes account of ambiguities in the values themselves; establishes priorities without ignoring any valid interest; and responds constructively to pervasive human frailty.

RESPONSIVE LAW AND THE RULE OF LAW

I turn now to a third—and perhaps the most important—pillar of communitarian jurisprudence. This is the idea that law should be responsive to changing circumstances and to the needs of the community. Here "law" refers to the whole system of legal norms and institutions, including judicial interpretation and administrative regulation as well as explicit legislation.

An ideal of responsive law is latent in the critique of positivism I referred to earlier; it is a latent theme in historical jurisprudence; and it can be clearly discerned in the perspectives of legal realism and sociological jurisprudence, including contemporary studies of "law and society."[7] These intellectual currents have argued that the contexts of law—political, cultural, economic, social, psychological—decisively affect the quality of justice. Failure to take account of these realities lends the legal order an excessive dignity, insulates it from needed criticism, and offers society inadequate leverage for change. If a legal system is inefficient, or indifferent to social needs, it will deliver a cramped, selective, and impoverished justice. Without responsive law, the community is shortchanged. Law is more just when it springs from the character and condition of the people, and when it is administered with due regard for the integrity of institutions and the vitality of civil society.

To fulfill this ideal, legal institutions must be redesigned, in various ways, to enhance law's capacity to deliver justice in light of prevailing social conditions. This requires strategies of *inclusion*, which increase access to the system in part by broadening the range of interests law acknowledges. It also requires strategies of *respect*, including respect for institutions close to the people. Thus responsive law takes seriously the claims of social, political, and legal pluralism; and it relies, as much as possible, on self-regulation rather than on imposed rules or commands.

These strategies demand openness, adaptation, and reconstruction. But legal institutions must be competent as well. A responsive legal order is not best understood as passively accommodating unregulated claims and interests; it is something more than a friendly, nonintrusive facilitator of private transactions. Responsive law is active, creative, and purposive.

Responsiveness could be a serious challenge to the *Rechtsstaat* or the rule of law. Compared to autonomous law, a responsive legal order is less rule-centered and less rights-centered; less preoccupied with the control of official discretion, including judicial discretion; less worried about the separation of law and politics, especially the "high politics" of principle and policy.

This blurring of boundaries is a hallmark of responsive law—as it is, I believe, in part at least, of all institutional morality. We have learned that to do justice we must recognize the continuities—the interdependence—of law, politics, economics, morality, and social practice. For example, social conditions may obscure the line between private and public morality, private and public government.

This is not to say that the autonomy of social spheres is irrelevant or unimportant. I am not claiming that "everything is political," as some contemporary writers do. Blurred *boundaries* do not erase all differences; they are compatible with recognizing that, for many purposes, different principles and logics prevail; or with the idea that one sphere may have moral primacy over others.

Responsive law does entail risks. We might even call it a high-risk strategy in the quest for justice. This should not be surprising: recall the point I made earlier that *communitarian* liberalism is in important respects more idealistic than classical liberalism; and moral idealism is always more risky than moral realism. It would indeed be folly to allow the vision of a richer ideal to distract us from the basic necessities and recurrent vulnerabilities of democracy, education, and doing justice. Even as it seeks reconstruction and renewal, responsiveness builds on foundations already laid. These include the idea that no official, however mighty, is above the law; the independence of the judiciary; and assurance that the law protects a substantial array of fundamental rights. When confidence in these achievements is justified, a broader vision can be framed; higher aspirations can be embraced. We may then ask whether the rule-of-law model, as hitherto understood, fully meets the community's needs; we may well conclude it is reasonable to accept some institutional risks in the interests of social justice.

THE CLAIMS OF PARTICULARISM

Finally we come to what may be the most vexing, most difficult issue for liberal thought and practice. This is the need to find a proper balance between universalism and particularism. A *strict* communitarianism celebrates diversity, inclines toward moral relativism, and treats moral experience as inescapably local and framed by special obligations. Modern liberals, on the other hand, impatient with parochial outlooks, are deeply suspicious of limited communities, which demand conformity and suppress individuality. The gift of enlightenment—the liberal ideal—is a *cosmopolitan* morality. Liberal community is found in comprehensive unities, which are created and sustained by universalist standards of equality and dignity. These are the foundations of critical morality; and for liberals critical morality is the only true morality.

The more synthetic vision of communitarian liberalism takes seriously the claims of local experience and cultural identity. It does so, however, while affirming a universalist ethic, as in the recognition of basic human rights. Communitarians recognize that the loss of cultural identity is a potentially disabling condition, a genuine source of suffering and alienation. Hence, in the jurisprudence of communitarian liberalism rights of cultural membership are acknowledged, as are the virtues of patriotism. In keeping with the spirit of liberalism, however, such membership must be voluntary, at least for adults, and the culture or subculture whose value is at issue must meet a threshold standard of critical morality.

Cultural particularity makes a positive contribution to the enrichment of community. There is much to be gained, in moral strength and subtlety, from intimate acquaintance with a distinctive culture. By experiencing a tradition from within, one can appreciate the nuances of conduct and the principles that underlie law and custom. Therefore, if a people's uniqueness has something worthwhile to offer, its agents should be faithful to their origins. In an international assembly of scholars or statesmen, we do not ask the participants to shed their distinctive identities. On the contrary, we hope to gain from their diversity.

From the standpoint of critical morality, however, parochial experience cannot be treated as an unqualified good. We try to draw from special histories a universal message. To do so is to find a basis for criticizing one's own heritage, not only from within but also in the light of other experiences and more comprehensive interests. This understanding must reject a radical moral or cultural relativism. We may conclude that critical morality entails respect for the particularity and diversity of human cultures. In this way, we make good the liberal commitment to toleration and to the rejection of ethnocentrism. At the same time, we give due weight to the claims of particularity.

NOTES

1. This chapter is in part adapted from *The Moral Commonwealth* (Selznick 1992; see also Selznick 2002).

2. See Selznick 1992, 360–65, where I discuss historicity, identity, mutuality, plurality, autonomy, participation, and integration as elements of community.

3. In Selznick 2002, 17, I refer to "the animating principle of community, which we may call 'the union of solidarity and respect.'"

4. When boundaries are *blurred*, they are not necessarily *eliminated*; and the blurring of boundaries may be quite compatible with specific forms of institutional autonomy. Thus we can uphold the independence of judges, or the special prerogatives of parents, even as we recognize that the boundary between law and politics, or between parenting and teaching, is less definite and more permeable than hitherto understood.

5. Such a view was recently expressed by the British philosopher Stuart Hampshire (1989, 68) who wrote, "one has to ask, in a Hobbesian spirit, what [justice] prevents rather than what it engenders."

6. For a relevant discussion of sociological jurisprudence, see Walker 1988, 368–69, where it is argued that, due to its embrace of "social engineering," "sociological jurisprudence has largely left behind the historical school's tenets and the democratic theory of law in general."

7. When we founded the Center for the Study of Law and Society at Berkeley in 1961, Lon Fuller criticized the name we chose. He preferred "law *in* society" rather than "law *and* society."

REFERENCES

Hampshire, Stuart. 1989. *Innocence and Experience*. Cambridge, MA: Harvard University Press.

Santayana, George. [1933] 1954. *The Life of Reason*. New York: Scribner's.

Selznick, Philip. 1992. *The Moral Commonwealth: Social Theory and the Promise of Community*. Berkeley: University of California Press.

———. 2002. *The Communitarian Persuasion*. Washington, DC: Woodrow Wilson Center Press; Baltimore, MD: Johns Hopkins University Press.

Walker, Geoffrey de Q. 1988. *The Rule of Law: Foundations of Constitutional Democracy*. Melbourne: Melbourne University Press.

2

Living Law Revisited: Communitarianism and Sociology of Law[1]

Roger Cotterrell

The concept of living law (*lebendes Recht*) was part of Eugen Ehrlich's ambitious "laying of foundations" (*Grundlegung*) for legal sociology (Ehrlich 2002). It is the seminal idea which most obviously takes us "back to the beginning in sociology of law" (Nelken 1984). At what seems the very start of the modern history of empirical socio-legal inquiry (Rottleuthner 1998, 227), Ehrlich used this concept to affirm a view of law that would be adopted in different ways by many other scholars: the view that law, even in the context of modern nation states, should be thought of as something more than, and in certain respects very different from, the regulatory products or techniques of the state and its judicial, legislative, or administrative agencies.

The idea of living law locates law's doctrinal sources, regulatory authority and normative essence in communal life, understood in some way as a realm of shared moral understandings or social interaction, and not primarily (if at all) in the purely political authority and coercive power of the state. Law "lives" insofar as it grows from, and is shaped, tested, and sanctioned by the collective experience of individuals interacting in particular social fields or contexts. The forms of social regulation that arise in the many different kinds of association in which people interrelate are forms of living law. The important implication is that, by contrast, state law is *not* alive except in so far as it directly expresses these forms of regulation. It is the hierarchically organized, centrally coordinated, and systematized official law of the state, promulgated and enforced only by its legislative, judicial, and administrative agencies. It may even be *morally dead*; existing not in citizens' moral consciousness and guiding their practices but found only in texts that document the norms guiding decisions (*Entscheidungsnormen*) by state agencies, including courts.

The concept of living law haunts sociology of law. Like a ghost it is neither actually present in contemporary debates nor spiritually absent from them. It expresses insights that have been considered important, perhaps central, to sociological inquiry about law and it is still referred to frequently in the literature. Yet it has been substantially banished from serious theoretical analysis in sociologically oriented writings about modern Western legal systems.

Why might there be profit now in reconsidering this "ghost" in the machine of socio-legal studies? One reason is that it helps to direct us toward alternatives to the dominant paradigm of law underpinning much socio-legal inquiry in contemporary Western (and many other) societies. Many writers, in different contexts and different ways, imply that this paradigm is gradually becoming exhausted. The paradigm of modern Western law has been the law of the nation state considered as a politically produced, rationally unified, normatively distinctive, and primarily instrumental system of regulation, and as a form of knowledge and understanding that is inevitably and appropriately monopolized by lawyers. But this focus now seems less satisfactory than in the past.

The reasons are many. Among them are uncertainties about the capabilities and technical suitability of state law as a directive instrument (see, e.g., Teubner 1987), about its identity, integrity, and relation to other kinds of regulation (Foucault 1991; Ewald 1990; Rose and Valverde 1998), and about the social foundations of its legitimacy (Habermas 1996, 427–46, 449–50). Hence, a consideration of forms of regulation beyond the paradigm case of state law seems increasingly important. Also notable are calls—reflecting felt moral and political needs—to reexplore relationships between law and culture so as to focus more clearly on issues about popular experience and consciousness of law (see, e.g., Merry 1995). It has seemed important, for example, to consider how in the face of the sometimes oppressive power of the state and its law, opportunities for resistance and assertion of freedom can arise from confrontations between professional and popular legal consciousness (see, e.g., Ewick and Silbey 1998; Yngvesson 1993; Merry 1990). Given such priorities, the legal arena may be viewed as extending far beyond the institutions or even the doctrine of state law itself. Finally, it is now generally recognized that old theoretical oppositions between "law" (as state law) and "society" are too simple to address many specific issues in socio-legal research (see, e.g., Nelken 1986). It is important to understand law *in* society (as an aspect of society, rather than an "external" force acting on it). But this may involve reconsidering the nature of law in broad terms. To treat law as an agency of the state seems inadequate, because that is merely to beg the question of the nature of the field of experience which law represents.

In this changing perspective on law, insights about legal pluralism, which the concept of living law helped to focus within sociology of law, and which legal anthropologists have long used in studying non-Western law, now seem increasingly important in studying the law of Western-style nation states. But pluralistic views of the law of contemporary political societies represented by nation states raise a difficult theoretical problem. What concept of *law*, what general view of law's nature, is appropriate to contemporary legal sociology?

The ambiguous position of the idea of living law in the literature of sociology of law is a symptom of this unresolved difficulty. I shall argue that the ambitions which underlay the development of the concept of living law are still important and that these are essentially *moral* ambitions which place questions of values close to the heart of the task of determining an appropriate sociological concept of law. For this reason some philosophical debates about the nature of community and the moral structure of contemporary Western societies are relevant to sociology of law's projects. I shall suggest finally that, despite its notorious vagueness and difficulty, the concept of community (implicit in the idea of living law) has to be returned in some form to the heart of the concept of law itself.

THE "GHOST" OF LIVING LAW

Around 1913, when Ehrlich fully elaborated the concept of living law (Ehrlich 2002), related ideas resonated in the work of many European critics of orthodox legal thought (Rottleuthner 1988; Nussbaum 1940; and see, e.g., Petrazycki 1955; Gierke 1955). But these ideas appeared in the literature at what might seem in retrospect to have been a very inappropriate historical moment. Thus, the advocacy of them often seems, in retrospect, tinged with nostalgia. Max Weber's major writings on sociology of law (Weber 1978) were published only a few years after Ehrlich's work. Weber's sociology was informed by an acute sensitivity to the nature of modern Western state power, and it adopted a sharply contrasting and seemingly far more realistic view of modern law. Weber made the relationship of law and state central to an understanding of modern law. He linked the basis of authority of the modern nation state with the development of modern, formally rational law and treated the relationship between modern law and modern state as essentially symbiotic. Weber associated law, in a "disenchanted" modern world, not with community and the interplay of social interaction and association but with the sort of formal rules that structure modern bureaucracy (in business enterprises no less than state agencies). Law's main link with social (especially economic) relationships was not as their expression but as a state-guaranteed framework of norms available to give them calculability and predictability.

Unlike Weber, Ehrlich offered no systematic sociology, despite his erudition. He presented social insights touristically, with the enthusiasms of the sightseer (Ehrlich 2002, 10–11; and see Ziegert 1979, 228). He may have had only limited appreciation of political and social circumstances beyond his local sphere (Ziegert 1979, 232). Above all, his view of social life was that of a lawyer (ibid., 228, 230, 231). And it has often been remarked that Ehrlich's sociology of law was guided by very practical lawyers' concerns. Immediate experience, for Ehrlich, was the experience of a law professor observing the complex coordination of vastly different social and ethnic groups in an isolated region of the dying Austro–Hungarian Empire at the beginning of the twentieth century. This experience suggested that overloaded expectations were attached to state law and should be reduced (Ehrlich 2002, 71–72; Nelken 1984, 167). The study of living law would assist state officials, including judges, in decision making (Rottleuthner 1988, 232). It would inform state law—the law that lawyers know and use—and help to make it more realistic and more meaningful when applied in everyday social settings.

Ehrlich (2002, 43) writes that sociology of law is not bound by practical considerations. It is a pure science quite different from lawyers' unsystematic methods of analysis. Yet, implicitly, it is a *lawyer's* social science of law. It passionately rejects the social and theoretical preeminence of state law (ibid., 71); yet is produced by a jurist in the service of that law. The German school of "free law finding" of which Ehrlich was a founder, attempted to find a more secure authority for creative development of law by courts, drawing on the social forces surrounding legal institutions, so as to escape mere reliance on the state bureaucratic tradition. It sought to reinforce the status of lawyers and especially judges (Rottleuthner 1988, 239) in circumstances in which the continental European judge's work seemed to have become "a nearly bureaucratic execution of statute orders and prefabricated, codified decisions" (Ziegert 1979, 227). And when Ehrlich's ideas were first promoted in the English-speaking world, it was for their apparent usefulness in showing how to reinvigorate the common-law judge's creativity, then perceived as somewhat moribund (Page 1914, 75). Indeed, Roscoe Pound, Ehrlich's American champion, saw sociology as just such an aid to common-law methods.

This situation—inside the world of state law, yet also outside it—explains many of the incoherences and inadequacies of the concept of living law. There is no way to delimit the concept's scope, except to recognize it as embracing all forms of social regulation, actually operative in any given social field, that are generally regarded as of great social importance and clearly obligatory (Ehrlich 2002, 164–65). Living law can develop in any kind of social association as its internal means of regulation. Such associations can include families, business firms, clubs, partnerships, contracting parties, social classes, corporations, cities, localities, churches, professions, political parties, nations, and international groupings of nations (ibid., 26–27, 54–55). No effort is made to distinguish theoretically these vastly different social and legal contexts (cf. Gurvitch 1973, 117, 121).

Thus, the concept of living law gains coherence only from its polemical purpose: that of setting alongside state law (especially private law) an infinity of types of informal regulation that parallel specific fields of state or lawyers' law. Living law is the ever-present *conscience* of state law; it is the normative evidence of moral life available to monitor lawyers' law and where necessary shake it from moral sterility or social irrelevance. The unity of living law is given only as the *alter ego* of lawyers' law. It has no theoretical unity or precision outside this context.

Before we dismiss the hopelessly incoherent idea of living law, however, we should recognize parallel problems in its contemporary offspring, the concept of legal pluralism—especially as applied to contemporary Western societies in what has been generally termed the "new" legal pluralism (Merry 1988). Legal pluralism emphasizes the diversity of normative systems or regimes interacting with state law and demands that, for purposes of analysis, at least some of these should themselves be recognized as kinds of law. In this context we still have to ask: "What is law and where is it?" (Santos 1987, 281) and "Where do we stop speaking of law and find ourselves simply describing social life?" (Merry 1988, 878). One writer suggests we might need a new Hohfeld or Kelsen to organize the insights of legal pluralism into a general legal theory (Chiba 1989, 3). The problem of living law—what a critic of Ehrlich once called the problem of "megalomaniac jurisprudence" encompassing everything without adequate theoretical discrimination (Allen 1964, 32)--may thus survive in contemporary form. Indeed, Ehrlich notes, with seemingly total unconcern, that the difficulty is like trying to catch a stream and hold it in a pond (Ehrlich 1922, 133; 2002, 488). And it *could* remain a matter of unconcern for a practical-minded jurist. An incoherent notion of living law could serve well enough to marshal critical resources around the lawyer's *coherent* understanding of legal doctrine applied in state courts. For Ehrlich, the only concept of law that needed to be genuinely rigorous was the lawyer's concept of state law.

Contemporary concepts of legal pluralism are, of course, not usually constrained by the lawyers' concerns that explain Ehrlich's situation. The traditions of legal pluralist analysis have been developed primarily by anthropologists, who have been, presumably, relatively free of professional allegiances to lawyers' views of law. The problem for contemporary legal pluralism has been different. Western anthropologists' (and sociologists') paradigm experience of law—suggesting its fully developed form—has usually been that of state law (Snyder 1981, 163–64); whether in settings where customary law has been officially subordinated, incorporated, adapted, or exceptionalized by state law (see Mastura 1994, esp. 474–75; and Chiba 1989); or in the pluralistic legal life of advanced Western societies to which anthropologists (and sociologists) have increasingly directed attention (see, e.g., Greenhouse 1982). To escape the "brooding omnipresence" of the state-law paradigm it has, indeed, often seemed appropriate to cease to talk in terms of law at all when analyzing nonstate forms of regulation (Roberts 1979, chap. 2; and see Snyder 1981, 66–67, 69). The issue, ultimately, is not one about defining law, but rather about the variety of moral settings and sources of regulation and about the kinds of authority that this regulation is able to command.

I want to conclude this brief discussion of the concept of living law on a positive note that will, I hope, suggest why, despite all its problems, the concept captures certain matters of enduring importance. Why was living law so important to Ehrlich that he declared its preeminence over state law even while directing all his work in the service of the latter? I think it was because the accident of the time and place in which he worked gave him an insight into moral and technical problems of state law, which may have seemed much less pressing to most lawyers in stable Western societies in his era than they did to him, but which have gradually come to seem increasingly important. At the time and place in which he wrote, on the edge of an empire whose state was about to disintegrate with the splitting apart of the extremely diverse national, cultural, and ethnic elements of that empire, Ehrlich was acutely aware of the fragility of state law as an effective regulator and of the *moral precariousness* of its authority. His parochial context gave him a very different view of the state and its law from, for example, Weber in Imperial Germany. But it was a view that might have received some sympathy from the other great contemporaneous founder of sociology of law, Émile Durkheim. Writing in a France wrecked by economic and cultural conflicts, Durkheim well understood the fragility of social solidarity and the moral authority of the state (Durkheim 1984, 291–328; Cotterrell 1999, chap. 2; Magraw 1983, chap. 3).

Ehrlich's situation allowed him to see, in a way that seemed archaic through most of the twentieth century but now appears prescient, the particular legal importance of the nation and the community as social associations and hence as moral entities. Ehrlich describes in detail the nation's social complexity as an association in which numerous smaller social associations (for example, economic, cultural, political, religious, and local) exist. Each association or community is portrayed as having its own legitimacy as a system of normatively ordered social relationships. Each has its own problems of maintaining internal integrity and external relations; of regulating its members' conduct in relation to each other and to the association as a whole; of maintaining their allegiance and ordering their participation within it. Ehrlich saw that social associations or communities, giving rise to their own structures of regulation, can exist beyond the scope of the nation, and hence the nation state. He recognized transnational regulation as part of the infinite variety of living law.

Most important is the idea that the state is to be conceptually distinguished from the nation and all other social associations. While allegiance to the state is a matter of the reach of its political authority, allegiance to the nation and other social associations depends on what we might call their broadly moral authority. This authority may be grounded in mutual recognition of congruent personal interests, in emotional attachments, in common traditions or environments, or in shared values or beliefs. But ultimately it is guaranteed by the member's need or wish to remain a part of the association, to stay within its jurisdiction. The ultimate sanction available to enforce the living law of social associations is the threat that the miscreant will be excluded from them. For Ehrlich, it seems, the nature of authority is inseparable from the nature of the types of social relations out of which authority arises. Implicit also are further difficult questions. If law is most truly the living law of social associations, and finds the moral basis of its authority in them, what authority does the lawyer ultimately serve? And where does the citizen's ultimate allegiance lie?

What remains disastrously missing from Ehrlich's picture of law is a specification of the theoretical relationship between the state and social associations. To theorize successfully this relationship would have been to alter lawyers' understanding of the nature of law (as state law) in the light of the sociological insights of living law. Through such an alteration Ehrlich would have cemented the importance of the study of living law for lawyers, as part of their essential intellectual world and professional outlook. But this did not happen. Living law did not disrupt juristic conceptions of law. Lawyers could dismiss Ehrlich's work by saying that living law, however sociologically interesting or relevant in legal policy debates, was simply not a matter of law as far as they were concerned, because it had no defined, specific, and invariant relation to the tasks of the state's legal agencies.

We can thus understand the ghostly presence and absence of the idea of living law in contemporary sociology of law. It is absent because lawyers can bypass it and sociologists are likely to find scant value in its conflation of many different social phenomena in a concept that almost wholly lacks sociological rigor. Nevertheless, the ambition remains for a radical reconceptualization of law in terms of its social conditions of existence and for the purpose of making it more morally responsive to those it purports to regulate. The concept of living law symbolizes that enduring ambition in sociology of law. It captures a part of the critical spirit of the research field. As such it remains powerfully present. The ghost is not likely to be exorcized; nor would it be good to banish it.

THE STATE, THE INDIVIDUAL, AND SOCIAL ASSOCIATIONS

Pluralist perspectives have begun to encourage a reconceptualization of state law in complex Western societies. To take one example from a wide literature, Peter Fitzpatrick (1984) has argued that the coherence of state law is, in certain respects, dependent on the parallel existence of certain other normative fields structured according to normative principles radically different from those of state law. The rule of law doctrine in state law may, for example, depend for its viability as a principle of social ordering on the very differently structured regimes of discipline existing in the workplace or in the prison, which influence the conditions of "docile citizenship" on which the operation of the rule of law depends. Thus state law and other techniques of normative ordering are mutually sustaining. They interpenetrate and shape each other in complex ways (see also Henry 1983; Cooper 1998).

But what principles should guide efforts to rethink state law by reference to other normative systems? We noted that the concept of living law emerged out of worries about the destiny of state law and the techniques, skills, and crafts (especially judicial) that went with it. The effort to import sociology into legal inquiry was an effort to change the direction of state regulation, to reinvigorate its methods of regulation, and make them more responsive to social context. The impulse was to confront state law with its necessary moral conditions of existence and, in the process, to show that, in the context of the modern nation state, these conditions could not sustain a state law with the regulatory ambitions that it had come to assume. Ehrlich associated the over-extended reach of state law in Western European societies with its individualist ethos: the "culmination of individualism is the principle that every man is an end unto himself. . . . The ideal of justice of individualism is the individual and his property, the individual . . . who recognizes no superior but the state, and is not bound by anything but the contracts he has freely entered into" (Ehrlich 2002, 235).

These impulses toward the rethinking of the nature of state law are, above all, moral impulses; to breathe moral life into law, to put it in touch with the sources of its normative authority in everyday moral experience. Similar impulses are found in Durkheim's work, as well as similar serious doubts about the capacity of the state, and of centralized or hierarchically structured state law, to provide morally meaningful regulation.[2] Such worries, linked to observation of state law's frequent remoteness and ineffectiveness, are reflected in some contemporary demands for responsive law (Selznick 1992, 463–76), the product of the state somehow acting in moral partnership with the regulated citizenry.

It is this kind of impulse to rethink the nature and scope of state law that the rest of this chapter seeks to pursue. But because the rethinking is largely motivated by the demand that law embody certain *values* (responsiveness, appropriateness to local contexts, respect for the integrity of community life in some sense, sensitivity to the diversity of moral experience of the regulated population), it easily moves outside the accepted scope of an empirically oriented sociology (and anthropology) of law. After all, value choices are involved in deciding how far to treat living law phenomena as "law"; how much attention to pay to these types of regulation in legal debates; how to think about the state in relation to law; how to conceptualize social associations. Legal sociologists and anthropologists have been prepared increasingly to structure and justify their empirical researches in terms of value-guided critique of law. But there has remained an understandable reluctance to engage in philosophical discussion of ideal social institutions.

Nevertheless, much social inquiry about law, developed within the shadow of the dominant paradigm of state law, *already presupposes* certain foundational values embedded in that paradigm. The paradigm reflects long centuries of lawyers' interpretations of legal ideas and theorization of the nature of law, as well as broader currents of political thought, moral understanding, assumptions about the fundamental character of social life, and reflections on specific historical experiences. It is a paradigm embedded in the modern history and intellectual traditions of Western societies, the societies in which the dominant orientations of sociological inquiry about law have been developed. Ehrlich tried to present living law as morally meaningful law that should force a reconsideration of the dominant paradigm of state law. We need to confront the intellectual resources that inform that paradigm if we are to pursue comparable aspirations.

One way of doing so is through elements of communitarian theory developed in contemporary political philosophy. I do not wish to suggest that communitarian theory as such should be adopted to guide the aspirations of sociology of law. Certainly, much of it inhabits realms of speculation distant from the careful empirical observation of particular conditions of social interaction that has typified the best sociology. But it provides certain valuable themes.

The starting point is a reconsideration of the political and moral situation of the individual citizen. Communitarianism examines analytically the structure of Western liberalism and its individualist legal orientations that Ehrlich noted. For communitarians, the individual is not, as Western liberalism asserts, a socially "unencumbered self" but a social being formed in association with others within communities (Sandel 1984; Taylor 1992, 45). On this view, autonomous individuals gain their very autonomy from the possibility of conceiving of alternative choices and courses of action. And these choices and possibilities are given by the social civilization in which the individual develops (Taylor 1992). Such a claim may entail the suggestion that the support of individual autonomy and freedom is found at least as much in community structures of some kind, as in the state's coercive powers. If the sustaining structures of community wither, the regulatory task entrusted to the state becomes unmanageable. Thus Michael Sandel (1984, 92), a prominent communitarian theorist, observes "what appear simultaneously as the power and powerlessness of the nation state," experienced as "an overly intrusive presence" yet "disempowered," incapable of discharging the regulatory burdens heaped on it. Solutions to problems of state regulation might, therefore, sometimes lie in strengthening structures of community on which the realization of individual autonomy depends.

At the level of individual life, communitarianism observes a sense of loss and longing (ibid., 94–95), so that people are more entangled yet less attached to each other than ever before. In this condition democracy itself becomes enfeebled and lifeless. Democracy becomes less meaningful as the centralization of the regulatory power of the state proceeds (ibid., 93–94). This is because democracy depends on a vital sense of community that makes participation in the processes of shaping regulation worthwhile and important (Selznick 1992, 363–64, 522–24). Hence the meaning of citizenship is a central focus for some communitarian writers (Miller 1992; cf. Bubeck 1999). Particularly important in this context are questions of allegiance and authority. We noted earlier how Ehrlich separated the concept of state from that of nation, seeing the latter as a social association that could thus be the creator of a living law contrasted with state law. Contemporary communitarians sometimes similarly distinguish allegiance to the nation as a community from allegiance to the state (MacIntyre 1985, 254; Miller 1992, 88). Philip Selznick, applying his long experience with issues of sociology of law to develop in detail a communitarian perspective, also stresses a certain moral primacy of community over state (Selznick 1992, 505–10).

From the wealth of communitarian ideas, one other theme is of major importance here. The view of the basis of individual autonomy that communitarianism encourages often entails a different view of rights from the view that predominates in liberal thought and informs much thinking in sociology of law and legal theory. Since the individual is, for communitarianism, not a presocial being but a being whose very essence is socially given through the character of the community in which the individual grows to personhood, it follows that social relations are not to be seen as structured solely or even mainly by the interplay of rights existing independently of some sense of communal good (Taylor 1992; but cf. Miller 1992, 94). Other connections between individuals are stressed by communitarians as reflecting more appropriately the communal structures within which individuality is formed. Hence friendship or care have been emphasized especially by feminist writers as more appropriate models of community relationships (Friedman 1989; Bubeck 1999). From another standpoint the idea of trust, and especially mutual interpersonal trust, might seem a basic element of community (Cotterrell 1995, 325–32).

What should socio-legal scholars make of these ideas? Is communitarianism essentially an idealistic but unrealistic response to the sense of "loss and longing" that its exponents notice and perhaps themselves feel? Empirically oriented legal sociologists are likely to point out the difficulty in treating community as a focus of regulation in the conditions of advanced societies. Contemporary societies are increasingly atomistic; at least, the complexities of legally regulating them seem frequently to involve assuming that they are. The concept of community is applied most easily to premodern social forms—the *Gemeinschaft* and the self-regulating guild, the isolated neighborhood and the clan. Perhaps, then, "'community' stands for the kind of world which is not, regrettably, available to us" (Bauman 2001, 3).

In much communitarian literature a fundamental vagueness about the scale and scope of the communities under discussion persists (Bauman 1993, 44). Sometimes analysis is in terms of the whole range of social associations that Ehrlich had in mind. Often, however, discussion focuses on the polity—the political society of the nation state—as the community. Sometimes it is asserted that no other focus of significant regulatory authority is really viable (Miller 1992). What is important, in this view, is to understand the moral nature of the nation as a focus of allegiance, and the means by which the nation is presented as a focus of moral allegiance.

Very important matters, clearly understood by Ehrlich, seem neglected in much communitarian literature. Is it really possible to think of the whole national political society as a community? Perhaps contemporary experience in many parts of the world confirms that it is; the deep emotions that can attach to the sense of nation are too often underestimated. In most Western nation-state political societies, however, it is difficult to think of the strong consensus on values that has often been associated with the idea of community in the past. Often what exists is a political rhetoric of community values (Cotterrell 1995, 242–43), community constructed or imagined for specific political projects. Alasdair MacIntyre links ideas of community with traditional virtues that he sees modernity as having undermined. MacIntyre (1985, 252) asserts: "our [Western nation-state] society cannot hope to achieve moral consensus"; there are simply too many competing moral concepts—views of justice—that cannot be rationally resolved. Thus, for MacIntyre, community—understood as the locus of morality—has to be thought of in terms of a different (if variable) scale from that of the nation state.

Communitarianism, nevertheless, usefully encourages a radical rethinking of the relationship between state and individual. It challenges the view of this relationship that underpins much Western philosophy and legal thought and has been carried into the paradigm informing much socio-legal scholarship. Communitarianism does not provide adequate resources for this rethinking partly because—as a philosophical movement—it lacks sufficient sociological commitment to the empirical examination of social differences, the sheer diversity of Ehrlich's social associations. But in its alternative view of rights, individual autonomy, and the location of regulatory authority, it challenges foundational assumptions about the character, functions, and limits of state law and the forms of justice it offers.

It is worth mentioning here the very important discussion in Michael Walzer's book *Spheres of Justice* of the complexity and variety of principles of justice and of their application that arise in different social spheres in complex modern societies (Walzer 1985). Walzer's concern is not with differences between localities or specific social or cultural groups, which have been the traditional focus of much pluralist writing about legal regulation. He looks rather at many different types of social goods (for example, commodities, offices of responsibility, work, leisure, education, respect and recognition, and political power) in connection with which a modern state must establish regulatory principles of justice for their distribution. Walzer addresses the important point that social relationships requiring regulation and the appropriate principles of their regulation may vary greatly as between these different spheres of distribution.

Where then do communitarian ideas take us if we introduce them into sociolegal studies? They carry into modern debate a sense of dissatisfaction with the unmediated relationship of state and individual: the same sense that made Ehrlich use the concept of living law to try to prise apart that relationship. In some forms they import a conservatism—a reverence for traditional ways and social forms—which is also present in some of Ehrlich's thinking. But, although critical thought in legal scholarship may be an effort to break away from some of the agendas of modernity, it cannot properly lead to efforts to return to the past. It may, indeed, be important to see law as an institution supporting communication across cultural diversity, as much as an instrument for politically steering society (Habermas 1986, 1996). But law today cannot be the law of some reinvigorated *Gemeinschaft*. In any case, few people would welcome such a possibility.

One way of avoiding a drift to conservatism is to affirm that, in general, community structures meriting legal protection or expression or even, in some cases, possessing a degree of regulatory authority of their own in partnership with that of the state, should be open and voluntary. Thus, they will allow, as far as possible, free movement into them and, certainly, out of them. Where unfettered freedom of entry is impracticable, qualifications for entry should be based on achieved merit, not ascribed status. Such general propositions are, however, not always applicable. At the very least, they require much elaboration not possible here. Indeed, it is a further virtue of some writing on communitarian ideas that it explores contrasting principles of group membership arising in such diverse social associations as clubs, families, neighborhoods, and nations.[3]

Another way to limit the conservative aspects of communitarian perspectives is to reduce the traditional emphasis on shared values as a central defining aspect of any community. Ehrlich's view of social associations has some continuing merit here, too. He focuses on mutual interaction as the essence of these associations, though, of course, that may involve—or be premised on—adherence to commonly held values or beliefs. Some modern communitarians stress that in seeking community bonds in national culture, "the common culture we are looking for must be of a relatively thin kind" (Miller 1992, 93). Unifying values may be limited.

If, for example, the idea of mutual trust is taken as central to community, then the shared values essential to community will only be those needed to enable this trust to exist and flourish. They will vary depending on the nature of the trusting relationships that characterize different types of community. From such a standpoint it is appropriate to think of communities not as social groups or populations but rather as *types of social relations* intertwined in often intricate ways to create social networks (Cotterrell 1997). Social life can be more or less communally organized depending on the extent of the development of mutual trusting relationships within it. And regulation—informed by the insights of socio-legal research—might be consciously shaped to foster and support such relationships.

A third way to counter the conservatism of some invocations of community is to stress that relations of community are always to be understood, from a certain standpoint, as relations of power. A focus on community cannot properly displace a concern with the analysis of power and its links to law, but makes this central. Communities are sites of conflict, as much as of harmony. The idea that they could be regulated to make them never the former and always the latter has often led, in practice, to unlimited repression (Bauman 2001, 4–5, 96–97). As relations of dependence, mutual trusting relationships are rarely evenly balanced. Nevertheless, solidarity and stability in relations of community, and the possibility that those relations can provide a source of moral authority for regulation, rely on a *limiting* of extremes of power and on the existence of *mutual* reliance and the recognition of *cross*-dependencies (Cotterrell 1995, 330). So power, productively pervading social relations but also giving rise to "major dominations" (Foucault 1979, 93–96), must be studied as an aspect of community.

Legal sociologists are accustomed to working with specific, concrete hypotheses. Abstract ideas in sociology of law are usually and properly developed not from general philosophical speculations but in relation to particular projects of empirical inquiry. The material introduced in this chapter may seem remote from such necessary foci of research. Nevertheless, it seems clear, from a variety of general discussions of socio-legal studies—especially perhaps from many recent assessments of American law-and-society research—that there is a sense of a need to reconsider directions of effort.

I certainly do not wish to suggest that socio-legal studies should incorporate the philosophical outlook of communitarianism; nor that they should shift their focus from the numerous pressing problems arising in the analysis of contemporary forms of state law in advanced nation states. As a field that has been shaped by the broad aspirations of social science, however, socio-legal scholarship has established its credentials in relation to particular paradigms of both science and law. These paradigms now seem to be changing fundamentally. The idea of science that has typified the modern age has been the idea of science overcoming nature, and so dispelling the dangers that unregulated nature presents for humankind. The comparable modern idea of law has been that of law overcoming culture, and so dispelling the ignorance and irrationality which modern thought has often associated with the traditional in culture.

Nowadays there is a tendency to emphasize a need to protect nature against science, and perhaps to protect culture against law. This tendency should not be allowed to weaken the commitment to a social science of law. But it should make us recognize that socio-legal studies must treat with great seriousness the need to nurture diverse moral conditions of human interaction and, indeed, of human interaction with nature. I have argued that a certain ambition was implied in the founding conceptions of modern sociology of law with which this chapter has been concerned. It was to require state law to cooperate pluralistically with other forms of regulation precisely in order to respect and regulate moral diversity and so preserve and enhance law's own regulatory authority. Such an ambition remains no less relevant today, nearly a century after the concept of living law began its complex intellectual history.

NOTES

1, This chapter is a substantially revised version of a paper originally presented at the meeting of the International Sociological Association Research Committee on Sociology of Law, Kobe, Japan, in August 1995.

2. See Cotterrell 1999 for detailed analysis of Durkheim's sociology of law and morality.

3. See especially Walzer 1985, chap. 2; and cf. the contrast drawn between genetic and voluntary associations in Ehrlich 2002, 28.

REFERENCES

Allen, Carleton K. 1964. *Law in the Making*. 7th ed. Oxford: Oxford University Press.

Avineri, Shlomo, and Avner de-Shalit, eds. 1992. *Communitarianism and Individualism*. Oxford: Oxford University Press.

Bauman, Zygmunt. 1993. *Postmodern Ethics*. Oxford: Blackwell.

———. 2001. *Community: Seeking Safety in an Insecure World*. Cambridge: Polity Press.

Bubeck, Diemut. 1999. A Feminist Approach to Citizenship. In *Gender and the Use of Time*, ed. Owlen Hufton and Yota Kravaritou, 401–28. The Hague: Kluwer Law International.

Chiba, Masaji. 1989. *Legal Pluralism: Toward a General Theory through Japanese Legal Culture*. Tokyo: Tokai University Press.

Cooper, Davina. 1998. *Governing Out of Order: Space, Law and the Politics of Belonging*. London: Rivers Oram Press.

Cotterrell, Roger. 1995. *Law's Community: Legal Theory in Sociological Perspective*. Oxford: Oxford University Press.

———. 1997. A Legal Concept of Community. *Canadian Journal of Law and Society* 12:75–91.

———. 1999. *Émile Durkheim: Law in a Moral Domain*. Stanford: Stanford University Press.

Durkheim, Émile. 1984. *The Division of Labour in Society*. Trans. W. D. Halls. London: Macmillan.

Ehrlich, Eugen. 1922. The Sociology of Law. *Harvard Law Review* 36:130–45.

———. 2002. *Fundamental Principles of the Sociology of Law*. Trans. Walter L. Moll [1936]. Repr. New Brunswick, NJ: Transaction Publishers.

Ewald, François. 1990. Norms, Discipline, and the Law. *Representations* 30:138–61.

Ewick, Patricia, and Susan S. Silbey. 1998. *The Common Place of Law: Stories from Everyday Life*. Chicago: University of Chicago Press.

Fitzpatrick, Peter. 1984. Law and Societies. *Osgoode Hall Law Journal* 22:115–38.

Foucault, Michel. 1979. *The History of Sexuality*, vol. 1, *An Introduction*. Trans. R. Hurley. London: Allen Lane.

———. 1991. Governmentality. In *The Foucault Effect: Studies in Governmentality*, ed. Graham Burchell, Colin Gordon, and Peter Miller, 87–104. Hemel Hempstead: Harvester Wheatsheaf.

Friedman, Marilyn. 1989. Feminism and Modern Friendship: Dislocating the Community. *Ethics* 99:275–90.

Gierke, Otto von. 1958. *Natural Law and the Theory of Society*. Trans. E. Barker [1934]. Repr. Cambridge: Cambridge University Press.

Greenhouse, Carol J. 1982. Nature Is to Culture as Praying Is to Suing: Legal Pluralism in an American Suburb. *Journal of Legal Pluralism* 20:17–35.

Gurvitch, Georges. 1973. *Sociology of Law*. Repr. [1947]. London: Routledge and Kegan Paul.

Habermas, Jürgen. 1986. Law as Medium and Law as Institution. In *Dilemmas of Law in the Welfare State*, ed. Gunther Teubner, 203–20. Berlin: Walter de Gruyter.

———. 1996. *Between Facts and Norms: Contributions to a Discourse Theory of Law and Democracy*. Trans. W. Rehg. Cambridge: Polity Press.

Henry, Stuart. 1983. *Private Justice: Towards Integrated Theorising in the Sociology of Law*. London: Routledge and Kegan Paul.

MacIntyre, Alasdair. 1985. *After Virtue: A Study in Moral Theory*. 2nd ed. London: Duckworth.

Magraw, Roger. 1983. *France 1815–1914: The Bourgeois Century*. London: Fontana.

Mastura, Michael O. 1994. Legal Pluralism in the Philippines. *Law and Society Review* 28:461–75.

Merry, Sally E. 1988. Legal Pluralism. *Law and Society Review* 22:869–96.

———. 1990. *Getting Justice and Getting Even: Legal Consciousness among Working-Class Americans*. Chicago: University of Chicago Press.

———. 1995. Resistance and the Cultural Power of Law. *Law and Society Review* 29:11–26.

Miller, David. 1992. Community and Citizenship [1990]. Repr. Avineri and de-Shalit, 85–100.

Nelken, David. 1984. Law in Action or Living Law? Back to the Beginning in Sociology of Law. *Legal Studies* 4:157–74.

———. 1986. Beyond the Study of "Law and Society": Henry's *Private Justice* and O'Hagan's *The End of Law*. *American Bar Foundation Research Journal*: 323–38.

Nussbaum, Arthur. 1940. Fact Research in Law. *Columbia Law Review* 40:189–219.

Page, William H. 1914. Professor Ehrlich's Czernowitz Seminar of Living Law. In Proceedings of the 14th Annual Meeting of the Association of American Law Schools, December 28, 29, and 30, 1914, 46–75. Chicago: Association of American Law Schools.

Petrazycki, Leon. 1955. *Law and Morality*. Trans. Hugh W. Babb. Cambridge, MA: Harvard University Press.

Roberts, Simon A. 1979. *Order and Dispute: An Introduction to Legal Anthropology*. Harmondsworth: Penguin.

Rose, Nikolas, and Mariana Valverde. 1998. Governed by Law? *Social and Legal Studies* 7:541–51.

Rottleuthner, Hubert. 1988. Three Legal Sociologies: Eugen Ehrlich, Hugo Sinzheimer, Max Weber. In *European Yearbook in the Sociology of Law 1988*, ed. Alberto Febbrajo, 227–59. Milan: Giuffrè.

Sandel, Michael. 1984. The Procedural Republic and the Unencumbered Self. *Political Theory* 12:81–96.

Santos, Boaventura de Sousa. 1987. Law: A Map of Misreading: Toward a Postmodern Conception of Law. *Journal of Law and Society* 14:279–302.

Selznick, Philip. 1992. *The Moral Commonwealth: Social Theory and the Promise of Community*. Berkeley: University of California Press.

Snyder, Francis G. 1981. Anthropology, Dispute Processes and Law: A Critical Introduction. *British Journal of Law and Society* 8:141–80.

Taylor, Charles. 1992. Atomism [1979]. Repr. Avineri and de-Shalit, 29–50.

Teubner, Gunther. 1987. Juridification: Concepts, Aspects, Limits, Solutions. In *Juridification of Social Spheres: A Comparative Analysis in the Areas of Labor, Corporate, Antitrust and Social Welfare Law*, ed. Gunther Teubner, 3–48. Berlin: Walter de Gruyter.

Walzer, Michael. 1985. *Spheres of Justice: A Defence of Pluralism and Equality*. Repr. [1983]. Oxford: Blackwell.

Weber, Max. 1978. *Economy and Society: An Outline of Interpretive Sociology*. Trans. Ephraim Fischoff et al. [1968]. Repr. Berkeley: University of California Press.

Yngvesson, Barbara. 1993. *Virtuous Citizens, Disruptive Subjects: Order and Complaint in a New England Court*. New York: Routledge.

Ziegert, Klaus A. 1979. The Sociology behind Eugen Ehrlich's Sociology of Law. *International Journal of the Sociology of Law* 7:225–73.

3

Law and Society in Japan[1]

Toon Peters

LAW IN A COMPARATIVE CULTURAL PERSPECTIVE

According to Alexis de Tocqueville (1856, 407–8n), governments show their true colors in their colonies. It is in the colonies that their characteristics can be observed in a pronounced way and on an enlarged scale. Therefore in order to study the character—and particularly the decadent character—of the government of France under Louis XIV, Tocqueville looked at Canada. It is my thesis that, if we want to get to know the characteristics of Western law, good and bad, the best country to study is Japan. Japan is the only example of a modern society that adopted all the institutions and ideas of Western law but treated them in a completely different, much more differentiated way. In Japan there has been a keener recognition of practical advantages and disadvantages, functions and malfunctions, as well as mental (rather than material) costs and benefits. To increase our insight into the ambiguous relationship between law and society, probably no other study would be more revealing than that of Japan's experience with modern Western law.

In the West, we are accustomed to considering law and society as mutually intertwined. Indeed, law is so much interwoven in our web of social relations—in the way we address social problems, deal with conflicts, shape personal and business relations, organize our activities, conceive authority, fight crime and deviant behavior, pursue policies, and "plan" the future—that it cannot be thought of as separate from our concept of social order. The same applies to our concept of the person: we conceive a person primarily as a *legal* person, as a holder of rights. Without exaggeration, I think we can say that law is not only an essential element of the social order, but that law in fact *constitutes* social order as we know it.

Studying the role of the law in *Japanese* society may help us understand the specifically *Western* nature of our legal concept of society. Law is not only an instrument of our will; it also forms the cultural context that conditions our will: it is a way of thinking and speaking about the reality in which we were raised; a reality that commits us to ideals of rationality, reasonableness, and individual freedom, which we did not invent ourselves. The same circumstance, however, that law is so much part and parcel of our concept of reality and of our moral consciousness makes it difficult for us to become aware of the limitations inherent in them, that is, the blind spots and taboos in our legal consciousness.[2] In modern Japanese society the law is much less interwoven with other aspects of culture and society; law has remained a separate entity, a *corpus alienum*, associated with *certain* principles of order that *compete* with other principles; associated also with a more limited practical value. It is, literally, an artificial language. Many Japanese legal terms have no counterparts in ordinary language, and their precise meaning can only be understood if one knows the terms in German jurisprudence with which these concepts are meant to correspond. It is a language in which only *certain* things can be thought of and expressed, and other things, more essential to the Japanese mind, cannot be expressed. In spite of, or perhaps thanks to, these limitations, Japanese law retains a very specific symbolic value; it articulates values that cannot otherwise be expressed, stresses the existential human interests that Japanese people have in common with non-Japanese, and constitutes the means of communication through which Japanese society, and thus Japanese people, participate in global society.

The circumstances that in the West created a rational system of law conceived in universalistic terms and, I want to stress this, a rational and universalistic frame of legal *thinking*, were nonexistent in the Japanese tradition. I shall briefly discuss the main contrasts. They show how deep was the cultural abyss that had to be bridged when Japan adopted Western law.

The Concept of Moral Order

A first difference lies in how the normative order is conceived. In the European tradition the moral order was thought to derive from transcendental authority, essentially universal, encompassing all of Christianity. All earthly power was subject to this higher moral and legal order, which could be appealed to in case rulers and laws were in conflict with it. The duty to obey was therefore basically provisional: subjects had the right to resist unjust authority. This notion—that all power is subject to law, and that obedience is due to the law and not to those in power—is an essential part of the Western concept of law. In traditional Japanese society such a notion did not exist. The normative dimension of social reality was inherent in the human relations that constituted this reality. Authority had a sacred and therefore "absolute" character; in his private life the individual's moral consciousness was tied to real-life contexts; and Confucianism, adopted from China, provided a moral philosophy that confirmed the existing order.[3]

The Nature of Government Authority

As has often been remarked, the feudal system, as it existed in Japan before the Tokugawa period, roughly corresponded to European feudalism in the Middle Ages (Bloch 1940; Reischauer 1956; Hall 1962; Hintze 1970a).[4] However, the specific features of the European feudal system that were so important for the emergence of modern law did not develop in the Japanese tradition. Firstly, the original, quasi-familial relationship of unquestioning personal obedience of the vassal to his lord, characteristic of the first, military phase of feudalism in Japan, remained largely preserved in the later, political phase.[5] In Europe this relationship evolved into a contractual form that was no longer exclusive and thus could be maintained with several lords, with clearly defined rights and duties. This contractual concept of political authority was highly significant for the development of modern constitutionalism in Europe. Secondly, the circumstance that the Japanese samurai were not able to develop into economically independent landed gentry, as the European feudal aristocracy did, contributed to the fact that in Japan, unlike in Europe, no strong, politically effective class of property owners emerged. Thus, in the Tokugawa period many important feudal lords were deposed or transferred by the supreme political authority, and debts owed by the nobility to the merchant class were annulled by political decree. Finally, the feudal struggle for power, characterized by the pursuit of political hegemony through techniques of exclusion, control, and cooptation, did not, as in Europe, crystallize into a constitutional sharing of powers.[6]

Civil Society

For the development of modern law, the significance of an independent sphere of civil freedom emerging from within the feudal system should not be underestimated. This civil freedom, which first arose in the corporate rights granted to cities, had to be respected by political authorities and could be experienced by the citizens as "innate." When the Japanese rulers sealed off the country from foreign traffic, the development of a politically strong merchant class, and thus also modern civil freedom, was nipped in the bud (Sansom [1961] 1977, chap. 4).

Law as an Independent System of Meaning

Finally, a circumstance that contributed greatly to the development of rational law in the West and for which no equivalent existed in Japan was the presence of a secularized, conceptually elaborated system of legal thought in the form of Roman law, as it was studied and taught at the universities of medieval Europe. Jurists educated at these universities were taught Roman law, and they became increasingly important in public administration and as legal advisers to the emergent middle class.

Certainly law broadly understood, as a way of providing for the maintenance of social order, especially punishing crimes and settling disputes, and for the organization of government, did exist in traditional Japanese society. But if we regard law as typically characterized by a formal articulation of such rules, creating an autonomous system of norms capable of being effective outside the contexts from which they arose, to which contending parties can lawfully appeal, and to which the supreme political authority is committed, then we must conclude that there was no *such* law in Japan before the reception of Western law.

Insofar as law existed in a weak sense, it was sustained by the rulers' interest in a regular tax income and in the maintenance of civil peace. They treated open conflict as in principle illegitimate. This system had no room for jurisdiction in our sense, i.e., settling disputes according to a formal and freely accessible procedure, by an independent judicial body that passes judgment on right or wrong, on the basis of general rules that are valid outside the context of the actual dispute. A dispute had to be settled as quickly as possible, and it was the responsibility of the person with actual authority, in the context at hand, to see to it that this occurred. There was no possibility of appeal beyond the given authority.

WESTERN LAW AND TRADITIONAL JAPANESE MORALITY

So far I have stressed the negative aspects: the absence of law in traditional Japan and of the conditions that could have led to its emergence. It would be wrong, however, to ignore the more positive moral characteristics of traditional Japanese social order, characteristics that may also have a universal significance when viewed from the standpoint of our present predicament (Peters 1989). (I will come back to this.) I want to point to the value of an immanent morality, inherent in social relations, situated in group life, which demands that we govern our actions by what social reality as a "going concern" requires of us. I want to draw your attention to the motivating force of the personal instead of the objective and business-like in social relations; to the dynamics of human relations when interactive reciprocity prevails over formal contractual bonds. Finally, I want to indicate also the moral value of the subordination of self-interest to the interest of the community.[7] These are certainly values whose cultural significance in our present situation cannot be denied. Awareness of those traditional values fed moral resistance against far-reaching restructuring of Japanese society on the model of Western law.

According to many Japanese, among whom are renowned politicians and scholars, such a restructuring, if unrestrained by a moral consciousness based on traditional values, would destroy the society as a *community*.

The first motive for taking over Western law was Japan's wish to lift the unequal trade agreements that the Western imperialist powers had forced upon Japan in the second half of the nineteenth century. Through these agreements Japan lost its autonomy with respect to tariffs, and had to accept extraterritoriality clauses, which removed subjects of foreign powers in Japan from the jurisdiction of the Japanese government. These concessions amounted to a serious breach of Japanese sovereignty in its own territory. Extraterritoriality clauses were common in the agreements between Western and non-Western nations, because the former did not want to entrust their subjects to a non-Western system of justice. It soon became clear to the Japanese that the Western states would not modify these unfavorable agreements if the Japanese did not first introduce a Westernized system of law.

The first two of many Japanese sent abroad to study Western law, Tsuda Mamichi and Nishi Amane, attended lectures at Leiden University (Feenstra 1981). Here, for the first time, they became acquainted with civil law and with the concept of individual entitlement to subjective, private rights. But the Japanese soon discovered that the Dutch had largely taken over their civil law from the French, and so their attention shifted first to France, later to Germany. The Japanese discovery of Western law is a fascinating and illuminating story. This reception of Western law is a spectacular example of large-scale cultural adaptation, one of the most far-reaching the modern world has seen. Because revising the agreements was evidently important for internal politics, the process was rushed and received a great deal of attention. In a formal sense one could say that the reception of Western law was settled within a few decades.

A second motive was added as the Japanese became better acquainted with Western law. The Japanese authorities discovered a practical benefit in this system of law: it could be used as a rational system for the organization of a modern, strong state, a state that, in Japan's part of the world, would be able to resist the pressures of Western powers. In other words, they discovered the instrumental meaning of the law—law as social technology.

Yet a third motive appeared when the Japanese that studied Western law became familiar with the ideals behind legal concepts and doctrines, as well as with the underlying social presuppositions. They realized that the concept of subjective rights was based on the notion of respect for the individual as an autonomous social and moral actor; that subjective rights guaranteed a sovereign freedom to the ordinary people of a nation, which was to be respected by the government; that Western constitutional law rested on the idea that government power should be limited and distributed over various independent bodies; that under a constitutional regime the people should participate in affairs of state through parliamentary representation.

The Japanese were unanimous with regard to the first aim, the lifting of the unjust agreements. They were also united with regard to the general desirability of strengthening the state by means of a modern legal system. A strong state was unanimously regarded as a precondition for national independence, and also for any further liberties people might be able to gain for themselves, within their political community. There was disagreement, however, on the third reason for accepting Western law—the ideals it generated and encouraged. The government elite favored a restricted use of Western law, as an instrument of government. In addition the traditional elites, and increasingly other groups as well, who were excluded from positions of power in the new Japanese state, welcomed the Westernized law insofar as it enhanced their own benefits and freedoms.

THE MEANING OF THE RECEPTION OF WESTERN LAW

The cultural significance of the reception of Western law in Japan can be summarized in four characteristics. First, it particularly concerned the introduction of a new language: a system of new meanings that gave expression to ideas and desires for which there formerly had been no words. Second, this new system of meanings was largely counterfactual, that is, gave expression to many things that did not yet exist and whose empirical preconditions had not yet been realized. Third, there was a paradox in the way Western law was introduced: new rights *against* the government were introduced *by* the government, which meant that from the beginning the practical significance of those rights was greatly limited. Fourth, there arose a normative dualism, a clash and competition of value systems, one embodied in the Westernized legal system, the other upholding traditional Japanese culture. We shall briefly discuss each of these characteristics.

Law as a New Language

The most important effect of the introduction of Western law in modern Japanese society lies in the fact that it established a system of concepts, principles, and meanings that did not exist in the Japanese cultural tradition. Western law brought with it a legal image of society. This entailed a new interpretation of society as constituted by formal rules and clearly delineated, that is, limited types of authority; social relations conceived in terms of individual rights; procedural regulations for the official exercise of power, as in maintaining order and in prosecuting and punishing criminals; and the legitimacy in principle of disputes and criticism. The law provided a new language in which new desires and new, modern ideals of freedom, equality, individualism, and protection against arbitrary use of power could be expressed. As stated before—and I will return to this point later—the governing elite was worried about this: Would everything turn out all right? Would government remain in control? Would the people remain obedient? Would they not, while primarily concerned about their rights, forget about their duties?[8]

Counterfactual Character

The introduction of the new law did not mean that it became a reality in social life. For that, it would have to be observed and used in practice; and an *awareness* of law was required, a consciousness of one's *rights*, a new political culture of citizenship. The clearest example of this understanding is found in a text by Ueki Emori (1927), the major advocate of a democratic constitution, on the freedom and the rights of the people:[9] it is essential that people claim and defend their rights; silently tolerating injustice is a source of misery. In another text, Ueki (1880) stressed the great importance of freedom of thought and speech for checking arbitrariness at the administrative level. In practice, of course, life in Japan remained largely controlled by the old principles and meanings, by a culture of hierarchical subservience. It was Fukuzawa Yukichi, Japan's leading intellectual in the initial period of the modern era, who showed the best understanding of this problem. He was critical of the movement that pleaded for a parliamentary system of government and of its tendency to focus political discussion on state power, for this consolidated the old idea that the government represented everything valuable. Instead he called for developing and strengthening the autonomous, private sphere, in which people think and act independently, and in which they defend their rights. An awareness of *private law* was, in his view, more important than participation in political power. I will briefly quote his last speech, delivered on September 24, 1898 (Fukuzawa 1962, 753–59; Oxford 1973, 187–93).

Fukuzawa started with the observation that there had been no law in the past: the feudal lords had ruled their people in the way they had wanted. Even if there was some kind of legislation, this was kept secret for the people. After the opening-up of the ports, and particularly after the Meiji Restoration, however, the political structure changed fundamentally. "Today's world," according to Fukuzawa, "is a world of law." At first this law was considered a matter for government only. But it became increasingly clear that law was also important for ordinary people, especially in business. Without knowledge of the law, people were not even able to manage their own households: "Before you're aware of it, other people will have stolen your money, land, and house."

Fukuzawa also spoke about the meaning of law in the protection of human rights: "Two or three months have passed since the civil law was introduced.

In the chapter on the family, there are about twenty articles describing the various grounds for divorce. Up to now, however, hardly anybody has made use of this right: only one woman in Tokushima . . . and one in Tokyo! These women are the only ones who have filed for a divorce on the grounds of cruelty by their husbands. They wanted a divorce, but their husbands refused. Therefore the women presented their cases to the judge. . . It is hard to believe that these are the only cases in this large country! There must be at least two thousand, perhaps twenty thousand cases of women who are beaten daily by their drunken husbands! Of all the families in Japan only these two cases of men beating their wives have been exposed. This shows that Japanese people know little yet about law." So far Fukuzawa.

Considering the Japanese customs at the time it is perhaps more remarkable that so soon after the introduction of civil law two women were so courageous as to enter into a lawsuit involving their husbands! Fukuzawa's message is clear, however: in order to realize the new law, the existing culture had to be transformed; people had to become aware of their rights, and they needed the courage to claim those rights. This *conception of law as a project*—a project of radical change of traditional society and culture—was, initially, only latent. It became, however, increasingly recognized, particularly in its negative implications for the traditional system of values, which in the thirties gave rise to strong rejection. But this conception of law as a project came into its own after World War II, when fundamental social reform became the *explicit purpose* of the law.

Half-Hearted Constitutionalism

The dominant role played by the government in the process of introducing Western law meant that an important function of law—fostering and enabling social criticism—remained mostly undeveloped. The government's role was in turn closely connected with the character of the Meiji Restoration as an "aristocratic revolution" (Smith 1966). After a group within the ruling elite seized power, changes in state and society were forced *top down*. This also applied to the new legal system, with its notions of civil autonomy and equality, horizontal rather than vertical solidarity, and restraint of government power. The importance the law would have for society was greatly determined by the authoritarian context of its introduction. This context explains how "innate" human rights, "granted by heaven," could at first, for example by Ueki Emori, be interpreted as rights granted by *the state* (Ishida 1975).

In view of the growing popularity of democratic and liberal ideas from the West, which gained momentum during the 1870s in the Movement for Freedom and the People's Rights (Ike [1950] 1969), the institution of a constitutional government was certainly not without risks for the ruling elite. The elite sought to minimize these risks. The constitution was not introduced before a system of laws and regulations had been developed giving all the power to the government. Particularly important were the extensive authority of the state police and the restrictions on freedom of speech, association, and assembly. The Japanese constitution of 1889 showed this inner contradiction, which indeed characterized most of the *European* constitutions of the Restoration period. A limited or half-hearted constitutionalism was accepted.

Normative Dualism

In the West we are familiar with the gap between law in theory and law in practice. From a comparative, cultural perspective we have to remark, however, that here such discrepancies are mostly understood against the background of an underlying continuity between the premises of formal law and the standards maintained in practice. After the introduction of Western law in Japan there were, however, *contradictory* principles of normative order. Western law brought with it a different, more universalistic conception of social order whereby sacredness was located in the individual rather than, as Japanese tradition would demand, in communal relations. Many people, especially those who had positions of power, found it difficult to accept the legal model of social order. They rejected its implications for criticism of authority and disliked its moral implications as well. To others the system had a strong appeal, for its promise of emancipation. Since their first acquaintance with the ideas of Western law, politicians and intellectuals have debated the validity of these ideas in the Japanese context. This always involved the clash of interests, including class-related interests. Therefore the struggle came to be seen as a fundamental social conflict—one that, incidentally, was more and more suppressed by those in power. The foreign system of law received formal acceptance, but the legitimacy of the ideals associated with this law remained controversial. At the same time, the national tradition lost its moral self-evidence. Often it took ingenious means to maintain those aspects of the tradition people wanted to preserve against the trends of the period. In its strictly instrumental sense the law could, to a certain extent, be given a place in the traditional system of values; in its ideal sense, however, it was mostly diametrically opposed. Since the French Revolution modern times have not witnessed a sharper confrontation of social ideas within one culture. I think this dualistic legal orientation, which has since characterized modern Japanese society, has created a certain moral schizophrenia, which I often noticed in my discussions with Japanese lawyers, and which was experienced by many Japanese Christians. Uchimura Kanzo's "Jesus and Japan"[10] comes to mind, but he was certainly not the only one. As a well-known senior professor of civil law recently told me: "We, Japanese jurists, have of course a juridical way of thinking, and we love the law, but deep inside we are also Japanese." I cannot imagine there being *one* among my present colleagues that experiences any tension at all between his being a jurist and his being Dutch.

LAW, POWER, AND MORALITY

Two themes can be distinguished in the normative issues described. First, the tension between legal ideals and power in the state and in other social contexts; and second, the moral character of modern society. In the minds of most protagonists these themes were intertwined, not separate. The government presented itself, mostly in good faith, as a moral authority. And those who sought a moral order supervised by government, fearing that an exclusive emphasis on rights would lead to social disintegration, almost always started from a benevolent conception of authority. For them, "power" was not problematic.

As I indicated above, the initial reactions to Western law—whose introduction was thought necessary to retain national independence—were by no means wholly negative. However, as the state became increasingly authoritarian, negative reactions gained more and more importance. This ideological rejection had two aspects, which should be distinguished for purposes of a modern understanding of law and society: a *repressive* posture and, at the same time, a *valid moral concern* for human well-being in modern society.

Law and Power

In the period prior to the proclamation of the Meiji Constitution in 1889, the confrontation between law and power took spectacular shape in the Movement for Freedom and the People's Rights. This movement, through its numerous political meetings, manifestations, petitions, publications,[11] and educational activities, created a *critical public* counterposed to government. A similar development took place in the constitutional politics of the period after World War II. (I will come back to this.) Demands and protests, using the language of law, evoked the political philosophies of Rousseau, Mill, Spencer, and others. But they were also fed—as the historian Irokawa Daikichi has stressed ([1970] 1985, esp. chap. 5; 1967; Bowen 1980, 200–1)—by an authentically democratic sense of justice. Since the state did not respond, the movement developed revolutionary characteristics, and a number of armed insurrections occurred. The government reacted with increasingly repressive measures by the police, and with further restrictions of the freedom of association and assembly. Subsequently these measures became hallmarks of the authoritarian state. The democratization movement circa World War I was not in a position to bring about any changes. Moreover, after World War I, the spirit of the times was soon determined by authoritarian tendencies in many countries. It was within this metaconstitutional, political context that the constitution, with its various elements of the rule of law, could be "given" to the people. Meanwhile, the government set itself the task of directing public opinion and suppressing criticism. A program of moral indoctrination, carried out by the schools, sought to turn all Japanese citizens into obedient, self-sacrificing subjects.

There was an element of truth in the opinion of the Japanese leaders that law was not the only important factor in social life, and that the state could only exist on the basis of a common moral awareness. A wholly autonomous law does not supply the moral conditions for its *adequate* functioning. A state under the rule of law can only exist *within a political community*, but it cannot create such a community. This was clearly understood by Ito Hirobumi, the most prominent politician at the time of the establishment of the constitution, who expressed it well in his famous speech to the secret council on July 18, 1888 (Inada 1987, 567–68; Pittau 1967, 177–78). The constitutional governments of Europe, he pointed out, were all based on the Christian religion, which pervaded the hearts of the people and created a fundamental unanimity. If, and here I paraphrase, such a fundamental, moral unanimity can be taken for granted, then government may confine itself to protecting civil liberties and creating guarantees against abuses of power. Ito thought that neither Buddhism nor Shinto could play the same role in Japan as Christianity did in Europe. Only the worship of the Imperial House could provide the necessary moral bond.

Law and Morality

Ito's views led to an ideology of the "family state." I want to suggest, however, a different way of thinking about law and morality, one that looks to the *opposition* of law and family. I have in mind the contrast between understanding human relations in legal terms or, on the other hand, as constituted by bonds of personal commitment. In this perspective authority has a special *function*, and is subject to evaluation in the light of that function. Shorn of that focus, the "state as family" readily degenerates into an ideological instrument of moral manipulation. In this context I would like to call attention to a discussion of "good faith," by one of the leading lawyers of modern Japan, Makino Eiichi (1926). According to Makino the law can only contribute to a viable human society if it is motivated, guided, and qualified by a sense of moral solidarity, as we find it in family relations. Families, he argued, are outstanding examples of natural moral communities, which nurture and support the most important traditional duties. When a concept of family law oriented toward individual rights was about to be introduced into the first draft of a civil code, there was fierce resistance. Many people considered a civil code based on individual rights a direct threat to morality.[12] The democratic reform of family law after World War II, in which the legal status of individual family members was improved, met similar resistance, particularly from Makino (Steiner 1987, 191ff.) who, by the way, was a declared opponent of *arbitrary* authority exercised by the paterfamilias (Tokoro 1974). In both cases the main point of resistance was the belief that the new law would impair the *full* and *moral* character of family relations. Here I should like to remind you of the fact that in our own times many people, including Jürgen Habermas (1981, 2:489–547), have pointed to the destructive consequences of the individualizing law of the welfare state on Western family life.

Makino began his treatise on good faith with an observation about the tension between law and morality—a tension also recognized in the Western tradition. As an example he presented the well-known controversy about the validity of the contract in Shakespeare's *The Merchant of Venice,* which required Antonio to forfeit a pound of his flesh to Shylock if he failed to pay his debt on time. Makino compared this case with a decree by the Japanese Supreme Court in 1920 concerning the repurchase of property. Shakespeare's case dramatically illustrated the contrast between a strictly *legal* attitude and a *moral* attitude, which would of course refrain from legal action that must lead to a barbarous act, in this case, a man's death.

As regards the second case mentioned by Makino, the Japanese civil code grants the repurchase of property by the seller if the right to do so has been claimed in the original agreement, and if the seller refunds the purchase price and transaction costs. Here the seller had met the conditions, but due to an error in calculating the costs he had paid the buyer only 527 yen instead of the 529 yen he owed. On this ground the buyer had refused to agree to the repurchase.

Invoking the principle of good faith, the Japanese Supreme Court ruled in favor of the seller. Of course the latter had to make up the difference, but when the buyer used this small difference to deny the validity of the repurchase, he acted contrary to the principle of good faith in contractual relations. As Makino put it: a strict conception of the law as shown by Shylock can only serve the interest of one party. Such a legal conception may be valid law in a *formal* sense, but it can never be just for *both* parties. With such a legal conception the other party always has to be alert. Society would become a painful affair if we should try to put such a law into practice! Nobody could tolerate a situation like that for a long time! For the legal system all contracts, certificates, statutory regulations, and legal instruments would be no more than weapons in the struggle for life. In the repurchase case, as decided by the Supreme Court, law and contract were not regarded as *weapons*, but as means of mutual help and cooperation.

Makino contrasted the individualistic legal mentality of modern civil society with the social and moral mentality of traditional feudal society. The relation between lord and vassal in feudal times—it seems Makino primarily had in mind the relation between lord and vassal in Europe, although later he also mentioned the "path of the samurai"—certainly had a contractual aspect, but this relation was more than a contract. It constituted a context in which the lord accepted and protected the vassal as a whole person, and the vassal owed unconditional obedience to the lord. In later times this bond was loosened, and reduced to a more purely contractual relationship: one independent, individual interest was linked to another independent, individual interest. The motto, according to Makino, became "individual independence and self-respect." The individual's new independence was undoubtedly a good thing, though it was antisocial in that it rejected the earlier conception of mutual protection. The notion that every human being should fend for himself also led to a greater reliance on *property*—as it were as a guarantee *against* others—and *contract* more and more became the preferred means of promoting self-interest. In that emerging context, a strict interpretation of rights and obligations came to seem appropriate.

In the 1920s and 1930s there was widespread reaction against this nineteenth-century liberal individualism. In Japan the trend harked back to older, more communal values. This development is of special interest to me, for it was far more than just another manifestation of the spirit of the times. The revival of those older values—Makino mentions feudal bonds of solidarity—is a quest for those intrinsically social and morally binding values that are weakened and even rejected by a legal system based on individualism.

According to Makino, some of that older, elementary solidarity was preserved in prewar Japanese family law. Under Japanese civil law there could be no contract between husband and wife: their relation was governed by a duty of mutual support. Also, according to the penal code, theft within the family was not a punishable act. This means that in the context of the family people could not engage in legal quarrels; the moral standard of mutual solidarity did not allow this. Makino did not plead *against* modern contract law and property law, but he did argue for their *moralization*—later called "socialization" in the West (see esp. Valkhoff 1938). Through the principle of good faith—derived from *Gemeinschaft*-type relations, such as the feudal bond between lord and vassal, and the family—legal relations could be understood as normatively embedded in a moral solidarity that precedes and transcends the legal relation and governs its interpretation. In such contracts the law is an *element*, an *aspect*, but does not *constitute* the relation.

In this plea for the family model as the standard for contractual and other relations, we discern a clear turn away from a social order based on *law* toward a social order based on *morality*. This also became manifest in the requirement of mediation in labor disputes, as well as in rent and lease cases. Here the family model became an ideological weapon in the class struggle, a means to save often repressive, patriarchal relations of authority where these were about to disappear as a result of developments in the capitalist economy. But the turn away from the law was also expressed *within* the law, in the preference for *certain* notions and doctrines adopted from European law, such as good faith, the prohibition of abuse of right, the doctrine of judicial activism, and, in penal law, the ideas of the Modern School, where the emphasis was not on legal protection against government power, but on correction and education of the criminal. As stated above, it is important to distinguish the repressive aspects discernible here, which became more and more prominent in the period prior to World War II, from the moral objections against the legal model of social order. What remained was the repressive law of the authoritarian state. Yet this was strongly imbued with moralistic ideas and policies. The emphasis was on *indoctrination* and, in the persecution of political delinquents—as is fit in a state understood as a religious community—on confession and reform.[13] The spirit of the repression was more moral than legal.

To conclude my discussion of the Japanese reaction to Western law, I shall briefly discuss the postwar developments.

POSTWAR DEVELOPMENTS

After World War II, inspired by the United States, a second reception of Western legal ideas gave Japanese law a strong new impulse. Most important was the introduction of a democratic constitution. In addition, an entirely new law of criminal procedure was introduced, based on accusation rather than inquisition; education was freed from the repressive ideology of state control; new labor law and a liberalized law of family relations were adopted. Judicial independence was strengthened, the police decentralized, local self-government reinforced, and many other democratizing measures were introduced. With the dismantling of the police state, a critical public sphere came into being, ready to claim and use the new liberties.

With its three principles of sovereignty of the people, pacifism, and respect for human rights, the new constitution was a radical rejection of the ideological structure of the prewar authoritarian state. The latter located sovereignty in the Emperor and thus raised government above the law; sacrified the well-being of its own citizens to a policy of military expansion; and frustrated law's potential for protecting citizens against the arbitrary power of government.

The new law supplied a normative foundation for a large-scale democratic reform of the political and social order. The changes were *initiated* by the American Occupation Forces,[14] but they were *adopted*, *executed*, and *maintained* by the internal democratic forces in Japanese society. Again there was an adoption of "foreign" institutions and ideas, but the majority of Japanese accepted these changes enthusiastically, as a set of ideals and as a program of social reform.[15]

I would like to draw attention to the fact that this time, as before, the country was adopting *counterfactual* law, that is, law embodying a critical alternative to established social practices. In many cases the changes had more to do with form than content, and some were partly canceled after the American occupation ended. An important circumstance is that sections of the government bureaucracy and the conservative party, which remained in power almost without interruption from 1955, rejected some principles of the new law and tried to make revisions, in both form and substance, by reinterpreting the law and by putting their own stamp on administrative practice. However, this revisionism encountered strong resistance from democratic forces and public opinion in Japanese society.

Furthermore, after the American-inspired reform, there continued to be considerable discrepancy between the legal model and the realities of political, administrative, judicial, and social practice. From this it should not be inferred, however, that law is of minor importance in Japanese society. Such a conclusion would overlook law's important role as a source of social criticism in the postwar period. Nowhere else has law had greater significance as a critical counterlanguage, a *counterpoint* (Wertheim 1953), to dominant practices. As a language of criticism the law worked from outside rather than from within the established system. Procedural legalities in parliament and the courtroom were often neutralized by power. Instead, legal ideals took effect in public opinion and political discussion, which could be strong and demonstrative, particularly in protests against rearmament, on behalf of the environment, and, by the Bar,[16] against the repressive character of criminal-law procedures.[17] In this way, law has been a resource for *external* control over prevailing powers and dominant practices.

CONCLUSION

In Japan the connection between law and society is less close, more distanced, than in Western culture. Legal rules and concepts have less importance. Rather, like traditional social relations in the Western past, social practices in Japan follow an immanent morality. The latter springs from and is situated in the dynamics of human interaction.

The Japanese experience shows that, in a modern society as well as in a traditional society, issues of social order can be addressed in ways that are not mainly or distinctively legal. Moreover, to those of us who come from the West, the objections raised to Western law can appear very plausible. They show concern for the precarious nature of social relations and for safeguarding, within those relations, the moral values of community and humanity. Where there is exclusive emphasis on rights and formal rules, those values are easily destroyed. Moreover, the critics often show better insight into human interaction and social structure than is revealed in the assumptions of the Western model of legal order. For the sake of our own Western society—nowadays characterized by a continuous expansion of "rights," which damages rather than serves human dignity; and by ever-increasing dependence on formal, legal, and bureaucratic structuring, without thereby establishing a genuine social order—it would be good for us to reconsider, in light of the Japanese experience, how the connection between law and society should be perceived and evaluated.

In the Japanese political context, however, objection to the rule-of-law model was largely a reaction against law-related ideals of human freedom, especially freedom from abuse of power. The lesson is that, in Japan as elsewhere, the most essential and valuable contribution of law lies in its critical and constitutional function. Law plays its most prominent role when brought into action against arbitrary and repressive rulers. It will be a real achievement, for us in the West as well as for Japan, to cultivate this corrective and restraining function and the legal language of objection and protest, while keeping in mind the limits of law as an instrument for attaining social order and well-being.

NOTES

1. This chapter is the English translation of "Recht en Samenleving in Japan," the 1992 inaugural lecture of the late Antonie A. G. (Toon) Peters at Leiden University (Peters 1993). Trans. Hildegard Penn. The editor is grateful to Masayuki Murayama for his help in checking the use of Japanese proper names, translations, and sources. Printed with permission from the publisher, Kluwer BV, a subsidiary of Wolters Kluwer Nederland.

2. There are vital aspects of human societal life that cannot adequately, or only with difficulty, be understood and appreciated in terms of our legal frame of thought that is premised on equality, individual autonomy, and order-oriented consciousness. Thus Doi Takeo (1973) showed how difficult it is for Westerners to appreciate the concept of "dependence." Also Louis Dumont (1966) showed how much trouble we in the West have with "hierarchy," for which, in his opinion, our modern egalitarian ideology is responsible. Jan Broekman ([1978] 1991, esp. part 3; 1979) brought this cognitive and moral inability back to the structural characteristics of the "legal discourse," which to such a large extent controls our understanding of social reality. Ongoing juridification of society might mean that this legal concept of reality gains more and more exclusive validity, and that thus we also grow more and more unable to appreciate values that are incompatible with the premises of that way of thinking.

3. In this context the sharp characterization of the traditional Japanese value system by Robert Bellah is relevant (1962, 32ff). See also Nakamura Hajime ([1964] 1971, chaps. 34 and 35).

4. Ishii Shiro (1972, chap. 1) also points to some, for the development of modern law salient, differences between Japanese and European feudalism.

5. Here I follow Hintze's distinction (1970a) of phases in the development of feudalism in which different elements were dominant in turn, consecutively (a) the bond of loyalty between warlord and followers, (b) independent rule by the vassal over the feudal estate, and (c) landownership. Hintze's characterization points to a development tendency inherent in the system, which took place in Europe, but not in Japan.

6. Europe saw the development from the feudal system to an estate society, in which the *meliores et maiores terrae* independently represented the land with the lord, and which is the basis of the modern rule of law; this development has *not* taken place in Japan (Hintze 1970b).

7. It is self-evident that this value orientation—*Gemeinnutz geht vor Eigennutz*—can easily take on pathological forms and can be abused, as the recent history of Japan and other (European) countries shows. The possibility of abuse should not blind us for the valid moral essence of personal effort, helpfulness, and sacrifice for the benefit of the common interest.

8. See Gluck (1985, esp. chap. 5), who summarizes the discussions on civil morality at the time.

9. On Ueki's opinions, see Ike [1950] 1969, 129–37; Bowen 1980.

10. "I love two J's . . . one is Jesus, and the other is Japan. I do not know which I love more . . . Jesus and Japan; my faith is not a circle with one center; it is an ellipse with two centers. My heart and mind revolve around the two dear names . . . Jesus makes me a world-man, a friend of humanity; Japan makes me a lover of my country, and through it binds me firmly to the terrestrial globe. . . ." (Uchimura 1967, 349–50).

11. Pittau 1967, 67: "With one or two exceptions the Japanese press had as its *raison d'être* the task of criticizing whatever the government did."

12. Of great importance was the resistance expressed by Japan's major conservative constitutionalist, Hozumi Yatsuka ([1891] 1943). In his opinion too much emphasis had been laid on the development of private law, which threatened to upset the balance between public and private law. Unlike Western, Christian society, where the individual human being was central and where the law originated from the relations between free individuals, Japanese society was based on the family system and ancestor worship. The civil code that was about to be introduced was very much oriented towards the individual and thus had an atmosphere diametrically opposed to this. It attacked the religious foundation of Japanese society. The traditional "path of *pietas*" would thus lose its foundation in law. On this issue see also Murakami 1974, esp. 32ff., 47ff., 52–58.

13. See esp. Mitchell 1992. Also everyday administration of criminal justice in postwar Japan is still characterized by a heavy emphasis on confession and repentence.

14. In the report of the Government Section of the Supreme Commander for the Allied Powers (1949), the democratization operation led by the Americans is documented in 1,300 pages. See also Ward and Sakamoto 1987.

15. The new principles of the postwar constitution were not "foreign" in the sense that they linked up with ideals that had already found their expression in the Japanese tradition, such as individual freedom. The "new" aspect was that these ideals were articulated in concepts and were granted formal, normative status. They were,

in the words of the well-known Japanese historian Ienaga Saburo ([1977] 1983, esp. chaps. 1 and 6), like seeds that fell in fertile soil.

16. In the Japanese judicial system, the Bar has a function of critical opposition to the Ministry of Justice. In a continuous flow of studies and pamphlets published by the Bar, repressive practices and tendencies in law and society are criticized, with reference to human rights.

17. This repressive character of the administration of criminal justice in Japan is closely connected with the institutionalized practice of preventive custody in police cells, and with the dominant position of the police and the Public Prosecutor in criminal investigations. Sharp criticism of this has been delivered by Japan's most prominent liberal criminal jurist, Professor Hirano Ryuichi (1989).

REFERENCES

Bellah, Robert N. 1962. Values and Social Change in Modern Japan. In *Studies on Modernization of Japan*, 13–56. Asian Cultural Series no. 3. Mitaka, Tokyo: International Christian University.

Bloch, Marc. 1940. La féodalité comme type social et son action. In *La société féodale*, vol. 2, *Les classes et le gouvernement des hommes*, 240–60. Paris: Albin Michel.

Bowen, Roger W. 1980. *Rebellion and Democracy in Meiji Japan*. Berkeley: University of California Press.

Broekman, Jan M. [1978] 1991. *Recht en antropologie* [Law and Anthropology]. Brussel: Story-Scientia.

———. 1979. *Recht en taal* [Law and Language]. Deventer: Kluwer.

Doi, Takeo. 1973. *The Anatomy of Dependence*. Tokyo: Kodansha International.

Dumont, Louis. 1966. *Homo hierarchicus: Essai sur le système des castes*. Paris: Gallimard.

Feenstra, R. 1981. Contacten op juridisch gebied tussen Nederland en Japan in de 2e helft van de 19e eeuw [Contacts in the Legal Domain between the Netherlands and Japan in the Second Half of the Nineteenth Century]. In *Gratia commercii*, Opstellen aangeboden aan A. van Oven [Essays in honor of A. van Oven], ed. P. Tuit et al., 57–69. Zwolle: Tjeenk Willink.

Fukuzawa, Yukichi. 1962. *Fukuzawa Yukichi Zenshû* [Collected Works of Fukuzawa Yukichi]. Vol. 19. Tokyo: Iwanami Shoten.

Gluck, Carol. 1985. *Japan's Modern Myths: Ideology in the Late Meiji Period*. Princeton, NJ: Princeton University Press.

Government Section of the Supreme Commander for the Allied Powers. 1949. Political Reorientation of Japan: September 1945 to September 1948. Washington, DC: U.S. Government Printing Office.

Habermas, Jürgen. 1981. *Theorie des kommunikativen Handelns*. Frankfurt am Main: Suhrkamp.

Hall, John W. 1962. Feudalism in Japan: A Reassessment. In *Studies in the Institutional History of Early Modern Japan*, ed. John W. Hall and Marius B. Jansen, 15–51. Princeton, NJ: Princeton University Press.

Hintze, Otto. 1970a. Wesen und Verbreitung des Feudalismus [1929]. In *Staat und Verfassung*, 84–119. 3rd ed. Göttingen: Vandenhoeck und Ruprecht.

———. 1970b. Weltgeschichtliche Bedingungen der Repräsentativverfassung [1931]. In *Staat und Verfassung*, 140–85. 3rd ed. Göttingen: Vandenhoeck und Ruprecht.

Hirano, Ryuichi. 1989. Diagnosis of the Current Code of Criminal Procedure. *Law in Japan* 22:129–42.

Hozumi, Yatsuka. [1891] 1943. Mimpô idete chûkô horobu [Fidelity and Pietas Will Be Lost after the Promulgation of the Civil Code]. In *Hozumi Yatsuka hakushi ronbunshû* [Collected Essays of Dr Hozumi Yatsuka], 223–27. Tokyo: Yuhikaku.

Ienaga, Saburo. [1977] 1983. *Rekishi no naka no kempô* [The Constitution in History]. 2 vols. Repr. Tokyo: Tokyo Daigaku Shuppankai.

Ike, Nobutaka. [1950] 1969. *The Beginnings of Political Democracy in Japan*. New York: Greenwood Press.

Inada, Masatsugu. 1987. *Meiji kempô seiritsushi* [The History of the Creation of the Meiji Constitution]. Vol. 2. Tokyo: Yuhikaku.

Irokawa, Daikichi. 1967. Freedom and the Concept of People's Rights. *Japan Quarterly* 14:175–83.

———. [1970] 1985. *The Culture of the Meiji Period*. Princeton, NJ: Princeton University Press.

Ishida, Takeshi. 1975. Fundamental Human Rights and the Development of Legal Thought in Japan [1968]. *Law in Japan* 8:39–66.

Ishii, Shiro. 1972. *Nihon kindai hôshi kôgi* [Discourses on the History of Modern Japanese Law]. Tokyo: Seirin Shoin Shinsha.

Makino, Eiichi. 1926. Kojinteki to shakaiteki [Individual and Social]. In *Sei no hôritsu to ri no hôritsu* [Living Law and Theoretical Law], 31–60. Tokyo: Yuhikaku.

Mitchell, Richard H. 1992. *Janus-Faced Justice: Political Criminals in Imperial Japan*. Honolulu: University of Hawaii Press.

Murakami, Junichi. 1974. *Einführung in die Grundlagen des japanischen Rechts*. Darmstadt: Wissenschaftliche Buchgesellschaft.

Nakamura, Hajime. [1964] 1971. *Ways of Thinking of Eastern Peoples: India, China, Tibet, Japan*. Honolulu: University of Hawaii Press.

Oxford, Wayne H. 1973. *The Speeches of Fukuzawa: A Translation and Critical Study*. Tokyo: Hokuseido Press.

Peters, Antonie A. G. 1989. Naar een herwaardering van het juridisch model van maatschappelijke orde [Towards a Revaluation of the Legal Model of Social Order]. In *Op zoek naar juridisch onderzoek in de jaren negentig* [Searching for Legal Research in the Nineties], ed. G. J. H. van Hoof et al., 189–223. Utrecht: Nederlands Instituut voor Sociaal en Economisch Recht [Netherlands Institute for Social and Economic Law Research], Utrecht University.

———. 1993. Recht en samenleving in Japan. Inaugural lecture, February 28, 1992, Leiden University. Arnhem: Gouda Quint.

Pittau, S. J., Joseph. 1967. *Political Thought in Early Meiji Japan*. Cambridge, MA: Harvard University Press.

Reischauer, Edwin O. 1956. Japanese Feudalism. In *Feudalism in History*, ed. Rushton Coulborn, 26–48. Princeton, NJ: Princeton University Press.

Sansom, George B. [1961] 1977. *Japan in World History*. Tokyo: Tuttle.

Smith, Thomas C. 1966. Japan's Aristocratic Revolution [1960]. In *Class, Status, and Power*, ed. Reinhard Bendix and Seymour Martin Lipset, 135–40. New York: Free Press.

Steiner, Kurt. 1987. The Occupation and the Reform of the Japanese Civil Code. In Ward and Sakamoto, 188–220.

Tocqueville, Alexis de. 1856. *L'Ancien régime et la révolution*. 2nd ed. Paris: Michel Lévy Frères.

Tokoro, Kazuhiko. 1974. Makino Eiichi. In *Nihon no hôgakusha* [Japanese Jurists], ed. Ushiomi Toshitake and Toshitani Nobuyoshi, 257–74. Tokyo: Nihon Hyoronsha.

Uchimura, Kanzo. 1967. Two J's [1925]. In *Sources of Japanese Tradition*, ed. Ryusaku Tsunoda et al., 349–50. Vol. 2. New York: Columbia University Press.

Ueki, Emori. 1880. *Genron jiyûron* [About the Freedom of Speech]. Osaka: Aikokusha.

———. 1927. Minken jiyûron [1879] [About the Rights of the People and about Freedom]. In *Meiji bunka zenshû* [Collected Works on the Culture of the Meiji Era], 181–96. Tokyo: Nihon Hyoronsha.

Valkhoff, J. 1938. *Een Eeuw Rechtsontwikkeling: De vermaatschappelijking van het Nederlandse Privaatrecht sinds de codificatie (1838–1938)* [One Century of Legal Development: The Socialization of Dutch Private Law since the Codification (1838–1938)]. Amsterdam: Arbeiderspers.

Ward, Robert E., and Sakamoto Yoshikazu, eds. 1987. *Democratizing Japan*. Honolulu: University of Hawaii Press.

Wertheim, W. F. 1953. Het contrapunt in de samenleving [The Counterpoint in Society]. In *Weerklank op het werk van Jan Romein* [Response to the Work of Jan Romein], ed. H. J. Pos et al., 210–17. Amsterdam: Wereldbibliotheek.

Part II

COMMUNITARIANISM IN THE EUROPEAN ARENA

4

The European Union as Community: An Argument about the Public Sphere in International Society and Politics[1]

Jos de Beus

THE POSSIBILITY OF EUROPEAN COMMUNITARIANISM

The communitarian case for European integration seems weak. On the one hand, communitarian philosophers and social scientists argue that the European scale is too large to engender common values and norms in society and coherent laws and policies in politics. On the other hand, historians and experts in comparative studies argue that the European Union is neither a community nor a state but a joint venture of governments for control of state rule and national passion in an expanding region. Member states may represent real communities in the spirit of representative and participatory democracy. But they cannot create an overarching community of communities, neither by democratic means nor by authoritarian ones.

Nevertheless, I will examine and defend a conception of the European public sphere as part and parcel of a communitarian view of European integration after the Treaty of Nice (2000), the Laeken Declaration (2001), the Convention on the Future of Europe (2002–2003), Eastern enlargement, the European Council's agreement on a new constitutional treaty, the European Council's decision to start bargaining on Turkey's entry (all in 2004), and the crisis of ratification of the constitutional treaty in 2005.

Valuable modes of integration, both old ones (free trade) and new ones (common foreign policy), require a combination of the supranational public sphere and national public spheres in which political parties are leading actors competing with each other with respect to rival views of European identity and sovereignty. My argument is a defense of the primacy of politics at the levels of European government and national government in member states. European law ought to be the two-level outcome of peaceful and open conflict and resolution of conflict between different social groups and their representative political organizations with separate views of the public interest, including views of European civilization, power sharing, and commitment.

I acknowledge that a hybrid polity such as the European Union sets limits to politics, particularly to party rivalry, as carrier of pacification and integration of European morals, rules, and records of performance. Such a polity involves consensus in many ways, in some cases moral consensus in the spirit of impartiality. The European Union always was, and will remain in the foreseeable future, a mixed government at the level of global regions, relying on interplay between intergovernmentalism and supranationalism, balance of power and abolition of international conflict, and plural sources of civil community and authority. Yet I will try to justify the bottom-up consensus of party compromise in the public sphere, after a demonstration of the failure of both interactive consensus in the political theory of multilevel governance and top-down consensus in the political theory of supranational constitution making. I argue that Etzioni's communitarian theory about European integration, stressing the role of convergence of interests, legitimacy of goals, and regime reinforcement of actions, needs a public sphere of associations and media that facilitates "megalogues," Etzioni's phrase for inclusive transnational debates linking elites and ordinary citizens across diverse national states (Etzioni 1996, 2001, 2004).

The composition of my argument is as follows. The next section is a brief discussion of the no-community thesis. According to this thesis, there is no European public (audience, crowd, people/nation, *demos/populus*, citizenry), notwithstanding some convergence of lifestyles and world views. The thesis also claims that the missing public is desirable in the light of the uniqueness of European integration (European union *sui generis*). Effective and stable unity of European policies and arrangements requires a departure from traditional modes of political-community building. Section three raises the question why, since Germany's Minister of Foreign Affairs Fischer's speech in May 2000, European politicians have stepped up their efforts to create a public sphere in order to connect with wider (electoral and moral) constituencies, while risking stagnation of European policies and definitive loss of their own privileges with respect to representation.[2] Section four spells out the task of political theory in this field of normalization of the postwar experiment of European integration. Political theory should continue its analysis of the moral determinacy and adequacy of old models, including federalism, institutionalism, and supranationalism. It should also examine new models that include the public sphere, such as European good governance, European constitutional patriotism, and European democratic space. Section five entails a critical review of the political ideal of multilevel governance, that is, output-oriented legitimacy via innovation of European administration by bringing in all affected levels of national government and all affected nongovernmental actors in civil societies. Section six entails a critical review of the political ideal of a constitution-based political union, that is, input-oriented legitimacy via a representative and deliberative convention that agrees on essentials (values, goals, rights, organizations, checks and balances). Section seven presents my own conception of a democratic political space, that is, throughput-oriented legitimacy via contestation among families and federations of political parties—old and new, moderate and radical, for or against European integration. Section eight is closely related to section seven. It discusses some practical objections against my solution. Do parties have the will to become European players in the face of two-level crisis in European party families? Is the European Union ready for partisan government? Why do parties in the European Parliament since 1979 gather nausea instead of affection? And what about the loss of authority of parties as tertiary associations: without ordinary members, yet with omnipresence in mass media—financed by either the state or the rich? The closing section is a concluding remark about Europe's public-sphere deficit and the precarious legitimization of the European project today.

My approach is mainly theoretical. It does not use case studies (see De Beus 2001a, 2001b on social democracy). It stands on the shoulders of other scholars (Haas 1958; Marquand 1978; Hix and Lord 1997; Mair 2000a; Schmitter 2000; Marks and Steenbergen 2004; Hix 2005, 175–207). It tries to fill a gap between the high politics of European integration of public policies and the low politics of Europeanization of peoples. The gap may be understood as a lack of throughput-oriented legitimacy, although that term has no fixed meaning in Eastonian systems theory. My approach deviates from the mainstream as to the concept of a compound public sphere, the prominence of political parties as transmission mechanisms between civil societies and states, and the politicization of issues related to European identity, sovereignty, and democracy in the spirit of liberal internationalism (more precisely, perhaps pompously, liberal communitarianism applied to the European Union).

THE NO-COMMUNITY THESIS

Let us define the European public as an encompassing set of citizens of all European member states that has free access to a common public sphere, that cultivates the institutions and practices of such a sphere (European culture), that develops an opinion of European policies as well as a belief in European unity and the dignity, trust, and solidarity among fellow Europeans (European public opinion and identity), and that is engaged in democratic self-determination of the European future (European sovereignty). According to conventional wisdom in the empirical literature, there is no such community (Therborn 1995; Crouch 1999; Guibernau 2001; Imig and Tarrow 2001; Hermann, Brewer, and Risse 2004). There is no transnational middle class committed to European citizenship. There is no wide debate and discourse beyond borders on major issues like trade policy, monetary union, enlargement, and institutional reform. There is no European civil society in the sense of forums in society and politics, created and set in motion by transnational journals, television channels, websites, political parties, interest groups, and social movements. There is no European public culture, marked off from national traditions as well as the Brussels policy culture of European officials (Middlemas 1995; Shore 2000). Finally, and most importantly, there is no European identity as a source of mass loyalty to the European Union as community, regime, framework of institutions, policy, and leadership.

The empirical literature covers a number of interesting phenomena. I recall the failure of the European Commission to shape a wider circle beyond vested interests; the strategy and impact of news media and their frames with regard to European topics; the Europeanization of high public culture such as in financial and academic circles; the dynamics of linguistic competences in European settings; the partly unintended influence of European networks and policies on the identity of producers and consumers (Common Agricultural Policy, environmental policy); and the convergence of private economic culture and public social culture, particularly after the introduction of the Euro (Laitin 1997; Dyson 2000; Norris 2000, 183–207; Schlesinger and Kevin 2000; Shore 2000; Liebert 2001; Mak 2001; Díez Medrano 2003). A new wave of studies leaves aside the stagnation of the supranational public sphere and examines the Europeanization of national public spheres as a consequence of European integration. This literature tries to explain variation in Europeanization by the general variable of adaptation pressure (goodness of fit between European requirements and national regulations) and specific variables, such as openness of the economy, duration of membership, persistence of old cleavages, and democratic structure (consensual or majoritarian systems). Most variables have positive as well as negative effects on Europeanization of the national public sphere (De Beus and Mak 2001, 2005; Green Cowles, Caporaso, and Risse 2001; Eder and Giessen 2001; Featherstone and Radaelli 2003; Van de Steeg 2005).

Before turning to the question of whether the missing European public implies a shared problem for politicians (section three) and political theorists (section four), I want to save an old account of it from oblivion in order to show that the desirability of a missing public is the normative part of the no-community thesis.

Part of the triumph of the postwar European movement after centuries of utopian pacifism in Europe concerns the unique character of organizations such as the European Coal and Steel Community and the European Economic Community. On the one hand, these organizations embodied supranational jurisdiction and capacity. Hence they differed from traditional international organizations. On the other hand, these organizations refrained from traditional methods of centralization and assimilation. In order to end destructive competition between democratic nation states and to start mutually beneficial cooperation between those states, European rulers tried to avoid classical methods like constitution making, language standardization, conscription, taxation, and a core area of control (defense, foreign policy, police, property rights, education, public utilities). The novelty of functionalist practice—Monnet's method—can be shown, by stressing some negative features of functionalist philosophy (Haas 1958, 1964; Duchêne 1994; Schmitter 2000, 1–22). European integration implies major change in the domestic and international relations of a number of states on the subcontinent of Western Europe *without*:

- precedents in local history (acceptance of commercial and democratic society in the Treaty of Rome of 1957);[3]
- claims to regional and global hegemony (acceptance of defensive alliances under American leadership as well as European priority of economic integration);
- prospects of social crisis and revolution (acceptance of the plurality and moderation of liberal democracies in an era of peace); and
- plans with respect to final objectives, competences, and boundaries (acceptance of institutional and strategic indirection).

In this philosophy, democracy remains so strongly connected to national self-determination that its immediate extension during the early stages of European integration would degenerate into trench diplomacy, deadlock, and intensified nationalism. Therefore, limited access and publicity are neither sins nor breaches of norms but indispensable means for integration in the best interests of ordinary Europeans. The time will not be ripe for politicization of European institutions and policies till integration has become irreversible and the sense of interdependence and community has become quasi-natural.

The upshot of this argument is that the well-known reference to the unique nature of European integration (a political system *sui generis*) is an integral part of the no-community thesis. The missing public is a desirable element of the process of European integration. Clearly, recurrent observations in the literature about the unique experiment of European integration reveal a substantial political view. It celebrates the European invention of soft power and extranationalistic authority (Laffan, O'Donnell, and Smith 2000; Rifkin 2004; Slaughter 2004; Leonard 2005).

WHY POLITICIANS NEED A EUROPEAN PUBLIC SPHERE

It is helpful to draw a distinction between a public-policy sphere and a public sphere in society and politics. A public-policy sphere is a court-like circle of interest groups around state organs with major regulatory and financial powers. The state organ creates its own constituency in order to attain control and legitimacy, while the interest group penetrates the state in order to gain influence and special advantages. A public sphere is a countrylike collection of voluntary associations distinct from the state. Such associations are engaged in the provision of collective goods as well as in public mobilization and communication that challenge government agencies, commercial firms, and other voluntary associations. Interest groups do not jeopardize representative democracy and democratic society generally, as criminal and extremist organizations tend to do. Yet a public sphere seems superior to a public-policy sphere from the viewpoint of political equality and functioning of the political system (Habermas 1962; Hirst 1994; Cohen and Rogers 1995; Warren 2000; Young 2000).

Gradual expansion of European policies and steady proliferation of activities by European institutions, such as the European Commission and the European Parliament, have been accompanied by the growth of lobbying of business groups, trade unions, subnational regions, consumer and environmental movements (Hix 1999, 208–34). I refer to this system of interest intermediation as the public-policy sphere of the European Union.

The formation of a public-policy sphere seems contrary to the raison d'être of independent regulatory authorities, to Monnet's ideal of experts (morally committed to the European point of view, independent and neutral, enterprising), and to the interest of national governments in containing autonomous growth of supranational agencies. It is not hard to see, however, why most politicians involved in European integration eventually facilitate or accept the public-policy sphere. It is an element of informal organization and management of goodwill without which formal delegation and differentiation of competences and responsibilities in a supranational setting will never work in the first place (Hooghe and Marks 2001, 69–80). It buttresses, on balance, the prominent role of politicians as arbitrators and sponsors. It is the inevitable response to the real and growing impact of European policies on legal arrangements and vital interests. And it is an arena in the European game of institutional competition. It is difficult for you to stick to the virginal liberal doctrine of professional autonomy while others build up their policy network, or to build up such a network while denying and blocking the rights of other politicians to do the same thing.

Hence, the extension of a fragmented public-policy sphere in Europe since the departure of freely floating pioneers like Monnet and Mansholt is not mysterious. There are lobbyists, consultants, academics, and spokespersons in quasi-corporatist arrangements in Brussels. This contributes to the workability of Europe's highly complex procedures without undermining what Dahl (1999) has called the politician's claim to "guardianship" and the civil servant's claim to "bureaucratic bargaining." The real issue lies elsewhere. Why would politicians, whether national or European, need a public sphere?

Such a sphere implies increasing contestability of decisions of political elites; increasing frictions in formal negotiations in the spotlights (peak conferences) and backstage (small committees); increasing resistance against European integration; increasing representation of differences between nations and national groups, such as classes, with respect to European unity; and increasing complexity and loss of control (see Warren 2000, 60–93, on public-sphere effects).

My hypothetical answer is based on the following distinction between two states of the (European) Union. State I: Politicians, particularly heads of government, articulate a strong common will and vision on the future of Europe; they are secure and self-confident with regard to their own position and role as representatives of public interests in international affairs; and they rely on passive and general support in large electoral constituencies (the so-called permissive consensus within and across national electorates). Under these circumstances they stick to an elitist repertoire: autonomous foreign policy between governments; consensual accommodation between the European Council/the Council of the European Union and the European Commission; and insulation from national public spheres. State II: Politicians are confused or divided about the future of Europe; they question their own credentials in representation and worry about their monopolies of representation; and they perceive decline of support in national electorates as well as hostility, ready to be exploited by populist movements. Under these circumstances they are willing to open a public political sphere in Europe.

One may interpret the general development of the European climate of opinion since the late 1980s as a transition from State I to State II (Pond 1999; Calleo 2001; Hitchcock 2002; Gillingham 2003; Tsoukalis 2003; Marks and Steenbergen 2004; Hix 2005).[4] The Single European Act (1986) on the liberalization and unification of a European market in 1992 is perhaps the last example of smooth top-down legitimization of major integration. The Treaty of Maastricht (1992) led to successful monetary integration (single currency, central bank, supranational monetary policy). Yet European politicians needed a lot of crisis management, imagination, and luck to handle new symptoms of alienation, such as party schisms, negative referendum votes, strikes against policies of retrenchment, and right-wing populism. Since 1997 (Agenda 2000), the European Union embarked on the next grand projects of Eastern enlargement and framing a political union. The unpopularity of these projects, mixed with sheer ignorance of most citizens in the present member states, is closely related to recent setbacks. One of them is the lack of unity and leadership in global issues (relations with the United States, Russia, and other great powers; control over global market failure; defense policy). Another one is absence of consolidation of the monetary union, lack of success in maintaining economic growth and social justice, and failure to support multiethnic tolerance (laborious coordination of fiscal, monetary, and social policies; postponement of common policies of immigration and integration of foreigners). Yet another one is the limited progress in relations between large and small states in institutional reform, and between net contributing and net receiving states in agricultural and regional policies.

This, then, is the backdrop of a stunning recent turn to the problem of the weak public sphere of the European Union. Many spectators used to agree with Weiler's point about Europe's quasi-constitutional treaties: "What Europe needs, therefore, is not a constitution but an ethos and *telos* to justify, if they can, the constitutional order it has already embraced" (Weiler 1996, 106). Today it seems as if politicians wrong-foot these spectators. The Treaty of Nice—itself incomplete and predictable in its reinforcement of consensual rules that weaken the Union's capacity to act—was preceded by an open and rich exchange of constitutional views by leaders of government and ministers of foreign affairs. The Laeken Declaration seems a laundry list of all questions that have been raised in the academic literature on the democracy deficit. The Convention on the Future of Europe looks like a new chapter in the political history of Europe that started with the French revolution and ended since 1989 with round tables and new liberal-democratic constitutions in Eastern Europe (Gillingham 2003, 313–56; Ludlow 2002; Norman 2003). Its widely contested draft treaty entails many new arrangements, such as the charter of human rights, the definition of European competences, and the nonrotating president as well as the minister of foreign affairs of the EU.

There is much more that can be said about all this. I did not deal with the endogenous decline of self-evidence of the European idea after effective pacification (new generations without vivid understanding of the evils of war), or with growth of civil distrust in most European democracies. Nor did I discuss concrete events, like corruption scandals in the European Commission and the European Parliament, miscarriage of the ban on Haider's Austria, and deterioration of American-European relations and intra-European relations during the presidency of George W. Bush (antiterror policy, invasion and occupation of Iraq, promotion of non-Western democracy by a Western empire). The following conclusions may be sufficient for my argument.

First, the clash between the good of European integration and the good of democracy has become a normal experience for European politicians, albeit an ambiguous one. On the one hand, these politicians suggest good reasons for cooperation in an open-ended series of sensitive files, such as corporate governance, energy, (military) technology, asylum, and police and criminal law. On the other hand, they suggest good reasons for avoidance of debates, elections, and referenda on such specific issues and the general issue of European federalism. An example is the loud disavowal of commissioner Verheugen by the European establishment, when this German commissioner aired the proposal of a German referendum on enlargement (September 2000). On the one hand, the establishment is convinced that a sophisticated information campaign will consolidate mass support of Eastern enlargement in the Western core. On the other hand, it fears spontaneous rejection of enlargement in national referenda.

Second, the motives of politicians at both levels (European and national ministers and members of parliament plus members of the European Commission) for launching a public politics of European constitution making are stronger than ever, yet mixed. They seem stronger now than in the high years of Kohl and Mitterrand. They also seem mixed. Some politicians are driven by idealism, although their principles and schemes differ substantively. Others go with the stream in order to preserve old interests and methods. Some leaders and followers act like madmen (Berlusconi). But most leaders and followers in the conflict on institutional reform since Amsterdam, Nice, Laeken, and Rome feel impotent. They do not fear a cosmopolitan coalition that demands and imposes publicity now, or a rise to power of radical nationalists who dismantle the European Union. They fear disunity, overload, and sclerosis of their own making, and the debilitating inability of all to bind themselves to collective rules that diminish such negativity in time.

Finally, the unique political system of the European Union is turning into a normal state of sorts. A normal state controls means of violence, allocates resources to lower levels of administration, and commands political loyalty (Etzioni 2001, xxii). Political scientists find it surprisingly hard to determine a dying hour of functionalism or the labor pains of federalism or the restoration of the nation state. The characteristic indeterminacy of European integration, the unintended consequences of European schemes, and the alternation of times of flourishing and times of arrest all seem related to the absence of a hegemonic member state, the absence of an archenemy after the collapse of totalitarianism, the diversity of political traditions, and the strange dialectics of conflicts that necessitate integration and second-order conflicts that are generated by such integration. Hoffmann (1995) refers here to the metaphor of the European Sisyphus.

Nevertheless, it is striking to observe emergent behavioral similarities between the European Union and the modern state. The Union is preoccupied with its own legitimization versus non-European states, rival authorities (national and regional governments), its personnel, and the civilian population on the entire peninsula. It augments its own role in the core process of public organization and administration of public goods (international, legal, economic, and social policies). Its core business is the complex ordering of security, (economic) liberty, and prosperity. Its self-reflection concerns best practices of public administration (European Commission 2001). Its discourse is full with normative references to citizenship. Like any state, the European political system is supposed to constitute its own power, resource base, and organizational capacity. These are deemed necessary to guarantee survival of European citizens in the global society and politics today, to transform European anarchy into peaceful order, to subordinate European order and government to the rule of law and enforcement of legal rules, to protect and promote the liberty and welfare of European citizens, to realize other elements of the European public interest, to minimize harm to others (foreigners in the widest sense), and to cooperate with others in cases of mutual benefits and global human benefits.

THE CONTRIBUTION OF EUROPEAN POLITICAL THEORY

In his authoritative treatise on contemporary political theory, Kymlicka (2002, 313) seems to deny the relevance of a European public sphere: "[F]ew people have any clear idea what principles of justice or standards of democratization or norms of virtue or loyalty should apply to transnational citizenship." He argues that there are two remedies against the European democracy deficit, namely, to increase the power and accountability of the European Parliament or those of national parliaments in member states. He tries to demonstrate that most Europeans prefer the second remedy. Replacement of the Council of the European Union (nationally nominated ministers) by the European Parliament as the major decision-making body would hollow out national parliaments. A pan-European public sphere in which Danish, Italian, and other citizens participate, is beyond imagination. The success (if any) of transnational democracies such as the European one depends on the ongoing achievement and health of national democracy, including the national public sphere (ibid., 312–15).

I concur with Kymlicka's point about the continuing relevance of national public spheres, but I disagree with his point about the irrelevance of the European public sphere "in the foreseeable future" (ibid., 315). Given the pervasiveness of international external effects, the democratic quality of a European Union in which Danish ministers and heads of government are accountable to Danish members of parliament and Danish voters, in which Italian politicians are accountable to Italian citizens, and so on, seems to require an additional mechanism that regulates the relation between Danish politicians and non-Danish citizens from all other member states. Kymlicka refers implicitly to the cultural mechanism of the moral constituency (Gutmann and Thompson 1996, 144–51; Thompson 1999, 120). Danish politicians are morally obliged to take (vital) interests of non-Danish citizens into account, while Danish voters are morally obliged to support candidates who take the European public seriously. This seems a much more daunting prospect than the formation of a public sphere in which a European Parliament can thrive on the basis of political accountability in the face of social and electoral constituencies.

Another objection concerns institutions. The obvious implication of Kymlicka's argument is abolition of the European Parliament and its replacement by a parliament of members of national parliaments. The new parliament should exercise rights to discussion, inquiry, petition, consultation, and advice. (It is up to national parliaments to strike down European legislation.) Combined with another implication, namely, degradation of the European Commission to a civil service of the Council of the European Union, such a design would even be more limited than the related design of the European Communities in the 1950s and 1960s. It is clear that some general actor, say an intergovernmental conference or a constitutional convention, should take a binding decision here. It is also clear that this actor needs much more argument for the radical restoration that Kymlicka proposes than a generalization of the Folketing model (Newman 1996; Smith 1996).

Finally, the outcome of Kymlicka's nationalization of European politics would be either freezing of the present *acquis communautaire* or an unraveling from the Economic and Monetary Union back to the Common Market, the Customs Union, and, finally, the Free Trade Area. Again, we need much more reason for European differentiation than the traditional foreign policy of Denmark before 1973.

Surely political theorists need to take the European Union more seriously than this otherwise magnificent textbook suggests (Eriksen, Follesdal, and Malnes 1995; Bellamy and Castiglione 1998; Pagden 2002; Dobson and Follesdal 2004). There are some old models of European integration on a democratic basis and some new ones. The model of federalism dates back to the early days of the European Movement. A new generation and vanguard ought to abolish destructive rivalry among nations and establish creative unity by founding a federal European state as one of the building blocks of a cosmopolitan world order. The model of institutionalism is the ideology of many European authorities today. Social institutions such as market exchange beyond national borders, political institutions such as the Brussels framework of bargaining, and legal institutions such as the European Court of Justice ought to produce and reproduce identification of national citizens with an emergent European polity. The model of supranationalism is both the ideal and self-image of a European establishment. At some point, the European identity of such an establishment ought to spill over to the identity of ordinary citizens, including immobile and poor nationals. The new models are much more explicit and demanding as to public justification of integration, standards of leadership and professionalism, the ideal of citizenship, and the solution to the democracy deficit. They include good governance at many levels, constitutional patriotism, and the democratic space of Europe. Political theorists should assess these models. They should give up the antiquated distinction between national state/national egoism and world state/global altruism and take the intermediate level of European society and politics into account.

In the following sections I will compare the new approaches in European political theory. The first is a neofunctionalist argument about multilevel governance, stressing democratic legitimacy of the output of European policies. The second is a neoconstitutionalist argument about citizenship, stressing democratic legitimacy of the input of European procedures. The third is a neocommunitarian argument about integration of societies, stressing democratic legitimacy of the throughput of European parties. My taxonomy is, of course, schematic. All approaches bring in the European public sphere as, respectively, the benign outcome of European regulation in public-policy cultures, the countervailing power against abuse of power at a European scale, and as political action that gives meaning and force to constitutional and administrative rules and understandings in the European Union.[5]

Two special risks have to be taken into account here, namely, Eurocentrism and politicization. Eurocentrism is the old fallacy of seeing European interests as universal interests without argument. Politicization concerns a bias of political scientists, that is, a predisposition to focus on politics as the source of European community and authority, while neglecting all other sources, such as religion, law, and technology.

EUROPEAN MULTILEVEL GOVERNANCE: AVOIDING THE PUBLIC SPHERE

As far as I know, Scharpf's case for multilevel governance in the European Union is the best formulation of a political theory of multilevel governance, on a par with the empirical work of Hooghe and Marks (Scharpf 1999; Hooghe and Marks 2001; Jordan 2001). Scharpf's point of departure is a distinction between input-oriented legitimacy and output-oriented legitimacy. Input-oriented legitimacy stands for mass participation, equality, popular identity, majority rule, passions, populism, and government by the people (general will). Output-oriented legitimacy stands for competition among elites, liberty, representation, separation of powers, interests, liberalism, and government for the people (public utility) (Scharpf 1975). Scharpf wants to demonstrate that the only viable strategy of legitimization of further European integration is promotion of output-oriented legitimacy of the European Union and protection of input-oriented legitimacy of its member states.

The first step in his argument concerns the impossibility of input-oriented legitimacy at the European level. Such legitimacy requires a preexisting sense of collective identity (thick popular identity), Europe-wide policy discourses, strong supranational institutions that assure accountability of office holders to a European constituency, and limited heterogeneity between member states. Most relevant circumstances for legitimization of the European Union along these lines have worsened. Scharpf (1999, 188) concludes that "all discourses that draw on input-oriented legitimizing arguments can only exacerbate the perception of an irremediable European democratic deficit."

The second step in Scharpf's argument concerns the possibility of output-oriented legitimacy of Europe. Such legitimacy depends on institutions that, on the one hand, hinder the abuse of public power of European agencies, and, on the other, facilitate the effective solution of a limited number of common problems of national governments and their constituencies. Scharpf refers here to public accountability of policymakers (particularly supranational policymakers, e.g., central bankers), independent expertise, corporatist and intergovernmental agreement, and pluralist policy networks. Recently, he added the open method of coordination to this list of policy-quality-enhancing institutions.[6] This is attainment of common targets through organized learning by national governments (De la Porte and Pochet 2002).

In the national case, electoral accountability and nonmajoritarian institutions are combined in order to create a sufficiently high level of output-oriented legitimacy, even of unpopular decisions. In the European case, the absence of electoral accountability is compensated by the pursuit of consensual goals among elites. Policymakers constrain themselves to a narrow range of problems. They remain below the threshold of political visibility. They search for conflict-minimizing solutions. Or they rely on the legitimacy resources of cooperative governments nationally and subnationally. Although public accountability of the European Commission, the Council, and the Court of Justice is weak, mutual dependency and control seem sufficiently strong to render abuse of public power a lesser concern. The real issue is the effectiveness of multilevel policymaking in Europe (Scharpf 1999, 189).

Scharpf's third step relates to the distinction between negative and positive integration. Negative integration refers to the removal of tariffs, quantitative restrictions, and other barriers to trade or obstacles to free competition. It includes liberalization and privatization. Positive integration refers to the reconstruction of a system of economic regulation at the European level. It includes market-correcting interventions. The effectiveness of negative integration relies on the legal tools of the Commission, the Court, and national judicial branches. By contrast, positive integration depends on agreement in the Council of Ministers and the European Parliament. This agreement is hindered by nonnegotiable conflicts between national states, rooted in differences with respect to ideology, economic self-interest, and institutions. Consequently, European effectiveness is strong in the field of negative integration (e.g., competition policy), and weak in the field of positive integration (e.g., proportional and progressive taxation).

The general issue in the perspective of output-oriented legitimacy is the vulnerability of national welfare states in an era of globalization, regulatory competition between states, steady negative integration of Europe, and lagging positive integration (unemployment, poverty, lack of fiscal reciprocity) (Scharpf 2003). The specific issue is political salience of similar national problems in the area where both European and national capacities for problem solving are weak: social policy, industrial relations, macroeconomic employment policy, and taxation of mobile factors of production.

The fourth step is a list of recommendations. National governments should invent policy mixes that increase employment in the service sector and maintain the tax base, taking into account the necessity of national competitiveness, their tradition of social protection, and the restrictive rules of the Stability and Growth Pact (see Scharpf and Schmidt 2000). The European Union should help these governments by limiting negative integration (protection of national public services); by coordinating national actions on employment (the first example of open coordination); by setting dual ecological standards for rich and poor member states; by setting a floor under welfare spending; and by allowing enhanced cooperation between member states with identical problems, like pension funding. To summarize this step: the future legitimacy of the European Union coincides in many ways with the effectiveness of economic policies in a wide sense. These policies should strengthen typically European variants of "embedded" capitalism (see Albert 1991; Crouch 1999, part 2; Hall and Soskice 2001).

The final step is an assessment of multilevel governance in the European Union. The quality of European policies should be improved by pluralism in transnational networks (open communication, countervailing associations, deliberation) and legal integration in the area of market-correcting regulations. The aim of positive integration is not politically salient. It is the completion of a truly European space for economic freedom, transaction, justice, and pleasure (Scharpf 1999, 203). In order to overcome the inefficiencies of multilevel governance due to veto points of many players, the design of positive integration should be delegated to the European Commission, the Committee of Permanent Representatives, and the European Court of Justice. These institutions are instrumental in supporting national governments to hold the promise of the welfare state, to join policy competition on the basis of fairness, and to make hard choices reflexively.

This theory is powerful. The vision of the European level of administration as an extra layer of protection of national democracies, partly as replacement of classical border control, belongs to the public philosophy of Europe (see my section two). Pursuit of consensus among leaders by consociational methods is an important feature of European integration in both domestic democratic politics and European bureaucratic politics (Lijphart 1999, 42–47; Schmidt 2002). Furthermore, multilevel governance is an emergent practice of public administration within member states. It is marked by diffusion of political power (many actors, sectors, and levels); horizontal acquisition and exercise of authority (networks); soft control by the legislative and executive branches (instead of violence and coercion); and invention of responsiveness, transparency, and accountability in political-administrative projects. It makes sense, then, to improve the coherence of governance in domestic and supranational policies of European integration (Pierre 2000; Pierre and Peters 2000). In addition, economic issues were—and still are—important in the perception of national electorates, national politicians, architects of the European Union, and policymakers. The legacy of American military guardianship after 1945 has been crucial here. It provided European governments with the opportunity, incentive, and means to concentrate on civil bread-and-butter issues. (Elster once noted that European economic growth since the 1950s resembles Prussian growth in the nineteenth century, and German-Japanese recovery after the Second World War. It is a by-product of constrained political emancipation and unlocked economic emancipation.) Finally, center-left and center-right governments have been involved since the mid-1990s in applying the open method of coordination to social policy and employment policy at the backdrop of the noncontroversial goal of modernization. The Lisbon conference of 2000 on the new economy symbolized this new challenge (De Beus 2001a; Visser 2002).

Yet, despite all these benefits, multilevel governance cannot replace the legitimization function of a European public sphere. First, the European Union needs a two-level public discourse to develop a common concept of positive integration. In a classic article, Hayek has claimed that lack of international agreement on moral principles would block the making of socialist and social-liberal policies in a European monetary union. He also argued that "classical" liberalism, akin to the Tinbergen-Scharpf concept of negative integration, is the only viable option that avoids both European egoism and inefficient planning by a European federal government (Hayek 1939, 255–72). Silent constitutionalization, driven by anonymous European judges, seems conceptually impossible in the minefield of market correction. A recent study shows that the basic idea of embedded capitalism is contested by a coalition that favors neoliberalism (Hooghe and Marks 2001). Its analysis of European policies of regional development also shows that multilevel governance is "weakest in the strategic planning stages" (ibid., 85). This supports my claim that the European

Union would need a public political struggle resulting in a stable binding choice to make output-oriented legitimacy work.

Second, the literature is eloquent as to multilevel governance as a response to failure of central government and its principles of representative democracy and bureaucracy, yet silent as to the response to democratic failure of multilevel governance itself. Such governance seems marred by blocking, parasitic, exploiting, excluding, meddlesome, and corrupt behavior (illustrative is the inability of European authorities to limit accumulation and detailing of policies). The pathology of many levels seems caused by a lack of centralism, constitutional rules, publicity, and popular participation. March and Olsen had to introduce the *deus ex machina* of the good governor to democratize multilevel governance (March and Olsen 1995; see also Peters and Pierre 2002; Van Tatenhove 2002). Scharpf (1997) is well aware of the issue. He regards it an unsettled question for scholars and a lesser concern for citizens, as far as European corruption is concerned (Scharpf 1999, 20, 189).

Third, the focus on economic issues may be less obvious than political economists think. In some cases, good economic performance does not contribute to the legitimacy of the European Union because of its low visibility, reinforced by the predisposition of national actors to take all the credit. In other cases, there is bad economic performance because of national errors—rather than errors of European commissioners, judges, or civil servants—while the European Union is blamed (blame avoidance). In certain cases the contribution of European coordination to the final performance of the economy simply cannot be determined. Finally, there are cases where the relation between the state of the economy and the popularity of policymakers is complex or simply absent (see Ferguson 2002, 224–52, on the myth of the feel-good factor). If national electorates worry about foreigners, criminals, and corrupt politicians, while being secure of their jobs and their social rights, then the strategy of effective economic integration may well be futile as far as European legitimacy is concerned. This is part of the story of the Dutch landslide elections of May 2002.

I am not arguing here against European "economism," and its alleged negative impact on geopolitical rationality, peace with Eastern Europe, civic culture in member states, and noneconomic policies of the European Union (Judt 1996; Siedentop 2000). I argue that even the crowded field of the politics of economic policy in the Economic and Monetary Union needs a public sphere to produce output-oriented legitimacy. Recent studies bear out that the open method of coordination becomes more effective by bringing in civil society (Zeitlin and Pochet 2005).

Finally, and most speculatively, we may wonder why politicians who celebrate the open method of coordination also approved the initiative of the Belgian presidency in the second half of 2000 to set up a constitutional convention. Perhaps they concur with Joschka Fischer's general point, apart from disagreement about his specific conception of federalism: a new mode of input-oriented legitimacy is needed in order to preserve output-oriented legitimacy in the present Union and to establish a minimum of output-oriented legitimacy in the Union after enlargement.

EUROPEAN CONSTITUTIONALISM: LEGALIZING THE PUBLIC SPHERE

Habermas is the leading political theorist of European constitutional democracy. Such praise applies to the sheer volume and continuity of his writings, and his monumental combination of discourse ethics, social and historical theory of public communication, republicanism, and a public intellectual's commitment to the Enlightenment, the center-left, and the European idea (Habermas 1985, 1990, 1992, 1996, 1998, 2001a, 2001b, 2004; cf. Höffe 1999; Weiler 1999; Ferry 2000; Siedentop 2000; Nicolaidis and Howse 2001). The next short exposition of Habermas's argument is focused on themes most relevant to my own argument. These are, respectively, the best reasons for further integration, exhaustion of functionalism, convergence toward constitutional patriotism, the catalytic constitution, and the cosmopolitan imperative.

Habermas favors reform and extension of European policies rather than conservation or contraction. His argument is both general and specific. The general argument concerns globalization of markets and media. According to Habermas, the recent wave of globalization undermines the conditions for effectiveness and legitimacy of the national state as the primary site of legal security, territorial sovereignty, political identity, and democratic citizenship. He refers here to global pollution; evasion of taxes by the best off; international governmental organizations with legitimacy deficits; intolerance with respect to immigrants and refugees; the end of political culture and its replacement by market culture (the state as a firm, electoral consumerism, timocracy). Both the closure of neonational protectionism and the openness of postmodern neoliberalism are inadequate responses to this broad tendency of deterioration. A third way is needed. Europeans should develop a sense of the peculiar balance of openness and closure. This has always marked the fortunate episodes in the history of European modernization. Construction of a European supranational entity with a distinct capacity of control and zone of authority is the proper answer to globalization.

Habermas draws a distinction here between the general argument of counterglobalization (grounds for or against postnational citizenship) and specific arguments (motives for or against political integration of Europe). He refers to an exchange of general arguments between European skeptics, European freetraders, European federalists, and supporters of political cosmopolitanism.

Their debate concerns the future of full employment, the trade-off between social justice and economic efficiency, the competence of a supranational organization, and the issue of loyalty and morality beyond national limits. Habermas sides with the federalists and cosmopolitans. Full employment requires European coordination. European regulation should widen markets and correct them from the point of view of European efficiency and justice. The supranational level of economic, social, and industrial policy should be strengthened. Finally, the European democratic state and civil society can be transferred from the national to the supranational level as the first stage in a sequence leading to world citizenship. All these points seem to enrich Habermas's view of European unification as a mode of globalization of democratic law and politics.

The specific arguments concern the end of warfare, the domestication of German expansion, and economic recovery. Habermas suggests an updated reformulation of these Cold War considerations in favor of European unity: legal pacifism under the sign of the United Nations, Eastern enlargement, and a "social-democratic" reading of the economic justification of the European project. That reading resembles Scharpf's image of embedded capitalism.[7]

The theme of exhaustion of the functionalist method of European integration since the 1980s and 1990s is rather implicit in Habermas's essays, partly because he seldom refers to the practice of European agricultural and competition policies. I take it that Habermas endorses the view that functionalism creates a democracy deficit, that it is self-defeating (the success of intergovernmental, judicial, technocratic, and bureaucratic initiatives provokes opposition and a call for democracy), that it faces structural overload, and that it cannot be used to create Habermas's ideal of political union.

The theme of constitutional patriotism is probably the most innovative element of Habermas's European philosophy. Constitutional patriotism implies that individuals and groups identify themselves with other individuals and groups as members of one people who endorse the values and norms of a liberal constitution. Habermas's point is conceptual, empirical, and normative. Conceptually, constitutional patriotism must be distinguished from the private and biographical sentiment of love of country as well as from ethnic or quasi-ethnic conceptions of nationhood, including descent, language, history, possession of land, religion, morality, and traditional ways of life. Such patriotism is a purely political phenomenon. It must also be distinguished from forms of civic nationalism like mainstream republicanism and communitarianism. These views of citizenship are equally political but much thicker. They include, *inter alia,* a shared language, history, and local standards of decent public policy.

Historically, constitutional patriotism is the good outcome of Europe's bad history of state making, religious strife, class struggle, and colonialism.

Habermas sees that the civic nature of European peoples is enmeshed with ethnic understandings, rivalry among elites with strategies of mass mobilization during early stages of national democratization, wars (hence deeply entrenched images of other nations as barbarians and enemies), state policies of assimilation, moral majority views, contingent communities of fate, and the ongoing formation of what Kymlicka (1995, 76–80) refers to as societal cultures. Habermas argues, however, that a process of decoupling and purification has occurred. Civic and political components of national consciousness became stronger, while ethnic and cultural components became weaker. He refers here to the turbulent struggles for peace, legal security, voting rights, social security, equality between the sexes, public control of the business cycle, and tolerance of individuality and minorities. Recent history of Germany and other European countries should be interpreted as the final stage of civilization of democratic nationalism and internationalism. Democracy and the nation state "jointly produced the striking innovation of a civic solidarity that provides the cement of national societies" (Habermas 2001b, 16).

Normatively, constitutional patriotism is sufficient as the legitimate source of truly European obligations (including distributive obligations) and as a stable mode of real unification of European peoples and states. Habermas draws a distinction between substance and process. Substance is about the rules and understandings of the formal constitution of the European Union. Process is about the emergence of a European civil society, the construction of a Europe-wide public sphere, and the shaping of a political culture that can be shared by all European citizens. Habermas adds that it is neither desirable nor possible that European peoples abolish themselves and merge into a thick, quasi-national sense of community at a larger scale.

The next theme is the catalytic role of a European constitution. Habermas (ibid.) argues that globalization, the pursuit of conservation of the great democratic achievements of diverse national states in Europe, learning behavior of European policymakers and officials, and convergence of Europeans toward a common political morality will not engender the right kind of European integration unless a constitution is made with a "catalytic effect." This is a constitution with explicitly federalist contents. It is simultaneously the stake, core, and enabling factor of Europe's civil society, public sphere, and political culture. Habermas spells out some elements of the constitution, such as tricameralism (chambers of representatives of citizens, states, and regions). He does not discuss the scenarios of "circular creation" of a European federation, except for a vague reference to an initial referendum.

The final theme of Habermas concerns the cosmopolitan imperative. European politicians and citizens ought to establish global domestic policy. Such a policy concerns the regulation of world markets, humanitarian intervention, and the pursuit of global criminal and social justice. The policies of the European Union should promote these long-term transformations, both in the present state of international politics and after reform of the United Nations, the North Atlantic Treaty Organization, the Organization of African Unity, and other such bodies (Habermas 1998, 165–69; 2004, 113–93).

This theory is in many ways a role model for European political theorists (see my section four). The underlying intuitions seem all right. Like Europe's member states, the European Union must watch over a balance between openness and closure. It can only ask from its citizens to join critical processes of scale enlargement and to assume global obligations if it remains credible in realizing the ideal of public protection and public self-determination within the Union's jurisdiction. Furthermore, democratic constitutionalism is a force of integration. Even in the hard case of secession threats, such as Catalonia or Scotland, it may turn out to be a practical method for controlled fragmentation (cf. Tully 1995). The theory injects the general concept of public sphere into specialized discussions among economists, sociologists, and political scientists about the optimal currency area, social convergence, and multilevel governance. Finally, Habermas brings the political dimension of European integration back in. He sees the analogy between political mobilization for national democracy and such mobilization for postnational democracy. His political view is a recognizable expression of the European center-left. He speaks directly to politicians and a general public of readers, rather than only to colleagues in the academic world. There is no doubt that this thinker with his dense style has influenced the Convention on the Future of Europe.

Nevertheless, there is something artificial in this entire approach of the European public sphere. My objections concern, respectively, the lack of a plausible argument about European crisis (that explains and justifies the constitutional moment), the thin view of political identity, neglect of the special role of political parties, and some lack of clarity with regard to top-down constitution making. I will disregard Habermas's protest against the war in Iraq (2003) and his dubious idea that anti-Americanism (in the sense of anti-imperialism) is an integral part of the coming shared identity of Western European and Eastern European states and peoples (Habermas 2004).

In general, theorists of constitutional democracy need an argument about the constitutional moment, that is to say, a story about big crisis, basic conflict, and new balance due to constitutional revolution. In particular, these theorists have to come to terms with the problem of meaningless constitutions. Constitutional conventions can ratify a new balance after protracted civil struggle, indeed after civil war, or after great disruption, such as foreign occupation. Even in those special circumstances of critical group consciousness, conventions only produce an illusion of order under the guardianship of lawyers, when old elites in society and politics are unwilling to commit themselves and new elites are unable to mobilize massive support. European constitutionalists today are bound to tell how a common repetition of the collapse of bourgeois constitutionalism in national and international affairs after 1918 is to be avoided (Mazower 1998, 1–39).

Habermas's arguments do not emphasize the prospects of European war, German expansionism, economic depression, or an overload crisis of the European Union. His main argument concerns globalization. Globalization destroys the nation state. European integration will save the best achievements of these states, such as social protection. European elites will recognize this. They will overcome their internal disagreements about the future of the European Union and represent European masses (because they must). Constitution making will become the catalyst. The weak part of this argument concerns the identity of friends and enemies of European integration. In order to explain the constitutional moment, Habermas needs to trace old elites and masses that hold on to national government against new elites and masses that demand European government. Hence, the entry of protectionists versus neoliberals, supporters of embedded capitalism versus its opponents, skeptics versus good Europeans, next to free traders versus federalists and cosmopolitans. None of these accounts gives the reader a clue as to the social conflict within and across countries that the European constitution is supposed to solve.[8]

My second objection concerns constitutional patriotism. In theory, such loyalty may travel lightly through a European space. Practically, it is hard to see how an abstract and ideal view of political civilization, stripped of all particularistic features (language, a sense of history, local sense of the good and the right), could have become the common postnational identity of the member states, and will become the future European identity. Like Habermas, I believe in a civic and quasi-national concept of European identity. Unlike Habermas, I do not think that constitutional patriotism will motivate citizens who do not belong to the class of constitutional lawyers and moral philosophers.

A republican like Habermas sees the written constitution as the dominant force of cohesion, both within and across member states. A democratic political union of Europe is instrumental to the build-up of world governance. Love of Europe is the outcome of the right kind of constitutional politics. It is also conditional, that is, dependent on the liberal contents of European law, particularly its social-democratic reading. The boundaries of the European polity should be open (Europe as migration society). A communitarian like myself sees the public culture as the dominant force of cohesion. As all such cultures, European culture must be the outcome of dynamic cultural accommodation, mutual economic advantage, interwoven history, and cultural policies (like the binding choice of a European standard language). A democratic political union of Europe is instrumental to continued pacification and to its flourishing in a wide sense. Love of Europe is the precondition of the right kind of politics, whether high (constitutional politics) or low (ordinary politics). It also constitutes the stake of European identity politics, as the present contestation about the future of European immigration and multiethnic tolerance shows. Liberal communitarianism welcomes a restrictive and selective immigration policy of the Union, based on legal, political, and economic principles. In short, Habermas leaves local political understandings, such as a historic party compromise on religious education or social security, out of the concept of political identity, while I include local political understandings (see De Beus 2001c).

In Habermas's analysis, political parties are one of the many actors in the public sphere, on a par with interest groups, social movements, and news media. He denies the special role of political parties.[9] Yet, unlike interest groups, parties articulate a coherent view of the public interest in all social domains. Unlike social movements, parties present candidates in general elections and accept responsibility for public policy after the arbitrage of voters. Unlike news media, parties change the law. They may turn democratic nationalism into the law of the land, causing domestic and international instability (Snyder 2000). They may also turn liberal internationalism into the law of the land, as they have in Europe since 1951. Furthermore, militant party competition in the public sphere is the functional equivalent of civil war and the functional alternative to usurpation by strangers. Since those modes of imposed European unification are unthinkable now, Europe is in need of political parties to define the constitutional moment. Orderly party competition has become the mechanism for creative compromise between old and new social elites. Habermas rightly points out that a European constitution will remain the business of elites, like the European treaties from Paris to Nice, without two-level moral dialogues in civil society and the public sphere. But without leadership of political parties, such dialogue has no point. The catalytic constitution that creates a new public sphere and a new political culture will fail to come. As Etzioni (2001, xxxvi), a colleague of Habermas, observes: "Even if tomorrow the European Union has a constitutional assembly and formed a democratic federation, emulating the founding assembly of the United States, moral dialogues would still be essential both for the assembly to succeed and for the people of Europe not to rebel against it. It should be noted that the American constitutional assembly occurred in a very small society, with a population smaller than quite a few single European cities now have. In addition, in those days, large segments of the population were not politically engaged. This is no longer the case."

This brings me to my final objection. To date, Habermas has looked away from third-order politics, that is, the politics with respect to the ideal or optimal conditions for democratic constitutional politics (Pogge 1997). He does not apply his famous model of deliberative democracy here. This makes a lot of sense from a pragmatic point of view, since there will be no escape from bootstrapping or "circular creation" (Habermas, following Offe) in the Union's present predicament. It also leads, however, to some lack of clarity with respect to the assessment of the Convention on the Future of Europe. On the one hand, Habermas celebrated this convention as an unexpected window of opportunity. On the other, Habermas's view of the public sphere implies that elitist constitutional engineering cannot create institutions that give birth to the practices of supranational democracy. A basic will of politicians who represent broad constituencies to join supranational society and politics must already be in place. The Convention, however, was in many ways (agenda, appointment of members, and so on) the result of intergovernmental bargaining among reluctant constitutionalists within a public-policy culture, failing to draw attention of mass media and national electorates (as its president conceded, without foreseeing the consequent problem of popular rejection in national referenda [*Le Monde*, July 23, 2002]). So top-down consensus among nominated members of a constitutional convention is an ambiguous phenomenon in the neoconstitutionalism of Habermas, as in political reality.

EUROPEAN PARTIES: VENTURING THE PUBLIC SPHERE

Effectiveness of multilevel governance in the European Union presupposes legitimacy of the Union's policies of integration. Legitimacy of the Union's policies presupposes a shared public political culture, oriented to the basic structure of government, as agreed upon in treaties or a constitution. Sharing a public political culture in a democracy, of itself a political mode of collective identification, presupposes a prominent role of political parties. Or so I argued in my comments on Scharpf and Habermas. This section raises two follow-up questions that are normative. Why ought parties to lead in the politics of European integration? How ought they to lead?

My arguments for European primacy of party politics concern the pursuit of consensus in a pluralist polity, representation of the public interest, and regulation of identity crises.

Generally, there are three modes of consensus in democratic politics. Consensus top-down (or assimilating consensus) is state-driven and paternalist. Public policy demands basic social change. Policy innovation is a matter of imposition of the elite's preferences. In the second half of (Europe's) nineteenth century, the role of the state in modernizing the market economy and protecting the working class was in many ways the result of *embourgeoisement* initiatives of tutelary state elites, eager to control destabilizing conflicts in civil society. Consensus bottom-up (or ratifying consensus) is society-driven and liberating. Public policy ratifies basic change of society (of power, scarcity, and morals) that is already taking place. Policy adaptation is a matter of compromise within and across old and new elites in society. In the second half of the twentieth century, the role of the state in stabilizing the business cycle and safeguarding social rights was the result of accommodation among elites in society, eager to close periods of polarization and collective self-help. Interactive consensus (or organic consensus) is public-driven and conservative. Public policy invents basic social change and covers its main risks simultaneously. Policymaking is a process of routine reform and a matter of permanent communication between state elites and social elites. During the 1990s, the role of the state in public-sector reform was the result of interaction among elites in public–private networks, eager to protect their constituencies and their own prerogatives from both market competition and majority rule.

From the standpoint of normative democratic political theory, top-down consensus on European integration is a nonstarter. Western Europe is the most democratic region in the world today (Ferguson 2002, 355). Guardianship of late-nineteenth-century social liberals cannot drive the coming rounds of integration in the new century, and guardianship of mid-twentieth-century functionalists ought not to.[10] Scharpf's reappraisal of the European Court of Justice as governor of positive integration will not be sufficient to tackle the legitimacy deficit.

Interactive consensus must also be rejected. On the one hand, interactive consensus within nation states seems defective because of a lack of structure-induced incentives to discourage virtual representation and to encourage real representation, marked by responsiveness, transparency, and accountability (see the criticism of good multilevel governance in section five). On the other hand, interactive consensus at the supranational level is impossible because of the missing European community. This leaves us with the principle of bottom-up consensus. National political parties should be in the middle of public contestation in their societies about globalization and Europeanization. Their compromise should guide the European line of conduct of national governments. Likewise, transnational political parties should be prominent in the public conflict and debate about the policy of supranational authorities in the emergent European society.

A second argument dates back to grounds of existence of democratic politics. Representation of the public interest by one actor, whether a natural or a corporate one, is beyond the limits of human reason. In order to determine the public interest as adequately as possible, humans need free intercourse on the basis of procedural equality between different actors who represent social groups and their particular views of the public interest. A democratic ordering of party formation, party competition, party discussion, and party government is an indispensable mode of such intercourse. In this modern perspective, the terms of social unity and neutral government are determined by continuous party rivalry in the public sphere of civil society and democratic politics (Manin 1997; Dunn 2000, 19–29; Fennema 2001, 169–201). This perspective implies, then, that the public interest of European integration, as well as the public interest of formation of European institutions and practices that settle the conflicts produced by European integration, ought to be the outcome of two-level party rivalry.

My final argument concerns the future of the European Union here and now. Political integration is necessary in order to preserve economic and legal integration. It is also necessary in order to control future widening and deepening of European membership. On the one hand, this is a process of redefinition of state sovereignty that goes in tandem with crises of national identity, related to an unavoidable pursuit of European identity (Anderson 1992, 267–68). Habermas's thesis about the reality of postnational identity in postwar national states is too optimistic, apart from being inconsistent with his emphasis on a constitutional moment. On the other hand, the European idea is incompatible with political strategies that provoke domestic and international crises in order to manipulate support for the European cause (or to manipulate demands for renationalization). Hence we need a mechanism to make or manage intermediate crises. Peaceful and open politics among parties provides us with such a mechanism. Party politics involves not only the revelation of collective preferences with regard to Europe's authoritative allocation of goods; it also involves forming conceptions of European identity (Pizzorno 2002).

How ought political parties to lead in the politics of European integration? The following moral requirements and examples may constitute a point of orientation here. The principle of peacefulness suggests that parties renounce all strategies of mobilization and communication that incite to violence for or against European integration. It follows from the idea that pacification is part and parcel of democracy and the project of European unity. It does not prohibit, however, public expressions of friendship and animosity with respect to nations and institutions. The principle of publicity suggests that parties defend their own proposals—particularly unpopular ones—and attack proposals of other parties—particularly popular ones—in the public sphere, in parliament as well as in mass media. Exceptions, such as secrecy in meetings of the constitutional convention, ought to rest on public reasons (Elster 1995; Luban 1996). The principle of leadership suggests that parties ought to take the initiative in criticizing and correcting flawed European policies, in formulating coherent and rival visions and scenarios, in breaking through stalemates, and in preserving the unity, effectiveness, efficiency, and comprehensibility of policies in "the most formalized and complex set of decision-making rules of any political system in the world" (Hix 2005, 3).

Finally, the principle of responsibility implies that politicians of all parties take the vital interests of Europe as a whole into account when certain nations and national groups harm or ignore these interests, while they also take the vital interests of nations and national groups into account when certain European majorities harm or ignore these interests. Furthermore, the principle requires that party politicians honor special moral obligations as candidates, heads of government, ministers, and members of parliament (supporting the governing coalition or opposing it). Candidates ought to shape and persuade constituencies by spelling out their concerns and promises with respect to the European question during campaigns. Heads of government ought to justify their planning and bargaining behavior publicly, at home and abroad. Ministers ought to clarify their mandate, to inform in early stages, and to account for their own share in joint policy-making in public forums (party meetings, sessions of parliament, interviews). Members of parliament ought to counterpoise European executive authorities, to create an arena for debate, opposition, and compromise between distinct and cohesive parties, and to function as a forum for public discussion on the design of the future European society.

Many philosophers are prepared to formulate more demanding rules for political parties for the sake of authentic deliberation and social justice (Christiano 1996; Gutmann and Thompson 1996; Cohen and Sabel 1997; Eriksen and Fossum 2000). I beg to differ here. In general, the parties' freedom of political imagination needs to be cherished. In many ways the retreat of political parties has already gone too far, owing to proliferation and the growing political assertiveness of news media, civil services, corporations, referendum movements, and policy consultants. In particular, the trouble with Europe's parties is not excessive politicization, but subordination of party views to the views of states (often multiparty governments), adaptation to short-term preferences of voters, bureaucratization, prevention of party schism, and avoidance of confrontation between parties in the middle supporting European integration, and Euro-skeptic challengers on the left and the right. Many politicians are prudent and evasive vis-à-vis expressions of national vulnerability and the sense of a lack of pan-European orientation in the current opinion climate. These are certainly not the times of militant European expansionism or stiff nationalism. While the postwar setting was marked by the fear of war and the dream of a unified Europe that would replace the failed nation states, the current setting is marked by the fading of postwar fears and dreams, and a sense of general disappointment and frustration about the capacity of both national and European authorities to keep the promise of public self-determination and protection (Buruma 1999, 304). The new demon is populism, rather than new fascism. It is the unintended consequence of the incapacity of center parties in power to come to terms with real concerns of middle and lower classes about foreigners of Eastern European and non-European descent and about the scale and complexity of European policies, which are perceived as interventions of foreign rulers. Freedom of imagination of the old people's parties in Europe seems a more intelligent answer to populism than moral regulation of free speech mixed with old-fashioned European elitism.

The real test for a party politics of European integration follows naturally from this characterization of the European question. Can and will political parties use their freedom to attain two-level consistency? The criterion of consistent party action in the dual public sphere of Europe is rather demanding. In the phase of party formation, it implies some goodness of fit between the constituency of party one in member state A and the constituency of its sister party one in member state B (a similar conclusion applies to sister parties two, three, etc.). In the phase of party competition, it implies a goodness of fit between campaigns during national and European elections. In the phase of party discussion in parliament, it implies a goodness of fit between national and European representation, both within the national party and across sister parties. In the phase of party government, it implies a goodness of fit between governments of identical hue, both internationally and supranationally. I will not discuss the proper solutions of problems of party coordination and cooperation in this chapter (see Hix and Lord 1997, 54–76). I should like to confine myself to two general conclusions about a common party space in the European Union.

The minor conclusion is that all parties with candidates in both national and European parliaments ought to strive for overall consistency instead of playing tactical two-level games, such as blame avoidance, shaping scapegoats, and rhetorical support of institutional reform (the familiar behavioral indicators of false Europeanism). In the case of parties with federalist manifestos, it is a point of honor to build federal parties.

The major conclusion concerns the distinction between principles of political fairness, such as peacefulness, publicity, leadership, and responsibility, and criteria of political rationality, such as two-level consistency. Political fairness should ban forms of gross inconsistency (say a promise in the European Council to join the Monetary Union before the next election and a promise to the national rank-and-file to call a national referendum on entry after the next election). It should not, however, determine consistency by some legal arrangement. The general pursuit of consistent two-level party strategies is essentially contested. It ought to be part of the stuff of open-ended democracy in a European political space.

ISSUES OF FEASIBILITY

Although I do not champion central party rule in a federal European Union, as Hix and Lord (1997, 198–220) have done, the case for two-level party prominence in a European public sphere is an idealist one that is bound to raise many issues of feasibility.

Mainstream political science states that so-called party families inhabit the European space by now. They include Christian democrats, social democrats, liberals, conservatives, and radicals (greens, radical right, radical left, regionalists, anti-Europeans). They hold distinct views of Europe and European integration, e.g., on the issue of "positive integration" (Scharpf) alias "embedded capitalism" (Habermas). They are organized in federations and factions (in the European Parliament). They compete in European and national elections. Their candidates hold offices in legislative and executive branches of European and national governments, some of them being directly elected by voters (members of parliament, presidents).

However, there are two major differences between parties at the European level and parties at the national level. First, European parties are relatively incoherent in terms of ideology, organization, campaigning, representation, policymaking, style, and reputation. Second, partisanship is relatively weak in European elections (second-order elections, determined by national frames), in national referenda on European issues (many parties cannot catch all members of their constituencies), and in procedures of the European Parliament (consensual, geared to technical agendas, common institutional interests, lobbies, and symbolic actions on global issues), procedures of the European Commission (consensual, geared to technical agendas, common institutional interests, strategic and symbolic European issues, bearing the mark of neutrality), and procedures of the European Councils and delegations of member states (consensual, geared to the international arguing and bargaining, bearing the mark of diplomacy).

The somewhat paradoxical results are that all politicians in Europe are party politicians, while their policies are neutralized as far as party difference is concerned; that parties have significantly more in common with parties in the same party family than they do with other parties from their own country, while their policies are nationalized as far as critical issues about state interests and national interests are concerned; and that institutional innovations, like the introduction of direct elections of the European Parliament in 1979, have a surprisingly limited impact on the formation of a European electorate, while national electorates are surprisingly similar as to outlooks, discourses, and principles of reasoning and choice (Middlemas 1995, part 2; Van der Eijk and Franklin 1996; Hix and Lord 1997; Schmitt and Thomassen 1999; Hooghe and Marks 2001, part 3; Hix 2002; Marks and Steenbergen 2004; Hix 2005, 133–87).

Against this backdrop, the following issues of feasibility with respect to European party politics arise: weakness of will of party families; their lack of power; discredit of European parliamentarism; and, most urgently, decline of popular roots of vested parties and the language barrier.

Political parties may have many prudent reasons to avoid Europeanization and denationalization of their rivalry in the public sphere. It involves the risk of party schism, the loss of political capital of older generations of leaders and activists, a struggle for power between politicians of large states and politicians of small states, an increase of transaction costs of politics and costs of campaigning, basic uncertainty about the relation between loss of old constituencies and gain of new ones, the danger of artificial divisiveness regarding European policies, and the familiar dark side of international public associations (lack of engagement, corruption, bureaucratization, irresponsibility in financial and economic matters, and hypocrisy in legal and moral matters).

Political parties may not have the means of power to drive out their secondary role in European politics. Within the European apparatus, they must challenge bureaucracies, judges, independent authorities, communities of experts, and, last but not least, traditional leaders in member states. Within European society, they must challenge big business, regional alliances, large trade unions, and interest groups and lobbies of producers and consumers. Within national public spheres, they must challenge social movements, mass media, and referendum voters.

The discredit of the European Parliament is persistent, as witness the structural decline of turnout in European elections. Notwithstanding its growth of formal competences, its control of European authorities, and its inventiveness in shaping the first European arena of deliberation, this parliament has failed so far to overcome the growing pains of postnational democracy (such as corruption) and to gather the affection and curiosity of ordinary citizens, journalists, scholars, artists, and intellectuals.

European parties, particularly the old people's parties, have lost their popular base. Among thirteen long-established democracies in Western Europe, including two nonmembers of the European Union (Norway and Switzerland), the mean level of party membership has fallen from 9.8 percent of the electorate in 1980 to just 5.7 percent today. This implies that party membership as a percentage of the electorate now averages less than 60 percent of the levels recorded just two decades ago. The only countries in Western Europe that record a growth in membership rates are Greece, Portugal, and Spain, in each of which the parties began more or less from scratch in the mid-1970s. This tendency is reinforced by a fall of activism of members and declining levels of turnout in national elections (Mair 2000b, 2; see Crouch 1999, 312–65; Gallagher, Laver, and Mair 2000). The numbers illustrate a recent party development. Parties are turning into tertiary associations, without members yet with private or public sponsors. They risk the loss of a popular base, indeed the loss of their monopoly of representation in matters of the state (Manin 1997, 218–35; Dalton 2004).

A final obstacle for the primacy of European party politics is the language barrier. Without a common European language and linguistic competence of the many, a flourishing European public sphere remains a chimera (Kymlicka

2001). I did not collect data on the development of skills, laws, and habits here. My impression is that only English-speaking individuals and groups have managed so far to imitate the vitality of national public spheres. One example is the role of the English journal *Financial Times* in the financial community of Europe. One expert presents the hopeful view of the European language community as a four-story house, with eleven languages (and in a decade more than twenty) on the floor of European institutions; English and French on the floor of informal bargaining between member states and European institutions; English in "civil Europe" (transnational society); and "robust" national languages plus English in ordinary domestic intercourse. Starting from the regularity "the more languages, the more English," he unfolds a cultural policy to de-anglicize English (De Swaan 2001, 174, 190–93; De Swaan in *de Volkskrant*, November 2, 2001).

A number of conclusions can be drawn from this concise survey. First, both the issue of legitimacy and the issue of feasibility should be taken seriously in works of political theory on the solution of the democracy deficit of the European Union. Second, the European Union may be ready for other forms of democratization than the creation of a political public sphere, but it certainly is not ready today for such creation if we mean party politics. Third, the politics of democratization of the European Union may avoid certain obstacles connected to high constitutional politics by turning to low party politics, but politicization of the European question along party lines certainly implies specific obstacles (such as the language barrier). Fourth, without a minimal popular base of parties, European integration cannot legitimize itself by ratifying consensus bottom-up. Assuming that interactive consensus is infeasible, this would leave us with all the possibilities and limits of assimilating consensus top-down. Finally, creation of two-level constituencies in a two-level public sphere requires Schumpeterian political imagination and entrepreneurship (a neglected topic in contemporary political science and political theory alike).

A CONCLUDING REMARK ABOUT EUROPE'S PUBLIC-SPHERE DEFICIT

The European Union suffers from a public-sphere deficit. On the one hand, it needs a connection between the macro-talk of European leaders in their networks and the micro-talk of European citizens in their houses and public places. This is Etzioni's point about "megalogues" that prevent alienation and revolt (Etzioni 1996, 106–10). On the other hand, recent research on the Europeanization of the public spheres of France, Germany, Italy, the Netherlands, Spain, the United Kingdom, and nonmember Switzerland shows that the central role of state actors has been reinforced while civil society actors remain weak (Koopmans 2005). Hence, the European gap between the democratic ideal and the real world has become larger since the 1990s rather than smaller.

Meanwhile, the future of the European Union turns into a race between elitist and populist forces, both armed with specific views of the European Union as guarded palace. The race can be won by democratic forces in a center that holds (Yeats) when moderates reconcile the demands of cultural security and open society (Cruise O'Brien 1994). Moderates should put their best resources—their generosity to begin with—not only in the design of European integration but also in the design of democratization. Institutions and practices that restore the primacy of the political in national states and introduce such primacy in the emergent European state, ought to be part of that design. In a broad sense, political primacy means that a free and sovereign people determines its own destination by means of a constitutional balance of power between several branches of government that promotes cooperative conflict between political parties for the sake of the public interest and the legitimate rights of citizens. A more narrow view of political primacy suggests that representative parties exercise authority and effective control in the government's relations and interactions with powerful actors in the market economy. The broad view stresses the need for a well-ordered political system in a cohesive union of European peoples. The narrow view stresses the need for popular credibility in public-policy coordination. While Habermas opts for the broad view and Scharpf for the narrow one, I argued that political parties ought to and may play a constructive role in both domains.

Surely, the idea of primacy of (party) politics should never suggest that politics is the sole foundation of social order, that political action is the highest stage of the good life, or that the will of the people may overstep moral and legal constraints related to a universal standard of decency. There are, fortunately from the perspective of humane and European pluralism, several sources of legitimacy and consent, which European politicians ought to exploit on a par with rational electoral choice: social conventions, principles of justice, procedures of rational organization, and the cash nexus (Held 1995, 161). Furthermore, there is something irreversible now to European integration, which means that legitimacy of national states and legitimacy of the European Union boil down to a similar historic experience: "No matter how efficient the tax system, no matter how representative the parliament, no matter how liquid the bond market and no matter how well managed the currency, in the end the legitimacy of a state is bound up with such intangibles as tradition (the memory of past benefits), charisma (the appeal of present leaders), popular belief (faith in future rewards, material or spiritual) and propaganda (the state's use of available media to bolster all these)" (Ferguson 2002, 422).

NOTES

1. This chapter partly derives from a larger research project entitled "The transformation of political mobilization and communication in European public spheres" (EUROPUB.COM), which is directed by Ruud Koopmans (Free University of Amsterdam) and sponsored by the European Commission in the context of its Fifth Framework Programme (project number HPSE-CT2000-00046). An outline of the project can be found at europub.wz-berlin.de.

2. Joschka Fischer, "From Confederacy to Federation: Thoughts on the Finality of European Integration," speech at the Humboldt University in Berlin, May 12, 2000, issued by the German Ministry of Foreign Affairs.

3. The Treaty of Westphalia of 1648 did not ring in commercial society, and the Treaty of Utrecht of 1713 did not ring in democratic society (Pocock 2002).

4. A Dutch study of public support of European integration in twelve member states in 1952–1998 concludes that the number of supporters of integration was constantly higher than the number of opponents, except for negative scores of the United Kingdom and Denmark. It also concludes that the 1990s was a decade of convergence of public opinion. In the mid-1980s support was highest in the founding member states and lowest in the United Kingdom and Denmark, while intermediate in Ireland, Greece, Portugal, and Spain. In the 1990s, support decreased in the founding-member states and Ireland, while it increased in the United Kingdom and Denmark. This result also confirms the meaning of Ireland's 2001 rejection of the Nice Treaty (Jansen 2001).

5. My notion of throughput-oriented legitimacy does not sit well with Easton's notions of input and output. Easton refers to parties as agents on the input-side, particularly involved in the structure of conversion of wants into demands, of regulation of such conversion (gatekeeping), and of regulation of support (Easton 1965, 95–97, 256–59). I am trying to explore a distinction between the input of European demands and support, the output of European policies, and the throughput of conversion of input into output. Party formation is related to the input of European interests, passions, and principles; party government is related to the output of European regulations, directives, decisions, and recommendations; party competition is related to conversion of the European idea into European unity.

6. Talk at the Workshop Governability in Post-Industrial Societies, Utrecht School of Governance, Utrecht University, April 26–27, 2002. The workshop discussed two comparative projects, namely, Scharpf and Schmidt 2000; Bovens, 't Hart, and Peters 2001.

7. Habermas refers to Therborn's statement (1995) that collective bargaining, trade unions, public social services, and rights of women and children are special features of the European model of society, marked off from the American model. He does not read this statement as a Swedish image of European integration.

8. One may also conceive labels such as protectionism as moral views. Perhaps Habermas wants to show that participation in constitutional politics is morally obligatory because such politics creates the kind of European integration that realizes basic human rights (a concern of legal pacifists in the EU, the United States, and everywhere else) and liberal equality (a concern of left-wing internationalists, federalists, and cos-

mopolitans alike). But Habermas does not present his analysis of grounds (general arguments) and motives (specific arguments) in terms of universal ethical reasons.

9. For example, Habermas never raises the issue of why Christian democrats, social democrats (including Third Way socialists), conservatives, and radicals in the European Parliament ought to approve or will approve his left-wing proposals. One possible answer is, of course, that embedded capitalism has become part of local political understandings of main parties within and across European member states (particularly in its most advanced form in a number of small countries). Habermas seems inclined to give this answer, but his thin concept of constitutional patriotism does not allow him to do so.

10. For a discussion on the interplay between top-down and bottom-up consensus in the first decade of European integration, see Anderson 1997.

REFERENCES

Albert, Michel. 1991. *Capitalisme contre capitalisme.* Paris: Seuil.

Anderson, Perry. 1992. *A Zone of Engagement.* London: Verso.

———. 1997. Under the Sign of the Interim. In Gowan and Anderson, 51–71.

Archibugi, Daniele, David Held, and Martin Köhler, eds. 1998. *Re-Imagining Political Community: Studies in Cosmopolitan Democracy.* Cambridge: Polity Press.

Bellamy, Richard, and Dario Castiglione, eds. 1996. *Constitutionalism in Transformation: European and Theoretical Perspectives.* Oxford: Blackwell.

———. 1998. Between Cosmopolis and Community. In Archibugi, Held, and Köhler, 152–78.

Bovens, Mark, Paul 't Hart, and Guy Peters, eds. 2001. *Success and Failure in Public Governance: A Comparative Analysis.* Cheltenham: Edward Elgar.

Buruma, Ian. 1999. *Voltaire's Coconuts.* London: Weidenfeld and Nicholson.

Calleo, David. 2001. *Rethinking Europe's Future.* Princeton, NJ: Princeton University Press.

Christiano, Thomas. 1996. *The Rule of the Many.* Boulder, CO: Westview Press.

Cohen, Joshua, and Joel Rogers. 1995. *Associations and Democracy.* London: Verso.

Cohen, Joshua, and Charles Sabel. 1997. Directly-Deliberative Polyarchy. *European Law Journal* 3:313–42.

Crouch, Colin. 1999. *Social Change in Western Europe.* Oxford: Oxford University Press.

Cruise O'Brien, Connor. 1994. *On the Eve of the Millennium.* New York: Free Press.

Dahl, Robert A. 1999. Can International Organizations Be Democratic? In Shapiro and Hacker-Cordón, 19–36.

Dalton, Russell. 2004. *Democratic Challenges, Democratic Choices.* Oxford: Oxford University Press.

De Beus, Jos. 2001a. Are Third Way Social Democrats Friends or Enemies of European Integration? In Magnusson and Strath, 361–88.

———. 2001b. Dutch Social Democracy and EMU. In Notermans, 225–52.

———. 2001c. Quasi-National European Identity and European Democracy. *Law and Philosophy* 20:283–311.

De Beus, Jos, and Jeannette Mak. 2001. The Missing European Public. *Acta Politica* 36:339–57.
———. 2005. European Integration without Europeanisation. *Acta Politica* 40, forthcoming.
De la Porte, Caroline, and Philippe Pochet, eds. 2002. *Building Social Europe through the Open Method of Co-ordination*. Brussels: P.I.E.-Peter Lang.
De Swaan, Abram. 2001. *Words of the World: The Global Language System*. Cambridge: Polity Press.
Díez Medrano, Juan. 2003. *Framing Europe: Attitudes to European Integration in Germany, Spain, and the United Kingdom*. Princeton, NJ: Princeton University Press.
Dobson, Lynn, and Andreas Follesdal, eds. 2004. *Political Theory and the European Constitution*. London: Routledge.
Duchêne, Francois. 1994. *Jean Monnet: The First Statesman of Interdependence*. New York: Norton.
Dunn, John. 2000. *The Cunning of Unreason: Making Sense of Politics*. London: HarperCollins.
Dyson, Kenneth. 2000. EMU and Europeanization. *Journal of Common Market Studies* 38:645–66.
Easton, David. 1965. *A Systems Analysis of Political Life*. New York: Wiley.
Eder, Klaus, and Bernhard Giessen, eds. 2001. *European Citizenship: National Legacies and Transnational Projects*. Oxford: Oxford University Press.
Elster, Jon. 1995. Forces and Mechanisms in the Constitution Making Process. *Duke Law Journal* 45:364–96.
Eriksen, Erik, Andreas Follesdal, and Raino Malnes. 1995. Europeanization and Normative Political Theory. Working paper 1, ARENA – Center for European Studies, University of Oslo.
Eriksen, Erik Oddvar, and John Erik Fossum, eds. 2000. *Democracy in the European Union: Integration through Deliberation?* London: Routledge.
Etzioni, Amitai. 1996. *The New Golden Rule: Community and Morality in a Democratic Society*. New York: Basic Books.
———. 2001. *Political Unification Revisited*. 2nd ed. Lanham, MD: Lexington Books.
———. 2004. *From Empire to Community: A New Approach to International Relations*. New York: Palgrave Macmillan.
European Commission. 2001. European Governance: A White Paper. Luxembourg: Office for Official Publications of the European Communities.
Featherstone, Kevin, and Claudio M. Radaelli, eds. 2003. *The Politics of Europeanization*. Oxford: Oxford University Press.
Fennema, Meindert. 2001. *De moderne democratie: De geschiedenis van een politieke theorie*. 2nd ed. Amsterdam: Spinhuis.
Ferguson, Niall. 2002. *The Cash Nexus: Money and Power in the Modern World, 1700–2000*. London: Penguin Books.
Ferry, Jean-Marc. 2000. *La question de l'état européen*. Paris: Gallimard.
Gallagher, Michael, Michael Laver, and Peter Mair. 2000. *Representative Government in Modern Europe*. 3rd ed. New York: McGraw-Hill.
Gillingham, John. 2003. *European Integration, 1950–2003: Superstate or New Market Economy?* Cambridge: Cambridge University Press.

Goodin, Robert E., ed. 1996. *The Theory of Institutional Design*. Cambridge: Cambridge University Press.

Gowan, Peter, and Perry Anderson, eds. 1997. *The Question of Europe*. London: Verso.

Green Cowles, Maria, James Caporaso, and Thomas Risse, eds. 2001. *Transforming Europe: Europeanization and Domestic Change*. Ithaca, NY: Cornell University Press.

Guibernau, Montserrat, ed. 2001. *Governing European Diversity*. London: Sage.

Gutmann, Amy, and Dennis Thompson. 1996. *Democracy and Disagreement*. Cambridge, MA: Harvard University Press.

Haas, Ernst. 1958. *The Uniting of Europe*. London: Stevens.

———. 1964. *Beyond the Nation-State: Functionalism and International Organization*. Stanford, CA: Stanford University Press.

Habermas, Jürgen. 1962. *Strukturwandel der Öffentlichkeit*. Neuwied: Luchterhand.

———. 1985. *Der philosophische Diskurs der Moderne*. Frankfurt: Suhrkamp.

———. 1990. *Die nachholende Revolution*. Frankfurt: Suhrkamp.

———. 1992. *Faktizität und Geltung: Beiträge zur Diskurstheorie des Rechts und des demokratischen Rechtsstaats*. Frankfurt: Suhrkamp.

———. 1996. *Die Einbeziehung der Anderen*. Frankfurt: Suhrkamp.

———. 1998. *Die postnationale Konstellation*. Frankfurt: Suhrkamp.

———. 2001a. *Zeite der Übergange*. Frankfurt: Suhrkamp.

———. 2001b. Why Europe Needs a Constitution. *New Left Review* 11 (September–October): 5–26.

———. 2004. *Der gespaltene Westen*. Frankfurt: Suhrkamp.

Hall, Peter A., and David Soskice, eds. 2001. *Varieties of Capitalism: The Institutional Foundations of Comparative Advantage*. Oxford: Oxford University Press.

Hayek, Friedrich. 1939. The Economic Conditions of Interstate Federalism. In *Individualism and Economic Order*, 255–72. London: Routledge.

Held, David. 1995. *Democracy and the Global Order: From the Modern State to Cosmopolitan Governance*. Cambridge: Polity Press.

Hermann, Richard, Marilyn Brewer, and Thomas Risse, eds. 2004. *Transnational Identities: Becoming European in the EU*. Lanham, MD: Rowman and Littlefield.

Hirst, Paul. 1994. *Associative Democracy: New Forms of Economic and Social Governance*. Cambridge: Polity Press.

Hitchcock, William I. 2002. *The Struggle for Europe: The Turbulent History of a Divided Continent, 1945–2002*. New York: Doubleday.

Hix, Simon. 1999. *The Political System of the European Union*. London: Palgrave.

———. 2002. Parties at the European Level. In Webb, Farrell, and Holliday, 280–309.

———. 2005. *The Political System of the European Union*. 2nd. ed. London: Palgrave.

Hix, Simon, and Christopher Lord. 1997. *Political Parties in the European Union*. London: Macmillan.

Höffe, Otfried. 1999. *Demokratie im Zeitalter der Globalisierung*. München: Beck.

Hoffmann, Stanley. 1995. *The European Sisyphus: Essays on Europe, 1964–1994*. Boulder, CO: Westview Press.

Hooghe, Liesbet, and Gary Marks. 2001. *Multilevel Governance and European Integration*. Oxford: Rowman and Littlefield.

Imig, Doug, and Sidney Tarrow, eds. 2001. *Contentious Europeans: Protest and Politics in an Integrating Europe*. Lanham, MD: Rowman and Littlefield.

Janssen, Joseph. 2001. Publieke steun voor de Europese Unie. PhD diss., University of Maastricht.

Jordan, Andrew. 2001. The European Union: An Evolving System of Multi-Level Governance . . . or Government? *Policy and Politics* 29:193–208.

Judt, Tony. 1996. *A Grand Illusion? An Essay on Europe.* London: Penguin Books.

Koopmans, Ruud. 2005. The Transformation of Political Mobilization and Communication in European Public Spheres. Final report. Berlin: WZB.

Kymlicka, Will. 1995. *Multicultural Citizenship.* Oxford: Clarendon Press.

———. 2001. *Politics in the Vernacular.* Oxford: Oxford University Press.

———. 2002. *Contemporary Political Philosophy.* 2nd ed. Oxford: Oxford University Press.

Laffan, Brigid, Rory O'Donnell, and Michael Smith. 2000. *Europe's Experimental Union: Rethinking Integration.* London: Routledge.

Laitin, David. 1997. The Cultural Identities of a European State. *Politics and Society* 25:277–302.

Leonard, Mark. 2005. *Perpetual Power: Why Europe Will Run the 21st Century.* New York: HarperCollins.

Liebert, Ulrike. 2001. Constructing EMU. In Magnusson and Strath, 271–300.

Lijphart, Arend. 1999. *Patterns of Democracy: Government Forms and Performance in Thirty-Six Countries.* New Haven, CT: Yale University Press.

Luban, David. 1996. The Publicity Principle. In Goodin, 154–98.

Ludlow, Peter. 2002. *The Laeken Council.* Brussels: EuroComment.

Magnusson, Lars, and Bo Strath, eds. 2001. *From the Werner Plan to the EMU.* Brussels: P.I.E.-Peter Lang.

Mair, Peter. 2000a. The Limited Impact of Europe on National Party Systems. *West European Politics* 23 (4): 27–51.

———. 2000b. Political Parties and Democracy. Paper presented at the Wiardi Beckman Stichting Seminar on The Futures of Political Parties, Amsterdam, July 5.

Mak, Jeannette. 2001. Selling Europe. PhD diss., European University Institute, Florence.

Manin, Bernhard. 1997. *The Principles of Representative Government.* Cambridge: Cambridge University Press.

March, James G., and Johan P. Olsen. 1995. *Democratic Governance.* New York: Free Press.

Marks, Gary, and Marco R. Steenbergen, eds. 2004. *European Integration and Political Conflict.* Cambridge: Cambridge University Press.

Marquand, David. 1978. Towards a Europe of the Parties. *Political Quarterly* 49:425–45.

Mazower, Mark. 1998. *Dark Continent: Europe's Twentieth Century.* London: Allen Lane.

Middlemas, Keith. 1995. *Orchestrating Europe: The Informal Politics of European Union 1973–1995.* London: Fontana.

Newman, Michael. 1996. *Democracy, Sovereignty, and the European Union.* London: Sage.

Nicolaidis, Kalypso, and Robert Howse, eds. 2001. *The Federal Vision: Legitimacy and Levels of Governance in the United States and the European Union.* Oxford: Oxford University Press.

Norman, Peter. 2003. *The Accidental Constitution: The Story of the European Convention*. Brussels: EuroComment.

Norris, Pippa. 2000. *A Virtuous Circle: Political Communications in Postindustrial Societies*. Cambridge: Cambridge University Press.

Notermans, Ton, ed. 2001. *Social Democracy and Monetary Union*. New York: Berghahn Books.

Nye, Jr., Joseph S. 2004. *Soft Power: The Means to Success in World Politics*. New York: PublicAffairs.

Pagden, Anthony, ed. 2002. *The Idea of Europe: From Antiquity to the European Union*. Cambridge: Cambridge University Press.

Peters, B. Guy, and Jon Pierre. 2002. Governance and Governability in the European Union. Paper presented at the Workshop Governability in Post-Industrial Societies, Utrecht School of Governance, Utrecht University, April 26–27.

Pierre, Jon, ed. 2000. *Debating Governance: Authority, Steering, and Democracy*. Oxford: Oxford University Press.

Pierre, Jon, and B. Guy Peters. 2000. *Governance, Politics, and the State*. London: Macmillan.

Pizzorno, Alessandro. 2002. The Impossibilities of Democracy. Stein Rokkan Lecture, European Consortium of Political Science, Turin, March 22–27.

Pocock, John. 2002. Some Europes in Their History. In Pagden, 55–71.

Pogge, Thomas W. 1997. Creating Supranational Institutions Democratically: Reflections on the European Union's "Democratic Deficit." *Journal of Political Philosophy* 5:163–82.

Pond, Elisabeth. 1999. *The Rebirth of Europe*. Washington, DC: Brookings Institution.

Rifkin, Jeremy. 2004. *The European Dream: How Europe's Vision of the Future is Quietly Eclipsing the American Dream*. New York: Tarcher/Penguin.

Scharpf, Fritz W. 1975. *Demokratietheorie zwischen Utopie und Anpassung*. Kronberg/Ts.: Scriptor Verlag.

———. 1997. *Games Real Actors Play: Actor-Centered Institutionalism in Policy Research*. Boulder, CO: Westview Press.

———. 1999. *Governing in Europe: Effective and Democratic?* Oxford: Oxford University Press.

———. 2003. The Vitality of the Nation State in 21st-Century Europe. In *De vitaliteit van de nationale staat in het Europa van de 21ste eeuw*, ed. WRR, 15–30. WRR-lecture 2002. Groningen: Stenfert Kroese.

Scharpf, Fritz W., and Vivien A. Schmidt, eds. 2000. *Welfare and Work in the Open Economy*, vol. 1, *From Vulnerability to Competitiveness in Comparative Perspective*; vol. 2, *Diverse Responses to Common Challenges in Twelve Countries*. Oxford: Oxford University Press.

Schlesinger, Philippe, and Deirdre Kevin. 2000. Can the EU Become a Sphere of Publics? In Eriksen and Fossum, 206–29.

Schmidt, Manfred. 2002. The Consociational State. *Acta Politica* 37:213–27.

Schmitt, Herman, and Jacques Thomassen, eds. 1999. *Political Representation and Legitimacy in the European Union*. Oxford: Oxford University Press.

Schmitter, Philippe. 2000. *How to Democratize the EU . . . and Why Bother?* Lanham, MD: Rowman and Littlefield.

Shapiro, Ian, and Casiano Hacker-Cordón, eds. 1999. *Democracy's Edges*. Cambridge: Cambridge University Press.

Shore, Cris. 2000. *Building Europe: The Cultural Politics of European Integration*. London: Routledge.

Siedentop, Larry. 2000. *Democracy in Europe*. London: Allen Lane.

Slaughter, Anne-Marie. 2004. *A New World Order*. Princeton, NJ: Princeton University Press.

Smith, Eivind, ed. 1996. *National Parliaments as Cornerstone of European Integration*. The Hague: Kluwer Law International.

Snyder, Jack. 2000. *From Voting to Violence: Democratization and Nationalist Conflict*. New York: Norton.

Therborn, Göran. 1995. *European Modernity and Beyond: The Trajectory of European Societies, 1945–2000*. London: Sage.

Thompson, Dennis. 1999. Democratic Theory and Global Society. *Journal of Political Philosophy* 7:111–25.

Tsoukalis, Loukas. 2003. *What Kind of Europe?* Oxford: Oxford University Press.

Tully, James. 1995. *Strange Multiplicity: Constitutionalism in an Age of Diversity*. Cambridge: Cambridge University Press.

Van der Eijk, Cees, and Mark Franklin, eds. 1996. *Choosing Europe? The European Electorate and National Politics in the Face of Union*. Ann Arbor: University of Michigan Press.

Van de Steeg, Marianne. 2005. The Public Sphere in the European Union. PhD diss., European University Institute, Florence.

Van Tatenhove, Jan. 2002. Policy Making in an Institutional Void. Paper presented at the XVth World Congress of Sociology, Brisbane, July 7–13.

Visser, Jelle. 2002. Is the European Employment Strategy the Answer? Paper presented at the Workshop Governability in Post-Industrial Societies, Utrecht School of Governance, Utrecht University, April 26–27.

Warren, Mark E. 2000. *Democracy and Association*. Princeton, NJ: Princeton University Press.

Webb, Paul, David Farrell, and Ian Holliday, eds. 2002. *Political Parties in Advanced Industrial Democracies*. Oxford: Oxford University Press.

Weiler, Joseph. 1996. European Neo-Constitutionalism. In Bellamy and Castiglione, 105–21.

———. 1999. *The Constitution of Europe*. Cambridge: Cambridge University Press.

Young, Iris Marion. 2000. *Inclusion and Democracy*. Oxford: Oxford University Press.

Zeitlin, Jonathan, and Philippe Pochet, eds., with Lars Magnusson. 2005. *The Open Method of Co-ordination in Action*. Brussels: P.I.E.-Peter Lang.

5

Deepening Social Europe through Legal Pluralism[1]

Anton Hemerijck

FROM A DIPLOMATIC TO A POLITICAL UNION

The European Union finds itself at an important political juncture. It could be argued that the EU is experiencing the painful transition from a *diplomatic* to a *political* union. Politicization of the EU polity in recent years is leading to growing distrust among finance ministers over the Stability and Growth Pact, which has a negative impact on economic performance of the European economy, widening the gaps in growth, employment, and R&D investments between the EU and the U.S. economy. Europe is going through a period of sluggish growth. Job creation has been elusive. Conservative governments came back into power in most member states. Many countries are in the process of implementing painful social reforms, which increasingly encounter stiff resistance, in the face of very high levels of unemployment. In addition, the debate over the accession of Turkey, tussle between the European Parliament and the new Commission, over the candidacy of Buttiglioni, in 2004, and, finally, the French and Dutch referenda over the draft Constitution in 2005—all this has put the EU into a severe legitimacy crisis. Feelings of political discontent not only undermine the European economic project, they also negatively affect the national welfare states that make up the EU. To the extent that European economic integration seemingly destabilizes national arrangements for social protection, this is likely to trigger defensive mobilization on the part of social and political actors aiming to restore national closure of their welfare state with strong elements of exclusion and xenophobia, putting into jeopardy the political space for the establishment of a legal framework for the integration of ten new member states, while at the same time creating the economic and social conditions for an integrated labor market with decent social protection across the enlarged European Union. To be sure, the accession of ten more member states to the European Union in May 2004 has brought about an enormous increase in the economic and social heterogeneity. As a result, agreement on binding employment and social standards, in line with traditional community legislation, will be ever more difficult to achieve. I hold, therefore, that social progress in Europe will have to rely more heavily on legal pluralism, on horizontal EU social dialogue and "soft-law" processes of open coordination, if it is to succeed. To be sure, this does not rule out gloomy scenarios of competitive retrenchment.

Notwithstanding the immanent legitimacy crisis, since the mid-1990s employment and social policy concerns have moved progressively toward the top of the European agenda. The realization of an internal market and the creation of a monetary union in a period of high unemployment have provided strong incentives for European employment- and social-policy initiatives. The incorporation of a separate employment chapter in the Treaty of Amsterdam (June 1997) marks a watershed in the Europeanization of social policy. Through the mid-1990s, the debate over the future of social Europe was couched in terms of "good intentions, high principles, and little action" (Lange 1993, 7). Today, EU social policy is no longer the "stepchild" of European integration. The completion of the internal market and the European Monetary Union seems to have made it increasingly difficult to exclude employment and social concerns from the European policy agenda. However, claims with respect to the emancipation of "social Europe" should not be exaggerated. By and large, European employment- and social-policy initiatives, triggered by "spillover" effects of the dynamic of single market and monetary integration, complement rather than replace entrenched national welfare commitments and policy legacies. Nevertheless, work- and welfare-policy issues have since the mid-1990s become ever more intertwined with the single market and EMU. As a consequence, the EU today is no longer a "single-purpose" economic intergovernmental organization or *Zweckverband*. With integrated markets and a single currency, proper social protection and a healthy labor market are no longer a mere matter for national governments. The question therefore is not *whether* the European Union has to play a role in social and employment policy, decided by some simplistic binary "subsidiarity" test, but *how* it can make its most effective and legitimate contribution to the ongoing process of (self-)transformation in Europe's highly diverse social-market economies (Hemerijck 2002).

Any adequate understanding of the state of social Europe, I argue, has to be built upon the interaction of highly entrenched national welfare regimes and the emergent reality of a deepening and widening EU employment- and social-policy profile. In this chapter I hope to show how national welfare states have over time come to be deeply embedded within a wider EU economic- and social-policy space. This contribution deals explicitly with the *dynamic* process of the Europeanization of employment and social policy through initiatives of legal pluralism. Europeanization creates new constraints and opportunities for both domestic welfare reform and EU social-policy innovation. Against the backdrop of profound changes in economic conditions, social problems, and political ambitions, together with consecutive waves of EU enlargement, European elements are incorporated into national welfare systems, and vice versa. Notwithstanding the increased importance of the EU, the nation state remains the principal site for welfare reform and the cornerstone of European institutions.

Before turning to the historical narrative, the chapter begins (section two) with a conceptual exposition of the shared patrimony of Europe's social-market economies in terms of a specific triad of common normative, cognitive, and institutional characteristics, which as I will show has its roots in both liberal and communitarian political, social, and legal thought. Next (section three), I continue with a theoretical exposition of what I would like to coin the "double bind of social Europe," resulting from the joint commitment to domestic social-policy intervention and European market integration. It is exactly this double commitment that makes it extremely difficult to unilaterally shift social competencies from the jurisdiction of national welfare states to the level of the European Union. At the same time, however, I believe that the double bind of social Europe triggered the "qualitative turn" of European employment and social policy in the 1990s, on the basis of innovative procedures of legal pluralism. Next, sections four and five deal with the empirical dynamic of social-policy Europeanization since the 1957 Rome Treaty. Section four concerns the period from the Golden Age of self-contained national welfare states to the launch of the Single Market Program. Section five focuses more explicitly on the innovations in the direction of legal pluralism in EU employment and social policymaking, since the mid-1990s, under the shadow of the EMU. In a piecemeal fashion, the launch of the social dialogue and experiments with the open method of coordination in employment, social-cohesion, and pension policy have enabled the member states to strike a new balance between the goals of competitiveness and solidarity, based on an explicit recognition of *legitimate diversity*. Next, section six discusses the substantive challenges and the likely impact of enlargement for Europe's national welfare states. How much diversity in policy design and economic development can the EU effectively absorb? The closing section tries to assess the robustness of the EU social-policy profile in terms of the institutional complementarities between "hard" community legislation, i.e., enforceable directives and regulation, bi- and tripartite social dialogue, and "softer" forms of *governance by objectives* through open coordination, based on recommendations and guidelines.

THE SOCIAL-MARKET ECONOMY

In the debate over the contribution of EU policymaking to employment growth, making work pay, gender equalization, fair and sustainable pensions, poverty alleviation, the promotion of social inclusion, and the pursuit of high-quality and sustainable health care, the expression of a distinctly "European social model" is increasingly used as a reference term (Falkner 1998; De la Porte and Pochet 2002; Hemerijck 2002; Scharpf 2001, 2002; Vandenbroucke 2002; Trubek and Mosher 2003; Offe 2003).

Despite various attempts of the European Commission to delineate the notion of a European social model, thus far descriptions and definitions have remained fairly general. In the wake of the ratification of the Maastricht Treaty (1992), the notion of a *social dimension* of the European Union gained prominence in EU publications. The White Paper of the Commission on Growth, Employment, and Competitiveness (European Commission 1993) for the first time delineated the "European social model" as a combination of economic performance and social solidarity, based on a mixed economy, with the participation of all citizens, which balances markets with state steering and social dialogue. The White Paper also underlined the importance of social-partnership support for the single market and the single currency to the development of a specific social dimension in cooperation with the member states. Employing a more declarative language, the *Comité des Sages* in 1996 in its position paper "For a Europe of Civil and Social Rights" declared that:

> Europe cannot be built on unemployment and social exclusion, nor on a shortfall in citizenship. Europe will be a Europe for everyone, for all its citizens, or it will be nothing. It will not tackle the new challenges now facing it—competitiveness, the demographic situation, enlargement and globalisation—if it does not strengthen its social dimension and demonstrate its ability to ensure that fundamental social rights are respected and applied (European Commission 1996, 23).

The Comité des Sages recognized the importance of a minimum income and repeatedly emphasized the dangers of increasing inequality. The 1997 Dutch presidency advocated reconsidering the welfare state as a "productive factor," while launching the common employment policy (Hemerijck 1998). In turn, employment growth should help to ensure the sustainability of Europe's high-quality social-protection systems. At the same time, the Commission endorsed this insight in its communication on "Modernising and Improving Social Protection in the European Union":

> The European social model is valued and should be consolidated. The model is based both on common values and the understanding that social policy and economic performance are not contradictory but mutually reinforcing. Highly

developed social protection systems are a major component of this social model (European Commission 1997, 1).

The Lisbon Summit in March 2000 came out in favor of a Europe with "more and better jobs and greater social cohesion." With respect to employment, the 2000 Lisbon Council set a target of a 70 percent employment rate, and a 60 percent employment rate for women, to be achieved in 2010. As a follow-up to Lisbon, the Nice European Council in December 2000 endorsed the crucial contribution of the "European social model" to the knowledge-based economy:

> The European social model, with its developed systems of social protection, must underpin the transformation to the knowledge economy. . . . People are Europe's main asset and should be the focal point of the Union's policies. Investing in people and developing an active and dynamic welfare state will be crucial both to Europe's place in the knowledge economy and for ensuring that the emergence of this new economy does not compound the existing social problems of unemployment, social exclusion and poverty (European Union 2000, annex 1, no. 7).

The Nice Council also witnessed the "solemn declaration" of the Charter of Fundamental Rights. The Charter broke new ground for social Europe by including a list of fundamental rights, not only civil and political rights but also social and industrial rights. However, it was not given a formal legal status.

The Belgian presidency in 2001 forged a political agreement on quantitative indicators for monitoring progress with respect to social inclusion across member states. It also endorsed, at the Laeken Council, in December 2001 common objectives for pension reform. Under the charismatic leadership of Vandenbroucke, Minister for Social Affairs and Pensions, the Belgian presidency pressed the European Union to support the member states to develop "active welfare states."

Many outstanding issues of how to rescue social Europe from its traditional "Cinderella status" (Shaw 2003) have been hotly debated in the Working Group on Social Europe of the European Convention, ranging from the normative principles to be included in a constitution and the legal status of the Charter, to policy objectives and instruments of regulation, the division of institutional competencies between EU institutions, the member states, and the social partners in the areas of employment policy and social protection, together with the coordination between EU economic and social policy more broadly. A central concern in the final report of the Social Europe Working Group (European Convention 2003a, 8) is that the pursuit of "social objectives" should be "equivalent, not subordinate, to economic objectives" in an enlarging Union: "The EU cannot be a credible force for good in the wider world if it is indifferent to questions of social justice and poverty in European society or to how its citizens are treated at work and in retirement" (ibid., 4).

My main reservation against the underspecified use of the concept of "the European social model" in the singular is that it suggests a large degree of *uniformity* across the political economies of Europe (Hemerijck 2002). Europe's social-market economies display substantial differences in development, political traditions, policy design, and institutional make-up. This is the consequence of the divisive experiences in European history of feudalism, Catholicism, rival military strife, absolutism, the Reformation, the Enlightenment, democracy, capitalist industrial development, working class protest, economic depression, and two dislocating twentieth-century world wars. The lesson of these experiences, as Offe (2003) has aptly put it, is that in an environment of international rivalry, class cleavages, and religious divisions any "winner-takes-all strategy" does not lead to stable and viable solutions.

If discontinuities, conflicts, and diversities (of interests, of identities, of ideas) can neither be escaped through "exit" nor repressed through state terror, the only remaining option is to institutionalize some viable form of coexistence of classes, states, and identities. This is the lesson on the learning of which both history and the territorial situation of Europe have put a high premium since the Westphalian peace settlement—the lesson of bridging, regulating, and constraining domestic and international conflict while at the same time recognizing the legitimacy and inescapability of diversity (Offe 2003, 440).

If there is anything distinctive about European societies, it is the recognition of *legitimate diversity* and the related high value placed on the *accommodation of interests* through mutual compromise rather than top-down imposition and adversialism. Likewise, postwar European integration is best understood as an attempt to design a supranational polity so as to manage economic interdependence and cultural diversity through negotiated policy coordination (Moravcsik 1998).

Normative, Cognitive, and Institutional Foundations

Respect for *legitimate diversity* and the political preference for *interest accommodation* in orderly fashion have left a large imprint on contemporary European political economies. Both the commitment to the welfare state and social-partnership participation in economic policymaking can be observed as distinctive outcomes of Europe's historical recognition of legitimate diversity, which set Europe's social-market economies apart from other geopolitical regions of the world, such as North America and Southeast Asia.

European social-market economies do share a number of common characteristics (Hemerijck 2002). We can think of a shared patrimony of social Europe, made up of a distinctive triad of normative, cognitive, and institutional characteristics. *Normatively*, there is a fundamental commitment to social justice, to basic social citizenship, to the pooling of social risks collectively across Europe. Social citizenship is the key organizing principle of the lives of several generations. It represents a deeply institutionalized social contract. In the words of Marshall, social citizenship holds out a promise of the enlargement, enrichment, and equalization of people's "life chances" (Marshall [1950] 1963, 107). This implied, practically everywhere in Europe, the expansion of mass education as an instrument for equal opportunities, together with the introduction of a universal right to real income "not proportionate to the market value of the claimant" (ibid., 100), as a means to equalize living conditions and eliminate social risks across the life cycle. Protecting the vulnerable and preventing the disadvantaged from becoming vulnerable lies at the heart of a European ethos of "equal social worth." "Minimum guaranteed resources" are widely accepted and expected by European publics and deeply entrenched in policy programs and institutions. A rights-based justification of the welfare state captures an empowerment strategy, sanctioned by law. It enabled all citizens to exercise their basic civil and political rights. The vocabulary of reform is in most member states couched in terms of a solidaristic commitment that society will not abandon those who fail. The welfare state revolved around three constitutive elements. First, citizenship is about the membership in a nation state and a "social contract" between the state and its citizens. Second, it delineates a bundle of universal rights. Third, it refers to a particular collective identity of a political community, within which citizenship rights can be exercised. In other words, social rights not only provide individuals with a sense of material security against the adverse effects of poverty, illness, disability, unemployment, and old age in a territorially bound state. In turn, social security encourages a sense of belonging and commitment to a kind of national society within which citizens live.

Rereading Marshall in the context of the debate between liberals and communitarians, I am tempted to reclassify his lectures for contemporary use as being communitarian-liberal in spirit. In line with the communitarian tradition, Marshall's lectures were empirically oriented, sociologically informed, based on a rather expansive conception of politics and society, and particularly concerned with the societal processes of inclusion. Unlike contemporary communitarians and more in line with the liberal political philosophy of Rawls (1971), Marshall's approach is far more political. Marshall's state-centered, universalist, rights-based justification of the welfare state captures an empowerment strategy, sanctioned by law, to enable all citizens to exercise their basic civil and political rights, rightly underscored in the welfare-liberal tradition, so as to let them share, in line with communitarian reasoning, "to the full" in the "social heritage" of the nation in accordance with the "standard prevailing in society."

The *commitment to the welfare state*, to basic social citizenship, to the pooling of social risks collectively, is deeply entrenched in postwar social and economic policymaking across Europe. The preference for high levels of employment, universal access to health care and education; adequate social insurance for sickness, disability, unemployment, and old age; and minimum resources of social assistance to prevent poverty and reduce social exclusion—this preference is widely accepted by European publics. The stigmatizing discourse of the "deserving" versus "undeserving" poor never really gained currency in the European Union, apart from the Thatcher era in the United Kingdom in the 1980s. Gender equality has become one of the linchpin objectives of EU employment- and social-policy regulation (Meehan 1993). In this respect, as Esping-Andersen (2002) observes, the European debate is close to the normative benchmark of Rawls, stipulating that substantial changes in the social status of citizens must be to the greatest advantage of the worst-off. In agreement with Rawls's "difference principle," the European social ethos prioritizes social inclusion, the welfare of the least advantaged, and the reduction of inequalities as essential ingredients in any strategy to boost competitiveness.

At the *cognitive* level, secondly, it is recognized that social justice can contribute to economic efficiency and competition. As a productive factor, a term coined during the Dutch presidency in 1997, social policy can minimize uncertainty, mitigate market downturns, and increase the ability and willingness to take risks, acquire more specialized skills, and pursue investment opportunities. Social policy also serves to create and stabilize collective goods, channel industrial conflict in periods of structural adjustment, and, in turn, foster political stability and social cohesion (Streeck 1997). A relatively equal distribution of incomes reduces dire poverty and social instability. If social cohesion and stability are thus recognized as productive resources, then surely the alleged contradiction between social justice and economic efficiency breaks down. Social policy can then no longer be perceived as consumption-related benefits, taken out of an efficient economy by distributive politics. From this perspective, social policy and economic performance are indissolubly interconnected. Comprehensive welfare states ensure that most income groups have reasonable access to education, which is good for overall productivity and, as a consequence, beneficial for high-quality investment decisions. By the same token, a well-developed system of social welfare and protection allows citizens to fulfill socially useful and prosperity-enhancing functions that are economically risky for individuals. The welfare state is regarded as a social investment. Against the neoliberal assumption of a big "trade-off" between economic efficiency and social justice, European policy elites agree that social policy is an essential factor in promoting economic adjustment, that there is no contradiction between economic competitiveness and social cohesion.

Finally, *institutionally*, European systems of industrial relations are marked by high degrees of interest organization and comprehensive negotiations between the government and the social partners over conflicts of interest in matters of economic and social policy. Compared to North America, industrial relations are stable; the majority of workers are covered by collective agreements determining working conditions, employment protection, and living standards. Social partnership, with "trust" as a constitutive element, moreover, encourages a problem-solving style of policymaking, as it provides collective actors with the necessary social capital and institutional resources to overcome sectionalist interests. Today's organization of production relies heavily on realizing gains from cooperation. Comprehensive systems of industrial relations, anchored in collective industrial rights—like the right to union representation, codetermination, and health and safety requirements—permit macroeconomically responsive wage setting (Streeck 1997). The institutions of collective bargaining, legal extension of collective agreements, and works councils foster long-term employer–employee relationship at the enterprise level. Institutions of social partnership encourage employers and trade unions to invest in and administer vocational education and training programs, contributing to the country's competitiveness by upgrading human capital.

Also at the level of European Union strategy, great weight is placed on the contribution of the "social partners" to policy formulation, execution, and evaluation. The EU is committed to an institutionalized social dialogue between the two sides of industry together with policymakers, as well as to other forms of concertation with the representatives of "civil society." Building on an earlier tradition of sponsored "social dialogue," the Maastricht Treaty gave the social partners the right to reach European collective agreements that could be translated into directives (see below). The European Commission very much sees social-partnership involvement as contributing to the legitimacy of its social and economic policymaking. In terms of workplace representation, the Directive of the Establishment of a European Works Council is now supplemented by the European Company Statute (Directive 2001/86/C).

The line of reasoning behind the potential positive effect of social policy on economic performance as a productive factor clearly also makes a virtue of institutions that support the argument that a strong economy requires a strong welfare state. The dimension of social dialogue and organized trust features prominently in communitarian social and legal thought (Handler 1990; Cotterrell 1995). Especially Cotterrell emphasizes the crucial importance of social interaction on the basis of interpersonal trust as the basic building block of any community. Moreover, an active and participative "civil society" is believed to contribute to the effectiveness and legitimacy of European public policy. However, it must be stressed that, in contrast to the possible adverse effects of social policy on economic performance, the reasoning behind the idea of social policy as a productive factor occupies a far more difficult intellectual and practical position. Any explanation of the interactive effects between social policy and economic performance is critically dependent on identifying institutional conditions under which it is possible to formulate and implement effective social and economic policy. Although comprehensive welfare states are surely not economically dysfunctional, certain policies do have a negative impact on economic processes. Excessively generous social-security benefits, not backed by activating labor-market policies, do undermine work incentives, contribute to a high tax burden, and lead to high gross labor costs. The analysis of social policy as a productive factor heavily relies on empirical data and case-by-case comparisons. We always need to consider the "fine" structures of the welfare state. There are no quick fixes. This makes the nature of policy prescriptions imminently conditional.

BEYOND THE DOUBLE BIND OF SOCIAL EUROPE

The welfare state, as it developed in Western Europe in the second half of the twentieth century, represents an extraordinary historical achievement. Never before in history, according to Scharpf (2003), had state authority been so fully under the control of democratic politics, and never before had it been used so effectively to ensure internal peace and public order, to promote economic growth and well-being, civil liberty, and social solidarity. The legitimacy and effectiveness of social and economic policy depended heavily on political authority over its citizens and control over economic resources within its territorial jurisdiction. This is no longer the case. Since the early 1980s, as a result of cumulative changes, the authority of the national welfare state over its own territorial and economic boundaries has been drastically reduced. The worldwide deconstruction of economic boundaries has especially inhibited the capacity of the national welfare state for effective social-problem solving (Hemerijck and Schludi 2000). Work- and welfare-policy issues have since the mid-1990s become ever more intertwined with the single market and EMU. The further European integration progresses, the more it infringes upon the basic features of national welfare regimes, the more economic integration will come to interact with the basic (re)distributional functions of the welfare state. While the Monetary Union has reduced the transaction costs of transnational trade and investment, for national governments presiding over expensive welfare states European economic integration has greatly increased the difficulties of managing national economies, regulating production processes, and financing social transfers and public services (Scharpf 2001).

When social problems can no longer be effectively resolved at national levels, it seems only natural to turn to the European level for effective and legitimate problem solving. However, benign European responses to "spillover" problems resulting from economic internationalization cannot be taken for granted in employment and social policy, for both technical and political reasons. First of all, EU member states not only differ in levels of economic development, also countries at the same level of economic development differ greatly in the levels and the structures of social-protection and public-service provision, with Ireland spending less than 35 percent of GDP for social protection and public services, and Sweden more than 58 percent. Secondly, the institutions of the European Union, which have been principally designed to seek market integration, are inadequate and ill-equipped for an expansion of social-policy competencies. The transposition of macroeconomic regulation from the level of the nation state to institutions of the European Union will not be matched by centralized social-policy initiatives. However much domestic reforms are constrained by the Single Market Program, EMU, and the Stability and Growth Pact, the territorial site of welfare reform remains the nation state. Expanding the reach of "positive integration"—to correct for "negative integration" of the removal of national barriers to trade and free competition—critically depends on unanimity within the Council of Ministers, which is even less likely to be forthcoming in a Union of twenty-five or more members with highly diverse social-policy repertoires and levels of economic development. Moreover, unpopular European solutions violating strongly held preferences of national electorates were impossible to uphold in national political arenas.

European welfare states today face the predicament of a "double bind." On the one hand, EU member states are unlikely to shed their welfare-state obligations, as this would jeopardize the political bases of their legitimacy. On the other hand, EU member states have, since the late 1970s, become irreversibly committed to a pervasive program of European economic integration. In the face of this double bind, EU member states cannot want to shed their welfare state function without undermining the territorial bases of their political legitimacy, while at the same time they cannot want to reverse the process of economic integration that increasingly exposes their now semisovereign welfare states to regulatory competition. From this pessimistic reading, the "uneven growth" between market-expanding "negative integration" and market-correcting "positive integration" will increasingly constrain national autonomy in politically salient areas of industrial relations, social security, labor-market regulation, and redistributive taxation, which make up the now semisovereign national welfare state (Leibfried and Pierson 1995, 44).

As a result of market integration, the loss of national exchange rates, interest-rate policies from EMU, and the accompanying budgetary restrictions of the Stability and Growth Pact, member states will increasingly be deprived of their capacity to maintain the kind of protective social-citizenship arrangements. They may find themselves in a vicious cycle of deflationary "beggar-thy-neighbor" strategies of internal devaluation, tax competition, "social dumping," and a "race-to-the-bottom" process of competitive retrenchment. To be sure, with a common monetary policy and the loss of exchange-rate flexibility, the burden of adjustment will be shifted onto labor markets and welfare regimes. Moreover, the agreement of the Stability and Growth Pact implies that fiscal policy can only play a limited role, as the 3 percent deficit limit obliges governments to cut social-security expenditure during an economic downturn. In addition, free mobility of goods, capital, and labor in the internal market has made it easier for economic actors to avoid legal restrictions, undermining the tax base necessary to finance national welfare states (Begg 2002). Ultimately, through the backdoor, European economic integration will forge a full-fledged, "disembedded," neoliberal European political economy.

I question the claim that the primacy of "negative integration" will inevitably overrun "positive integration." In the dynamic interaction between the EU market-making commitments and domestic social-protection arrangements, new forms of "embeddedness" have emerged over the past decades as a consequence of "political," not per se "functional," spillover effects of European economic integration. With the intensification of economic integration, political elites have come to realize that in order to maintain popular support for the European project, the EU must be able to present itself to its citizens as a credible institution of economic protection, and certainly not as a threat to established social rights (Offe 2003). European citizens expect that certain services will be provided by their national welfare states. If these expectations remain largely unfulfilled, the fundamental "social-citizenship contract," and hence the democratic legitimacy of both the national welfare state and the European-integration project, could be in jeopardy.

For an adequate understanding of the more benign dynamics at play, it is critically important to separate, as suggested by Ferrera (2002), two relevant dimensions. In order to bring out the interactive dynamic between very different national welfare systems vis-à-vis ongoing deepening and widening of EU employment and social policy, we need to set apart, on the one hand, (the diversity of) national welfare regimes, and on the other, the characteristic features of the emerging EU employment- and social-policy profile.

Following Esping-Andersen (1990) and Ferrera, Hemerijck, and Rhodes (2000), three or four distinct types of welfare state are distinguished. But even within each family cluster, there is considerable variation. The comprehensive Scandinavian welfare states are characterized by citizenship-based universal entitlements; generous replacement rates in transfer programs; general-revenue financing; a broad supply of social services beyond health and education; active family policy encouraging gender egalitarianism and women's integration in the labor market; low (Denmark) to high (Sweden) levels of employment protection, with a strong emphasis on active policies and training programs linked to general education; and corporatist industrial relations with peak-level bargaining, strong unions, and high levels of collective bargaining coverage.

The Anglo-Saxon welfare cluster, including Ireland and the United Kingdom, is characterized by a bias toward targeted, needs-based entitlements; low replacement rates in transfer programs; general-revenue financing; underdeveloped public social services beyond health and education; poor family services; low levels of employment protection, largely confined to ensure fair contracts, and no legacy of active labor-market policy, nor vocational training and education; and uncoordinated industrial relations with moderately strong unions, decentralized wage bargaining, and low levels of collective-bargaining coverage.

The Continental European welfare state, historically influenced by a combination of etatiste, corporatist, and familialist traditions, is characterized by occupationally distinct, employment-related social insurance; very unequal levels of generosity in transfer programs, combining generally very high pension-replacement rates; a contribution-biased revenue dependency; very modest levels of public social services beyond health and education, and often a considerable reliance on "third-sector" and private delivery; passive family policies premised on the conventional male-breadwinner family; generally strict levels of employment protection, meant to protect, once again, the male breadwinner combined with passive labor-market policies, but comprehensive systems of vocational education and training, especially in Germany, Austria, and the Netherlands; strong social partnership that extends into the administration of social insurance; and coordinated industrial relations, with a predominance of sectoral wage bargaining, with high levels of bargaining coverage and moderately strong unions.

Finally, the Southern European welfare family institutionally resembles the Continental welfare states, but provides more checkered and unequal coverage in terms of public services and social insurance, with disproportionately high expenditure on retirement. Holes in the social-safety net are patched by family members in countries such as Italy, Greece, Portugal, and Spain (Ferrera 1996).

Turning to the European Union, it should at the outset be emphasized that EU social-policy initiatives, for the most part, address a different set of questions than national welfare states do. As argued above, EU social-policy initiatives mainly deal with the "spillover" problems that arise from European market integration.

The European Union is primarily a community of rights that acts essentially by lawmaking. EU laws apply throughout the territory of the Union. They take precedence over the national laws of the member states. The competencies of the European Union arise from the founding treaties and always relate to a single authorization as laid down in art. 5 (1) EC. As a consequence, EU member states transfer part of their sovereignty to the European level. The result of this transfer of legal competencies has been the development of "multilevel governance," i.e., codecision making at different levels: the European Union and the member states, as well as regions and municipalities. Most decisions in primary law are taken by the European Council and the European Parliament, on the basis of proposals put forward by the European Commission. The Council can only act if the Commission sets an agenda with appropriate proposals. Thus a dominant role in the legislative process is delegated to the European Commission. The participatory rights of the European Parliament in the legislative process vary from issue area to issue area, which is separately regulated in the individual chapters of the Treaty. The European Court of Justice (ECJ) has to ensure that the application and interpretation of European Community law is in accordance with art. 220 EC.

The prevalent EU social- and employment-policy profile has four components (Ferrera, Hemerijck, and Rhodes 2000). First, on the level of *constitutional principles*, art. 2 EC explicitly mentions the promotion of high rates of employment and social protection, equality of men and women, high standards of living for EU inhabitants, and social cohesion and solidarity between member states as tasks of the Union, as core *normative principles* guiding Community action.

Secondly, *binding community legislation* (regulations and directives), following the logic of the Community method by which the Commission has the exclusive right of initiative, and the Council decides (preferably by qualified majority) with participation of the European Parliament (ideally codecision), subject to the jurisdiction of the ECJ, is now in place in many areas of social policy. The Treaty of Rome's market-compatibility requirement (largely related to the free movement of workers) lies at the heart of an elaborate set of supranational rules and jurisprudence, ensuring the transferability across member states of nationally defined entitlements and promoting the interpenetration of national social systems. Equal-treatment and gender-opportunities directives—spurred by ECJ case law deriving from them—have consolidated a binding set of rights for men and women across national borders. Various aspects of EU citizenship left their imprint on the Maastricht Treaty in 1992 (arts. 17–22). The debate in the Convention was about whether the Charter of Fundamental Rights "approved" of during the Nice Summit in December 2000, should be incorporated in the new Constitution.

Thirdly, a number of *institutional complementarities,* more in line with the basic tenets of legal pluralism, next to the traditional "community method," have in recent decades emerged to promote cooperation of member states on the politically sensitive aspects of social-security and employment policy. The bipartite social dialogue that is now included in the EC Treaty (art. 138), allows the social partners to conclude agreements on the community level, which may be transformed into (framework) directives. In addition to these relatively "hard" forms of coordination, many "softer" forms of cooperation and coordination have recently emerged, including the so-called "open method of coordination" (OMC) and the looser macroeconomic dialogue known as the Cologne process, bringing together the Council, the Commission, the European Central Bank, and the social partners with a representative of the monetary authorities outside the Eurozone (1999). The Cologne process is important in the development of a shared cognitive framework of the emergent EMU macroeconomic policy regime through a dialogue, in which the social partners can better anticipate the consequences of their strategies of collective action.

Finally, there exists a relatively autonomous *policy network*, *above and beyond the nation state*, of policy institutions and committees, such as the Social Protection Committee, the Employment Committee, the Economic Policy Committee, the Social Affairs and Labor Council. Many of the participants in these forums are capable of making alliances with nongovernmental actors, such as the European Trade Union Confederation (ETUC) and the European employers organization (UNICE), in shaping European policy developments (Falkner 1998; Ferrera, Hemerijck, and Rhodes 2000; De la Porte and Pochet 2002).

SOCIAL EUROPE IN HISTORICAL PERSPECTIVE

Over the past fifty years, at various stages of the process of European integration, depending on prevailing social and economic conditions, policy actors at various levels of decision making have tried to launch domestic and EU-level employment- and social-policy intervention. Moments of fundamental political change, often associated with consecutive waves of enlargement of the European Union, provided important windows of opportunity for policy redirection toward further Europeanization but also, at times, tendencies toward (re)nationalization. A case in point is the extent to which EMU convergence criteria, a clear example of Europeanization, acted as a catalyst in the resurgence of national "social pacts" in the 1990s. Economic conditions, political ambitions, enlargement dynamics, in interaction with the path-dependent imprint of national social-policy legacies, thus channel and shape the idiosyncratic institutionalization of social Europe in the enlarging European Union. The interactive dynamic between national welfare arrangements and European social-policy constraints and ambitions, in the second half of the twentieth century, can generally be divided into four periods (see table 5.1): (i) economic modernization and expansion of the national welfare state (1950–1973);

Table 5.1 Development of European Social Policy

Period	*National Level*	*European Level*	*Europeanization of Social Policy*	*Governance Method*	*Enlargement-Related Diversity*
1950–1973	Economic modernization; expansion of the welfare state; proactive Keynesianism; moderate social partners	EEG Council of Europe	Free movement of workers Equal pay for men and women Common social security of migrant workers European Social Fund European Social Charter	Harmonization: Pushed by intra-European labor mobility and political ambitions for market-driven social-policy convergence High ambitions for universal social rights	The Six: Continental welfare states and Southern European model (Italy)
1974–1983	Stagflation; polarization; social conflict; national crisis management		Protection of workers' rights Equal treatment of men and women Protection and safety at work	Harmonization ambitions result in "Eurosclerosis"	Denmark, UK, Ireland (1973) and Greece (1981): Scandinavian, Anglo-Saxon, and Southern welfare states enter European policy space

1984–1994	Neoliberal moment; deregulation; economic internationalization; market integration	Single European Act (SEA) Social Protocol Maastricht Treaty (TEU)	Health and safety at work Social Protocol Decision of the European Court to protect national systems of solidarity Collective interest representation and codetermination Employment of third country nationals Gender equality for labor force	Minimum standards decided by a qualified majority (QMV); British opt-out; driven by deepening of market integration QMV extended; driven by economic internationalization, deregulation of markets, budgetary and debt constraints imposed by EMU	Spain and Portugal (1986): reinforcing presence of Southern European model

(*continued*)

Table 5.1 Development of European Social Policy (*continued*)

Period	*National Level*	*European Level*	*Europeanization of Social Policy*	*Governance Method*	*Enlargement-Related Diversity*
1995–2003	Social-democratic moment; social pacts; diverse policy response in different institutional settings	Amsterdam Summit Nice Summit	European Employment Strategy Social dialogue Basic rights maintained OMC introduced at Lisbon as complementary method of EU governance	Social dialogue (fundamental guidelines concerning employment opportunity, social inclusion, retirement) Open method of coordination; driven by structural unemployment, aging population, constraints imposed by EMU (Stability and Growth Pact) in context of strong welfare heterogeneity	Sweden, Finland and Austria (1995): reinforcing presence of high-standard Scandinavian and Continental welfare model

(ii) social conflict and national crisis management (1974–1983); (iii) economic internationalization and market integration (1984–1994); and (iv) matching common concerns with legitimate diversity (1995–2003) (Asbeek, Brusse, and Hemerijck 2002). With each wave of enlargement, the institutional diversity of social Europe increased. In this section, I concentrate on the first three periods; in the next section I focus more explicitly on the recent period since the Amsterdam Treaty.

Economic Modernization and the Expansion of the National Welfare State

During the era of economic modernization and expansion of the national welfare state (1950–1973), the foundations were laid for new ground rules of national unity, economic order, collective action, and social citizenship in a large number of Western European countries. In the wake of the reconstruction boom, postwar democratic governments in Western Europe strove for economic growth, full employment (especially for men), and a higher level of social security, health care, and education through the implementation of an active and interventionist socioeconomic policy. By and large, we observe an expansion of the welfare state from targeted policies for the poor and the needy toward more universal schemes. Moderate forces within the trade unions and business organizations supported the welfare state and the Keynesian mixed economy of managed capitalism, which offered the prospect of a positive spiral of full employment, high wages, rising demand, increased productivity, and, finally, a higher standard of living (including social protection) for everyone (Hall 2001).

The ambitious social policy laid out in the Treaty of Rome, signed in March 1957, establishing "an ever closer union among the European peoples," was the product of postwar optimism and the "historical compromise" between the moderate representatives of labor and capital. The preamble of the EC Treaty established economic and social advance and the continual improvement of lives and labor environments as essential goals of the EC (Barnard 2000, 6). Still, national policymakers, with the exception of the French, believed that European social authorities should be limited to establishing only the basic conditions of free movement of labor and harmonization of social-security rights. The fact that, despite this, the treaty referred to "closer collaboration between member states" in the areas of education, employment, labor conditions, labor relations, and social security can be explained by the Franco-German compromise that occurred at the last minute of the Treaty negotiations, when the French proposal for increased harmonization of social legislation and regulation encountered resistance from Germany, Italy, and the Benelux states (Hantrais 2000, 2–3). Nevertheless, the road toward harmonization was not blocked by this setback. On the contrary, considering that the first member states, with the exception of Italy, belonged to the group of Continental welfare states, a process of "spontaneous" convergence as a pendant of economic advance was not considered unthinkable. In this period, it was expected that national welfare states would tend toward uniform, qualitatively high standards of social protection in the long run. At a later stage, positive spillover effects of this partial convergence could still lead to further harmonization. The belief was that, whatever happened, it would be a "race to the top" rather than a "race to the bottom."

With the Treaty of Rome, the European Social Fund (ESF) was established (arts. 123–28), the importance of which increased with successive rounds of enlargement. It aimed to simplify the employment of workers, increase their geographical and occupational mobility within the Community, and facilitate adaptation to change, particularly through vocational training and retraining. Today, ESF expenditures cover 9 percent of the EU budget.

In the course of the 1960s, among European businessmen the aspiration for a level playing field in the social domain within a free internal market began to emerge. This wish was an important driving force behind the Commission's agenda concerning health and safety in the workplace. With reference to the authority of the Community, as far as working conditions were concerned, the Treaty of Rome did little more than require the member states to promote these aims (art. 117). The Commission was given the task of coordinating the member states' activities in the social sphere, including working conditions (arts. 51 and 118). Gender equality in wages and workers' freedom of movement was mandated in the Treaty (arts. 119 and 48–50 respectively) (Leibfried and Pierson 2000, 274; Barnard 2000, 1–3). This implied the prohibition of discrimination against workers with respect to employment, remuneration, and working conditions. Another crucial item of legislation from this period was Regulation 1408/71. In the Treaty of Rome, it had already been determined in art. 42 that, after the completion of the customs union, the free movement of employees had to be realized. Regulation 1408/71 established the social-security rights of migrant workers. Through this regulation, national governments lost a degree of control over "their" working citizens, so that ever since we can speak of "semisovereign welfare states" (Leibfried and Pierson 2000).

Social Conflict and National Crisis Management

Following 1974, European social integration progressed more slowly. The member states of the European Community experienced the worst economic crisis since the 1930s. They entered a new phase of social conflict and national crisis management (1974–1983), partly due to the continuing high wage demands of the strong national unions. Waves of international recessions led to divergent national responses in which each member state of the EC pursued its own crisis-management policy. This period of stagflation, low growth, widening economic divergence, and political divisions brought new protectionist pressures and tensions in the EC. The naive expectations of spontaneous social convergence within the EU, supported by intensified policy coordination, dissipated rapidly.

Disregarding the striking renationalization of social and economic policy, the Commission creatively used its limited power to promote the social dimension of the labor sphere. Based on the general fundamentals of harmonization contained in art. 100a EC (now art. 94 EC), guidelines that pertain to conditions in the workplace were agreed upon. When the governments of the Six decided to put the Werner plan (1970) for monetary union on the agenda against a background of economic decline and industrial conflict in a number of member states, a window of opportunity presented itself. Starting that year, the Commission launched a series of Social Action Programs that served as a basis for a boom in their legislative initiatives.

Eventually the aim of harmonization encountered the strong opposition of three member states that joined in 1973: the United Kingdom, the Republic of Ireland, and Denmark. Because their welfare traditions and institutions differed fundamentally from the dominant Continental model, policymakers particularly in Denmark and Britain rapidly became outspoken opponents of every form of European legislation that could be seen as detrimental to national autonomy in social policy (Hantrais 2000, 24). The creativity of the Commission and the Court in the development of the social *acquis* was continuously challenged because of this resistance to further deepening of the Union in the 1970s and 1980s.

Economic Internationalization and the Deepening of Market Integration

Despite economic recovery in the latter half of the 1980s, unemployment remained high in most European states. Many abandoned the neocorporatist experiments that initially had seemed so effective. One exception to this was the Netherlands, where the Accord of Wassenaar of 1982 ushered in a new period of "responsive corporatism" (Visser and Hemerijck 1997). Most Continental welfare states combatted unemployment in part by lowering the effective retirement age and tolerating an increase in the number of people on temporary and permanent sick leave (Ebbinghaus 2000).

In the political arena, it is significant that at this time European electorates turned their backs on social democracy to join the supply-side-focused neoliberal solutions of deregulation and privatization. The position of trade unions was weakened by processes of deindustrialization, rapid technological advance, and expansion of the service sector. Keynesian economic policy was supplanted by a more stringent macroeconomic variant, focusing on fiscal stability and hard currency. The ability to influence employment hereby shifted from macroeconomic policy to the adjoining domains of wage, social security, and labor-market policy. In the sphere of labor relations, a reorientation took place toward market-conforming wage moderation.

At the EU level, this dynamic period of economic internationalization and the deepening of market integration (1983–1995) found its rejoinder in the launch of the "1992 program," introduced in 1985, and intended to complete market integration, leading to a major Treaty revision in 1986. The completion of the internal market was very much a project of internal economic development and external economic assertiveness in the face of flourishing Japanese and American economies, and decisively not a program of internal social intervention. A key element of the Single Market Program was the complete liberalization of intra-EC and extra-EC capital movements. The Single European Act of 1986 was based on political consensus over the twin principles of *subsidiarity* and *proportionality*, stipulating that Community action should only take place where it is necessary or more effective than action at the level of the member states; and Community action should be as limited as possible and leave as much flexibility as possible. The internal market—which, however, is far from complete—was made possible not only by qualified-majority voting but also by the move away from detailed European harmonization through *mutual-recognition* and *framework-directive* approaches, in areas such as health and safety at work, leaving detailed technical specifications to standardization bodies.

With the entry of Greece (1981) and of Portugal and Spain (1986), the Southern European welfare state made its debut in the political arena of the European Union, although (southern) Italy already represented this category to some extent. Divergence was facilitated partially because the member states were able to implement guidelines in very different ways, and because the EC could exert little control over whether directives were upheld. In the more developed economies of Northwestern Europe, this led not only to fear of possible objections to decisions regarding new initiatives, but also to a fear of social dumping. The perception was that unequal levels of social protection and the very different traditions among the member states could make social rights detrimental to competitiveness. Countries with higher standards of social protection would be at a great financial disadvantage compared to those with lower standards. Generous welfare states unable to respond adequately to the extremes of policy and tax competition would have to pay a high price in terms of economic stagnation and unemployment.

The expected social dumping never occurred. In the first place, social costs turned out to be only one of many factors considered by enterprises making investment decisions, in addition to productivity, education and training, innovative potential, infrastructure, business climate, and labor relations stability. Secondly, the proclivity of Southern European member states to engage in a "race to the bottom" was mitigated by EU cohesion policy as a kind of quid pro quo. The relatively easy expansion of the cohesion policy, compared with the small steps made in the areas of labor-market regulation, labor relations, and social security, can be partly explained by the fact that the cohesion fund, although costly for those making net payments, did not threaten the policy autonomy of the generous welfare states.

When the single market came into force in 1987, national welfare policy, in essence, became subject to the principles of free competition. The Single European Act reflects a confirmation of national as opposed to European responsibility for social policy. One important exception was made for minimum harmonization concerning health and safety of workers as a safety valve of the unanimity agreement, so as to prevent "unfair" competition (art. 118a). For the first time in European social policy, it allowed directives to be adopted on the basis of qualified-majority voting in the Council. In the wake of the completion of the single market, there were proposals with respect to the unification of social protection in a single European system, through the introduction of an additional shared thirteenth (and what would now be a sixteenth) state system. Yet actual measures were very limited: the two 1992 texts on minimum protection and social protection were merely given the status of Council Recommendations, and, as such, remained at the "softest" end of the legal spectrum. The Council Recommendation 92/442/EEC of July 1992 aimed at promoting convergence between the social-protection policies of the member states in order to reduce differences in social-protection levels that might inhibit the free movement of persons and to prevent any type of mutual undercutting between the systems of social protection of the member states.

TOWARD JOINT PROBLEM SOLVING THROUGH LEGAL PLURALISM

In the wake of the Single European Act, the prospects for ambitious EU social-policy initiatives were bleak. The overall reluctance of the member states to take social-policy measures at the EU level resulted in the paradox whereby the member states, by asserting their sovereignty, were unwittingly losing their autonomy in social policy (Leibfried and Pierson 2000). It was increasingly felt as imperative to legitimize the integration process in terms of social policy considerations. However, it also became overwhelmingly clear that the accommodation of so many policy traditions, systems of finance and enforcement, and decision-making styles was no longer feasible on a European basis. This stimulated the development of more innovative and flexible institutional solutions in the 1990s. Ultimately, it was not the competition between the policies of the Southern European and the Continental and Scandinavian welfare states, but the political confrontation between the European Commission and the United Kingdom (with other "unwilling" countries in its wake) that forced the issue of the necessity of institutional flexibility in the EU. Moreover, German unification in 1990 produced a new mini-enlargement, with the absorption of the GDR into the German Federal Republic, with major consequences for the European political economy.

Following these considerations, the Social Charter was adopted in 1989. The Charter, despite being a not legally binding declaration, represented a considerable step in a new direction. The Treaty of the European Union (TEU) and especially its Protocol are the basic landmarks of this period. The Agreement on Social Policy based on the Protocol on Social Policy and concluded within the realm of the Treaty of the European Union at Maastricht, brought about further extension of EC competencies in the social field, insofar as the Council was given the right to decide on minimum norms for social policy.

During the negotiations for the Intergovernmental Conference (IGC) preceding the Treaty of Maastricht, attempts to include the objectives of this Charter as art. 117 in the text of the Treaty failed because of the British veto (Cullen and Campbell 1998, 264). The final result of the negotiations was a separate binding Protocol for each of the eleven member states concerning social policy (the Protocol on Social Policy) relating to work environments, and a unanimous vote concerning the development of working conditions and social security (Brinkmann 1998, 239; Hantrais 2000, 27). With this compromise over the closer coordination of eleven countries, acceptable to all twelve member states, it was possible for the group of eleven to impose guidelines concerning labor conditions, consultation of employees, and equal opportunities for men and women by a qualified majority. This constituted a remarkable extension of the competencies of the EU into a wide range of policy issues. Market-correcting interventions remained, however, dependent on unanimity within the Council. In a sense, the British opt-out marked the first step toward greater differentiation in European social-policy development.

A second institutional innovation that sprang from the Social Protocol pertains to the formalization of the European social dialogue between the social partners at the Community level. The idea of anchoring the social dialogue dates back to the 1985 "Val Duchesse" initiative of Jacques Delors to promote industrial relations at the European level in which the Union of Industries of the European Communities (UNICE), the European Centre of Public Enterprises (CEEP), and the European Trade Union Confederation (ETUC) participate as representatives of the social partners. The Social Protocol allows the European social partners to sign collective agreements. Through decisions of the Council, these agreements could attain the status of fundamental guidelines, with minimum standards that permit much freedom of policy at the national and sectoral levels (Brinkmann 1998, 241–42). According to art. 4 of the Protocol, it is also possible to assign to the social partners, at their own request, the task of implementing specific guidelines. Ultimately the social dialogue was introduced into the body of the Treaty (new arts. 138 and 139) at Amsterdam in 1997, stating that "[t]he Commission shall have the task of promoting consultation of management and labour at the Community level and shall take any relevant measure to facilitate their dialogue by ensuring balanced support for the parties." This new status of the social partners is an example of "horizontal flexibility." Wage setting and collective bargaining were, however, exempted from this regulatory competence.

The results of the social dialogue (intersectoral or intrasectoral) have not entirely fulfilled expectations. Since Maastricht, the social dialogue, an example of horizontal subsidiarity, has led to only four relatively meager accords on parental leave (1995), part-time work (1997), fixed-term work (1999), and telework (2002). With respect to the last, the European social partners chose, for the first time in the case of an intersectoral agreement, to implement the 2002 Framework Agreement on Telework by the "voluntary route," rather than through a Council directive backed by legal force. Also, the Work Programme of the European Social Partners for 2003–2005, presented in November 2002, revealed a preference to develop "a more autonomous social dialogue," indicating a desire to come out of the shadow of Community legislation. With the encouragement of the Commission, at the sectoral level some twenty-seven sectoral social-dialogue committees have been established. Despite a lack of distinct progress in reaching a better balance between social-protection objectives and economic-policy considerations in the EU, the social dialogue, established in arts. 138 and 139 of the new Treaty, provides an important institutional infrastructure for tripartite coregulation and bipartite self-regulation as central features of the institutional architecture of social Europe. The framework agreements reached in the EU social dialogue and transformed into EC directives are explicitly regarded by the social partners as contributing to social Europe. A pressing political problem that remains is how far the social dialogue between nonstate representatives of management and labor, consulted by the Commission, is acceptable in terms of democratic legitimacy, since neither the European Parliament nor national parliaments have any formal role.

As I pointed out in the previous section, in 1992 agreement was reached over a rather weak commitment on the part of the member states to seek convergence on social protection objectives (Council Recommendation 92/442/EEC), in an attempt to bolster the legitimacy of social-policy ambitions: from the goal of harmonization to that of convergence. Proposals for solutions to the problem of coordination—the "thirteenth" or "sixteenth state" and the "European social snake"—on the other hand, were never enacted due to lack of political support.

In 1995, three new members—Austria, Sweden, and Finland—presiding over fairly advanced welfare states and social-partnership institutions, joined the EU. On the road to EMU, from the second half of the 1990s, we are witnessing a quality leap in EU employment- and social-policy initiatives, trampling the received wisdom of market-making supremacy over market-correcting policy concerns, European Court of Justice bias toward negative integration, and political immobility at the level of EU decision making. The pace of change in European employment and social policy clearly also rebuts the bias toward policy immobility at the level of the EU. Moreover, rulings of the ECJ, i.e., the Brentjens and Albany cases, reveal that principles of national solidarity have become recognized as one of the basic objectives of the European Union. This juridical recognition might open the way for more socially inspired case law and, indirectly, for political pressure on the Commission at large and the Council to agree on a political recognition of the principle of national solidarity to protect domestic welfare policies. With respect to gender equality, the ECJ had already been a central actor as it endorsed a broad interpretation of art. 119 on domestic measures to ensure equal pay and equal treatment, also with regard to social security. In short, we are recently observing a shift toward taking market-correction policy interventions more seriously.

In the run-up to the Treaty of Amsterdam, we are able to observe timid steps toward the constitutionalization of social policy. By reformulating art. 117 of the Treaty, the European Union has come to embrace the promotion of employment, the improvement of living conditions, and combatting social exclusion as core European policy objectives. The Amsterdam Treaty transferred the Social Agreement into the main Treaty. In order to achieve the free movement of workers, and especially to ensure payments of benefits from country to country, the ECJ has interpreted regulations for migrant workers expansively and imposed the principle of nondiscrimination in all aspects of social security, except for social assistance. Many more directives were enacted in the 1990s, including those on worker information, conditions of work contracts, atypical workers, and parental leave.

At the time of the European Council in Amsterdam, in June 1997, thirteen of the fifteen member states had social-democratic or socialist governments, giving the Europeanization of social policy a vital impulse. With so many social-democratic parties back in government in the late 1990s, the central question was what the European Union could do by way of shelter for national welfare states, given that European solutions could not be adopted for both technical and political reasons (Scharpf 2002). While they recognized the need for a flexible approach to social problems (particularly high unemployment, exceeding 10 percent in 1993), they also knew that, at both the national and the European level, room for uniform strategies was foreclosed. Moreover, effective implementation of Community legislation was seen to demand new forms of implementation, as Community policy increasingly touched on sensitive social-policy issues (Best 2003). At Maastricht, the doubling of resources for the structural funds was already accompanied by new forms of partnership with substate and private stakeholders. EU employment and social policy had to come to terms with the increasing diversity and political sensitivities of welfare provisions in an enlarging Union. As a response to this dilemma, a policy approach was adopted that left decision making largely with the member states, but gave greater weight to EU institutions in goal setting, benchmarking, monitoring, and policy coordination. By explicitly recognizing the legitimate diversity of national welfare states at the European level, new ways of coordinating national reform trajectories based on broadly formulated common social goals were ventured.

The launch of the Economic and Monetary Union prompted new forms of policy coordination aimed at convergence of national policy toward common objectives on the basis of nonbinding, multilateral surveillance. This began with the Broad Economic Policy Guidelines (BEPGs), but soon this method of more open policy coordination spread to key areas of social and employment policy.

At the Amsterdam Summit, a renewed European social-policy agenda emerged, based on the principle of respect for the integrity and divergence of national systems. The European Council unanimously supported the creation of a separate chapter on employment in the Treaty (arts. 125–30 EC [formerly art. 109n–109s]). In addition, the United Kingdom, under New Labour, signed the Social Protocol (arts. 136–43 EC [formerly arts. 117–20]), which made it an integral part of the EC Treaty. The adapted social chapter introduced codecision-making authority for the European Parliament, decision making by a qualified majority in the Council, explicit reference to fundamental social rights, and a new provision for the development of social-inclusion programs.

Equally critical to the new EU social-policy profile has been the change in tune of the ECJ in recent rulings. In a number of cases the Court has upheld national social regulation against the principles of market integration at the EU level. This has led the Court to develop the "principle of national solidarity" as a legitimate exemption from competition law (Barnard 2000). This principle, when applied, indicates a certain primacy of social protection over market integration. In the Albany case, dealing with compulsory affiliation in a Dutch pension scheme, the Court ruled:

> It follows that the social security schemes, as described, are based on a system of compulsory contribution. . . Organisations involved in the management of the public social security system fulfill an exclusively social function. That activity is based on the principle of national solidarity and is entirely non-profit-making. Accordingly, that activity is not an economic activity. . . .

Apparently, the Court ruled that the EU could not turn a blind eye to the social problems competition law created for national welfare states. The ECJ, as a court of last resort, has, in its rulings concerning social regulation and the internal market, often shied away from endorsing the legalistic primacy of "negative integration" in this politically sensitive area, where endorsing was in theory possible.

The introduction of a separate employment chapter in the Treaty of Amsterdam is best understood not so much as a "functional" spillover, but as an effect of "political" spillover of the EMU (Van der Meer and Van Riel 2002). It was forcefully championed by the European Commission and most center-left governments. Through their combined efforts to tackle unemployment, these governments, in terms of policy content, wanted to show that Europe is about more than just "market and money," and that its social dimension is also important to the average European citizen. In a political sense, this employment policy can therefore be seen as a "correction" of Maastricht. In both substantive and institutional respects, the European Employment Strategy (EES), launched under the Luxembourg presidency in the second half of 1997, concerns a coordination process, based on a management-by-objectives approach with respect to national employment and social-policy traditions, which since have come to serve as an example of governance in other areas of European policymaking.

The EES was accepted on condition that no national authority would be transferred to Brussels, there would be no extra cost, and EMU rules would be fully respected. The EES consists of four priority pillars: employability, entrepreneurship, adaptability, and equal opportunities, in a manner consistent with the BEPGs. The aim of the EES is to raise employment participation throughout the European Union, allowing for different national strategies to contribute to this aim. All this through a procedure of "learning by monitoring," bent on strengthening, activating, and informing national reform debates and strategies through peer review without binding objectives. Every member state agreed to develop an annual National Action Plan (NAP) for employment to translate the common guidelines into clear-cut national policy measures, supplemented by—often multi-annual—policy goals.

There is also an annual multilateral inspection procedure, in which member states evaluate each other's NAPs (peer review—see art. 128 EC). The social partners on the national and European levels are involved in developing plans to improve employment on their respective levels. The Commission plays a facilitating role by defining indicators, exchanging information, and producing comparative analyses. The (Social) Council can make recommendations to member states based on qualified-majority voting and at the proposal of the Commission, but it cannot impose sanctions. The Council can also adjust EES pillars and guidelines on the basis of the insight and suggestions of the Commission. These guidelines have increasingly been made more specific: at the Lisbon Summit, agreement was reached on an overall employment level of 70 percent (60 percent for women) by 2010. In Stockholm, the EES was further strengthened by the setting of interim objectives and the introduction of a target employment rate of 50 percent among older employees (55–64 years of age) in 2010 (Goetschy 2003). In 2003, the employment guidelines were revised. They now aim at the three overarching and interrelated objectives of full employment, quality and productivity at work, and social cohesion and inclusion.

Since the first employment experiments began in Luxembourg, the open method of coordination (OMC) has quickly spread to other social-policy areas. It is now used, for example, in social exclusion (Lisbon 2000), the modernization of pension provisions (Gothenburg and Laeken 2001), and the implementation of framework directives on lifelong education and teleworking. The European Council at Lisbon on March 23–24, 2000, formally recognized OMC as a legitimate form of European governance. OMC exemplifies, as Visser and Hemerijck (2003) put it, a "contextualized" method of benchmarking, allowing consultation over guidelines and national action plans, with ongoing feedback on implementation. This in sharp contrast to one-size-fits-all "decontextualized" benchmarks, which often characterize OECD and IMF recommendations. OMC facilitates policy progress in areas where EU competencies are relatively weak, where regulation is infeasible and impracticable. Open coordination has the potential to develop into a valuable addition to the modes of governing now available in the European polity. It is eminently more flexible than "joint decision procedures" or "intergovernmental negotiations." Moreover, in contrast to "mutual adjustment," it can provide useful safeguards against an unintended "race to the bottom" (Scharpf 2000). Successes achieved through OMC are likely to enhance the legitimacy of the EU as a social union, which in turn would allow policy-makers to translate the much-discussed but underspecified "European social model" into a set of agreed upon policy objectives. This procedure potentially goes well beyond the "usual solemn but vague declarations at European Summits" (Vandenbroucke 2002).

Based on evaluations of the EES, we are able to draw a few tentative conclusions with respect to the effectiveness of the open method of coordination (cf. Best and Bossaert 2002; Zeitlin 2003). Most important, Europe's employment ambitions are far more lofty and concrete than ever before. Employment policies are being discussed at the highest level. Ministers and civil servants are being kept alert, and an activating approach toward social policy is diffused. National ambitions have been raised and translated into a large number of concrete targets concerning employment, education and training, reduction of poverty, access to resources, literacy, and integration. Much more attention is paid to activation, and there is a strong focus on increasing labor participation and better adjustment between work and household responsibilities in young families. There is ample evidence of increased *policy direction*, with employment objectives now firmly anchored as a central goal of the Union, *policy coherence* between different policy areas at the national level, together with more *policy coordination* between the member states and more *policy integration* between national and EU policies.

Second, the Luxembourg process seems to have contributed to the establishment of a *learning network* beyond the borders of national welfare states. EES not only expanded the scope for countries to learn from each other, the benchmarking process was also exploited to reveal weaknesses and thus enhanced the potential for better policy delivery. In addition, EES seems to have contributed to improved *social and economic policy coordination* within the EU.

With respect to legitimacy concerns, the "openness" of EES should be questioned. The limitation is that OMC has remained an isolated process. The audience for learning remained very limited, mainly to the participants who were directly involved. This is against expectations and against the hope of rising cross-national pressures via "naming and shaming," while the public resonance of the European Employment Policy in the public debate remains muted. EES has thus far lacked transparency. Moreover, it enhanced the political importance of the European Council, at the expense of the European Parliament, national parliaments, and the ECJ. Most countries have tried to involve the social partners in formulating the NAPs. However, this has often failed because of lack of time and bureaucratic rigidities. More important, national parliamentarians and policymakers know little about what happens behind the scenes of OMC processes, principally because they seldom discuss European issues in any serious manner.

This lack of anchoring of the EES in national political debate makes it a rather precarious *convergence-of-objectives* cum *governance-by-objectives* approach, critically dependent on the willingness of national policymakers to learn from each other and voluntarily coordinate and adapt their policies rather than to sabotage the process by freeriding. OMC is fragile in the sense that it is highly contingent on the extent to which national policymakers see themselves as pursuing convergent or parallel goals. Any process of "open coordination," exactly because of its openness and, hence, its ambiguity, needs a strong political engine for it to work as a free and noncommitting process of deliberation over problems and solutions. Without substantive consensus and a sense of urgency, there is a danger that OMC ends up to be a ritual of "dressing up" existing policies (Ferrera 2002). However, with the shift to the conservative right in recent years, employment ambitions were not watered down.

In June 2000, the Council established the Social Protection Committee, which was given a legal basis in the EC Treaty (new art. 144) at Nice. Also the Nice proclamation of the Charter of Fundamental Rights (a European Bill of Rights) gave social Europe more visibility. The Social Protection Committee developed as a series of common objectives, which were endorsed by the European Council at Nice in December 2000 (revised in December 2002).

A telling example of improved European economic- *and* social-policy coordination is the Joint Commission and Council Report on pensions, prepared by the Economic Policy Committee together with the Social Protection Committee, presented at the 2003 Spring European Council, embracing the twin goals of economic sustainability and social adequacy, while meeting changing societal needs (European Commission 2003b).

During the Convention on the Future of Europe in 2003, an in-depth discussion took place on how to introduce the open method of coordination in the draft constitution. The final solution that was adopted in the Treaty establishing a Constitution for Europe (European Convention 2003b), which was signed on October 29, 2004, by the twenty-five EU Heads of State and Government, consisted in introducing, not a general definition of OMC, but rather a more specific reference to four policy areas which relied on OMC as a mode of policymaking under article III-107:

> To this end, the Commission shall act in close contact with member states, delivering opinions and arranging consultations both on problems arising at the national level and on those of concern to international organisations, in particular initiatives aiming at the establishment of guidelines and indicators, the organisation of exchange of best practices, and the preparation of the necessary elements for periodic monitoring and evaluation. The European Parliament shall be kept fully informed. Before delivering the opinions provided for in this article, the Commission shall consult the Economic and Social Committee.

Today it is unlikely, given the recent French and Dutch referenda in which the draft treaty was voted down, that the Constitution for Europe will be ratified.

THE IMPERATIVE OF ENLARGEMENT

Is the mixture of "hard" community legislation, social dialogue, and "soft law" forms of open coordination, established in the late 1990s, capable of coping with the new social-policy challenges of an EU of twenty-five member states in the first decade of the twenty-first century? How much system diversity can effectively be "absorbed" through OMC processes? Are peer reviews and benchmarking feasible in a union of twenty-five? The entry of so many new members with significantly less sturdy social-protection systems and labor-market regimes clearly is a daunting challenge for the European Union. The question is whether the outlook for social policy will be affected by the impending enlargement in a predictable and manageable way. To be sure, substantial budgetary, administrative, and operational burdens will accompany the EU's expansion to Central and Eastern Europe (CEE). This is true of both the new member states and the old EU of Fifteen.

The enlargement of the EU to twenty-five or more member states implies a growth of the population of 28 percent, but at the same time a significant decline in average income levels by no less than 18 percent. In short, enlargement will go together with a serious increase in income inequality in the EU. Under a common macroeconomic policy framework, it is very likely that the eastward enlargement will aggravate economic disparities and social exclusion for any given overall EU growth rate. In part this is a straightforward arithmetic inference: when the instruments of macroeconomic policy are set for a broader economic area, the probability that particular segments and regions will find the overall stance of policy less helpful is increased with each enlargement. Thus, if a particular region is adversely affected by a loss of competitiveness of a prominent sector of economic activity, it is unlikely that monetary policy set for the Eurozone as a whole will be effectively responsive. The region thus has to adjust by other means, some of which may lead to income and employment losses that could engender social exclusion. It may well be true that adding new member states to the EU will benefit current and new members alike. But there will be a specific sectoral and local or regional impact that is likely to lead to new social problems. Following this logic of reasoning, in the EU of Fifteen we observe a resurgence of the fear of the "social-dumping" thesis in the West, coupled with right-wing populism and xenophobia (Mayes, Berghman, and Salais 2001).

When we take account of the specific social problems that confront CEE countries, a more nuanced perspective emerges. The accession states face a much greater economic-development challenge than their predecessors, while the social *acquis* is more extensive than during earlier rounds of enlargement. Although the Commission's progress reports indicate that the bulk of the social *acquis* has now been transposed, some gaps remain, especially with regard to "hard" social legislation. Furthermore, due in part to a lack of governmental administrative and financial capacity, as well as the social partners' unfamiliarity with the social *acquis*, implementation is a problem in most countries. For a long time, the EU has been offering technical assistance and organizing international conferences for experts from current and candidate member states. However, part of this is connected with an underlying fear of the possible negative effects of this hard *acquis* on the competitiveness of small- and medium-size enterprises in Central and Eastern Europe (Draus 2001). Implementation of the *acquis* in the coming years will doubtlessly still fall short and in some sectors hinder catch-up growth (WRR 2001). In the worst-case scenario, this will lead to conflicts over unfair policy competition and a general lack of trust in the observance of social legislation.

State socialist social policy contained a number of distinct and internally consistent qualities, sufficient to warrant the attribution of a particular type of "service-heavy" and "transfer-lean" welfare regime, practically the opposite of the Continental welfare regime, from which most of the CEE countries originally descended (Manning 2004). Hospitals and schools were run by the central state, income support was handled by trade unions, and the majority of housing was allocated by industrial enterprises to their own (and other) favored workers. Unemployment did not officially exist because the constitution guaranteed work for all, and social care (of small children and older people) was heavily institutionalized. Since the government controlled almost all of domestic production, taxation was unnecessary.

Alongside this idiosyncratic policy legacy, the inheritance of an egalitarian communist-era political philosophy is a favorable circumstance, in that social payments in the candidate countries are already high in relation to their level of economic development. The new tax systems, introduced in recent years, are, to be sure, inferior to those of the current member states, but the composition of income from taxes and social contributions is very similar. Furthermore, the development of the European social-policy regime shows that widening and deepening the social *acquis* can occur simultaneously. I see no reason why this should end with the inclusion of ten or more countries from Central and Eastern Europe.

The social problems of the countries of Central and Eastern Europe are definitely more intense, but not wholly different from those of current member states (Clark-Dageville 2002, 123). Persistent unemployment in an unfavorable macroeconomic climate, pension systems overburdened because of an aging population, health problems, and increasing social inequality also figure prominently on national and European policy agendas elsewhere. In addition, the particular kind of social-gender equality has disappeared in the process, with women increasingly taking on the double burden of paid work and family responsibilities (Manning 2004). Enlargement of the EU will bring in new member states with significantly lower labor costs, and even if the enlargement is ultimately of mutual benefit, it can be expected to have local and sectoral effects that will constitute new causes of unemployment, with the attendant risk of intensified social exclusion. Aging of the population because of its demographic profile is a well-documented trend that will simultaneously increase the proportion of the traditionally vulnerable elderly in the population and lower the taxpaying base of working individuals. In addition, and notwithstanding the recent bursting of the "dotcom bubble," the phenomenon of the new economy will continue to reshape productive processes.

The CEE unemployment crisis has its origins in extensive economic restructuring (Stark and Bruszt 1998). There is an exodus of labor from the public to the private sector and from heavy industry and agriculture to light industry and services. In the fight against unemployment growth, many CEE governments in the 1990s introduced passive labor-market measures such as early retirement and disability payments, thus putting even more pressure on employment. As a result, many workers have withdrawn from the job market (to the shadow economy).

With respect to welfare reform in the transition period, the EU has been a relatively weak transnational actor, in comparison to the IMF and the World Bank. CEE countries have at first been keen to pursue neoliberal reform strategies, especially in pensions, in return for support from the IMF and the World Bank. More recently, many governments have begun to resort to more active labor-market instruments, such as special programs for education and training, and subsidized employment for the disadvantaged, more in line with EU policy ambitions. As part of the EU accession process, many CEE countries have been shadowing the European Employment Strategy, including the four-pillar framework (Keune 2003). The so-called National Action Plans for Adoption of the Acquis require them to develop long-term strategies in preparation for the more detailed annual action plans to be developed within the framework of the EES. In an attempt to guide this process and to "socialize" the member states' policymakers, the Commission is drawing up so-called Joint Assessments of Employment Policy (JAP) in cooperation with the candidate countries. In countries like the Czech Republic, Bulgaria, Estonia, Poland, and Slovenia, employment policy is also increasingly modeled on the EES's four-pillar structure. The EES thus seems to promote policy developments in the CEE countries, despite their limited financial and institutional capacities. This allows them to experiment with policy innovations that match their own labor market challenges, both among themselves and in the company of more "experienced" EU member states. A similar positive picture emerges from the CEE policy experiment modeled after the EU social-inclusion OMC process. There is certainly room for criticism. The JAPs report minimal involvement of the social partners in Central and Eastern Europe. Not only are trade unions usually politically weak and employers' organizations slow to develop, but there is often also a paternal attitude on the part of governments and a lack of preparedness on the part of employers to organize and represent themselves collectively.

The majority of empirical studies dealing with enlargement and social policy highlight deficient institutional capacities for effective employment and social policy as the single greatest weakness facing the CEE welfare states (Wagener 2002). A robust institutional framework, able to channel, enforce, and implement the much-needed consensus over welfare reform in post-communist societies, is lacking (Keune 2003). This is especially problematic with respect to the social dialogue. While the social partners at the European level have virtually become legislators, many studies reveal that the social partners in CEE countries have been largely marginalized by their national governments (Lendvai 2004). In the face of weak governance capacities, conflicts of economic integration and social disparities could easily become explosive.

Hence the direction in which the CEE welfare states will develop after their entry into the EU cannot be foreseen (Deacon 2000). On the one hand, harking back to policy legacies rooted in the 1930s, they show similarities in terms of policy development with the Continental welfare states (Germany and France). Social policy today is largely financed by workers' premiums and contributions. Furthermore, a multipillar pension system is rapidly being implemented (Denmark and the Netherlands). Labor-market regulations show many similarities with the most flexible job markets in Western Europe (United Kingdom and Ireland). Trade unions and employers' organizations are in general poorly represented in the new private sectors. These policy developments suggest that welfare state models are becoming increasingly mixed or "hybridized" (Zeitlin 2003). Nonetheless, institutional fragmentation hinders the development of an effective social dialogue and a much-required political consensus over necessary reforms. In this area of institution building, the EU can step in with support.

THE INSTITUTIONAL COMPLEMENTARITIES OF SOCIAL EUROPE

The European social-policy agenda has come a long way since six Continental welfare states set out to establish a common market. The development of EC social legislation has increased since the late 1950s, with the 1990s being the most active period. With each wave of enlargement, EU employment- and social-policy initiatives have had to come to terms with the increasing diversity of national welfare states. Although social policy is deeply entrenched in national politics, the social dimension of the European Union no longer merely holds a "Cinderella status" of good intentions (job growth, social dialogue), high principles (improving living standards, working conditions, solidarity, and adequate social protection), but little action. However, EC social policy largely remains regulatory, with key areas for regulation being working conditions, gender equality, and health and safety in the workplace. To be sure, the fundamental economic freedoms entrenched in the Treaty establishing the European (Economic) Community and in European economic policies that have sought to liberalize markets and deregulate state intervention in the economy, have constrained the autonomy of national governments in macroeconomic policy. In addition, European economic integration has reduced the range of member states' interventionist instruments and limited the spending powers for social policy by demanding strict adherence to the criteria of the Stability and Growth Pact. However, European economic integration did not signify the demise of the welfare state.

In the past, with every wave of enlargement, it was argued that widening the EU would enfeeble the prospects for deepening, especially in the politically sensitive employment- and social-policy areas. With the benefit of hindsight, the notion that widening goes at the expense of deepening of the EU cannot be upheld. Widening and deepening has occurred in tandem. This is not to say that reaching consensus over issues of fiscal, social, and employment policy will become easier in a more heterogeneous Union of twenty-five member states. On the contrary, we have observed a three-pronged development characterized by: (1) a gradual emancipation of the social- and employment-policy agenda at the European level; (2) a geographical expansion of membership; and (3) a qualitative change in the nature of EU governance needed to manage the greater political salience of state and policy diversity across member states (Tsoukalis 2003). Today, the EU finds itself at an important constitutional juncture. With the twenty-five members of 2004 there was a clear need for a new Constitutional Treaty laying down the ground rules for economic- and social-policy coordination. The accession of ten more states to the European Union in May 2004 brought about an enormous increase in the economic and social heterogeneity among member states. Therefore, it seems fair to conclude that, in the future, agreement on binding standards will be even more difficult to achieve. At the same time, the social-policy consequences of European economic integration will become more poignant. If community legislation is more difficult, social progress will have to rely more on horizontal EU social dialogue and "soft-law" processes of the open method of coordination, where state policymakers remain the central actors embedded in a larger European economic- and social-policy space.

The verdict is still out on whether the recent innovations of open coordination, officially adopted at the Lisbon European Council in March 2000, encourage member states jointly to mitigate "negative" integration, through enhanced social- and economic-policy coordination, while making room for differentiated "positive" integration, by way of effective joint policy learning (WRR 2003). The discovery of legal pluralism through social dialogue, opt-outs, and open coordination was triggered by difficulties of European initiatives in areas where EU competencies are relatively weak and where regulation by community law was unachievable and impractical. As alternatives to "hard law," i.e., the so-called rule-based method of regulation, these "soft-law" instruments have become preferable to and more effective than "watered-down" directives. While allowing for diversity in domestic policy responses, social dialogue and, especially, open coordination nonetheless "exert pressure on laggards and offer best practices to poor performers" (Dauderstädt 2004, 10).

We live in a period of far-reaching societal and economic transitions. Most European welfare states are in the process of renegotiating the terms of the postwar social-citizen contract, including a reconfiguration of the role of government, levels of decision making, and actors that are or should be involved in the governance of social policy (Ferrera, Hemerijck, and Rhodes 2000; Ferrera and Hemerijck 2003). One of the most distinctive institutional features of the European welfare *state* has been its public, legalistic nature: the responsibility of ensuring social solidarity and cohesion lies with the government—ultimately the national (i.e., central) government. Public funds, public schemes, and public bureaucracies have traditionally been the main pillars of the welfare edifice. Various developments have challenged this state-centric paradigm in recent years—a challenge often summarized in the emergence of new forms of "governance" beyond the traditional territorial state. The ongoing redefinition of the territorial state is apparent in two ways (Supiot 2003). National governments no longer monopolize welfare provision. Increasingly, states and EU institutions focus on laying down the institutional ground rules and social principles shaping multilevel governance. Hereby the state is withdrawing, while at the same time reaffirming its role as the guardian of the "goodness of fit" of economic competitiveness and social solidarity. Striking in this respect is the resurgence of national "social pacts," agreed to by functionally organized interests and domestic policymakers, and the widening of the scope of a "governance-by-objectives" approach at the level of the EU, epitomized by the social dialogue and, even more so, by the open method of coordination in the areas of employment, social exclusion, and pension, which also—albeit at a distance—engages the social partners. While many countries (especially the larger ones) have been experimenting with decentralization of competencies to subnational (regional and local) governments in response to numerous pressures—from increased international competition to fiscal overload at the state level—the European Union, as shown above, has been gradually emerging as an autonomous suprastate level of social regulation and to some extent redistribution (through the structural funds), creating a complex system of multilevel interactions that has turned national welfare states from fully sovereign to semisovereign entities (Leibfried and Pierson 2000). Patterns of decision making in European social policy have been transformed in the process. Qualified-majority voting has been introduced in treaty reforms and has extended into day-to-day practice. Furthermore, at the European level, labor and industry groups have become key players in European social policy, able to decide on the content of new directives. While over time the "hard" social *acquis* has surely "deepened," more recently new "softer" forms of EU involvement, such as the social dialogue and the open method of coordination, have become institutionalized so as to balance common concerns and legitimate diversity, i.e., respect for institutional differences of formerly self-contained territorial welfare states.

Multilevel Europe continues to depend on democratic legitimacy derived from and mediated through national legislatures, which remain the primary focal point of political identity in Europe and the cornerstone for further policy integration. Less binding and legal-pluralist modes of governance, i.e., social dialogue and open coordination, should, therefore, not be viewed as *alternatives* to the Community method but as necessary or indispensable *complements*. It is arguably a sign of good health that fifty years of European integration has developed such a wide range of modes of governance for European cooperation (Best 2003).

In recent years the movement toward incremental social supranationalism has been put in jeopardy, due to the loss in momentum of the Lisbon agenda, the lack of visibility of the independent tiers of the Lisbon strategy, and ambiguity with respect to the causal relations between growth, employment, and social protection. This shows the political limits of integration by policy coordination. Social progress has to be built on a "doubly engaging" political logic, with the commitment of both the European and national parliaments, to harden OMC processes in the shadow of the Charter of Fundamental Rights, which was attached to the Nice Treaty. However, in the face of the 2005 French and Dutch referenda over the draft constitution, gloomy neonationalist scenarios of defensive closure and zero-sum subsidiarity cannot be ruled out!

NOTE

1. This chapter is a product of a wider comparative study of the future of welfare in Europe that I started with Maurizio Ferrera and Martin Rhodes in 1999, in the framework of the Portuguese presidency of the European Union in the first half of 2000. Our joint collaboration resulted in the book *The Future of Social Europe* (Lisbon: Celta Editora, 2000), which will be completely revised for publication in 2005 by Oxford University Press. Separate from Maurizio and Martin, I further elaborated, with Jos Berghman, my ideas of the EU dimension of social policy in a study for the Greek presidency, published under the title *Connecting Welfare Diversity within the European Social Model* (ed. Theodoros Sakellaropoulos and Jos Berghman) in 2004 by Intersentia. The present chapter constitutes a revised, expanded, and updated version of the paper "The European Social Patrimony: Deepening Social Europe through Legitimate Diversity," written for the Greek presidency, in which I have introduced a special focus on the movement toward institutional flexibility and legal pluralism since the early 1990s. Many colleagues and friends have given me excellent comments on earlier drafts over the past five years. I would especially like to thank Maurizio Ferrera, Martin Rhodes, Wendy Asbeek Brusse, Jos Berghman, Jelle Visser, and Jonathan Zeitlin, next to Paul van Seters, the editor of the present book.

REFERENCES

Asbeek Brusse, Wendy, and Anton Hemerijck. 2002. Deepening Social Europe in an Enlarged Union. In *Work and Welfare in the Enlarging Euroland*, ed. Michael Dauderstädt and Lothar Witte, 113–33. Bonn: Friedrich Ebert Stiftung.

Barnard, Catherine. 2000. *EC Employment Law*. 2nd ed. Oxford: Oxford University Press.

Begg, Iain. 2002. EMU and Employment: Social Models in the EMU: Convergence? Co-Existence? The Role of Economic and Social Actors. Working paper 42/02, One Europe or Several? Working Papers, University of Sussex.

Best, Edward. 2003. Alternative Regulations or Complementary Methods? Evolving Options in European Governance. *Eipascope*, no. 1:2–11.

Best, Edward, and Danielle Bossaert, eds. 2002. *From Luxembourg to Lisbon and Beyond: Making the Employment Strategy Work*. Maastricht: European Institute of Public Administration.

Brinkmann, Gisbert. 1998. Lawmaking under the Social Chapter of Maastricht. In Craig and Harlow, 239–61.

Brusis, Martin. 1998. Introduction: Residual or European Welfare Model? Central and Eastern Europe at the Crossroads. In Central and Eastern Europe on the Way into the European Union: Welfare State Reforms in the Czech Republic, Hungary, Poland and Slovakia, ed. Martin Brusis, 1–22. Working paper, Centrum für angewandte Politikforschung, Munich.

Clark-Dageville, Hélène. 2002. The Employment Strategy and the Enlargement of the Union. In Best and Bossaert, 121–27.

Clasen, Jochen. 2001. Managing the Economic Risks of Unemployment in the UK. Paper presented at the conference Welfare Systems and the Management of the Economic Risk of Unemployment, European University Institute, Florence, 10–11 December.

Cotterrell, Roger. 1995. *Law's Community: Legal Theory in Sociological Perspective*. Oxford: Clarendon Press.

Craig, Paul, and Carol Harlow, eds. 1998. *Lawmaking in the European Union*. The Hague: Kluwer Law International.

Cullen, Holly, and Elinor Campbell. 1998. The Future of Social Policy-Making in the European Union. In Craig and Harlow, 262–84.

Dauderstädt, Michael. 2004. Conflicting Distributive Interests in a Deepening and Widening Europe: A Challenge to the Emerging Europolity. Bonn: Friedrich Ebert Stiftung.

Deacon, Bob. 2000. Eastern European Welfare States: The Impact of the Politics of Globalization. *Journal of European Social Policy* 10:146–61.

De la Porte, Caroline, and Philippe Pochet. 2002. Supple Coordination at EU Level and the Key Actors' Involvement. In *Building Social Europe through the Open Method of Co-ordination,* ed. Caroline De la Porte and Philippe Pochet, 27–68. Brussels: P.I.E.-Peter Lang.

Draus, Franciczek. 2001. Social Dialogue in European Union Candidate Countries. Working paper, www.euractiv.com (accessed April 22, 2002).

Ebbinghaus, Bernhard. 2000. Any Way out of "Exit from Work"? Reversing the Entrenched Pathways of Early Retirement. In Scharpf and Schmidt, vol. 2:511–53.

Esping-Andersen, Gøsta. 1990. *The Three Worlds of Welfare Capitalism*. Cambridge: Polity Press.

———. 2002. Towards the Good Society, Once Again? In Esping-Andersen, Gallie, Hemerijck, and Myles, 1–25.

Esping-Andersen, Gøsta, ed., with Duncan Gallie, Anton Hemerijck, and John Myles. 2002. *Why We Need a New Welfare State*. Oxford: Oxford University Press.

European Commission. 1993. White Paper on Growth, Competitiveness, and Employment: The Challenges and Ways Forward into the 21st Century. Luxembourg: Office for Official Publications of the European Communities.

———. 1996. For a Europe of Civil and Social Rights. Report by the *Comité des Sages*, chaired by Maria de Lourdes Pintasilgo. Luxembourg: Office for Official Publications of the European Communities.

———. 1997. Modernising and Improving Social Protection in the European Union. Luxembourg: Office for Official Publications of the European Communities.

———. 2003a. Joint Report by the Commission and the Council on Adequate and Sustainable Pensions. Luxembourg: Office for Official Publications of the European Communities.

———. 2003b. Strengthening the Social Dimension of the Lisbon Strategy: Streamlining Open Coordination in the Field of Social Protection. Luxembourg: Office for Official Publications of the European Communities.

European Convention. 2003a. Final report of the Working Group on "Social Europe." Luxembourg: Office for Official Publications of the European Communities.

———. 2003b. Draft Treaty Establishing a Constitution for Europe. Adopted by consensus on June 13 and July 10, and submitted to the President of the European Council in Rome on July 18. Luxembourg: Office for Official Publications of the European Communities.

European Union. 2000. Presidency Conclusions: Nice European Council Meeting. Luxembourg: Office for Official Publications of the European Communities.

Falkner, Gerda. 1998. *EU Social Policy in the 1990s: Towards a Corporatist Policy Community*. London: Routledge.

Ferrera, Maurizio. 1996. The Southern Model of Welfare in Social Europe. *Journal of European Social Policy* 6:17–37.

———. 2002. The European Social Model and the Open Method of Coordination. *Revue Belge de Sécurité Sociale* 44:469–72.

Ferrera, Maurizio, and Anton Hemerijck. 2003. Recalibrating Europe's Welfare Regimes. In Zeitlin and Trubek, 88–128.

Ferrera, Maurizio, Anton Hemerijck, and Martin Rhodes. 2000. *The Future of Social Europe: Recasting Work and Welfare in the New Economy*. Lisbon: Celta Editora.

Genschel, Philipp. 2001. Globalization, Tax Competition and the Fiscal Viability of the Welfare State. Working paper, MPIfG, Cologne.

Goetschy, Janine. 1999. The European Employment Strategy: Genesis and Development. *European Journal of Industrial Relations* 6:117–37.

———. 2003. The European Employment Strategy, Multilevel Governance, and Policy Coordination: Past, Present, and Future. In Zeitlin and Trubek, 59–87.

Hall, Peter. 2001. The Evolution of Economic Policy-Making in the European Union. In *From the Nation State to Europe? Essays in Honour of Jack Hayward*, ed. Anand Menon and Vincent Wright, 214–45. Oxford: Oxford University Press.

Handler, Joel F. 1990. *Law and the Search for Community*. Philadelphia: University of Pennsylvania Press.

Hantrais, Linda. 2000. *Social Policy in the European Union*. 2nd ed. Basingstoke: Macmillan.

Hemerijck, Anton. 1998. Social Policy and Economic Performance: Employment, Activating Welfare State and Economic Competitiveness. The Hague: Ministry of Social Affairs and Employment.

———. 2002. The Self-Transformation of the European Social Model(s). In Esping-Andersen, Gallie, Hemerijck, and Myles, 173–214.

Hemerijck, Anton, and Martin Schludi. 2000. Sequences of Policy Failures and Effective Policy Responses. In Scharpf and Schmidt, vol. 1:125–228.

Hemerijck, Anton, and Jelle Visser. 2003. Policy Learning in European Welfare States. Working paper, AIAS, University of Amsterdam.

Keune, Maarten. 2003. Labour Market Flexibility in Central and Eastern Europe: An Analysis of Non-Standard Employment and Working-Time Arrangements in the Czech Republic and Hungary. Working paper, Department of Political and Social Sciences, European University Institute, Florence.

Kovács, János Mátyás. 2002. Approaching the EU and Reaching the US? Rival Narratives on Transforming Welfare Regimes in East-Central Europe. *West European Politics* 25:175–204.

Lange, Peter. 1993. Maastricht and the Social Protocol: Why Did They Do It? *Politics and Society* 21:5–36.

Leibfried, Stephan, and Paul Pierson. 1995. *European Social Policy: Between Fragmentation and Integration*. Washington, DC: Brookings Institution.

———. 2000. Social Policy: Left to Courts and Markets? In *Policy-Making in the European Union*, ed. Helen Wallace and William Wallace, 4th edition, 267–92. Oxford: Oxford University Press.

Lendvai, Noémi. 2004. The Weakest Link? EU Accession and Enlargement: Dialoguing EU and Post-Communist Social Policy. *Journal of European Social Policy* 14:319–33.

Manning, Nick. 2004. Diversity and Change in Pre-Accession Central and Eastern Europe since 1989. *Journal of European Social Policy* 14: 211–32.

Marshall, T.H. [1950] 1963. *Citizenship and Social Class and Other Essays*. Cambridge: Cambridge University Press.

Mayes, David G., Jos Berghman, and Robert Salais. 2001. *Social Exclusion and European Policy*. Cheltenham: Edward Elgar.

Meehan, Elizabeth. 1993. *Citizenship and the European Community*. London: Sage.

Moravcsik, Andrew. 1998. *The Choice for Europe: Social Purpose and State Power from Messina to Maastricht*. Ithaca, NY: Cornell University Press.

Offe, Claus. 2003. The European Model of "Social" Capitalism: Can It Survive European Integration? *Journal of Political Philosophy* 11:437–69.

Rawls, John. 1971. *A Theory of Justice*. Cambridge, MA: Harvard University Press.

Sabel, Charles S., and Jonathan Zeitlin. 2003. Networked Governance and Pragmatic Constitutionalism: The New Transformation of Europe. Working paper, Columbia Law School, New York/University of Wisconsin, Madison.

Scharpf, Fritz W. 1999. *Governing in Europe: Effective and Democratic?* Oxford: Oxford University Press.

———. 2000. The Viability of Advanced Welfare States in the International Economy: Vulnerabilities and Options. *Journal of European Policy Studies* 7:190–228.

———. 2001. Democratic Legitimacy under Conditions of Regulatory Competition: Why Europe Differs from the United States. In *The Federal Vision: Legitimacy and Levels of Governance in the United States and the European Union*, ed. Kalypso Nicolaidis and Robert Howse, 355–74. Oxford: Oxford University Press.

———. 2002. The European Social Model: Coping with the Challenges of Diversity. *Journal of Common Market Studies* 40:645–70.

———. 2003. The Vitality of the Nation State in 21st Century Europe. In *De vitaliteit van de nationale staat in het Europa van de 21ste eeuw*, ed. WRR, 15–30. WRR-lecture 2002. Groningen: Stenfert Kroese.

Scharpf, Fritz W., and Vivien A. Schmidt, eds. 2000. *Welfare and Work in the Open Economy*, vol. 1, *From Vulnerability to Competitiveness in Comparative Perspective*; vol. 2, *Diverse Responses to Common Challenges in Twelve Countries*. Oxford: Oxford University Press.

Shaw, Jo. 2003. A Strong Europe Is a Social Europe. Working paper 05/03, The Federal Trust for Education and Research, London.

Stark, David, and László Bruszt. 1998. *Postsocialist Pathways: Transforming Politics and Property in East Central Europe*. Cambridge: Cambridge University Press.

Streeck, Wolfgang. 1997. Beneficial Constraints: On the Economic Limits of Rational Voluntarism. In *Contemporary Capitalism: The Embeddedness of Institutions*, ed. J. Rogers Hollingsworth and Robert Boyer, 197–219. Cambridge: Cambridge University Press.

Supiot, Alain. 2003. Governing Work and Welfare in a Global Economy. In Zeitlin and Trubek, 376–406.

Trubek, David M., and James Mosher. 2003. New Governance, Employment Policy, and the European Social Model. In Zeitlin and Trubek, 33–58.

Tsoukalis, Loukas. 2003. *What Kind of Europe?* Oxford: Oxford University Press.

Vandenbroucke, Frank. 2002. Foreword: Sustainable Social Justice and "Open Coordination" in Europe. In Esping-Andersen, Gallie, Hemerijck, and Myles, viii–xxiv.

Van der Meer, Bart, and Marc van Riel. 2002. De "advocacy coalition" voor het Europese werkgelegenheidsbeleid: Het Europese integratieproces sinds EMU. *Beleid en Maatschappij* 29:123–33.

Visser, Jelle, and Anton Hemerijck. 1997. *"A Dutch Miracle": Job Growth, Welfare Reform and Corporatism in the Netherlands*. Amsterdam: Amsterdam University Press.

Wagener, Hans-Jürgen. 2002. The Welfare State in Transition Economies and Accession to the EU. *West European Politics* 25:152–74.

WRR (Wetenschappelijke Raad voor het Regeringsbeleid). 2001. *Naar een Europabrede Unie*. Den Haag: Sdu Uitgevers.

———. 2003. *Slagvaardigheid in de Europabrede Unie*. Den Haag: Sdu Uitgevers.

Zeitlin, Jonathan. 2003. Introduction: Governing Work and Welfare in a New Economy. In Zeitlin and Trubek, 1–30.

Zeitlin, Jonathan, and David M. Trubek, eds. 2003. *Governing Work and Welfare in a New Economy: European and American Experiments*. Oxford: Oxford University Press.

6

A Liberal Critique of Communitarian Economics

Paul de Beer

I guess most economists feel quite uncomfortable when they hear about something called "communitarian economics." "Community" is something economists are not really familiar with. Either they are concerned with individual economic agents (in microeconomic theory) or with macroeconomic aggregates. Even when economists study the behavior of groups, e.g., large corporations or trade unions, these are either considered as individual entities or as aggregates of individual agents, but not really as communities.

Still, I suppose, most economists wouldn't deny that "communities" really exist. But if one concedes that individual behavior is at least partly shaped or influenced by the community the individual belongs to, then it seems inevitable that "community" is a relevant variable in explaining economic phenomena. So it seems worthwhile to explore what communitarianism can add to "standard" (neoclassical) economic theory.

On starting this exercise one is immediately confronted with the fact that there is not anything like a coherent and comprehensive communitarian theory. It is my impression that different communitarian ideas are not so much characterized by what they have in common as by what they are opposed to, namely purely individualistic "liberal" thinking.

To start with, I think one should discriminate between communitarian ideas that have a mainly "positive" ("scientific" or "objective") character and those that have a mainly "normative" ("ethical" or "subjective") character. (Of course, one may dispute whether such a strict distinction between "facts" and "values" can really be made. Nevertheless, I think it is still a useful analytical distinction.) After having passed judgment on communitarianism as both a positive and a normative economic theory, I conclude with an overall assessment of communitarianism by comparing it with its European counterpart, the "Third Way," and with welfare liberalism.

COMMUNITARIANISM AS A POSITIVE THEORY

As a positive theory, the most elementary criticism communitarians may have regarding mainstream economic thought is that economic phenomena cannot be explained merely by reference to the behavior of individual economic agents. In fact, this may be nothing but the well-known criticism of the "fallacy of composition" which lies at the heart of Keynesianism or, more generally, macroeconomic theory. As Heilbroner (1972, 131) defines it: "The fallacy consists of assuming that what is true of the individual case must also be true of all cases combined. The flaw in reasoning lies in our tendency to overlook 'side effects' of individual actions . . . which may be negligible in isolation but which are very important in the aggregate."

This criticism, though being far from new, is, I think, very relevant in a period that neoclassical microeconomic theory and supply-side economics (which, in my opinion, are really the same thing) have a hegemonic position in economics. It is often startling to see how easily, almost casually, microeconomic causal relations are generalized to macroeconomic phenomena these days. For example, the ubiquitous pleas for a reduction of tax rates are mainly based on the asserted positive impact of lower tax rates on the behavior of individual persons or firms. Workers are expected to exert a greater effort if allowed to retain a larger share of their earned income. Hence, a tax reduction will increase total labor effort and result in a higher national product, it is argued. Whenever there is high involuntary unemployment, however, the extra effort of one worker may hurt the chances of an unemployed worker to find a job. The incentive from a tax reduction will then simply result in the crowding out of some workers by others. Besides, a tax reduction will have to be financed by a cut in public expenditure, which might result, for example, in some civil servants being laid off and a worsening of public services. Only after a careful assessment of all positive and negative effects *at the macro level* can one pass a balanced judgment on the merits of a tax reduction.

A more "sophisticated" communitarian criticism to standard economic thought may be that individual agents do not act in a kind of void, but that their behavior is at least partly shaped by the institutions that guide their actions and by their (social) relations with other individuals. Bellah et al. (1991, 19, 29) express this criticism as follows: "The individualistic assumptions of our culture lead us to believe that we can live as we choose, using the big institutions . . . for our own ends, without fundamentally being influenced by them." And: "The major blind spot in the economic theory . . . is that it sees only disaggregated individuals, not the institutions that give them meaning and a place in the world. In the theoretical perspective . . . there are only the goods or interests of individuals, assumed to be fixed preferences which can only be aggregated but not discussed."

This criticism too is not very original. In fact, it seems to amount to something like institutional economic theory or socioeconomic theory. Etzioni (1988, 185), for example, states that, in contrast to neoclassical theory, "it is a core assumption of socio-economists that social collectivities (such as local communities, ethnic and racial groups, and social movements) are pivotal actors; and that the qualities of most decision-making *and* deliberation . . . are deeply affected and can be explained to a significant extent by collective processes and structures (institutions and organizations)."

Perhaps institutions and communal values might even be incorporated into neoclassical theory, as has been attempted by Akerlof (1984) in his "theory of social custom." He simply adds some social elements (values, reputation) to the individual utility function and supposes the individual's utility is not only influenced by "traditional" economic factors as income and leisure, but also by his reputation, which in turn depends on his compliance to generally accepted "codes of behavior" in the community. His utility may also be directly positively influenced by the fact that he acts in accordance with values and norms he himself believes in. Akerlof then shows that people may behave in a way that conflicts with their financial interests. This fact may lead to a stable macroeconomic equilibrium in which the norms are obeyed by most economic agents.

Institutions also are of central interest in the so-called new institutional economics (e.g., Williamson 1975, and Furubotn and Richter 1998). Institutional economists recognize the crucial role of institutions in shaping human (and *a fortiori* economic) behavior. However, new institutional economics is still firmly rooted in the neoclassical maxim of methodological individualism, which means that it starts from rationally acting individual agents. Institutions are then conceptualized as "external" factors that influence the costs of transactions between individual persons or organizations. In contrast to neoclassical economics, which regards legal restrictions on the free market as impediments to economic efficiency, new institutional economists acknowledge that market regulation may sometimes improve market performance, for example if information asymmetries are an obstacle to realizing the theoretical optimal market outcome.

A third kind of communitarian criticism of standard economic theory might be that the "homo economicus"—economic man who is only rationally pursuing his (financial) self-interest and who is central to neoclassical theory—is not a real phenomenon but a theoretical artifact. However, this is in fact not criticism of neoclassical theory, but only of a common interpretation of it or of the way it is often elaborated in empirical research. This communitarian critique mainly draws attention to the (too often neglected) fact that in reality the utility function of most individuals also contains other-regarding interests. This fact is also acknowledged by some economists who work within the standard neoclassical framework. E.g., Sen (1987, 9) "would like to argue that economics, as it has emerged, can be made more productive by paying greater and more explicit attention to the ethical considerations that shape human behavior and judgment." Consequently, he denies that there is any logical connection between the assumption of "rational" behavior and of self-interest maximization. "To see any departure from self-interest maximization as evidence of irrationality must imply a rejection of the role of ethics in actual decision making" (Sen 1987, 15).

Etzioni (1988, chap. 3) suggests that the traditional "mono-utility" assumption of neoclassical economics, which represents some sense of pleasure or self-satisfaction, should be replaced by a "bi-utility" conception that, apart from "pleasure," also contains a *moral* dimension. Moral commitment cannot be simply traded for "material" interests. One does not simply decide to commit a crime as soon as the material rewards of crime become larger than the perceived costs, calculated as the product of the probability of being caught and the expected monetary value of the punishment, as is suggested in Gary Becker's theory of crime. Etzioni states that human behavior cannot be understood as a simultaneous optimization of both moral commitments and material interests. These motives are fundamentally distinct factors that guide individual behavior and cannot be collapsed into one utility concept.

Khalil (1997) supports Etzioni's contention that personal interests cannot smoothly substitute commitments, but criticizes Etzioni for neglecting the fact that commitments and interests cannot be considered as completely independent from each other either. He explains his position by comparing gifts (e.g., a birthday present) with grants (e.g., a donation to a charitable organization). Although it is clear that receiving a gift is not equivalent to receiving a grant of the same monetary value, it is also clear that the utility one derives from a gift is not independent of (though neither equivalent to) the "material" satisfaction it produces. So it seems best to merge moral commitments and material interests in the same utility concept, while acknowledging that this does not imply that both elements are smoothly substitutable (hence, the utility function might not be continuously differentiable in both arguments, as is usually assumed in theoretical and empirical analyses).

Although the criticism of the assumption of the self-interested, egocentric individual is very relevant to understanding economic behavior, it is usually very hard to incorporate these nonselfish interests in empirical economic research, mainly because of lack of reliable data.

To summarize my observations on "communitarian economics" as a positive theory: although the communitarian criticism of standard economic theory as it is often (especially during the last two decades) applied is, in my opinion, quite correct and very relevant, the communitarian perspective does not add any really new element to economic analysis, but mainly embroiders on well-known "alternatives" to neoclassical theory within economic theory (Keynesianism, institutional economics) or outside economic theory (sociology). It seems that communitarianism as a positive theory is in fact an attempt of sociologists to recapture some of the ground they have lost by the "imperialist" attempts of economists (of whom Gary Becker is perhaps the most influential representative) to explain more and more aspects of human behavior by "economic" motives.

COMMUNITARIANISM AS A NORMATIVE THEORY

Although communitarianism clearly opposes standard neoclassical theory, it is my impression that most communitarians are even more critical of what is often regarded as the normative counterpart of this, namely liberal political philosophy. However, since political liberalism is quite diverse in character, this criticism too may have widely divergent interpretations. The common element of these diverse interpretations is, I think, that they insist on the existence of certain "communitarian" (or "common") values. But they differ in the exact interpretation of these common values.

Most directly related to the criticism of neoclassical economic theory seems to be the communitarian criticism of the *moral* superiority of the free market or laissez-faire policy. Communitarians criticize libertarian views according to which there is no other common good than the unrestricted (negative) freedom of all individuals, as suggested by Hayek, Friedman, Nozick, and others. For example, Bellah et al. (1991, 6) say: "If philosophical liberals are those who believe that all our problems can be solved by autonomous individuals, a market economy, and a procedural state, whereas communitarians believe that more substantive ethical identities and a more active participation in a democratic polity are necessary for the functioning of any decent society, then we are indeed communitarians." This criticism of libertarianism is of course far from unique for communitarianism, but is shared with many other political philosophies, ranging from welfare liberalism to Marxism.

Communitarian economics might also criticize another branch of liberal thought, namely utilitarianism, which contends that the common good (or the social-welfare function, as economists might prefer to call it) is simply the sum total of all individual utilities or interests. As Bellah et al. (1991, 95) say: "Our individualistic heritage taught us that there is no such thing as the common good but only the sum of individual goods. But in our complex, interdependent world, the sum of individual goods, organized only under the tyranny of the market, often produces a common bad that eventually erodes our personal satisfactions as well."

More specifically, communitarians seem opposed to (or even offended by) a specific application of utilitarian thinking, namely using cost-benefit analysis in all fields of socioeconomic policy, because it reduces the interests of individual citizens to monetary figures. Cost-benefit analysis can amount to calculations according to which the lives of people should be sacrificed because their monetary value is less than the costs to save them. "The technique of cost-benefit analysis leads to the construction of a market, with incentives and costs, where none naturally exists. . . To create such a fictive market requires one to set a price on everything, from human lives to scenic vistas, so that trade-offs among these goods can be calculated as costs and benefits." And: "There is simply something about human lives that cannot, and should not, be evaluated in economic terms" (Bellah et al. 1991, 28, 121). This criticism comes quite close to the well-known dictum that economists know the price of everything but the value of nothing. In the words of Bellah et al. (1991, 117): "[Cost-benefit economists] define the value of life abstracted from any particular life. In doing this they ignore an essential meaning of life as we commonly understand it—that each life is unique and irreplaceable."

However, communitarians seem to overlook that the refusal to talk about human lives in monetary terms does not change the fact that in reality one has to make financial decisions and trade-offs that may determine the life chances of people. For example, by deciding how much tax money will be spent on different public services that may affect the chance of survival of citizens, politicians implicitly put a price tag on individual lives, even though they often do not seem to be conscious of that fact. If a certain amount is spent on a costly treatment of a rare but killing disease that will save a specific number of lives, then the value of an individual live *is* in fact expressed in monetary terms. By not talking about the monetary value of saving a life, however, one runs the risk of completely arbitrary decision making. Suppose, for example, that spending the same amount of money on a preventive measure (e.g., a vaccination program) would save far more lives, although the specific individuals that survive thanks to the vaccination are less easily identified. Then knowing the cost-benefit ratio of these different measures can lead to a more rational and balanced weighing of the alternatives. But, of course, applying cost-benefit analysis does not *force* politicians to choose the measure with the most favorable cost-benefit ratio. That would reduce politics to a purely technocratic exercise. There might be perfectly rational reasons to prefer the more costly treatment (e.g., because of the particular population group that is susceptible to the illness). But at least one should be aware of the extra cost that is involved in this decision—not only in monetary terms but also in terms of other lives that are not being saved. Hence, as long as cost-benefit analysis is not used as a mechanical device to surpass political deliberation, there is nothing inhuman in calculating the implicit monetary value of human lives.

Nevertheless, much of communitarian criticism of utilitarian thinking is, in my opinion, quite correct. But again, this criticism has been put forward by others long before communitarianism was *en vogue*. Most renowned, though certainly not original either, is perhaps the criticism of utilitarianism by John Rawls (1971, esp. chaps. 3 and 9) and the many who have elaborated or amended his "theory of justice." This liberal criticism of utilitarianism is mainly individualistic, in the sense that it criticizes the utilitarian thesis that the interests of the individual may be sacrificed for the greater interests of the community at large or the aggregated interests of other people. As an alternative to utilitarian thought, Rawls formulated his two principles of justice, of which the first says that "[e]ach person has an equal right to a fully adequate scheme of equal basic liberties which is compatible with a similar scheme of liberties for all," and the second, that social and economic inequalities between people must be "attached to offices and positions open to all under conditions of fair equality of opportunity" and must be "to the greatest benefit of the least advantaged members of society" (the so-called "difference principle," as most recently formulated in Rawls 1993, 7).

The thinking of some communitarians, like Selznick (1992, esp. chap. 16), seems to be largely in accordance with this welfare liberalism. Others however, do not seem to criticize utilitarianism because it neglects the interest of the individual, but because it gives the wrong account of the common good. They go even a step further than utilitarians in claiming that the individual interest is not only subordinated to the common interest, but that the common good is something quite different from the aggregation of all individual interests. In their opinion, the common good cannot be formulated exclusively in terms of individual utilities or interests; the common good contains some really *common*, supraindividual elements, e.g., a common culture or a shared tradition (see, e.g., Sandel 1982, esp. chap. 4). These communitarians are so-called perfectionists, who regard a specific conception of "the good life" as superior to other conceptions and find it desirable that this specific conception of the good life be promoted, irrespective of whether most or all people share this conception. In this sense "perfectionist" communitarians are fundamentally antiliberal.

My main objection to this perfectionist thought is that it is impossible to give a satisfying account as to who is to decide what the preferable conception of the good life should be. It seems unavoidable that either a minority elite group or the majority will impose its opinion on the remaining citizens. However, as Kymlicka (1990, 203–4) has pointed out, "no life goes better by being led from the outside according to values the person does not endorse. My life only goes better if I am leading it from the inside, according to my beliefs about value."

Only if a specific conception of the good life (or part of it) is shared by literally all members of a specific community, is it unproblematic to promote this conception consciously. But in that case, the promotion of a shared conception is not in conflict with liberal neutrality, which is only concerned with alternative *contested* conceptions of the good life. So Rawls—and in fact practically all liberals—assumes that there is an "overlapping consensus" between all "reasonable" conceptions of the good, which enables him to formulate his list of "primary goods" that are essential for the promotion of all these different conceptions (Rawls 1993, lecture 4).

Nevertheless, it should be emphasized that, even if there is a consensus on a specific conception of the good life, this does not mean that this conception should be fixed once and for all. Individuals should be free to revise their conception in the light of new experiences or information (Kymlicka 1990, 202–4).

CONCLUSION: A MARRIAGE BETWEEN COMMUNITARIANISM AND THE THIRD WAY?

Communitarianism is first and foremost an American phenomenon. In my opinion, its "rise" should be understood as a reaction to the prevailing conservative ideology in the United States in the 1980s: neoliberalism, monetarism, supply-side economics, Reaganomics. In short: the canonization of the free market. As it became more and more apparent that this ideology was not only far less successful in economic terms than its proponents asserted but also that it resulted in deep cracks in societies' texture (e.g., sharply increasing income disparities), some Americans turned to Western Europe hoping to find in the European welfare state an alternative for the harsh American system. So communitarianism could be seen as an attempt to incorporate some elements of continental European welfare states into the American free-market economy, while making this alternative acceptable by casting it in American terms, for example by emphasizing the role of communities instead of the role of the state.

If one interprets communitarianism in this way, it is not surprising that it did not obtain a foothold in Europe: after all, why seek a duplicate if you already have the original? In fact, at about the same time that communitarianism rose in the United States, in Europe just the opposite development took place, especially among social democrats. Since the 1980s Europeans became more and more critical of their welfare states—or at least of the way they were functioning. Many Europeans were tempted to turn to the dynamic and flexible American economy as an example for Europe. The main offspring of this European reflection on the welfare state has been the reformulation of social-democratic ideology under the heading of the "Third Way." Some social-democratic thinkers, among whom sociologist Anthony Giddens (1998), have tried to formulate the theoretical underpinnings of the Third Way. In their view the Third Way means a shift in emphasis from equal outcomes to equal opportunities. It entails a government that leaves more room for market forces and directs public spending to productive social investments, especially education, to equip people with the resources to operate as self-reliant and responsible citizens, instead of to passive income transfers (e.g., unemployment benefits and social assistance). Nevertheless, these ideas can hardly be considered a comprehensive and coherent alternative for existing political programs. It is no coincidence that the name "Third Way" merely indicates what it is not—neither pure capitalism nor state socialism—but does not really give a clue as to what it does embrace. In this respect it resembles its American counterpart communitarianism, which is also more easily characterized by what it criticizes than by what it advocates.

Both communitarianism and the Third Way can be considered as signals that people in the United States *and* in Europe are tired of having to make a sharp choice between a rough but dynamic capitalist system and a soft but inefficient state-socialist system. They hope to find a middle way that combines the strong points of the free market and the welfare state, while avoiding their weaknesses. However, it is far from evident that by steering such a middle course one will really find oneself in the best of both worlds. It is also possible that the hoped-for synergy will not materialize and instead one will wind up with the weak points of both alternatives.

It might therefore be wiser not to throw away the baby with the bathwater and join the older tradition of social-liberal or welfare-liberal thought, as represented by political philosophers as Rawls, Dworkin, Ackerman, Sen, and Van Parijs. This liberal tradition in fact also attempts to combine a capitalist free-market economy with the social objectives of equal opportunities, an equitable income distribution, and decent public services. And although there are numerous differences of opinion concerning the practical implications of such a welfare-liberal approach, compared to communitarianism and the Third Way it is built on more solid theoretical ground. As Nobel laureate Amartya Sen in particular has shown, it is very well possible to start from classical economic theory and combine this with different kinds of social objectives in order to arrive at an attractive ideological program that exceeds neoliberal thought, based on a purely individual interpretation of the common good. So perhaps the best thing communitarians can do is to give up their pretension of a self-contained comprehensive ideology and join forces with welfare liberals in their fight against neoliberal laissez-faire politics.

REFERENCES

Akerlof, George A. 1984. A Theory of Social Custom, of Which Unemployment May Be One Consequence. In *An Economic Theorist's Book of Tales*, 69–99. Cambridge: Cambridge University Press.

Bellah, Robert N., Richard Madsen, William M. Sullivan, Ann Swidler, and Steven M. Tipton. 1991. *The Good Society*. New York: Knopf.

Etzioni, Amitai. 1988. *The Moral Dimension: Toward a New Economics*. New York: Free Press.

Giddens, Anthony. 1998. *The Third Way: The Renewal of Social Democracy*. Cambridge: Polity Press.

Furubotn, Eirik G., and Rudolf Richter. 1998. *Institutions and Economic Theory: The Contribution of the New Institutional Economics*. Ann Arbor: University of Michigan Press.

Heilbroner, Robert L. 1972. *Understanding Macroeconomics*. 4th ed. Englewood Cliffs, NJ: Prentice-Hall.

Khalil, Elias L. 1997. Etzioni *versus* Becker: Do Moral Sentiments Differ from Ordinary Tastes? *De Economist* 145:491–520.

Kymlicka, Will. 1990. *Contemporary Political Philosophy: An Introduction*. Oxford: Clarendon Press.

Rawls, John. 1971. *A Theory of Justice*. Oxford: Oxford University Press.

———. 1993. *Political Liberalism*. New York: Columbia University Press.

Sandel, Michael J. 1982. *Liberalism and the Limits of Justice*. Cambridge: Cambridge University Press.

Selznick, Philip. 1992. *The Moral Commonwealth: Social Theory and the Promise of Community*. Berkeley: University of California Press.

Sen, Amartya. 1987. *On Ethics and Economics*. Oxford: Basil Blackwell.

Williamson, Oliver E. 1975. *Markets and Hierarchies: Analysis and Antitrust Implication*. New York: Free Press.

Part III

THE SOCIAL VALUES OF LAW

7

Protection or Prohibition of Aggressive Speech? Arguments from the Liberal and Communitarian Perspectives[1]

Winfried Brugger

AGGRESSIVE SPEECH: THE ENDURANCE TEST FOR LIBERALISM AND THE FREEDOM OF SPEECH

Freedom of speech is a centerpiece of liberal thought.[2] Immanuel Kant spoke of the palladium of citizen rights and regarded publicity and public acceptance as the legitimacy tests for all legal regulations (Kant [1795] 1968, 381–86). As such, the modern state has incorporated these principles. It protects the relevant freedom of communication through the means of fundamental rights. One may view such a constitutional guarantee as a natural development of liberalism. However, a closer look reveals that the establishment of free speech contains an additional aspect of practical experience: it is only necessary when the danger of oppression looms—either by the state or by the community which is capable of implementing political decisions through the majority (Mill [1859] 1973, 490–530, summarized at 528). Even in liberal societies, an open and unimpeded political discussion among societal groups and political parties is by no means an automatic law of nature. Rather, a constitutional guarantee reflects the permanent seducing danger of collectively suppressing opinions that are unreasonable, irritating, outrageous, or shocking to the spirit of the times.[3]

Perhaps liberal instinct and the spirit of tolerance are sufficient to tolerate moderately critical opinions of persons or groups. However, tolerance becomes fragile when criticisms turn more radical. It is precisely at this point that liberalism is put to the test: should tolerance and patience extend to speech that is regarded as outrageous, incorrect, unjust, or immoral? For example, imagine a demonstrator who advocates the following positions: (1) "Immigrants who apply for social welfare are parasites!"[4] (2) "Stop the invasion and alienation of our country by criminal immigrants who are threatening our freedom and property, and deluging us with drugs!"[5] (3) During the public appearance the commentator displays insignia that represent ideologies of racial superiority and inferiority: e.g., the swastika in Germany, and the Ku Klux Klan cross in the United States.[6] How should a legal system respond to such aggressive or even hateful speech within the public domain?[7] It is here that opinions divide.

Consider a short overview of the methods in which modern states nationally and internationally handle this type of speech. One group of countries, primarily led by the United States, protects aggressive hate speech in an extensive manner, at least to the extent that relevant public issues are addressed. The second group of states includes Germany, members of the European Council,[8] as well as signatories to International Human Rights Conventions.[9] Regarding the examples mentioned above, all utterances are prohibited according to the German view and protected under the American perspective. Thus, roughly speaking, there exists a certain competition between the American viewpoint and that of Germany, Europe, and International Conventions.[10]

The crux of the disagreement is whether a state has the right to impose legal restrictions based on the *content of the speech*. Such a "regulation of opinion" is generally suspect in a liberal state. German constitutional law takes this into account by stipulating that restrictions are only possible when promulgated by a "general law" as opposed to a regulation targeting specific opinions. Moreover, the German state is also constitutionally bound to neutrality in relation to opinions expressed in the public domain.[11] If—within such clauses or analogous doctrines—the freedom of speech is recognized to take priority over other values potentially at risk from a particular type of speech, the prohibition of content-specific regulations and adherence to state neutrality are strictly applied. Infractions against these standards then are in most cases considered unconstitutional. Comparatively, in the United States, laws specifically prohibiting the expression of certain views are colloquially (but fittingly) characterized as "cardinal sins" against free speech or the principle of neutrality (Sullivan 2001, 9). If priority is, however, not generally granted to free speech, as in Germany, content-specific laws are allowed in several cases. Moreover, the state may be partial, and may even influence the processes of building societal opinions.[12] This leads us to the next question: which forms of objectionable speech can or should be subject to legal sanctions? From the point of view of Germany, Europe, and International Conventions, but in contrast to that of the United States, particularly objectionable, aggressive hate speech may be prohibited and criminally sanctioned. Usually[13] such sanctions are to be found in norms punishing (1) individual and collective insults, (2) the incitement of hatred and violence against minorities, (3) racial propaganda, and (4) discrimination.[14]

This chapter does not provide an analysis of the various legal provisions.[15] Rather, the arguments shall be discussed and the values introduced that are typically at odds in the case of aggressive speech. This will be done in a dialectical way. After a brief characterization of the types of arguments (section two), a description of the specific arguments presented by liberal, American proponents urging the utmost priority of free speech will follow (section three). Next, the contrary viewpoint that reverses the priority will be considered. Many commentators have characterized this perspective as communitarianism (section four). Finally, this characterization will be analyzed and a mediating view under the framework of "liberal communitarianism" will be presented (section five). Moreover, two charts in the appendix will illustrate the differences between the two opposing viewpoints outlined here and the three main versions of communitarianism.

STRUCTURE OF THE ARGUMENTS

Relevant arguments for and against granting priority to free speech over other competing values (Rosenfeld 2003, sec. 1; Post 1991, 271–77) can roughly be divided into those that regard the consequence of an utterance as crucial, and those that, independent of possible or likely consequences, focus on the autonomy of the speaker in the broadest sense of the term.[15] There is a general agreement that these two forms may be analytically distinguished; however, when weighing the value of free speech against other competing values, both arguments should be considered. While arguments based on the autonomy of the speaker tend to be framed individualistically, so that an unjustified infringement is viewed as "injustice," arguments based on the consequence of speech tend to be strongly probabilistic and are categorized by their suitability or unsuitability in the promotion of a specific collective goal. Particular forms of speech or specific messages are then "good" or "bad" for the political climate as well as for civilized public discourse. Furthermore, one may extend the reference point from micro to macro by comparing how aggressive speech relates to overarching ideals of the human person, societal order, and governmental functions. Moreover, communication is always a relationship between the speaker, recipients, and the general public.[17] For the argument based on the consequences of speech, this relationship is self-evident. For the arguments based on the status of the speaker, this is not necessarily taken for granted—the conception may be solipsistic or strongly oriented toward the rights of the speaker.[18] Whatever right to autonomy a speaker may have when expressing opinions, one should not ignore the potential costs of a damaged reputation or the potential harm to societal expectations of civilized discourse. Finally, attention must be given to if and how historical experiences of domination and exploitation should be considered in the above-mentioned arguments—particularly with regard to determining the dangers of aggressive speech for vulnerable groups that may require special state protection.

ARGUMENTS FOR GRANTING PRIORITY TO AGGRESSIVE SPEECH

Let us first consider the arguments of the liberal[19] American advocate, who supports the extensive protection of aggressive speech addressing relevant public issues (Weinstein 1999; 2001, 146–49; Bracken 1994; Sullivan 2001, 9):

1. *Autonomy*. Freedom of speech is relevant *only* to human beings but yet *to all* human beings. It is through communication that humans can develop into what they are—namely, beings only partially driven by instinct and hence free to form moral orientations and develop individual personalities.[20] From the capacity of moral discourse follows human dignity. Personality in turn is expressed through the process of shaping an individual into a distinct person through communication. Because actions are the mere expression of human personality and individuality, and the capacity to engage in moral discourse is the prerequisite for the action to follow, priority is given to the formulation of personality through communication. For this reason, the freedom of communication deserves special status.

Due to the fact that humans not only *have* opinions but *are* what is embodied in those opinions (Kaleb 1996, 223), freedom of expression is a fundamental right related directly to the individual. Conflicts between the individual person and collective preferences are not only possible, but in light of previous experience likely. Therefore, freedom of speech should not only be protected against domination by the majority but also, due to its relationship with individual autonomy, should be granted preference. Infractions against free speech are typically violations against liberty and equality. The former occurs because the state, with the force of criminal sanction, dictates to the individual *what* he or she should or should not think and *how* he or she should or should not pass judgment. The latter occurs because certain individuals or groups are free to form and defend opinions, while others who contradict the predominant viewpoint are prohibited from doing so. Infringements of freedom and equality are also suffered by the speaker's listeners. Such results are impermissible paternalism.[21]

2. *Opinions, arguments, and emotions*. Aggressive speech must be treated like all other forms of conformist, mainstream speech or civilized expressions of criticism. Strong value judgments are typically indicators of deeply seated conflicts the speaker has experienced with prevalent conditions of society. Emotions—ranging from mild criticism to rejection and hate—must either be respected as expressions of personal judgments[22] or at least accepted as a side effect of the critical attitude of the speaker.[23] This does not exclude the possibility that social institutions and state authorities support civilized interaction and communication. However, this may be accomplished only in an instructive and facilitating manner and not through the means of criminal

sanctions that have the inherent tendency of decimating the message rather than merely improving its style.

3. *First consequentialist argument.* Aggressive speech can admittedly infringe upon the recipient's claim to respect and dignity. However, it may also be justified to the extent that aggressive judgments are explicitly or implicitly related to actual or presumed facts and thus allow for free discussion. For example, the speaker may mistakenly assume certain facts that are exposed during open discussion. Here, the opportunity exists to revise the stated opinion. Contrarily, assumed facts may indeed be accurate, leaving no reason for revision. As such, truths concerning societal or politically relevant issues should always be expressed or even filtered out through the course of discussion.[24]

Consider the two examples mentioned above. When a speaker characterizes immigrants entitled to social welfare benefits as "parasites," or chastises the criminality rate among immigrants on the basis of incorrect or exaggerated figures, open discussion can clarify these mistakes and cause the speaker to revise the original viewpoint. However, if the figures prove in fact to be correct, the opinion cannot be revised in light of mere factual numbers.

4. *Second consequentialist argument.* In the event that value judgments are professed without factual basis, as in the above-mentioned example of displaying symbols of racial superiority, the dispute does not concern facts but rather values between individuals and groups. Such value conflicts are to be carried out in public discourse and may not be suppressed by means of state authority. It is only in this manner that the learning process is facilitated and more pointed arguments can develop. However, only in a moderately enlightened society is this possible.[25] Moreover, it is argued that aggressive speech is a means by which aggressors can let off steam (Kretzmer 1987, 487; Coliver 1992, 374). In the majority of cases, aggression evaporates or at least is partially deflated—thereby reducing the likelihood of aggressive physical actions.

5. *Third consequentialist argument.* In the event that violent acts are taken or are threatened to be taken with "fighting words," then, legally, either *speech* no longer exists but rather *action* (which clearly may be punished); or the recipient is confronted with the immediate danger of violence and the state is obligated to protect that person from bodily harm as well as to reestablish law and order.[26] In contrast, statements that may only indirectly harm society in the long term may not be criminally sanctioned in a liberal state that respects free speech.[27] The determination of such unclear and indirect damage to the life and limb of concrete individuals requires an uncertain prognosis that may be subject to the prejudices of the dominant class. The predicted damage may eventually occur, but it is not certain. What, however, is certain is that state-imposed sanctions restricting the freedom of speech curtail the dignity, personality, freedom, and equality of the speaker.

In such a conflict, the certain damage to the individual rights of the speaker must be avoided, and the uncertain damage to the public must be accepted. Moreover, one may argue that objectionable speech may always be countered with rebuttal. As such, the liberal motto, "when in doubt, more speech is preferable to less speech," is affirmed.[28]

6. *Attacks against personal honor and defamatory statements.* In regard to the legal rights of individuals and groups to dignity and protection from rhetorical attacks, statements devoid of factual assertions—that is to say, value judgments of one group against another—must be respected as a distinct personal expression of the speaker. Such statements may lead to societal unrest, but a closer look reveals that such unrest may actually be productive. For instance, a statement, which at first glance appears to be a mere value judgment, may upon closer examination turn out to be based on factual assumptions made consciously or unconsciously. Thus, the confirmation or perhaps revision of opinion through contact with contradictory facts is possible and in turn serves the process of discovering truth. Consider such statements as "Italians are members of the Mafia," "Germans are Nazis," "Poles are thieves," as well as other views expressing racial inferiority or superiority. Such claims can be rebutted by comparing relevant criminal statistics with those of other groups and countries. Supposing that the claims contained a grain of truth, one may still point out factors unrelated to nationality and ethnicity that may lead to higher statistical rates. As for the alleged superiority of one race over another, it is often possible to refer to factual similarities between members of different races. Admittedly, in a polarized field of discussion, facts concerning the equality of all human beings (Selznick 1992, 96–104) will not necessarily change the mind of a convinced racist.

Pure value judgments in the form of derogatory statements do not necessarily result in a defamation of character. This is only possible if the recipient's individual or group definition of self is mainly determined through the evaluation of others.[29] This is not necessarily the case, especially due to the fact that derogatory statements not supported by corresponding facts or statements of truth often reveal more about the speaker than the recipient, especially in cases of aggressive speech.

7. *Collective defamation of character.* This area requires an additional consideration. Expressions that defame individual character are easily recognized: one knows the perpetrator as well as the object of attack. In the case of collective defamations against Germans, Italians, Poles, etc., the identity of the victim is less clear. Derogatory value judgments may simply mean that, according to the speaker's judgment, too many members of the group in question correspond with the negative characteristics expressed. It would rarely be assumed that such statements address all members of the group without exception. The generalization of a reproach ("all people designated as . . . may be characterized as . . .") can often be understood as an expres-

sion of indignation, which always tends to be subject to exaggeration and therefore stereotypes. "Against a background of sharp disagreement, efforts at persuasion sometimes proceed through exaggeration, vilification, and distortion" (Cohen 1996, 193). The reasonable individual knows that one cannot take stereotypes at their face value. Summary characterizations of people are inevitable aspects of human communication (Luhmann 1998, 104–6). One cannot do full justice in every instance to every person's individuality and peculiar circumstances.[30]

Even if a judgment is meant to address all members of a particular group and a negative value is ascribed to a particular person due to that person's membership in that group, this remains an expression constructed through the personality of the speaker and not through the exclusive or primary characteristics of the recipient. The addressee has the right to say, "I am a member of the group which you have rhetorically attacked. But above all, I am an independent person, and I am not concerned or affected by your remarks against this group. I may be attached to this group, but in the end, I am more than and different from this group."[31] Whether one is affected by a statement or not, rebuttal always remains an option.

Therefore, in regard to the individual and collective protection of character, there are many considerations that argue against sanctioning value judgments of a derogatory nature, if the statements address important public issues. Such value judgments are not—or at least not inevitably—detrimental to the reputation of the recipient. The speaker, by contrast, risks the danger of isolation and defamation in social life if judgments are sufficiently extreme and/or shocking.

However, the situation is different in cases in which derogatory statements are recognizably based on purported facts that, if true, are sufficient to damage the social and professional standing of the recipient. Because such reputations are often gained through long-term efforts, their protection is a matter of justice.

This viewpoint of free speech, which protects aggressive speech in issues of public relevance, corresponds with a specific understanding of human nature, society, and state, as well as of neutrality and integration.

8. *Human nature.* The human being is a moral person, as well as a unique and irreplaceable individual. In communication, his or her status as an expressive subject is at stake.[32] Social norms and restrictions placed on free speech by the state must be justified to the speaker, and not vice versa.[33] One may designate this as "legitimizing individualism" (Höffe 1999, 45–48). Expressing one's mind need not be aggressive—often its exercise will not be offensive at all. However, it must be permissible that a person express himself or herself in a fundamentally critical manner due to the fact that such statements are a constitutive part of the speaker's personality and should be regarded as a personal contribution to matters of public interest.

9. *Society*. According to this view, societal interaction need not be negative or aggressive—solidarity, cooperation, and civility are not excluded but rather included. Yet conflicts and disputes are viewed as conceivable and likely and should be openly voiced. Sometimes, or even often, such conflicts are carried out in a civilized manner; however, when heated conflict occurs, it must be tolerated by the legal system to the extent that the line to imminent violence is not crossed. "To be sure, civility has its place in public deliberation. But so have anger, disgust, bitter criticism, and open expressions of hostility" (Cohen 1996, 188n62).

10. *State*. The state may, and must, protect the physical integrity of its citizens. A peaceful and secure coexistence should be provided by preventing violence between citizens. Nonetheless, the state may not attempt to suppress each form of unrest, judgmental exaggeration, or rhetorical aggression. Life in society, especially in a multicultural society, means life in a state of unrest.[34] This unrest is an expression of the capacity of reflection and articulation among differing individuals and groups and must be upheld in a liberal state.[35] Otherwise, the duty of the state to maintain peace suddenly spills over into maintaining graveyard silence.[36] To sum up, the individual stands before society and the society, with its mechanisms of self-regulation, stands before the state with its monopoly over the forces of coercion.[37] Coercion is only legitimate under the premise of democracy when all citizens and groups enjoy equal rights of participation in the discussions and decisions formulating regulations that apply to all (Post 1991, 325–27).

11. *Neutrality and integration*. The state must remain neutral in relation to the spectrum of opinions held by its individual citizens.[38] Only in this manner can the state safeguard the dignity, freedom, and equality of all citizens and thus realize—if realization is possible at all—genuine *integration*. This is defined in terms of unobstructed *societal recognition* of all individuals and groups as equals[39] as well as *political recognition* that all opinions of all citizens may be expressed and that judgments may not be excluded before they are expressed (Post 1997, 480–81; 1991, 280–85; Weinstein 2001, 147, 150). Those who violate this principle commit a cardinal sin against the freedom of speech[40] and thus have taken the first step from a liberal toward an authoritarian, tyrannical polity.[41]

ARGUMENTS FOR THE RESTRICTION OF AGGRESSIVE SPEECH

Now consider the advocate inspired by the viewpoint prevalent in Germany, Europe, and International Conventions, who strives to protect the critical potential of free speech while allowing state restrictions against aggressive and/or hate speech:[42]

1. *Autonomy*. Freedom of speech is indeed important to everyone. Communication is the vehicle for moral reflection and personal development and therefore the basis for human autonomy. Through the expression of views, the individual shapes and presents him- or herself to other human beings and establishes relationships with them. However, legitimate individualism may not be exaggerated and, in particular, turned against the mediation between individuals and society.[43] It is true that the individual must be defended against collective paternalism. However, not every reference to community should be understood as collective domination. The freedom to fully develop one's personality depends upon mutual understandings between individuals and groups. Peaceful engagement requires that the state respect and protect the various groups in society. Aggressive or hateful speech directed toward individuals or groups denies the right of the recipients to participate freely and equally in the effort to develop and define a common good. If the state restricts aggressive speech, it does not violate the freedom and equality of the individual or collective speakers, but rather *secures the unobstructed development and equal recognition of the recipients*. Restricting the rights of hate instigators cannot be viewed as paternalism, but is rather a means of securing the equal status of citizenship for all members of society by eliminating messages from the public domain that would detract from that status. The freedom of speech is indeed a particularly important right, but yet still more fundamental is the status as a member of the community deserving "equal concern and respect" (Dworkin 1978, 180–83 272–78).[44]

2. *Opinions, arguments, and emotions*. Such restrictions of aggressive speech do not necessarily prohibit the speaker from expressing criticism of public affairs. Normally, it is possible to make statements that deeply move a person without aggression or attacking another person's character. One only has to choose a civilized form: *fortiter in re, suaviter in modo*.[45] This has the additional advantage that citizens may count on a certain measure of civility in the public and political spheres. Certainly citizens would be more willing to enter and be active in areas in which the communicative climate is not so brutal as to make only the most robust and insensitive personalities willing to expose themselves to attacks by opponents (Bull 2001, 185–90). Moreover, by reducing the emotionality of discussion, rationality is thereby promoted.

3. *First consequentialist argument*. Insofar as aggressive speech implicitly or explicitly refers to factual matters, it should be possible to assert the truth through a process of public discussion. However, thoughtless assertions of facts connected with aggressive rhetoric damage the peaceful coexistence of individuals and groups. Therefore, the speaker carries the burden of exposition and proof when relying on assertions of defamatory facts.[46] In particular,

measures should be taken against the propensity to justify defamations of character by alleging facts that are so general that they are neither subject to proof nor counterproof (Kriele 1994, 1900). Regarding the examples mentioned above, it would follow that if a speaker claimed that immigrants receiving social welfare are parasites, this comes with the obligation to disclose the data supporting this judgment. Furthermore, the speaker may express this view without diminishing the recipient's status as a human being. Therefore, the use of the word "parasite" should also be punished appropriately.[47] The same burdens of exposition and proof would also apply to the characterization of immigrants as criminals.

4. *Second consequentialist argument.* Insofar as the third message of displaying racist symbols constitutes pure value judgments that are not based on assumptions of fact, these statements cannot be scientifically disproved. Such expressions are matters of personal value judgments of the speaker, which should be protected under freedom of speech in a liberal state. However, a contrary conclusion must be made regarding value judgments that solely defame the recipient to the degree that basic fundamental rights and equalities are denied. Such expressions do not contribute to the societal learning process. On the contrary, it has been demonstrated that such slogans can be employed to justify ethnic cleansing, genocide, exploitation, and oppression (Kretzmer 1987, 447–48). In this case, the best arguments do not always prevail. Therefore, the state has the right and obligation to exclude clearly malicious and inhumane arguments from public discourse.[48]

The "letting-off-steam" argument is also not convincing. A speaker may conceivably "cool down" as a result of uttering hate speech, but this is not necessarily the case. On the contrary, the speaker may be even more engulfed in hatred. One cannot simply assume that the "steam" has vanished into thin air without further consequences. Instead, this kind of rhetorical aggression may—and is intended to—have an effect on the general public: to win followers of xenophobia or to incite hatred of asylum seekers and other minorities. This can and often will have fatal consequences for the peaceful coexistence in society. Such speech creates conflict instead of harmony, oppression instead of equality, aggression instead of peace. It is therefore justified to prohibit hate-instigating speech.[49] Education alone is not enough; the symbolic and deterring authority of criminal law is needed (Jones 1998, 152–53).

5. *Third consequentialist argument.* The task of the state is not limited to securing the physical integrity of citizens against imminent physical violence. This task is certainly indispensable, but it is too narrowly related to the micro situation of violence and neglects the equally important, if not predominant situation of preventing *violence on the macro scale.* It is precisely the messages of hatred and aggression that, in the medium and long term, sooner or later spill over into large-scale hate crimes, violence, murder, and

even ethnic expulsion. Effective action against public disturbances should be directed against such a tremendous potential of aggression that may be summoned at any time. Not only should the state penalize the "imminent" dangers of physical violence, but also the abstract likelihood that hate speech may turn into hate crimes. Even the mere danger of "brushfire" violence should be eliminated.[50] Thus, the state must control this gray area in the political climate.[51]

6. *Attacks against personal honor and defamatory statements.* Regarding defamation of character in the form of value judgments, whether or not supported by factual assertions, one may not single-mindedly focus on the speaker's interest of self-expression. Defamation and incitement to hatred have consequences that must also be made part of the deliberation. Merely pointing out that aggressive speech does not constitute criminally relevant physical violence—bodily harm or wrongful death—falls far short of the mark. Words can, if they are aggressive and expressive of hatred, turn into violent actions that can be equivalent to simple violations of physical integrity, if not more.[52] One cannot lose sight of the fact that physical integrity is but one side of the entire person. On the other side lies psychological integrity. Self-confidence and confidence in one's place in the world are only possible when a person enjoys equal rights and equal respect in the society in which that person lives and contributes. Rhetorical aggression toward individuals and groups far too often silences the voices of the recipients. This is especially true if the addressees belong to minority groups.[53] In the long run, derogatory messages from powerful groups toward weaker groups remain in their minds long after the message is expressed, thereby narrowing life options and lessening the status of equality.

7. *Collective defamation of character.* There is no real difference between defamations of individuals and defamations of collectives. Human beings are not primarily isolated individuals. Membership in a particular group often determines self-identification. Defamation of a respective group may be typically regarded as defamation against every individual member of that group.[54] Regardless of whom the speaker intends to defame when directing an aggressive message toward a group—whether only a few, many, or all of its members—one thing is certain: on the side of recipients all may feel injured in their character. This is more likely in the case of minorities than in the case of majority groups. Hate speech is admittedly a message conveyed by a particular speaker, which reveals much about his or her personality. However, for the purpose of legal assessment, it would be fatal to abstract this right to self-expression from the concrete consequences of the speech to the self-esteem of the recipient group. Moreover, aggressive speech forces weak minorities into a defensive position.[55] To the extent that messages involve assumptions of fact, the recipient group is compelled to disprove the statement. If the messages contain long-standing derogatory

judgments, minorities are forced to fight for equal respect that should be granted regardless. In addition, some or many of the members may not be up to this challenge and, due to the negative evaluations of others, will not be able to develop their personalities freely and genuinely. What will follow is "self-hatred, humiliation, isolation, impairment of the capacity to form close interracial relationships, and adverse effects on relationships within a given group" (Kretzmer 1987, 466). As such, the stereotypes placed upon them may not be effectively challenged. Lastly, by allowing all forms of speech, the legal order places a premium on the side of the aggressor. However, victim protection should have priority over protecting the perpetrator.

Therefore, it is incorrect to limit legal liability to damages to one's reputation based on assumptions of fact. Such damages should indeed be deterred and punished by the legal order. However, the legal claim to dignity and respect also encompasses value judgments that cause internal rather than external bleeding.[56] All individuals and groups should enjoy equal protection in society against aggressive words or physical actions, regardless whether caused by the state or private individuals. It is moreover desirable that minimal standards of civility be maintained and legally safeguarded. Lack of civility in mutual interaction is the first step toward explicit aggression against unfavorable persons or groups.[57]

The preceding arguments translate into a consistent conception of human nature, society, and state, and also lead to an understanding of neutrality and social integration different from the American view.

8. *Human nature.* Individuality is indeed the starting point for the conception of human nature, but individuality is strongly intertwined with social relations and societal identities. Every person is the son or daughter of concrete parents, a citizen of a particular country, and in the course of his or her life develops loyalties as a member of a particular community. These associations are as important to self-understanding and self-respect as the single, isolated self—if in fact not more important. This unavoidable, sometimes harmonious, sometimes conflict-laden interrelatedness between the individual and his or her associational life-spheres may be referred to as communitarianism.[58] The freedom of speech is also an aspect of this tension. It guarantees the expression of one's individuality, but it is also rooted in the common linguistic understandings of how to live one's life. Communication does not only enable a person to criticize others, but also serves to maintain a common framework for understanding and interaction. This presupposes, however, that the basic conditions of a peaceful and productive interaction are respected and legally protected.

9. *Society.* Similar to the American viewpoint, societal life is regarded as molded by cooperation and conflict so that not only affirmation but also criticism must be possible and legally guaranteed. But with respect to the extent and intensity of criticism toward other persons and groups, it is disputed that

in a society of well-intentioned people serious conflicts between groups will necessarily occur.[59] When such conflicts do occur, appropriate or at least minimal standards of civility and mutual respect are demanded and legally sanctioned in order to strengthen the self-confidence of persons and groups under attack, as well as to prevent an asymmetrical distribution of social power.

10. *State*. State authority is not only competent to secure peace in the sense of physical integrity, but it is also competent to protect the psychic integrity of individuals and societal groups to the extent that these are threatened by rhetoricai aggression. A "good climate" among all citizens should reign supreme.[60] If that goal turns out to be utopian, at the very least a climate of animosity or hatred must be avoided by punishing hate speech and exaggerated, factually unsupported criticisms against sections of the community.[61] Sooner or later such a climate will spill over into actions motivated by hatred, lead to persecution, and contribute to maintaining the suppression of minorities. To prevent this, legal measures in the primary stages of violence are justified against messages that, in the long run, threaten a productive and egalitarian coexistence in state and society.

11. *Neutrality and integration*. The state must be neutral vis-à-vis viewpoints put forward by its citizens. However, when criticism threatens elementary conditions of civility, equality, and the self-determination of disadvantaged groups, the state can and must be partial. In particular, it must stand on the side of the poor, weak, and suppressed.[62] Long-term integration presupposes that messages threatening this very goal are prohibited and punished.

Faced with these two lines of arguments, one cannot fail to be astonished that both appear plausible, even convincing, yet contradictory in substance.[63] Each argument may claim a corresponding constitutional basis for its tenets due to the fact that the values of autonomy, dignity, freedom, equality, and democracy are explicitly, or at least implicitly, anchored in the U.S. Constitution, the German Basic Law, many modern constitutions, as well as International Conventions. Moreover, it is undisputed that the legitimate functions of the state include securing peace and fostering integration. Yet, as demonstrated above, there exist clear and dramatic differences in the understanding of these values. Sharp, exaggerated criticisms of immigrants or asylum seekers and the propagation of racist theories are allowed in the United States but prohibited in Germany, as well as in member states of the Council of Europe and International Conventions. Here we face a clear piece of evidence supporting the thesis that the relevant constitutional provisions do not sufficiently determine the understanding of the subject material—cultural and historical preconceptions still play an important role. This is particularly evident when German attorneys express a lack of understanding when first confronted with American regulation of free speech—and vice versa. However, as the two competing lines of argumentation have demonstrated above, neither one is entirely unreasonable. Once one has fully reflected on the reasons supporting each respective argument, it is indeed difficult to decide between them. The fundamental disagreement among modern states on this question demonstrates that consensus is unlikely. How then should one decide? One possible starting point is discussion of this dispute within the framework of the conflict between liberalism and communitarianism.

AGGRESSIVE SPEECH AS AN EXAMPLE OF THE CONFLICT BETWEEN LIBERALISM AND COMMUNITARIANISM?

The tension between both conceptions of free speech cannot be described only in terms of a geographical and comparative-law dispute between the United States on the one hand and Germany, Europe, and International Conventions on the other. One can also analyze these differences in terms of the current debate between American *liberals* and *communitarians*—a debate that is also practiced within other progressive legal systems.[64] In this view, the method by which governments regulate aggressive speech is an illustration of the more general opposition between liberalism and communitarianism (Note 1988, 683–84; see also Symposium 1997). Is it not correct to say that the U.S. view is based more on the isolated individual asserting his or her liberty against society and the state,[65] while the competing view relies more on communal bonds in the life and communication of human beings?[66]

As plausible as this may sound, one should not too hastily assume that a necessary antagonism exists between liberalism and communitarianism. Both "liberalism" and "communitarianism" comprise a family of theories with several branches that, depending on the particular variety, to a greater or lesser degree exemplify the contradictory relation between the two philosophies. Liberalism, for instance, can focus either on the single individual[67] or on associational bonds.[68] The latter variety of liberalism certainly shares a close affinity with communitarianism, which indeed emphasizes the individual's relationship with groups of all kinds; however, it does not advocate a total subjugation or complete assimilation of the individual in preconceived and fixed ways of life. Rather, integrity and integration is the motto (Selznick 1992, 369, on the related notion of "independence and interdependence"). "Integrity" embraces the core liberal ideas of the independent individual as well as freedom of choice (Brugger 1999, 172), albeit with varying emphases, depending on the particular conception of communitarianism.[69]

(1) *Conservative communitarianism* views human beings as greatly, though not exclusively, influenced by their social, cultural, and political environment. "Freedom of choice" to some extent is socially acknowledged and legally recognized as a fundamental right.[70] However, the realization of

this right is mainly accomplished through identification with the traditional "life forms" of a particular community. This includes the occasional conscious withdrawal from and reconfiguration of those communities in terms of goals, structures, and requirements of membership.

(2) *Liberal communitarianism* presupposes a close relationship between the individual's autonomy, the goal of leading a rich and fulfilling life, and the rights and duties attached to membership in a particular community. Liberal communitarianism takes a closer look at the various forms of association and analyzes communities ranging from fleeting ad hoc associations to those with an extensive degree of member identification. Moreover, the theory analyzes their historical continuity or discontinuity; if a given association or mode of living preserves its goals and structures over a long period of time, without manipulation or coercion, one can presuppose its intrinsic worth for the well-being of its members. Liberal communitarianism also distinguishes between narrow and wide-ranging communities. In political life, these communities range from the local level to the regional, national, continental, international, or supranational (in the case of the European Union) level. In all these diversified communities, what is viewed as the common good must first be internally defined and separated from external concerns. Second, priorities must be established in order to balance internal and external interests Whereas conservative communitarianism advocates a clear priority for the smaller, local, and traditional communities, liberal communitarianism does not espouse such an a priori hierarchy; instead, it supports spheres of responsibility that range from the local context to universal concerns and strives to develop a gradation of reciprocal obligations that do justice to the near horizon as well as the far horizon of mankind as a whole.

(3) *Egalitarian communitarianism, universalism, or liberalism* claims that humanity as a whole is the most important, decisive community affiliation. Morality and justice should be constructed mainly on the basis of the similarities characterizing all members of humankind—the capacity to communicate, reason, and morally reflect as well as common human needs and vulnerabilities. The whole range of human associations and all lifestyle choices should be allowed to develop equally and freely. As for governmental action, all forms of association should be equally respected and promoted with the exception that impoverished or disadvantaged groups may receive particular attention.[71]

Regarding the legal regulation of aggressive speech, there are commonalities as well as differences. As to commonalities, liberalism and communitarianism both respect individual freedom to communicate and form associations. They consider civilized and informed discourse a politically desirable goal toward which individuals and groups should work and that the state may propagate. Beyond that, however, the role of the state is a matter of contention. According to the liberal view in the United States, the role of the state in political discourse, especially with respect to the sanctions of criminal law, is limited to securing physical integrity and the prevention of physical violence in cases of clear and present danger.[72] Civilized public discussions are desirable, but may not be enforced through the vehicle of criminal sanctions.[73] In a free society, conflicts between individuals and groups are to be expected that are often accompanied by emotions and sharp, defamatory words. Possible loss of civility in mutual interaction is the price of freedom and equality in an open political discourse of public matters.[74] However, the general limitation of state authority can also be viewed as a communitarian tenet due to the fact that, according to this theory, it is the primary function of intermediary organizations of society to promote the development of individual personalities and societal integration. In cases of doubt, the state's authority to impose sanctions is likely to be limited rather than extended (Nisbet 1962; Brugger 1999, 257).

Liberalism as well as communitarianism can accept the notions that *human beings are born and raised in communities* and that self-evaluation as individuals and members of various groups is strongly influenced through cultural values. However, the U.S. perspective places greater emphasis on the possibility of conflicts than on expectations of harmony between the individual and society or between different communities. In some or many cases, such conflicts are bound to lead to rhetorical provocation and aggression. This view is certainly realistic. The desired consequence of counterspeech is not only an argumentative struggle for a solution that is right or acceptable to all parties but also a promotion of one's personal independence and creativity. In the case of conflict, the necessary independence requires a particularly robust personality, which is admittedly difficult to develop for sensitive constitutions or disadvantaged groups compared with naturally strong personalities[75] or dominant groups. However, the American liberal view remains steadfast in its support of unfettered communication in cases of public conflict. Strong individualism is the guiding light: without effort and courage one cannot build a person that one can be proud of. The requirement to meet aggressive speech with civilized or sharp rebuttal without being able to rely on criminal repercussions against the aggressor corresponds with the motto of the American pioneers: "Go west, young man!" This expressive and active individualism is certainly "liberal," but this, in itself, does not necessarily express antipathy toward communities. Depending on the situation, communities can enable or suppress human development (Selznick 1992, 360), and in cases of conflict, they are—and should be—subject to the judgments of their members. As such, this may be viewed as liberal communitarianism.

Should collective defamations and hate speech against groups be criminally sanctioned even if they address political issues? The U.S.-liberal view delivers a clear "no," while the competing view renders the contrary verdict.

Both arguments move within the framework of communitarian conceptions. First, communitarianism emphasizes the identity-creating function of group membership (Post 1997, 475–76; Selznick 1992, 357–65). This appears to support the thesis that group defamation also affects the group's members—that is to say all of them.[76] However, this is a thesis of conservative communitarianism and not of its liberal branch. This latter view holds that the formation of identity has to resolve the tension between groups and individuals. The individual is not, for the purposes of self-identity and self-evaluation, inseparably bound to membership in a particular community,[77] and certainly not in the case of external derogatory judgments.[78] Second, one should differentiate between communities involving the core aspects of one's identity (Selznick 1992, 184–92) and others of a more fleeting nature. It is more difficult to distance oneself from core communities than from ad hoc associations. But even vis-à-vis core communities, such as family or religious groups, the individual is more than just an indistinguishable member. Hence a uniform treatment of individual and group defamation is not necessary. Liberal communitarianism is more likely to reject collective defamations due to the fact that the final decision regarding the level of identification with or detachment from a group rests with the individual. Finally, one cannot equate the assignment of personal characteristics by others with personal self-appraisal. In any case, this should not be fostered by the legal order.

Is the viewpoint of a legal regime rejecting collective defamation antithetical to a proper historical understanding? Is it not overly idealistic? Does it not deny or overlook the real existence of oppression and exploitation of disfavored groups through symbolic and rhetorical harassment?[79] Should not a historically sensitive conception of communitarianism be guided by the notion of equal respect and promotion of all human beings and groups? And does this not mean that disadvantaged groups should be supported by imposing criminal sanctions, based on norms against collective defamations and incitements to racial persecution, on rhetorical attacks against self-worth? Not necessarily. Permitting aggressive speech does not in every instance support or strengthen existing hierarchies or structures of domination. The reverse is also possible: argumentative counterattacks, whether civilized or aggressive, can be the first step toward liberation from oppression![80] Segregation, for instance, can be abolished and replaced by integration.[81] This would certainly be in accordance with liberal communitarianism. In most cases it is impossible to determine in advance if such developments are likely. It would also be unreasonable to characterize aggressive speech a priori as exploitative, oppressive, and unjustifiable or to believe that damages to the collective feelings of self-worth or even physical integrity will inevitably occur.[82]

Communitarianism indeed bears an affinity with the view that honor and reputation are important values worthy of protection. Humans are immersed in the concrete world of language, norms, and culture in which they are raised. This cultural world might be viewed as an advantage or as a burden, depending on whether it helps or obstructs living a fulfilling life. In any case, participation and recognition within one's reference groups is clearly important for the formation of identity and gaining the respect of others. Personal honor presupposes a physical existence, but it only gains concrete reality through mutual respect—as a "human being" (in contrast to an animal), a "person" (with the potential for moral reflection), and/or a "personality" (in various social roles). Personal honor and social status are important to most people, but they are also fragile assets that can be easily destroyed.[83] The interdependence between self-evaluation and the real or assumed negative or positive evaluation by others is complex and often obscure. Therefore, an expression of derogation or lack of personal respect or perhaps an aggressive denial that a person is worthy of respect, can certainly inflict considerable psychological wounds, which may be no less harmful than an actual physical injury.[84] It is not a coincidence that in the German language terms such as *Rufmord* (character assassination) and *Ehrabschneider* (calumniator) use a reference to a physical violation.

Still, one should not jump to the conclusion that extensive legal protection of honor through the vehicle of criminal sanction is necessary in all cases in which aggressive speech "hurts."[85] The relevant reasons have already been mentioned: societal mechanisms should come before state regulation;[86] an extensive legal definition of personal honor leads to legal uncertainty and may produce exaggerated sensitivity; excessive claims based on personal honor may make it more profitable to be a victim than to defend oneself actively. Also, arguments based on the consequences of speech, pessimistically maintaining that every public attack on a person's honor inevitably leads to isolation and loss of a previously enjoyed level of respect, do not necessarily hold water.[87] "Character assassination," for instance, does not lead to death. The rhetorical attack may backfire on the reputation of the "murderer." A person who refers to a handicapped person as a "cripple," for instance, may make him- or herself appear to be something of a "cripple"—at least in the moral sense of the term.[88]

Much depends on the type of personal attack being made. Purely derogatory messages devoid of factual assertions will be recognized by the public—if it is not already prejudiced—as a primary judgment of the speaker, and will not necessarily be ascribed to the recipient. If an assault is based on factual claims, it is possible in the United States as well as in Germany and most other modern states to defend oneself legally. Admittedly, the situation is precarious when very broad and general claims of fact are expressed to support criticism or to raise suspicion, that is to say, when these claims are not specific enough to be proved or disproved.[89] In such cases, it is indeed possible to create the impression that a judgment has a factual basis if the listener is not sensitive enough to distinguish between a specifically or only vaguely fact-based or even pure value judgment. Nevertheless, one cannot simply assume that the public is "naturally trusting"[90] and believes everything it reads in newspapers or sees on television. Rather, the public possesses a "natural skepticism." Depending on which camp the listener belongs to or from where the attack is launched, one can guess what is coming: the opposition party is bickering against the government's political agenda and calling the head of government a hypocrite and villain who is trying to defraud the voters. Did anyone expect anything else? This is not to deny that there are cases in which a person's sense of honor cannot be adequately defended and the recipient ends up walking away with injuries. But what would be the consequence if the law had to prevent and deter all such defamations?

In public matters an extensive, criminally sanctioned regime against defamation of character would effectively create the danger of eliminating politically relevant criticism. Seen from the guidelines of liberty and equality, public criticism is a necessary component of politics, if the general regulations "of the people"—that is to say, every citizen—as "authors" of the law are to be accepted and abided "by the people."[91] Indeed, there is an irresolvable tension between civility and openness in political discourse. This conflict, however, represents an intrinsic tension within liberal communitarianism and does not stand outside of it.

What stance does communitarianism take toward xenophobia and racism, as themes of aggressive speech? Communitarianism is concerned with the criteria that create commonalities between people and life forms in state and society into which individuals can be integrated and develop without loss of integrity. At the same time, communitarianism is not a uniform, monolithic theory. It analyzes all types of life forms in their internal structures as well as the interactions between them. It may have a preference for smaller communities (conservative communitarianism) or the community of humankind (egalitarian, universalistic communitarianism). Liberal communitarianism regards all community affiliations as significant, and seeks to construct balanced relations between the near and far horizons of human interaction. Questions of membership can arise internally within the community but also in the relationship between communities. Outside of the single universal community of humankind there will always be questions about the conditions of inclusion and exclusion, and about differing degrees of identification and solidarity. Who should or should not—due to birth, particular characteristics, actions, or relationships—automatically or by choice be considered a member of a specific community (i.e., family, religion, profession, nation, etc.)? Who should be expelled from a group and in which instances? This discussion and the answers to such questions are an integral part of human life and belong to the preservation of specific cultures and forms of association. It would be foolish to discount these considerations entirely as instances of xenophobia or racism or to sustain the premise that everyone can or should be integrated into everything.

This is also true of the communities constituted by nation states—and more generally of all forms of political organization. These also require discussion and decision as to conditions of acquisition and loss of membership, as long as they are based on a definite territory with a particular people, for whose well-being the organization has a specific responsibility. Despite a general trend toward delegating many responsibilities to international political actors, nation states are still expected to care for the well-being of their citizens, for instance in matters of social welfare. Yet many do not agree that the discourse concerning membership or disassociation should take place in a robust and unrestrained manner. Proponents of egalitarian and universalistic communitarianism consistently draw a parallel between the group of the "internal weak and oppressed" and "the weak and suppressed of the world" who need effective assistance in their countries or who are willing to immigrate. According to egalitarian communitarianism, discourse regarding the social and political equality of all members of humankind should be carried on in a civilized, and not a robust or aggressive, manner. But the discussion should also lead to the predetermined "egalitarian" conclusion: considerable differences between citizens and foreigners, insiders and outsiders, are viewed as unacceptable and categorically labeled as "racism" or "ethnocentrism" against the many immigrants who want to live and work, for instance, in the European Union.

How do conservative and liberal communitarians respond to this view? Both varieties would generally prefer a civilized discussion but would rule out legal sanctions of sharply or aggressively worded positions. As a result, both would reject the view that "considerable inequality" in treatment between citizens and foreigners or residents and willing immigrants should be prohibited. The conservative communitarians have a particular preference for smaller communities over larger ones—in this context, the community of the nation state over the world community. Liberal communitarians are concerned with mediating near and far relationships, without having an a priori preference for one over the other.[92] In the end, both theory types believe it is legitimate to defend the distribution of benefits and burdens differently among citizens and noncitizens. Immigration could be extensively (conservative communitarianism) or at least significantly (liberal communitarianism) restricted without necessarily equating such a policy with "xenophobia." Rather, the distinctions between the closer and more distant responsibilities are regarded as "natural" and legitimate expressions of gradations of loyalty and identification with the community in which one was raised. Not to take these differences into account would be immoral and unjust.

But these viewpoints concur with egalitarian and universalistic communitarianism that the status of every individual as a human being also must be considered, and may not be entirely neglected as a factor.[93] The common characteristics of all human beings are the predominant criteria for morality and justice among the universalistic communitarians. According to the conservative communitarians, the hierarchy of reference points for reciprocal obligations is reversed: close communities and their internal common good prevail, but some consideration has to be given to universal human needs and rights. Liberal communitarians mediate this point with stricter levels of responsibility. Thus, depending on the variety of communitarianism chosen, immigration or foreign aid to a vast, limited, or substantial extent must be possible. As to treating citizens and noncitizens differently, certain elementary rights—a standard of human rights to be more clearly defined—must be guaranteed without exception (Walzer 1994, chap. 1). Moreover, depending on the type of communitarianism, the requirement of equal treatment varies considerably. In the extreme case, a wholly equal treatment and rapid naturalization of noncitizens factually living in the political community are advocated without expectation of loyalty or identification; acting within the limits of the law suffices. This is the view of egalitarian communitarianism.

How is racism viewed? Racism may take various forms. It may range from defending a theory of racist superiority of one group over another, to unspecified calls for action, to the propagation or actual execution of expulsion and genocide. Modern communitarianism has always maintained a basic component of integrity and integration of all people. Its perspective rejects all aforementioned forms of racism in the narrow or genuine sense of the term.

However, caution should be exercised as well: not all differentiated treatment of citizens and noncitizens is a form of racism. Only egalitarian or universalistic communitarianism would lean toward this view. The other two theory varieties maintain that disputes concerning political inclusion and exclusion as well as contentious debates about the extent and criteria for equal or unequal treatment should be permissible in a liberal society. Moreover, these criteria can take on different meanings in different contexts. All such exclusions or unequal treatments lead, one may argue, to the "reduction," "devaluation," or "denial" of the status of human beings as equals and thus represent "racism" in the broader sense of the term (i.e., as understood by egalitarian universalists). By contrast, conservative communitarianism and liberal communitarianism maintain that while rhetorical racism in the broader sense does not promote civilized dialogue, it must be accepted in a free society in which there are no "speech police." Such discussions should not automatically trigger legal sanctions by means of norms gauged toward racial hatred and defamation, nor should these regulations be used as a deterrent. Otherwise, one would be confronted with the situation that egalitarian/universalistic communitarians claim to have the only correct conception of community, integration, and justice. With this, one would be on the path to an authoritarian state: even though all citizens should enjoy equal freedom and protection, the task of interpreting moral and legal standards would be arrogated by one side and excluded for the other.

NOTES

1. For their generous help with the translation from German, I would like to thank Eva Pils, University College London, and Mark C. Tracy, University of Heidelberg.

2. See Häntzschel 1932, 652: "The freedom to speak one's mind is a child of liberalism. It comes from the time when citizens were still facing the state as its subjects, when they could not yet say: 'The state is us.'" [All translations from German mine.] With this latter phrase Häntzschel implicitly refers to the preamble of the U.S. Constitution, which begins with "We the People."

3. On the "impulse to censor" see Trager and Dickerson 1999, 33–36; Kaleb 1996, 221; Mill [1859] 1973, 490–530; Justice Holmes, dissenting, in *Abrams v. United States*, 250 U.S. 616, 630 (1919): "Persecution for the expression of opinions seems to me perfectly logical. If you have no doubt of your premises or your power and want a certain result with all your heart, you naturally express your wishes in law and sweep away all opposition." Holmes then goes on to argue against this view.

4. Modelled on Oberlandesgericht [Appellate Court] Frankfurt, decision of August 15, 2000, *Neue Zeitschrift für Strafrecht–Rechtsprechungsreport* 2000, 368–69.

5. This statement is modeled on a German and an American case. See Verwaltungsgericht [Administrative Court] Frankfurt, resolution of February 22, 1993, *Neue Juristische Wochenschrift* 1993, 2067–69 (on the exclusion of an election campaign brochure from national mail service, and on criminal liability for this message as an instance of "incitement to racist persecution" [*Volksverhetzung*]), and *Beauharnais v. Illinois*, 343 U.S. 250 (1952). On this case see Brugger 2003, 391–93.

6. The use of the swastika is prohibited by criminal law in Germany, according to secs. 86 and 86a of the German Criminal Code. In the United States, the claim of the superiority of the white or Aryan race as expressed by the Ku Klux Klan cross is not prohibited, if it does not amount to a "threat" or "intimidation." See the so-called "Skokie controversy," on planned Neo-Nazi demonstrations in a Jewish residential area, which has been vividly described by Downs 1985. See also *RAV v. St. Louis*, 505 U.S. 377 (1992); *Virginia v. Black*, 538 U.S. 343 (2003).

7. This chapter only deals with "political" and not with private or business-related controversies. The first and second of the above-mentioned statements are characterized by their combination of value judgment and assertion of facts, whereas the third statement constitutes a purely normative derogatory message, not supported by any factual claims.

8. See Appleman 1996; Coliver 1992; Douglas-Scott 1999; with further references, Brugger 2002.

9. See in particular the *International Convention on the Elimination of Any Form of Racial Discrimination* of March 7, 1966. On this convention and on further legal norms and legal literature in this area of international law, see Zimmer 2001.

10. See notes 5, 6, 8, and 9 above, and note 14 below. Also, Rosenfeld 2003, 1541: "If free speech in the United States is shaped above all by individualism and libertarianism, collective concerns and other values such as honor and dignity lie at the heart of the conceptions of free speech that originate in international covenants or in the constitutional jurisprudence of other Western democracies."

11. See, for instance, the characteristic restrictions of free speech as "general laws" in art. 5, sec. 2, of the German Basic Law. Sec. 1 reads: "Every person shall have the right freely to express and disseminate his opinions in speech, writing, and pictures and to inform himself without hindrance from generally accessible sources. Freedom of the press and freedom of reporting by means of broadcasts and films shall be guaranteed. There shall be no censorship." Sec. 2 reads: "These rights shall find their limits in the provisions of the general laws, in provisions for the protection of young persons, and in the right to personal honor." See also art. 3, sec. 3, of the German Basic Law that states: "No one may be disadvantaged or preferred on account of his religious or political views. . . ."

12. This is the case in Germany, as numerous prohibitions of aggressive speech show. They are categorized as restricting freedom of speech, but do not count as unjustified infringements of it. Rather they are considered as "general laws," or norms for the protection of "personal honor" or "young people" that are specifically mentioned in art. 5 of the Basic Law as limitation clauses—see note 11 above.

13. Other methods to impose legal sanctions include, in the realm of civil law, duties to desist, restitute, or pay damages, or, in the sphere of administrative law, withdrawing a license from public broadcasting institutions, disciplinary measures against certain public servants, etc. For the sake of simplicity, in what follows I discuss primarily criminal sanctions.

14. For the first group of cases, see secs. 185ff. of the German Criminal Code, for the second and third example secs. 130ff. of the German Criminal Code. Generally on cases of "group defamation, breach of peace, and incitement to hatred," see Kretzmer 1987, esp. 494–506. For a study in comparative law, see Roth 1993, esp. 192–201.

15. See Brugger 2003, 2002; Zimmer 2001.

16. On this common distinction—already used by Häntzschel (1932, 652)—see Brison 1998, esp. 321–22, who further examines different conceptions of autonomy. The German Federal Constitutional Court uses this distinction. See the much-quoted following passage from its *Lüth* decision, BVerfGE 7, 198, 208: "The fundamental right to free expression of opinion is, as the most direct expression of human personality in society, one of the foremost human rights of all. . . . For a free democratic state system, it is nothing other than constitutive, for it is only through it that the constant intellectual debate, the clash of opinions, that is its vital element, is made possible. . . ."

17. In legal terms this differentiation is mirrored by the fact that criminal offenses of libel have the purpose of protecting those individuals concretely attacked, whereas public peace-related offenses are punished to protect the public as a whole.

18. Glendon (1991) regards this as an essential characteristic of the predominant American political culture. Her telling chapter headings are "The Land of Rights"

"The Illusion of Absoluteness," "The Lone Rights Bearer," "The Missing Language of Responsibility," "Rights Insularity."

19. The terms "American" and "liberal" here refer to the dominant free-speech doctrines and court practices; they are not to be confused with "liberals" in the American party sense, i.e., members of the Democratic Party. Some scholars in the United States would characterize this free-speech position as "libertarian," whereas most American, German, and European legal experts would use the term "liberal." I follow the latter characterization and hope that no misunderstandings for American readers occur. Against this dominant "liberal" view, fierce criticism has been leveled by the American minority, whose view is summed up in section four of this chapter, with some references to further authors (note 41 below). This minority in the United States is basically defending the view inspired by German, European, and International Law, and its adherents fall under the American headings of "egalitarians," "feminists," or "critical race theorists." They often are members of the Democratic Party and thus "liberals" in the political-party sense, not "libertarians."

20. This description addresses two or even three different conceptions of autonomy: one of equality as a person or moral subject, one emphasizing differences among individual people, and one of expressive individualism.

21. See Wells 1997, 174: "Distrust of the ability of citizens to make decisions is antithetical to autonomy. . . ." At 174n62, Wells quotes from the decision *First National Bank v. Bellotti*, 435 U.S. 765, 791ff. (1979): "[T]he people in our democracy are entrusted with the responsibility of judging and evaluating the relative merit of conflicting arguments. . . . [I]f there be any danger that the people cannot evaluate the information and arguments advanced . . . it is a danger contemplated by the Framers of the First Amendment."

22. See *Cohen v. California*, 403 U.S. 15, 26 (1971): "[M]uch linguistic expression serves a dual communicative function: it conveys not only ideas capable of relatively precise, detached explication, but otherwise inexpressible emotions as well. In fact, words are often chosen as much for their emotive as their cognitive force. We cannot sanction the view that the Constitution, while solicitous of the cognitive content of individual speech, has little or no regard for that emotive function which, practically speaking, may often be the more important element of the overall message sought to be [communicated]." On this, and on the "essential connection between the form and content of speech," see Weinstein 2001, 154. See also BVerfGE 81, 278, 291, where the German Federal Constitutional Court views the protection of works of art as follows—and essentially the same standards must apply to stating one's political views: "The outrageousness of a form of presentation does not deprive a work of its status as art. Art cannot be subjected to a state control of style or *niveau*."

23. James Madison put it thus: "Some degree of abuse is inseparable from the proper use of everything." Cited from Cohen 1996, 191.

24. As already noted in note 7 above, I am only addressing publicly relevant matters. Different principles may have to be applied in cases of making private and intimate, even though "true," information public.

25. This, at least, is the U.S. view. See Roth 1993, 180, on the "full reliance on the power of the 'free market of ideas' in which [it is held] the good is bound to win over the evil."

26. "Fighting words" according to the U.S. view may legally be restricted or punished, as long as the law authorizing to do so is neutral toward the view expressed by the words in question. They comprise words that by their very utterance inflict injury or tend to incite an immediate breach of the peace.

27. See Justice Holmes, dissenting, in *Abrams v. United States*, 250 U.S. 616, 630 (1919): "[E]very year if not every day we have to wager our salvation upon some prophecy based upon imperfect knowledge. While that experiment is part of our system I think that we should be eternally vigilant against attempts to check the expression of opinions that we loathe and believe to be fraught with death, unless they so imminently threaten immediate interference with the lawful and pressing purposes of the law that an immediate check is required to save our country."

28. See the famous dictum by Justice Brandeis, concurring, in *Whitney v. California*, 274 U.S. 357, 375–76 (1927): "[T]hose who won our independence by revolution were no cowards. They did not fear political change. They did not exalt order at the cost of liberty. To courageous, self-reliant men, with confidence in the power of free and fearless reasoning applied through the process of popular government, no danger flowing from speech can be deemed clear and present, unless the incidence of the evil apprehended is so imminent that it may befall even before there is opportunity for full discussion. If there be time to expose through discussion the falsehood or fallacies, to avert the evil by the processes of education, *the remedy to be applied is more speech, not enforced silence*." (Emphasis added.)

29. See Butler 1997, 4: "One is not simply fixed by the name that one is called. In being called an injurious name, one is derogated and demeaned. But the name holds out another possibility as well: by being called a name, one is also, paradoxically, given a certain possibility for social existence, initiated into a temporal life of language that exceeds the prior purposes that animate that call. Thus the injurious address may appear to fix or paralyze the one it hails, but it may also produce an unexpected and enabling response. If to be addressed is to be interpellated, then the offensive call runs the risk of inaugurating a subject in speech who comes to use language to counter the offensive call." See also ibid., 163; note 75 below.

30. So if, for instance, a German Chancellor says that "teachers are lazy," we know what is meant. "Too many teachers are lazy," in his view.

31. See Sullivan 2001, 12, on the American tradition as one "that views civil rights and civil liberties as supporting social fluidity rather than entrenchment in fixed groups. . . . [W]e should not be stuck in group identities that are ascribed to us—through, for example, the operation of prejudice or selective disregard or indifference. Instead we should be able to join or exit our interest group memberships and our expressive and intimate associations relatively easily." Sullivan here addresses one of the core theses of associative liberalism: that association is important, but should offer "join and exit" conditions. See Brugger 1999, 217; Post 1991, 294.

32. A good example for this view is the position of the late Justice Brennan, which still represents the dominant view within the U.S. Supreme Court. His view has been summarized in Marion 1997, viii–ix. Marion mentions the following as key phrases: "autonomous individualism," "committed to freeing people from the constraints of 'collective society,' whether rooted in nature, tradition, history or majority preferences, so that they may define themselves in the image of their own

choosing," "enhancement of self through expressive activity, ideally resulting in complete individual differentiation," "freeing people to enjoy the maximum of self-expression and self-determination."

33. See note 21 above and Post 1991, 281: "In America, the censorial power is in the people over the Government, and not in the Government over the people." This refers to *The New York Times Co. v. Sullivan*, 376 U.S. 254, 274 (1964).

34. This point is well put in Sullivan 2001, 6: "In the [Supreme] Court's view, government may regulate the clash of bodies but not the stirring of hearts and minds."

35. See Roth 1993, 179–80: "The United States regards the more conspicuous strength of ethnic groups as an expression of greater pluralism, an acceptance of being 'beyond the melting pot,' and feels that their greater strength makes laws for the protection of these racial groups unnecessary. In Europe, the contrary view prevails: greater pluralism is seen as making protective laws imperative."

36. See *Cohen v. California*, 403 U.S. 15, 24 (1971): "To many, the immediate consequence of this [broad freedom of speech] may often appear to be only verbal tumult, discord, and even offensive utterances. These are, however, within established limits, in truth necessary side effects of the broader enduring values which the process of open debate permits us to achieve. That the air may at times seem filled with verbal cacophony is, in this sense, not a sign of weakness but of strength."

37. Rosenfeld (2003, 1529) mentions three components of the U.S. conception of the relationship between politics and freedom of speech: "strong preference for liberty over equality, commitment to individualism, and a natural rights tradition derived from Locke which champions freedom from the state—or negative freedom—over freedom through the state—or positive freedom."

38. See Justice Marshall in *Police Department of Chicago v. Mosley*, 408 U.S. 92, 95–96 (1972): "[A]bove all else, the First Amendment means that government has no power to restrict expression because of its message, its ideas, its subject matter, or its content."

39. This view was expressed by the dissenting Justice Harlan in *Plessy v. Ferguson*: "If the two races are to meet upon terms of social equality, it must be the result of natural affinities, a mutual appreciation of each other's merits and a voluntary consent of individuals. . . . [Legislation] is powerless to eradicate racial instincts or abolish distinctions based on physical differences, and the attempt to do so can only result in accentuating the difficulties of the present situation." 163 U.S. 537, 551–52 (1896).

40. See Sullivan 2001, 9: "[V]iewpoint discrimination by the government is the cardinal First Amendment sin, all the more when it is directed against political dissent."

41. The Colombian representative at the conference for the formulation and ratification of the Convention against Racial Discrimination (note 9 above) criticized the draft provision for penalizing racist speech (art. 4) in the following way: "[P]unishing ideas, whatever they may be, is to aid and abet tyranny, and leads to the abuse of power. . . . As far as we are concerned and as far as democracy is concerned, ideas should be fought with ideas and reasons; theories must be refuted by arguments and not by the scaffold, prison, exile, confiscation or fines." Quoted in Kretzmer 1987, 457.

42. In the United States there have been vociferous protests against the view described in section three. For examples, see Matsuda et al. 1993; Jones 1998; Delgado and Stefancic 1997. As these titles indicate, many of the arguments are addressed not

only against aggressive or hate speech, but against pornography as well. The latter area is not discussed here.

43. See BVerfGE 7, 198, 205: "This value system [of the German Basic Law] has its center in the individual person and in the human dignity of the individual freely thriving within his social community . . . ," and the Court's corresponding conception of human nature: "The Basic Law does not conceive of human beings as isolated, sovereign individuals; rather, regarding the tension individual–community, the Basic Law has come down in favor of a conception of the individual person as integrated in a community, and obligated towards it, without however detracting from the individual worth of each person."

44. The phrase can be used on both sides in this dispute. Dworkin himself views its significance primarily as justifying protection of the speaker, even of a speaker uttering aggressive (or pornographic) speech. See Dworkin 1996, chaps. 8–10. Jones (1998) puts forth a view congenial to the one expressed in the main text above.

45. On this phrase see Bull 2001, 172–73n44. At 184, Bull warns against "wholesale rejection of a 'decent' form." Also see Stark 1996, 210–11, thesis no. 10: "Contrary to the principles developed by German courts in last instance, the form of a value judgment is relevant. . . It is therefore necessary to examine [in concrete cases] if it was necessary for expressing some view, to use the specific words. If one concludes that it would have been possible convincingly to articulate the statement in question by using different, less invasive words, then the statement [actually made] is not protected by [the free speech clause in] article 5, section 1."

46. Thus Kriele 1994, 1899–1900, 1902; Stark 1996, 219, thesis no. 8; 221–22, thesis no. 19.

47. And indeed, in Germany it is punished. See note 4 above.

48. According to art. 4 of the Convention against Racial Discrimination (note 9 above), the member states have to penalize racist statements and organizations. On the concept of "racism," see sec. V.7. A duty to outlaw such speech can also result from constitutional law insofar as the text of the constitution (or a pertinent doctrine developed by the constitutional court) includes positive governmental obligations to "protect" dignity. The German Constitution does exactly that in art. 1, sec. 1.

49. Indeed, it is prohibited in Germany, insofar as it constitutes "*Volksverhetzung*," incitement to racist persecution, in the sense of sec. 130 of the German Criminal Code.

50. This, precisely, is the conception inherent to sec. 130 of the German Criminal Code. See Wandres 2000, 212: "The terrifying ghosts of incitement to racist persecution are called 'pogrom,' 'massacre,' and 'genocide.' The criminal offence of incitement to hatred therefore is essentially directed against forms of conduct, which might, if things go very badly, contribute to another crime against humanity being perpetrated in Germany." In a similar vein, Jones 1998, 152. A standard work in this context is Allport [1954] 1979, 14–15, 48–63, on the stages of 1. antilocution, 2. avoidance, 3. discrimination, 4. physical attack, and 5. extermination.

51. See note 47 above; Kübler 2000, 127: "[I]n any case [of criminal actions based on hatred] a specific climate of opinion . . . a complex coincidence of popular assumptions and convictions leading to the exclusion and stigmatization of certain groups is the *conditio sine qua non*."

52. In Anglo-American literature there are studies of the kinds of harm occurring in this context. See chap. 1, "Words that Wound," in Delgado and Stefancic 1997,

3–26, and the book with the same title by Matsuda et al. 1993. This book begins with the following sentence: "This is a book about assaultive speech, about words that are used as weapons to ambush, terrorize, wound, humiliate, and degrade" ("Introduction," ix).

53. American writers in particular frequently point out the role of derogatory "labeling" and the "silencing" that may result from it. See the first two essays in chap. 3 of Lederer and Delgado 1995: "Cross-Burning and the Sound of Silence," 114–21; "Silencing Women's Speech," 122–130. The title of the second essay refers to the consequences of pornography.

54. Kretzmer (1987, 446) quotes Riesman (1942, 731): "It is only through strengthening the protection of the groups to which an individual belongs that his own values and his own reputation can be adequately safeguarded."

55. See Isensee 1997, 17: "One who claims the right of honor for himself is necessarily already in the defensive position—is a victim."

56. The narrower conception of honor is defended in the United States, the wider one in Germany. See Whitman's instructive comparisons in 1997, 1295–1312, 1372–84.

57. See Jones 1998, 152: "Group defamation is a condition precedent to more aggressive and violent forms of racial discrimination"; Rosenfeld 2003, 1567: "It would of course be preferable if hate could be defeated by reason. But since unfortunately that has failed all too often, there seems to be no alternative but to combat hate speech through regulation in order to secure a minimum of civility in the public arena."

58. See Note 1988, 689: "Communitarians argue that human agency cannot be intelligibly abstracted from the ends and purposes that an individual has as a member of society. It is only as residents of particular regions, as practitioners of certain callings, as adherents to particular religions, and, ultimately, as citizens of particular regimes that individuals arrive at determinate choices about who they are."

59. Bull (2001, 164, 168) points out that Germany is "shy" of conflicts.

60. See Hofmann 1992, 164: "The objective of article 131 of the [German] Federal Criminal Code [in its previous version] is the maintenance of social harmony to which incitement to racial hatred is considered to pose a serious threat."

61. According to this understanding, sec. 130 of the German Criminal Code—which provides for punishing "incitement to racist persecution"—is a "climate offense," not only in substance but also in verbal form. For the expression "climate protection" is indeed used in this context. See Wandres 2000, 213. This is also true of prohibitions of aggressive and hate speech. See the many references to "climate" in Zimmer 2001. Moreover, in sec. 130 of the German Criminal Code the criterion of defamation is used precisely to distinguish impermissible and punishable forms of harsh criticism of foreigners or immigrants—incitement to racist persecution—from permissible ones.

62. From the German viewpoint, the principle of social welfare in art. 20, sec. 1, and the principle of equality in art. 3 can be read to require this attitude. Then both norms create an obligation to create equal conditions for the socially disadvantaged. For a similar American view, see Rosenfeld 2003, 1535–41, 1561.

63. Mill ([1859] 1973, 510) had already contemplated this case: "But on every subject on which difference of opinion is possible, the truth depends on a balance to be

struck between two sets of conflicting reasons." I hope to have presented the two opposed views in their "most plausible and persuasive form" (ibid., 511).

64. As to the understanding of the terms "liberal" and "libertarian," see note 19 above. For a general discussion of communitarianism and its relation to liberalism without reference to aggressive speech, see Mulhall and Swift 1992; Höffe 1999, 130–34, 296–303, 354–56; Brugger 1999, 253–84.

65. See for this characterization Rosenfeld 2003, 1529: "strong preference for liberty over equality, commitment to individualism, and . . . freedom from the state. . . ."

66. See Kriele 1994, 1897, for a representative way of putting this: "Human beings are made for [life in] community, not for lives as isolated individuals. 'Murdering' one's reputation and thus depriving the individual of his social environment is, besides murder, inflicting physical injuries, and robbery of one's entire belongings, among the worst that can be done to a person."

67. See Dietze 1985, 5: "Pure Liberalism is the idea of an unlimited, insatiable desire for freedom"; 62: "As a drive to gain more freedom, liberalism is egoistic and egotistic in a way similar to liberty itself." Also see note 18 above.

68. This is what John Stuart Mill and Alexis de Tocqueville do, for instance. One may also call associative liberalism "constitutional liberalism." See Brugger 1999, sec. 7.

69. On the three following types see Brugger 1999, 258–69, and the chart at the end of the main text.

70. Here one can distinguish between premodern, pre-Enlightenment, or totalitarian community thought on the one hand, where this "liberal" core element is not existent or is marginalized, and modern, enlightened communitarianism on the other hand, which even in its conservative variety acknowledges that, to use Kant's terminology, every human being should be seen as an end in himself or herself. So, in a wide, weak sense, even conservative communitarianism is "liberal," though not in the strong and narrower sense of "liberal communitarianism."

71. Referring to the key phrases used in the text before note 69 above, one could say that conservative communitarianism is concerned primarily with "integrity, integration, particularity," liberal communitarianism with "integrity, liberty, integration," and universal communitarianism with "integrity, integration, equalization."

72. See nos. 5, 9, and 10 in the section "Arguments for Granting Priority to Aggressive Speech" above.

73. The competing view based on German, European, and International Law is different: its aim is to provide the criminal law's protection for physical and psychic integrity, and to extend the concept of "violent deed"—words are regarded as deeds when one cannot evade them nor forestall the damage they do by launching a verbal counterattack.

74. See notes 6 and 22 above on *RAV* and *Cohen*.

75. See notes 28, 29, 31, and 32 above; Mill [1859] 1973, 507. Also see Ernst Bloch's parallel conception of "uprightness," showing backbone [*aufrechter Gang*], which can be applied to communicative situations too: Bloch 1961, 12, 14.

76. See Note 1988, 683: "This note argues that communitarianism provides a compelling justification for group libel laws."

77. See Sullivan 2001, 9, on the "tradition of constitutional law [as] one that views civil rights and civil liberties as supporting social fluidity rather than entrenchment in

fixed groups." Sullivan provides a historical explanation for this, and says, at 12–13, that the situation in societies under strong influences of religion or other traditions might be different.

78. But the opposite is argued in Note 1988, 690: "[The] offense that the members of [the attacked groups] take at group vilification reflects a *constitutive component* of their identities. It is not possible . . . as liberalism supposes, to disregard such sensibilities while still respecting the personhood of the individuals who experience them." The author expresses himself in a similar way at 691, 699n110, but more cautiously at 695n85: "In linking individual dignity to reputation—to a person's estimation in the opinion of others—this formulation recognizes that a person's identity is *in part* comprised of his or her standing in the community." (Emphasis added.)

79. Feminist legal literature claims that this is happening. See, for instance, Baer 2000, who follows Catherine MacKinnon, at 79 ("the grand liberal theories behind speech law lack an adequate recognition of power") and 91ff. (Baer's sec. 4 is entitled "An Alternative Point of View: Speech and Hierarchy").

80. Conversely, the prohibition of aggressive speech (for instance, speech damaging a person's honor or inciting to national or racial hatred) can be leveled against groups seeking to emancipate themselves and to give voice to messages of liberation. Note 1988, 692n71, quotes from an American court decision as follows: "[If] Nazi speech can be restricted because of its offensiveness, then 'the anti-racist himself could be oppressed.'" For similar arguments, see Roth 1993, 184; Rosenfeld 2003, 1525; Coliver 1992, 373; Post 1991, 297, 297n161; Kretzmer 1987, 511; Weinstein 1997, 462–71.

81. Proponents of the American view keep referring to the example of aggressive speech as it was used to bring about equal rights for different races in the 1960s and 1970s. See the preceding note and Greenawalt 1995, 151–52; Allport [1954] 1979, 510.

82. Take a married couple for an example. One spouse shouts at the other: I hate you! This is hate speech—pure hatred, it seems. But a closer look quickly reveals that the person shouting has some other, material, and specific concern (You don't love me, neglect me, spend too much money, or the like), which at that moment he or she deems so urgent that he or she cannot help shouting: I hate you! This example can be used to explain public disputes as well. Often, an expression of dislike or hatred will disguise a substantive message or concern that should be addressed.

83. According to Arthur Schopenhauer, personal honor is "objectively understood, others' opinion of one's value, and subjectively understood, our fear of that opinion." Cited in Isensee 1997, 16.

84. The former German President Friedrich Ebert, after a libel case in which he was not able fully to clear his name of the charge of "betraying" his country, is reported to have said: "The mental pain is worse. They have taken me out politically; now they want to murder me morally. I won't survive this." Quoted in Senfft 1994, 7.

85. This does not rule out the communitarian insight that civilized values are created over a long time and require constant care, and that an assessment of how to do so, and how to prevent dangers to them, requires a long-term perspective. One must not be limited to looking at damages imminent in the present. But as the discussions between the American and the German/European views demonstrate, it is often unclear what the long-term consequences of either allowing or prohibiting aggressive speech would be.

86. Even Isensee (1997, 46) emphasizes this, while otherwise advocating a stronger state protection of personal honor: "The sensitive issues of the protection of honor are primarily taken care of by extralegal norms, morality, ethos, convention, tact, and one's social sensory apparatus." He goes on to warn against conjoining political correctness with legal sanctions.

87. But see Kriele 1994, 1897: "[The] media should be placed under a special duty of care. 'Character assassination' perpetrated by the media can completely destroy its victim's entire social network [of relationships]."

88. See the German Federal Constitutional Court's decision BVerfGE 86, 1, from which this illustration is taken.

89. One may think of such criticisms as "dubious transactions" or "verging on the criminal."

90. This, however, is argued by Kriele (1994, 1903): "This is all the more true because people are naturally confident towards the media."

91. See note 43 above. These arguments do not rule out or discount as undesirable stronger protection of personal honor in nonpolitical matters—for instance, in private disputes. But in this area, too, one must not jump to the conclusion that any attempt to damage someone's honor will be successful.

92. However, liberal communitarianism also assumes, as a matter of moral development, a "priority of the particular" that needs to be reflected properly in any moral theory, and that is considered to provide an argument against exaggerated degrees of worldwide solidarity. See Selznick 1992, 193–201. According to this view, differential treatment of those nearer and those further to oneself is morally, and legally, legitimate.

93. See notes 68–71 above on this Enlightenment or liberal element in all types of modern communitarianism.

REFERENCES

Allport, Gordon. [1954] 1979. *The Nature of Prejudice*. Cambridge, MA: Addison-Wesley.

Appleman, Bradley A. 1996. Hate Speech: A Comparison of the Approaches Taken by the United States and Germany. *Wisconsin International Law Journal* 14:422–40.

Baer, Susanne. 2000. Violence: Dilemmas of Democracy and Law. In *Freedom of Speech and Incitement against Democracy*, ed. David Kretzmer and Francine Kershman Hazan, 63–100. London: Kluwer Law International.

Bloch, Ernst. 1961. *Naturrecht und menschliche Würde* [Natural Law and Human Dignity]. Frankfurt am Main: Suhrkamp.

Bracken, Harry M. 1994. *Freedom of Speech: Words Are Not Deeds*. Westport, CT: Praeger.

Brison, Susan J. 1998. The Autonomy Defense of Free Speech. *Ethics* 108:312–39.

Brugger, Winfried. 1999. *Liberalismus, Pluralismus, Kommunitarismus*. Baden-Baden: Nomos.

———. 2002. Constitutional Treatment of Hate Speech. In *Stocktaking in German Public Law*, ed. Eibe Riedel, 117–51. Baden-Baden: Nomos.

———. 2003. Verbot oder Schutz von Haßrede? Rechtsvergleichende Beobachtungen zum deutschen und amerikanischen Recht [Prohibition or Protection of Hate Speech? Comparative Observations on German and American Law]. *Archiv des öffentlichen Rechts* 128:372–411.

Bull, Hans Peter. 2001. Freiheit und Grenzen des Meinungskampfes [Freedom and Limitations of the Battle of Ideas]. In *Festschrift 50 Jahre Bundesverfassungsgericht* [Essays in Honor of the 50th Anniversary of the Federal Constitutional Court], vol. 2, ed. Peter Badura and Horst Dreier, 172–91. Tübingen: Mohr Siebeck.

Butler, Judith. 1997. *Excitable Speech: A Politics of the Performative.* New York: Routledge.

Cohen, Joshua. 1996. Freedom of Expression. In *Toleration: An Elusive Virtue*, ed. David Heyd, 173–225. Princeton, NJ: Princeton University Press.

Coliver, Sandra, ed. 1992. *Striking a Balance: Hate Speech, Freedom of Expression and Non-Discrimination.* London: Article 19, International Centre Against Censorship.

Delgado, Richard, and Jean Stefancic, eds. 1997. *Must We Defend Nazis? Hate Speech, Pornography, and the New First Amendment.* New York: New York University Press.

Dietze, Gottfried. 1985. *Reiner Liberalismus* [Pure Liberalism]. Tübingen: Mohr Siebeck.

Douglas-Scott, Sionaidh. 1999. The Hatefulness of Protected Speech: A Comparison of American and European Approaches. *William and Mary Bill of Rights Journal* 7:305–47.

Downs, Donald A. 1985. *Nazis in Skokie: Freedom, Community, and the First Amendment.* Notre Dame, IN: University of Notre Dame Press.

Dworkin, Ronald. 1978. *Taking Rights Seriously.* Cambridge, MA: Harvard University Press.

———. 1996. *Freedom's Law: The Moral Reading of the American Constitution.* Cambridge, MA: Harvard University Press.

Glendon, Mary Ann. 1991. *Rights Talk: The Impoverishment of Political Discourse.* New York: Free Press.

Greenawalt, Kent. 1995. *Fighting Words: Individuals, Communities, and Liberties of Speech.* Princeton, NJ: Princeton University Press.

Häntzschel, Kurt. 1932. Das Recht der freien Meinungsäußerung [The Right to Free Speech]. In *Handbuch des deutschen Staatsrechts II* [Handbook of German Constitutional Law], ed. Gerhard Anschütz and Richard Thoma, sec. 105, 651–75. Tübingen: Mohr Siebeck.

Hensley, Thomas R., ed. 2001. *The Boundaries of Freedom of Expression and Order in American Democracy.* Kent, OH: Kent State University Press.

Höffe, Otfried. 1999. *Demokratie im Zeitalter der Globalisierung* [Democracy in the Age of Globalization]. München: Beck.

Hofmann, Rainer. 1992. Incitement to National and Racial Hatred: The Legal Situation in Germany. In Coliver, 159–70.

Isensee, Josef. 1997. Grundrecht auf Ehre [The Fundamental Right to Honor]. In *Staatsphilosophie und Rechtspolitik: Festschrift für Martin Kriele* [Political Philosophy and Legal Policy: Festschrift in Honor of Martin Kriele], ed. Burkhardt Ziemske, Theo Langheid, Heinrich Wilms, and Görg Haverkate, 5–48. München: Beck.

Jones, Thomas D. 1998. *Human Rights: Group Defamation, Freedom of Expression, and the Law of Nations.* The Hague: Nijhoff.

Kaleb, George. 1996. The Freedom of Worthless and Harmful Speech. In *Liberalism Without Illusion*, ed. Bernard Yack, 220–40. Chicago, IL: University of Chicago Press.

Kant, Immanuel. [1795] 1968. Zum ewigen Frieden [On Eternal Peace]. In *Kants Werke VIII: Akademieausgabe* [Kant's Writings: Academy Edition], app. 2, 381–86 Berlin: de Gruyter.

Kretzmer, David. 1987. Freedom of Speech and Racism. *Cardozo Law Review* 8:445–513.

Kriele, Martin. 1994. Ehrenschutz und Meinungsfreiheit [Legal Protection of Honor and Freedom of Speech]. *Neue Juristische Wochenschrift*: 1897–1905.

Kübler, Friedrich. 2000. Rassenhetze und Meinungsfreiheit [Incitement to Racial Hatred and Freedom of Speech]. *Archiv des öffentlichen Rechts* 125:109–30.

Lederer, Laura J., and Richard Delgado, eds. 1995. *The Price We Pay: The Case against Racist Speech, Hate Propaganda, and Pornography.* New York: Hill and Wang.

Luhmann, Niklas. 1998. Meinungsfreiheit, öffentliche Meinung, Demokratie [Freedom of Speech, Public Opinion, Democracy]. In *Meinungsfreiheit als Menschenrecht* [The Right to Free Speech as a Human Right], ed. Ernst-Joachim Lampe, 99–110. Baden-Baden: Nomos.

Marion, David E. 1997. *The Jurisprudence of Justice William J. Brennan, Jr.: The Law and Politics of "Libertarian Dignity."* Lanham, MD: Rowman and Littlefield.

Matsuda, Mari J., Charles R. Lawrence III, Richard Delgado, and Kimberle Williams Crenshaw. 1993. *Words that Wound: Critical Race Theory, Assaultive Speech, and the First Amendment.* Boulder, CO: Westview Press.

Mill, John Stuart. [1859] 1973. *On Liberty*. Repr. in Jeremy Bentham and John Stuart Mill, *The Utilitarians*, 490–530. Garden City, NY: Anchor Books.

Mulhall, Stephen, and Adam Swift. 1992. *Liberals and Communitarians.* Oxford: Blackwell.

Nisbet, Robert. 1962. *Community and Power.* New York: Oxford University Press.

Note. 1988. A Communitarian Defense of Group Libel Laws. *Harvard Law Review* 101:683–701.

Post, Robert. 1991. Racist Speech, Democracy, and the First Amendment. *William and Mary Law Review* 32:267–327.

———. 1997. Community and the First Amendment. *Arizona State Law Journal* 29:473–84.

Riesman, David. 1942. Democracy and Defamation: Control of Group Defamation. *Columbia Law Review* 42:727–80.

Rosenfeld, Michel. 2003. Hate Speech in Constitutional Jurisprudence: A Comparative Analysis. *Cardozo Law Review* 24:1523–67.

Roth, Stephen J. 1993. The Laws of Six Countries: An Analytical Comparison. In *Under the Shadow of Weimar: Democracy, Law, and Racial Incitement in Six Countries*, ed. Louis Greenspan and Cyril Levitt, 177–212. Westport, CT: Praeger.

Selznick, Philip. 1992. *The Moral Commonwealth: Social Theory and the Promise of Community.* Berkeley: University of California Press.

Senfft, Heinrich. 1994. *Schmäher vor Gericht: Persönlichkeitsschutz und öffentliche Meinung in Deutschland* [Libellers in Court: Protection of Honor and Public Opinion in Germany]. Göttingen: Wallstein.

Stark, Ralf. 1996. *Ehrenschutz in Deutschland* [The Legal Protection of Honor in Germany]. Berlin: Duncker und Humblot.

Sullivan, Kathleen. 2001. Freedom of Expression in the United States: Past and Present. In Hensley, 1–16.

Symposium. 1997. Free Speech and Community. *Arizona State Law Review* 29:459–584.

Trager, Robert, and Donna L. Dickerson. 1999. *Freedom of Expression in the 21st Century*. Thousand Oaks, CA: Pine Forge Press.

Walzer, Michael. 1994. *Thick and Thin: Moral Argument at Home and Abroad*. Notre Dame, IN: University of Notre Dame Press.

Wandres, Thomas. 2000. *Die Strafbarkeit des Auschwitz-Leugnens* [The Criminality of Denying Auschwitz]. Berlin: Duncker und Humblot.

Weinstein, James. 1997. A Brief Introduction to Free Speech Doctrine. In Symposium, 461–71.

———. 1999. *Hate Speech, Pornography, and the Attack on Free Speech Doctrine*. Boulder, CO: Westview Press.

———. 2001. Hate Speech, Viewpoint Neutrality, and the American Concept of Democracy. In Hensley, 146–69.

Wells, Christina E. 1997. Reinvigorating Autonomy, Freedom and Responsibility in the Supreme Court's First Amendment Jurisprudence. *Harvard Civil Rights–Civil Liberties Review* 32:159–96.

Whitman, James Q. 2000. Enforcing Civility and Respect: Three Societies. *Yale Law Journal* 109:1279–1398.

Zimmer, Anja. 2001. *Hate Speech im Völkerrecht: Rassendiskriminierende Äußerungen im Spannungsfeld zwischen Rassendiskriminierungsverbot und Meinungsfreiheit* [Hate Speech in International Law: Racially Discriminatory Statements and the Tension between the Prohibition of Racial Discrimination and Freedom of Speech]. Frankfurt am Main: Lang.

Appendix 7.1 Protection or Prohibition of Aggressive Speech? Two Opposed Views

	United States of America. Dominant American Free Speech Liberalism	*Germany, Europe, International Conventions. Communitarianism?*
1. Autonomy of the speaker	Normative and expressive individualism, priority of "freedom from" communal bonds	Moderate individualism, equal emphasis on "freedom from" and "freedom to" joining communities
2. Arguments and emotions	They are connected. Civilized forms of interaction are desirable but will not be legally enforced. Words are not deeds	Emotions can be separated from arguments. Duty to avoid uncivilized communication. Aggressive words as harmful deeds
3. First consequentialist argument	It must be permissible for fact-based aggressive speech to be uttered. Goal: discovery of truth	Same, but more burdens of exposition and evidence are placed on the speaker
4. Second consequentialist argument	Derogatory value judgments can encourage learning processes. Better arguments will normally prevail	Derogatory value judgments rarely initiate learning processes. Malicious arguments sometimes, or often, prevail. Rhetorical aggression fosters conflict and leads to an increase in criminal behavior
5. Third consequentialist argument	No freedom of speech where physical violence is imminently threatened, where clear and present danger exists	Even an abstract, nonimminent danger, i.e., the danger of a danger, can justify restrictions of the freedom of speech
6. Competing value of personal honor	Legally protected only as reputation, protection from false derogatory judgments	A person's honor extends to basic forms of civility, independent of whether a derogatory judgment of a person is fact-based or purely evaluative
7. Protection of "collective honor"?	No protection of collective honor, because the individual member is more than and different from the collective	Yes, if an insulting message is directed toward all individual members of a collective, or toward core groups

(continued)

Appendix 7.1 Protection or Prohibition of Aggressive Speech? Two Opposed Views (*continued*)

	United States of America. Dominant American Free Speech Liberalism	*Germany, Europe, International Conventions. Communitarianism?*
8. Conception of the person	The individual has priority. "Upright posture," backbone in communicative processes, expected. More speech preferable to less speech	Equal respect toward every individual has priority. No duty on the part of the verbally attacked to launch verbal counterattack
9. Conception of society	Consensus and discord, cooperation and conflict. It must be possible for communicative conflicts to be carried out	Denial that existential conflicts are bound to occur. Or "reasonable persons" ought to be able to reach a compromise
10. Conception of the state	The state is only responsible for securing the absence of physical violence and protecting bodily integrity. No state control of the political climate	The state is also responsible for protecting the psychic integrity of individuals and groups, especially with respect to minorities
11. State neutrality and integration in society	Strict principle of viewpoint neutrality. Integration into society is to occur through voluntary mutual recognition	The state must be on the side of the poor and weak minorities. Control of the political climate as a means of encouraging societal integration

Appendix 7.2 Three Versions of Communitarianism

	1. *Conservative Communitarianism*	2. *Liberal Communitarianism*	3. *Egalitarian-Universalistic Communitarianism*
1. Anthropology, conception of human nature	Individual needs strong roots in the community	Individual needs to live in multiple communities	Autonomous individual endowed with reason
2. Conception of freedom	"Freedom to" lead a fulfilled life in one's community	"Freedom" and fulfillment "in" one's communities	Fulfillment through option of "freedom from" one's community
3. Importance of traditional lifestyles for how one should live	Constitutive role; one lives for "ends prior to one's self"	Range from instrumental to constitutive	Primarily instrumental, free choice of lifestyle, "self prior to ends"
4. Conception of morality	Priority of traditions, ethical practices, conventional morality	Mutual references between conventional and reflexive, critical morality	Priority of reflexive, critical morality over conventional morality
5. Justification of moral norms; *principium diiudicationis*	Recourse to "is" as the concrete substance of good and just; particular justification; internal perspective; may be only marginally generalized	Recourse from "is" to "ought" through master ideals; particular and general justifications; from "inside" to "outside" arguments; graded responsibilities	Recourse to "ought" through abstraction; proceduralization; discourse from "outside" to "inside"; extensive generalizations
6. Compliance with moral norms, *principium executionis*	Individual is integrated and bound by existing relationships of solidarity	Immanence and transcendence of existing relationships of solidarity	Appeal to reason; all human beings are ends in themselves
7. Relationship between community and justice	Community tends to replace or define justice	Community and justice have to be balanced out	Universal justice tends to replace or take priority over particular communities
8. Relationship between collective goals and individual rights	Collective goals tend to have priority	Collective goals and individual rights have to be balanced out	Individual rights tend to have priority

(*continued*)

Appendix 7.2 Three Versions of Communitarianism (*continued*)

	1. Conservative Communitarianism	*2. Liberal Communitarianism*	*3. Egalitarian-Universalistic Communitarianism*
9. Conception of the common good	Traditional lifestyles primarily respected and promoted; constitutional rights to freedom and equality secondary	Balance between the respect and promotion of particular lifestyles and constitutional rights to equality and freedom	Equal respect and promotion of all people and groups; neutrality toward particular lifestyles
10. Status of minority rights	Priority placed on status of majority	Open and civilized struggle for recognition	Priority placed on status of minority
11. Mutual responsibility among individuals	Near horizon of morality takes precedence	Theory of responsibility spheres graded from near to far horizons of morality	Far horizon of morality takes precedence
12. Primary focal point of human beings	Concrete personality	Concrete personality and abstract legal person	Abstract legal person
13. Political integration, stability through	Substantial consensus and/or participation in the democratic process	Participation in the democratic process and at least partial substantial consensus	Democratic participation and rights to freedom and equality

8

The Tension between the *Law of Justice* and the *Law of Love*[1]

Dorien Pessers

In the first chapter of this book, Van Seters contends that liberalism and communitarianism both contain ambiguities. Denial of these ambiguities leads to the disappearance from sight of the fundamental continuities between these two currents. His general thesis can be supported, if we take the "rights discourse"—one of the central elements of the liberalism–communitarianism debate—into consideration. Thus, the critique of many communitarians involves the claim that today we speak only three languages: the language of individual uniqueness and self-realization, the language of subjective rights, and the language of economics. Together these languages confirm and reinforce the selfish nature of humankind. The consequence of these barren languages, moreover, is that they limit our powers of perception—and with it our intellectual horizon. Important moral dimensions of life and of living together, therefore, remain hidden from view.

But is our language really as barren as it is made out to be? Can we not claim with equal right that we also know the language of duty, of moral and social obligation to others? It is undeniably true that in a culture like ours, with its strong individualistic and even narcissistic traits, the language of entitlement rings louder than the language of obligation. Yet, that does not alter the fact that in everyday practice also the morality of duty—in different variations and intensities—is adhered to. People do not comply only with their narrowly defined legal duties, but also, in their interaction with family members, friends, neighbors, and colleagues, with their moral and social duties. Indeed, people apparently feel an obligation even toward strangers and persons that are distant, as is shown by the extensive inheritances, donations, and contributions that are received by charities (Schuyt 2001a, 2001b). The many practices of the ethics of duty generate just as many forms of social cohesion and solidarity. Does an author like Selbourne (1994, 167) not exaggerate, when he writes that in our society duty is "the great neglected rule"? Long-term processes of modernity, such as liberalization, rationalization, secularization, and individualization, have not completely depleted the premodern sources of the morality of duty. On the basis of tradition, religion, gratitude, love, and charity, or on the basis of precepts such as "*noblesse oblige,*" people will continue to feel an obligation toward others. Other, contemporary sources have developed, moreover, like the duties of citizenship, civil society, and brotherhood/solidarity. The problem of the relation between rights and duties, therefore, is not so much a matter of the decline of values, but rather a matter of the balance between values. This chapter will call attention to that balance in light of the dialectical tension between the *Law of Justice* and the *Law of Love.*[2]

THE *LAW OF JUSTICE* VERSUS THE *LAW OF LOVE*

It is not easy to come to grips with the varied notion of "duty." Is it about enforceable legal duties? Or is it about moral and social duties that are not enforceable and are often seen as virtues? Is it about virtues like, for instance, generosity, helpfulness, hospitality? Is it about duties to others, to oneself, to God? Is it about civic or communal duties? Is it about duties deriving from social status? And what are the sources of these duties? Are they based on the law? Do they proceed from a sense of guilt? Do they ensue from a feeling of responsibility? Do they depend on gratitude, or on love and charity? Or do they follow, partly, from enlightened self-interest?

A common classification is the distinction between *determinate* and *indeterminate* duties. Certain duties are strictly defined legal duties that correspond with strictly defined and enforceable rights. They belong, therefore, to what is known as the "rights discourse." The indeterminate duties, however, have not been strictly defined and, in principle, cannot be legally enforced. The interested party is dependent on the sense of duty of others.

Schneewind (1998) connects the distinction between determinate and indeterminate duties with the distinction between the *Law of Justice* and the *Law of Love.* With regard to both types of law a long tradition of legal philosophy exists that considers the compliance with these two types of law as a precondition for a just society. To substantiate this claim Schneewind quotes, among others, Grotius, Pufendorf, and Kant. According to Grotius, legal duties are the minimal requirements for social life. Hence, it is important that they can be enforced. This minimal justice has to be supplemented with indeterminate duties that raise the quality of social life. Pufendorf lists help, support, good advice to others, the gratitude one shows, and the services that are extended selflessly. Kant prefers not to speak of love, but of benevolence (*benevolentia*), which stems from a sense of moral duty and belongs to the realm of the virtues. With Kant the legal duties are also minimal preconditions for a well-ordered society. The duties that proceed from virtue, on the other hand, are aimed at the happiness and well-being of others and through these also of our own.

That justice is out of the question when only strictly specified legal duties are adhered to, is obvious from the position of children. Children are especially vulnerable when they are treated hard-heartedly or unkindly and when their interests are not promoted conscientiously. They cannot assert any rights to an affectionate upbringing and loving care, but the absence of these can have far-reaching consequences for their chances in life and their happiness (O'Neill 1988).

Not only children are dependent on the morality of duty of others. The moral quality of society as a whole drops when only legal obligations are observed. In every relationship that is of any permanence or relies on trust more is expected than a merely legal, instrumental morality. Take, for instance, home care. Care measured with a stopwatch is experienced as unfeeling and unjust, because in the relationship between care-giver and patient only strictly defined legal obligations are fulfilled. Similarly, it is experienced as unjust when a doctor only pays strictly professional attention to his patients, but lacks a bedside manner. The same applies to education. A good teacher should do more than what one is legally required to do. He, or she, should get to know the student as far as that is necessary to make a contribution to the intellectual and moral education of that student. From employees, in general, it is expected that they are loyal to the company or institution they work for, and observe a duty to provide for it that goes beyond the literal wording of the employment contract. Compliance with indeterminate duties is valued to such a degree within society, that such indeterminate duties have even been assimilated into positive law in the shape of the open norms of equity and tort law. Under certain circumstances, therefore, indeterminate duties can also be enforced by law.

THE MORALITY OF DUTY AS A MORALITY OF GIVING

What is the source of the *Law of Love*, or, in other words, of loyalty, compassion, and generosity? Why do people comply with their indeterminate duties? Various philosophical authors explain the morality of duty from the notion of the gift. Thus, Ricoeur (1995) resolves the observance of legally unenforceable duties into what he calls "the economy of the gift." According to Ricoeur, the economy of the gift has its religious origins in the "givenness of the world." The world that we find obliges us to preserve it, maintain it, and pass it on. The gift is the source of the duty. This notion is also inherent in the rule "*suum cuique tribuere*": "to each his own" implies that something already belongs to someone, which has to be returned. Ricoeur connects the morality of duty with the commandments concerning love in the Testament. "Love me, for I am your Creator," God says. A bigger gift than creation is scarcely possible. And "thou shalt love thy neighbor as thyself," because he is part of creation and therefore of the gift. As a commandment of love, the givenness of the world and of life is, according to Ricoeur, prior to every human relation and communication.

We also come across Ricoeur's ethics of the gift with an author like Arendt. She treats life, and the world we encounter at birth, as a gift that commits us to the act of receiving and passing on (Arendt 1968, 22). In feminist ethics this notion is also prominent and influential. Held, for instance, claims that what represents the crucial human experience is not the *zum Tode sein*, the finiteness and death wish—that male Western philosophy is drenched in—but the act of being born. Living, giving, passing on, the intergenerational aspect, and, especially, the responsibility for future generations determine the moral perspective in equal measure. Life is given to children. This gift obliges to give back in the form of passing life on. The combination of the primary gift of life and the love that is given in unison creates the capacity for loyalty, generosity, and compliance with indeterminate duties in the child (Held 1989).

Yet the command of love and the morality of duty ensuing from it can also go too far and give rise to pathological relations that jar with the notion of justice. The mother who always gives and believes that her only task is to serve, will lose self-respect. He who believes that he should also love his enemies and, therefore, observe indeterminate duties toward them, might possibly be losing sight of the distinction between courage and cowardice. Hence, Ricoeur (1995) points to the importance of determinate, well-defined obligations that introduce a degree of equivalence in the exchange of services and, thereby, correct a limitless sense of duty. He concludes, therefore, that "justice is the necessary medium of love." In the same sense, a feminist author like Gilligan (1982) also claims that the principle of equality should establish a balance between what is given and received.

The gift as the source of the morality of duty looms much larger in anthropology than in philosophy. In his famous *Essai sur le don* Mauss (1923–1924) describes how the gift underlies all peaceful coexistence and generates cohesion and solidarity exactly because of its binding character. The heart of his argument is that along with the gift—contrary to the contract—the person is also given. For, in the gift, or in the service provided, the spirit of the giver is always present, for instance in the care with which the gift was selected or the service performed, in the intention with which the gift was given, or in the personal indebtedness for which the gift or the service is a redemption. To give is to connect oneself with the gift. It is this connection with the self that is so obliging and compels the reciprocation of the gift, in the shape of a return gift or service. To settle a bill too late with an anonymous, contractual party, one time only, will lead to a fleeting sense of guilt, at the most. But not to return a favor, not to support the neighbors that did support you, not to help a colleague that did help you, or, only to give a puny present to those who honored you with a princely gift: all that can give us a deep sense of guilt due to the betrayal of the duty to reciprocate. The gift, therefore, creates an enduring, intersubjective tie, i.e., social cohesion and solidarity, between giver and recipient. Their relation is not determined by the contractual and instrumental rule "*do ut des*" but by the moral and social rule "*do quia mihi datum est*": I give because I was given to.[3] As moral debtor and creditor the parties permanently succeed each other in alternating inequality.

The notion of the gift is also present in the rule of "*noblesse oblige*": he who has received many talents, privileges, and wealth, ought to pass some of this on to others. Also charity can be resolved into a duty to give of those who have received much. The social mechanism of the gift also joins together the generations. That which we received as cultural heritage from our forebears, we should maintain as good stewards and pass on to later generations.

Yet, here, there is also a threat of pathological relations. Exactly because a gift puts such moral obligations on us, there is always a possibility of abuse. Excessive giving, such that it is clear in advance that the receiver will never be able to give back in the same degree, maneuvers the receiver into a permanent and irredeemable relation of indebtedness that is susceptible to blackmail. The possibility of manipulation through the use of the gift explains the biblical expression, "it is better to give than to receive." This same insight is attested to in a statement by a French politician: "Why does this man hate me so? Have I ever done him a service?" Bribes and promotional gifts also take advantage of this feeling of guilt and the sense of duty that ensues from it. Not infrequently a promotional gift creates a bigger sense of obligation than a contract.[4] Moreover the chain of permanent mutual obligation can be experienced as suffocating and unfree. This oppressiveness is often attributed to family relations or to small, tight communities within which everybody owes everybody else.[5] Hence contractual relations in which people perform reciprocally and are then relieved from any obligations, can be experienced as liberating. Here, also, the determinate legal duty can serve as a correction on the indeterminate social duty—for the sake of just relations.

We can recognize the same dialectical relation between determinate and indeterminate duties in the fault lines of our legal history. Feudalism was characterized by enduring relations of dependency in which everybody had an obligation to everybody else. The vassal to the king, and the king to the vassal. The serf to the lord, and the lord to the serf. The master to the apprentice, and the apprentice to the master. The congregation to God and the Church, and the Church to the congregation. Duties deriving from status, duties to one's neighbors, religious duties, and family and kinship duties determined daily existence and the course of life. These duties, moreover, were indeterminate and were founded on customary law, on religion, on tradition, or on magic. To be sure, the expectation that mutual obligations would be honored was often violated, but was nonetheless of great importance. Failure to comply, after all, led to loss of reputation or banishment from the community. The morality of duty was, in part, preserved by a bleak Christian mood of personal guilt.

From the sixteenth century onward, the feudal social structure started to break down. Innumerable developments—e.g., economic, scientific, demographic, political, and religious (religious wars)—had an influence on this (Pessers 1999, 152–56). Within the framework of this chapter it is mainly their culmination in the eighteenth century that is important: the Enlightenment. The processes of rationalization, secularization, and individualization that were then set in motion put an end to the gloomy mood of being obligated and changed it into an optimistic attitude of being entitled. Being entitled vis-à-vis the world. The world could be scrutinized and controlled scientifically, processed economically, and changed politically. Entitled, also, with respect to others and with respect to the sovereign and the state. Feudal relations were declared taboo and thought to be at odds with the liberty and equality that each individual could claim as his or her natural rights. The individual became the center of the new, positive law. As a carrier of subjective rights—set against the legal duties of others—each person could "stand up like men, look others in the eye, and feel himself in some fundamental way the equal of anyone" (Feinberg 1980, 143). The new self-confidence increased people's self-respect. The human rights that were proclaimed promised that the serf could buy his freedom from the lord, the apprentice from the master, and the vassal from the king. People no longer needed to stay imprisoned in a network of constraining relations of dependency, but could determine themselves who they wanted to associate with and under what conditions. The "rights discourse" came into being and, from that moment onward, would become a weapon in the struggle against humiliating dependency and oppression. Citizens, workers, women, blacks, and gays have benefited from it in the course of the last few centuries.

Criticism of what is known as the "rights discourse," therefore, is not aimed at its historic and emancipatory consequences, but at the dominance of the contract or ownership model that was implicit in it from the start. In the emerging market economy of the eighteenth century, social relations were represented as contractual relations between owners (Macpherson 1962). People no longer needed to commit more, or for a longer period, than was determined by the terms of the contract. Outside of the contractual relation they had no responsibilities toward each other. The reduction of social relations to contractual relations was defended by Enlightenment philosophers like Hobbes, Locke, and particularly Smith, with the argument that the individual was the best advocate of his own interests. The individual will only enter into agreements freely and equally. He will not let himself be forced into relations of dependency, with an imbalance between rights and duties. Autonomy, property, and freedom of contract are, therefore, considered synonymous with justice. The effect was that—unlike the premodern law of custom—modern, positive law (with its corresponding, determinate duties) was primarily seen as an instrument to keep people out of each other's way, to make their freedom, their possessions, their life, their private space, and their autonomy inviolable to others. Even though this inviolability is in keeping with the tenor of human rights, it also undermines the preconditions for social cohesion and solidarity. Marx was one of the first who—in *On the Jewish Question*—articulated this critique on the "rights discourse": "the right of man to freedom is not based on the union of man with man, but on the separation of man from man. It is the right to this separation, the rights of the limited individual who is limited to himself" (Marx 1977, 53).

THE MORALITY OF DUTY AS A MORALITY OF RECIPROCITY

Central to the *Law of Justice*, as well as to the *Law of Love*, are relationships of exchange. In the first case, this concerns a brief exchange of determinate services according to a strict complementarity of rights and duties. The relationship is dominated by a contractual *do ut des* morality. Not the person, but the deal is central. In the second case, the primary concern is an enduring exchange of indeterminate services, which are experienced as a moral or social duty, and which are not set against enforceable rights. This relationship is dominated by the morality of giving, according to the rule *do quia mihi datum est*. Not the deal, but the person is central.

The noncompliance with determinate, positivized, legal duties results in a default or a wrongful act. The deal ought as yet to be settled, through compliance or compensation. The noncompliance with indeterminate duties—on the contrary—can lead to feelings of deprivation, broken trust, underestimation, and alienation in those who believe to be the rightful claimants of those moral and social duties. There are no legal remedies they can turn to, only social sanctions like the dissolution of friendship and trust.

In both cases, the noncompliance with duties means a breach of either a manifest or a latent expectation of reciprocity. Hence, it is the principle of reciprocity that lies at the basis of both rules. The French anthropologist Lévi-Strauss is credited for the insight that the gift is indeed the source, but not also—as Mauss believed—the explanation of the morality of duty. That explanation has to be sought on a deeper level, in the mechanism of reciprocity, which, as a fundamental principle, structures our thinking, feeling, and acting (Lévi-Strauss [1949] 1967).

First of all, Lévi-Strauss reduces the principle of reciprocity to our mental structure—following the famous studies by Piaget. This mental structure operates through reciprocity, i.e., what is perceived is first turned back (reflected) on itself, and then brought into the cognitive apparatus. Thereafter, the cognitive apparatus is capable of recognizing the physical environment. For, in that which is perceived, something of the self(-realized) returns. Through the same mechanism of reciprocity, a relationship to the other is established. People appear to acknowledge the other, only when they recognize that other. That is, when one's individuality is reflected in that other. Yet one's individuality is never reflected directly through the other. For that, a third, mediating agency is necessary. This could be a blood relationship, because of which family traits and family customs are reciprocally reflected. The stronger the recognition, the more people are prepared to show responsibility and solidarity. One feels "one's brother's keeper." Also, social relations can be this third agency. Through shared experiences, memories, work, or living environment, one's individuality is reflected in the other. People see their own conditions reflected in the other and are prepared to recognize those others.

In the recognition the structure of reciprocity is extended. For recognition is also a recurring cycle of giving, receiving, and returning of words, services, presents, care, and goods. What is always at issue is that what is given, in due course, has to be settled with a material, immaterial, or symbolic equivalent—in accordance with the expectation of reciprocity. This permanent, circular process in which the goods and services exchanged are subordinate to the family or social tie, we call reciprocity (from Latin *reciprocare*, which means "flowing to and fro"). Naturally, self-interest plays a part. The one who gives, is confident that in due course he will be given (back) to. Incidentally, this return service can take countless forms, which means that the self-interest is not directly evident. Prestige gained, thankfulness, a reward in the hereafter, the feeling of "doing good," can all be considered as a return favor.

Reciprocity, therefore, is not only a mental and psychological state of being, it is also a social (background) expectation and—in the true meaning of reciprocity—a fundamental norm of the social order, which is often articulated in a more detailed form in other normative systems, like religion.[6]

Where people no longer recognize each other, because little or nothing of their individuality is reflected, the willingness to recognize the other in a moral way also appears to decrease.[7] The other is a stranger, who, because of his strangeness, instills skepticism and fear rather than trust. This fear all too often turns out to be the source of aggression. If a certain bond—and therefore a beginning of social cohesion—is to develop between these strangers, then, here also, a third mediating agency is necessary. The law is preeminently the agency that can mediate between strangers. The law performs this classical function of keeping the peace by creating boundaries (of ownership), coordinating expectations and actions, and determining precisely defined rights and duties. Thanks to such a common legal order, strangers can know each other as people invested with rights. In that case, they develop a willingness to recognize each other, by mutually observing the strictly defined legal duties. This minimal reciprocity in which parties—because of their suspicion—make an equal exchange, and then go their separate ways, we call mutuality (from the Latin *mutuus*, which means from both sides). Thus, reciprocity—in the restricted sense of mutuality—is also a fundamental norm of the legal order.

If the mutuality of the *Law of Justice* is a first and minimal precondition for bonding between strangers, then it can also be the first step toward the reciprocity of the *Law of Love*. If a society succeeds in regulating the social relations between strangers in a principled way according to legal principles and fundamental rights—and thereby seeks to avoid unequal relationships of exchange—trust can grow between strangers. Because of that trust one is more likely to have the courage to break out of the "Beschränkung" (the limitation Marx spoke of), and to have the courage to start noncontractual, and even long-term relationships, with others, in the secure knowledge that—thanks to the mediating function of law—the services exchanged will even out in the long run. On this—self-enhancing—trust within reciprocal social relations, the solidarity arrangements of the welfare state, for instance, are based. What is given on behalf of strangers in the shape of social-security contributions, will sooner or later return—when one's own need arises—in the social contributions of others.

It goes without saying that not only the institutions of the rule of law and democracy, but also schools, unions, sports societies, churches, etc. here play an important—for an also mediating—role. They reinforce the norm of reciprocity—through internalization—on the social level. In short, a strong rule-of-law tradition, a democracy and *civil society* with permanent institutions, and a capacity for reciprocity acquired within the family and social sphere, together make up the preconditions for strong social cohesion and solidarity (Putnam 1993).

THE DELICATE BALANCE BETWEEN THE *LAW OF JUSTICE* AND THE *LAW OF LOVE*

With the mechanism of reciprocity a decrease in solidarity can also be explained. Such a decrease can occur when the preconditions for reciprocity are no longer met and the characteristics of reciprocity are no longer observed. For instance, in societies that become heterogeneous in a relatively short period of time (the problem of European multicultural societies), insufficient mediating agencies are present. Recognition of the other does not occur, because in the stranger little or nothing of one's own individuality returns. Moreover, when a common social substrate is absent, the legal recognition of the other as a co-carrier of common (human) rights appears to lead only to a limited acknowledgment of the other. At most, clearly defined duties are complied with. Other than that, exclusion and discrimination are often evident. The mechanism of reciprocity only turns out to lead to recognition in more or less homogeneous societies. Therefore, it is of the utmost importance that between the established and the newcomers mediating agencies are created. Education, work, and sports can play that mediating role. In education, the language and the jointly acquired knowledge will return in the other. In the workplace, common skills are developed. In sports, common rules are observed. What is crucial in every instance is that an exchange takes place. Because only through exchange can the social mechanism of reciprocity, and thus the development from skeptical, mutual relations to trust-based, reciprocal relations, get started. All this under the precondition that the process is embedded in the structure of the rule of law, of course.

Yet, also within homogeneous societies with a high level of solidarity, there can be a deterioration of solidarity. We can see that happen, for instance, in places where family and social relations are recast into legal relations, in the sense that they are mutualized. Where at first the "rights discourse" in family law was aimed at the emancipation of women and children, now the strict definition of rights and duties seems to have become an aim in itself. The norm that in relationships of love there has to be a to and fro of support, depending on individual needs and wants, in some important respects has been replaced by a contractual conception of the relationship of love. Within the "negotiating household" of modern-day families, detailed rules are often arrived at concerning the division of income, goods, and child care. The indeterminate nature of the services provided, which is so characteristic of the morality of duty, disappears. The *Law of Justice*, in that case, undermines the *Law of Love*.

We see the same thing occurring in education. The indeterminate duties of the teacher and student are replaced with a contractual relation. Teachers are no longer valued for their professional ethics, which requires them to share the knowledge they received with their students, as best they can and as widely as possible. On the contrary, the pursuit of their profession is subordinate to credits, to the requisite size of the study material, to contact hours, and to output figures. A calculating attitude is instilled in the student.

Also in health care the morality of reciprocity is increasingly replaced with a morality of mutuality. The relationship between doctor and patient is seen, less and less, as a relationship of trust, in which the doctor, by definition, observes the indeterminate duties of good health care. The treatment agreement that doctor and patient are supposed to arrive at, the standardization of, and growth of protocol within, medical treatment, the increasing tendency of patients to take doctors to court—all of these contribute to the mutualization of relationships of care.

The relation between civil servants and citizens is changing as well. As a result of large-scale privatization and incorporation of public utilities and other parts of the public sector, civil-service morality recedes into the background. This morality consisted of serving the common good in an impartial and disinterested fashion. What society as a whole has realized in terms of collective goods and institutions, has to be saved and guarded with good stewardship in order to pass on its fruits to citizens and coming generations. As soon as collective goods are privatized, their administrators enter into a different "frame of mind." They have to learn another language: the language of profit projections, short-term planning, and stockholder value. Strict legal and contractual duties take the place of the civil service's indeterminate duty of care.

The general trend in our society to impose contractual relations, business-organization models, and market forces on fields that have traditionally been characterized by the morality of indeterminate duties, or morality of reciprocity, has made the legal order absolute at the expense of the social order, and mutuality absolute at the expense of reciprocity. But a legal order always functions—and can only function—within a social order. The morality of reciprocity and the morality of mutuality that have been set against each other in this chapter as two ideal types—for the sake of conceptual clarity—actually fade into each other in real life. And, only when they reach a balance, can we speak of individual and social justice.

NOTES

1. This chapter is previously published in Dutch as "De *Law of Justice* versus de *Law of Love*," in Cliteur and Ten Napel, 31–42. Trans. Wouter de Been. Reprinted with permission of Ars Aequi Legal Publishers.

2. This tension is sometimes also stated in terms of an ethics of right versus an ethics of duty; a morality of justice versus a morality of care; a narrow morality versus a broad morality; a morality of mutuality versus a morality of reciprocity. This last distinction will be discussed further on in this chapter.

3. For further elucidation of this rule, see Pessers 1999.

4. Much has been written about the manipulative character of gifts. See, for instance, Komter 1996.

5. Such oppressiveness has often been described in novels. For a fascinating academic approach, see Kruijt 1968.

6. A classic essay is Gouldner 1960. See also Pessers 1999.

7. This has been confirmed time and again by empirical research. For this "relational-distance theory," see Black 1976.

REFERENCES

Arendt, Hannah. 1968. *Men in Dark Times*. New York: Harcourt.

Black, Donald. 1976. *The Behavior of Law*. New York: Academic Press.

Cliteur, Paul, and Hans-Martien ten Napel, eds. 2003. *Rechten, plichten, deugden*. Nijmegen: Ars Aequi Libri.

Feinberg, Joel. 1980. The Nature and Value of Rights. In *Rights, Justice, and the Bounds of Liberty: Essays in Social Philosophy*, 143–58. Princeton, NJ: Princeton University Press.

Gilligan, Carol. 1982. *In a Different Voice: Psychological Theory and Women's Development*. Cambridge, MA: Harvard University Press.

Gouldner, Alvin W. 1960. The Norm of Reciprocity: A Preliminary Statement. *American Sociological Review* 25:161–78.

Held, Virginia. 1989. Birth and Death. *Ethics* 99:362–88.

Komter, Aafke, ed. 1996. *The Gift: An Interdisciplinary Perspective*. Amsterdam: Amsterdam University Press.

Kruijt, J. P. 1968. Gemeenschap als sociologisch begrip: Een kritiek op Tönnies. In *Zoeklicht en kompas*, Bundel prof.dr. J. P. Kruijt aangeboden bij zijn afscheid als hoogleraar aan de Rijksuniversiteit te Utrecht, ed. Sj. Groenman et al., 180–202. Assen: Van Gorcum.

Lévi-Strauss, Claude. [1949] 1967. Le principe de la réciprocité. In *Les structures élémentaires de la parenté*, 66–86. Paris: Mouton.

Macpherson, C. B. 1962. *The Political Theory of Possessive Individualism: Hobbes to Locke*. Oxford: Clarendon Press.

Marx, Karl. 1977. *Karl Marx: Selected Writings*. Ed. David McLellan. Oxford: Oxford University Press.

Mauss, Marcel. 1923–1924. Essai sur le donne: Forme et raison de l'échange dans les sociétés archaïques. *Année Sociologique*, n.s., vol. 1:30–186. Repr. in *Sociologie et anthropologie*, 143–279. Paris: Presses Universitaires de France, 1950.

O'Neill, Onora. 1988. Children's Rights and Children's Lives. *Ethics* 98:445–63.

Pessers, Dorien. 1999. *Liefde, solidariteit en recht: Een interdisciplinair onderzoek naar het wederkerigheidsbeginsel*. PhD diss., University of Amsterdam.

Putnam, Robert D. 1993. *Making Democracy Work: Civic Traditions in Modern Italy*. Princeton, NJ: Princeton University Press.

Ricoeur, Paul. 1995. Love and Justice. *Philosophy and Social Criticism* 21 (5/6): 23–39.

Schneewind, Jerome B. 1998. *The Invention of Autonomy: A History of Modern Moral Philosophy*. New York: Cambridge University Press.

Schuyt, Theo N. M., ed. 2001a. *Geven in Nederland: Giften, legaten, sponsoring en vrijwilligerswerk*. Houten: Bohn Stafleu van Loghum.

———. 2001b. *De filantropische sector en "philanthropic studies" in Nederland: Wetenschappelijke belangstelling voor een maatschappelijke sector in wording.* Houten: Bohn Stafleu van Loghum.

Selbourne, David. 1994. *The Principle of Duty: An Essay on the Foundations of the Civic Order.* London: Sinclair-Stevenson.

9

The Appeal to Common Tradition: Its Progressive Potential[1]

Sanne Taekema

The most successful claim of communitarianism is the idea that individuals should be understood as deeply rooted in their social environment, an idea for which Selznick (1992, 201) uses the elegant term of "the implicated self." The individual is a primarily social being, shaped by family, community, and society. From this basic insight, the theory of what it means to be embedded in social relations—morally, politically, legally—can be developed. One particularly interesting issue related to the theme of embeddedness is what exactly the individual is part of: the issue of the identity and historicity of community itself (ibid., 361). What makes a community is in important respects determined by the historical background of that community, by the fact that the present group of people feels connected through its shared past. This chapter starts from the idea that, if we wish to understand what constitutes a shared history, a profitable approach is to study traditions. Because a focus on tradition is primarily associated with the theory of conservatism, I will discuss tradition and conservatism together in this chapter. At the background of this discussion is the worry that communitarian theory that takes traditions seriously is easily misinterpreted as romanticizing the past and supporting reactionary viewpoints. My aim is to show how traditions can be sources for development and change, especially in the field of law.

In a nutshell, the argument of the chapter is as follows. When traditions of common value are appealed to in legal or political debates, the first impulse is to understand such an appeal as conservative, i.e., as a claim to a heritage that has long been the same and that can explain what people share. In this chapter I want to explore the other side of tradition: my claim is that the appeal to tradition is actually an effective way to develop practices of law or politics in new directions. To show how this progressive potential of tradition can be realized, I will draw on ideas about creativity of interpretation and the ideal side of values. I will use the Dutch debate on multiculturalism as an illustration.

APPEALS TO TRADITION

"Because this is the way we have always done things." In this phrase, all the elements of an appeal to tradition can be recognized. First of all, there is the central element of continuity with the past. There is no tradition without the understanding that this way of behaving was not invented anew but was practiced before by others in the same way. The second element that is important is the particular community to which the tradition belongs. An appeal to tradition depends upon a "we" for whom the tradition is important. A tradition is always particular to a recognizable community, although this community can be larger or smaller and is not always clearly definable. We speak of the English political tradition, the Western legal tradition, the Buddhist religious tradition without a clear notion of the community involved.[2] Nevertheless, a tradition depends on being sustained by a community. This is connected to the third element: a tradition is a pattern of behavior, a way of doing things, which implies that a tradition has to be practiced (Oakeshott 1991, 26). If nobody acts as the tradition prescribes anymore, it vanishes, because its existence is in its use. The pattern of behavior makes up the typical content of the tradition: the actual wearing of a certain costume, the activity of singing particular songs.

What is behind an appeal to tradition? What makes it a convincing argument to use? The interesting thing to note is that it does not always convince; the appeal to tradition is acceptable only to particular groups and movements. Appeals to tradition have done well to support the formation of national identities, so well that this motive even gave rise to many occasions of inventing national traditions.[3] They have particular force, however, in conservative politics. Since Edmund Burke's *Reflections on the Revolution in France*, the appeal to tradition has served to counter revolutionary politics. To point out the dangers of political change by revolution, Burke aimed to show the value of existing political and social institutions and the need to retain them. Transcending the particulars of the time, Burke's are still the more convincing among conservative arguments. The main points are that it is impossible to gain knowledge of a working political order in the abstract and that it is extremely difficult to assess the effects of a practical decision. Society is too complex to be governed by a few abstract principles (Burke 1955, 69–70). Tradition can be regarded as the accumulated wisdom of earlier generations, which should be used, not cast aside. It finds support in a distrust of the power of abstract reasoning: no individual mind can think through the consequences of an action completely.

The conservative argument for traditions is supported by a realistic, or even pessimistic, view of human nature that sees mankind as incapable of acting without relying on prejudice (in the sense of engrained habitual judgments) and prone to failure. Especially the individual is mistrusted: the idea of one person alone is usually not interesting or worthwhile, and if it is, it has probably already been thought of by others before. The individual is too easily led astray by his own will and emotions, so that the traditional order of society is necessary to keep these sentiments in check.

I do not propose to adopt the conservative position wholesale, I merely wish to point out that the conservative background of an appeal to tradition resonates with basic communitarian ideas: an eye for variety and complex social relations and a critical view of both abstract reasoning and the divorce of individuals from their social context.

The conservative defense of tradition is best known as part of a political movement, but it has been more successful in the context of law. Appeals to tradition are more generally accepted in a legal context, especially in common law countries. In politics there is always a tension between tradition and ideology, to use Oakeshott's terminology (1991, 58), that is, a tension between arguments based on accepted patterns and arguments that appeal to an independent system of ideas. In law, that tension is absent: the ideas are seen as emanating from the legal tradition. The authority of tradition is needed to make legal arguments convincing. That authority of long-established ideas is most apparent in adjudication, in judicial argument for legal change. Reforms are hardly ever presented as something completely new and supported by abstract justice; they are presented as a recovery of ideas that were always there but acquire a new dimension in present circumstances. We may consider judging as a branch of legal argument that is committed to tradition by the very nature of the institution: the judiciary derives its legitimacy to a large extent from its adherence to the separation of powers and its reluctance to give (openly) political decisions. However, even in other legal activities, such as statutory reform, the appeal to tradition can be recognized. For instance, the Dutch recodification of civil law was presented as a necessary step to bring the statutory rules in line with the substance of the law as it had developed in case law throughout the twentieth century (Hondius 1982, 363).

Arguably the most central tradition in Dutch legal theory and practice is the tradition of the *Rechtsstaat* (Witteveen 2004b, 76–77).[4] As the idea that the state and all government action should be bound by law, it has served as the background for political and legal development in the Netherlands for centuries. It is a tradition that is invoked in almost any contemporary debate on legal reform, which is not so surprising because it contains a wide range of legal values and principles. Usually, the ideas of the *Rechtsstaat* are seen as falling into four main groups: legality, basic rights, *trias politica* (separation or balance of powers), and democracy. Depending on the importance attached to particular elements, the principle of equality and that of judicial review are sometimes mentioned separately. Most of the elements of the Dutch tradition have their origin in common European traditions of law and politics, in which Enlightenment ideas are maybe the most prominent, although there are many earlier ideas from the Western legal tradition that have continued to exert their influence, such as the distinction between law and politics, and the idea that law has supremacy over the political authorities (Berman 1983, 8–9).

Because of the combination of established tradition with ideological ideas, legal traditions such as that of the *Rechtsstaat* are also good examples of a type that I would like to call traditions of common value. Although it is difficult to make a sound typology of traditions, a distinction can be made between generally local traditions of a superficial nature, such as traditional dress, music, and celebration, and larger traditions of which the core is adherence to a set of values, such as the conservative political tradition or the common law tradition.[5] The idea of a tradition of common value is related to MacIntyre's concept of a tradition (1984, 222): ". . . when a tradition is in good order it is always partially constituted by an argument about the goods the pursuit of which gives to that tradition its particular point and purpose." MacIntyre sees all traditions, as he does the practices for which traditions form the context, as defined by the pursuit of specific goods. Although I think of traditions as a broader category, including smaller traditions, I will retain the idea that certain traditions are related to practices and that these are partly constituted by value-orientation. Traditions of common value are important for my purposes because the explicit reference to values makes possible the reinterpretation and development of the ideal side of the tradition (but I will turn to that argument below).

Many people feel uneasy about the appeal to tradition because of the lack of substance of such an argument. The claim that something should be because it has always been like this seems empty, not a real reason. Thus we see that traditional arguments are often backed by claims that the tradition should be followed because it is right, because the values embodied in it are the truth. Muller (1997, 4–5) makes a useful distinction between orthodoxy and conservatism that can be applied here: a defense of existing institutions based on the belief that they correspond to some ultimate truth is orthodox, while "the conservative defends existing institutions because their very existence creates the presumption that they have served some useful function." Although the need to support appeals to tradition with more substantive claims is apparent, the orthodox position is dangerous to the development of traditions. Its truth claim makes it impossible to admit discussion about traditions or change of traditions. It is precisely the possibility of these two i.e., discussion and change, that gives living traditions their progressive potential. And, perhaps surprisingly, the conservative argument for traditions gives many openings to bring out that potential.

INTERPRETING TRADITION

One of the main problems of orthodoxy is that the tradition is treated as closed. To take orthodox religion as an example, arguments are premised on a holy text as the source of the tradition, which is infallible and contains the answers to every problem. There is only one true interpretation of the tradition, and usually there are only a small number of people with the authority of giving that interpretation. In combination, these two features of orthodoxy obstruct the renewal and adaptation of the tradition.

In itself, there is nothing in a tradition that prevents it from reforming, but there are certain conditions that can stimulate such reform that are not always in place. If we return to the basic conservative notion of a tradition, the main feature of a tradition is its history. For conservatives, its historical survival is not only what makes it a tradition but also the argument for its value: the tradition would not have survived if it did not have some, apparent or implicit, usefulness. However, the way a tradition survives is in its being practiced by people: it is passed on through generations by every person who acts it out. In order to do that, the tradition needs to be interpreted: what should I do to act in accordance with the tradition? Usually, there is an overlap between generations so that the older generation can tell the younger how they practice the tradition, but somehow traditions slowly change. Such change is made possible by the individual act of interpretation, needed because the history of the tradition does not speak for itself. The reform of a tradition can take place when the reinterpretations of individuals are accepted as part of the tradition. It is necessary, however, to clarify what exactly an individual's contribution to a tradition is.

At this point, it is helpful to turn to the view of traditions of Oakeshott (1991, 12), who stresses the aspect of traditions being habits of behavior and connects this with the concept of practical knowledge. Practical knowledge, in his view, is to be distinguished from technical knowledge. The latter is the knowledge of techniques that can be precisely formulated, written down, and learned deliberately, while the former exists only in use, by performing certain patterns of behavior, and is not reflective. The important point Oakeshott makes is that all human activity makes use of these two kinds of knowledge at the same time. His example of cooking makes this clear: there are rules in the cookbook that can teach the technical knowledge of making a sauce, but there is practical knowledge involved as well to make a really good sauce. Such knowledge is transferred and trained in use: "the only way to acquire it is by apprenticeship to a master" (ibid., 15).

Practical knowledge can be regarded as traditional knowledge, and Oakeshott criticizes rationalist, or ideological, politics for denying that such knowledge is relevant or even that it is knowledge at all. Thus, Oakeshott (ibid., 61) claims that traditions of behavior are sources of knowledge that can be transmitted only through social interaction. Precisely because the knowledge of a tradition cannot be completely formulated but is visible in the traditional activity, it is dependent upon the interpretation of individual practitioners for its continuation. Traditions are fluid and lack a changeless center; they have continuity, because their elements never all change at the same time. Although Oakeshott does not highlight the role of the individual in a tradition, two aspects of this role can be distinguished.

The role of an individual participant in any tradition is twofold: the basic role of carrier of the tradition and the more demanding role of developer of the tradition. A tradition is like a language (ibid., 62), and in the development of language we can see the same things. First, people are needed to carry on the use of the language: when nobody speaks it any longer, the language is dead. Second, individuals contribute new words and expressions that can become part of the language: by their creative use the language evolves. Although the first aspect is easily acknowledged in relation to traditions, the importance of the creativity of individuals is easily overlooked, yet it is crucial for exploring progression.

For understanding individual creativity in a social context, we need a different theory than conservatism: John Dewey's pragmatism. Although it may seem strange to connect Dewey, the prototypical advocate of radical change and rationalistic scientific experiment, to the idea of tradition and Oakeshott's conservatism, there are good reasons for doing this. The most important reason is that Dewey (1984, 29) stresses the idea of knowledge as a practical matter: knowing is a form of doing. A second reason is that Dewey (1960, 99–100) has an eye for the context of thought, in which he includes traditions: one cannot think or analyze without a background of (cultural and theoretical) tradition, which one cannot possibly question completely all in one inquiry.

In pragmatism, a tradition is only the background for practical problem solving, in which new ideas can be tried and experimentally tested.[6] Other than in conservative theorizing, in which traditions are to be respected as the accumulation of wisdom, pragmatist thinking has no objection to consciously trying to reform traditions that are no longer practically relevant. Traditions are the necessary context for our practical activities but they should not be revered. Because the aim of practical activities is the solving of problems, the question for the role of traditions is how they can become tools for tackling problems. As I have said before, a tradition does not speak for itself, and, moreover, it does not apply itself to a problem. The connection between the tradition and the problematic situation at hand needs to be made, consciously or implicitly. The more serious the problem, the less obvious the knowledge to be gathered from the tradition will be.

Without the recognition that creative solutions can be derived from a tradition, one natural reaction to a difficult problem is to declare the tradition no longer relevant. Another obvious reaction is to apply the tradition in an orthodox manner, i.e., to deny that the problem is difficult by simply repeating the solution that has always been applied without considering its relevance in present conditions. An example of this type of reaction is a common (European) approach to genetic modification of food sources: not considering the pros and cons in a balanced way but declaring it to be unnatural and therefore dangerous.[7] In order to avoid both extremes, i.e., either the irrelevance of tradition or the orthodox interpretation of it, creative reinterpretation of tradition is necessary.

For such creative reinterpretation, conscious manipulation of the tradition to apply it to the problem at hand is inescapable. Here, the conservative view of traditions as implicitly passed on from generation to generation, from master to apprentice, reaches its limits. Innovation of the tradition depends on the inventiveness of a practitioner who is not satisfied to do things exactly as taught by the earlier generation but, for instance, applies a known method to a different field. Although a complete mastery of traditional methods or arguments is necessary to function in any practical endeavor, as was Oakeshott's argument, it is necessary to move beyond simple mastery to reform in order to excel. A cook who simply repeats what he has learned from the chefs to whom he was apprenticed will never earn a Michelin star. The pragmatist insight is that reform comes naturally when the connection between a practical problem and its traditional background is consciously examined in the search for a solution. For example, when the Palm House in London's Kew Gardens was being built, Richard Turner, the ironfounder responsible for the iron and glass construction, found that traditional cast iron could not span such great width, and he successfully made use of the wrought iron beams previously used only in shipbuilding.[8]

Although individual creativity is the start for progressive reform, it is not sufficient to achieve it. It needs to be followed by a social response for the new interpretation to take hold. The difficulty lies in the perception of the tradition's identity: even though traditions do not have an unchangeable core, they change only gradually and are implicitly understood by their communities as having a meaning and identity. When a proposal for reform departs sharply from the line of the tradition, that implicit understanding is challenged, and the proposal is in danger of being rejected as not in keeping with the tradition. The argument that the creative solution can be understood as following from the tradition needs to be accepted by the community to which the tradition belongs. Thus, reform of a tradition is an interactive process with a historical dimension: only over time can one be sure that a progressive interpretation has been incorporated as part of the tradition.

One area in which we can clearly see the struggle for reinterpretation is in the confrontation of the law with problems of multiculturalism. To illustrate the point, I will discuss two cases in Dutch law that show the importance, and pitfalls, of interpretation of the Dutch tradition of basic civil rights. The first case concerns the statements of a Muslim imam, El Moumni, about homosexuality, for which he was prosecuted on the basis of a criminal law article that forbids discriminatory insult of groups (article 137c Criminal Code). The second case concerns a woman applying for a job as clerk in a court who refused to take off her headscarf during work in the court. She brought her case before the Equal Treatment Commission, which hears cases concerning article 1 of the Dutch Constitution, containing the right to equal treatment and nondiscrimination. Both the Criminal Court and the Equal Treatment Commission had to address the issue of the meaning of basic rights: in the first case, the right to free speech and the freedom of religion, in the second, the right to equal treatment. Both rights are seen as central to the Dutch understanding of the *Rechtsstaat*, as guarantees of the values of freedom and equality that form the core of that concept (cf. Witteveen 2004b, 82).

The imam, El Moumni, had given an interview broadcast on Dutch national television in which he had spoken about homosexuality as damaging to society and a "disease"[9] that is likely to spread. Both the Court of First Instance and the Court of Appeal judged that his utterances were not a discriminatory insult in the sense of the Criminal Code.[10] The Court of Appeal judged that the utterances were not an insult primarily because they reflected his opinion about the sinfulness of homosexuality *as anchored* in the Islamic faith. The Court's assessment that his utterances simply expressed the Islamic faith was supported by the opinion of an expert witness (a Dutch professor of Islam) that the utterances were based on the texts of the Koran and other fundamental Islamic texts. This interpretation reflects the Protestant framework of tolerance, as described by Van der Burg (1998, 242): "In concrete discussions of tolerance, we can sometimes see an even more distinctly Protestant emphasis when religious beliefs are reduced to the doctrinal contents of sacred texts." Because El Moumni's utterances are a direct expression of an established religion as is evident from the main religious texts, his words are protected by the freedom of religion and to be tolerated.

In this case, the court uses a standard interpretation of the freedom of religion to support its decision: it looks for and finds a basis in a text. This is a basic type of argument both in the Dutch legal and the Dutch religious tradition: a literal source is the prime evidence of the existence of a religious doctrine. Moreover, freedom of religion is protected to a greater extent than freedom of speech; religious expression has a special status and stronger protection than, for instance, political expression.[11] Thus, the court fails to be creative in two ways: first, because it treats religion as orthodoxy, and second, because it fails to acknowledge the continuity of different kinds of expression and the need for a similar constitutional protection. The reduction of religion to text-based belief only allows for the protection of religions that have such a textual basis; this is problematic, for instance, in the case of Hinduism, the practices of which are not strictly based on texts (see Van der Burg 1998, 244). Separating religious expression from other kinds of expression obscures the fact that there is a general tension between the freedom of expression and the principle of nondiscrimination. Moreover, it leads to the strange consequence that a political party with a religious inspiration is allowed to discriminate more than a nonreligious political party.[12]

The case of the clerk with a headscarf concerned the conflict between the right to equal treatment of minorities and the neutrality of the judiciary. The woman concerned had applied for a job as clerk to the District Court of Zwolle; in the job interview she indicated that she was willing to wear the robe prescribed for both clerks and judges, but that she would not take off her headscarf during work. For that reason, she was not hired: the Court argued that a clerk with a headscarf was contrary to the neutral appearance of court officials. She filed a complaint with the Equal Treatment Commission.[13] The question before the Commission was whether the refusal to hire (because of the headscarf) constituted an unjustified distinction in the sense of the statute on equal treatment, the statute that elaborates article 1 Constitution. In the statute, making a direct distinction on the basis of, among other things, religion is forbidden, while an indirect distinction is forbidden in principle unless there is an objective justification for the distinction. The Commission argued that, in this case, the distinction was indirect because the reason for disallowing the headscarf in the courtroom was the protection of the neutrality of the judiciary, while it had the consequence of discriminating against women of the Islamic faith. It judged that this indirect distinction was unjustified, because in its opinion the dress code for clerks does not serve a true need. It pointed to the fact that there are even judges, for instance in family law cases, who refrain from wearing a robe in court. Moreover, the judiciary considered itself committed to having members from different groups in society. The refusal to consider applicants wearing a headscarf was deemed a disproportionately heavy measure.

The Commission simply accepted the argument of the woman that her headscarf was an expression of her religion without further investigation about the necessity of wearing a headscarf in the Islamic faith. Other than the judge in the El Moumni case, the Commission followed the standard case law that judges should not try to decide theological debates.[14] While discussing the right to equal treatment, the Commission also balanced two other basic values of the *Rechtsstaat*: the basic freedom of religion and the impartiality of the judiciary. Both fundamental freedoms and the independent position of the judiciary (in the context of the *trias politica*) are seen as central principles of the Dutch state under the rule of law. The Commission argued that the impartiality that the courts should convey toward citizens did not require a neutral appearance, without religious symbols, of the court clerks. The Commission stressed that there should be as much room for pluriformity in the court system as is compatible with impartiality.

To my mind, the Commission shows the possibilities of a creative reinterpretation of the tradition of the *Rechtsstaat* in a multicultural society. What is important is that it made explicit how it weighed the different values of that tradition, thus enabling an open discussion about the extent to which its interpretation could be seen as reflecting these values. It was by no means uncontroversial: many jurists, members of Parliament, and media commentators argued that allowing headscarves in the courtroom was an unacceptable departure from the visible impartiality of the judiciary. However, the fact that a genuine debate was possible is an indication of the viability of the Dutch rule of law tradition.

IDEAL-ORIENTED TRADITION

The key to a living tradition is the capacity of the tradition to change without losing its identity. Apart from the people involved in interpretation, there is a second source present in traditions that can prevent the fall of a tradition into decay or orthodoxy: the tradition's values. As I indicated above, many traditions can be characterized as traditions of common value, deriving an important part of their identity from the values contained in their practices. Such values can serve to promote the dynamic side of traditions if they are seen as ideals.

The main characteristic of ideals, and the essential one in this context, is that they are not completely realizable in practice (Rescher 1993, 130–31; Taekema 2003, 40–41). Ideals present possibilities for improvement that can be pursued in action, but that tend to elude full actualization. Ideals are open-ended: it is difficult to formulate them exactly in such a way that it is clear what the ideal demands and how this is best achieved. The ideal of legality, for instance, is a leading ideal of the legal system, the meaning of which changes along with the relations between law and society from autonomous to responsive law (Nonet and Selznick 1978, 107–8). Such an ideal is also complex: it encompasses different values that pull in different directions. In the case of legality understood as the reduction of arbitrariness, there is a tension between, on the one hand, clarity—having clear rules that are constant over time—and, on the other, consistency—the avoidance of contradictory rules.[15] This complexity contributes to unrealizability: there are always dimensions of the ideal that are overlooked and that will suddenly become apparent (again) in a new situation.

Because of their incomplete realization, ideals are well-suited to stimulate change. Whenever the lack of realization of the ideal is perceived, the ideal also indicates a direction for improvement by which the practice can be brought closer to the realization of the ideal. Because ideals are open-ended and complex, encompassing different dimensions of value, they continue to make development and change possible.

Often, orientation toward ideals is regarded as opposed to an orientation toward tradition. Oakeshott (1991, 40), for instance, criticized the morality of rationalism as "the morality of the self-conscious pursuit of moral ideals" because it treats ideals as part of a self-contained ideology. This is a view of ideals that can indeed be recognized in ideological social movements that advocate radical changes of society on the basis of ideals such as equality and freedom. Ideals are then seen as abstract ideas separate from social reality, while tradition is portrayed as containing old values that have become obsolete.

However, a more fruitful way of understanding ideals is to regard ideals as immanent in the practices of the tradition, which makes it much easier to connect ideals to traditions.[16] A view of ideals as immanent sees them as latent in social reality (Selznick 1961, 90): they are an implicit part of social interactions and experiences. More specifically, we can connect ideals to practices, understood as complex forms of socially established, cooperative human activity (MacIntyre 1984, 187). Ideals are an inherent element of practices because they partly determine what the point of a practice is and what we can achieve by it: practices are ideal-oriented. In this view, ideal and tradition can be closely linked because we can understand a tradition as a historically extended version of a practice in which ideals have long been implicitly present. If the ideals of a practice have been governing that practice over an extended period of time, keeping their guiding role despite, or thanks to, continued reformulation, the practice has acquired the history characteristic of a tradition.

Because ideals form a dimension of practices and traditions that points to the pursuit of value that is not present yet, i.e., their unrealizable character, they provide a reason for acting, for striving toward a better version of the practice in which the ideal is fulfilled. Ideals thus give practices a dynamic quality, and they are the main source for internal criticism. Ideals can be used to improve a practice or tradition from the inside because an appeal to the ideal entails an appeal to an unrealized aspect of the value inherent in the tradition. In the context of law: if justice is appealed to in criticism of a legal decision or legal rule, this is not an appeal to an external standard that is found without reference to existing law. The more accurate understanding of justice is to see it as one of the central ideals toward which the practices of law are oriented, but which they fail to realize completely (Taekema 2003, 191–94). New dimensions of justice appear when the problems of everyday practice are confronted, often appearing in the negative: when one realizes that straightforward application of an existing rule would lead to an unjust situation, the understanding of the ideal of justice is deepened in the effort made to find a just resolution to the problem.

A similar analysis can be made of the examples of El Moumni and the headscarf in court if we focus on the ideals present. First, freedom of religion can be fruitfully understood as a central ideal of the *Rechtsstaat* tradition, which played an important role in the Western European and Dutch development of liberal rights. Conceived as the freedom of conscience and the freedom to hold private religious ceremonies, it was recognized in the Union of Utrecht in 1579 (Van der Burg 1998, 229), the start of the move toward the Dutch Republic. Since then, the freedom of religion has been a constant in the Dutch catalogue of fundamental rights; in the present Constitution, it is article 6, just ahead of the freedom of expression. In the two cases, the freedom of religion has an uneasy relationship with the different, more recent ideal of equality, which has pride of place as the first article of the Constitution.

In the case of El Moumni, there is a conflict between the public dimension of the freedom of religion and the right to nondiscrimination of homosexuals, who are targeted by El Moumni's words. As I mentioned already, this is a problem of religious expression rather than religious conscience. The freedom of conscience may be said today to form the unproblematic core of the ideal of religious freedom, but that is only an aspect of the ideal. It is in the other aspects, such as expression, rituals, and moral claims, that religions clash with the liberal values of the rule of law. Or more specifically, they show the tensions between these liberal ideals: how far can freedom of expression be extended without endangering equal respect? Is the tolerance of minorities' religious and cultural practices more important or the protection of vulnerable groups such as women or homosexuals? In the case of discriminatory speech, the ideals involved fuel the dynamics of the debate because attempts to reconcile the ideals give rise to criticism: the El Moumni decision can be criticized for inadequate recognition of the importance of the freedom of expression in itself. The interaction between ideals and specific solutions in the practices of law thus stimulates the continuous (re)development of a tradition of legal and political thinking on the issue of fundamental rights.

In the case of the headscarf in court, the ideal of equality appears on the same side of the conflict as the freedom of religion: the woman involved claims recognition as a Muslim woman wearing a headscarf who is equal to other applicants to the job of court clerk. The conflict is about the fundamental right to equal treatment versus the impartiality of the court, in which both are ideals whose meaning is contested. The meaning of legal equality here takes on the dimension of equal recognition (Taylor 1995), raising the question of whether particular identities such as that of a Muslim woman can be recognized in the context of a neutral liberal state. From the other side, the impartiality ideal of the court is tested: can the semblance of partiality be avoided when outward appearances clearly show court officials' private identities? At the center of the conflict, the big question then arises whether it is possible to conceive of a pluralist state and to make legal institutions themselves pluralist. I can only raise and not answer this question in the scope of this chapter, but the connection between the question itself and such specific legal problems as that of the wearing of headscarves in court can serve to show that a debate about a specific problem can hardly avoid reassessing central ideals of the tradition of the *Rechtsstaat*.

Thus, the ideals present in traditions can ensure the tradition's relevance to new problems, stimulate its development, and contribute to a progressive interpretation. However, in the other direction, connecting traditions and ideals has important advantages too. Ideals have to be interpreted realistically (Witteveen 2004b, 132): an argument based on an ideal that strays too far from the tradition is easily recognized as utopian, involving too many changes with an insecure outcome. By asking whether acting upon the ideal can still be seen as an activity within the tradition, the ideal remains anchored in social reality.

CONCLUSION: CHALLENGING INTERPRETATIONS

Living traditions support the sense of community that enables individuals to feel they belong, but there are two dangers to guard against. The first is the danger of orthodoxy: of interpreting the tradition as the only right way of life enshrining the true values of life. The best way of avoiding orthodoxy and its standard reactions to legal and political problems is to make sure that the creative interpretation of individuals working within the tradition is appreciated. Having meaningful debates about such interpretations can ensure an open vitality of the tradition. The second danger is that of stagnation and decay: a tradition that no longer reacts to new problems, out of touch with society. Interpreting the tradition's values as ideals, as open-ended and not completely realizable directions for improvement, opens up the tradition's potential for change. In combination, recognition of the individual's contributions to interpreting ideals in the practices of law and politics can provide the kind of internal criticism of traditions that has a good chance of slowly but really moving them onward.

This argument on the interaction of individuals and traditions brings a specific perspective to the communitarian claim that the individual is inherently social. Not only are individuals profoundly shaped by their community's traditions, they are also capable of shaping their traditions and, by implication, their communities. This capability entails moral responsibility for one's membership of the larger whole.

NOTES

1. Many thanks to Wibren van der Burg for his valuable suggestions.

2. Of course, this is not a problem generated by the idea of a tradition: communities are fluid and notoriously difficult to define. Maybe an approach of community like Cotterrell's is the only feasible strategy: distinguishing types of community as ideal types which are not to be found in pure form in social reality (Cotterrell 2003, 259).

3. For striking examples of such inventions, see Hobsbawm and Ranger 1983.

4. I use the term *Rechtsstaat* instead of rule of law, because it is a broader concept including not only principles of legality and the separation of powers but also basic rights and (according to most authors) democracy; see Witteveen 2004b. The question whether rule of law and democracy are opposites or companions has been decided in favor of the latter characterization in the Dutch debate, in which reference is usually to the "democratic *Rechtsstaat*."

5. We could then maybe characterize a traditional community as a community in which the different kinds of tradition are felt to be integral parts of the community's culture, often because they are all seen as belonging to the common religion. Cotterrell (2003, 259) uses a looser definition: "traditional community is based on shared customs, traditions, experiences or history, or just living in the same environment or speaking the same language."

6. Problem solving should be understood broadly to include curiosity about theoretical problems: the physicist wanting to find out the behavior of elementary particles is involved in practical problem solving, working against the background of the natural sciences with their methods and values.

7. Of course, this is not the only current approach to genetic modification, but it is an important one in the political discourse. See, e.g., the Greenpeace article "Genetic Engineering: Too Good to Go Wrong?" archive.greenpeace.org/comms/97/geneng/getoogoo.html (accessed June 14, 2004).

8. www.rbgkew.org.uk/ksheets/palmhouse.html (accessed June 15, 2004).

9. Actually, the word he used was "marat," which is more correctly translated as "aberration" according to an Islam expert consulted by the court.

10. See the judgment of the Court of Appeal (Gerechtshof's-Gravenhage 18-11-2000, LJN nr. AF0667).

11. On the basis of the same article 137c Criminal Code, a candidate in local elections with a racist program was convicted for discriminatory insult (Hoge Raad 14-03-1989, *Nederlandse Jurisprudentie* 1990/29).

12. The leader of one of the Christian parties in Parliament, Leen van Dijcke, was also acquitted in a criminal trial concerning antihomosexual remarks (Hoge Raad 9-1-2001, *Nederlandse Jurisprudentie* 2001/203).

13. Decision 2001-53 Commissie Gelijke Behandeling (22-06-2001).

14. The Commission refers to Hoge Raad 15-2-1957, *Nederlandse Jurisprudentie* 1957/201.

15. I have used Fuller's principles of legality which can conflict (Fuller 1969, 45) to fill in the ideal of legality as formulated by Selznick, for whom conflict between constitutive values of the ideal is less of an issue (Selznick 1961, 94). See also Taekema 2003, 181–83.

16. For a more detailed account of an immanent concept of ideals, see Taekema 2003, 28–40; on the connection between ideal and practices, see ibid., 174–78.

REFERENCES

Berman, Harold. 1983. *Law and Revolution: The Formation of the Western Legal Tradition*. Cambridge, MA: Harvard University Press.

Burke, Edmund. 1955. *Reflections on the Revolution in France*. Ed. Thomas H. D Mahoney. New York: Liberal Arts Press.

Cotterrell, Roger. 2003. *The Politics of Jurisprudence: A Critical Introduction to Legal Philosophy*. 2nd ed. London: LexisNexis.

Dewey, John. 1960. Context and Thought. In *On Experience, Nature, and Freedom. Representative Selections*, ed. Richard Bernstein, 88–110. New York: Liberal Arts Press.

———. 1984. *The Quest for Certainty*. Vol. 4 of *The Later Works: 1925–1953*. Ed. Jo-Ann Boydston. Carbondale: Southern Illinois University Press.

Fuller, Lon L. 1969. *The Morality of Law*. 2nd ed. New Haven, CT: Yale University Press.

Hobsbawm, Eric, and Terence Ranger, eds. 1983. *The Invention of Tradition*. Cambridge: Cambridge University Press.

Hondius, E. H. 1982. Recodification of the Law in the Netherlands: The New Civil Code Experience. *Netherlands International Law Review* 29:348–66.

MacIntyre, Alasdair. 1984. *After Virtue*. 2nd ed. Notre Dame, IN: University of Notre Dame Press.

Muller, Jerry Z., ed. 1997. *Conservatism: An Anthology of Social and Political Thought from David Hume to the Present*. Princeton, NJ: Princeton University Press.

Nonet, Philippe, and Philip Selznick. 1978. *Law and Society in Transition: Toward Responsive Law*. New York: Harper and Row.

Oakeshott, Michael. 1991. *Rationalism in Politics and Other Essays*. Indianapolis, IN: Liberty Press.

Rescher, Nicholas. 1993. *The Validity of Values*. Vol. 2 of *A System of Pragmatic Idealism*. Princeton, NJ: Princeton University Press.

Selznick, Philip. 1961. Sociology and Natural Law. *Natural Law Forum* 6:84–108.

———. 1992. *The Moral Commonwealth: Social Theory and the Promise of Community*. Berkeley: University of California Press.

Taekema, Sanne. 2003. *The Concept of Ideals in Legal Theory*. The Hague: Kluwer Law International.

Taylor, Charles. 1995. The Politics of Recognition. In *Philosophical Arguments*, 225–56. Cambridge, MA: Harvard University Press.

Van der Burg, Wibren. 1998. Beliefs, Persons, and Practices: Beyond Tolerance. *Ethical Theory and Moral Practice* 1:227–54.

Witteveen, Willem. 2004a. Realist Idealism and the Rule of Law. In *The Importance of Ideals: Debating Their Relevance in Law, Morality, and Politics*, ed. Wibren van der Burg and Sanne Taekema, 117–45. Brussels: P.I.E.-Peter Lang.

———. 2004b. Inhabiting Legality: How the Dutch Keep Reconstructing their "Rechtsstaat." In *Understanding Dutch Law*, ed. Sanne Taekema, 75–101. Den Haag: Boom Juridische uitgevers.

Conclusion

Toward a "Communitarian" Concept of Law: The Case of the Questionable European Constitution

Willem Witteveen

COMMUNITARIAN LIBERALISM AND THE DOMAIN OF LAW

The debate over liberalism and communitarianism can be construed in oppositional and in cooperative terms. After an oppositional phase of the debate, there followed a more constructive one (Mulhall and Swift 1996). The idea of communitarian liberalism or liberal communitarianism emerged as an integrative enterprise seeking to gain from an exploration of the continuities, the differences, and the tensions between liberal and communitarian intellectual traditions. This book has brought this exploration from the arenas of political theory into the domain of law. The expectation was that this would be a meaningful thing to do, since contemporary law has been both deeply influenced by liberal assumptions and practices and can also be viewed as the expression of the values and principles of distinct communities. As Van Seters formulated it in the first chapter: "Much of contemporary jurisprudence . . . is rooted in the soil of liberalism. . . . At the same time, the legal tradition may be read as the historical reflection of community, of its various manifestations, its evolving values and aspirations, its recurring vicissitudes and pitfalls." Seeing that the domain of law is the meeting ground for both liberal and communitarian positions, Van Seters raises the following very broad question: "To the extent that communitarianism can be understood as an effort to reconstruct liberalism . . . what good is to come of this for legal theory and legal practice?"

In this chapter we will return to this question. What do the authors of this book have to say about the consequences for our understanding of law (in both its theoretical expressions and its practical manifestations) from lines of reasoning taking communitarian liberalism seriously? The consequences are many and varied. The authors in this book clearly do not speak from one theoretically unified position and they do not have the same views on the relationship between community and law. It is not even apparent that they have a shared understanding of a concept of law that is congenial to the communitarian–liberal debate. It would therefore not be profitable to try to squeeze their diverse views of law and community into something resembling a definition. Rather, let us see what prospects the authors see for future work on community and law, and what they take law to be in this connection.

PROSPECTS AND REMINDERS

Law and Community in Socio-Legal Studies

Of all the authors in the book, Selznick is perhaps most outspoken in his considerations on the prospects for law of a turn toward communitarian liberalism. His jurisprudence of communitarian liberalism promises both better politics and better law. In politics, a focus on communitarian liberalism "extends and enriches liberal ideas in that it seeks *effective* freedom, *substantive* rationality, and *social* justice," Selznick claims programmatically. In the domain of law, communitarian liberalism means a resistance to the ontological separations advocated by positivism (of law and morality, law and history, law and politics, law and society). Law will draw form and substance from the experience of community, Selznick believes, seeking a balance between rights, responsibilities, and values. In conclusion, Selznick envisages the emergence of responsive law. The whole system of legal norms and institutions, including judicial interpretation and administrative regulation as well as explicit legislation, should be responsive to changing circumstances and to the needs of the community.

Like Selznick, Cotterrell is also strongly in favor of turning toward community in law and jurisprudence. Legal sociology should come to terms with the heritage of Ehrlich's idea of "living law," locating "law's doctrinal sources, regulatory authority, and normative essence in communal life, understood in some way as a realm of shared moral understandings or social interaction, and not primarily (if at all) in the purely political authority and coercive power of the state." Also like Selznick, who stresses that communitarianism is not necessarily conservatism and can serve the progressive elimination of arbitrariness from social life, Cotterrell thinks a drift into conservatism must be avoided. He emphasizes liberal values such as the open and voluntary nature of community ties, the mutuality of interactions rather than the fixation of communal values, and a critical awareness of power and its links to law.

If we call the kind of approach to communitarian liberalism exhibited by Selznick and Cotterrell the socio-legal one, Peters can also be included here.

But his focus is different in being thoroughly comparativist; for Peters studying the role of law in a non-Western society (in his case Japanese society) is needed to better understand the specifically Western nature of law and community. Law, for him, is "a way of thinking and speaking about the reality in which we were raised; a reality that commits us to ideals of rationality, reasonableness, and individual freedom, which we did not invent ourselves." The liberal nature of our community, conceived in legal terms, can be better understood by becoming aware of other cultural possibilities. While in the Western world law has become a language for imagining and structuring communal life, in Japan law and society are more distanced and issues of social order are not necessarily addressed through law. This raises serious questions about the proliferation of rights in Western legal culture and about the "ever-increasing dependence on formal, legal, and bureaucratic structuring, without thereby establishing a genuine social order."

Communitarianism in the European Arena

After these chapters, which can be loosely labeled as socio-legal and conceptual studies into the relations between law and community, we next come to a second group of chapters in which the express focus is on political, economic, and social problems in the context of the European Union. The question of a communitarian understanding of law and society is present at most in the background. This does not mean the authors have nothing of interest to say about law and community. Indirect insights, gained as a byproduct of efforts directed at another target, can be very valuable. Moreover, these authors engage with political, economic, and social matters in an awareness that all of these concerns in some way and at some moment involve legal practices, such as legislation, regulation, administration, and conflict resolution, and that this legal dimension in its turn influences the set of available responses to political, economic, and social problems.

De Beus argues that the European Union can only become a political community through the emergence of a public sphere in its unique system of mixed government; this public sphere will have to be constituted by the democratic contests between political parties operating across the boundaries of the member states. De Beus rejects Scharpf's idea of multilevel governance as too technocratic and finds Habermassian constitutionalism on the other hand too high-strung. Transboundary party politics should be the main driving force for European integration, not bureaucracy or constitution making. This position implies the rejection of some traditional notions of public law (positivist lawmaking through regulation vis-à-vis natural-law-inspired forms of constitutional deliberation) and the acceptance of another one, visible only in its contours. Political parties should adhere to certain principles in their endeavors to create a European public sphere: principles of political fairness (such as peacefulness, publicity, leadership, and responsibility) and principles of political strategy (consistency in policies within and across national boundaries). These principles for political action mentioned by De Beus, if transposed to the field of legal theory, could translate into legal concepts of interactionist lawmaking, such as those advocated by Dewey, Fuller, and the American legal realists, in which norms of fairness for interactive lawmaking are derived from principled notions such as the ones mentioned here (especially transparency and reciprocity).[1]

For Hemerijck, the crucial issue is how Europe can achieve effective social values and social policies through legal methods that are characterized as "legal pluralism, horizontal EU social dialogue, and 'soft-law' processes of open coordination." The emphasis in this approach (which seems to be situated in the multilevel-governance camp) is thus more explicitly on interactionist lawmaking. Joint problem solving by the member states requires various forms of legal pluralism, Hemerijck argues, such as the social dialogue following on the Maastricht Treaty, the European Employment Strategy, and the coordination and benchmarking strategy of the Open Method of Coordination (OMC). This legal pluralism, recognized as official forms of European governance, has been instrumental in making progress toward a social Europe but remains "critically dependent on the willingness of national policymakers to learn from each other and voluntarily coordinate and adapt their policies rather than to sabotage the process by freeriding." Processes of open coordination are vulnerable because of their openness and ambiguity to disruptions and so need strong political support. Therefore, Hemerijck advocates the use of soft law (law not limited to hard and fast rules and commands but shaping itself through deliberation, consultation, negotiation, and coordination and using a wide variety of linguistic forms) but recognizes its dependence on the kinds of established authority relations that are derived from more positivist notions of law and sovereignty. There is an ambiguity here as to the projected concept of law.

In De Beer's liberal critique of communitarian economics, issues of understanding law in society move much further to the background, while yet not being entirely irrelevant to his argument. In discussing communitarianism as a normative theory, De Beer takes issue with those "perfectionist" communitarians who take the common good to be more than the aggregation of all individual interests (but instead posit a common culture or a shared tradition). Who is to decide what the preferable conception of the good life should be, De Beer asks, before concluding that minority elites or majority rule will impose a decision on the remaining citizens. At most an overlapping consensus between reasonable conceptions of the good can be reached, but this brings communitarianism back to the liberalism of John Rawls. This whole discussion assumes the availability of authoritative and effective legal arrangements to implement the overlapping consensus in the form of legal rights and duties, while remaining silent as to the nature of the law needed to fulfill these community-shaping functions. While most economic liberals will have an affinity to legal positivism and instrumentalism, viewing the law as a more or less neutral instrument for political decisions, it is conceivable that Selznick's communitarian notion of responsive law would be used to establish exactly where the boundaries of the overlapping consensus model are to be drawn, reckoning with the expressed views and needs of the population. But this is a mere speculation, since the kind of argument De Beer (like many economists) employs simply gives no indication of a preference either way.

The Social Values of Law

The third group of chapters in this book concerns values and ideals (in ethics, in social relations, in traditions and practices). Conceptions of law and community are clearly relevant to these concerns, and the authors accordingly address these more directly than the authors of the second group of chapters. Comparative work need not only concern whole societies and cultures, it can also be done within a common culture by differentiating between different strands of liberal and communitarian perspectives that are all expressions of the culture's value system. Brugger, going deeply into the discourse relating to the prohibition or protection of aggressive speech (this ancient test case of liberalism), in the end distinguishes three different versions of communitarianism: substantive, conservative communitarianism; liberal communitarianism; and egalitarian-universalistic communitarianism. They differ on a number of dimensions, such as their conceptions of freedom and of morality and their views on the justification and compliance of moral norms. When it comes to communitarian conceptions of law, Brugger sees clear differences. Whereas the conservative tendency favors community over justice and gives priority to collective goals over individual rights, liberal communitarians seek a balancing out between community values and individual justice and also between collective goals and individual rights. The egalitarian-universalistic communitarians accord priority to universal principles of justice over the convictions of particular communities and tend to award priority to individual rights over collectively defined goals.

Communitarian liberalism seeks a balance between rights and duties, between freedom and responsibility, between an ethics of duty and an ethics of care. Pessers adds to these familiar dualisms her own contrast between the morality of mutuality and the morality of reciprocity, which she then explicitly connects to the domain of law: the "law of justice" as the prerequisite for the "law of love." Mutuality is the relationship between strangers who enter into a transaction and make an equal exchange. This is only possible thanks to the establishment of a common legal order ("the law as the agency which can mediate between strangers"). This mutuality between strangers (the law of justice) can then develop into relationships of reciprocity following the social logic of seeing oneself in the other and of the recognition of the other through the recurring cycle of giving, receiving, and returning of words, services, presents, care, and goods (the law of love). As a result of this cyclical process, the commonality of the legal order changes its quality as well, coming to encompass the solidarity arrangements of the welfare state. Pessers contrasts this positive scenario with a negative one, leading to the loss of solidarity and relationships of reciprocity. She sees the trend to impose contractual relations, business organization models, and market forces on fields traditionally defined by the morality of reciprocity (a morality of indeterminate duties) as the cause of a perversion of the legal order by which it comes to be separated from the social order and to dominate it, while mutuality is raised at the expense of reciprocity. The balance of rights and duties is disturbed. In fact, the nature of law changes as the nature of the community changes. "A legal order always functions—and can only function—within a social order."

In Taekema's chapter, the community of law is characterized in terms of its traditions and practices, and of the prospect of a pragmatist progression (Dewey) toward the ideals embedded in them. Legal traditions are traditions of common value that are not necessarily conservative in nature; through the reinterpretations of interacting individuals the tradition can be reformed from within, and when the problematic situation can thus be better handled, we can speak of pragmatist progression. "The key to a living tradition is the capacity of the tradition to change without losing its identity," Taekema argues, showing that apart from individuals interacting to find in a pragmatic way new solutions for problems the "old" understanding of the tradition cannot manage, it is the dynamic articulation of ideals related to the practices of the tradition that promotes dynamic change without loss of identity (an example being the transformations in the practices and ideals of the rule of law). "Because of their incomplete realization, ideals are well-suited to stimulate change. Whenever the lack of realization of the ideal is perceived, the ideal also indicates a direction for improvement by which the practice can be brought closer to the realization of the ideal."

A Plethora of Understandings

As this brief tour d'horizon makes clear, there is a wide variety of understanding of law and community to be found in the chapters of this book. It would, indeed, be a mistaken hermeneutical strategy to try to squeeze them all into the basket of one or other particular "communitarian" concept of law. Is not the diversity in these understandings and interpretations of law itself an indication of the present predicament of law-and-community studies?

Does it not point at the fractured nature of the liberal–communitarian debate? Apparently the authors are engaging in specialized dialogues involving a wide variety of communities of researchers and practitioners. They make use of theories and research methods, coming from a broad range of disciplines studying social life. All of these disciplines tend to have somewhat different concepts of law, even if implicitly so. It would be a very communitarian move to make if in this predicament we could postulate a concept of law that all discourses can subscribe to. But this might be comparable to the vision of the Tower of Babel, to the pursuit of the perfect language understandable by all speakers. And notice the different strategies employed in the three groups of chapters of the book. While the socio-legal authors are indeed looking for a communitarian concept of law (Selznick's responsive law, Cotterrell's living law), the authors on political, economic, and social problems have less need of a unified concept of law and of legal practice, and we can only tentatively infer the kind of understanding of law they have in mind. Perhaps the need for a communitarian concept of law is not so great for these authors? Then again, the authors dedicating themselves to questions of value do articulate visions of the communitarian nature of law, but they tend to put different emphases than the socio-legal authors, conceptualizing law as an ongoing conversation or as a moral bonding or as a tradition of common value. This suggests their kinds of debates also have different conceptual needs.

And yet, if there is no straightforward answer to the question of what a communitarian concept of law entails, there is a clear tendency away from the most common concept of law, which is a positivist concept of law limiting law to rules and commands, relating it to the authorized state agencies, and separating the domain of law from all other value-laden domains such as morality, politics, history, and society. The avoidance of positivism is a step into the direction of another concept of law altogether. Does this have to be its alleged counterpart, natural law, with its emphasis on high ideals that are always imperfectly realized in rules and practices? Or is there still another direction in which the search can move? Judging by the chapters, the new communitarian concept of law must satisfy a number of requirements:

- include nonstate law;
- address a wide variety of sources of law;
- cover many forms of commitment to the law of the community;
- be open to the elaboration of values or ideals in ongoing practices;
- provide normative orientation to participants.

All of these requirements raise new questions, such as: How to identify "nonstate law" in a positive manner? Which other sources of argumentation besides rules and commands to include and which to exclude? What socially recognized forms does commitment to the law take (and what, exactly, is a practice of law)? How do ideals relate to other sources of law, such as rules or principles? If there is a shared internal aspect of law, how much scope for individual reservations and dissents must this offer to count as both a communal and a liberal practice? What a welter of questions! It is unrealistic to expect a broad consensus on this range of issues. Clearly, a communitarian concept of law does not automatically arise by enlarging the scope of the positivist concept of law to embrace all of the requirements listed, since these are too open-ended; new limits must be drawn. But how?

THREE ELEMENTARY MODELS

One way to proceed is by answering this question: What elementary notions of law are already prevalent in the family of legal cultures of the Western world? If we for a moment forget about the theoretical sophistication of the science of jurisprudence, which has managed to complicate matters in the many centuries it has pondered the nature of the concept of law, what do we find? It is my contention that on the basis of a cultural analysis of law, there is not one but a limited number of elementary notions of law present in any legal culture.[2] We can take these notions up as elementary models that, explicated as models, may be used as machines generating arguments about law. By switching in a perspectivist way between some such models, we can compare different lines of argumentation on a given topic requiring to be approached with some kind of concept of law in mind.[3]

To keep this dialogical procedure manageable, we will postulate just three of these models of law: a positivist one, a natural-law model, and an interactionist understanding of law (see also Witteveen 2001, 45–70). The perspectivist changes afforded by these three elementary models already allow for a network of arguments and counterarguments that can be of use in a rhetorical procedure for the formation of judgment. Since judgment always requires a case in which it can be exercised, we will also have to provide such a case for application of the models. This will be the case of the making of a Constitution for the European Union.

According to the simple model of *positivism*, law consists of the collection or system of rules that have been called into being by the competent lawmaking authorities. Law is seen to be contained in authoritative texts: in treaties, constitutions, statutes, regulations, judicial opinions, contracts; in short, in documents that are binding on some audience they rightfully address. By thus limiting its sources, the positivist model effects a separation of spheres: the legal domain is an entity in itself, demarcated from other "spheres," such as morality, religion, politics, economics, or social life. Positivism opens a procedural window on the law; it highlights the activities of jurists and officeholders in shaping, adapting, and applying law, in the service of the community at large. The law itself is conceived in instrumental terms; it is seen as the expression of individual and collective intentions to achieve certain aims, and its documentary nature is supposed to be instrumental in bringing these aims about. All in all, in its bare essentials, this is a model of law readily recognizable in all of the really existing legal cultures of the Western world.

The simple model of *natural law*, on the other hand, is neither procedural nor instrumentalist, and it rejects emphatically the separation between law and morals. The model conceives of the rules of law as imperfectly realized interpretations of universal ideals and principles of justice. Rational human beings everywhere and at all times can by critical reasoning discover the demands of justice, especially by confronting injustice. Over and above the collection of rules that positivism declares to be all the law there is, in the model of natural law is postulated a system of ideal law, which allows for critical comparisons. This view of law is broader than the textual view of law. The ideal rules are not always enacted in binding legal documents but are unwritten ("written in the hearts of men," writes Cicero). The force of natural law precepts does not derive from their recognition by competent authorities at all but from their value and validity for all human beings that live together under a system of law. Like the model of positivism, traces of natural law can be found in all Western legal systems, maybe not as a dominant concept of law but at least in the background to formalist and instrumentalist concerns, as counterpart to the positivist world view.

It is often thought that positivism and natural law, in presenting such opposing pictures of law, exhaust the possibilities for a meaningful conceptualization of law. But in fact there is a third culturally based model of law which does not occupy some middle ground but articulates an entirely different understanding of what characterizes the enterprise of law. The focus of this third model is on the interactions between people that become legally binding on them. For *interactionism*, law is a human activity. Law is always constructed, effectuated, and disbanded by the actions of people in social settings. Law is a particular way of organizing human groups; it can be defined as the continuous generation and adaptation of interactional expectancies. The interactionist model does not focus on authoritative documents alone, as does positivism, and it does not posit an ideal world of rational and universalist norms, as does natural law. It considers all of these as aspects of interaction. The rules of law are in this view certainly important, as are principles of justice. Their importance derives from human activities, from what people do to each other. Not the law in books, but the law in action is what counts here. Rather than separating law from other domains, interactionism stresses both the boundaries and their possible transgressions. Instead of making universal comparisons between ideals and principles on the one hand and rules and practices on the other, the interactionist model stresses the cultural construction of ideals and principles and relates these to rules and practices. While the third model is usually not the dominant one in official legal ideologies, it is important in all Western legal systems at all points where local knowledge, power relationships, and gradual evolutionary change are at issue.

The three models sketched here in such bare outlines are not intended as mature theories of law. They are precisely models, deliberately simplified accounts of conceptions that are in practice often vaguely defined. Their strength is to clearly bring out a limited but valuable perspective on law and society: the perspective of rule making and rule following versus the perspective of imperfect but perfectable justice versus the perspective of ongoing interaction in law's practices. But the three models have corresponding weaknesses. The textualism, proceduralism, and instrumentalism of positivism are drawbacks when implementation, content, and resistance to change are the issues. The critical potential of natural law may be offset by the undecidability of presumably rational debates about what the universal principles mean in a controversial problem. The empirical flexibility and wide scope of normativity in interactionism can be criticized as a lack of firm grip on reality and as ethical relativism. There are two sides to every aspect of each model of law.

This is why debates between adherents of these three positions are interminable. Neither side can offer arguments that are absolutely compelling when they are interpreted from within the perspective of their opponents. But in this inconclusiveness lies a greater strength of the simple models of law. When debates between the models in fact take place—something that does not demand great theoretical sophistication but can occur during the course of moderately hard law cases—important topics of the legal culture are recirculated. The models perform as the old rhetorical idea of *inventio*, as a machine for the generation of arguments on opposing sides of a topic. In the process, considerable refinement of the theories is a possibility, but, interestingly, this sophistication does not do away with the simple versions. Precisely the elementary models show their practical usefulness in legal reasoning, since they generate plausible lines of argument that must be addressed in the formation of considered judgments. Contradictions and tensions between these lines of argumentation are an advantage for a rhetorical process of judgment formation rather than a drawback.

THE THREE MODELS AND THE CONSTITUTION OF THE EUROPEAN UNION

In order to show the merits of this perspectivist approach to concepts of law that are part and parcel of community life, a case study is needed. For this we turn to the question of a Constitution for the European Union. After many changes in the treaties constituting the institutional structure of the European Union (Maastricht, Amsterdam), it was widely felt that the resulting governmental structures were too complicated to work properly (especially the unanimity requirement was an obstacle for efficient governance) and that the legal infrastructure of the legal and political organs of the Union had become too complex to be understood by the citizens of the member states (thus hampering the democratization and the transparency of the European polity). It was time for a new start in the form of a Constitution for Europe. At the same time, the movement toward expansion of the European Union, if pursued on the basis of the old institutional logic of the European institutions, would lead to serious disruptions of the processes of governance and would threaten to undermine the vitality of the European Union. This contributed to a sense of urgency regarding such a Constitution. While these concerns in most member states were felt to be good reasons for establishing some kind of Constitution, there was no clear idea either of what the Constitution for Europe should contain or of the way in which it should be established as not only a legal document (another treaty) but also the living law of the Union. The three models can now be used to generate some obvious lines of argument relevant to these concerns.

What should a Constitution for Europe be about? The positivist answer is clear-cut: a constitution is a binding document creating a clear structure of authorities and competencies for a legal community; it is about democratic self-governance of the constituting units through their representative agencies and on the basis of rules and regulations; and it should result in legal certainty as to the command structure accepted as the backbone of the European Union. Surely, the Union is not identifiable as belonging to a class of legal systems, it is sui generis, and so it will develop further and require adaptations of its institutional structure. In a positivist model, it is first of all important to use the constitution as a document providing a formal structure that is transparent and authoritative; all subsequent changes should be included through the proper amendment procedures that are to be part of any constitution. Once the constitution is in place, positivism advises against continual adaptations through ongoing negotiations and against using methods of soft law (soft law, on a positivist account, isn't law at all). Positivism thus emphasizes proceduralism and instrumentalism, and it advocates legal certainty and transparency as constitutional values. It is compatible with the idea of multilevel governance, but only if the structure of competencies regulating multilevel governance is clearly articulated and is not subject to permanent renegotiations. As to the second question—how to establish a Constitution for Europe as both a legal document and as living law—the positivist model focuses exclusively on its first part, framing a constitution in a strictly legal sense as only a legal document of a certain kind and leaving the issue of its practical working or its ideal content to other spheres of discourse.

From the perspective of natural law, the European Constitution must be judged on whether it contributes to the articulation of the right kind of normative and legal order for Europe and whether the ideals it expresses are amenable to realization. The constitution should offer an institutional structure that expresses the ideals of democracy and the rule of law, and it must in this regard be faithful to various traditions that have developed in its member states but take these only as the starting point for a debate about a truly European democracy and a veritable European rule of law, improving upon their contributing traditions and coming close to those kinds of democracy and rule of law that all rational human beings can assent to. The model of natural law also lays great stress on the inclusion of a catalogue of human rights, and it raises the issue of whether it would not be best to see these as rights pertaining not only to the citizens of the European nations but to all people. As this example shows, the high aspirations of the model can be put to critical use; no actual constitutional proposal is likely to accommodate all of them. The constitution must be more than a binding legal document. The natural law model is interested in the question of how its lofty ideals and rational procedures can become a reality, in how constitutional norms can become living law. Apart from all kinds of practical obstacles and interfering power relationships, which are acknowledged but do not form part of the explicit concern of the model, it is seen as important that all constitutional provisions can be defended on the basis of rational considerations all people can adhere to; this will ensure their acceptance by rational participants in the social practices under its normative reach.

According to the model of interactionism, a constitutional document for Europe can be useful as a way of giving expression to mutual interactional expectancies in the processes of governance of the European Union. The crucial question is then how adequate these interactional expectancies are captured in the document. Is the European Union for instance rightly moving away from consensus decisions toward majoritarian decisions? Does this move reflect merely a practical compromise between political leaders, or does it rest on a broader normative consensus in the member states? Interactionism will be wary of placing too much confidence in the language of the constitution, since its provisions will after all be a fixation of constitutional meanings at a certain moment in time and cannot reflect changes in the development of European constitutional norms, especially not since the European Union is only just emerging as a meaningful political and legal system. Because it values social dynamism, the interactionist model does not focus exclusively on binding documents such as the constitution, but favors a wide range of sources of constitutional norms and has an open eye to the changes taking place in a broadly conceived constitutional conversation of Europe. While agreeing with positivism that the constitution should attempt to provide for authoritative and practical institutional arrangements and with natural law that it should express community values relating to democracy, the rule of law, and human rights, interactionism is neither procedural and instrumentalist nor universalist and rationalist in its expectations of these tasks. What matters most is how provisional constitutional documents (such as the constitution itself but also all subsequent treaties) gradually change to reflect better the constitutional norms of ever-larger parts of the European Community. In taking the ideal of living law seriously, the interactionist model advocates a multiplicity of normative sources, it is in favor of soft law and of horizontal coordination methods, and it generally claims that the constitutional structure must not be dictated from above by a small elite but must be seen in a bottom-up perspective, as expressing the emerging convictions European citizens discover through public debate.

Already in these brief elaborations of the three models and their application to the debates about the European Constitution, some of the topical effects of the models can be discerned. Each model affords a view of the Constitution that is valuable in its own terms. It raises relevant questions that should be part of a critical debate of the subject. By putting questions and providing answers according to the limited frames implied by the models, a series of different considerations becomes available. How to integrate them in a considered judgment? The answers do not converge since the starting points of the models are so different. The perspectivist use of the three models leads to separate lines of argumentation that are on many points incompatible, and it clearly shows contradictions and tensions between the elementary notions of law the models articulate. But this is not a drawback but an advantage, since it prevents too early closure of processes of opinion formation and stimulates the search for chains of arguments at a higher level of inclusiveness.

THEORETICAL ELABORATIONS FROM THE RHETORICAL TRADITION

The three simple models sketched above have the advantage of generating lines of argumentation that can then be used in a dialogical and perspectivist way to provide reasoned judgments. It is surprising how many interesting questions and critical assessments follow from such simple models. But there is a limit to what such elementary models of law and community can do. They offer simplified pictures of their subject matter and are lacking in theoretical sophistication. It seems attractive to pursue empirically richer and intellectually more stimulating approaches. After all, legal, social, and political traditions of thought offer a wide array of theories that may be relevant for issues of law and community. Theoretical elaboration also has its drawbacks, however. By moving away from the elementary assumptions about law and community found in a culture, these theories will tend to be more controversial and perhaps, because of this controversiality, will be less effective in providing a "communitarian" (and so a shared) concept of law. And how to choose from among a wide array of theories in different domains of the social sciences? We can perhaps best limit the risks of controversiality by concentrating on those approaches that are consonant with the dialogical and perspectivist method used in relation to the simple models. This refers us to the rhetorical tradition that in fact lies at the basis of the whole idea of perspectivist argumentation through *inventio*.[4]

What is meant by "the rhetorical tradition" (Witteveen 1988, 23–49)? The art of rhetoric was developed in Athens and perfected in Rome. Beginning from the technical arts of persuasion of the sophists that came under philosophical attack by Plato, developed into practical arts of argumentation by Aristotle and Isocrates, revitalized and extended by the Roman rhetoricians (Cicero, Quintilian), the art of rhetoric established itself as a vital force in Western culture (Kennedy 1980). Through the ages, the classical writings of the art of rhetoric have been read and interpreted, and many new arts of persuasion were written, for both general and specific purposes (embracing for instance legal practices of advocacy and judging). Rhetoric has all this time not only been a practical art, it was also a body of theoretical considerations fed from culturally embedded practices of speaking and writing for an audience. Its conceptualizations of the elements of persuasive speech and writing came to be the general cultural categories of communication (think of the whole set of figures of speech). Its more specific advice on strategies of persuasion has been translated into practical maxims for ethics, politics, and law. Not surprisingly, there are to this day theoretical approaches to law and community that have their roots in the rhetorical tradition.

The perspectivist method involving simple models that are confronted with each other in a public debate between protagonists or in an internal dialogue of the theorists is a direct offshoot of the rhetorical method for arriving at a persuasive argument and of the traditional structure of the rhetorical situation (i.e., the typical situations within which practical eloquence can flourish). Rhetorical method in the classical authors progressed through various stages: the search for all possible relevant arguments (called *inventio*), the structuring of these arguments so as to present a partial plea but reckoning with what is to be expected from the adversary (*dispositio*), the craft of finding the proper stylistic expression of the argument (*elocutio*), the art of commemorating the argument in such a way as to be able to present and to improvise on it (*memoria*), and finally the art of oral presentation (*actio*). These five stages of the rhetorical process are anchored in the method of *inventio*, which recommends the bringing together of as many realistic or imagined lines of argumentation that can be relevant for the issue at stake in the debate. It works by choosing the point of view of your own side and then switching to the point of view of the opposing side, and back again. In perspectivism as applied to models of law, this traditional division of intellectual labor has been extended somewhat to add a third point of view, interacting with the other two.

The rhetorical situation of the legal process is traditionally structured in a way that reflects the dynamics of the rhetorical method. Two protagonists typically confront each other before an impartial judge. While both advocates are free to use all available rhetorical methods to make their case as strong as can be and in the process may follow all kinds of strategies of persuasion, the judge compares the arguments from both sides and plays the one advocate out against the other, thus maximizing the chance of coming to a qualitatively acceptable judgment as to what happened and as to the applicability of the law in the dispute. The dynamics of the rhetorical situation stimulates a kind of theoretical reflection on its potentialities finding expression in a series of handbooks on the topics for debate, both general and specific ones, organized in a dialectical way to provide arguments for and against a thesis; this is called a *Topica*. The rhetorical situation is always geared to a controversy; the perspectivist method is imitating this in its application to a controversial issue (such as the questions concerning the Constitution for Europe).

In the following sections, we will look at three theoretical approaches of law and community that can be related to the rhetorical tradition: James Boyd White's vision of law as a culture of argument and of translation as a model for legal practice; Giambattista Vico's idea of *sensus communis* and its consequences for the concept of law; and Philip Pettit's republican notion of freedom as nondomination and all this entails for citizenship and legislative strategy. In each instance, we will also return to the case of the Constitution for Europe, asking what the theory helps us bring more sharply into focus. In this way, a *Topica* for constitution making is shown to be a possibility.

JUSTICE AS TRANSLATION

White, one of the originators of the Law-and-Literature movement, has a distinctly communitarian concept of law. To him, law is both a social practice and a culture of argument. Indeed: "The law is at once a social activity—a way of acting with others—and a cultural activity, a way of acting with a certain set of materials found in the culture. It is always communal, both in the sense that it always takes place in a social context, and in the sense that it is always constitutive of the community by which it works. The law is an art of persuasion that creates the objects of its persuasion, for it constitutes both the community and the culture it commends" (White 1985, 35). When lawyers argue a hard case, when judges interpret a constitution, when legislators debate a new law, and in countless other instances of engaging in the legal arts of persuasion, White speaks of a "constitutive rhetoric," because through all these social activities the law as a culture of argument is built and rebuilt.

This raises the question of how to understand the nature of the communicative processes involved in this cultural and communal lawmaking. At this point, White takes issue with those (also situated within the field of the rhetorical tradition) who conceive of communication as a flow of information from a source to a destination and of the message as a vehicle delivering its content at the end of the line. This is a false picture of communication. The expression is rather "a gesture, the meaning of which is indissolubly tied to its immediate and unique context: to its language and culture, to the social relations out of which it emerges and upon which it acts, to the prior texts that its author and audience use to establish and understand its terms, to its location in a particular place in the physical world, and so on" (White 1990, 236). The responses to such gestures are, still according to White, to be understood on the model of translations. An act of translation can never be a mere replication of the original expression or a straightforward conveying of the original "message." Rather, it is indeed a kind of gesture in acknowledgment of the limits of communication, seeking to respond adequately to the expression under translation. When translations succeed, as they sometimes do, they are not so much literal renditions or faithful renderings as appropriate responses (in this stress on appropriateness we meet again with the rhetorical concept of *decorum*, developed under the traditional rubric of stylistics or *elocutio*). It is White's contention that the model of translation is a suitable one for understanding all those speech acts and persuasive activities the people of the law engage in when they perform the many and varied tasks of the law as a culture of argument.

The acts of translation at the back of the rhetorical activities of jurists give expression to an ethical attitude appropriate to the domain of law. The good translator attempts to be herself "in relation to an always imperfectly known and imperfectly knowable other who is entitled to a respect equal to her own" (White 1990, 258). Since the text dealt with has no fixed meaning and there is always an untranslatable element in it, the gestures in response to the text must be ethically motivated reconstructive efforts. In this way, the discourse of the law can perform a mediating function between other discourses and remain at the same time reflectively aware of the power exercised by the discourse of law in its social context (ibid., 261–62). (A good translator, we can infer from this, does not only have respect for the other as author and for the text under translation but is also aware of the power relationships involved in the act of translation itself and adopts an attitude of service instead of one of domination.)

Surely, White's theory of justice as translation is both more sophisticated and more controversial than the three elementary models of law. We are now in a position to ask what justice as translation can add to the lines of argumentation already posited for the emerging discourse on the European Constitution. The theme of communication as translation, drawing attention to the inherent difficulties in reaching an understanding between interacting persons and the ethical aspects of dealing with these difficulties, is highly relevant for the design of an institutional structure for the European Union. European institutions at all levels of governance have to grapple with the fact that there are now twenty-five member states and that in these member states over forty different languages are spoken. All meetings, whether open or closed to the public, have to employ translators to facilitate communication between the participants from different national and cultural backgrounds. Misunderstandings are to be expected on a massive scale; the problem of communication is even institutionalized in the very decisional structures of the Union where the preference for unanimity in decision making protects minority languages as well as minority positions.

There is a fascinating gap between the law in the books and the law in action here. Officially, all languages are equal, and the European Commission furthers also the protection of minority languages within national cultures. But because translation into all available languages would be an enormous obstacle to effective and speedy decision making, in practice there is one dominant language (English), and there is also an important position for French in the diplomatic circuits. All citizens and representatives and officials for whom English is not their first language are at a disadvantage in the day-to-day interactions making up the practices of community decision making. While this is a strong incentive for all influence-seeking actors to improve upon their knowledge of English, it widens the gap between the official decision-circuits, productive of enormous amounts of regulations, and the ordinary citizens of the member states who, simply put, perceive the European Union as a distant and alien bureaucracy and who do not consider themselves to be citizens of Europe.

There is no easy way out of the language problem. While the institutional structure for effective governance is helped by making English the only official language of the European Union (a decision that will never be accepted by a number of member states, notably France), the legitimacy of the European Union would be strengthened by opening up more of its business to speakers of a very large variety of languages (which would of course make effective decision making an impossibility). Precisely in this predicament, well described by De Swaan (2002), it is fruitful to turn to the idea of justice as translation for its honest acknowledgment of the predicament and for the ethical attitude recommended by the model of translation. What then would be needed is a vocabulary of responsive "gestures"; an ensemble of strategies for dealing with serious cases of miscommunication within the institutional structures themselves but especially between the European institutions and the citizens. Not only is it at the moment unclear what such a "vocabulary of gestures" would consist of, since the European institutions do not really attempt to communicate with the citizens in a serious way, it is also not clear what powerful actors would be willing to press for steps in this direction. Perhaps, De Beus's proposal for institutional change through political parties could make a difference because presumably effective European political parties would have to mediate between many languages and would in the first place have to speak the language of their supporters in order to be legitimate and effective. The idea of justice as translation can best be seen as a new frame for the institutional politics of Europe, one that serves to raise issues and suggest directions for answers. In this, it is heir to the topical approach of the rhetorical tradition that also draws attention to important structural issues and provides useful general considerations without fully determining the process of judgment relating to actual problems.

Another element of White's approach, his idea of law as a culture of argument, highlights the problem of subsidiarity under the European Constitution. The idea of the subsidiarity principle is that the European institutions are competent to act in those areas of policy not exclusively reserved to them, if and only if the collective purposes of a particular policy area cannot sufficiently be achieved by the member states on their central, regional, or local levels of decision making. The idea is one of decentralization and local autonomy whenever feasible. The European institutions should especially act in those areas where the scope of the policy or its effects surpass the capabilities of lower-level authorities. This subsidiarity principle is hard to reconcile with the practical dynamics of institutionalization, which has led to very large areas of policy being centralized, while it is not evident that national, regional, or local levels could not deal with the problem adequately. Because of this tension between the ideal and practical realities, subsidiarity deserves a place in the Constitution where it will be one of the central topics in debates over the further development of the European Union. What the idea of law as a culture of argument reminds us of is, in this respect, that proper demarcations of the reach of the subsidiarity principle as a counterforce against bureaucratic centralization must be supported by the factual existence of cultures of argument (where people actually debate the law) on all the levels mentioned: the European, the national, the regional, and the local. And this precondition for meaningful debate and decision making over the reach of subsidiarity, the existence of what we might call a "multilevel living law," is often lacking.

SENSUS COMMUNIS

The history of rhetorical theory has produced at least one explicitly communitarian concept of law, Vico's idea of the *sensus communis* animating law as cultural expression. Sensus communis is not the same as common sense as we now understand it. Indeed, Vico rejected the most common meaning of common sense in circulation today, the Cartesian equation of common sense with practical judgment (as in the knowledge of how to do something in an expedient, practical manner). Against the rationalist view of common sense, Vico defended the Greek and Roman notions of common sense developed in the rhetorical tradition (an example of a Greek notion being Aristotle's *doxa*, or the common opinion of mature men; and an example of a Roman notion being Seneca's sense of propriety, the shared but unstated mores of a community). During the Renaissance and the subsequent Enlightenment, the idea of common sense had developed considerably from these classical roots. In Vico's lifetime, the eighteenth century, sensus communis "had become the locus of a whole cluster of meanings: an organizing sense, an unreflective opinion shared by most people, the manners or social values of a community, the first principle of reflection, an innate capacity for simple, logical reasoning" (Schaeffer 1990, 3).

Out of this jumble of available conceptual materials, Vico fashioned his highly innovative understanding of sensus communis by joining common sense as practiced in the arts of rhetoric with common sense as a constructive element in the science of law. Summarzing Schaeffer's patient reconstruction of how Vico effectuated this innovation, we can say that the sensus communis of rhetoric is both the major resource (common knowledge) of speakers and audiences alike and the goal of eloquence (creatively changing and improving shared knowledge). Practices of rhetoric, of which the law courts are a main example, take shape through performances and in this way educate all participants, thus keeping all actors in the public arena in touch with common knowledge and social values. There is a dynamic potential in common sense. As Vico himself put it (1990, 13), "common sense, besides being the criterion of practical judgment, is also the guiding standard of eloquence." When we turn to the role of common sense in law, there is a comparable dynamic at work, as we will see.

But first something must be said about Vico's reasons for writing about sensus communis in law. The Kingdom of Naples did not have a written law, no Code guiding legal practice, but depended on oral arguments between opposing counsel, on the jurisprudence developed by judges balancing conflicting interests, on complicated and unsystematized customary law, and it was accessible only to the elite of lawyers conducting all their business in Latin. Law in Naples was crucially dependent on an oral tradition of legal rhetoric. Rationalist reformers, mobilizing the philosophy of Descartes and the rational natural law systems of Grotius and Pufendorf, tried to modernize the legal system and found support with the Royal Court and administration officials who wanted more control over legal practice. Vico opposed these forces and in his defense of eloquence had to contend especially with the rationalist reformers' attack on the doctrine of *communis opinio* or *consensus gentium*, the stock of common knowledge referred to by the lawyers as the ground for probable truth in their case law (and making use of such *consensus gentium* arguments was of course of central importance in the absence of a written code). As Schaeffer (1990, 51–52) notes: "Communis opinio provided the link among customary law, legal tradition, and rhetoric conceived as dealing with probability. . . . By substituting Cartesian rationality for consensus the reformers were able to shift the whole basis of legal theory from tradition to the present. Cartesian theory offered a justification for innovative social change achieved through the courts and administration, an ability to adapt the law to changing social conditions by making the basis for legislation 'rational' rather than 'traditional.'" Countering this powerful mix of motives, Vico had to find a way of uniting common law with natural law. He had to show that the traditional, customary law embodied in the rhetorical practices of the court system could be based in natural law, in some kind of "natural" normative order that was accessible to human reason and exhibited a set of constructive principles.

How could Vico do this? He created a "constructivist" theory of knowledge, using two principles: *verum-factum* (truth can be known when the human mind makes it) and *verum-certum* (the facts of the social world change as practical decisions create certainty in it). Especially the latter principle is important for the reconciliation of common law and natural law. Bypassing the idea of a purely rational basis of natural law, Vico took as his concept of natural law the universal law of the Romans: *jus gentium*, the common element to be found in the laws of all civil societies. This universal law could never be the mere product of abstract reasoning; it would be established by customs emerging in reflection of the sensus communis. The sensus communis is then defined by Vico (1970, 21, no. 141) as "judgment without reflection, shared by an entire class, an entire people, an entire nation, or the entire human race." It is the ground of practical decisions, "that which makes human choice certain with respect to needs and utilities." The *verum-certum* principle is at work, turning natural law into common law. This is effected by Divine Providence. Sensus communis thus becomes the criterion for social judgment within the scale of a community (within a class, a people, a nation, or the human race). At the same time, it is an ideal to strive for in lawmaking. Wise legislators adapt the customs of their society to what they perceive as the sensus communis, bringing the law of the community into harmony with universal law. "Laws are the embodiment of a gradual and collective response on the part of an entire society."[5] And so Vico arrives at his synthesis: *jus gentium naturale*.

From this far too brief synopsis it might seem that there is just one natural law that can be turned into various common law systems through sensus communis. But this would be to overlook Vico's most original accomplishment, his theory of the historical progression of mankind through various stages and according to a poetic logic that has left its traces in the metaphors and other figures of speech that have been delivered from ancient times (the times before history could be written) (Goetsch 1995). It is precisely the different historical trajectory of nations that explains why there have to be different legal systems, even if they reflect in an imperfect way through sensus communis, elaborated in the rhetorical practices of the community, the dictates of universal law. And this is also why Cartesian rationalism and rational natural-law thinking are wrong, since they do not allow for the history of conceptual development.

The sensus communis was defined by Vico as a "judgment without reflection." It is a basis of judgment, not the focus of argument itself. Yet the historical theory of Vico, with its idea of a cycle of national cultures, stimulates not only reflection on the sensus communis but also interpretation of its meaning in the context of a certain community's public life. Interpretation of the sensus communis can be used to effect reforms of a system of laws and institutions from within, through the available rhetorical methods. But these are reforms that are intended to be faithful to the dictates of *jus gentium naturale*. Vico himself (1990) advocates this method in his essay *On the Study Methods of Our Time* in a discussion of the history of the Roman republic. The jurist should engage in a comparative study of the many contexts shaping laws and institutions:

> I would have the jurist study the origin, the consolidation, the growth, the culmination, and the dissolution of a great polity like the Roman Empire. Let him draw a parallel between the Roman Empire and the monarchic system of our age, in order to investigate whether the same beneficial effects spring from both of them. I will have him scrutinize the cause of public utility underlying and explaining each particular group of rules of Roman law and constituting the necessary basis of it. The purpose should be to ascertain which provisions were issued for an aim profitable to private individuals, or to monarchy; to point out those not harmful, and therefore deserving of being allowed to stand, and those which, being perceived as detrimental, should be rejected (Vico 1990, 66–67).

Immediately after this exhortatory passage, Vico formulates the sensus communis as this jurisprudential study should interpret it, as those judgments about law that are certain because being made by humans in the course of their history. In doing this, Vico achieves no less a rational exposition of natural law precepts as did Grotius or Pufendorf:

> What is justice? It is constant care for the common good. In what does the science of law consist? In the knowledge of the best government. What is law? It is an art of watching over the public interest. What is law, or "the just"? It is the useful. What is natural law? The private interest of each one of us. What is the law of nations? The common good of all nations. What is civil law? The good of the commonwealth. What are the sources of law and why did the law of nature

originate? That man may live in any way soever. Why did jus gentium arise? That man might live in security and ease. What reason accounts for the establishment of civil law? The attainment of a happy and prosperous life. Which is the highest law, the standards we are to follow whenever we interpret any legal enactment? The greatness of the state, the preservation of our ruler, the glory of both (Vico 1990, 67).

SENSUS COMMUNIS AND THE EUROPEAN CONSTITUTION

Vico's system of thought is fascinating but also obscure, appealing and yet distant, and it seems to be very far removed from the debates over the Constitution for Europe. But precisely because he makes the common understandings of the community into his central category for understanding the argumentative practices, the discourse, going on in the legal and political institutions of a state, his ideas may be more relevant than would seem at first sight. Vico's jurisprudence, applied to the question of the European Constitution, immediately gives rise to a number of troubling questions. Can there be a sensus communis on the scale of Europe as a political and legal entity? Does each member state possess, as a separate culture, its own sensus communis? Can a union of member states have one overarching sensus communis? Is it possible, in drafting a Constitution, to explicate at least part of what is meant by this European sensus communis or common heritage? When in the European member states there are different religions and Christians, Jews, and Mohammedans have to live in peace with each other and with those who are not religiously inclined, how does this cultural heterogeneity reflect in the collective wisdom of the Union as a whole?

These questions are perhaps too large to be answered conclusively. But they are, each and all, to the point, bringing out some of the really troubling problems with European unification. A Constitution that, in time, itself becomes part of the common knowledge of the citizens of Europe, must aspire to answer them or at least to provide inspiringly worded principles that are amenable to future interpretation, and that may generate new meanings in an as yet unclear future. Realizing this, it becomes especially worrisome that the proposed Constitution for Europe does not manage to provide an illuminating and inspiring preamble. The text as proposed by the drafters already was a conceptually confused jumble of categories. The preamble reads like a political speech mixing humanist values with vague references to cultural, religious, and humanitarian traditions; suggesting that the history of the European nations has culminated in a general respect for human rights; making policy declarations about the desirability of progress, welfare, culture, and science; committing itself to democracy and transparency, and to peace, justice, and solidarity on a world scale; expressing faith in the common will to overcome the old oppositions between the nations of Europe; praying that a unity of diversities will offer people the best chances to live their own lives while also respecting the rights of future generations; allegedly continuing with the great European adventure. . . Yes, this was a text expressing many basic convictions but no "unreflective judgments." Immediately on the publication of the preamble, in various member states a political debate ensued about the contents of the European sensus communis. In the process, there were proposals to mention God, the Christian God to be precise, and these proposals were fiercely resisted by humanists or unreligious speakers. The strange invention of the "Judeo-Christian tradition" made its entrance. (Vico would have had great difficulty understanding this notion. Were there not in historical time two traditions, a Christian and a Jewish one, and had they not been at war with each other?) No proposals were made to include a reference to Islam, very likely as a result of the war on terror, in which the religion of Islam is conflated with the extremism of political Islamists. But how can a declaration about the common values and traditions of Europe fail to mention the large part of the European population adhering to the religion of Islam?

Vico's communitarian concept of law thus generates questions that are of great relevance but remain underdiscussed; this is already enough to expect from a topical approach. But there is a constructive message in Vico's project as well. Vico believes that human lawgivers labor under enormous limitations and can never, on the basis of science and rationality, devise a perfect state. He would have been very critical of the regulatory bureaucracy of modern welfare states. Yet we can see that despite human limitations there is sometimes progress in constitutional and political history and improvement of economic, social, and legal systems. This is due to Providence. "There are forms of order which, without human discernment of intent, and often against the designs of men, Providence has given to this great city of the human race" (Vico 1970, 60, no. 342). An example is that from the struggle between kings and nobles over domination, a balance of powers arose and with it an ideal of the rule of law. Isaiah Berlin (1992, 75) reckons Vico among those political thinkers who, like Herder, Schelling, and Hegel, believe in "a cosmic, purposive tendency which moulds men's passions and desires into institutions and forms of social life in an intelligible pattern" and as a corollary of this conviction "that this cannot be done by the conscious control of intelligent experts who know how to canalize human weaknesses either for the society's advantage or for their own selfish ends." Controversial though this thesis no doubt is, it is an articulation of a topos that is part and parcel of the history of the Europe now submitting to unification, and it opposes the rationalist and bureaucratic assumptions concentrated in the European institutions. What, exactly, is here common sense?

REPUBLICAN LAWMAKING

The political theory of (neo)republicanism has historical roots in the rhetorical tradition. The old (as well as the new) idea of the republic as the best democratic form of political life combines the ideal of autonomous yet communal citizenship with values such as freedom, equality, and justice, while making the process of lawmaking through participation and deliberation into its central institution of governance. This potent combination of elements is also present in the rhetorical tradition. We can think of the ancient notion of the rhetorical situation, for instance, as a truly republican form of the legal process. Autonomous and free advocates are equal in their standing and in their chances for persuasion and they are confronting a judge who is neither their better nor their ruler but, like them, belongs to the people. All of the participants in the rhetorical situation are bound to the community's ideals of justice and fairness and are guided by the customs and rules evolved through its legislative history. In the writings of the Roman jurist Cicero, these rhetorical and republican ideals already can be seen to come together. With the rediscovery of the republican conception of politics and democracy now underway in political theory, there is bound to be a fuller appreciation of the value of public eloquence.

Republicanism pictures a legal community of free and equal citizens as both the precondition and the end result of democratic self-governance. In this communitarian concept of law and lawmaking, freedom is understood in a certain way: as nondomination. According to Pettit, nondomination is neither negative liberty ("the area within which one is free from interference"), nor is it positive liberty ("individual autonomy, being one's own master").[6] Republicans do not condemn all interference overstepping a fixed boundary, and they do not think of autonomy merely as individual autonomy. They value positively the efforts of collective and deliberative autonomy, in which the public domain is given shape, and they think democratically deliberated interferences with individual lives can be justifiable as long as these do not result in domination and dependency. For free citizens the worst situation is one of slavery or bondage, being delivered to the good or bad intentions of a master and to a tyranny of intentions. Modern bureaucracy may foster just such social relationships of dependency or bondage; it tends toward domination. Pettit (1997, viii) defines the republican ideal of freedom as nondomination as follows: "Freedom as nondomination is a condition under which a person is immune, and more or less saliently immune, to interference on an arbitrary basis." This is the kind of freedom the laws should protect. But nondomination as an ideal of freedom does not mean that there cannot be strong legislative interventions in social life, encroaching if need be on individual (negatively or positively defined) freedoms; nondomination does not mean noninterference. The republican conception of politics sets great store by the possibility of collective decision making through legislation and believes this will be possible without using techniques of domination, and preferably using methods empowering individuals rather than making them dependent. As Pettit (ibid., 66) concludes: "There will be systems of law available, at least in principle, which are entirely undominating and entirely consistent with freedom: not only will they inhibit potential dominators and reduce unfreedom, they will do so without representing a form of domination in their own right."

Can such nondominating systems of law also be envisaged for the European Union, and can they be awarded constitutional status? Notice first the kinds of European regulation that are on principle rejected by the republican project. All regulatory interference on an arbitrary basis must be banished. Also, the effect of regulation may not be that people or groups or organizations are made dependent on others; regulation by the European Union may not be an instrument for domination by some actors over others. This represents two practical tests that can be applied to all regulations of the *acquis communautaire*. A legislative-rationality test asks whether the proposed rules are justified by reasons that are strong enough in themselves and are proportional to the issue at hand. A social-power test inquires whether the rules avoid creating or sustaining situations in which one person or group or organization is made dependent on another. This is not the place to apply such tests to a range of European regulations; it is enough to argue the originality and relevance of the republican project in this respect.[7] The economic ideology of the European regulators tends to present all rules as necessary conditions that all market parties must submit to equally, thus circumventing the problem of whether the rules are too detailed and whether they are proportional to the purposes they are intended to regulate. Bureaucratic overregulation is from the standpoint of participants in social practices a form of arbitrary interference. The consultation process at the back of most European regulation makes interest groups into coauthors of regulation to which all actors in a field are subjected; this procedure easily leads to the situation in which a group or an interest that has managed to dominate the consultations also comes to dominate other social interests through the allegedly neutral European regulation.

In a more positive vein, the republican project attempts to formulate a legislative strategy that may be used for the regulation of collective problems, as these are defined by deliberative democratic procedures, in the hope of achieving nondominant regulation. Pettit argues that, facing a choice between deviant-centered regulation and complier-centered regulation, the republican preference is for the latter kind of regulation. Most regulation is of the first kind: it concentrates on influencing the behavior of those people who will tend to deviate in the absence of controls ("the knaves"). This leads to a massive use of sanctions and rewards, punishing bad behavior and stimulating good behavior. This strategy works on the level of individual motivation, while not making much use of another regulatory mechanism: screens or filters. Screens filter agents to a position where they make the choices (an example is the selection process for membership of a jury), or they structure the availability of options, trying to affect opportunities rather than incentives. Pettit criticizes the deviant-centered strategy for treating all actors as knaves and thus underusing the tendency toward cooperation on the part of those (the majority of citizens) who are willing to behave in a socially acceptable way and even undercutting their motives for being good.[8]

The complier-centered strategy, on the other hand, is not designed to deal with the most corrupt person but with "the more ordinary individual who mostly deliberates, where it is appropriate, in a public-spirited way." The ordinary individual can be corrupted, she can also turn out to become a knave, but in the first instance it is supposed there is a willingness to behave in a socially desirable manner. In this strategy, sanctions are not applied indiscriminately from the actual motivations of the individual actor. Pettit argues that in this regulatory strategy there are three principles that are ranked in order of priority:

- screen before sanctioning;
- sanction in a complier-supportive way;
- structure sanctions to cope with possible knavery.

Screening can have the effect of putting actors with positive motivations in places where the important decisions are made that help achieve the purpose of the regulation. Complier-supportive sanctions appeal to communally shared notions of approval and disapproval, using the motivation of the individual actors to be in good standing with their peers. For the knaves who do not comply under the first two strategies, one can think of sanctions in an escalating hierarchy, punishing repetitive offenders heavier, in the hope of pushing them back into the category of more compliant citizens.[9]

The complier-centered regulatory strategy is a republican strategy, which conceives of the actor as a citizen rather than on the model of the potential knave, seeking to enforce socially constructive motivations rather than merely trying to fight deviant tendencies. In a background paper to *Republicanism*, Pettit (2002, 276) describes the problem of republican-spirited institutional design as of having to ensure that the institution is discourse-compatible: "An institution will be discourse-compatible so far as it can be explained and justified among members, and its demands articulated, consistently with those people relating to one another as co-reasoning citizens: that is, as agents who make a claim only to that sort of mutual influence that occurs when each is given a relevant and acceptable reason to act as required." Republican regulation will always have to be discourse-compatible, is the corollary, always assuming the actors addressed by the norms to be "co-reasoning citizens."

What about European regulation, as conceived under the proposed Constitution, in the light of this republican idea of a complier-centered and discourse-compatible legislative strategy? Well, the first thing to notice is the absence of any notion of regulative strategy in the European context and in the document of the European Constitution. It is quite a challenge to formulate one on the constitutional level and then also to think of a practical way of moving the many regulatory committees in the direction of adopting it. The Constitution now limits itself to enumerating a number of different types of European regulation but does not set out qualitative criteria to be followed in the adoption of the one or the other kind. Also when subsidiarity is cited as a principle (and this is no doubt compatible with republican ideals), it is left to the negotiations between national and European authorities to draw the line of what falls under the scope of the subsidiarity principle, and the Constitution again does not give normative orientation on how to translate this abstract notion into workable regulatory institutions and practices. The republican theory of democratic governance by and for free citizens could be the beginning of a constitutional debate on European institutional design and regulatory practices, but there are up to now no signs such a debate has reached the public arena.

TOWARD A COMMUNITARIAN CONCEPT OF LAW?

We have come a long way from the initial question of what communitarian liberalism has to offer for legal theory and legal practice. Have we also made progress toward a "communitarian" concept of law? In our search, we have returned to the rhetorical tradition with its dialogical and perspectivist methods for the articulation of topics for argumentation. The value of the questions raised through this method and the answers tentatively put forward have been tested in a case study, that of the debate on a Constitution for Europe. All in all, our search for a communitarian understanding of law has followed the path rhetoricians like Aristotle or Cicero would have recognized as the procedure leading to a *Topica*: a collection of relevant commonplaces for argumentation.

There were two stages in this "topical" undertaking. First, we posited three models of law and community (positivism, natural law, and interactionism), which in all their elemental simplicity and dialectical tension were said to be part of the culture of law. Using these models for a perspectivist dialogue, we showed they generated a surprisingly broad set of questions that could be meaningfully applied to the case of the European Constitution. In the second stage, we brought together three theoretically more refined and richer (but also more controversial) theories of law and community with roots in the rhetorical tradition, making use of these theories for the same topical and perspectivist ends. This led to more specific questions about the European Constitution and also to more incisive lines of argumentation concerning them.

White's cultural approach to law brings out the processes of translation at the heart of legal practices, and it raises questions about the design of European institutions adequate to the challenges of translation between languages and between cultures. Justice as translation is an ideal that requires a different conception of the subsidiarity principle, demanding it to develop into a method for multilevel living law. Vico's explicitly communitarian and rhetorical concept of law (as sensus communis) lends itself to a critique of constitutional references to the European heritage as something all member states have in common, and it exposes the shallowness of the invocation of shared values and traditions in the Constitution's preamble. His view of the limits of human control over the destiny of nations, while controversially based on Providence, is a reminder of a powerful way of thinking about the limits of nation building and democratic-bureaucratic governance. Pettit's revitalization of republicanism, consonant with the citizenship ideal enshrined in the rhetorical tradition, aligns political freedom as nondomination with processes of democratic governance. A discourse-compatible regulatory strategy that is complier-centered rather than deviant-centered is proposed as a model for regulation that may well be valuable in the context of the European Union; in the light of this legislative strategy, the passages on legislation and regulation in the proposed Constitution seem both too instrumentalist and too formalist, omitting all reference to qualitative criteria for judging the appropriateness of regulation.

The rhetorical method, in these two stages, has indeed brought out a large number of pertinent questions and relevant considerations. It is, as it were, a *Topica in statu nascendi*. But it has to be concluded also that this rhetorical procedure brings a plethora of understandings of law, not a unified communitarian concept. There is at this stage of the journey simply no fixed formula in sight, no definition of law and community which is generally applicable in all contexts and all situations, not even in the special case of the debate over a Constitution for Europe. Do we have to be sorry about this, or does it simply characterize the predicament we are in? It is remarkable that this open-endedness, this inconclusiveness, this ability to again and again take up new frames and models, is also to be found in those chapters in this book that are most explicitly concerned with the development of a communitarian view of law: Selznick's ideal of responsive law and Cotterrell's exhortation to pursue living law. As long as the practices of law in a society are responsive to human needs, and in doing so satisfy a number of qualitative criteria, they count as communitarian liberalism's ideal of law. This is an inspiring thought, but it does not provide clear limitations on what can count as meaningful responsive law, and it consciously leaves open the possibility that in social interactions new forms and methods of lawmaking will emerge. Living law amounts to an overall change in perspective, to viewing legal practice from the bottom upwards instead of from the top downwards; it seeks to connect the practices of law to the outlooks and values of communities. Again, the forms of law seem to be of less relevance than the general drift of the movement to make living law more effective. In fact, both Selznick and Cotterrell put their definitions of law to use for sociological analyses of specific themes and problems and adapt the choice of definition to the analytical need. This undogmatic attitude to the concept of law is commendable. Perhaps we should all be able to unite around Cotterrell's most liberal definition of law (1995, 3): "Law in its broadest sociological sense is a field of experience shaped and structured by problems of government, social control, and social order."

The debates about law and society to which communitarians and liberals and communitarian liberals have contributed so much during the last decades show a shift toward more careful attention to what is actually happening in the practices in which legal and other values are made to work, which is perhaps even a kind of pragmatist turn in political theorizing. A rhetorical and perspectivist method is supportive of this general trend. We are, indeed, moving toward a communitarian concept of law, but this title can be read in two ways, as being about the "concept of law" but also as mentioning the way to get there; it asks our full attention for the roads taken in search of it.

NOTES

1. On Dewey, see Taekema 2003, 227–32. On Fuller, see Witteveen and Van der Burg 1998. On American legal realism, see Horwitz 1992; Tamanaha 1997.

2. On cultural analysis generally, see Douglas 1987.

3. On the method of perspectivism, see Witteveen 1998a.

4. The rhetorical program of inventio in the service of argumentation and judgment has been taken up by scholars developing a rhetoric of inquiry for the sciences. See Simons 1990, 1–31; Nelson 1998, 3–33.

5. As Isaiah Berlin (1992, 86) captures Vico's idea of legislation.

6. This is the influential typology of Isaiah Berlin's "Two Concepts of Liberty," reprinted in Berlin 2002, 166–217.

7. For an example of an EU regulation failing on both counts, see Witteveen 1998b, 334–39. The analysis there uses a different analytical frame, however: Fuller's internal morality of legislation.

8. For the full argument, see Pettit 1997, 212–19.

9. For the full argument, see ibid., 219–30.

REFERENCES

Berlin, Isaiah. 1992. *Vico and Herder*. London: Hogarth Press.

———. 2002. *Liberty*. Ed. Henry Hardy. Oxford: Oxford University Press.

Cotterrell, Roger. 1995. *Law's Community: Legal Theory in Sociological Perspective*. Oxford: Clarendon Press.

De Swaan, Abram. 2002. *Woorden van de wereld*. Amsterdam: Bert Bakker.

Douglas, Mary. 1987. *How Institutions Think*. London: Routledge and Kegan Paul.

Goetsch, Jr., James Robert. 1995. *Vico's Axioms: The Geometry of the Human World*. New Haven, CT: Yale University Press.

Horwitz, Morton J. 1992. *The Transformation of American Law, 1870–1960: The Crisis of Legal Orthodoxy*. Oxford: Oxford University Press.

Kennedy, George A. 1980. *Classical Rhetoric and Its Christian and Secular Traditions from Ancient to Modern Times*. Chapel Hill: University of North Carolina Press.

Mulhall, Stephen, and Adam Swift. 1996. *Liberals and Communitarians*. 2nd ed. Oxford: Blackwell.

Nelson, John S. 1998. *Tropes of Politics*. Madison: University of Wisconsin Press.

Pettit, Philip. 1997. *Republicanism: A Theory of Freedom and Government*. Oxford: Oxford University Press.

———. 2002. *Rules, Reasons, and Norms*. Oxford: Clarendon Press.

Schaeffer, John D. 1990. *Sensus Communis: Vico, Rhetoric, and the Limits of Relativism*. Durham, NC: Duke University Press.

Simons, Herbert W. 1990. *The Rhetorical Turn: Invention and Persuasion in the Conduct of Inquiry*. Chicago: University of Chicago Press.

Taekema, Sanne. 2003. *The Concept of Ideals in Legal Theory*. The Hague: Kluwer Law International.

Tamanaha, Brian Z. 1997. *Realistic Socio-Legal Theory: Pragmatism and a Social Theory of Law*. Oxford: Clarendon Press.

Vico, Giambattista. 1970. *The New Science of Giambattista Vico*. Trans. Thomas Bergin and Max Fisch. Ithaca, NY: Cornell University Press.

———. 1990. *On the Study Methods of Our Time*. Trans. Elio Gianturco. Ithaca, NY: Cornell University Press.

White, James Boyd. 1985. *Heracles' Bow*. Madison: University of Wisconsin Press.

———. 1990. *Justice as Translation*. Chicago: University of Chicago Press.

Witteveen, Willem J. 1988. *De retoriek in het recht*. Zwolle: W. E. J. Tjeenk Willink.

———. 1998a. Great Webs and Tapestries and Fabrications. In *New Approaches to Semiotics and the Human Sciences*, ed. William Pencak and J. Ralph Lindgren, 265–76. New York: Peter Lang.

———. 1998b. Laws of Lawmaking. In Witteveen and Van der Burg, 312–45.

———. 2001. *De geordende wereld van het recht*. Amsterdam: Amsterdam University Press.

Witteveen, Willem J., and Wibren van der Burg, eds. 1998. *Rediscovering Fuller: Essays on Implicit Law and Institutional Design*. Amsterdam: Amsterdam University Press.

Index

About the Editor and Contributors

Paul de Beer is Henri Polak Professor of Industrial Relations at the University of Amsterdam. His inaugural lecture is entitled *Tien geboden voor de vakbeweging* (Ten Commandments for the Labor Union Movement). He is affiliated with the Amsterdam Institute for Advanced Labour Studies (AIAS) and De Burcht (Dutch Trade Union Museum). His most recent book is *Perspectief op de arbeidsmarkt* (Perspective on the Labor Market).

Jos de Beus is professor of political theory at the University of Amsterdam. His inaugural lecture is entitled *Een primaat van politiek* (A Primacy of Politics). A new book, *Nederland Europeaniseert (maar niet van harte)* (The Netherlands Europeanizes—But Not Wholeheartedly), with Jeanette Mak, is forthcoming.

Winfried Brugger is professor of public law and philosophy of law at the UniVersity of Heidelberg and Fellow at the Max Weber Institute in Cultural and Social Sciences at Erfurt University in Germany. Some of his recent books are *Liberalismus, Pluralismus, Kommunitarismus* (Liberalism, Pluralism, Communitarianism); *Freiheit und Sicherheit* (Freedom and Security); and *Das anthropologische Kreuz der Entscheidung in Politik und Recht* (Four Anthropological Perspectives in Deciding Hard Cases in Politics and Law).

Roger Cotterrell is Anniversary Professor of Legal Theory in the School of Law at Queen Mary and Westfield College, University of London. He was elected a Fellow of the British Academy in 2005. His recent books include *Law's Community: Legal Theory in Sociological Perspective*; *Émile*

Durkheim: Law in a Moral Domain; *Sociological Perspectives on Law*, 2 vols.; and *The Politics of Jurisprudence: A Critical Introduction to Legal Philosophy*, 2nd ed.

Anton Hemerijck is director of the Wetenschappelijke Raad voor het Regeringsbeleid (Dutch Scientific Council for Government Policy). He is the coauthor of *'A Dutch Miracle': Job Growth, Welfare Reform and Corporatism in the Netherlands*, with Jelle Visser, and the coeditor of *Why We Need a New Welfare State*, with Gøsta Esping-Andersen, Duncan Gallie, and John Myles.

Dorien Pessers is professor of legal foundations of privacy at the Free University of Amsterdam. Her inaugural lecture is entitled *Big Mother: Over de personalisering van de publieke sfeer* (On the Personalization of the Public Sphere). She is the author of *Liefde, solidariteit en recht: Een interdisciplinair onderzoek naar het wederkerigheidsbeginsel* (Love, Solidarity, and Law: An Interdisciplinary Investigation of the Reciprocity Principle), and *Verdwaalde seksen: Over sperminators, metroseksuelen en autocopieën* (Lost Sexes: On Sperminators, Metrosexuals, and Autocopies).

Toon Peters (†1994) was professor of legal sociology at Utrecht University and professor of law and society of Japan at Leiden University. A collection of his essays is published under the title *Recht als kritische discussie* (Law as Critical Discussion).

Philip Selznick is Professor Emeritus of Law and Sociology in the School of Law and the Department of Sociology at the University of California, Berkeley. In 2003 he received the Law and Society Association's Harry J. Kalven Jr. Prize. His most recent books are *The Moral Commonwealth: Social Theory and the Promise of Community* and *The Communitarian Persuasion*.

Paul van Seters was professor of legal sociology at Tilburg University, the Netherlands. Currently he is director of Globus, and professor of globalization and sustainable development in Tias Business School at Tilburg University. He is the coeditor of *Globalization and Its New Divides*, with Bas de Gaay Fortman and Arie de Ruiter.

Sanne Taekema is assistant professor of law at Tilburg University, the Netherlands. She is author of *The Concept of Ideals in Legal Theory*, editor of *Understanding Dutch Law*, and coeditor of *Verbeeldingsmacht: Wat juristen moeten lezen* (Power of Imagination: What Jurists Ought to Read), with Willem Witteveen, and *The Importance of Ideals: Debating Their Relevance in Law, Morality, and Politics*, with Wibren van der Burg.

Willem Witteveen is professor of jurisprudence at Tilburg University, the Netherlands. His books include *De denkbeeldige staat: Voorstellingen van democratische vernieuwing* (The Imaginary State: Images of Democratic Innovation); *De geordende wereld van het recht: Een inleiding* (The Nomos of Law: An Introduction); and *Rediscovering Fuller: Essays on Implicit Law and Institutional Design*, coedited with Wibren van der Burg.

www.ingramcontent.com/pod-product-compliance
Ingram Content Group UK Ltd.
Pitfield, Milton Keynes, MK11 3LW, UK
UKHW041632031026
15587UKWH00001B/244

9 780742 522701

AF837247

Literature of Crisis

Literature of Crisis

Spain's Engagement with Liquid Capital

Olga Bezhanova

Lewisburg
Bucknell University Press

Published by Bucknell University Press
Copublished by The Rowman & Littlefield Publishing Group, Inc.
4501 Forbes Boulevard, Suite 200, Lanham, Maryland 20706
www.rowman.com

Unit A, Whitacre Mews, 26-34 Stannary Street, London SE11 4AB

Copyright © 2017 by Olga Bezhanova

We gratefully acknowledge permission to reprint the following:

Excerpts from Antonio Muñoz Molina, *Todo lo que era sólido*, Editorial Sex Barral, S.A.
Excerpts from *Crematorio* by Rafael Chirbes: Copyright 2007 by Rafael Chirbes. Used by permission of Editorial Anagrama, S.A.
Excerpts from *Marca(da) España. Retrato poético de una sociedad en crisis*: Copyright 2014 by participating writers. Used by permission of Amargord Ediciones, S.L.
Borges Blázquez, Lola. Personal interview. 7 August 2015.
Excerpts from *En legítima defensa. Poetas en tiempos de crisis*, Bartleby Editores, LLC, 2014.

All rights reserved. No part of this book may be reproduced in any form or by any electronic or mechanical means, including information storage and retrieval systems, without written permission from the publisher, except by a reviewer who may quote passages in a review.

British Library Cataloguing in Publication Information Available

Library of Congress Cataloging-in-Publication Data Available

ISBN 978-1-61148-836-4 (cloth : alk. paper)
ISBN 978-1-61148-837-1 (electronic)

Printed in the United States of America

To Klara

Contents

Acknowledgments

As I attempted to demonstrate in this book, the fluidity that is eroding so many of the certainties that used to underpin our lives can be felt in all areas of existence. Work, relationships, politics, and academia are changing as a result of being constantly battered by flows of liquid capital. If it is not in our power to stop this liquefaction, we can use some of its aspects to our advantage. The erosion of borders between nations and fields of knowledge and the shortening of all manner of distances between human beings offered by the Internet allowed me to find an unexpected and still somewhat nontraditional audience for the ideas that I developed in this book. The readers of my blog accompanied me on this intellectual journey from the very beginning, taking me to task for every inconsistency in my argument and pointing out blind spots in my reasoning. Their intelligent and unforgiving comments were of invaluable assistance to me in this project.

My URCA assistant, Derek Drew, offered valuable help in the early stages of conducting research for this book. Dr. Bill Retzlaff, the associate dean of the College of Arts and Sciences of Southern Illinois University at Edwardsville, and Dean Gregory Budzban helped fund the editing of the manuscript, which is quite a feat at a time when funding for public universities is at a low ebb. Dr. Marcia Eppich-Harris of Marian University provided efficient and reliable editing services.

I started working on this project soon after experiencing the most devastating loss in my life. The love and support provided by my friend Regina VanOverschelde helped me face this tragedy. My parents, Nadiya Byezhanova and Michael Blekhman, never wavered in their belief in my success. The most inspiring person I know, my sister Marina Byezhanova, helped me find meaning in the midst of apparent senselessness. My husband, Nikita Tuzov, never stopped amazing me with his kindness, strength, and capacity to love.

Introduction

The Crisis That Will Not End

> "We cannot call ourselves modern, nor even postmodern, which implies a relationship of dependency on and opposition to modernity, but are inhabitants of a world that is changing, who call this change 'crisis.'"[1]

"I can assure you that Spain is already emerging from the crisis," Spain's head of government, Mariano Rajoy, announced at the Ibero-American Summit in Panama in October 2013.[2] A little over a year later, in December 2014, Rajoy felt confident enough to ensure the business leaders who had gathered to listen to his speech, dedicated to the achievements of his first three years in office, that in many ways, the crisis was already a thing of the past.[3] By August 2015, up to 70 percent of Spaniards were expressing the belief that the worst of the crisis was over,[4] and experts at Banco Bilbao Vizcaya Argentaria, the second largest banking group in Spain, predicted that Spain's economy would grow by 2.3 percent in 2017.[5] A new crisis, however, was looming ahead. In the general elections held on December 20, 2015, none of the political parties gained a large enough majority to allow them to form a government. An ensuing political stalemate could not be resolved even by a second election held in June 2016. Only at the end of October was Mariano Rajoy confirmed as head of government. In his investiture speech, Rajoy echoed the optimism of the speeches he had given à propos the economic crisis: "Hoy comienza [esta historia]. Hoy trazamos el camino del futuro." [Today this story begins. Today we are charting our future path.][6] Yet another crisis seemed to be resolved.

This triumphalist approach—of which Rajoy is far from being the only proponent—is based on the belief that Spain's political and economic crises of the first two decades of the twenty-first century are unconnected events of a relatively short duration that, at some point, are bound to end. This narrative aims to preclude the discussion of the permanent changes to the economic and political space brought by these crises. In the words of Carlo Bordoni, "[A crisis] is perceived by everyone as an event of limited duration, which we can soon leave behind and without too much damage, thanks to the drastic measures taken to deal with it. Sacrifices are more easily endured if they are short-lived, if the purpose and end are seen in the near future. However, crises, even induced ones, can no longer be considered temporary."[7] Framing the economic crisis as temporary made it easier to justify the unpopular austerity measures that had an especially painful effect on the countries of Southern Europe. Spain's parliamentary crisis, in turn, diverted much of the public's attention from the discussion of whether the damage done to the welfare state by austerity could be repaired. Rajoy's investiture speech of 2016 made it clear that he considers austerity measures to be an unqualified success and in no need of being walked back.[8] Those who have been impacted by the transformations experienced by the global economy in recent years have to content themselves with assurances that the crisis is over and there is nothing left to discuss.

The vocabulary we use to talk about the events that have shaped the global economy since 2008 suggests that what Americans know as "the Recession" and Spaniards refer to as "la crisis" is generally expected to be temporary in nature. The *Oxford English Dictionary* defines the economic term "recession" as "a temporary decline or setback in economic activity or prosperity."[9] *Diccionario manual e ilustrado de la lengua española* bases its definition of the word "crisis" on a medical term that refers to a turning point in the course of an illness and notes that, by extension, the word means "momento decisivo de un negocio grave y de consecuencias importantes" [a decisive moment in a serious issue of grave consequences].[10] The vision of a crisis as a moment in time that has a specific beginning and, more importantly, a definitive ending is the one that has currency today. However, there is a different meaning that this term has carried since its earliest origins. The word "crisis" originates from the Greek "κρισις," which *A Greek-English Lexicon* defines as "decision, judgement; choice, election; interpretation of dreams and portents."[11] This definition deemphasizes the temporary nature of a crisis and, instead, stresses the importance of the decisions that originate from it. Covarrubias's dictionary of 1611 does not list the word "crisis," yet the article dedicated to the word "crítico" not only draws a distinction between "días críticos" [critical days] and "enfermedades crónicas" [chronic illnesses] but also points to a connection between the words "crisis" and "crítico" (Greek "κριτικος"), which means "judicial o judiciario . . . y de aquí se dixeron críticos los que juzgan y examinan con rigor las poesías y las escrituras y obras de otros" [judicial or related to jurisprudence . . . and this is why those who judge and examine with rigor the poems and the writing and the works of others are called critics].[12] In this book, I provide a critical analysis of the literature that has been created in Spain in response to the global economic collapse of 2008. Such an analysis allows for greater insights into the nature of the crisis than the ones offered by the celebratory pronouncements on the part of Spain's government and the media.

Spain has been experiencing the crisis in a particularly painful way, and the artistic response to these traumatic events has been powerful and abundant. Crisis literature is pointing to the probability that the crisis is not a temporary problem that can be finally resolved if correct economic measures are taken. To the contrary, there is every reason to believe that the losses in long-term stable employment, the growing precariousness of work, the increased economic insecurity, the citizens' disillusionment with the capacity of democratic governments to withstand the pressures of global capital, the erosion of the welfare state, and the explosive growth in inequality that have characterized the first decade and a half of the twenty-first century are not likely to disappear any time soon. Spanish artists are exploring the reasons behind Spain's particularly painful experience of the crisis and, at the same time, are placing the suffering that the crisis is causing in Spain within the context of global developments that are ensuring its durability. The works of literature that have been created since the rise of the anti-austerity movement in Spain often incorporate the experiences of the protesters and strive to serve as an extension of discussion spaces that characterize the movement. The ubiquitous narrative of the crisis as "a technical problem [that] had to be solved by experts"[13] is questioned in these works of art, albeit with varying degrees of success.

Spain's position at the margins of Europe was not fully overcome after the country's entrance into the European Union, and the global economic collapse has made it clear that slipping into the position of an outsider to the European project is always within reach for Spain. Throughout the crisis, the dismissive acronym of PIGS was often used in the English-speaking media to refer to the countries of Southern Europe (Portugal, Italy, Greece, and Spain) that found it especially hard to overcome the consequences of the 2008 collapse of the real estate market.[14] From a model member of the EU, Spain moved, within just a few years, to the ranks of states that are seen as dispensable to the European project. Spain's marginalization within Europe marks the country as the perfect locus from which a critical approximation to the crisis can be conducted:

> The tendencies at full swing in the "centre" are, as a rule, most promptly spotted and most clearly articulated in places temporarily relegated to the "fringes." Living at the outskirts of the civilizational centre means being near enough to see things clearly, yet far enough to "objectify" them and so to mold and condense the perceptions into concepts.[15]

Spanish essayists, novelists, and poets analyzed in this book approach the crisis from perspectives that are inspired by their generational, political, and artistic differences. Still, all of these writers see the crisis not as an isolated occurrence but, rather, as one of the stages in a far-reaching societal transformation that represents "a structural threat to the welfarist domestication of capitalism"[16] that is making a profound impact on the very concepts of participatory democracy, work, political engagement, and community in all developed countries.

At the same time, most of the writers I analyze believe that the acutely painful effects that the global economic crisis of 2008–2012 has had on Spain cannot be understood without considering the legacy of the Spanish Civil War and the dictatorship of Franco, which put in place the mechanisms that are making it especially hard for Spain to process the consequences of the global transformations that are occurring today. As Antonio Muñoz Molina pointed out in his essay *Todo lo que era sólido,* the crisis is "la emergencia más grave que hemos tenido desde la Guerra Civil" [the most serious emergency we have had since the Civil War],[17] and as a result, it is impossible to avoid using the war as a frame of reference in a discussion of the current crisis. Even the writers who, like Muñoz Molina himself, are opposed to making the Civil War part of the discussion about the crisis find that an analysis of the war and its legacy is unavoidable if one is to understand the severity of the impact that the crisis has had on Spain. There was barely an attempt, during Spain's transition to democracy, to question the system of property relations inherited from the dictatorship of Franco,[18] but the economic collapse of 2008–2012 has made many in Spain wonder whether such questioning can be put off any longer. Today, it has become clear that only the most superficial analysis of the crisis can avoid turning to the decades that preceded it in search for the roots of the current troubles.[19]

Questioning the way in which the Transition era approached the legacy of the Civil War and the dictatorship is common to the writers who are publishing works of literature about the crisis. The rejection of what Guillem Martínez has termed the Culture of the Transition (or CT), defined as "una cultura cuyos intelectuales están absolutamente comprometidos, contra lo problemático y con el Estado" [a culture whose intellectuals are politically committed against what's problematic and in favor of the State],[20] is central to crisis novels by Rafael Chirbes, Benjamín Prado, and Luis García Montero. Antonio Muñoz Molina, on the other hand, carries out an analysis of the crisis from the position of one of the clearest representatives of the CT ideology.[21] The limitations of Muñoz Molina's crisis essay that I analyze in the first chapter of this book point to the failure of the CT to offer a compelling response to the crisis. The narratives that CT produces resist any insights that might threaten the system of economic and political relations constituted by the Transition. Many of the crisis writers realize, however, that the current situation does not call for cosmetic changes but rather for a profound critical engagement with the existing reality that does not shirk from the need to hold nothing as too sacred to be questioned and, if needed, rejected.

Spain's crisis literature does not exist in isolation from the social resistance movements that have consolidated in the aftermath of the crisis.

The 15-M movement (also known as "Indignados") that surged in 2011 in response to what many in Spain perceived as governmental mishandling of the crisis attempted to create "a language ecosystem expressive of new subjectivities"[22] because there was a widespread feeling that no meaningful transformation could be achieved without making space for new forms of subjectivity that would reflect the changing reality. Literature of the crisis contributes to the task of putting into words the emotions that arise in response to the devastation of the crisis. Novels by Rafael Chirbes, Luis García Montero, Benjamín Prado, and Belén Gopegui; essays by Antonio Muñoz Molina and Lucía Etxebarria; and poetry by the artists who contributed to the collections titled *En legítima defensa. Poetas en tiempos de crisis* and *Marca(da) España. Retrato poético de una sociedad en crisis* point to the necessity of expanding our vision of the crisis from the purely financial to a broader definition that will include the changes the crisis augurs for the areas of human existence that lie outside the strictly economic realm. The era of "'primacy of the economy' (and of the economists)" that began in the late 1950s and has existed in an uncontested form until today[23] is being questioned by the writers who approach the current economic crisis in their work. It is becoming increasingly clear that the mystique of high finance that has positioned this sphere as being too complex for understanding has made resisting the consequences of the crisis more difficult:

> Knowledge of the economy, the mechanism of the markets and their operation would be essential to counteract power. Their strength is, once again, rooted in the people's ignorance: the operations and decisions that governments implement for and in relation to markets are passively accepted in a spirit of resignation that is very similar to fatalism. Without the possibility of reply and criticizing, there is no more than a dull and confused protest.[24]

Writers of the crisis take upon themselves the task of demystifying the situation by placing a discussion of the economic causes and consequences of the crisis within a familiar and nonthreatening network of literary production.

In their efforts to access the issues that lie at the core of the crisis, Spanish artists assert their right to interpret and, hence, define the ways in which economic structures make themselves felt in all areas of human endeavor. In the words of Alain Touraine, "the current crisis is based on a breakdown in the relationship between the financial economy and all other sectors of society."[25] Literature can serve as a conduit through which those who have no control over the world of high finance may travel toward reclaiming a measure of control over the flyaway financial economy. The consequences of allowing the financial sector to become a world unto itself that accepts no input or supervision on the part of the citizenry or even national governments have been dire. There is a shared conviction among the authors I discuss in this book that the belief in the economists' capacity to understand and control the functioning of global financial markets has been misplaced. In this respect, Spanish writers echo the words of the German sociologist Ulrich Beck, who pointed out that "the crisis is not purely a matter of the economy (and of thinking about the economy) but is also one of society and politics and our prevailing ways of thinking about them. . . . Economics has lost sight of the society it is analysing."[26] Artists are not alone in thinking that the economic measures taken in response to the crisis have been counterproductive. In 2011 a group of Spanish economists founded an organization called Economistas Frente a la Crisis [Economists Against the Crisis] to offer a vision of the economy that contradicts the neoliberal program of austerity adopted by the Spanish government.[27] The activities of Economistas Frente a la Crisis demonstrate that there is a clear need for a public debate about economic issues.

Spain's literature of the crisis attempts to counter the belief that finance is too complex for anybody but professional economists to understand and calls on everybody to participate in analyzing what went wrong and how or whether the broken economy can be repaired. As Moreno-Caballud points out, the greatest danger to the achievements of Spain's protest movements does not originate from the outdated and less-than-capable institutions of the establishment but from the fact that the hierarchy "of those who know and those who don't know tends to constantly resurface."[28] The works of literature analyzed in this book strive to break down the hierarchies that exclude most of the people impacted by global transformations from a small coterie of experts allowed to opine on the crisis. While the authors who address the crisis within the confines of the essay genre do not escape from the temptation to appoint themselves as an authority to be listened to, the novelists and the poets of the crisis refuse to occupy the position of those in the know who dispense the kind of wisdom that those who are not in the know are incapable of accessing on their own.

On the eve of the global economic crisis, it seemed as if Spain's economy could not be in a better shape.[29] In his crisis essay *Todo lo que era sólido*, Muñoz Molina quotes a litany of talking points used by Spain's politicians who, as late as 2008, relied on statistical data to demonstrate that Spain's economy was booming.[30] What these numbers concealed, however, was that the country's seeming prosperity was built on a bubble.[31] The celebratory reports about Spain's economic growth were based on the belief that numbers speak for themselves and require no further analysis. The primacy of numbers over words came into question once the crisis began:

> La creencia en la locuacidad de las cifras forma parte de tus creencias hasta que no caes en que es una metáfora que te está pensando a ti,

> cuando estabas creyendo que eras tú quien la usaba para pensar por ti mismo [The idea that numbers can speak forms part of your beliefs until you begin to realize that this is a metaphor that is thinking you up while you believed that you were the one who used it in order to think for yourself].[32]

As Luisa Elena Delgado points out, the idea that everything needs to be quantified resulted in a reduction of social reality to lists of numbers and made even political protests depend for their measure of viability on numbers and not on the ideas expressed by protesters.[33] The unqualified trust in numbers that inspired the creation of the bubble economy needs to give way to a recognition that words matter as much or even more. The need to reclaim the primacy of the word inspires many of the works of literature created in response to the crisis.

These novels, essays, and poems share the vision of the crisis that is perfectly encapsulated by Gramsci's famous definition: "The crisis consists precisely in the fact that the old is dying and the new cannot be born: in this interregnum, morbid phenomena of the most varied kind come to pass."[34] The economic crisis of 2008–2012 is one of several that have occurred recently in a world where crises of all kinds have become the norm. There is a growing tendency to refer as "a crisis" to developments whose understanding would gain from an avoidance of this particular term.[35] The feeling of living in a world that is constantly being shaken by crises comes from the often-unacknowledged fact that the very state model we inhabit is undergoing a profound change: "We live in a constant state of crisis, and the crisis also involves the modern state, whose structure, functionality, effectiveness (including the system of democratic representation) are no longer suited to the times in which we live."[36] National governments are less and less capable of resolving problems visited upon citizens by faraway developments. As a result, voters lose confidence in the capacity of democratic institutions to address their most pressing concerns. The growing popularity of political movements that used to be confined to the fringes and the electoral success of nontraditional candidates testify to the increasing restlessness of electorates that are disillusioned with the existing democratic structures.

Spain's tortuous path to representative democracy finally culminated, after the death of dictator Franco, in an establishment of a stable, functioning democratic state. Today, however, it is becoming clear that, from the very start, this achievement carried the seeds of its own disruption because the foundations of the current global economic crisis were being laid during the same time in the 1970s when Spain's democracy was consolidated:

> The origins of the present global economic crisis . . . may be traced to the 1970s and the capital logic and concomitant global restructuring that expressed the attempt by core capital to circumvent the limits to

> capital accumulation imposed in the advanced capitalist societies, in order to raise again the rate of profit. This new globalized capital logic took the form of the globalization of production, the financialization of capital and the globalization of finance, accompanied by ideologically driven economic doctrines emphasizing new extremes of self-regulation and de-regulation of capital and market.[37]

Spain's newly democratic state fully subscribed to these economic policies, and even left-wing political parties agreed not to question the neoliberal economic precepts that have dominated the world economy since the 1970s.[38] Because of the close identification of Spain's democracy with this economic philosophy, the current crisis has created a crisis of confidence in the very political system that has demonstrated its incapacity to protect citizens from the depredations of deregulated markets.[39] Time and again, the authors of crisis literature question the value of Spain's self-identification as a democratic society if the country's democratic institutions are dedicated to defending the interests of transnational financial interests to the detriment of voters.

The sustained growth of the country's economy before 2008 had left little space for questioning the neoliberal economic mechanisms in post-Transition Spain, given that these economic policies were credited with the capacity to produce an unprecedented enrichment of Spaniards.[40] The promise of finally overcoming Spain's marginalization within Europe that was implicit in adopting the economic policies shared by the members of the European Economic Community put too high a premium—economically, but also emotionally and psychologically—on avoiding any deviation from the economic path set by the leaders of deregulation policies. In the words of Manolo Monereo, a member of the Political Counsel of Izquierda Unida,[41] Spain's desire to overcome the myth of its insufficient modernity, the contemporary version of its Black Legend, pushed the country into an uncritical acceptance of EEC's and, later, EU's economic policies:

> El "ya somos como ellos" y el "somos europeos" se confundieron: atrás quedaban definitivamente el atraso económico y el complejo de inferioridad de un pueblo en busca de una modernidad perdida y casi nunca encontrada [There was a confusion between "we are now just like them" and "we are Europeans": we were finally leaving behind the economic backwardness and the inferiority complex of a modernity that had been lost and almost never found].[42]

The belief that unprecedented economic prosperity was bound to follow an integration into the union of European nations was supported by the improvement in Spaniards' well-being after the 1986 entrance into the EEC and the creation of a robust welfare state in Spain.[43]

By the time the twenty-first century began, Spain comfortably inhabited its newly acquired image as a model member of the European Union that had managed to shed its undemocratic past to achieve explosive economic growth. These gains cast doubt on the necessity of looking for an alternative to the political and economic status quo.[44] The crisis, however, has shattered Spaniards' confidence in the stability of their position as valuable participants in the European project and removed the obstacles to questioning the results of the Transition. Moreover, the very value of "Europe" as an ideological construct and an object of emotional attachment is now being questioned, given that the policies of economic austerity that are dictated to Spain by Brussels are increasingly blamed in Spain for the suffering of the country's citizens affected by the crisis: "Europe is very quickly losing, at the street level, the attraction that it used to have in Spain. Europe, which during the fascist dictatorships led by General Franco was perceived by the democratic forces as the dream to be reached once democracy had been established, has become a nightmare."[45] Literature of the crisis voices a profound disillusionment with the way in which the political and the economic realms in the post-Franco era were constituted and proposes to undertake an analysis of the past that will help create solutions to the problems of today. The works of literature analyzed in this book were published before Spain's political system was shaken by the failure of the political parties to constitute a functioning government between December 2015 and the end of October 2016. Still, a conscience of the insufficiency and even impotence of Spain's democratic institutions is already present in many of them.

Spain's political right has been sensitive to the subversive potential implicit in questioning the past and has used the crisis as an excuse to subject the growing interest in the country's past to an exercise in austerity: " The crisis in Spain has been appropriated by the right to deprioritize historical memory as they argue that the gravity of the present situation obviates a concern with the past, and that the scarcity of resources makes funding destined for historical memory unsustainable."[46] Spain's Historical Memory Law adopted in late 2007 as a result of efforts by the Socialist government of Rodríguez Zapatero was, from its very beginning, rejected by the Partido Popular.[47] The opponents of the law insisted that it undermined the legitimacy of the Transition and, consequently, cast doubt on the entire constitutional system that arose from it.[48] During the municipal elections of 2007, José María Aznar, the former president of Spain's government, gave a talk in Calatayud, Zaragoza, suggesting that the recovery of historical memory of the war and the dictatorship would somehow undermine the country's capacity to build a better future:

> España no necesita mirar hacia atrás ni remover huesos, ni tumbas, ni hablar de guerras civiles. España lo que necesita es mirar más que nunca al futuro y tender puentes pero no volver a etapas absurdas de divisiones y de confrontaciones." [Spain doesn't need to look backwards or dig up bones and graves or talk about civil wars. What Spain

needs is, more than ever, to look to the future and build bridges instead of going back to the absurd times of divisions and confrontations.][49]

The Transition-era belief that inquiries into the crimes of the Franco dictatorship would bring Spain to the brink of another civil conflict has thus reappeared in Aznar's precrisis discussion of historical memory. Aznar positioned the need to forget the past as a necessary precondition to entering a better future and dismissed the Civil War of 1936–1939 as one of many indistinguishable and unimportant "civil wars."

The economic crisis made it harder to evoke the need to preserve the gains of the Transition as an argument against the recovery of historical memory, given that the Transition was rapidly losing its hallowed status.[50] Instead, Spain's political right relied upon the crisis itself to construct a narrative of the past that would erase the Civil War and the dictatorship from the list of subjects fit for discussion during the difficult times. For instance, during a talk given at the Foro Agrario in Valladolid in October 2015, Isabel García Tejerina, Spain's Minister of Agriculture, used the idea that the crisis had been overcome to promote a vision of Spain's history that represents a linear path from one success to another: "La historia de España y los españoles es la de un éxito colectivo. Juntos hemos vencido a la peor crisis" [The history of Spain and of the Spaniards is that of a collective success. Together we have achieved a victory over the worst of crises].[51] The forum was sponsored by Caja España-Duero, a banking entity whose leadership was investigated in 2014 by the National Court[52] "por 'idear' la emisión de preferentes y deuda subordinada como un instrumento para capitalizar las entidades 'a costa y en perjuicio de los clientes'" [for coming up with the idea to issue preferred stock and subordinated shares as an instrument to capitalize the entities "at the expense and to the detriment of clients"].[53] The minister's vision of the country's history as being defined by unmarred shared success excludes both those who were victimized by the war and the dictatorship and those who are struggling with joblessness and economic privations in today's Spain. This narrative is useful to the large financial concerns that are benefiting from the EU-mandated policies of propping up the banking industry with state money, yet it is less comforting to those who fail to perceive the current state of affairs in Spain as a great collective success.

The leaders of Partido Popular had made it very clear during the party's struggle to displace PSOE from power in the first years of the crisis that, in case of being elected, they would make every effort to cripple the recovery of the Republican memory of the Civil War and the dictatorship. At the time of the electoral campaign of 2008, Mariano Rajoy promised that if his party won the elections, "ni un solo euro del erario público" [not a single euro from public funds] would be invested into funding the provisions of the Historical Memory Law.[54] It has become clear since then, however, that Rajoy's contention that the state does not have resources to invest into maintaining historical legacy applies only to the Republican memory of the war. In October 2015, for instance, Rajoy did not manage to answer the question of journalist Pepa Bueno as to the selective nature of austerity measures administered by his government to the legacy of the Civil War. Rajoy insisted that he had no knowledge of the fact that the last four state budgets had included no funding for the disinterment of the bodies of Republicans from unmarked mass graves yet had subsidized the Francisco Franco Foundation.[55] Spain's literature of the crisis resists the attempts to use the crisis as an excuse for silencing the narratives of the war and the dictatorship that do not serve the purposes of the country's austerity government. In this, the crisis writers are responding to the wishes of those who are not prepared to sacrifice their interest in recovering the memory of the war to the austerity measures promoted by the Partido Popular.[56]

The authors analyzed in this book approach history in a way that is quite different from that which inspired the "memory boom" of the first decade of the century. The many works of literature on the subject of the Civil War and the dictatorship published in the years before the crisis often promoted a sentimentalized vision of that era, emptying it of any subversive potential.[57] The historical memory genre has enjoyed very good sales and is fully integrated into the consumerist culture that uses history to create the illusion that no alternative to the status quo is possible:

> A cultural market has capitalized on the historical memory by offering television series and films as well as novels to satisfy a perceived need by the general public to come to terms with the tragedy of the civil war, which expressly commercialize the memory with sentimental and even melodramatic stories. . . . The past may continue to be gone and unreachable, while the illusions of the market present us with a timeless succession of the same.[58]

Literature of the crisis, on the other hand, is looking for ways to disinter the disturbing potential of the war's legacy with the goal of mining it for solutions to Spain's current problems. The writers of the crisis literature refuse to see history as a commodity that, to be profitable, is emptied of any content that might prove even slightly subversive. Instead, they suggest relying on the past in order to approach the present in a critical manner. History is explored in these works of literature in a way that connects the patterns of economic exploitation created in the postwar era with today's economic troubles.

The need to come to terms with Spain's Francoist past is especially pressing given that the crisis has awakened fears that the growing impoverishment of Europeans might lead to the return of fascism.[59] Because of its history and the recency of its transition from the undemocratic dictatorship of Franco, Spain is often seen as especially likely to backslide from democracy.[60] Many of the works of literature analyzed here point to the possibility that an increasing presence and visibility of immigrants in Spain might be used by conservative political forces to promote narratives that are both undemocratic and hostile to the gains of the Western European welfare state. It was not until the 1990s that Spain transformed from a country of emigration to one of immigration, which is why the existing mechanisms of integrating immigrants are still deficient.[61] The economic hardship created by the crisis often leads to an exploitation of anti-immigrant fears in order to distract the public from the austerity measures administered to Spain's welfare programs. To offer a single example, the reduction in health spending has been explained as driven by the need to prevent the alleged abuse of Spain's health care system by immigrants:

> In 2012 as the current economic crisis becomes more dramatic . . . the Spanish government's announcement that they were going to make budget cuts in health spending has made clear the discriminatory discourses towards immigrants, and the argument that they take advantage of the welfare state has gained strength, aided also by the official political discourse in which this argument has been stated without any hesitation.[62]

Literature of the crisis attempts to humanize the image of an immigrant, pointing to the commonalities in the way the crisis is experienced by everybody in Spain, regardless of their country of origin. At the same time, these novels, essays, and poems do not sentimentalize the image of immigrants, demonstrating that an immigrant deserves to be engaged with as a complex and nuanced human being capable of both kindness and cruelty.[63]

Normally, immigrants do not possess a sophisticated knowledge of Spain's history when they come to the country. As a result, the task of making known to them the difficulties Spaniards had to overcome on their way to constructing a stable democracy becomes urgent.[64] Writers of the crisis ponder the ways in which memory of the Civil War can be made relevant to immigrant experiences in a manner that does not aim to erase the immigrants' own cultural and historical legacies. At the same time, soaring unemployment within Spain has forced many Spaniards to leave the country in search of employment. They find themselves in a position of immigrants who are striving to adapt to other cultures while connecting Spain's experience of the crisis to that of their new countries of residence.[65] Among the works of literature that I analyze, there are both those that were created by Spanish writers residing overseas and those that feature characters forced to move abroad in search of opportunities denied them at home by the harsh circumstances created by the crisis.

The increasing migratory flows of the late twentieth and early twenty-first centuries have weakened the capacity of national governments for sovereign decision making.[66] Growing migration is characteristic of a world in flux where borders are being rendered permeable and the form of statehood that relied on exercising control over national borders is being eroded. In the words of Zygmunt Bauman, "we are witnessing the revenge of nomadism over the principle of territoriality or settlement."[67] The profound transformation of the entire way of being of advanced capitalist societies that Bauman refers to as the "fluid stage of modernity"[68] is central to the experience of the era referred to as "the crisis." An emotional attachment to a particular territory—a neighborhood, a village, a city, or a country—that individuals might see as crucial to their sense of self is giving way to capital's need to have access to a rootless labor force that is ready to sever all attachments and move anywhere at a short notice in search of increasingly precarious employment. In a world dominated by liquid capital, few individuals can expect to practice the same profession throughout their entire adult lives or live among the people, the scenery, and the objects that are familiar to them since childhood. The need to mimic the fluidity of capital geographically, professionally, psychologically, and in every other way comes at a high cost. All that one can expect to gain in return for abandoning any kind of rootedness is a promise of an even greater fluidity in the future.

Spain's crisis literature strives to make sense of the increasing fluidity of existence. The high frequency of references to fluidity or liquidity is mirrored, in these works of art, by the writers' exploration of fluid narrative forms or their experimentation with fluid genres. For instance, Rafael Chirbes's novel *En la orilla* is centered around the image of the stagnant waters of a swamp that symbolize the protagonist's incapacity to adapt to the growing fluidity of economic and interpersonal relationships that have an impact on his life. Lucia Etxebarria's essay *Liquidación por derribo* relies upon an unstoppable flow of the author's writing to sweep away the readers' resistance to accepting the changes that are taking place. The collection of poetry *Marca(da) España* is organized on the basis of creating a continuous flow between the photography of the German journalist Reiner Wandler and the Spanish poets who used it as inspiration for their poetry.

The emergence of "light, free-floating capitalism, marked by the disengagement and loosening of ties linking capital and labor"[69] is leaving many workers unmoored and lost in the world where their hold on productive employment becomes increasingly more precarious. The erosion of stable employment in favor of short-term contract work has been taking place in Spain for years. Spain's explosive job growth during the economic boom of the second half of the 1980s inspired optimistic accounts of the state of the country's economy that concealed the growing difficulty of finding stable, long-term work.[70] Since 2008, the crisis of

Spain's job market became impossible to conceal.[71] The destructive nature of unemployment or underemployment is at the center of most of the works of literature analyzed in this book. Their characters overcome the shame implicit in unemployment to discuss the ways in which the new reality of a growing number of people failing to escape the cycle of short-term contracts transforms the very concept of work. Joblessness often leads to an identity crisis which, in spite of the pain it entails, allows these characters to observe that their individual crises are part of a larger transformation that is impacting the very nature of the society they inhabit.

Amidst the growing fluidity of capital and permeability of national borders, national governments are weakened by their incapacity to place any significant obstacles in the path of capital flows that are ravaging national economies and leaving great numbers of citizens outside of productive employment. The "global neoliberal order" that began to emerge during the 1970s entails "dismantled national productive systems and globalized agents, alongside weak national governments and insufficient, uncoordinated supranational authorities that operate along their fringes."[72] National governments have little power to control the capital flows that have an enormous impact on the lives of citizens. Instead, they look for ways to mitigate the effects of the global economic collapse in a manner that will be beneficial to large financial concerns. The crisis has made it clear that when faced with a choice between helping the citizens and rescuing the country's financial entities, national governments would choose the latter.[73] The problematic nature of this newly constituted global order was laid bare by the crisis of 2008 when citizens started to realize that national governments were impotent to impose their authority on capital flows. This development added a problematic dimension to political activism on the national or local levels: "Much of the power previously contained inside the borders of the nation-state evaporated and flew into the no-man's land of the 'space of flows,' whereas politics has remained as before territorially fixed and constrained."[74] In order to signal their disillusionment with the capacity of either of the two major political parties in Spain to oppose the power of the banks, the protesters of the 15-M movement used slogans like "Ni PSOE ni PP," "Nuestros sueños no caben en vuestras urnas," "Ni cara A, ni cara B, queremos cambiar de disco" ["Neither PSOE nor PP," "Our dreams don't fit into your ballot boxes," "Neither side A nor side B, we want to change the record"].[75]

At the time when it emerged, the 15-M movement did not ally itself with any existing political party and proposed to draw attention to the incapacity of Spain's political establishment to speak to the needs of the voters. In 2013, many of the movement's participants came together to organize a political party that would offer an alternative to the Socialist

Party (PSOE) and the Popular Party (PP). The new party was called Podemos, and the party's official website defined its goals as follows:

> Podemos was born with the conviction that change is possible and with the certainty that this change will not be created by other political parties (especially by the ones that have led us to the present situation) but by the people who work or are looking for work every day and demand, with complete legitimacy, a future that is more prosperous and equal for themselves and their families.[76]

By the end of 2015, the party's membership was close to 400,000,[77] which testifies to the eagerness of many Spaniards to step outside of the confines of Spain's "politics as usual." As the party started losing ground to the centrist Ciudadanos, however, the leadership decided to modify Podemos's more radical positions and withdrew the suggestion to rewrite Spain's constitution, recognizing that "the political pact of 1978 had 'positive elements' and achieved 'a difficult accord in very complex circumstances.'"[78] Podemos's journey toward an increasingly centrist and pro-establishment position once again raises the question of the extent to which the political process on a national level can address globally generated problems. At the elections of December 2015, Podemos gained slightly over 20 percent of the vote. In May 2016, an alliance between Podemos and Izquierda Unida was created and named Unidos Podemos [Together We Can]. This measure, however, failed to bring an increase in voter support in the repeat elections of June 2016. A record low voter turnout for these elections and the political stalemate that lasted until late October 2016 and kept the country in suspense as to which party would form the government demonstrated that none of the existing political options were ready to offer a convincing path out of the crisis.

The capital's liberation from being tied to any specific territory erodes confidence in the nation-state model and the state's capacity to defend the interests of its citizens: "As markets drive out politics, the nation-state increasingly loses its capacities to raise taxes and stimulate growth, and with them the ability to secure the essential foundations of its own legitimacy."[79] As the preface to the collection of poetry *Marca(da) España* points out, nation-states are forced to market themselves to global corporations to attract capital, fickle as the companies' allegiance to the nations in question might be. The efforts of national governments to turn the nation into a product that private commercial entities will find appealing undermines the very concept of national sovereignty:

> El nuevo orden mundial basado en la globalización de la economía y la interconexión de los mercados ha dejado prácticamente obsoletas muchas de las nociones asociadas al estado-nación independiente y soberano, a la vez que presenta nuevas demandas sobre los mecanismos de auto-presentación y representación nacional en el mercado global. [The new world order based on the globalization of the economy and inter-

> connectedness of markets has rendered practically obsolete many of the notions associated with an independent and sovereign nation-state, as well as positing new demands related to mechanisms of self-presentation and national representation on the global market.][80]

The erosion of authority commanded by a nation-state has a strong negative impact on the nation's capacity to guarantee the continued existence of a robust welfare system. The conflict between the interests of transnational corporations and citizens who expect their national governments to privilege their well-being over the profit-making capacity of these companies is experienced especially acutely by the countries located on the geographic and symbolic margins of the European project.[81] There is little reason to believe that the social programs that were eliminated or slashed as part of the anticrisis austerity measures will be reestablished in full now that the crisis is declared to have been overcome.

The weakening, or in Habermas's words, "the disempowerment,"[82] of the nation-state will not result in the erasure of political separatism or in the ebbing of the need to mount spectacles of passionate rejection of the Other that lies at the basis of national identification. To the contrary, anxieties over the fraying social safety net translate into an increasingly vocal and even violent rejection of migrants who are seen as competition for already dwindling resources. Virulent nationalism is on the rise in the developed countries whose citizens channel the rage they experience as a result of being left behind by the fluid economy into anti-immigrant *ressentiment*. The retreat of the nation-state can be observed not in a greater tolerance toward the Other but, rather, in the growing unwillingness or incapacity of national governments to fulfill "the promise to better the material welfare of [its] citizens."[83] The relentless assault of the flows of liquid capital sweeps away the controls, limited as they might have been, over social and economic stratification: "The globalization of the economy destroys a historical constellation that made the welfare state compromise possible. Even if this compromise was never the ideal solution for a problem inherent within capitalism itself, it nevertheless held capitalism's social costs within tolerable limits."[84] As the state retreats from its welfare obligations, new ways of articulating the links among the members of smaller and larger communities will have to be found to prevent the growing economic inequality from exacerbating ethnic and religious tensions in the heterogeneous Western societies.

The global transformations that hide under the label of "the crisis" will do away with many of the certainties that have informed the relationship between state and citizens since the consolidation of the nation-state model of state organization: "Under threat in the West appears to be the centrality of large industrial complexes, blue-collar work, full employment, centralized bureaucracies of management, mass markets for cheap standardized goods, the welfare state, mass political parties and the centrality of the national state as a unit of organization."[85] The welfare state, aptly described by García Recio as "esa gran fiesta a la que nos dijeron que estábamos todos invitados y de la que ahora nos expulsan a patadas" [this great feast to which we were told we were all invited and from which we are now being kicked out],[86] is crumbling, and there is no reason to believe that the privatization of the services it used to provide is likely to be reversed.[87] In spite of its self-congratulating rhetoric as to the end of the crisis, Partido Popular proposed a state budget for 2016 that continued the trend of defunding public education and health care and signaled the state's support for private alternatives for these crucial services.[88]

The major societal transformations that we are witnessing do not take place solely in the sphere of the economy. Post-Fordism, as the emerging societal form is often termed,[89] "is as much a description of cultural as of economic change. . . . Culture has ceased to be, if ever it was, a decorative addendum to the 'hard world' of production and things, the icing on the cake of the material world. The word is now as 'material' as the world."[90] Works of literature are creating a new language that will allow discussion of these new realities. Literature produces concrete images and ideas that can anchor the reader in the world of flows and, in this way, provide a foothold from which to engage in resistance to the liquefaction that capital visits on institutions and relationships alike. The rapid changes we are witnessing can be traced if we pay special attention to the transformation of language: "This acceleration becomes especially apparent at the level of language. . . . Many key political and social concepts are becoming anachronistic and are even becoming so hollowed out from within that they no longer disclose anything. . . . Everywhere we find deflated linguistic formulas, broken coordinates and hollowed-out institutions."[91] Crisis literature points to the erosion of meaning of such familiar concepts as, for instance, "democracy" and "welfare" and invites readers to participate in a shared construction of meaning, refusing to outsource this task to the corporate world. To give an example, the artists who contributed to the volume *Marca(da) España* reject the idea that the main task of the weakened nation-state should consist in assisting large companies in branding their products. Crisis poets attempt to rescue the word "Spain" as a space of collective identification that exists for purposes other than selling goods. National governments cannot be expected to withstand the pressures of fluid capital and preserve a welfare safety net to the extent that will prevent an increasing pauperization of large swathes of society. Jürgen Habermas believes that only "the consciousness of an obligatory cosmopolitan solidarity" can lead to the creation, on a global level, of mechanisms that will mitigate the effects of the erosion of the nation-state model.[92] Spain's literature of the crisis breaks through the country's manufactured isolation within Europe and points to its enmeshment in and responsibility for the global processes known as "the crisis."

Many of Spain's leading writers have participated in popular protest movements and pointed out that creating works of literature is a crucial component of the resistance to the destruction of the welfare state. For instance, Marta Sanz and Benjamín Prado read the statement of the manifestation against welfare cuts in July 2013. In Sanz's words, "En este momento convendría que cada escritor escribiera su propia novela de la crisis" [At this time, every writer should write a novel of the crisis].[93] Many of the Spanish writers are of the same mind as Sanz and have been creating works of literature that discuss the crisis. Not only novels but also essays, short stories, works of theater, and poetry of the crisis have been published in Spain, and there is no indication that the crisis genre is likely to lose its relevance any time soon. The writers of the crisis have already produced a significant number of valuable works of literature that refuse to adopt the definition of the crisis as a small contretemps of short duration that has already been partly or entirely overcome. It would not be possible to provide an in-depth analysis of all these works within a single volume. Instead, I have selected the ones that have enriched, more than others, my own understanding of Spain's experience of the crisis. Such a selection is always based on individual readerly tastes and interests and does not necessarily speak to the artistic quality and cultural impact of the texts that have been excluded from the analysis.

The fluidity that is eroding the economic, political, professional, and intellectual certainties that underpin our lives did not find a way into this book. I have adopted a fairly rigid structure of subdividing the works of literature I analyze into chapters according to their genre. There are clear differences in the ways in which essayists, novelists, and poets approach the crisis and conceptualize fluidity. Some, like Antonio Muñoz Molina and Lucía Etxebarria, believe that we have no choice but to sever all roots and liquefy ourselves with the hopes of becoming useful to liquid capital. Others, like Belén Gopegui and Isabel Pérez Montalbán, insist that forming networks of solidarity is crucial to stop the flows that are destroying our welfare protections and isolating us in the mentality of personal responsibility for the suffering that the crisis causes us. I coincide with those of the Spanish crisis writers who warn that an enthusiastic embrace of fluidity serves the needs of capital and facilitates exploitation. Pockets of resistance to the devastation wrought by liquid capital will appear in the spaces where those affected by the crisis come together in a refusal to dissolve the links of rootedness and solidarity that ground us in our shared reality. The structure of this book mimics the resistance to fluidity that characterizes the vision of the crisis shared by most of the authors I analyze.

Many essays that attempt to explain the causes of the crisis and point to ways of overcoming it have been published in Spain since 2008. For the purposes of this study, I concentrated on book-length essays by two of Spain's best-selling novelists, Antonio Muñoz Molina and Lucía Etxebarria. For now, they are the only renowned writers of fiction who have decided to explore the essay genre as a way of addressing the crisis. The first chapter of this book contrasts the manners in which these authors approach the concept of fluidity that is central to the experience of the crisis. Muñoz Molina's *Todo lo que era sólido* (2013) warns the readers that the gains of the Western European welfare state are under threat as a result of the unstoppable currents of capital. The writer suggests that Spaniards embrace the austerity measures proposed by the government of Mariano Rajoy and apply "cuts" to the intensity of their own political opinions and their interest in Spain's past. The writer allies himself with the position expressed by the representatives of Spain's political right who insist that dwelling on the country's history is likely to aggravate tensions and maybe even lead to another civil conflict. Like Muñoz Molina, Etxebarria locates the central causes of the severity of Spain's crisis in the Spaniards' presumed incapacity to overcome corruption. *Liquidación por derribo* (2013) enacts a welcoming approach to fluidity in its structure and the style of writing. In spite of their political differences, Muñoz Molina and Etxebarria arrive at a similar position that consists of condemning the excesses of Spanish consumers while advocating for a greater psychological and economic agility in embracing austerity on both societal and personal levels.

The second chapter of this book is dedicated to the novel of the crisis and begins with two novels by Rafael Chirbes, the writer whose name, more than any other, has been linked to the emergence of the genre of crisis literature.[94] Chirbes's *Crematorio* [*Crematorium*] was published in 2007, a year before the September 15, 2008, declaration of bankruptcy by Lehman Brothers, considered to mark the symbolic beginning of the crisis. The writer's *En la orilla*, published in English in 2016 with the title *On the Edge*, appeared at the pinnacle of the crisis in 2012. The novel points to the consequences of the corrupt business practices depicted in *Crematorio* and explores the devastation that the soaring unemployment has brought. Both novels remind readers that the foundations of the economic system that is collapsing were laid during the Civil War and the dictatorship of Franco and question the possibility of articulating an ideology of resistance in view of the discredited Socialist alternative to capitalism. The task of integrating Spain's historical memory into the narrative of anticapitalist struggle is complicated by tensions between Spanish-born characters and immigrants. The need to make any effort at political resistance meaningful to Spain's growing immigrant populations is also central to Luis García Montero's 2012 novel *No me cuentes tu vida* [*Don't Tell Me Your Life*]. The novel's middle-aged protagonist hopes to transmit his interest in Spain's history to his son and strives to overcome his fear that immigrants might not be receptive to the memory of the anti-Franco struggle that holds such a central meaning to the generations of Spaniards who ushered in the Transition to democracy. Benjamín Prado's *Ajuste de cuentas* [*Settling of Scores*] (2013) questions the value of Spain's democracy now that the crisis has laid bare the extent to which the country's democratically elected governments are beholden to global economic interests. The novel's protagonist, a journalist and a scholar of literature, finds in his writing a possibility of withstanding the pressures of ruthless market forces. The characters of Belén Gopegui's *El comité de la noche* (2014) also turn to writing as a way of creating a space where strategies of resistance can be articulated. The disillusionment with the capacity of the nation-state model to resist the devastation wrought by fluid capital prompts the characters of Gopegui's novel to create a clandestine resistance movement. The protagonists of this novel answer the question posed by Rafael Chirbes, the eldest of the writers analyzed here, as to the likelihood of an emergence of a resistance narrative that would offer the readers concrete possibilities of anticapitalist political engagement.

In the third chapter, I turn to poetry and discuss two poetic anthologies that were published with the specific intent to create a space for poets to share their experiences of the crisis. *En legítima defensa (Antología). Poetas en tiempos de crisis* [*In Self-Defense (Anthology). Poets in Times of Crisis*] and *Marca(da) España. Retrato poético de una sociedad en crisis* [*Branding Spain. A Poetic Depiction of Society in Crisis*] were published in 2014 and feature poetry by writers who belong to different generations and artistic movements. The specter of the Civil War is as present in these poems as in the novels and essays of the crisis. For instance, in her poem "La sorprendente vida" ["Amazing Life"] published in *En legítima defensa,* Francisca Aguirre evokes her personal memories of the war to issue a warning about the possibly violent consequences of allowing the exploitation of workers by the very rich to continue. "Dictadura financiera" [Financial Dictatorship], a poem that Isabel Pérez Montalbán contributed to *Marca(da) España,* echoes the idea expressed by Benjamín Prado in his novel of the crisis that the economic goals of the 1936 uprising of Spanish Nationalists are being achieved today through the seemingly peaceful austerity measures that benefit large financial concerns and foster economic inequality. The poets who contributed to these anthologies believe that the fluidity can be arrested through a creation of concrete images that will stop, albeit temporarily, the flows and allow for a moment of reflection needed to create strategies of resistance to the forces of global capital.

The short story genre is yet to produce a response to the crisis that, in terms of its artistic and intellectual value, would rise to the level of the novels, essays, and poems analyzed here. For instance, the publishing house Ediciones Atlantis initiated a project titled "Mayo temático" that the webpage introduced as follows:

> Una iniciativa editorial que recopila en seis tomos seis antologías centradas en la crisis, pero no solo en la económica, sino también en la social, ideológica, religiosa o afectiva. . . . Andalucía, Galicia, País Vasco, Castilla León, Valencia y Madrid verán recogida la interpretación literaria que sus autores hacen de la crisis. [A publishing initiative that gathers in six volumes six anthologies centered on the crisis but not only on the economic one but also on the social, ideological, religious, or affective. . . . Andalusia, Galicia, the Basque Country, Castile and Leon, Valencia and Madrid will see a collection of the literary interpretations that their authors have made of the crisis.][95]

Many of the motifs that appear in the prose and poetry of the crisis appear in these short stories. In the collection titled *Castilla-León: Golpe a la crisis. (Cinco narradores en clave del cuento)* [*Castile and Leon: A Blow to the Crisis (Five Narrators in Short Stories)*], four out of the five stories feature unemployed protagonists who look for ways to soothe the trauma of an unexpected expulsion from productive life. In the short story "Ciudades de plástico" ["Plastic Cities"] by Jairo Prieto Fernández, Ella, the protagonist whose lack of a name underscores the commonality of her experience of joblessness, arrives at a realization that the crisis represents much more than a malfunction of the economy:

> El problema ya no sólo parecía económico, sino que se estaba convirtiendo en un problema de salud pública. La crisis se había incrustado en la sangre, en los huesos, en las venas y en el sistema nervioso de las personas como un veneno invisible que los iba matando poco a poco. [The problem no longer appeared to be only economic. It was turning into a public health issue. The crisis had lodged in the people's blood, in the bones, in the veins and in the nervous system like an invisible poison that was killing them little by little.][96]

In José Villalba's "Que retumbe la fragua otra vez" ["Let the Forge Thunder Once Again"], a group of friends struggling with unemployment and marginalization expresses lack of trust in the kind of freedom that Western democracies can offer their citizens and arrives at a conclusion that the crisis cannot be addressed without remembering that "tenemos un pasado que ha dejado mucho lastre" [we have a past that has left a lot of baggage].[97] Still, more than works of art, the short stories published by Ediciones Atlantis as part of this project seem to constitute a contribution to the self-help genre that seeks to soothe tensions produced by the crisis through the creation of an escapist fantasy capable of providing a cathartic experience to the readers. Most of the short stories featured in the collection by authors from Andalusia, for example, have at their center a male protagonist who is crushed by unemployment and a consequent incapacity to provide for the family to which he is invariably devoted.[98] After experiencing great suffering and considering suicide, the unemployed male is miraculously saved by a stranger, a sibling, a priest, a child, and even an angel.

In April 2015, Cristina Fernández Cubas, one of Spain's leading authors working in the short story genre, published a collection titled *La habitación de Nona* [*Nona's Room*].[99] One of the stories in the collection, "Hablar con Viejas" ["Talking with Old Women"], allows the readers to hope that literature of the crisis will soon be enriched with contributions from short story writers. Alicia, the protagonist of Fernández Cubas's short story, discovers that the monstrosity awakened in her by the suffering she experiences as a result of the crisis has become greater than anything she can hope to contain. Alicia is imprisoned by the monster who reflects her own degradation and leaves her no hope of escaping and rebuilding her life. The past, represented in the story by the old woman referenced in the story's title, reveals itself as too powerful to be dismissed as nonthreatening. Alicia's greatest mistake consists in relying on her capacity to cheat the old woman and failing to recognize that caducity is not synonymous with weakness. The impossibility of establishing a genuine human contact untainted by financial considerations that lies at the heart of "Talking with Old Women" echoes the feelings of alienation that dominate the lives of the characters of crisis novels analyzed here. Unlike the short stories published by Ediciones Atlantis, Fernández Cubas's "Talking with Old Women" offers no possibility of catharsis and leaves it to the readers to find a way to come to terms with the monstrosity of the crisis. The complexity of the societal and economic transformations that hide beneath the label "the crisis" makes adapting the short story genre to the needs of the crisis literature a challenging task. There is no reason to believe, however, that Spanish writers will not be able to rise to this challenge.

Theater, on the other hand, has been inspired by the many collective initiatives arising from the 15-M protest movement to produce a wide variety of new formats of creative expression. A great number of independent theatrical groups and projects were created in response to the crisis, exploring the participatory possibilities of theater that could bring together artists and spectators in a search of a shared program of action. A theatrical collective Kubik Fabrik, for instance, made its mark as a space where artists could demonstrate parts of their work to spectators and receive their input on how the play should develop. Kubik's website makes it clear that creating a bastion of stability in a sea of fluid labor relations is a crucial part of its mission.[100] Kubik's loss of its performance space in Madrid's Usera district has been interpreted as a symptom that the effervescence of theatrical creativity in the past five years has been nothing but another bubble that has finally burst.[101] However, Kubik has turned the loss of its physical locale into an opportunity to explore new forms of artistic expression. The theater's last show in Usera, for instance, was based on a text created as a result of a collaboration between playwrights and the inhabitants of the neighborhood with the goal of rescuing from oblivion the collective memory of Usera.[102] A national tour of

"Historias de Usera" aims at bringing the experiences of this Madrid neighborhood to the rest of the country.

Teatro del Barrio shares with Kubik Fabrik the goal of reaching out to the inhabitants of the neighborhood where it is located. The theater offers a series of cultural and educational activities to adults and children who live in the Madrid neighborhood of Lavapiés and strives to foster community engagement.[103] On its website, Teatro del Barrio defines its mission as follows:

> Se trata de una iniciativa cultural para crear un proyecto denso, profundo, pluridisciplinar, destinado a cuestionar de forma radical la política, la sociedad, la economía y el arte. Sin ánimo de lucro. Sin propiedad. Asamblea. Ágora. Inteligencia colectiva. Radical." [This is a cultural initiative aimed at creating a dense, profound, pluridisciplinary project that will radically question politics, society, economy, and art. Nonprofit. Assembly. Agora. Collective intelligence. Radical.][104]

In 2014, Teatro del Barrio premiered *Ruz/Bárcenas*, a play created by Jordi Casanovas on the basis of the second deposition of Luis Bárcenas, the former senator and the treasurer of Partido Popular, conducted by Judge Pablo Ruz on July 15, 2013. In the short foreword to the text, Casanovas points out that his goal was to isolate the text of the deposition from the unstoppable torrent of news items about corruption in Spain and ground it in an environment of a theatrical performance where the spectators' attention would not be eroded by "el espectáculo mediático diario saturador" [the saturating daily spectacle of the media].[105] The changes that Casanovas introduced into the text of the deposition were limited to editing its length and breaking it into scenes.[106] The play reveals staggering levels of corruption among the leading figures of Partido Popular, including Mariano Rajoy and María Dolores de Cospedal, the party's Secretary General. The last words of the play are "Mariano Rajoy es el actual Presidente del Gobierno de España" [Mariano Rajoy is currently the president of the government of Spain].[107] Since the play premiered, Mariano Rajoy once again managed to be elected—albeit not without difficulty—to this position.

In the same year when *Ruz/Bárcenas* premiered, K Producciones, a theater company with a great interest in plays that touch upon subjects of political and social importance, brought to the stage the eminently successful *Ejecución hipotecaria* [*Foreclosure*] by Miguel Ángel Sánchez. Charly, the protagonist of the play, shares with many of the characters of crisis literature the disillusionment with the kind of society that was constituted as a result of Spain's transition to democracy:

> Te dicen que vives en un país libre, que estás en un estado de derecho. . . , les mola mucho lo del estado de derecho. ¡Un estado de derecho donde no tienes derecho a nada! ¡Ni a una vivienda digna! ¡Me cago en la puta constitución! [They tell you that you live in a free

> country, that there is rule of law. . . . They really dig all that about the rule of law. A rule of law where you have no rights! Not even the right to a decent place to live! I shit on the damn constitution!][108]

When a bank sends its representatives to evict Charly from his foreclosed apartment, he takes them hostage in a desperate attempt to resist the injustice of being denied a place to live. Charly is well aware of the narrative dictating that everybody should embrace fluidity to serve the interests of capital: "En estos tiempos hay que estar preparado para el cambio. Hay que ser flexible. ¿No es lo que dicen los ejecutivos?" [These days one has to be prepared for change. One has to be flexible. Isn't that what the executives say?].[109] Charly's is a solitary rebellion, however. He is isolated in his foreclosed apartment and has nobody to share his insights and develop a joint program of action. As a result, he fails to achieve anything and wreaks his vengeance on people who are as helpless in the face of the sweeping change brought by liquid capitalism as he is. The emergence, since the birth of the 15-M protest movement, of a great variety of theatrical groups that foster community engagement is aimed precisely at precluding such solitary tragedies. The importance of crisis theater lies not only in the texts that are written for the stage but, to an even greater degree, in the effervescing environment of political activism and collective engagement that gave rise to these theatric endeavors. This vibrant cultural scene cannot be covered in a single chapter and deserves to have a study dedicated to it that would explore the participatory and activist facets of the cultural initiatives arising from the crisis.

The genre of crisis literature has produced outstanding works of art that have greatly enriched Spanish letters and facilitated the readers' understanding of the crisis. The developments that are inspiring the writers of the crisis to create these novels, poems, and essays will not be undone irrespective of how politically expedient it might be to celebrate the end of the crisis. The works of literature discussed in this book serve as a space where private experiences and public concerns meet in a way that disrupts acquiescence with the narratives that serve the interests of the increasingly liquid capital. Despite the ideological, generational, and stylistic differences between the writers who have contributed to the literature of the crisis, their work relies on shared imagery, concepts, and concerns. This allows one to posit the existence of a genre of crisis literature, as opposed to isolated works of art that discuss the crisis.

NOTES

1. Zygmunt Bauman and Carlo Bordoni, *State of Crisis* (Cambridge: Polity, 2014), 108.

2. In the original: "Puedo asegurarles que España está saliendo ya de la crisis." See "Rajoy, ante los líderes iberoamericanos: 'España está saliendo ya de la crisis,'" *El*

Mundo, October 19, 2013, www.elmundo.es/elmundo/2013/10/19/espana/1382201074.html (accessed March 27, 2015).

3. "En muchos aspectos, la crisis ya es historia." See Carlos E. Cué, "Rajoy: 'La crisis ya es historia,'" *El País*, December 11, 2014,http://politica.elpais.com/politica/2014/12/11/actualidad/1418305803_331591.html (accessed September 2, 2015).

4. Gumersindo Lafuente and Silvia Bravo, "El paro y la desigualdad no dejan ver la recuperación," *El País*, August 1, 2015, http://politica.elpais.com/politica/2015/08/01/actualidad/1438444946_541840.html (accessed August 5, 2015.

5. Jeannette Neumann, "Why Is Spain's Economy Expanding So Robustly Without a Government?" *Wall Street Journal*, August 25, 2016. www.wsj.com/articles/why-is-spains-economy-expanding-so-robustly-without-a-government-1472136858 (accessed November 7, 2016).

6. "Discurso de Mariano Rajoy. Sesión de Investidura," Partido Popular, Oficina de Información, *El Mundo*, October 29, 2016, http://estaticos.elmundo.es/documentos/2016/10/29/discurso_investidura_rajoy.pdf, 2 (accessed November 8, 2016).

7. Bauman and Bordoni, *State of Crisis*, 59.

8. "No tiene ningún sentido liquidar todas las reformas. Mejoremos lo mejorable, pero no impidamos que España siga siendo el país que más crece en Europa y el que más empleo crea. ¿Acaso esto es malo?" [It makes no sense to liquidate all of the reforms. Let us improve what can be improved but let us not prevent Spain from continuing to have the fastest growing economy in Europe that creates the most jobs. Or is this a bad thing?] See "Discurso," http://estaticos.elmundo.es/documentos/2016/10/29/discurso_investidura_rajoy.pdf, 4 (accessed November 8, 2016).

9. "Recession," Definition 4. *Oxford English Dictionary*, second edition, Vol. IV (Oxford: Clarendon Press, 1989).

10. "Crisis," *Diccionario manual e ilustrado de la lengua española* (Madrid: Espasa Calpe, 1950), 464.

11. Henry George Liddell and Robert Scott, *A Greek-English Lexicon* (Oxford: Clarendon Press, 1996), 997.

12. "Días críticos llaman los médicos aquellos en que se puede hazer juyzio y discurso de la enfermedad del paciente. . . . Otras enfermedades ay que se llaman chrónicas, que quiere dezir temporales, porque no tienen cuenta los médicos de sus días, y en su cura no saben más de ciencia que una vieja por experiencia" [Medics refer as critical to the days when it is possible to judge and name a patient's illness. There are other illnesses called chronic, which means temporal, because doctors do not know how long they last and know less science that could cure them than an experienced old woman]. See Sebastián de Covarrubias, *Tesoro de la lengua castellana o española*, ed. Martín de Riquer (1611; repr., Barcelona: Horta, 1943), 372. The global economic crisis that began in 2008 seems to resemble more the illnesses that Covarrubias defines as chronic, rather than the ones in which he sees a potential for critical moments (i.e., the times when a definitive judgment as to what is happening can be made).

13. Luis Moreno-Caballud, *Cultures of Anyone: Studies on Cultural Democratization in the Spanish Neoliberal Crisis*, trans. Linda Grabner (Liverpool: Liverpool University Press, 2015), 26.

14. The crisis of 2008–2012 demonstrated that countries of Southern Europe never truly enjoyed the status of fully equal participants in the European project. The readiness evinced by the nations located at the geographic and symbolic center of Europe to consider an expulsion of Greece, Portugal, and Spain from the European Union because of the difficulties these countries experienced in addressing the consequences of the crisis is a sign of their marginalized position within Europe whose origins precede, by far, the current economic developments: "The PIGS were not made peripheral by the crisis—historically, they were already in the periphery. Although they were not part of the third world, their asymmetries with France, Germany, and the UK were very great. Although the Structural Funds of the EU allowed these countries to increase their standard of living, they also concealed their position on the periphery. In many ways, integration worsened their position by dismantling their productive sys-

tems and furthering deindustrialization." See Arturo Guillén, "Europe: A Crisis Within a Crisis," *International Journal of Political Economy* 41, no. 3 (Fall 2012): 60.

15. Zygmunt Bauman, *Liquid Modernity* (Cambridge: Polity, 2000), 141.

16. Jürgen Habermas, *The Postnational Constellation: Political Essays*, ed. and trans. Max Pensky (Cambridge, MA: MIT Press, 2001), 48.

17. Muñoz Molina, *Todo lo que era sólido*, 244–45.

18. J. Martínez-Alier and Jordi Roca, "Spain after Franco: From Corporatist Ideology to Corporatist Reality," *International Journal of Political Economy* 17, no. 4 (Winter 1987/1988): 57.

19. The crisis has demonstrated that many of the issues that were central during the years of the Second Republic and the Civil War still have not been resolved in a satisfactory manner. One such issue, for instance, is land ownership: "The economic crisis also reignited old social conflicts over the land. Jobless farmworkers, led by union leaders . . . started occupying uncultivated land properties in Andalusia, adding a new volatile dimension to the crisis. The confrontation over land ownership was one of the factors leading to the Spanish Civil War in the 1930s, when the elite resisted land reform. Agrarian reform (or the lack thereof) was one of the missing elements in the country's transition to democracy." Sebastián Royo, *Lessons from the Economic Crisis in Spain* (New York: Palgrave Macmillan, 2013), 8.

20. *CT o la Cultura de la Transición. Crítica a 35 años de cultura española*, ed. Guillem Martínez (Barcelona: Random House Mondadori, 2012), 18.

21. Sara Santamaría Colmenero, "El peso de la nación en Antonio Muñoz Molina: patriotismo constitucional y el consenso de la Transición," *Journal of Spanish Cultural Studies* 17, no. 2 (2016): 182.

22. Manuel Castells, *Networks of Outrage and Hope: Social Movements in the Internet Age* (Cambridge: Polity, 2012), 125.

23. Martínez-Alier and Roca, "Spain after Franco," 66.

24. Bauman and Bordoni, *State of Crisis*, 31.

25. Alain Touraine, *After the Crisis*, trans. Helen Morrison (2010; repr. Cambridge: Polity Press, 2014), 37.

26. Ulrich Beck, *German Europe*, trans. Rodney Livingstone (2012; repr. Cambridge: Polity Press, 2013), viii.

27. The organization's website defines its mission as opposing the deregulation and the dismantling of the welfare state that are being justified by the severity of the crisis. See "¿Quiénes somos?," *Economistas Frente a la Crisis*, http://economistasfrentealacrisis.com/.

28. Moreno-Caballud, *Cultures of Anyone*, 279.

29. "Spain was in 2008 in its 15th year of uninterrupted growth and was benefiting from the longest cycle of continuing expansion of the Spanish economy in modern history." See Sebastián Royo, "Reforms Betrayed? Zapatero and Continuities in Economic Policy," *Spain's "Second Transition"? The Socialist Government of José Luis Rodríguez Zapatero*, ed. Bonnie N. Field (Oxon: Routledge, 2011), 62.

30. Muñoz Molina, *Todo lo que era sólido*, 29.

31. Carsten Humlebæk points out that Spain's construction industry was twice as large, in relative terms, as that of other Western nations, being responsible for 20 percent of jobs created in the country since 2000. See Carsten Humlebæk, *Spain: Inventing the Nation* (London: Bloomsbury Academic, 2015), 210. Once the construction industry collapsed, it became clear that the economy was much weaker than what the glowing reports had led Spaniards to believe.

32. Emmánuel Lizcano, "Sin los cuentos sobre la crisis, a los de arriba no les salen las cuentas," *Fuera de lugar: conversaciones entre crisis y transformación*, ed. Amador Fernández-Savater (Madrid: Machado Libros, 2013), 144.

33. Luisa Elena Delgado, *La nación singular: fantasías de la normalidad democrática española (1996–2011)* (Madrid, España: Siglo XXI de España, 2014), 15.

34. Antonio Gramsci, *Prison Notebooks*, ed. and trans. Joseph A. Buttigieg, Vol. II (New York: Columbia University Press, 1996), 32–33.

35. For instance, as the most painful effects of the 2008–2012 collapse of financial markets started to wear off, Western media began discussing "the Ukraine crisis," which was the term of choice to refer to Ukraine's Revolution of Dignity and the ensuing war between Russia and Ukraine. When the hostilities in Ukraine somewhat subsided, news reports about "the Ukraine crisis" were displaced by a deluge of articles on the subject of the so-called "refugee crisis." It is clear that neither the armed conflict between Russia and Ukraine nor the demographic transformations in Europe are likely to be of short duration, yet the need to refer to them as "a crisis" persists. As I write these words, the media are filled with references to "the Syrian crisis." None of the situations described as "crises" have been resolved, yet the velocity of the public discourse moving from one "crisis" to the next creates an impression that these are unconnected occurrences rather than components of a larger phenomenon.

36. Bauman and Bordoni, *State of Crisis*, 27.

37. Barry K. Gills, "Going South: Capitalist Crisis, Systemic Crisis, Civilisational Crisis," *Third World Quarterly* 31, no. 2 (2010): 171.

38. Martínez-Alier and Roca, "Spain after Franco," 57.

39. Óscar J. Martín García, "A Country on a Tightrope: The Economic Crisis and the End of an Era in Spanish Politics," *Insight Turkey* 15, no. 3 (Summer 2013): 95.

40. Isidro López and Emmanuel Rodríguez, *Fin de ciclo. Financiarización, territorio y sociedad de propietarios en la onda larga del capitalismo hispano (1959–2010)* (Madrid: Traficantes de Sueños, 2010), www.traficantes.net/sites/default/files/pdfs/Fin percent20de percent20ciclo-Traficantes percent20de percent20Sue percentC3 percentB1os_0.pdf, 20 (accessed February 11, 2013).

41. Izquierda Unida, or United Left, is a coalition of several of Spain's left-wing parties, including the Communist Party of Spain, Revolutionary Workers' Party, the Feminist Party of Spain, and others. Since May 2016, Izquierda Unida is part of Unidos Podemos, a political alliance between IU and Podemos.

42. Manolo Monereo, *De la crisis a la revolución democrática* (Madrid: El Viejo Topo, 2013), 79–80.

43. Alfred Tovias, "Spain in the European Community," *Democratic Spain: Reshaping External Relations in a Changing World*, eds. Richard Gillespie, Fernando Rodrigo, and Jonathan Story (London & New York: Routledge, 1995), 95.

44. Luis Martín Cabrera, "Contra la suspensión de la mirada crítica: reflexiones sobre la persistencia del conflicto capital/trabajo en la cultura contemporánea española," *Arizona Journal of Hispanic Cultural Studies* 14 (2010): 119.

45. Vicente Navarro, "The Social Crisis of the Eurozone: The Case of Spain," *International Journal of Health Services* 43, no. 2 (2013): 191–92.

46. Lorraine Ryan, " The Economic Degeneration of Masculinity in Rafael Chirbes's *En la orilla*," *Romance Quarterly* 62, no. 2 (2015): 84.

47. The full name of this piece of legislation in Spanish is "Ley 52/2007, de 26 de diciembre, por la que se reconocen y amplían derechos y se establecen medidas en favor de quienes padecieron persecución o violencia durante la Guerra Civil y la Dictadura." See "Ley 52/2007, de 26 de diciembre, por la que se reconocen y amplían derechos y se establecen medidas en favor de quienes padecieron persecución o violencia durante la guerra civil y la dictadura," *Boletín Oficial del Estado* 310 (December 27, 2007): 53410–16, www.boe.es/buscar/pdf/2007/BOE-A-2007-22296-consolidado.pdf (accessed November 10, 2012).

48. Rafael Escudero, Patricia Campelo, Carmen Pérez González, and Emilio Silva, *Qué hacemos por la memoria histórica* (Madrid: Ediciones Akal, 2013), 38.

49. Quoted in Marina Llorente, "Exile and Erasure: A Poetic Reconstruction of the Spanish Past in Antonio Crespo Massieu's *Elegía en Portbou*," *Sites of Memory in Spain and Latin America: Trauma, Politics, and Resistance*, eds. Aída Díaz de León, Marina Llorente, and Marcella Salvi (Lanham, MD: Lexington Books, 2015), 73, note 15.

50. At the height of the crisis in 2012, journalist Guillem Martínez coordinated the publication of a collection of articles titled *CT o la Cultura de la Transición. Crítica a 35 años de cultura española* [*CT or Culture of the Transition. Critique of 35 Years of Spanish*

Culture]. Writers, journalists, and sociologists who contributed to the collection agreed that the severity of the crisis and Spain's incapacity to find a solution to the many problems revealed by the economic collapse was, to a great extent, a consequence of the decision to avoid discord that characterized the Transition. See Amador Fernández-Savater, "Emborronar la CT (del «No a la guerra» al 15-M)," *CT o la Cultura de la Transición. Crítica a 35 años de cultura española*, ed. Guillem Martínez (Barcelona: Random House Mondadori, 2012), 37–38.

51. "Tejerina: 'En el Gobierno hemos trabajado como mulas contra la crisis,'" *El Norte de Castilla*, October 15, 2015, www.elnortedecastilla.es/castillayleon/201510/15/tejerina-gobierno-hemos-trabajado-20151015103610.html (accessed November 5, 2015).

52. Spain's National Court, or Audiencia Nacional, is a centralized juridical body that has jurisdiction over the entire country.

53. "La Audiencia Nacional investigará a las cúpulas de Caja España y Caja Duero," *El País*, October 29, 2014, www.elmundo.es/economia/2014/07/29/53d7cc4c22601d15558b459d.html (accessed November 11, 2015).

54. "Rajoy cierra la Oficina de Víctimas como prometió en el 2008: 'Ni un solo euro para recuperar el pasado,'" *Elplural.com*, March 2, 2012, www.elplural.com/node/47953 (accessed November 11, 2015).

55. "Rajoy, sobre la subvención a la Fundación Francisco Franco: 'No lo sabía,'" *El Periódico*, October 28, 2015, www.elperiodico.com/es/noticias/politica/rajoy-desconoce-subvencion-fundacion-francisco-franco-4624649 (accessed November 11, 2015).

56. In the electoral campaign of 2015, the issue of historical memory was used by political forces that wanted to emerge from relative obscurity and speak to the issues that are likely to attract voters. For instance, Ciudadanos, a party that has been trying to make itself relevant on the national level, has spoken of its support for the provisions of the 2007 Historical Memory Law: "Albert Rivera, candidato de Ciudadanos a la presidencia del Gobierno, se ha comprometido este martes a apoyar la exhumación de los cadáveres que permanecen en las cunetas de los caminos y carreteras de España desde la Guerra Civil. 'Un país se mide por la dignidad con la que trata a sus muertos,' ha dicho el líder de la formación emergente" [Albert Rivera, the Ciudadanos' candidate to the presidency of the government, promised this Tuesday to support the exhumation of the bodies that remain buried at the roadsides of Spain since the Civil War. "A country is known by the dignity it accords to its dead," said the leader of the emerging political force]. See Juan José Mateo, "Rivera se compromete a apoyar las exhumaciones de la Guerra Civil," *El País*, November 18, 2015, http://politica.elpais.com/politica/2015/11/17/actualidad/1447796568_381704.html (accessed November 20, 2015). Rivera's efforts to signal support for the Historical Memory Law in the midst of an electoral campaign testifies to the continued importance of the recovery of historical memory to Spaniards.

57. Antonio Gómez López-Quiñones, *La guerra persistente. Memoria, violencia y utopía: representaciones contemporáneas de la Guerra Civil española* (Madrid: Iberoamericana, 2006), 15.

58. Francisco J. Sánchez, "From Neo-Francoist Memory to Political Feeling in Narratives of Unearthing: Sánchez Dragó's *Muertes Paralelas* (2006) and Andrés Trapiello's *Ayer no más* (2012)," *Romance Quarterly* 62, no. 1 (2014): 13.

59. Beck, *German Europe*, 14–15; Touraine, *After the Crisis*, 2.

60. Ewan Harrison and Sara McLaughlin Mitchell, *The Triumph of Democracy and the Eclipse of the West* (New York: Palgrave Macmillan, 2014), 116.

61. Rosa Aparicio and Andrés Tornos, "Towards an Analysis of Spanish Integration Policy," in *The Integration of Immigrants in European Societies: National Differences and Trends of Convergence*, eds. Friedrich Heckmann and Dominique Schnapper (Stuttgart: Lucius & Lucius, 2003), 213; Kitty Calavita, "Immigration, Law, and Marginalization in a Global Economy: Notes from Spain," *Law & Society Review* 32, no. 3 (1998): 538.

62. Antonio Bañón Hernández, Samantha Requena Romero, and Ma Eugenia González Cortés, "Health, Immigration and the Welfare State in Times of Crisis: A Critical Discourse Analysis," *Discourses on Immigration in Times of Economic Crisis: A*

Critical Perspective, ed. María Martínez Lirola (Newcastle upon Tyne: Cambridge Scholars, 2013), 129.

63. In the late 1990s, the figure of an immigrant was mined for the possibilities that it opened for the exploitation by the crime novel genre. This did not create a nuanced vision of Spain's immigrant communities. In her analysis of recent Spanish fiction that features immigrant characters, Maja Zovko points out that the stereotype linking immigrants to growing criminality appears in such recent novels as *Tánger* (1997) by Juan Madrid, *Ramito de hierbabuena* (2001) by Gerardo Muñoz Lorente, *Canciones de amor en Lolita's Club* (2005) by Juan Marsé, *La mala espera* (2009) by Marcelo Luján, *o Harraga* (2002), and *Donde mueren los ríos* (2003) by Antonio Lozano. See Maja Zovko, "Algunas peculiaridades de la narrativa actual sobre la inmigración extranjera en España," *Grup de Recerca sobre Migracions*, Galería de Investigación sobre Migraciones 3 (2014): 5–6. http://geografia.uab.es/migracions/eng/workingpapers.htm(accessed November 15, 2015). The displacement of immigrants toward marginalized and often criminalized spaces is explored in the crisis novels by Rafael Chirbes and Luis García Montero. These writers abandon the facile sensationalism of the approach present in the mystery novel genre and explore the political and historical reasons behind the marginalization of immigrants.

64. Mikel Azurmendi, "Diez tesis sobre el multiculturalismo," *Cuadernos de Pensamiento Político* 8 (October–December 2005): 100.

65. "Since 2009 . . . the number of Spaniards in their late teens, twenties, and early thirties leaving the country increased by 52%. . . . The flight is starting to include members of the country's educated and entrepreneurial elite." See Royo, *Lessons from the Economic Crisis in Spain*, 8.

66. Stephen Castles, Hein de Haas, and Mark J. Miller, *The Age of Migration: International Population Movements in the Modern World*, 5th ed. (London: Palgrave Macmillan, 2014), 16–17.

67. Bauman, *Liquid Modernity*, 13.

68. Ibid., 13.

69. Ibid., 149.

70. "During the high-growth period of 1986-90, over two million new jobs were created in Spain, more than in any other European country. . . . According to one study, 75% of work contracts in 1996 were for three months or less, with 50% lasting only one month (Mazuelos 1997:17). As a result of this trend, the labor force is increasingly split between older, long-term workers whose job security is ensured by government regulations and union contracts, working side by side with contingent employees with fixed-term contracts." See Calavita, "Immigration, Law, and Marginalization in a Global Economy," 534–36.

71. The unemployment figures used by the Spanish government to support its claim that the crisis has ended conceal the growth in part-time employment at the expense of stable, full-time work. In 2015, for instance, the number of part-time workers grew by 13.2%, while the number of long-term job contracts was reduced by 0.4%. See Alejandro Bolaños, "Las grandes empresas solo crean trabajo temporal en 2015," *El País*, November 24, 2015, http://economia.elpais.com/economia/2015/11/24/actualidad/1448368671_571076.html (accessed November 25, 2015). In response to the 2014 assertions of Spain's Minister of Employment and Social Security that the country's employment statistics showed positive trends in economic development, Inmaculada Cebrián, economics professor of Alcalá de Henares University, pointed out the importance of taking into consideration the growth in precarious employment: "Pese a la gravedad de la crisis y el sufrimiento que conlleva, no estamos arreglando ninguno de los problemas estructurales del mercado de trabajo. De hecho, la temporalidad no solo se ha mantenido sino que ahora empieza a aumentar (roza el 24% de los contratos); se ha introducido con fuerza el tiempo parcial no querido por los trabajadores (crece a ritmos del 9% interanual) y el empleo autónomo, que se promociona desde el Gobierno" [In spite of the gravity of the crisis and the suffering it brings, we are not fixing any of the structural problems of the job market. In fact, part-time employment

not only remained at the same level but is now starting to grow (it constitutes 24% of contracts); part-time employment that is unwanted by workers has a strong presence (it grows 9% per year) and self-employment that is being promoted by the government]. See Manuel V. Gómez and Carmen Sánchez-Silva, "La precariedad laboral va para largo," *El País*, March 8, 2014. http://economia.elpais.com/economia/2014/03/07/actualidad/1394227355_704422.html(accessed November 18, 2015).

72. Guillén, "Europe: A Crisis Within a Crisis," 63–64.

73. In Spain, as in many developed countries, the finance industry had to be "rescued" with public funds that often were borrowed from supranational banking entities and will need to be returned at the cost of dramatic cuts to social programs. The loan that the EU offered to the failing Spanish banks was given on condition that the state would assume the payments if the banks failed to repay the loan. Josep Manel Busqueta, et al., *Desentrañando la Unión Europea. Informes de economía crítica* 10, Seminari d'Economia Crítica: TAIFA, 2014, http://seminaritaifa.org/pdf/Informe_10_ES.pdf, 43 (accessed November 20, 2015).

74. Bauman and Bordoni, *State of Crisis*, 20.

75. A selection of slogans used by the protesters can be found at www.movimiento15m.org/2013/07/las-frases-y-lemas-del-movimiento-15m.html(accessed November 15, 2015).

76. This description comes from the English-language version of the party's website, https://podemos.info/conoce/?lang=en (accessed November 15, 2015).

77. *Podemos*, https://participa.podemos.info/es (accessed November 15, 2015).

78. Francesco Manetto, "Iglesias renuncia a una reforma integral de la Constitución," *El País*, November 20, 2015, http://politica.elpais.com/politica/2015/11/20/actualidad/1448052762_141488.html (accessed November 21, 2015).

79. Habermas, *The Postnational Constellation*, 79.

80. Alfredo Martínez Expósito, *Cuestión de imagen: cine y Marca España* (Vigo: Academia del Hispanismo, 2015), 24.

81. Navarro, "The Social Crisis of the Eurozone," 189.

82. Habermas, *The Postnational Constellation*, 69.

83. Philip Bobbitt, *The Shield of Achilles: War, Peace, and the Course of History* (New York: Anchor Books, 2003), xxvi.

84. Habermas, *The Postnational Constellation*, 52.

85. Ash Amin, "Post-Fordism: Models, Fantasies and Phantoms of Transition," *Post-Fordism: A Reader*, ed. Ash Amin (Oxford: Blackwell, 1994), 2.

86. Javier García Recio, "Mirar sin adornos," *La Opinión de Málaga*, March 23, 2013, www.opinionmalaga.com/especiales/libros/2013/10/04/mirar-sin-adornos/, 46 (accessed February 12, 2015).

87. The austerity measures adopted by Spain in the years of the crisis have been aimed at dismantling the welfare state piece by piece. Spain's public health care system, for instance, is already suffering a worsening in the quality of care it provides because of the recent privatization of some of the services associated with health care. A report published in *El País* in November 2015, for instance, demonstrates that the privatized laundry system leaves doctors' scrubs in a state that is significantly less capable of corresponding to the necessary hygienic standards than the public laundry system that was used before the crisis. See Elisa Silió, "Las batas de los hospitales públicos tienen hasta 80 tipos de bacterias," *El País*, November 19, 2015, http://ccaa.elpais.com/ccaa/2015/11/19/madrid/1447954475_929623.html (accessed December 3, 2015). In her crisis novel *El comité de la noche*, Belén Gopegui discusses the dangers of an increasingly powerful push, on the part of private medical companies, for a privatization of socialized health care in the countries of the European Union.

88. Elisa Silió, "El PSOE y Podemos rechazan los presupuestos del PP por antisociales," *El País*, December 3, 2015, http://ccaa.elpais.com/ccaa/2015/12/03/madrid/1449157351_631072.html (accessed December 3, 2015).

89. The new state form that is currently in the process of being consolidated has also been referred to as "postnational state" (Habermas, *The Postnational Constellation*, 61)

and "market-state" (Bobbitt, *The Shield of Achilles*, xxvii). In Spain, César Molinas, an economist and a former Merrill Lynch CEO, published an essay titled *Qué hacer con España* (2013) that is heavily indebted to Francis Fukuyama's *The End of History and the Last Man* (1992) and Philip Bobbitt's *The Shield of Achilles* (2003) and that relies on the term "la sociedad post-Histórica" (115) to refer to the series of transformations that are eroding the nation-state model. The ideas expressed in Molinas's volume overlap with those of Muñoz Molina's crisis essay *Todo lo que era sólido*.

90. Stuart Hall, "Brave New World," *Marxism Today* (Oct 1988): 28, www.unz.org/Pub/MarxismToday-1988oct-00024 (accessed September 30, 2015).

91. Ulrich Beck, *The Metamorphosis of the World* (Cambridge: Polity Press, 2016), 56–57.

92. Habermas, *The Postnational Constellation*, 55.

93. Javier Rodríguez Marcos, "La alicantina Francisca Aguirre, Premio Nacional de Poesía," *El País*, November 17, 2011, http://cultura.elpais.com/cultura/2011/11/17/actualidad/1321484405_850215.html (accessed July 23, 2015).

94. For instance, reviews of Chirbes's *En la orilla* by poet Javier Rodríguez Marcos and literary critic Fernando Valls were published in *Babelia* under the heading of "the great novel of the crisis in Spain." See "Material de derribo," *Babelia* 1, no. 110 (2 marzo 2015): 3. In a review of *En la orilla* in *La Razón*, Jesús Ferrer had the following to say about the novel: "Ésta no es sólo una novela sobre la crisis, porque aborda también algunos lacerantes aspectos de nuestra desorientada época . . . síntomas . . . de una moderna, árida deshumanización del presente" [This is not only a novel about the crisis because it also addresses some of the painful aspects of our disoriented epoch . . . symptoms . . . of a modern, arid dehumanization of the present]. See "Chirbes no está en crisis," *La Razón*, March 7, 2013, 65, www.anagrama-ed.es/view/11771/Chirbes percent20NH percent20512 percent20-percent20La percent20Razon.pdf (accessed February 2, 2015). A tribute published by Antonio Lucas in *El Mundo* after the writer's death in 2015 was titled "Fallece Rafael Chirbes, la letra y la rabia de la crisis" [Rafael Chirbes, the words and the ire of the crisis, has died]. Lucas points out that Chirbes's last two novels present the crisis as an unending state of affairs that is not likely to change. See Antonio Lucas, "Fallece Rafael Chirbes, la letra y la rabia de la crisis," *El Mundo*, August 16, 2015, www.elmundo.es/cultura/2015/08/15/55cf71bd46163f45298b4577.html (accessed November 24, 2015).

95. Edicionesatlantis.com: Catálogo, Ediciones Atlantis, December 1, 2015, www.edicionesatlantis.com/catalogo/12/andalucia-golpe-a-la-crisis/680 (accessed December 1, 2015).

96. Jairo Prieto Fernández, "Ciudades de plástico" in *Castilla-León: Golpe a la crisis. (Cinco narradores en clave del cuento)* (Madrid: Ediciones Atlantis, 2012), 29.

97. José Villalba, "Que retumbe la fragua otra vez" in *Castilla-León: Golpe a la crisis. (Cinco narradores en clave del cuento)* (Madrid: Ediciones Atlantis, 2012), 14.

98. Curiously, female unemployment is rarely mentioned in these short stories. The role of the female characters is to react to male joblessness in ways that are presented as either laudably supportive or egotistically critical.

99. In 2016, *La habitación de Nona* was awarded the Premio Nacional de Narrativa [National Narrative Prize].

100. "¿Qué es LaZonaKubik?" *La Zona Kubik*, Kubik Fabrik 2016, http://lazonakubik.com/que-es-lzk/ (accessed December 13, 2016).

101. José Luis Romo, "La escena 'off' se desinfla," *El Mundo*, January 9, 2016, www.elmundo.es/madrid/2016/01/09/569164de268e3e4f238b4624.html (accessed January 9, 2016).

102. "Historias de Usera," *Historias de Usera*, Kubik Fabrik 2016, www.historiasdeusera.com/las-historias (accessed December 15, 2016).

103. Cristina Oñoro Otero, "Otras maneras de habitar el espacio urbano: los Nuevos Espacios y Formatos teatrales de Madrid (2008–2014)," in *Espacios urbanos en el teatro español de los siglos XX y XXI*, ed. Cerstin Bauer-Funke (Hildesheim: Georg Olms Verlag, 2016), 384.

104. "Proyecto Barrio," *Teatro del Barrio,* http://www.teatrodelbarrio.com/full-width/ (accessed December 15, 2016).
105. Jordi Casanovas, *Ruz/Bárcenas,* Teatre Lliure y Teatro del Barrio: 2014, www.scribd.com/document/285590025/RUZ-BARCENAS, ii (accessed December 9, 2016).
106. Ibid., iii.
107. Ibid., 50.
108. Miguel Ángel Sánchez, *Ejecución hipotecaria* (Madrid: Fundación SGAE, 2014), 37.
109. Ibid., 51.

ONE

Essay

A Defense of Fluidity

There is a long and rich tradition in Spain of writers producing essays that address "the central, most controversial and long-debated issue in Spanish culture: the so-called 'Problem of Spain.'"[1] The eighteenth-century project of nation building produced an explosion of essays by the leading Spanish thinkers who were eager to construct a narrative of the country's past and, by doing so, mold its future. As "the first post-hegemonic European nation-state,"[2] Spain had to construct the myths of its national identity at a time when the new balance of power within Europe was relegating Spain to the margins. The notorious article "Espagne" ["Spain"] published by Nicholas Masson de Morvilliers in *Géographie Moderne* [*Modern Geography*] in 1783 provoked outrage in Spain with its question "Depuis deux siècles, depuis quatre, depuis dix, que doît-on à l'Espagne?" ["Two hundred, four hundred, ten hundred years later, what do we owe to Spain?"] and led to the publication of many essays that defended Spain from accusations of irrelevance within the changing European context.[3] Some of the most notable essays of the Spanish Enlightenment that address the issue of Spain's perceived decadence and outline the possibilities of the country's development are *Desengaños al teatro español* [*Disenchantments of the Spanish Theater*] by Nicolás Fernández de Moratín (1862–1863), Juan Cristóbal Romea y Tapia's *El escritor sin título* [*Writer Without a Title*] (1763), Clavijo y Fajardo's "Pensamientos" ["Thoughts"] published in his 1763–1767 periodical *El Pensador*, Javier Lampillas's *Ensayo histórico-apologético de la literatura española contra las opiniones preocupadas de algunos escritores modernos italianos* [*A Historical Apologetic Essay Against the Prejudiced Opinions of Some Modern Italian Writers*] (1786), Gaspar Melchor de Jovellanos's *Elogio de Carlos III* [*Praise *for Carlos III*] (1788), and Cadalso's *Cartas marruecas* [*Moroccan Letters*] (1789).

In his *Oración apologética por la España y su mérito literario* [*Apologetic Statement for Spain and Its Literary Merit*] (1786), Juan Pablo Forner insisted that Spain's marginalization within Europe was unfair. According to Forner, other European nations were never targeted by the kind of animosity that was reserved for Spain:

> ¿Qué nación hay hoy sobre cuya constitución, sobre cuyo saber se dispute más, se dude más, se calumnie más, se falte más a la razón, a la verdad, a la justicia, al decoro? A nadie hemos provocado, y furiosamente nos acometen cuantos del lado de allá de los Alpes y Pirineos constituyen la sabiduría en la maledicencia. [Which nation is there whose constitution and knowledge are more debated, more doubted, more calumnied with a complete disregard for reason, truth, and decorum? We have provoked no one, yet we are being furiously attacked by those who, on the other side of the Alps and the Pyrenees, believe that slander constitutes wisdom.][4]

Forner's position was shared by many of the eighteenth-century Spanish thinkers who wrote essays to defend the country from charges of cultural and intellectual decadence. In Spain, the myth of the country's exceptionalism, which is crucial to any nation-building project, was erected on the idea that Spain was persecuted and libeled more than any other European nation. The belief that the present victimization was a consequence of Spain's former hegemony in Europe oriented the country's nation-building essay genre toward attempts to elucidate the reasons for Spain's loss of its former glory and suggestions as to how a position of primacy within Europe could be recaptured.

In the first half of the nineteenth century, the invasion of the Napoleonic troops and the subsequent reactionary regime of Ferdinand VII produced the need to rearticulate the different scenarios of the country's future development. The heated polemic between Juan Nicolás Böhl de Faber, José Joaquín de Mora, and Antonio Alcalá Galiano (1814–1820) and Mariano José de Larra's voluminous body of essays published between 1828 and 1837 posit the myths of Spain's national identity as problematic and in need of further negotiation. The loss of the last remaining colonies of the Spanish Empire in 1898 intensified the perception of Spain as a problem that had to be debated. In the next fifty years, an entire literary genre formed around the discussions of "the problem of Spain."[5] Unamuno's *En torno al casticismo* [*Around Reason*] (1895) anticipates the preoccupation with Spain's loss of status as a world power that will later inspire Ángel Ganivet's *Idearium español* [*Spanish Idearium*] (1897), Ramiro de Maeztu's *Hacia otra España* [*Toward a Different Spain*] (1889), and Joaquín Costa's *Reconstrucción y europeización de España* [*Reconstruction and Europeanization of Spain*] (1900).

The first decades of the twentieth century did not dispel the perception that Spain was experiencing a crisis that needed to be addressed. In the prologue to the second edition of his *España invertebrada* [*Invertebrate Spain*] (1922), for instance, Ortega y Gasset defines the purpose of his essay as exploring "la grave enfermedad que España sufre" [the grave illness Spain suffers from][6] and analyzing "el estado de disolución a que ha vuelto la sociedad española" [the state of dissolution in which Spanish society has found itself].[7] Ortega y Gasset's student, María Zambrano, relies on the imagery suggested by the philosopher to underscore the gravity of Spain's identity crisis. In her autobiographical essay *Delirium and Destiny*, Zambrano points out that she and her colleagues at the Institución Libre de Enseñanza imagined Spain as sick and in need of being healed: "Spain was still not visible, we felt Spain more than we saw her, and we were yearning to see her, and it was necessary, absolutely necessary, that she become visible to the world once more, healed, whole, and self-possessed; she must be young and awake after her centuries-long sleep, whole despite her history."[8] In Zambrano's words, several generations of Spaniards "had grown up with the bitter taste of Spanish decadence mixed with an ancient pride in Spain's grandeur and with an inkling that the grandeur had been squandered."[9] The Spanish Civil War that exiled Zambrano from the country in 1939 demonstrated that the conflict between the different narratives of what path Spain should take could no longer be addressed peacefully.

The Franco era was marked by passionate debates as to whether there was a possibility of solving the problem of Spain. Pedro Laín Entralgo, one of the most authoritative public intellectuals of the dictatorship, published in 1948 an essay titled *España como problema* [*Spain as a Problem*]. According to Laín Entralgo, since the end of the seventeenth century, Spain was defined by a conflictive relationship between its "authentic" Hispanic values and the requirements of European modernity:

> Nuestro magno y constante problema [es] la relación entre la Hispanidad y la Modernidad, el diálogo entre una España fiel a sí misma y la Europa consecutiva a la paz de Westfalia. [Our great and persistent problem is the relationship between Hispanidad and Modernity, the dialogue between a Spain that is loyal to itself and the way Europe has been since the Peace of Westphalia.][10]

Spain's role as the locus from which European modernity originated in 1492[11] is disregarded in Laín Entralgo's analysis in favor of a vision that posits modernity as deeply anti-Hispanic. Instead of imitating the attempts to prove Spain's worth to Europe that inspired the writings of Forner, Lampillas, and other eighteenth-century thinkers, Laín Entralgo articulates a vision of *Hispanidad*, a cultural concept that includes Spain and Latin America and within which the values of premodern Europe can be preserved.[12] In response not only to Laín Entralgo but to the entire genre of elucidating "the problem of Spain," Rafael Calvo Serer published in 1949 a volume titled *España, sin problema* [*Spain Without a Problem*]. The military rebellion of 1936 put an end, according to Calvo Serer, to any further need to debate the issue:

> Por fortuna, de dos siglos en que España fue tema a discutir, hemos salido los españoles mediante un acto enérgico, tajante y claro, en 1936; desde 1939 España ha dejado de "ser un problema," para adquirir conciencia de que está enfrentada con "muchos problemas." [Fortunately, we, the Spaniards, have come out of the two centuries when Spain was a topic for discussion by virtue of an energetic, definitive and clear act in 1936; since 1939 Spain has stopped "being a problem" in order to realize that it faces "many problems."][13]

For Calvo Serer, after Franco's victory in 1939, Spain's mission resided in offering a Christian alternative to Sovietization and Americanization, both of which the writer perceived as decadent and destructive.[14]

Despite Calvo Serer's belief that it was time to abandon the vision of Spain as an inherently problematic entity, essays that addressed "the problem of Spain" continued to appear. Historian Sánchez-Albornoz published, while in exile in Argentina, *España, un enigma histórico* [*Spain, a Historical Enigma*], a two-volume response to *España en su historia* by Américo Castro. Sánchez-Albornoz still believed it was necessary to answer, a century and a half later, Masson de Morvilliers's question of what was owed to Spain. "No hemos sido un pueblo deudor, sino un pueblo acreedor de Europa" [Our country has not been a debtor but, rather, a creditor of Europe],[15] declared the historian at the beginning of his magnum opus, and he proceeded to trace the development of a peculiarly Spanish national character that, according to Sánchez-Albornoz, had already been visible in the drawings of the Altamira Cave and could still be felt in the twentieth century. The conscience of "nuestra crisis nacional" [our national crisis][16] imbues the historian's argument and leads him to an exaltation of Castilian Middle Ages that brings the beliefs of a Republican scholar Sánchez-Albornoz curiously close to those of a Francoist ideologue Laín Entralgo.

After the Transition, "the enigma of Spain" as a topic of essayistic production did not lose its relevance for thinkers and writers. Essayists began to reject the belief in Spain's exceptionality and pointed to the many ways in which the country's experience was neither unexpected nor unique. In 1997, Juan Pablo Fusi and Jordi Palafox published *España: 1808–1996. El desafío de la modernidad* [*Spain: 1808–1996. The Challenge of Modernity*], an essay that rejects the idea that Spain's economic and political development is a result of "una particular forma de ser de los españoles" [a particular way of being Spanish].[17] In 2006, Antonio-Miguel Bernal, a scholar of economic history, was awarded the Premio Nacional de Historia de España [National Prize for Spanish History] for his book *España, proyecto inacabado: los costes / beneficios del imperio* [*Spain, an Unfinished Project: Costs and Benefits of Empire*].[18] Bernal suggests that Spain has not yet been fully understood in spite of the voluminous essayistic output dedicated to solving the mystery of why Spain is the way it is:

> Hay que convenir, al menos, que "algo" debió ocurrir en nuestro devenir histórico que ayude a comprender por qué España protagonizó durante siglos una trayectoria impar en la historia universal y, al mismo tiempo, dejó en el camino tantas cosas por hacer cuando eran necesarias por la exigencia de los tiempos. [We have to agree, at least, that something must have occurred in our history that will help us understand why Spain, for centuries, played an incomparable role in the universal history and, at the same time, failed to do so many things that the times required.][19]

Bernal recognizes that the intensity of efforts to explain why "Spain is different" contributes to reinforcing the myth of Spain's difference.[20] Still, Bernal does not abstain from participating in the favorite national pastime of strengthening the mystique of "Spain" as an exceptionally opaque and incomprehensible entity.

A crisis that lasts for two and a half centuries and a decline that is lamented for equally as long beg the question of whether there really is a status quo that is being disturbed by this supposedly exceptional critical moment. Few things in Spain's essay genre can be relied upon as securely as the conscience that, at any given moment, the country can be said to be experiencing an especially severe crisis. Any essay about the current situation will have to position itself vis-à-vis this history of the genre. One possibility is to define today's predicament as a replay of one of the crises that Spain experienced in the past. To give an example of this way of framing the crisis, in his 2012 collection of articles titled *Otro 98 es necesario* [*Another 98 Is Necessary*], Pedro Jesús de la Peña, a scholar of Spanish literature, points out the similarities between the traumatic experiences of 1898 and "la actual crisis que ennegrece la silueta de todos los españoles" [the actual crisis that casts a pall over the image of all Spaniards].[21] Antonio Muñoz Molina and Lucia Etxebarria, the two writers whose essays I analyze in this chapter, take a different approach. Their writing on this subject is imbued with the consciousness that the erosion of Spain's welfare state is a result of transformations that are occurring on the global level. Neither author shies away from condemning the outrageously high levels of corruption in Spain that have aggravated the country's painful experience of the crisis, yet both realize that the decline of the welfare state model is not happening exclusively in Spain. The current crisis is finally not uniquely Spanish, yet Spain is positioned exceptionally well to understand and address it due to the country's belated adoption of a democratic welfare state model that is in danger because of this crisis.

Spaniards, Muñoz Molina and Etxebarria insist, have a reason to value their democracy because their road toward it was especially complex and often painful.

Muñoz Molina is only ten years older than Etxebarria, yet the writers belong to different literary generations. At the time of Franco's death, Muñoz Molina was nineteen years old and, as the author tells his readers in *Todo lo que era sólido* [*Everything That Was Solid*], was participating in clandestine activities and had been briefly jailed for taking part in a political protest in 1974.[22] In that year, Etxebarria was only eight and could not have had any experience of actively resisting the dictatorship. Etxebarria is often placed among the writers of Generation Kronen, Spain's equivalent of Generation X, which was named after José Angel Mañas's best-selling 1994 novel *Historias del Kronen* [*Stories of Kronen*].[23] Still, despite their generational, political, and artistic differences, Muñoz Molina and Etxebarria turned to the essay genre to discuss Spain's experience of the crisis. Both writers are sensitive to the growing fluidity that is sweeping away the familiar institutions and ways of life and believe that these changes must be embraced if one hopes to exercise a measure of control over their impact.

MUÑOZ MOLINA'S *TODO LO QUE ERA SÓLIDO* (2012): THE CRISIS OF THE WELFARE STATE

"All that has been regarded as solid, crumbles into fragments; all that was looked upon as holy is profaned; at long last, people are compelled to gaze open-eyed at their position in life and their social relations"[24] wrote Marx and Engels in *The Communist Manifesto* in 1848. Antonio Muñoz Molina uses the beginning of this famous phrase as a title to his 2013 book-length essay where he proposes to look "with sober eyes" at the situation in Spain. The epigraph to *Todo lo que era sólido* is taken from Joseph Conrad's *Lord Jim* and points to willful blindness: "It is extraordinary how we go through life with eyes half shut, with dull ears, with dormant thoughts."[25] Muñoz Molina believes that the crisis in Spain was caused by a drawn-out collective refusal of Spaniards to abandon the realm of illusion and acknowledge that a long-term mismanagement of the country's economy was taking place. The writer does not spare himself and accepts his share of responsibility for avoiding the truth. In the conclusion to the book, Muñoz Molina makes an impassioned plea to his readers, asking them to see things as they are:

"Ya no nos queda más remedio que empeñarnos en ver las cosas tal como son, a la sobria luz de lo real" [We have no choice but to make an effort to see things as they are, in the sobering light of reality].[26] With *Todo lo que era sólido*, the writer aims to awaken the people of Spain from a self-contented slumber of reason because, as he argues in the essay, it falls to artists like himself to bring about this awakening.

Muñoz Molina always creates complex titles for his work that transmit layered networks of meaning. *Todo lo que era sólido* is no exception. Aside from *The Communist Manifesto,* the title also echoes the ideas expressed by Zygmunt Bauman in *Liquid Modernity* (2000). Bauman points out that the melting of everything solid discussed in *The Communist Manifesto* differs from the liquefaction of all kinds of societal institutions that we can observe today. Marx and Engels were not planning to destroy all existing certainties and leave nothing in their place. Instead, Bauman argues, they expected a better class of solid certainties to arise in place of the ones that would be swept away because of their deficient nature.[27] After modernity demolished the constraints of the past, however, no new lasting, solid institutions arose where the old ones used to be. The technological revolution of the second half of the twentieth century freed capital from any attachment to a specific locale while the informational revolution liquefied borders, making it increasingly hard for national governments to exercise any control over the movements of capital.[28] Muñoz Molina's essay operates with the concept of fluidity that is much more Bauman's than Marx and Engels's.

In 2013, the year when Muñoz Molina's essay appeared in print, the author was awarded Premio Príncipe de Asturias de las Letras for his contribution to world literature. He is one of the leading Spanish writers, rising to international prominence with his novels *Beautus Ille* (1986), *Beltenebros* (1989), *Sefarad* (2001), *La noche de los tiempos* (2009), and others. *Todo lo que era sólido* is Muñoz Molina's first long essay on current affairs,[29] and the author begins it by explaining why he considers himself well-equipped to analyze the roots of the crisis and offer solutions. In the opening pages of the essay, Muñoz Molina tells his readers about a meeting he attended, shortly before the global economic collapse, with an executive of Merrill Lynch. The author reports feeling awed by the businessman's aura of expertise and his apparent insight into the workings of the world economy:

> Para mí había . . . en sus explicaciones nebulosas sobre los flujos económicos, una sugestión de omnisciencia alimentada a la vez por su solemnidad y por mi desconocimiento, por mi complejo de inferioridad de literato. [For me, there was . . . in his vague explanations about economic flows, a suggestion of omniscience that was nourished, simultaneously, by his solemnity and my ignorance, my inferiority complex of a man of letters.][30]

The book's readers are unlikely to be ignorant of the collapse of Merrill Lynch in 2008 and will measure the writer's 2006 impressions of the company against their ex post facto knowledge of its fate. Muñoz Molina adds poignancy to the anecdote by building up a contrast between his own powerlessness and the executive's self-possession: "Tenía muchas ganas de orinar y no me atrevía a levantarme o a preguntar con naturalidad dónde estaba el baño. Mi anfitrión me miraba desde el otro lado de la mesa con una benevolencia episcopal" [I really needed to urinate but didn't dare to get up or ask in a casual way where the bathroom was. My host observed me from the other side of the desk with an episcopal benevolence].[31] The experience of the crisis will make it easy for many to identify with the feeling that the most basic functions of their bodies are controlled by the representatives of financial institutions. With this anecdote, Muñoz Molina accesses the shared sensation of helplessness in the face of the complex world of finance and suggests that his "complejo de inferioridad de literato" [inferiority complex of a man of letters] in an encounter with the executive was not justified.[32]

The writer points out that the economists who led the global economy to the collapse relied upon rhetorical devices to explain to the public what was happening. According to Muñoz Molina, the gurus of high finance managed their metaphors as poorly as they did the financial institutions under their tutelage:

> El lenguaje de los economistas . . . consistía en la reiteración de unas cuantas metáforas simples: la desaceleración de un vehículo que ha avanzado a gran velocidad durante mucho tiempo; el aterrizaje confortable de un avión. Ésas eran las metáforas respetables. [The language of economists . . . consisted in reiterating a number of simple metaphors: the deceleration of a vehicle that has been moving at a high speed for a long time, a comfortable landing of an airplane. These were the respectable metaphors.][33]

If economists make use of metaphors to explain the functioning of the economy and fail as spectacularly as they did in the years immediately preceding the crisis, it follows that writers—whose command of rhetorical devices is more sophisticated—might be better equipped to discuss the global economic collapse. While the economy was booming, nobody was willing to observe the flaws in the metaphors used to reassure the public that the real estate bubble was unlikely to explode.[34] Muñoz Molina believes that the time has come for artists and intellectuals to regain control over metaphors, especially the kind that have such an enormous importance for the fate of the entire country.

Muñoz Molina is not alone in the belief that rhetorical devices have been used by economists and governmental agencies to downplay the responsibility that specific financial entities bear for the crisis. Sociologist Emmánuel Lizcano has conducted an analysis of the way metaphors are used to portray the crisis as a natural disaster and not something caused by human agency:

> Cuando se habla del *tsunami* provocado por el *desplome* de los fondos monetarios, de la *sequía* crediticia o de la *fuerza* del *huracán* financiero,

> se nos están presentando fenómenos propiamente económicos como si fueran fuerzas desatadas de la naturaleza. El primer efecto retórico consiste en anular toda responsabilidad por la crisis. Nadie es responsable de los tsunamis o las sequías, luego nadie es responsable de la crisis. Una vez construida así la irresponsabilidad particular, queda el terreno abonado para declararnos responsables a todos en general. [When we hear references to a *tsunami* caused by a *collapse* of monetary funds, the credit *drought*, or the strength of a financial *hurricane*, we are being led to see economic phenomena as if they were natural forces unleashed against us. The primary rhetorical effect consists in removing any responsibility for the crisis. Nobody is responsible for tsunamis or droughts, so nobody is responsible for the crisis. Once we posit that nobody in particular is responsible, we prepare the ground for declaring us all responsible in general.][35]

Despite his undoubted talent in the use of rhetorical devices, however, Muñoz Molina's analysis of the crisis in *Todo lo que era sólido* remains trapped in the idea that all Spaniards (and only Spaniards) are collectively and equally responsible for the severity of the crisis affecting Spain. For a writer who is so proud of his cosmopolitanism, Muñoz Molina offers a surprisingly parochial view of the crisis.

Not only does the writer blame his compatriots for remaining blind to the state of the country's economy, he also holds against them their reluctance to embrace the increasing fluidity of existence. Muñoz Molina holds up his own cosmopolitan lifestyle of an internationally best-selling author as an example for everybody in Spain to follow and laments what he considers an excessive attachment of Spaniards to their places of birth.[36] In the end, the writer's analysis of the crisis benefits the very financial institutions whose representatives Muñoz Molina accuses of being careless with metaphors. His insistence that one should sever all roots and move wherever one can better serve the momentary interests of capital is based on the writer's own blindness to the reasons this suggestion is impracticable for an overwhelming majority of Spaniards affected by the crisis. The accolades that Muñoz Molina's essay received from Spain's cultural establishment[37] point to a growing chasm between the standard-bearers of the Culture of Transition, of whom Muñoz Molina undoubtedly is one, and the many Spaniards who are questioning the value of the CT ideology.

Todo lo que era sólido consists of 104 sections that are between one and four pages long and are narrated in the first person. The author confesses to not having created any structure for his essay as he is grappling with finding an explanation for the disaster. The narrative moves back and forth, following the narrator on his journey of remembrance that will help him understand both the country's trajectory and his own: "Escribo dejándome llevar. El propio acto de escribir desata a la vez los argumentos y los recuerdos" [I write, letting myself go. The very act of writing unleashes arguments and memories].[38] The readers encounter a youthful Muñoz Molina as he huddles together with his friends for a secret perusal of *The Communist Manifesto* in Úbeda during the last years of the dictatorship, follow him to the 1974 protests in Madrid, witness his attempts to make a living as a lower-lever bureaucrat in the city council of Granada in 1981, and observe his work as the director of the Cervantes Institute in New York. In his struggle to recover the past, the writer realizes that a personal memory of events cannot always be trusted.[39] As he goes through his store of memories and pores over the pages of newspapers published several months before the onset of the crisis, the writer observes that there was always a plethora of evidence that nobody managed to interpret correctly at the time and that pointed to the inevitability of the crisis.

Muñoz Molina does not absolve himself from blame when he levels accusations of willful blindness on Spaniards. To the contrary, he believes that being a writer imposes upon him an obligation to see what is happening and organize his work around a clear-sighted analysis of reality.[40] The idea that the world experienced a bout of blindness that prevented anybody from seeing the approaching collapse of the global economy is not specific to Muñoz Molina. For instance, José Luis Segovia Bernabé, a professor of the Madrid campus of the Universidad Pontificia de Salamanca, offers a vision of the crisis that is like Muñoz Molina's:

> Una de las mayores lacras que impide acercarse a la verdad no es la mentira, sino algo tal vez menos reprobable moralmente pero igualmente peligroso como la ceguera. Resulta sorprendente la inexistencia de vigías y profetas dentro del sistema mismo que hubiesen alertado de la crisis que se venía encima. [One of the greatest vices that prevents us from approaching the truth is not lying but something that is probably less morally reprehensible but just as dangerous, which is blindness.][41]

Curiously, Segovia Bernabé teaches at a religious university funded by the government, which is precisely the kind of institution whose existence Muñoz Molina decries as "uno de los mayores expolios y de los mayores escándalos de la democracia española" [one of the greatest acts of pillage and the greatest scandals of Spanish democracy].[42] The writer considers the expenditure of public funds on religious schooling to stem from a refusal to see that this practice was inherited from Franco's era. Muñoz Molina asks his readers to consider how recent the establishment of a functioning democracy in Spain is and to recognize that the country's achievements since 1975 are fragile and need to be protected.

The idea of the fragility of civilization constitutes one of the essay's central motifs. The erosion of all certainties to which the title of *Todo lo que era sólido* points is part of the increasingly fluid nature of existence in late capitalist societies. Zygmunt Bauman, the sociologist who coined the term "liquid modernity," talks of "the harrowing and alarming uncertainty that was to become the major bane of liquid modern living."[43] In his essay, Muñoz Molina insists that this uncertainty is an inescapable condition of life today. The writer does not attempt to trace the origins of this precariousness and concentrates, instead, on searching for ways to mitigate its effects. Muñoz Molina strives to create a sense of urgency that will convince his readers of the need to act to prevent the tide of unstoppable change from sweeping away everything that makes life worthwhile: "Lo que hoy es más indiscutible y más sólido y nos importa más mañana puede haberse desmoronado" [What today is considered indisputable and completely solid and what matters to us the most can be dismantled tomorrow],[44] "lo que existió durante siglos desaparece en el curso de unos pocos años" [what existed for centuries disappears in the course of just a few years],[45] "nada es para siempre. Nadie prevé nada" [nothing is forever. Nobody foresees anything],[46] "nada es para siempre, nada ni nadie es de una sola pieza" [nothing is forever, nothing and nobody is made out of one piece],[47] "nada está a salvo. Nada valioso puede descuidarse ni durante un minuto" [nothing is safe. Nothing valuable can be neglected even for a minute],[48] "nada es seguro nunca" [nothing is ever certain].[49] The repetition of the words "nothing" and "nobody" intensifies the feeling that the crisis Muñoz Molina is addressing in the essay is much greater than the bursting of the real estate bubble and the collapse of financial markets in 2007–2008. The writer wants to bring to his readers' attention an existential danger to civilization at large.

The familiar dichotomy of civilization versus barbarity is crucial for Muñoz Molina's argument in *Todo lo que era sólido*. Everything of merit that humanity has managed to create is in danger of collapsing at any time if we do not remain vigilant.[50] For Muñoz Molina, a state with representational democracy and a strong social safety net is the greatest achievement of civilization that is in danger of being eroded by the fluidity of constant change. In the closing pages of the essay, the writer expresses a profound admiration for the Netherlands, a country where Muñoz Molina worked on parts of *Todo lo que era sólido* and that he sees as a model that Spain should follow. Amsterdam, "esta ciudad tan acogedora para mí" [the city that was so welcoming toward me],[51] carries both the scars of a much less tolerant and democratic past and the seeds of a dangerous and confusing future. For Muñoz Molina, the Netherlands represents a symbolic heart of Europe that Spain should observe closely if it is to avoid returning to a position on the margins of Europe that has characterized so much of its history.

The writer recognizes that the welfare state is in danger not only in Spain but everywhere it exists because there are global forces dedicated to dismantling it to derive profits from the services that now comprise the social safety net.[52] Muñoz Molina is reluctant to admit that the current crisis was not brought about solely by the wastefulness and obliviousness of Spaniards. Other than pointing out that the world is growing increasingly hostile to the gains of the welfare state,[53] the writer offers no analysis of the global developments that are threatening the welfare state model. Muñoz Molina's goal in the essay is to provide what Zygmunt Bauman calls "local solutions to global problems"[54] because he believes that his Spanish readership can realistically put these suggestions into practice. The writer's refusal to discuss in greater detail the international forces that threaten the welfare state is one of the instances of a silence that is more powerful than any number of words. Muñoz Molina positions the global dangers to the welfare state as so obvious that they require no further proof. The author's position is eminently logical: if the erosion of the nation-state leads to the dismantling of the social safety net, addressing the people of Spain as a group with a shared, unique destiny and a capacity to forge a common response to the issue is the only effective strategy. Muñoz Molina believes that the gains of the nation-state model can be preserved only by bolstering the national consciousness of Spaniards. The tension that exists between this idea and Muñoz Molina's suggestion that his compatriots embrace the fluidity of cosmopolitanism and sever their ties with the land of their birth remains unresolved.

Muñoz Molina is highly critical of the Spanish functionaries who squandered public funds on traveling to New York to promote the cultural heritage of the different regions of Spain.[55] He sees regionalism as a threat to an already weakened nation-state and maintains a steady focus on Spain as a totality in his argument. In this, Muñoz Molina is firmly on the side of Spain's political and cultural establishment that has made every effort to distract the public's attention from the crisis by inflating the danger posed to Spain's nationhood by regional separatist movements.[56] As a result of the media's focus on regional nationalisms, it is very rare that anybody manages to articulate that the true danger to the nation-state model resides in the incapacity of national governments to harness the flow of liquid capital. The Catalan and the Basque separatist movements are a familiar scapegoat that can syphon off some of the anxieties generated by the weakening of social guarantees. To "redeem, against, all odds, their seriously lopsided and steadily sinking *raison d'être*,"[57] weakened national governments direct the citizens' anger against a convenient Other, be it an immigrant, a separatist, or somebody equally easy to blame for the state's incapacity to address the people's most pressing concerns.

From Muñoz Molina's point of view, Spain's fraught entrance into modernity situates the country in a privileged position in terms of anticipating the impact of the erosion of the welfare state. The sensory displacement that accompanies globalization and that occurs "microscopically through everyday accretion"[58] is something that Spain experienced in a much more concentrated form than many other developed countries. Muñoz Molina is well aware of the trauma caused to his generation of

Spaniards by the rapid substitution of the agrarian society, where scarcity was the norm, with a late-capitalist Spain of exuberant consumption.[59] He does not doubt that the democratic Spain of the early twenty-first century represents a dramatic improvement over "la mezquina fealdad franquista" [the miserable Francoist ugliness],[60] yet the trauma of this swift transformation cannot be denied. Muñoz Molina warns against allowing the current state model to collapse as swiftly as it was introduced because the wounds left by its excision will be too deep to heal. It is no longer possible to recover the strategies that allowed one to exist within the scarcity model of the underindustrialized Spain of the 1950s. If the welfare state disappears, it will not be possible to turn to the past for useful lessons on how to adapt to the new reality.

In the writer's opinion, the only way to preserve the fragile gains of the welfare state resides in austerity. Muñoz Molina believes that the precrisis years saw excessive spending not only of money but also of words. The author whose preceding work was the 960-page-long *La noche de los tiempos* [*In the Night of Time*] (2009) calls for treating words as parsimoniously as one should approach Spain's rapidly dwindling financial resources.[61] The words that Muñoz Molina would like to subject to austerity cuts are the ones that question the Transition-era consensus of what the democratic Spain should be like. The writer's fear of discord is perfectly in keeping with what journalist Amador Fernández-Savater considers to be one of the central characteristics of the Culture of the Transition:

> La CT es una cultura profundamente «desproblematizadora»: no se pueden hacer preguntas sobre las formas de organizar la vida en común por fuera de lo posible autorizado. Los conflictos y los problemas son fisuras potenciales en el *statu quo* y su reparto de lugares, tareas y poderes. . . . Por tanto, es una cultura profundamente «despolitizadora», porque la política consiste precisamente en hacer preguntas sobre los modos de estar juntos. [CT is a profoundly "deproblematizing" culture: you can't ask questions about ways of organizing shared existence outside of what has been allowed. Conflicts and problems represent potential cracks in the *status quo* and its distribution of places, tasks, and powers. . . . As a result, this is a profoundly "depoliticizing" culture because politics consists precisely of asking questions about the ways of being together.][62]

Muñoz Molina's reluctance to accept that disagreement is a necessary component of living in a democratic society belies his oft-repeated asseverations as to his allegiance to democracy. His analysis of the crisis stalls because of his incapacity to question any of the tenets of the CT ideology.

Words are not the only resource that Muñoz Molina would like to subject to an exercise in austerity. The writer also sees memory in economic terms and believes that the attention paid to the recovery of historical memory in recent years exacerbated the crisis because time and energy dedicated to debating history were not invested elsewhere. According to the writer, the collective blindness that made the crisis possible is a side effect of an unhealthy fixation on the past, which is a disease that had afflicted Muñoz Molina, as well:

> Como tanta gente en España, yo también estaba enfermo de pasado. . . . Para escribir una novela leía con más atención los periódicos de 1936 que los de 2007. [Like so many people in Spain, I was also sickly obsessed with the past. . . . To write a novel, I paid more attention to newspapers from 1936 than those from 2007.][63]

The novel that the writer was working on in 2007 was *La noche de los tiempos,* set at the beginning of the Civil War. As the country descends into the war, Ignacio Abel, the novel's protagonist, is leaving Spain and trying to comprehend what led to this violent explosion. Muñoz Molina finds himself in a position like that of his protagonist as he sits down to write his next book, *Todo lo que era sólido.* At the time of writing his essay, however, Muñoz Molina seems to have repented the writing of the novel because of its engagement with history.

There was never any shortage of the novels on the Spanish Civil War, yet the closing years of the twentieth and the first decade of the twenty-first centuries saw a veritable explosion of literary works that explored every facet of Spain's civil conflict.[64] In the words of Nathan Richardson, "in the decade 2000-09 remembering became not simply a trend but *the* trend. . . . One writes a novel of the Spanish civil war, therefore one is a Spanish novelist—or at least a remunerated one."[65] The experience of the economic crisis allows Muñoz Molina to find an explanation for the intensity of the interest that novelists, filmmakers, and literary critics and their audiences had in the war during the precrisis years. According to the writer, accessing the memory of the war was a way of exploring the sense of unease caused by the approaching collapse that many in Spain could sense. Muñoz Molina confesses to being one of many artists who did not manage to see that, in talking about the past, they were searching for a way to speak about the worrisome aspects of the present.[66] The Spain at the brink of descending into the civil war that the writer recreated in *La noche de los tiempos* suffered, in Muñoz Molina's view, from the same incapacity to face reality that caused the current economic crisis.[67]

La noche de los tiempos is not, of course, Muñoz Molina's first novel that engages with history. The writer's novelistic output has been quite consistent in its interest toward the Civil War and Franco's dictatorship.[68] The writer's 1986 novel *Beatus Ille* is an early precursor of the "memory boom" that inspired the publication of dozens of Civil War novels after 2000. In *Todo lo que era sólido,* however, Muñoz Molina laments the "obsession . . . por el pasado" [obsession . . . with the past][69] and "fijación en el pasado" [fixation on the past][70] that characterized Spain before the real estate bubble burst and insists that "el pasado es un lujo que ya no podemos permitirnos" [the past is a luxury that we can no longer afford].[71] The interest in the past that produced "a 'memory boom' with regard to the Spanish Civil War"[72] becomes one of the luxury goods, which, according to Muñoz Molina, should be subjected to austerity measures. In this, the writer mimics the narrative on historical memory proposed by the conservative Partido Popular.[73]

In Muñoz Molina's opinion, discussions of the Spanish Civil War not only monopolize resources that could be invested into the fashioning of a less wasteful model of society, but also recreate "la sucia pelea civil" [the dirty civil fight][74] in today's Spain. The impassioned debates of Spain's "memory wars"[75] are consuming energy and trapping their participants in a vicious circle of repeating history instead of looking toward the future. As the battles of the Civil War are recreated in the verbal attacks that grow increasingly heated, the probability that the "two Spains" model will finally be put to rest diminishes. Muñoz Molina points out that discussing the war sharpens the divisions between the groups that base their identity on a sense of loyalty to either the Republican or the Nationalist cause. The belief that Spaniards are characterized by a predilection to violence, which makes them incapable of coexisting peacefully in a democratic society, was promoted by the Franco regime to justify its own existence.[76] Muñoz Molina accepts this Francoist argument as valid and takes it even further when he suggests that the mere discussion of the Civil War is likely to bring forth eruptions of violent hatred. The writer suggests that an emotional investment into the exploration of the past should be curtailed to divert the limited stock of Spaniards' energies toward addressing the economic challenges of the moment. Muñoz Molina's insistence that there is a limited quantity of resources that can be dedicated to addressing the crucial issues of the day points to an unquestioning acceptance of the austerity discourse that accompanied the anti-crisis measures of the Partido Popular government.

In keeping with his newfound admiration for a parsimonious treatment of resources, Muñoz Molina is convinced that even identities should be subjected to an exercise in austerity.[77] The writer uses the vocabulary of discounts and percentages in a discussion of identities to signal a new reality where economic considerations should prevail over ideological concerns. He believes that the Spaniards' approach to identities has been as wasteful as their treatment of credit flows that inundated the country in the last decade of the twentieth century. In the words of Zygmunt Bauman, "the search for identity is the ongoing struggle to arrest or slow down the flow, to solidify the fluid, to give form to the formless."[78] Muñoz Molina recognizes the futility of the struggle against fluidity and suggests that no energy should be wasted any longer on clinging to an illusion of stability that identities provide. The reason identities, convictions, and ideological postures should be scaled down is that they hinder a full acceptance of fluidity. Muñoz Molina argues that the only way of adapting to an increasingly fluid world is to make the self as fluid as possible. The habit of passionate adherence to political opinions is, according to the writer, one of the more unfortunate aspects of the legacy left by the Civil War and Franco's dictatorship. As the effects of the economic crisis intensify, the need to relinquish solidity, a process that Muñoz Molina calls "dejarse influir y dejarse fluir" [let oneself be influenced and let oneself flow],[79] becomes more pressing.

The way in which the writer structures his essay exemplifies the fluidity that he believes should guide everybody's response to the crisis. The 253-page book lacks a table of contents, and the fluidity of the argument is not interrupted by chapter titles. Muñoz Molina's "escribo dejándome llevar" [I write, letting myself go][80] points to the way in which, he insists, Spaniards should respond to the crisis. In an increasingly fluid world, letting go of every certainty, identity, and attachment and allowing the constant flow of ideas and events to carry one wherever it shall is the only approach that, in the author's opinion, will allow Spain to overcome the crisis. Muñoz Molina proves his own dedication to fluidity with a seemingly effortless exploration of a genre that is new to him. The culmination of the author's mastery of relinquishing what he used to hold dear comes when Muñoz Molina qualifies his preceding novel as escapist and informed by a refusal to face reality. This matter-of-fact dismissal of the enormous effort that undergirds the creation of a novel as complex as *La noche de los tiempos* illustrates the reality of the liquid world where "durability loses its attraction and turns from an asset into a liability."[81]

Still, fluidity is not invariably easy to adopt even for an author as dedicated to this goal as Muñoz Molina claims to be. Despite his insistence that an interest toward the past is a luxury that can no longer be afforded in Spain, the Civil War still constitutes Muñoz Molina's frame of reference in the essay. There are numerous allusions to the war that help the author articulate his ideas in a way that would be meaningful to his readers. For instance, to emphasize the gravity of the crisis, Muñoz Molina points out that it is the worst emergency Spain has experienced since the Civil War.[82] This is a way for the writer to sharpen his condemnation of pro-independence movements that, in his opinion, "siembran discordias que nos perjudicarán a todos, también a ellos, al rebajar más aún el crédito internacional de nuestro país" [sow discord that endangers us all, including themselves, by lowering even more our country's international credit ratings].[83] Once again, the language of economics makes its way into a discussion of unaffordable luxuries that have to be sacrificed if the crisis is to be overcome. At the same time, the reference to the war makes the discord that is supposedly sown by the supporters of Catalan independence appear more threatening. At the height of Spain's economic collapse in 2012, anxieties about pro-independence manifestations in Catalonia were being used by politicians and media to distract the public's attention from corruption scandals and the reduction in welfare services.[84] Muñoz Molina contributes to the narrative that posits the Catalan independence movement as the greatest danger to Spain and displaces the blame for the state of the economy onto the peaceful protesters in Catalonia.

The specter of the Civil War appears in Muñoz Molina's condemnation of the nostalgic attachment to the Republican legacy that dominated the public discourse in Spain in 2006.[85] The author suggests that the existing democracy in Spain is deserving of a greater respect than "la república más soñada que recordada de 1931" [the republic of 1931 that was more of a dream than a memory].[86] Still, Muñoz Molina does not always find it easy to follow his own advice. One of the most poignant anecdotes he shares in the essay is the story of the two Socialist mayors of his native city of Úbeda. José Gámez, the first mayor of the post-Franco Úbeda, spent decades waiting for democracy to arrive, but once it did, he realized that there was no place in it for him.[87] After a single term in office, Gámez was substituted by a younger, less principled member of the Socialist party.[88] In Muñoz Molina's account of the two mayors, there is an undeniable sense of nostalgia for the ideological purity of the old-school Socialists, especially when it is contrasted with the profligate dishonesty of today's PSOE. Despite his condemnation of Spaniards' supposedly excessive attachment to the mythology of the Republican Spain, it proves difficult for the author of *Beatus ille* and *El jinete polaco* to relinquish his admiration for Republican idealism and the contrast it offers with today's cynicism and disillusionment.

In November 2014, Muñoz Molina published a novel titled *Como la sombra que se va* [*A Disappearing Shadow*] that explores both the author's personal recollections of the past and the historical memory of events that took place in the United States and Portugal in the 1960s. The novel traces the attempt made by James Earl Ray, the murderer of Martin Luther King Jr., to flee to Africa by way of Lisbon in 1968. As he imagines Ray's time in Lisbon, Muñoz Molina remembers his own visit to the capital of Portugal in 1987, the year when he was working on his novel *El invierno en Lisboa* [*Winter in Lisbon*]. Several layers of history come together in *Como la sombra que se va,* a novel whose author referred to the past as an unaffordable luxury in an essay published only a year earlier. It is yet unclear whether Muñoz Molina has grown disillusioned with the view of the past he offered in *Todo lo que era* sólido or if the writer considers the United States, a country that recovered from the bursting of the real estate bubble faster than Spain, to be less in need of subjecting its history to an exercise in austerity.[89] During the presentation of the novel in Úbeda, the writer referred to the assassination of Dr. King as "una tragedia política americana que nos toca muy de cerca" [an American political tragedy that touches us very closely].[90] The United States has a great importance to Muñoz Molina, and a significant part of *Todo lo que era sólido* is dedicated to the author's experiences in this country. The writer shares fond memories of his work as the director of the Cervantes Institute in New York and believes that there are many lessons Spain can learn from the United States. At the same time, Muñoz Molina insists that imitation of the United States should never go too far, given that Spain is part of a kinder, less aggressive European tradition.[91] The writer traverses with great ease both the physical and the imaginative distance between Spain and the United States and seems unaware that few of his compatriots can imitate this fluid existence because they lack the resources that are accessible to a writer of Muñoz Molina's stature.

Still, Muñoz Molina struggles with fluidity. The seamless nature of the writing in *Todo lo que era sólido* and the author's call to all Spaniards to embrace fluidity stand in conflict with Muñoz Molina's incapacity to vanquish his own fascination with the past and renounce a parochial approach to the crisis. Even though the writer recognizes that the crisis is not a local but a global phenomenon, he blames Spain's difficulties on the Spaniards' incapacity fully to embrace the values of the Western civilization. *Todo lo que era sólido* is weighed down by being part of the tradition of essay writing that attempts to elucidate the "enigma of Spain" through the lens of the country's exceptionality. Muñoz Molina's essay does not offer any especially valuable recipes for overcoming the economic crisis, yet *Todo lo que era sólido* suggests, albeit unwittingly, a possible solution to the crisis of the Spanish essay genre. As sociologist Isidro López points out, the problems we are experiencing "cada vez tienen menos posibilidades de formularse en términos 'españoles'" [have fewer and fewer possibilities of being formulated in 'Spanish' terms],[92] and the essay genre will only gain from effecting a departure from the ideologically suspect slogan "Spain is different."[93] There is nothing exceptionally Spanish in the struggle to preserve at least some vestiges of the formerly robust welfare state. Muñoz Molina's struggle with fluidity can be equally relevant to his readers in and outside of Spain, even if his recipes as to the need to embrace austerity will not.

LUCÍA ETXEBARRIA'S *LIQUIDACIÓN POR DERRIBO* (2013): PRACTICING FLUIDITY

Etxebarria's crisis essay was published at a time when the writer was experiencing a crisis in her own career. At the age of thirty-two, Lucía Etxebarria had joined the ranks of Spain's most promising young writers after being awarded the Premio Nadal for her novel *Beatriz y los cuerpos celestes* [*Beatriz and Celestial Bodies*] (1998). After publishing several novels and receiving a variety of prestigious literary awards (including the Premio Planeta in 2004 for *Un milagro en equilibrio* [*A Miracle in Equilibrium*], a novel that explores the same theme of a woman's resistance to maturity as *Beatriz y los cuerpos celestes*), Etxebarria announced that she was abandoning her writing career. *Liquidación por derribo* begins with the author's explanation of the decision she made in 2011 to stop publishing her work. According to Etxebarria, this decision came as a result not only of her feeling exhausted from a struggle with Internet piracy, as she had indicated at the time,[94] but also because she refused to self-censor her views on the crisis any longer. In the introduction titled "Por qué rompí una promesa" [Why I Broke My Promise] the writer explains that her views on the economic crisis can only appear in the format of a book since no mainstream periodical would accept them for publication as articles.[95] Etxebarria positions her decision to write the essay as an instance of choosing "una libertad peligrosa" [a dangerous freedom] over "una servidumbre tranquila" [tranquil servitude],[96] demonstrating her skill at marketing her own work as an exercise in daring and subversion.

Liquidación por derribo did not attract as much attention as it could, however, because its release coincided with Etxebarria's brief yet scandalous appearance on the reality show "Campamento de verano" in the summer of 2013. After abandoning the show, the writer filed a lawsuit against several of the participants of two television programs produced by the Telecinco channel.[97] Etxebarria's stint on "Campamento de verano" and her fraught relations with the media figures connected to the show diverted the public's interest from the essay toward the writer's controversial public image. Since the time when she first appeared on Spain's literary scene, Etxebarria has "invited like no other the critics' wrath" and has often seen her work "easily brushed aside as either 'bad taste' or lacking of 'authentic literary value.'"[98] The writer's appearance on the reality show has made it even easier for her detractors to dismiss her published work as lacking in gravitas.

Etxebarria has a strong presence in the social media, and her online persona is often subjected to harsh criticism by journalists and the followers of her Twitter and Facebook accounts. In January 2012, for instance, Etxebarria attracted media attention when a nude photo of the writer was published on her Facebook page. Etxebarria felt compelled to pen an essay for *Vanity Fair Blogs* explaining what happened and insisting that her Facebook account had been hacked.[99] In March 2015, Etxebarria was criticized for her tweet about the crash of flight A320 in which she provided erroneous information without taking some time to verify her sources.[100] The sense of immediacy implicit in the activities conducted on social media makes this a mistake that few of their habitual users manage to avoid. Etxebarria's status as a famous writer and a media celebrity, however, invites a far greater scrutiny than that experienced by most of those who use Twitter and Facebook. Like many opinionated women with a strong presence in the public space, Etxebarria has had to deny rumors that her active stance is a result of mental illness. As I am writing these lines, the most recent status update on the writer's Facebook page is dedicated precisely to this issue:

> Acabo de quedarme blanca cuando en una conversación con un periodista me dice que él sabe de sobra que yo soy bipolar y que haría un enorme favor a los bipolares si lo admitiera en público. Pero no, resulta que no soy bipolar. Y no padezco trastorno alguno." [I experienced great shock when a journalist mentioned in a conversation that he knows very well I'm bipolar and that it would help bipolar people a lot if I acknowledged it publicly. But no, it turns out I'm not bipolar. And I'm not suffering from any disorder.][101]

Everything that Etxebarria writes is likely to be viewed at least by some of her readers through the lens of what they believe they know of her based on the relentless exposure of the writer's actions on social media, and both the author and her publishers are well aware of this.

The Planeta publishing group used the following statement to promote *Liquidación por derribo* on its website:

> Lucía Etxebarria, con el desparpajo que le caracteriza, se ha propuesto analizar rigurosamente lo que está pasando en España para explicárselo al ciudadano medio, que ya no puede más con esta tomadura de pelo." [With her habitual cheekiness, Lucía Etxebarria has tried to provide a rigorous analysis of what is happening in Spain in order to explain it to ordinary citizens who can't take any more of this practical joke.][102]

The short blurb centers on the contrast between a rigorous analysis of the economy and the "desparpajo" [cheekiness] that supposedly constitutes such a crucial characteristic of the author that it merits being included in the promotional material. The reference to "tomadura de pelo" [a practical joke] tips the balance in the description of the essay toward the ludic aspect of the book. In contrast, the same website described Muñoz Molina's *Todo lo que era sólido* as "un ensayo directo y apasionado . . . al más puro estilo de los ensayos de George Orwell o de Virginia Woolf" [a direct and passionate essay . . . in the purest tradition of essays by George Orwell or Virginia Woolf].[103] This way of marketing the two essays is misleading, however, given that *Liquidación por derribo* relies much more than Muñoz Molina's book on the use of specialized terminology from the field of economics and provides a significantly heavier amount of numerical data. The readers who come to Etxebarria's essay expecting to find "cheekiness" and "a practical joke" will discover that *Liquidación por derribo* is a much more complex and serious text than what the publishing house has suggested. The gender bias that has haunted Etxebarria throughout her literary career follows the writer even into the promotional materials dedicated to attracting readers to her work.

Without a doubt, Etxebarria is conscious of the obstacles that her gender and public persona create for the reception of an essay on the functioning of the economy published by her. A brief biographical note located at the beginning of *Liquidación por derribo* and written in Etxebarria's recognizable authorial style offers the readers the following information about the book's author:

> Lucía Etxebarria es hija de un abogado y economista, hermana de tres economistas (dos de ellos catedráticos en prestigiosas universidades) y ex cuñada de quien es considerado uno de los economistas más importantes de España. . . . Es capaz de explicar a cualquiera qué es la Curva de Kondratieff, la Ley de Say o el Teorema de la Telaraña sin pestañear. [Lucía Etxebarria is a daughter of a lawyer and an economist, a sister to three economists (two of whom are professors at prestigious universities) and a former sister-in-law to somebody who is considered one of the most important Spanish economists. . . . She can explain to anybody with ease what a Kondratiev wave, Say's Law or cobweb theory are.][104]

The same information is reiterated at the beginning of the second chapter, titled "La crisis financiera" [The Financial Crisis]. The writer explains that the reason she did not follow her father and brothers into the field of economics was the sexist belief that women lack the intellectual capacity to make a valuable impact on this branch of knowledge.[105] With this statement, Etxebarria offers her readers a choice between perpetuating the approach that dismisses women as incapable of opining on the economy or accepting the contribution that she has to make to the discussion of the economic crisis in Spain.

Once again, the contrast between Etxebarria's defense of her right to discuss the economic crisis and the ease with which Muñoz Molina launches into constructing his argument is very significant. Where Muñoz Molina abstains from listing the qualifications that authorize him to talk about the economy, Etxebarria feels the need to reiterate every aspect, including her familial connections, that might lend weight to her analysis of the crisis. *Liquidación por derribo* ends with a twelve-page bibliography enumerating print and online sources that the author used in her writing. There are also footnotes that explain the terminology that readers might find unfamiliar and listing bibliographical sources that do not appear in the final list of works cited. Aside from the bibliography, the table of contents includes an introductory note, a prologue, nine titled chapters, an epilogue, and an appendix. This places Etxebarria's essay significantly closer than Muñoz Molina's to the genre of academic writing.

Still, the essays by Muñoz Molina and Etxebarria share important similarities. Etxebarria frames her approach to the writing of this essay in a way that is nearly identical to that of Muñoz Molina's. The writer finds it important to point out that the text of the essay was produced in a highly fluid manner: "Este libro está escrito del tirón, casi por impulso" [This book was written all at once, as if by impulse],[106] "estas páginas . . . escritas del tirón" [these pages . . . written all at once].[107] The unverifiable impulsivity of the text's creation offers the readers a comforting encounter with Etxebarria's notoriously impulsive public persona. At the same time, this way of describing the process of the text's creation corresponds to the author's desire to jolt her readers out of their refusal to see what is going on. The theme of willful blindness that is so crucial to Muñoz Molina's argument reappears in *Liquidación por derribo*. Etxebarria points out that an article she published in 2006 was greeted with incredulity because nobody was ready to see and acknowledge what was really happening.[108] The writer hopes that *Liquidación por derribo* will sweep away the resistance to accepting the need for the kind of changes that will help mitigate the effects of the crisis.

Etxebarria explains her decision to write an essay analyzing the causes of the economic crisis in a way that is reminiscent of Muñoz Molina's in *Todo lo que era sólido*. The writer points out that the tendency of the public to believe in the infallibility of economists is misplaced.[109] This refusal to consider economists a group that is best qualified to explain the causes of the current crisis has been characteristic of much of the essayistic production published since 2008–2009. Ulrich Beck, for instance, points out in his essay *German Europe* that economists suffer from grave limitations that do not allow them to place their reasoning on the economy within the proper social and political framework:

> We might also say that the economists' viewpoint is politically and socially blind, that it blinds others too and that the economic advice that dominates discussion is based on political and social 'illiteracy.'. . . The general blindness may stem from the fact that the world's economists always base their opinions on some model or other and, if the models do not fit, you have a problem.[110]

At the same time, even within the field of economics there is a realization that the painful consequences of the crisis could have been softened had the analysis of the economy not been conducted solely in terms of its quantitative dimension: "A large group of eminent economists, including several Nobel Prize winners . . . have criticized the narrow vision, prompted by a superficial quantitativism, of a statistical and economic approach which reduces the situation of any one individual or social category to the level of their income in dollars."[111] The disillusionment with the capacity of the economists to predict the crisis or explain how to mitigate its effects has prompted not only sociologists like Alain Touraine or Ulrich Beck but also novelists and poets to engage in an analysis of the crisis.

Etxebarria does not deny that artists might be as prone to be swayed by their political beliefs as economists. However, she believes that the writers' capacity to express themselves clearly and in a way that their readers are likely to understand offers them an advantage over the scholars of economics.[112] In *Liquidación por derribo*, the author proposes to make use of her undoubted skill of creating beautiful prose to explain the workings of the financial markets to the readers. Instead of placing limitations on her capacity to discuss economics, Etxebarria claims that not being an economist by profession qualifies her to offer the kinds of insights into the crisis that those who work in the field have not been able to provide. In an increasingly fluid world, barriers between professions and fields of knowledge are being eroded, and Etxebarria makes use of this aspect of the crisis to advance her narrative of its causes. The title of her essay not only reminds the readers of a phrase that can be heard all too often in today's Spain, but also hints at fluidity.[113] "Liquidación" [liquidation] and "derribo" [demolition] are words that point to Spain's problematic construction industry and, at the same time, convey a sense of liquefaction and collapse that characterize the transformative and fraught era we call "the crisis." Fluidity is present in the essay in a variety of ways. Amid a discussion of Spain's corruption scandals, for instance, Etxebarria veers into an analysis of Barack Obama's victory in the 2012 presidential election in the United States. Obama's successful campaign serves as an example of how Spain's PSOE could make itself more relevant to voters in Spain.[114] *Liquidación por derribo* also contains a discussion of different forms of corruption and nepotism that exist in India, West Bengal, China, Russia, and Africa. The writer believes that an analysis of the traditions of corruption that exist in these regions can be used to explain the difficulties implicit in routing out Spain's own traditions of corruption.[115] The ease with which Etxebarria's argument moves between countries and continents illustrates the most cherished skill of today's worker: a capacity to embrace "lightness and speed"[116] that are crucial if one is to succeed in a world in flux.

The writer understands that the economic terminology she uses in the essay can prove confusing and even off-putting to the readers. For this reason, she creates a shared environment of lighthearted banter at the expense of the jargon-ridden writings of professional economists. Etxebarria intersperses her argument with asides like "atención al término de argot económico" [careful with a term of economic jargon][117] and "es decir, y en cristiano" [that is, to put it in a normal language][118] and offers facetious analogies, such as a comparison between toxic assets and toxic boyfriends: "Tienen muy buen aspecto y son muy prometedores. Al principio, parece que te van a cambiar la vida para bien, pero te la acaban cambiando para mal." [They look very nice and promise a lot. At the beginning, it looks as if they are about to change your life for the better but they end up changing it for the worse.][119] The reference to "toxic boyfriends" not only alleviates the text's complexity but also recalls Etxebarria's self-help book *Tu corazón no está bien de la cabeza* [*Your Heart Isn't Right in the Head*], which was published in the same year as *Liquidación por derribo* with the subheading of "How I Left a Toxic Relationship." In this way, Etxebarria points to the continuity within her artistic output and prevents *Liquidación por derribo* from being dismissed as not belonging among the rest of her books.

The narrative flow of the essay is interrupted with illustrations drawn by Javirroyo (Javier Royo Espallargas), a noted cartoonist and the editor of the online cartoon magazine *El Estafador*. The illustrations bring a note of levity to the narrative of the many tragic consequences of the crisis and relieve the succession of figures and facts offered by Etxebarria to illustrate her statements. The writer also makes every effort to prevent her argument from becoming monotonous and difficult to follow. The use of different fonts, lists, a variety of headings and subheadings, and the anecdotes demonstrating how Etxebarria and her friends are adapting to the crisis allows the author to make the text more accessible to the readers who might not have a sophisticated understanding of the workings of the global economy. At the same time, Etxebarria is careful to point out that her analysis of the economy, especially in what pertains to the financial markets in the United States, is based on simplification. In a single, short paragraph dedicated to the issue, Etxebarria qualifies her discussion of global finance various times with "simplificando . . . para resumir y a muy grandes rasgos . . . repito que estoy simplificando" [to simplify . . . to summarize and in very broad strokes . . . once again, I'm simplifying].[120] The writer anticipates the criticisms her essay will receive and attempts to respond to her future critics as she is preparing her text for publication.

Etxebarria dedicates a significant portion of the essay to enumerating the instances of corruption in Spain's government and business circles. By necessity, this requires the writer to provide a great number of figures in support of her argument. The use of colloquialisms and television-style cliffhangers aims to hold the readers' interest throughout the litany of facts and figures:

> Si lo de las estaciones y los aeropuertos fantasma . . . les ha dejado ojipláticos, esperen a leer los desmanes arquitectónicos cometidos por arquitectos estrella para los "edificios icónicos" españoles. [If the ghost train stations and airports . . . shocked you, just wait until you read about the architectural excesses carried out by the star architects of "iconic Spanish buildings."][121]

Etxebarria demonstrates the same zeal in offering as much factual proof for her assertions about the state of the economy as Muñoz Molina did in his essay. Still, the two writers belong to different generations, which is clear from the way they conduct research for their books. While Muñoz Molina bases a considerable part of his argument on the transformations experienced by print versions of newspapers, Etxebarria prefers to use online periodicals.

Politically, Muñoz Molina has long abandoned his youthful interest in Marxist theory and moved significantly to the right in terms of his politics.[122] Etxebarria, on the other hand, has no interest in the right-wing ideas that inspire much of Muñoz Molina's work.[123] In spite of their differing ideological positions, however, both Etxebarria and Muñoz Molina insist that the return of the rhetoric that dates back to the Spanish Civil War is exacerbating the troubles created by the collapse of the economy. After reassuring her readers that she does not consider herself "red" and supporting this statement with a condemnation of Stalin (as jarring as a reference to Stalin might appear in an essay on the current state of Spain's economy), Etxebarria explains why she does not want to be identified with either of the country's two largest parties:

> Dividir un país en dos y darte a elegir entre un bando u otro es un juego manipulador en el que se olvida que entre el blanco y el negro puede haber muchísimos matices de gris, un juego que conviene al sistema, pero que no me conviene a mí. A nosotros. [Dividing a country in two and letting you choose between one side or the other is a manipulative game that requires you to forget that there can be many shades of gray between black and white. This game serves the needs of the system but it doesn't serve mine. Ours.][124]

The echoes of the Spanish Civil War that are present in the image of "dos bandos" [two sides] are reinforced by the references to violence and aggression that, according to the writer, have come to dominate the discussions of the crisis. It might be true that, among the Spanish writers who have been writing about the crisis, Etxebarria is the one who "most thoroughly historicizes the crisis"[125] by pointing out the vestiges of franquismo in today's Spain.[126] Still, her way of framing the Civil War is not that different from Muñoz Molina's.

Allusions of varying degrees of obliqueness to the Civil War and the violence it produced have a long history of justifying the post-Transition status quo. Many of the political decisions made during the country's transition to democracy were motivated by the fear of another armed conflict:

> El *leitmotiv* de la transición española fue el "nunca más," pero dicho eslogan, lejos de referirse como en Argentina o en Brasil a la experiencia dictatorial, se circunscribe, exclusivamente, a la guerra civil. [The *leitmotiv* of the Spanish transition was "never again," but this slogan, far from being used to refer, like it did in Argentina or Brazil, to the dictatorship, is reserved exclusively for the civil war.][127]

This approach tacitly recognizes as true one of the favorite slogans of the Franco dictatorship. In 1964, the twenty-fifth anniversary of the Nationalist victory was celebrated, and the phrase "25 Años de Paz" [25 Years of Peace] was used extensively to promote "peace" as one of the greatest achievements of the regime. The belief that Franco brought peace to Spain remains controversial in a country where there are still streets and neighborhoods named "25 Años de Paz" [25 Years of Peace]. To give a single example among many, the Royal Mint came under criticism in

2015 for a 200-euro coin it released that seemed to give credence to the vision of the dictatorship as a peaceful time in the country's history:

> España incluye el franquismo dentro de los "70 años de paz." Emite monedas de 200 euros del fin de la Segunda Guerra Mundial, que obvian los 40 años de dictadura de Franco, lo que ha provocado polémica en las redes sociales donde también se ha cuestionado que el lema de "70 años de paz" evoca los "25 años de paz" utilizado por el franquismo. [Spain includes the dictatorship of Franco in "70 years of peace." It releases 200-euro coins commemorating the end of World War II that omit the 40 years of the Franco dictatorship. This has provoked a polemic in social networks where it has been pointed out that the slogan of "70 years of peace" alludes to the slogan of "25 years of peace" that was used by the dictatorship.][128]

This way of framing the dictatorship of Franco obviates the perspective of those who did not perceive it as peaceful and object to the use of one of the most memorable slogans of the Franco era.

In *Todo lo que era sólido*, Muñoz Molina makes a point of reminding his readers that "una de las metáforas de [los años de la Transición] fue el 'ruido de sables': el rumor continuo de la amenaza de un golpe" [one of the metaphors of the Transition was "saber-rattling": a constant noise threatening a coup].[129] This reminder allows the writer to make his argument in defense of the Transition and the political and economic structures that it produced. The Transition should not be placed under critical scrutiny, Muñoz Molina seems to suggest, since the measures taken by the political leaders of the Transition prevented another civil conflict from occurring after the dictator's death. Like Muñoz Molina, Etxebarria evokes the violence of the Civil War to signal her allegiance to the economic model accepted as the only possible one during the Transition. At the same time, she is more willing than Muñoz Molina to accept that Spain's "democracia de baja calidad" [low-quality democracy][130] is a result of mistakes made in the years following Franco's demise. The closed-list electoral system that was created to guarantee societal stability after the end of the dictatorship is one example that Etxebarria offers of a flaw in Spain's democratic system that the country inherited from the Transition.[131] The question to be asked today is whether the fear of a return to the ideological divisions that inspired the war will not, yet again, thwart the much-needed reforms. After the dictator's death, "fear of a right-wing coup, even a return to civil war, that might be provoked by democratization strategies that were too quick or too conflictual was . . . an ever-present feature of the transition and one that led Spaniards to prioritize peace, order and stability over other values such as justice, freedom, and democracy."[132] The greatest flaw in Etxebarria's argument stems from the writer's unconscious imitation of the Transition-era tropes even as she condemns the results of the Transition policies.

Etxebarria believes that the main problem in Spain today is that a fully democratic political system has not yet been created and suggests that there are still too many vestiges of *franquismo* in Spain. For instance, the writer qualifies the system of relations within Spain's political parties as "completamente dictatorial" [completely dictatorial][133] and reminds her readers that the only reason Spain did not become a republic after Franco's death was the dictator's decision to appoint Juan Carlos Borbón as his successor.[134] At the same time, traces of Francoist ideology (of which the writer seems to be unaware) are present in Etxebarria's text. For instance, the writer quotes Antonio Vallejo-Nágera's belief in "unemployment neurosis"[135] to support her argument about the dangers of long-term unemployment that was affecting over a quarter of Spaniards at the time *Liquidación por derribo* was written. Vallejo-Nágera is hardly a respected psychologist, however. In 1938, Vallejo-Nágera wrote to General Franco to suggest the creation of the Office of Psychological Research with the goal of conducting clinical studies on the Republican prisoners of war. Vallejo-Nágera's plan to search for "las raíces biopsíquicas del marxismo" [biopsychological roots of Marxism] was based on his belief that Marxism was a disease that affected those who fought on the Republican side of the conflict.[136] Vallejo-Nágera had created his theory of unemployment neurosis before the start of the Civil War, in 1935.[137] Yet even then the psychiatrist was preoccupied with

> el porvenir de nuestra raza, raza depauperada física y psíquicamente, raza que parece agotada por la pobreza de un suelo que apenas subviene a las necesidades biológicas más perentorias de sus habitants [the future of our race, a race that has been impoverished physically and psychologically, a race that seems exhausted by the poverty of the soil that barely provides for the most pressing biological needs of its inhabitants].[138]

There can be no doubt that Etxebarria shares neither Vallejo-Nágera's belief in eugenics nor his vision of Republicans as mentally deficient, yet his reputation as a legitimate scholar that was inherited from the dictatorship has not yet been placed under a critical scrutiny often enough for Etxebarria to be aware of it.[139]

Neither Muñoz Molina nor Etxebarria suggest any profound transformations to Spain's political or economic space or address in an in-depth way the global nature of the transformations we are witnessing. Both writers believe that only cosmetic changes are needed to address the crisis, and they make it clear that the main goal they envision for Spain is the preservation of the welfare state within the current neoliberal model. The greatest difference between their arguments lies in the authors' approach to austerity. While Muñoz Molina believes that only through cutting down spending might some form of welfare state manage to remain in existence, Etxebarria is opposed to governmental cuts in spending on social services and welfare benefits.[140] She supports those who choose to limit their personal consumption[141] yet believes that this is not a choice that anybody should be forced to make through austerity measures that are impoverishing the country's population and destroying its most valuable institutions. Unlike Muñoz Molina, Etxebarria realizes that heated discussions of the possibility of Catalonia's independence are being used by all political forces involved to distract the public's attention from the erosion of the welfare state.[142] The writer not only condemns the blindness that led Spaniards into their current predicament but also refuses to allow herself to be blinded by the propagandistic efforts of Mariano Rajoy's government.

Etxebarria's trajectory as a writer and a public figure says more about the nature of the crisis than the entire 310 pages of *Liquidación por derribo*. While the essay only hints at the need to liquefy the self as much as possible to achieve a semblance of financial security, the author's life is a clear example of how crucial it is to turn oneself into a "sellable commodity"[143] if one is wants to be financially and professionally successful within today's neoliberal model. Etxebarria moves with an apparent ease from publishing critically acclaimed novels to starring on reality TV, from penning self-help manuals to positioning herself as an expert on polyamory in her 2016 book *Más peligroso es no amar* [*It's More Dangerous Not to Love*], from analyzing the crisis to waging Twitter wars against her detractors. Unlike Muñoz Molina's version of fluidity, the incessant mobility practiced by Etxebarria is not about physical displacement from one country and one continent to another but, rather, about the constant refashioning of the self aimed at better suiting the needs of the fickle market. The readers of the essay are left with the question of what chances they have to stay afloat in this unforgiving system of economic relations if even somebody as gifted and as comfortable with fluidity as Etxebarria is struggling with unpaid bills and crushing debt.[144]

CONCLUSION

Essays by Antonio Muñoz Molina and Lucía Etxebarria theorize artists' responsibility for elaborating ways of preserving at least some remnants of the welfare state from the ravages of liquid capital. Both essays signal that fluidity is to be embraced rather than resisted and enact the skills that one needs to develop to succeed in fluid global societies composed of isolated individuals who exist in a state of "dismantled togetherness."[145] Muñoz Molina, for instance, creates a narrative where the authorial voice is disconnected from any community and speaks from a place of intellectual and emotional isolation:

> Si uno de los encantos del libro es su tono íntimo, personal e introspectivo, también constituye un discurso curiosamente monológico y solita-

rio, casi ensimismado. En un contexto donde la crisis ha fomentado la solidaridad, las cooperativas y la colaboración comunal, llama la atención que Muñoz Molina no cite a casi nadie: ni a ciudadanos, ni a intelectuales o expertos. [If one of the book's most charming qualities is its intimate, personal, and introspective tone, it also constitutes a curiously monologic and solitary, even self-absorbed, discourse. In the context where the crisis has encouraged solidarity, cooperatives, and communal collaboration, it is significant that Muñoz Molina quotes almost no one: not the citizens, nor the intellectuals and experts.][146]

Whether we see Muñoz Molina in a darkened room of an archive, in the streets of Amsterdam, or at the functions organized by the Cervantes Institute in New York, the writer appears solitary and disconnected from his environment. There is no place in his worldview for a dialogue with the people who are directly affected by the crisis. Muñoz Molina's goal is the opposite of the efforts of the participants in the 15-M movement to establish "a space to collaboratively manage everybody's 'cultural needs.'"[147] The writer hopes to displace the existing cohort of experts who have the right to opine on the crisis and occupy their place in a hierarchy of cultural authority that he is not prepared to question. In the end, his approach reinforces the neoliberal mentality that privileges a solitary voice of an authoritative knowledge broker.

Etxebarria's way of conceptualizing her role as an expert on the crisis is like Muñoz Molina's. The writer adopts a chatty tone of easy camaraderie with her readers, yet the solutions she offers belie the writer's attempts to create a vision of the crisis as a shared challenge that can be overcome collectively. For instance, Etxebarria offers anecdotes that illustrate the ways in which the crisis can be used to foster a personal "despertar espiritual" [spiritual awakening][148] in those who have substituted a sense of belonging to a community with constant efforts at self-improvement, rejecting anything that "resists being engulfed within the self and dealt with by the self's facilities."[149] Individual frugality and a partial retreat from consumerist goals substitute, in Etxebarria's worldview, the need for communal political action. Etxebarria's position vis-à-vis protesters is exemplified in her discussion of mass protests in Madrid that opens *Liquidación por derribo*. The writer repeats that she is in no way opposed to the existing system[150] and observes the protesters' clashes with the police from a distance. The tone that she adopts is that of an irate middle-class consumer who is upset that the tranquility of her prestigious residence in the center of Madrid was disturbed by the excessive violence of the authorities' response to the manifestations.

Not only does the genre of the crisis essay miss the opportunity to open itself up to a dialogue with protest movements; it is also failing to integrate an analysis of the legacy of the Civil War into the discussion of the crisis as well as the novel and the poetry of the crisis do. The war and the dictatorship are present in these essays as an inescapable frame of reference, yet the historical roots of today's troubles are not explored in much depth. Muñoz Molina and Etxebarria prefer to expand their analysis geographically rather than chronologically, and as a result, their crisis essays move more easily between continents than between times in history. The result of this approach for Muñoz Molina is a failure to identify traces of Francoist mentality within his own philosophical framework. For instance, the writer fails to see a connection between his lack of confidence in the capacity of his compatriots to remedy the situation through collective action and "la correspondiente necesidad de tutela, con lo que la historiadora Helen Graham ha identificado como uno de los 'Franco effects' que han venido sobreviviendo hasta el presente" [the corresponding need of tutelage, which historian Helen Graham has identified as one of the "Franco effects" that have survived until present].[151] Etxebarria's analysis of the crisis would also gain from a deeper engagement with the legacy of the dictatorship if the author were to take her argument beyond a conclusion that Spain's structures of corruption are rooted in the country's history.

The ideas expressed in *Todo lo que era sólido* and *Liquidación por derribo* have been echoed in the discussions of the crisis produced by the very economists whose capacity to provide a useful analysis of the crisis is put in doubt by both Muñoz Molina and Etxebarria. For instance, César Molinas, a holder of a doctoral degree in economics and a former CEO of Merrill Lynch in London, published in 2013 an essay titled *Qué hacer con España* [*What to Do with Spain?*] that is curiously similar, in what concerns its argument if not its style of writing, to the ideas expressed in *Todo lo que era sólido.* Molinas echoes Muñoz Molina's belief that the erosion of the welfare state is one of the most painful facets of an ongoing transformation of the nation-state model[152] and argues in favor of Spanish citizens abandoning an excessive reliance on the state to preserve some of the most basic programs of social welfare.[153] A self-imposed exercise in austerity is crucial, in the opinion of both the former Merrill Lynch CEO and the novelist, to keeping in existence a few remnants of the shredded social safety net. Molinas is aware of the similarities between his own argument and that of Muñoz Molina's and, in one of his tweets, recommended the writer's essay to his own readers: "Prueba también 'Todo lo que era sólido' de Muñoz Molina. Son dos maneras de escribir el mismo libro." [Try also Muñoz Molina's "Todo lo que era sólido." His and mine are two different ways of writing the same book.][154]

It is no coincidence that a former Merrill Lynch CEO and a writer who ridiculed the leadership of this very company in his essay arrived at such similar visions of the crisis. César Molinas's thinking is heavily indebted to *The Shield of Achilles: War, Peace, and the Course of History*, published in 2002 by Philip Bobbitt, a constitutional scholar and an advisor to the presidential administrations of Carter, H. W. Bush, and Clinton. In *The Shield of Achilles*, Bobbitt discusses, at great length, the profound societal transformations bound to arise "from the friction between the decaying nation-state and the emerging market-state"[155] and points out that there exists "a grotesque disparity between the rapid movement of international capital and the ponderous and territorially circumscribed responses of the nation-state, as clumsy as a bear chained to a stake, trying to chase a shifting beam of light."[156] Bobbitt and Molinas could not be more politically distant from Zygmunt Bauman and Jürgen Habermas, yet their ideas are very like those expressed in Bauman's discussion of liquid modernity and Habermas's vision of the postnational state model. In the same way, Muñoz Molina's conservatism does not prevent his understanding of the crisis from coinciding with the one that, as we will see in the next chapter, lies at the center of not only Etxebarria's *Liquidación por derribo* but also of Prado's *Ajuste de cuentas* and Gopegui's *El comité de la noche*. These writers are accessing a shared pool of ideas about the critical transformations experienced by Western societies and are creating a conduit toward these ideas for readers who are unlikely to follow the work of Bauman or Habermas but will be interested in perusing essays by their favorite novelists. Despite the clear limitations of the crisis essay, the value of the genre resides in illustrating the insufficiency of an approach that posits the crisis as a problem that can be addressed by isolated individuals.

NOTES

1. Thomas Mermall, "Culture and the Essay in Modern Spain," *The Cambridge Companion to Modern Spanish Culture*, ed. David T. Gies (Cambridge: Cambridge University Press, 1999), 165.
2. Michael Iarocci, *Properties of Modernity: Romantic Spain, Modern Europe, and the Legacies of Empire* (Nashville: Vanderbilt University Press, 2006), xi.
3. José Álvarez Junco, *Mater dolorosa. La idea de España en el siglo XIX* (Madrid: Taurus, 2001), 113–15.
4. Juan Pablo Forner, *Oración apologética por la España y su mérito literario* (1786; repr., Madrid: Publicaciones Españolas, 1956), 14.
5. Álvarez Junco, *Mater dolorosa. La idea de España en el siglo XIX*, 588.
6. José Ortega y Gasset, *España invertebrada, Bosquejo de algunos pensamientos históricos*, 8 ed. (1921; repr., Madrid: Revista de Occidente, 1952), 2.
7. Ibid., 5.
8. María Zambrano, *Delirium and Destiny: A Spaniard in Her Twenties*, trans. Carol Maier (1953; repr., Albany: State University of New York Press, 1999), 22.
9. Ibid., 42.
10. Pedro Laín Entralgo, *España como problema* (Madrid: Seminario de Problemas Hispanoamericanos, 1948), 26.
11. Enrique Dussel, "Beyond Eurocentrism: The World-System and the Limits of Modernity," trans. Eduardo Mendieta, *The Cultures of Globalization*, ed. Fredric Jameson and Masao Miyoshi (Durham and London: Duke University Press, 1998), 5.
12. Laín Entralgo, *España como prolbema*, 162–63.
13. Rafael Calvo Serer, *España, sin problema*, third ed. (1949; repr., Madrid: Ediciones Rialp, 1957), 14.
14. Ibid., 33–34.

15. Claudio Sánchez-Albornoz, *España, un enigma histórico*, Vol. I, second ed. (1956; repr., Buenos Aires: Editorial Sudamericana, 1962), 16.
16. Ibid., 11.
17. Juan Pablo Fusi and Jordi Palafox, *España: 1808–1996. El desafío de la modernidad* (Madrid: Espasa Calpe, 1997), 12.
18. This prize is awarded on a yearly basis by Spain's Ministry of Culture.
19. Antonio-Miguel Bernal, *España, proyecto inacabado: costes / beneficios del imperio* (Madrid: Marcial Pons, 2005), 34.
20. Ibid., 35.
21. Pedro J. de la Peña, *Otro 98 es necesario* (Madrid: Huerga y Fierro, 2012), 9.
22. Antonio Muñoz Molina, *Todo lo que era sólido* (Barcelona: Seix Barral, 2013), 66, 77.
23. Silvia Bermúdez, "Let's Talk About Sex?: From Almudena Grandes to Lucía Etxebarria, the Volatile Values of the Spanish Literary Market," *Women's Narrative and Film in Twentieth-Century Spain: A World of Difference(s)*, ed. Ofelia Ferrán and Kathleen Mary Glenn (New York: Routledge, 2002), 224.
24. Karl Marx and Friedrich Engels, *The Communist Manifesto*, ed. D. Ryazanoff, (1848; repr., New York: Russell & Russell, 1963), 63.
25. Muñoz Molina, *Todo lo que era sólido*, 7.
26. Ibid., 253.
27. Zygmunt Bauman, *Liquid Modernity* (Cambridge: Polity, 2000), 3.
28. Ibid., 150.
29. The writer has been contributing articles to various newspapers since 1982. His journalistic output, however, does not focus on politics and economy aside from an interest in Basque terrorism and references to figures like Eichmann and Pinochet (Jean-Pierre Castellani "Antonio Muñoz Molina entre literatura y periodismo: las columnas." *Olivar* 2, no. 2 (2001): 5). *Todo lo que era sólido* is unlike anything the author had published before, and the essay's very existence testifies to the gravity of the crisis in Muñoz Molina's eyes.
30. Muñoz Molina, *Todo lo que era sólido*, 25.
31. Ibid., 25.
32. In his crisis essay "El capitalismo funeral," Vicente Verdú echoes the belief that economists are less likely than writers to provide a useful explanation of what caused the crisis: "La economía . . . es la ciencia humana más atrasada. Y ello obedece a que con frecuencia se abstrae de las condiciones sociales, históricas, políticas, psicológicas y caóticas, que son inseparables de las actividades mercantiles. Como consecuencia, los expertos económicos resultan especialmente incapaces para interpretar las causas y las consecuencias de las perturbaciones monetarias o bursátiles. . . . Obedientes al cálculo, ignoran lo que no es calculable ni mensurable, como la vida, el sufrimiento, la alegría, el amor, el honor, la magnanimidad, la moda, la emulación, las comunicaciones y el mal humor" [The economy . . . is the most backward of social sciences. This happens because it frequently isolates itself from the social, historical, political, psychological, and chaotic conditions that are inseparable from commercial activities. As a consequence, the experts in economics prove to be completely incapable of interpreting the causes and the consequences of monetary or stock-market disturbances. . . . They obey calculations and pay no heed to things that cannot be calculated or measured, such as life, suffering, joy, love, honor, generosity, fashion, emulation, communications, and moodiness]. Vicente Verdú, *El capitalismo funeral. La crisis o la Tercera Guerra Mundial* (Barcelona: Anagrama, 2009), 17.
33. Muñoz Molina, *Todo lo que era sólido*, 9.
34. Ibid., 10.
35. Emmánuel Lizcano, "Sin los cuentos sobre la crisis, a los de arriba no les salen las cuentas," *Fuera de lugar: conversaciones entre crisis y transformación*, ed. Amador Fernández-Savater (Madrid: Machado Libros, 2013), 144.
36. Muñoz Molina, *Todo lo que era sólido*, 168.

37. Ignacio Sánchez-Cuenca, *La desfachatez intelectual: escritores e intelectuales ante la política* (Madrid: Catarata, 2016), 152.
38. Muñoz Molina, *Todo lo que era sólido*, 36.
39. Ibid., 139.
40. Ibid., 149.
41. José Luis Segovia Bernabé, "La realización del orden justo en la sociedad: responsabilidades," *Corintios XIII: Revista de teología y pastoral de la caridad*, 134 (2010): 42.
42. Muñoz Molina, *Todo lo que era sólido*, 72.
43. Zygmunt Bauman, *Liquid Love* (Cambridge: Polity, 2003), 51.
44. Muñoz Molina, *Todo lo que era sólido*, 197.
45. Ibid., 200.
46. Ibid., 213.
47. Ibid., 216.
48. Ibid., 224.
49. Ibid., 227.
50. Ibid., 198–99.
51. Ibid., 247.
52. Ibid., 218.
53. Ibid., 223.
54. Bauman, *Liquid Love*, 135.
55. Muñoz Molina, *Todo lo que era sólido*, 110–11.
56. Luisa Elena Delgado, *La nación singular: fantasías de la normalidad democrática española (1996–2011)* (Madrid, España: Siglo XXI de España, 2014), 23–25.
57. Zygmunt Bauman, *Strangers at Our Door* (Campridge: Polity, 2016), 32.
58. Nadia C. Seremetakis, "The Memory of the Senses, Part I: Marks of the Transitory," *The Senses Still: Perception and Memory as Material Culture in Modernity*, ed. Nadia C. Seremetakis (Chicago and London: University of Chicago Press, 1996), 30.
59. Muñoz Molina, *Todo lo que era sólido*, 201.
60. Ibid., 45–46.
61. Ibid., 231.
62. Amador Fernández-Savater, "Emborronar la CT (del «No a la guerra» al 15-M),' *CT o la Cultura de la Transición. Crítica a 35 años de cultura española*, ed. Guillem Martínez (Barcelona: Random House Mondadori, 2012), 37–38.
63. Muñoz Molina, *Todo lo que era sólido*, 150.
64. Isabel Cuñado, "Despertar tras la amnesia: guerra civil y postmemoria en la novela española del siglo XXI," *Dissidences* 3, no. 1 (2007): 1.
65. Nathan Richardson, "'No pensar,' or Does the Contemporary Spanish Novel of Memory Really Want to Know?: *Tiempo de silencio, Corazón tan blanco, Soldados de Salamina* and Beyond," Letras Hispanas 7, no. 1 (2010): 6.
66. Muñoz Molina, *Todo lo que era sólido*, 151.
67. Ibid., 151.
68. Olga López-Valero Colbert, *The Gaze on the Past: Popular Culture and History in Antonio Muñoz Molina's Novels* (Lewisburg: Bucknell University Press, 2007), 178.
69. Muñoz Molina, *Todo lo que era sólido*, 13.
70. Ibid., 14.
71. Ibid., 17.
72. Jo Labanyi, *Spanish Literature: A Very Short Introduction* (Oxford: Oxford University Press, 2010), 73.
73. Lorraine Ryan offers one of many examples of how representatives of the Partido Popular manipulate the crisis narrative to shut down any discussion of historical memory: "In the midst of debates about the transfer of Franco's grave from Valle de Los Caídos to his residence, El Pardo, PP politician Eduardo González Pons asserted that historical memory did not interest the Spanish populace, who were far more interested in reducing unemployment (Agencias). In April 2012, the PP commenced its fiscal abandonment of the recuperation of historical memory. It first budget reduced the annual amount conceded to the recuperation of memory from 6.2 million to 2.5

million, a drastic cut of 59.6 percent." Lorraine Ryan, " The Economic Degeneration of Masculinity in Rafael Chirbes's *En la orilla," Romance Quarterly* 62, no. 2 (2015): 84.

74. Muñoz Molina, *Todo lo que era sólido*, 11.

75. Helen Graham, "Coming to Terms with the Past: Spain's Memory Wars," *History Today* 54, no. 5 (May 2004): 29.

76. Carsten Humlebæk, "Creating a New Cohesive National Discourse in Spain after Franco," *Post-Authoritarian Cultures: Spain and Latin America's Southern Cone*, ed. Luis Martín-Estudillo and Roberto Ampuero (Nashville: Vanderbilt University Press, 2008), 197–98.

77. Muñoz Molina, *Todo lo que era sólido*, 226–27.

78. Bauman, *Liquid Modernity*, 82.

79. Muñoz Molina, *Todo lo que era sólido*, 228.

80. Ibid., 36.

81. Bauman, *Liquid Modernity*, 126.

82. Muñoz Molina, *Todo lo que era sólido*, 244–45.

83. Ibid., 245.

84. Delgado, *La nación singular: fantasías de la normalidad democrática española (1996–2011)*, 265–66.

85. The writer uses 2006 as his point of reference because that year witnessed not only the culmination of the precrisis wastefulness but also the commemoration of the seventy-fifth anniversary of the proclamation of the Second Republic and the seventieth anniversary of the beginning of the Civil War. Muñoz Molina, *Todo lo que era sólido*, 14.

86. Ibid., 15.

87. José Gámez's disillusionment with the long-awaited democracy is very similar to the story of Matías Bertomeu, the protagonist of Rafael Chirbes's novel *Crematorio* analyzed in the next chapter.

88. Muñoz Molina, *Todo lo que era sólido*, 68–69.

89. The realization that the countries of the EU have not weathered the crisis as well as the United States is often reflected in the Spanish media. For instance, *El País* published, in March 2015, an article titled "Una nueva primavera en Estados Unidos" [A New Spring in the United States] that speaks with great admiration of the success that the United States achieved in reversing the effects of the Great Recession . See Marc Bassets, "Una nueva primavera en Estados Unidos," *El País*, March 15, 2015. http://economia.elpais.com/economia/2015/03/13/actualidad/1426278977_656369.html(accessed March 15, 2015). The article was published several months after Muñoz Molina's novel, yet the contrast between the postrecession economies of the United States and Spain had been evident for quite a while. Bassets attributes the differences in today's state of the Western European and the US economies to the opposing approaches that their leaders took to repairing the damage wrought by the collapse of the real estate market. However, the long-term effects of globalization on the economic and political space of the United States remain outside the scope of Bassets' s analysis.

90. Ginés Donaire, "Antonio Muñoz Molina viaja al centro de su imaginario," *El País*, January 8, 2015, http://ccaa.elpais.com/ccaa/2015/01/08/andalucia/1420712798_259802.html (accessed November 2, 2015).

91. Muñoz Molina, *Todo lo que era sólido*, 181–82.

92. Isidro López, "Consensonomics: la ideología económica en la CT," *CT o la Cultura de la Transición. Crítica a 35 años de cultura española*, ed. Guillem Martínez (Barcelona: Random House Mondadori, 2012), 88.

93. In 1964, Manuel Fraga, Franco's Minister of Information and Tourism, placed this slogan at the center of a promotional campaign that aimed to attract tourists to the country. The slogan reflected the ideas as to "Spain's difference, peculiarity, exceptionality, and, at times, its 'abnormality' [that] have been circulating since the late eighteenth century in Spanish discussions of national identity and in accounts of Spain written by foreign travelers and tourists" (Afinoguénova and Martí-Olivella, xi). One of Fraga's goals was to normalize the dictatorship of Franco in the eyes of Europeans.

94. Tommaso Koch, "Las tensas relaciones de Lucía Etxebarria en la Red," *Cultura El País*, December 20, 2011, http://cultura.elpais.com/cultura/2011/12/20/actualidad/1324335603_850215.html (accessed March 27, 2015.
95. Ibid., 7–8.
96. Ibid., 20.
97. "Lucía Etxeberría denuncia a integrantes de 'Sálvame' y de 'Campamento de Verano' por acoso y maltrato," *La voz de Galicia*, August 1, 2013, www.lavozdegalicia.es/noticia/television/2013/08/01/etxeberria-denuncia-integrantes-salvame-campamento-verano-acoso-maltrato/00031375346977884762705.htm (accessed March 28, 2015).
98. Silvia Bermúdez, "Let's Talk About Sex?: From Almudena Grandes to Lucía Etxebarria, the Volatile Values of the Spanish Literary Market," *Women's Narrative and Film in Twentieth-Century Spain: A World of Difference(s)*, ed. Ofelia Ferrán and Kathleen Mary Glenn (New York: Routledge, 2002), 224.
99. Lucía Etxebarria, "Por qué está corriendo un desnudo mío por la red," *Vanity Fair Blogs, Vanity Fair*, January 24, 2012, http://blogs.revistavanityfair.es/vanityshow/2012/01/24/lucia-etxebarria (accessed March 28, 2015).
100. "Lucía Etxebarria la lía en Twitter con el teléfono de información sobre el accidente aéreo," *ABC*, Diario Abc, S.L., March 24, 2015, www.abc.es/estilo/gente/20150324/abci-lucia-etxebarria-twitter-telefono-201503241835.html (accessed March 28, 2015).
101. Lucía Etxebarria, "Acabo de quedarme." *Facebook*. Facebook, March 30, 2015.
102. www.planetadelibros.com/libro-liquidacion-por-derribo/92231 (accessed March 30, 2015).
103. www.planetadelibros.com/libro-todo-lo-que-era-solido/90928(accessed March 30, 2015).
104. Lucía Etxebarria, *Liquidación por derribo* (Barcelona: Planeta, 2013), 3.
105. Ibid., 72.
106. Ibid., 21.
107. Ibid., 221.
108. Ibid., 96.
109. Ibid., 73.
110. Ulrich Beck, *German Europe*, trans. Rodney Livingstone (Cambridge: Polity Press, 2013), 13.
111. Alain Touraine, *After the Crisis*, trans. Helen Morrison (Cambridge: Polity Press, 2014), 2.
112. Etxebarria, *Liquidación por derribo*, 73.
113. The English translation of the expression "liquidación por derribo" is "demolition sale."
114. Etxebarria, *Liquidación por derribo*, 277–79.
115. Ibid., 46–51.
116. Bauman, *Liquid Love*, 49.
117. Lucía Etxebarria, *Liquidación por derribo*, 83.
118. Ibid., 84, 100.
119. Ibid., 77.
120. Ibid., 76.
121. Ibid., 112.
122. In an analysis of Muñoz Molina's trajectory as a novelist, Jacqueline Cruz points out that there is a growing sense of nostalgia for the Franco era in the writer's novels: "Muñoz Molina's novels constitute a repeated attempt to embellish the Francoist past, whose negative elements are depicted as mere chance of fate, rather than the result of concrete socio-economic forces and international alliances. . . . There is almost a perverse complacency in his repeated allusions to the Republic's defeat." Jacqueline Cruz, "Of Good Torturers and Evil Workers: Antonio Muñoz Molina's *Plenilunio*," *Traces of Contamination: Unearthing the Francoist Legacy in Contemporary Spanish Discourse*, ed. Eloy E. Merino and H. Rosi Song (Lewisburg: Bucknell University Press, 2005), 209. In

his crisis essay, Muñoz Molina makes it clear that he believes that only the defeat of every emotional attachment to the Republican cause will guarantee a tranquil future for Spain.

123. In March 2016, Etxebarria accused Podemos of organizing a campaign of harassment against her on Twitter. In an open letter that she addressed to the party and to the digital periodical Público, the writer pointed out that she found it especially painful to be targeted by Podemos in spite of being "la izquierda de toda la vida" [a lifelong leftist] . Lucìa Etxebarria, "Carta abierta al diario Público y a Podemos de Lucía Etxebarría," *Público,* March 12, 2016, www.publico.es/culturas/carta-abierta-al-diario-publico.html (accessed November 21, 2016).

124. Etxebarria, *Liquidación por derribo,* 25.

125. Lorraine Ryan, " The Economic Degeneration of Masculinity in Rafael Chirbes's *En la orilla,*" 85.

126. Etxebarria, *Liquidación por derribo,* 56–62, 140.

127. Paloma Aguilar Fernández, "La presencia de la guerra civil y del franquismo en la democracia española," *Pasajes* 11 (Primavera 2003): 92.

128. Xavier Lladó, "España incluye el franquismo dentro de los '70 años de paz,'" *elMón* Totmedia, September 8, 2015, http://elmon.cat/noticia/107092/index.html (accessed December 28, 2016).

129. Muñoz Molina, *Todo lo que era sólido,* 39.

130. Etxebarria, *Liquidación por derribo,* 184.

131. Ibid., 184.

132. Madeleine Davis, "Is Spain Recovering Its Memory? Breaking the 'Pacto del Olvido,'" *Human Rights Quarterly* 27, no. 3 (August 2005): 864.

133. Etxebarria, *Liquidación por derribo,* 193.

134. Ibid., 141.

135. Ibid., 217.

136. Ricard Vinyes, Montse Armengou, and Ricard Belis, *Los niños perdidos del franquismo,* trans. Daniel Royo (Barcelona: Plaza & Janés, 2002), 31–32.

137. The transcription of the psychiatrist's last name varies from one source to another from Vallejo-Nágera to Vallejo Nájera.

138. Antonio Vallego-Nágera, "Neurosis y problemas médicos del paro obrero," *Anales de la academia nacional de medicina* LV, no. 1 (1935): 200.

139. Among the sources that discuss Vallejo-Nágera's beliefs and the manner in which they were used to strengthen the dictatorship, the collection of testimonial accounts titled *Los niños perdidos del franquismo* [The Lost Children of Francoism] (2002) by Ricard Vinyes, Montse Armengou, and Ricard Belis and the novel *Mala gente que camina* [Bad People Walking] (2006) by Benjamín Prado stand out.

140. Etxebarria, *Liquidación por derribo,* 19, 250.

141. Ibid., 33–36.

142. Ibid., 254.

143. Bauman, *Strangers at Our Door,* 110.

144. In 2013, the same year when *Liquidación por derribo* was published, Etxebarria confessed that she saw no way of repaying her debt to the Internal Revenue office without appearing on a reality TV show. Rebeca Cortés, "Lucía Etxebarría entra en 'Campamento de Verano' para pagar una deuda con Hacienda," *ABC.* Diario Abc, S.L., July 17, 2013.

145. Bauman, *Liquid Love,* 119.

146. Sebastián Faber, "Review of Antonio Muñoz Molina, *Todo lo que era sólido*" (Barcelona: Seix Barral, 2012), *ALCES XXI* 1 (2013): 739.

147. Luis Moreno-Caballud, *Cultures of Anyone: Studies on Cultural Democratization in the Spanish Neoliberal Crisis,* trans. Linda Grabner (Liverpool: Liverpool University Press, 2015), 191.

148. Etxebarria, *Liquidación por derribo,* 34.

149. Bauman, *Liquid Modernity,* 39.

150. Etxebarria, *Liquidación por derribo,* 17, 18–19.

151. Faber, "Review of Antonio Muñoz Molina, *Todo lo que era sólido*," 743–74.

152. César Molinas, *Qué hacer con España: del capitalismo castizo a la refundación de un país*, (Barcelona: Destino, 2013), 78.

153. Ibid., 114–16.

154. César Molinas (Cesar_Molinas), "Prueba también 'Todo lo que era sólido' de Muñoz Molina. Son dos maneras de escribir el mismo libro," September 24, 2013, 10:41 p.m., tweet.

155. Philip Bobbitt, *The Shield of Achilles: War, Peace, and the Course of History* (New York: Anchor Books, 2003), xxiii.

156. Ibid., 221.

TWO

Novel

Revisiting History

Traumatic occurrences usually take time to appear reflected in novels, yet the genre of crisis literature in Spain already has produced a significant number of novels by the country's leading writers.[1] The reason novels of the crisis started appearing in print so early is that there were already novelistic warnings about the unviability of the existing economic system. In 2005, for instance, a group of artists that publishes under the name Todoazen Collective released *El año que tampoco hicimos la revolución* [*Another Year We Failed to Make a Revolution*], a novel that consisted entirely of news items, which, taken together, traced the country's growing corruption that required governmental complicity on every level in order to be possible.[2] The novel's authors propose to arrest "un flujo continuo de narraciones" [the continuous flow of narratives] that we might not always notice but that have a great impact on the way we perceive the world around us.[3] The news items that the Todoazen Collective includes in the novel often fail to attract attention when published in newspapers. It is only when readers see them gathered in a single volume that the destructive potential of capital's insertion into governmental institutions becomes clear.[4]

Like the writers who have contributed to the later genre of crisis literature, members of the Todoazen Collective point to the threat posed by the increasing fluidity of capital to the gains of the Spanish welfare state and expect the text they create to serve as a space where readers can pause to question the developments they might accept uncritically during their daily lives. The narrative format that the Todoazen Collective chooses for this novel vindicates the role of literature as a vehicle of political change:

> *El año* no es simplemente una colección de estadísticas ni un libro escrito con el lenguaje de las ciencias sociales para reducir la complejidad de nuestras sociedades capitalistas a una serie de ecuaciones matemáticas e investigaciones cuantitativas. *El año* es claramente un experimento narrativo, que busca en la escritura toda su potencia política. [*El año* is not just a collection of statistical data or a book written in the language of social sciences to reduce the complexity of our capitalist societies to a series of mathematical equations and quantitative studies. *El año* is clearly a narrative experiment that finds all of its political power in writing.][5]

This is an approach shared by the authors of the crisis novels analyzed in this chapter. Unlike the authors of crisis essays, Rafael Chirbes, Luis García Montero, Benjamín Prado, and Belén Gopegui refuse to write depoliticized literature or support austerity. They question what Moreno-Caballud refers to as the "system . . . supported by the authority of experts and intellectuals who are heirs to the long tradition of cultural elites who pedagogically guide the people toward 'modern progress.'"[6] Instead of positioning themselves as figures of intellectual authority who dispense wisdom to the masses, these writers express the same rage, confusion, and despair that are experienced by everybody in Spain whose life has been impacted by the crisis. Novelists of the crisis do not dictate solutions because the hierarchical system of cultural relations constituted during the Transition has proven to be incapable of addressing the crisis and these writers see no reason to attempt to rescue this format of engaging with readers.

The authors of crisis novels discussed here belong to different generations, and the aesthetic conceptions within which they work vary greatly. All of them, however, believe that the recovery of historical memory is crucial for arriving at an understanding of the crisis. Rafael Chirbes, the oldest among this group of writers and the author who started writing about the crisis earlier than others, offers the bleakest perspective of Spain's situation, which does not allow for a single glimmer of hope. On the other hand, Belén Gopegui, the youngest of the writers I analyze in depth, advances the possibility that an effective resistance to the power of capital can arise amid the devastation wrought by the crisis. Art appears in these novels as a weapon of resistance that allows characters who engage in creative work to break through alienation and hopelessness. This vision of art is supported by the trajectory of the genre that starts with Chirbes's existential desperation, travels through the rage that inspires Prado's novel and the nostalgic musings of García Montero's text, and later develops into a more hopeful, albeit still mindful of the tragic aspects of the crisis, novel by Gopegui. Novels of the crisis continue to appear in print, and such writers as Javier López Menacho, Almudena Grandes, Eduardo Iglesias, and Pablo Gutiérrez have contributed to the genre of crisis literature.

RAFAEL CHIRBES

Rafael Chirbes was writing about the approaching disaster before it arrived and continued doing so after its shattering consequences became clear to everybody. Moreno-Caballud talks about "resonancias casi proféticas" [an almost prophetic resonance] of Chirbes's 2007 novel *Crematorio,*[7] and it is, indeed, tempting to credit the author of the novel with prescience, given his powerful depiction of the corruption in Spain's construction industry. Chirbes was awarded Premio de la Crítica de Narrativa Castellana in 2007 for *Crematorio* and again in 2014 for *En la orilla* which is a significant development in the career of an author who, until recently, was considered to be of interest only to a small minority of readers[8] and was better known outside the country (especially, in Germany[9]) than in Spain.[10] *En la orilla* also received Premio Nacional de Narrativa and Premio Francisco Umbral awarded by the Francisco Umbral Foundation to the best book of the year. The novel's popularity is "indicative of its resonance with readers whose lives, or those of their immediate family members, have been directly affected by the recession, a large demographic in a country with six million unemployed and one million families in which all members are unemployed."[11] In an interview he granted to *El Mundo* in 2013, Chirbes mentioned a possibility of writing a novel that would form a trilogy with *Crematorio* and *En la orilla*. The writer suggested that the creation of the third novel was contingent on there occurring a meaningful change in Spain's situation but was pessimistic as to whether that was possible.[12] Chirbes died of lung cancer on August 15, 2015, and admirers of his talent will not see a companion novel to *Crematorio* and *En la orilla* appear in print. Had the author lived, it is hard to imagine his seeing Spain's current situation as a great improvement on the tragic reality he depicted in his novels.

Chirbes has long been a critic's writer, and his popularity with readers outside of academia has been limited. According to a 2014 article in *El País,* until recently, Chirbes was "un escritor minoritario, de culto" [a writer who appealed to a minority of faithful followers].[13] The writer was conscious of the difference in the reception of the two most recent novels and his previous, less popular (albeit extraordinarily talented) work:

> Hasta *Crematorio* tenía buenas críticas y vendía y no tenía la sensación de estar majara. Pero esta novela me ha expuesto mucho al público. Pero ya es irremediable. [Before *Crematorio,* I had good reviews and my books sold and I didn't have a feeling of being crazy. But this novel exposed me a lot to the public. But that cannot be helped.][14]

The surge in readers' enthusiasm for Chirbes's more recent novels does not stem from a break with the thematic and narrative concerns that have been present throughout the writer's literary career. Calvo Carilla proposes that we approach *Crematorio* as a chapter in the author's "coherente proyecto de narración e interpretación crítica de la generación llamada a protagonizar el momento histórico más decisivo desde la sublevación militar franquista" [coherent project of a narrative and critical analysis of the generation called to protagonize the most decisive historic moment since the Francoist military uprising].[15] Chirbes is one of the most inventive writers, in terms of the narrative strategies he employs, among Spanish authors writing today. Yet Calvo Carilla is right in his assertion that, despite their obvious differences, all Chirbes's novels share an interest in the legacy of the Spanish Civil War and *franquismo* and are written in a very distinctive and recognizable authorial style. Chirbes's novels constitute a whole where narrative strategies draw attention to the ways in which the country's past remains alive in the present.

Within Chirbes's lifelong novelistic project, *Crematorio* and *En la orilla* form a diptych that, to a degree, sets the novels aside from the writer's preceding work.[16] Rodríguez Marcos suggests that *En la orilla* is "la cara B" [side B] of *Crematorio* and that the two novels are indissolubly linked by their thematic concerns.[17] In these novels, Chirbes speaks to the generation that came of age on the eve of Spain's transition to democracy and was seduced by the promise of prosperity in the newly democratic country. *Crematorio* offers a striking depiction of the culture of corruption pervasive in Spain's real estate industry in the opening decade of the twenty-first century. A highly successful TV series based on the novel aired on Canal+ in March–April 2011. The eight-episode series was written and directed by Jorge Sánchez-Cabezudo and captured a 6.1 percent share of the market with an average of 1,112,000 viewers for each episode.[18] Rafael Chirbes was not very enthusiastic about the series but the show's popularity testifies to the importance of the discussion that the writer initiated with this novel.[19] By the time *En la orilla* came out, it was clear that there was no discussion in Spain that was more worth having. The novel became an instant hit with the readers, has been translated into ten languages, and was turned into a play by *K Producciones*,[20] a theater company that specializes in "hacer teatro de autores vivos y con un fuerte compromiso político y social" [making theater of living writers with a strong political and social stance].[21] Rafael Chirbes is no longer physically alive, yet his crisis novels remain as relevant as they were at the time of their publication.

In his analysis of the literary response to the crisis, Ignacio Sánchez-Cuenca points out that Chirbes's *En la orilla* offers a more valuable approach to analyzing the causes of the crisis than Muñoz Molina's essay:

> Así como el objetivo literario de Chirbes resulta factible y, de hecho, queda admirablemente resuelto, sin que haya quizá mejor formato que la novela para conseguirlo. *Todo lo que era sólido*, en cambio, adopta una forma ensayística y se mete en un terreno pantanoso, careciendo de los medios para salir de la ciénaga. [Chirbes's literary goal turns out be feasible and, in fact, is achieved admirably since there is probably no

> better format than a novel to do so. *Todo lo que era sólido,* on the other hand, adopts an essay form and gets on marshy ground, lacking means to get out of the bog.][22]

The tongue-in-cheek references to marshes and bogs point to the centrality of this imagery that was introduced by Chirbes to the discussions of the crisis. Muñoz Molina remains mired in a bog of Transition-era myths that Chirbes described so well in his novels. Despite his insistence that fluidity must be mastered if one is to adapt to globalization, Muñoz Molina boxed himself into a format that did not allow him to escape from the constraints of the "Spain as a problem" genre. Chirbes, on the other hand, opened a discussion that was soon joined by other writers. The early date of publication of *Crematorio* and the popularity of both crisis novels by Chirbes did not fail to make an impact on the writers who contributed to the emerging genre of crisis literature. *Crematorio* and *En la orilla* make it clear that all areas of life are being affected by painful transformations, and it would be a mistake to talk exclusively about the economic ramifications of the crisis. Chirbes's contribution to crisis literature is not based solely on a devastating depiction of the tragic effects of the economic collapse. The writer attempts to indicate if not a path out of the current predicament then, at least, a possibility that such a path will one day be found.

In the pause between the publication of *Crematorio* and *En la orilla*, Chirbes released *Por cuenta propia* (2010), a collection of essays in literary criticism. The collection brings together essays and articles written by the writer between 2002 and 2009. It is hardly accidental that the writer should have decided to turn to literary analysis at a time when unstoppable information flows were making true political engagement feel outdated. In the writer's words,

> Los noticiarios de la televisión, las páginas de los periódicos, nos dejan la sensación de que somos sólo lectores o espectadores. Ninguna de las batallas de las que se nos informa parece ser la nuestra. [Television newscasts, newspaper pages leave us with a feeling that we are nothing but readers or viewers. None of the battles we are being informed about seem to be ours.][23]

The art of literary criticism allows one to engage in a dialogue with words on a page on a more active level. In the degraded world of *Crematorio,* the novel that marks the beginnings of the genre of crisis literature, in literary criticism is a space that harbors a possibility of conceiving an alternative to the desperation and cynicism engendered by the fluid capitalism of today. Chirbes does not idealize literary critics or place them outside the pale of his acerbic sarcasm. He makes it clear, however, that the relative unprofitability of literary scholarship allows the field to develop the kind of distance from the capitalist accumulation of profit that is necessary to create a meaningful critique of the status quo. Even if the literary critics of today are too apolitical to offer working alternatives, they can create, within the consumerist societies they inhabit, intellectual pockets where a memory of alternative discourses will be preserved. Even this limited sense of hope is absent from the writer's second novel of the crisis, however. The protagonist of *En la orilla* does not manage to find a haven from the devastation of the crisis either in literature or in history. Chirbes's novels will not offer any sense of respite to the readers, but they constitute a space where the reasons for the painful nature of the crisis can be analyzed.

Chirbes's entire literary trajectory is marked by the author's dedication to dispelling the myths of the Transition. The writer chronicles in his novels the betrayal, immediately after the death of Franco, of the revolutionary ideals that had inspired the clandestine struggle against the dictatorship. His crisis novels *Crematorio* and *En la orilla* make it clear that there can be no effective analysis of the economic collapse without taking into consideration the way in which the foundations of Spain's neoliberalism that had been laid during the last two decades of the Franco regime were protected by the Transition-era consensus. The current crisis is, for Chirbes, a logical development of the economic policies that were eagerly embraced by the politicians of the Transition. The missed opportunity for political and economic change that the Transition represents for the writer[24] has come to haunt Spaniards once it became clear that the model adopted during the Transition was built on unaddressed and unquestioned social and economic inequities. In the talk that Chirbes hoped to give at the reception for the Premio Nacional de Narrativa and that was published posthumously,[25] the writer speaks of the irony implicit in his receiving the award from the hands of the very political and cultural institutions that had been inherited from the Transition and that were responsible for the crisis that he denounced in his books.[26] Chirbes was planning to give the €20,000 that constitute the Premio Nacional de Narrativa to a beneficent organization called la Casa de la Caridad de Valencia. In the writer's words, the people who line up for the free dinners offered by la Casa are as devastated by the crisis as the characters of his novel, and his greatest hope is that his words will help them fight against those who rob them of their dignity.[27] The writer addressed his talk to Spain's Royal Family, the Minister of Culture, and the entire political and cultural establishment that he accused of complicity with the transnational business interests that caused the global economic collapse. Even after Chirbes's death, his words constituted a challenge to the existing political and economic order.

Crematorio *(2007): On the Brink of Collapse*

The editors of the collection of articles on Rafael Chirbes that was published in 2011 point out that the world of *Crematorio* is more tragic, more hopeless than anything the readers could have encountered before within the corpus of Chirbes's novelistic production:[28]

> Ahora ya no se trata, como en las novelas precedentes, de fracaso generacional, sino . . . de fracaso *tout court*, el fracaso cósmico leopardiano . . . la vida entendida como una cadena de pérdidas, de derrotas, de pequeños o grandes infiernos que, unas veces con lentitud y otras con apremio, nos queman. [It is no longer about a generational failure, like in the preceding novels . . . but about a failure *tout court*, a cosmic, Leopardian failure . . . life understood as a string of losses, defeats, small or large infernos that, sometimes slowly and sometimes rapidly, burn us.][29]

The idea of a fire where the final remains are burned appears in the very title of *Crematorio*. It refers to the crematorium where the body of Matías Bertomeu awaits cremation while the novel's characters ponder about their lives in the wake of Matías's death. Matías is a political activist who fought against Franco's dictatorship in the early 1970s, was disappointed by the Transition, and searched for ways to continue his struggle against capitalism and exploitation until his death. In the final years of his life, Matías becomes an organic farmer whose goal is to live a simple, self-sufficient life far from the rapid gentrification of his native town of Misent. Even that small escape is denied to him, however. To make ends meet, Matías is forced to sell his produce to gourmet restaurants and stores that cater to the growing tourism industry, the same industry that is destroying the natural beauty of Misent.[30] After Matías's death, even the meaningless and formulaic kind of protest that he tried to engage in ceases to be possible. The readers never hear Matías's voice, but he haunts other characters of the novel who mourn his passing and perceive it as the end of an era where a different future could still be imagined. Matías's death symbolizes the expiration of an alternative political project that could at least attempt to challenge the consumerist ideology of late capitalism. His body will be cremated, and nothing but dust will remain from the alternative way of thinking that Matías represents to the novel's characters.[31]

In an inner monologue addressed to Matías, Rubén Bertomeu, his brother and erstwhile comrade in the revolutionary struggle who abandoned activism to become a successful real estate developer, explains that Matías's political project failed because the form of democracy practiced in Spain turned out to be incompatible with what Matías and his comrades considered politics.[32] The post-Transition Spain has no use for people like Matías and rejects those who cannot embrace the country's all-consuming pursuit of the neoliberal dream. There is no place in it for a collective project of any kind, unless it exists for money making.[33] In 2007, when the novel was published, it was impossible to predict the massive mobilization that the protest movement of 15-M would achieve only four years later, and the reality that the novel depicts is still that of alienated consumers who are incapable of forming meaningful connections. The characters of *Crematorio* exist in a state of profound loneliness and do not even manage to come together during the shared time of grieving over Matías's death. The memories of the past that are tormenting Chirbes's characters are standing in the way of any meaningful connection they could form with each other. It is as if the only actual, solid relationship these characters can establish was the one they have with the past.

Ernesto, Matías's son, underscores the extent of his father's failure to make space in Spain for alternatives to neoliberalism. Ernesto becomes "tiburoncito de las finanzas" [a financial shark],[34] an assiduous reader of Milton Friedman and Alan Greenspan and an admirer of the Chicago School of Economics. As the novel went into print, the world was about to experience a global economic crisis brought about by the policies championed by Greenspan and his fellow believers in the rationality of free markets.[35] Chirbes's novel captures the moment immediately before the collapse, and it is not surprising that there should be such a great interest in *Crematorio* on the part of the readers. *Crematorio* offers a possibility for a reflection upon the causes of the existential crisis experienced by the country. Even though the characters of the novel never manage to come together to discuss what is tormenting them, the novel's readers have the experience of participating in or witnessing the mass mobilizations of the 15-M movement and can use the knowledge they gained to consider the alternatives to the way of being that Chirbes describes in the novel.

There are thirteen sections in *Crematorio*. Three of them are narrated in the first person by Rubén Bertomeu, a millionaire who made his fortune in the construction business on the coast of Valencia. With a single exception, the rest of the sections are narrated in the free, indirect style and introduce the perspectives of Mónica (Rubén's second wife who is almost fifty years his junior), Collado (Rubén's former employee whose life has been unraveling since Bertomeu refused to continue working with him), Silvia (Rubén's daughter who despises her father's way of making money but enjoys the luxury his wealth provides), Federico Brouard (a writer whose most famous novel Rubén considers to be a thinly veiled personal attack), and Yuri (an associate of a Russian mafioso Traian who took Collado's place by Rubén's side). The only character aside from Rubén whose voice the readers hear in a direct, first-person narrative is Juan Mullor, Rubén's son-in-law and a literary critic who is writing Federico Brouard's biography. There is also a short final section titled "Estampa invernal de Misent" [A Winter Postcard of Misent] that is narrated in a detached omniscient third-person voice. Understanding this complex narrative structure, a feat that has eluded several of the novel's reviewers,[36] is crucial for an analysis of *Crematorio*. In his 2013 interview with

Carmen de Eusebio, the writer reminded literary critics that the use of a great variety of narrative strategies in his novels corresponds to a purpose other than a mere display of writerly skill:

> Sé que a muchos profesores y críticos les parece como lo más destacable en un libro la exhibición de esa variedad estilística y la solvencia de su autor en el arte de utilizarla. . . . Pero yo creo que eso no es precisamente así. Cada novela te pide una técnica, y esos recursos son apenas nada (puro fuego de artificio) si no surgen como exigencias en la búsqueda de sentido. [I know that to many professors and critics it seems as if the most noteworthy thing about a book is an exhibition of stylistic variety and the author's mastery in using it. . . . But I believe that this is not exactly true. Every novel requires a technique, and these means are nothing remarkable (just fireworks) if they don't arise as unavoidable in a search for meaning.][37]

Chirbes's narrative techniques comprise the heart of the novel. Not only do they help, as the author suggests, to find the work's meaning; they constitute the meaning itself.

Rubén Bertomeu, the central character of the novel, amasses his fortune by tearing down old buildings and erecting luxury vacation chalets and apartment complexes in their place. Bribing local politicians and bureaucrats allows him to acquire building permits for land that used to be protected for ecological reasons. He is the only one among the novel's cast of characters who can transform reality, leaving others to react to the transformations he has wrought. There is no possibility left of meaningful change aside from the physical alteration of the landscape carried out by Rubén. He is incapable of changing the past that torments him and has lost faith in transforming society through politics. He attempts to conceal the spaces that bring back the recollections of the unprocessed trauma of the war and Franco-era repression, or, to use the term introduced by Pierre Nora, his *lieux de mémoire*,[38] underneath the mass-produced chalets that make the Levantine coast look like any other vacation zone. At the same time, Bertomeu's capacity to make a fortune can be traced back to the dictatorship of Franco, whose housing policies ensured a continued shortage of available housing and set in place mechanisms of speculation that came to dominate the country's construction industry.[39]

Even the limited power to transform reality that Rubén possesses is denied to other characters in the novel. All that Silvia, Collado, and Brouard can do is seethe with resentment behind Rubén's back while being irresistibly drawn toward his uncontrollable consumerism. These characters do not speak in the first person because they have abrogated their individuality to Rubén. In his discussion of indirect free style, Louis Bueler points out that "to appreciate the worldview of a novel narrated in indirect free style, readers must enter it through the character's thoughts and emotions, often emotions and thoughts too intimate or too tentative ly formed to be spoken or written by the character herself."[40] This narrative style, according to Bueler, signals "an interiority too embryonic or disturbing even to be capable of expression by the character."[41] Contrasted with Rubén's self-assured use of the first-person narrative, the free, indirect discourse of these characters sounds tentative and shaky. They are reduced to listing their grievances against Rubén and the reality he constructed while remaining incapable of leaving Rubén's orbit.

Bertomeu's dedication to building a new reality—and working in the construction business offers him the perfect opportunity to do just that—stems from his rejection of both his personal history and the country's past. Rubén and his erstwhile business partner, Collado, belong to the generation of "niños de la guerra" [children of the war], that is, people who grew up in the aftermath of the Spanish Civil War. Rubén is tormented by the memories of those who starved to death in the postwar years: "Y aquí, no hace tantos años, la gente se moría de hambre. Yo la he visto." [And here, not that long ago, people starved to death. I saw it.][42] This time in Spain's history is known as the "hunger years," and historians estimate that as many as 200,000 Spaniards died of starvation between 1939 and 1945.[43] Rubén was too small during the Civil War to remember it, but he can never forget the stories his father told him of trying to console his infant son who was terrified by the sounds of Misent being bombarded.[44] Collado shares with Rubén the memories of growing up during the harsh postwar years and hearing about the war from his father who was part of the victorious Nationalist troops in the battle of the Ebro in 1938 and who fought, as part of the División Azul, on the losing side during the Battle of Stalingrad in 1942–43.[45] The legacy of the war is not something these characters discuss openly, yet it informs much of what they do.

Collado, for instance, sees his work in the construction business as a way to exorcise the past that is haunting both him and the region where he lives:

> La ciudad, en ese nervioso descubrir y cubrir, parecía librarse precipitadamente de su pasado. Él, contemplando aquella excavación, también había tenido esa impresión de ordenar, clasificar y almacenar su pasado antes de librarse de él. [In this nervous discovering and covering up, the city seemed to be liberating itself from its past in a hurry. As he looked upon this excavation, he also had the impression of organizing, classifying and storing his past before liberating himself from it.][46]

Rubén agrees with Collado's belief that the frantic movement needed to succeed in the capitalist world helps to keep time at bay.[47] Rubén is heaping material possessions on top of the memories that torment him and expects the tumult of ceaseless activity to protect him from the past. He is hoping to transform even memory itself into a private possession that he will be able to control completely.[48] Rubén believes that a struggle against memory is the central purpose of his construction business: "El olvido. Olvidar la vida. Volver al olvido. Derribos Bertomeu. Que no quede ningún monumento conmemorativo de todo esto." [Forgetfulness. To forget life. To return to forgetfulness. Bertomeu Demolitions. Let there remain no monument commemorating any of this.][49] Construction is not possible without a preceding act of destruction: Rubén needs to demolish the buildings that connect him to his country's history and his own past to free the space for erecting his mass-produced chalets.

Other characters in the novel are as obsessed with the past as Rubén and Collado are. They perceive the past as the only space where the answers to their questions about the problems that haunt them in the present can be found. Yuri, an employee of Bertomeu's business partner Traian, is trying to preserve the memories of his native city of St. Petersburg but discovers that movie images of life in Russia have been superimposed over his recollections.[50] Yuri inhabits the world of criminality that seems far removed from the way of life of the solidly bourgeois Bertomeu family. The way Yuri and his associates are introduced reinforces this perception:

> La manera abrupta con que Chirbes clausura los avatares de algunos personajes: Irina, Traian o Yuri (el bloque ruso) [les confiere] una subalternidad que acaba por desgajarlos de los conflictos sobre los que se construye la novela. [The abruptness with which Chirbes closes down some of the characters' names: Irina, Traian o Yuri (the Russian block) confers upon them a subalternity that splits them off from the conflicts that undergird the novel.][51]

Yuri's and Traian's subalternity and apparent insignificance (which have led some of the novel's reviewers to confuse the two characters or to forget to list Yuri as one of the narrators[52]) are illusory, however. Rubén's construction empire would not be as prosperous if it were not for these members of organized crime who permit Bertomeu to preserve his image of a respectable businessman while they take it upon themselves to manage the more unsavory side of his business.

While Matías Bertomeu's death symbolizes the expiration of a political alternative to neoliberalism within Spain, Yuri and Traian remind the reader of the failure of such an alternative political project outside the country. Traian is a grandson of a Romanian railroad worker who, in 1922, fled to the USSR to serve the cause of the workers' revolution.[53] Traian and Yuri witnessed the collapse of the USSR, and their shared cynicism underscores the extent of the failure of the Communist project in Eastern Europe. Traian enjoys sharing nostalgic accounts of his grandfather's revolutionary activities, but he is convinced that there is no longer a place for this kind of idealism. The degradation of Traian, Yuri, and their lover, Irina, is symbolic of the devaluation of Eastern Europe as a region that could provide an alternative to capitalism. The countries of the former Soviet bloc are in a rush to catch up with the capitalist model from which they had been excluded until the collapse of the USSR:

> En Rusia y en todas esas naciones que se le han desgajado, acabará ocurriendo lo mismo [que en España] dentro de unos años. Ahora aún están en la fase de acumulación primitiva, ese momento en el que las sociedades necesitan devorarlo todo. El momento cannibal. [What is happening in Spain will in a few years take place in Russia and all these nations that split off from it. Now they are still undergoing the phase of primitive accumulation, this moment when societies need to devour it all. A cannibalistic moment.][54]

Traian, Yuri, and Irina serve as emissaries of an earlier, "less civilized" model of capitalism, providing a contrast with Spain's advanced neoliberalism.[55] For Rubén, Traian is not only a convenient business partner. In his conversations with Traian, Bertomeu is desperate to reject the younger version of himself that belonged to Spain's Communist Party and believed in the power of art to propel social change.[56] Rubén needs for Traian to confirm that, even in the USSR, there was social and economic stratification.[57] Rubén is looking for reassurance that social justice cannot be achieved, and Traian, as somebody who experienced life in the USSR and witnessed its collapse, represents, in Bertomeu's eyes, living proof that abandoning class struggle was the right thing to do.

Despite Bertomeu's apparent confidence in the decision to dedicate his life to ruthless money making, he constantly seeks proof that there were, indeed, no alternatives to this way of being. This need for reassurance sours Rubén's relationship with his only daughter. Silvia tries to resist her father's relentless drive to accumulate ever newer and shinier possessions and becomes, to his great dismay, a painting restorer. In his daughter's choice of profession, Rubén perceives a silent condemnation of his own attempts to destroy the past.[58] Bertomeu is tormented by a suspicion that his frenzy to rebuild Misent will not protect him from the advent of a more fluid form of capitalist relations than the one he has mastered so well. In the words of Zygmunt Bauman, "today's business organization has an element of disorganization deliberately built into it: the less solid and the more fluid it is, the better."[59] Bertomeu is aware of this and feels disturbed by the suggestion that the very solidity of the construction business might make it dispensable in the new era of liquid capital:

> Tío, es la hora de saltar de la pesadez del hormigón a la ligereza de la economía pura, me decía como si hablara con un patán. Me pareció que la voracidad de mi sobrino, que no paraba de engullir aperitivos . . . mientras hablaba, me ayudaba a detectar dentro de mí mismo una lamentable falta de energía. [Uncle, it is time to jump from the drag of concrete to the lightness of pure economy, he was telling me as if talk-

> ing to a yokel. It seemed to me as if the voracity of my nephew, who couldn't stop devouring appetizers . . . while he talked, allowed me to detect within myself a deplorable lack of energy.][60]

Crematorio was published in the autumn of 2007, the time when the world was about to witness the devastation of the construction industry by the unstoppable movement of liquid capital.[61] Bertomeu's battle against memory cannot prevent his way of making money from being relegated to the past, as well.[62]

Juan Mullor, Bertomeu's son-in-law, realizes that there is an enormous destructive impulse behind Rubén's need to keep building: "Fuera de la charca del egoísmo, del sálvese quien pueda, no hay nada. Nada está exento de eso. No hay ningún lugar neutral, ni un tiempo de tregua." [Aside from the puddle of egotism, from every man from himself, there is nothing. Nothing is exempt from it. There is no neutral place, no truce.][63] Despite Juan's pessimism, however, the novel does offer space to an alternative to Bertomeu's destructive construction. That space can be glimpsed in the segment narrated by Mullor himself in the only part of the novel with a first-person narrator who is not Rubén Bertomeu. Mullor is very dismissive of his own work as a literary critic and a professor of literature:

> Somos un capricho que se pagan las sociedades ricas y que a las pobres apenas si se les ocurre plantearse. Somos putas, flores de loto que se abren sobre la charca maloliente de la opulencia. [We are a whim that rich societies pay for and that poor ones don't even consider. We are whores, lotus flowers that open over a malodorous puddle of opulence.][64]

Still, the act of reading that is central to Mullor's profession provides a respite from the constant movement, from "ese nervioso descubrir y cubrir" [this nervous discovering and covering up],[65] "este frenético no parar" [this frenetic movement],[66] that defines the activities of Rubén and Collado. It is precisely the "uselessness" of literary criticism and its incapacity to bring a profit that turn Mullor into the only real antagonist to Rubén. Literature itself has been fully integrated into the logic of the market, and only a field of knowledge that is somewhat removed from the realm of profit making can offer a space for quiet reflection from which a vision of an alternative may one day arise. This is not to say that Mullor somehow manages to avoid the degradation that has affected all the novel's characters.[67] The literary critic is incapable of offering any resistance to Rubén and makes full use of the privileges that accrue to him because of being married to the millionaire's daughter. The time he spends with Federico Brouard is aimed less at talking to the writer than at ensuring that Brouard bequeaths his archives to Mullor's university, which will help Mullor in his research and solidify his position at his department.[68]

Rubén Bertomeu is disdainful of his son-in-law's profession yet he is also wary of Mullor's work, which, in Bertomeu's words, "resucita esos cuerpos a los que el tiempo ya había rendido" [resuscitates the corpses that the time had already vanquished].[69] The corpses that, in Rubén's opinion, should not be resuscitated are the social realist and proletarian novels of the 1950s.[70] This is precisely the literature that Bertomeu must have found inspiring in his political activism during the last years of Franco's regime. While he is also scornful of his daughter's work of preserving the artistic production of the past, Rubén is not as bothered by Silvia's efforts as he is by Mullor's. In part, this is evidence of Bertomeu's *machismo,*[71] yet it is also clear that Rubén is eager to destroy not all the past but, rather, the past of which he was a participant. Mullor's writing of Federico Brouard's biography reminds Bertomeu of everything he lost once he severed his contact with the idealistic friend of his youth and abandoned their shared project of political struggle. For Rubén, the loss of Brouard's friendship is akin to losing a limb and later realizing that the severed limb remained alive and healthy because of being separated from a diseased body.[72] In Mullor's work, the long-abandoned plan of architect Bertomeu, writer Brouard, and painter Montoliu to use art as a form of political activism is remembered and made public. Rubén is disturbed by the writing of the biography that reminds him of his friend's lifelong allegiance to the project that Rubén abandoned long ago.[73]

Mullor's section is narrated in the first person because, as materialistic and shallow as he is, Mullor represents the only existing challenge to Rubén's philosophy of destroying memory. In his conversations with the literary critic, Federico Brouard points out that the greatest danger present in the seemingly prosperous Spain of the first decade of the twenty-first century is the placid acceptance that no alternative is possible to the existing system.[74] Francis Fukuyama's belief that "the ideal of liberal democracy could not be improved on"[75] lies at the root of the worldview that does not posit any but purely cosmetic changes as either possible or desirable. It is not within Mullor's—or any single person's—power to change this state of affairs. However, Mullor can preserve the memory of the past and of the competing visions of Spain's future that used to inspire the anti-Francoist political struggles of the preceding generations. Mullor imagines himself as a doorman who protects the entrance into the "salón de baile en el que [los escritores] giran, seducen, se deslizan y saltan" [the ballroom where writers spin, seduce, glide and leap].[76] This imaginary ballroom is a space of memory where the alternative visions are stored until the time when there appears an opening in the monolithic structure of today's society.

The single first-person section narrated by Mullor does not, however, manage to subvert Rubén's dominance of the text. Bertomeu is the narrator of three long sections in the novel located at the beginning, in the middle, and almost at the end. His voice encircles the story and seeps into the sections narrated from the perspectives of other characters. Rubén's dominance of the novel has led critics to dismiss the section narrated by Juan in the first person.[77] It is true that Juan's voice does not manage to drown out Rubén's. A literary critic who studies the proletarian novels of the 1950s is not likely to be able to compete in terms of power and authority with a millionaire. Chirbes believes that novels should be informed by the reality they describe[78] and, unless the writer decided to explore the fantasy genre, readers should not have expected from him a novel where a professor of literature enjoyed a greater power to mold reality than a successful businessman.

The last section of the novel, titled "Estampa invernal de Misent" [A Winter Picture Card of Misent], is removed from the rest of the narrative not only chronologically (the events in the novel take place in the heat of summer) but also in terms of its tone. The highly emotional narratives of the novel's characters offer a contrast with the detached voice that describes, in the third person, how the beach near Misent looks on a winter night: "Es de noche. En esta época del año la playa aparece oscura y silenciosa." [Nighttime. At this time of year the beach looks dark and silent.][79] In contrast with the long, complex sentences that constitute the sections representing the viewpoints of the characters, this very short last section is broken into shorter, often staccato-like utterances. This is the only section of the novel that has a title, which sets it even further apart from the previous sections. The sense of eeriness created by an impersonal, detached description of an empty beach, the darkness, and a stray dog is reinforced by a strange stain that appears on the horizon: "Mar adentro vuelve a formarse la mancha espesa, como de brea, que ocupa todo el horizonte." [A thick tar-like stain begins to appear out at sea, occupying the whole horizon.][80] Of course, a reading of *Crematorio* carried out after the global economic collapse of 2008–2009 is in danger of falling into the temptation of seeing the threatening stain as a premonition of the tempest to come. Chirbes could not have predicted the collapse of the economy that was to take place soon after the publication of his novel. However, the cynicism and the disillusionment that permeate the narrative point to the unsustainable nature of the situation. The only logical development is an explosion that will disturb the status quo. *En la orilla*, the novel that Chirbes published after a six-year pause in novelistic production he took after *Crematorio*, describes the consequences of this collapse.

En la orilla*: An Existential Crisis*

Within the corpus of Chirbes's work, *En la orilla* (2013) offers the most desperate and tragic depiction of Spain's reality that the writer has ever produced. Chirbes's worldview was never overly optimistic, imbuing with pessimism almost all his characters, irrespective of their place in the political or social hierarchies.[81] The confusion in the face of the erosion of the patriarchal system experienced by both those who lost the Civil War in *La buena letra* and those who managed to turn the war's aftermath to their economic advantage in *Los disparos del cazador*, the disillusionment and cynicism of those who abandoned their youthful political struggle in *Los viejos amigos*, the degradation of the expiring dictatorship in *La caída de Madrid*, and the corruption and criminality that infect every area of life depicted in *Crematorio* contribute to the creation of a narrative universe that is both tragic and hopeless. Still, the harrowing story of a dying world in *En la orilla* is in a different order of magnitude in terms of its sheer desperation from anything the author had written before. "Es mi novela más amarga" [It is the most bitter among my novels], said Chirbes in his interview to Rodríguez Marcos,[82] and the readers did not fail to notice the darkness lying at the core of the novel.

The corruption and unbridled spending of the *años de pelotazo* described in *Crematorio* have led to the economic collapse that has devastated the country. The novel's characters are trying—and failing—to process the trauma of the crisis and adapt to the new reality of austerity, unemployment, and hopelessness. However, the crisis that haunts every page of the novel does not unfold solely in the realm of the economy. Chirbes offers a depiction of a society whose every aspect is experiencing a profound transformation. The destruction wrought by the economic crisis lays bare the rotten foundations of the society of consumers. Once life has been stripped of the superfluous, the degradation of all forms of human relationships becomes evident. The characters of the novel can no longer engage in the unbridled spending of the previous years, and the frenetic activity of the *años de pelotazo* stops. In the ensuing silence, the characters of *En la orilla* are forced to face the emptiness that was hiding beneath the consumer goods they had been accumulating frenetically in the years leading up to the collapse.

The concept of "la orilla," the word that can mean both "an edge" and "a shore" is not new to Chirbes's work and has always been linked, in the author's novels, to old age, caducity, and disintegration.[83] The characters of Chirbes's novels use the expression "en la orilla" to discuss something grander than their individual struggles with getting older. The flow of history sweeps them aside and makes them feel irrelevant and incapable of finding a place in a changing world. In the writer's 2000 novel *La caída de Madrid*, for instance, the seventy-five-year-old José Ricart tells his friend Maxi that observing the physical deterioration of the dictator Franco makes him feel abandoned on the shore of history:

> Creía que todo iba a ser seguro, para siempre marcado por un orden, y descubro a mi edad que, de repente, cambian las circunstancias y la vida te echa a la orilla. [I thought everything was going to be certain, forever orderly, and at my age I discover that, all of a sudden, circumstances change, and life casts you out onto the shore.][84]

José Ricart is aware of the enormous transformations that the country is likely to undergo after the dictator's death and fears them.[85] Ricart and Maxi managed to inscribe themselves very successfully into Franco's Spain and are convinced the changes that are coming will leave them stranded and unable to adapt.

There is a similar use of the concept of being stranded on a shore in *Crematorio*. Federico Brouard also feels defeated by history and turns to the image of "la orilla" to express these feelings:

> La otra orilla, Matías, ahora sé que ya la he abandonado para siempre, es definitivo, me refiero a la orilla de la salud. Estoy del otro lado del río, en la orilla del río en la que se meten en el agua los cuerpos deformes, feos, la orilla sin sexo. [The other shore, Matías, now I know that I have already left it forever, it's certain, I'm talking about the shore of good health. I'm on the other side of the river, on the shore where all the deformed, ugly bodies get into the water, a sexless shore.][86]

The shared political project of Brouard and his late friend Matías Bertomeu has come to nought. The hopes that Brouard had for a new society that would be built after the death of Franco never materialized. Brouard is mourning his physical frailty that makes it impossible for him to do anything but observe the consumerist frenzy that has come to substitute any form of political engagement. Brouard and Ricart belong to opposing ideological camps: while Brouard was imprisoned for his dissidence during the *franquismo*, Ricart embraced the regime and prospered. The dictator's death made people like Ricart doubt their capacity to adapt to the post-Franco Spain, but dissidents of Brouard's ilk did not find a place for themselves in the Spain of the Transition either.[87]

Esteban, the protagonist of *En la orilla*, can no longer be inscribed into the "two Spains" dichotomy embodied by Ricart and Brouard. Despite growing up with a Republican father who listens to the Pirenaica radio station[88] and treasures portraits of Marx and Dolores Ibárruri,[89] Esteban has little interest in politics. His closest friend, Francisco Marsal, the son of a wealthy Falangist, feels a greater curiosity, during the years of his youth, toward Leftist politics than Esteban.[90] Still, Esteban shares with Ricart and Brouard the feeling of being stranded "on the shore." The economic crisis sharpens his consciousness of a life wasted, but the roots of Esteban's existential angst lie in the past that is much more distant. Esteban's personal crisis, as well as Spain's economic collapse, is part of the legacy of the Spanish Civil War. The war is always present in Esteban's analysis of his own life, and his suicide is an attempt symbolically to erase the road that he (and, in larger terms, the country) has traveled since the war.

Like *Crematorio* (and all of Chirbes's longer novels), *En la orilla* has a complex narrative structure. Most of the novel is narrated in the first person by Esteban, a seventy-year-old carpenter who lives with his elderly father and was forced to close the family carpentry shop because of the crisis. In his narrative, Esteban reveals the reasons for his decision to end the life of his father and then his own. The flow of Esteban's monologue is interrupted by short narratives (marked by italic script) told from the perspectives of the people impacted by the closure of Esteban's business: his former employee Julio; the wife of Álvaro; another of Esteban's former employees; and Joaquín, another worker left unemployed because of Esteban's bankruptcy. These monologues are closed off from one another and convey the sense of loneliness that these characters experience. Their troubles are similar, yet every one of them is locked in his or her own world, incapable of forming a meaningful connection with others.

Aside from these monologues, there are three more sections that illustrate the impossibility of a dialogue in a society where profound alienation has set in. One of these sections represents a conversation between Joaquín's wife and a gas station worker, both of whom are lonely yet incapable of relating to each other without suspicion.[91] There is also a section consisting of the diary entries made by Esteban's father on the back of a calendar for the year 1960. As a former Republican soldier, Esteban's father takes refuge in silence from the reality of Franco's Spain, where his political convictions put him in danger. He is terrified of making his beliefs known to his wife and children because he does not want to cause them harm.[92] In the diary, Esteban's father expresses a hope that one day he will be able to share his experiences of the war and of the postwar persecution with his son.[93] In a postscript to the diary, a detached third-person voice informs the readers that the calendar will be lost when, several days after Esteban's suicide, officials will arrive to take possession of his house.[94] Esteban dies without reading his father's diary or even knowing of its existence.

Like the rest of the characters, Esteban suffers from loneliness, but his efforts to connect with his father fail. All he can do now is address an internal monologue to the elderly man who is no longer capable of having a conversation with his son.[95] In the years when Esteban worked by his father's side in the carpenter's shop, neither man tried to reach out to the other and share his thoughts. Now that Esteban is finally aware of the enormous impact that his father's legacy of being on the losing side of the Civil War had on his own life, the older man has retreated into senility and cannot be reached. The tragic alienation between father and son reaches its culmination in the scene where Esteban washes his infirm father's body, preparing him for their last journey to the marshes where Esteban will end their lives.[96] As his father's caretaker, Esteban helps him with his most intimate bodily functions, but there is no possibility of true closeness between the two men. Neither their physical proximity to each other nor the intertwining of their fates enables them to break through their profound alienation from each other.

In his loneliness, Esteban develops an attachment to Liliana, an immigrant from Colombia who works in Esteban's house providing care to his elderly father. Esteban considers his childlessness to be one of the greatest tragedies of his life and cherishes the possibility to act as a surrogate father to the young woman. However, his fantasy of a loving relationship with Liliana collapses when Esteban is no longer capable of paying Liliana for her company. Liliana mocks Esteban for his attempt to take his interactions with her outside of the realm of financial relations.[97] In the degraded world of *En la orilla,* the concept of caretaking has been emptied of meaning, and the care that Liliana provides is nothing but a series of entirely mechanical manipulations in exchange for money.[98] It is only Esteban's profound loneliness that allows him fleetingly to mistake Liliana's willingness to provide caretaking services in exchange for money for actual caring. All human interactions in the novel suffer from the characters' incapacity to fill them with meaning that goes beyond monetary exchange. Esteban's musings about the sister and the brother he has not seen for years revolve around the amounts borrowed and owed. The only event that can bring every family member back to the family home is the death of the father, which will imply the division of the property he owned. Esteban expects that encounter to resemble a civil war in miniature.[99] The Spain of today is very different from that of the Second Republic, however, and ideas do not cause animosity any longer. Wars between brothers and sisters are now waged over a tenuous prospect of acquiring a share in a very small estate that the father is assumed to possess. The children of the elderly Republican make a mockery of their father's anticapitalist ideals with their casual indifference to anything but money.

One of the sections in the novel constitutes a dialogue between Liliana and Susana, another immigrant from Colombia. The exchange between the two women makes it clear that Esteban's attempts to make Liliana see him as more than a paying customer have failed. According to Bauman, "the precariousness of social existence inspires a perception of the world around as an aggregate of products for immediate consumption. But perceiving the world, complete with its inhabitants, as a pool of consumer items makes the negotiation of lasting human bonds exceedingly hard."[100] Liliana's capacity to keep her family's finances afloat is tenuous at best, and she cannot allow herself to develop any emotional attachments that will not result in financial profit. Susana shares her friend's belief that it is crucial "not to fall prey to any emotions that defy translation into monetary gains."[101] She disapproves of Liliana's visits to a clairvoyant who promises to put Liliana in touch with her dead ancestors.[102] According to Susana, an activity that does not help one inscribe oneself more successfully into the logic of capitalist relations has no right to be pursued.

The deterioration of all forms of human relationships that we see in the novel is mirrored by the degradation of the political dream that inspired Esteban's father to fight on the side of the Republicans during the Civil War: "Decir ruso era decir Unión Soviética, la madre de todos los obreros del mundo. . . . Ahora, dices ruso y piensas en lo peor: extorsión, mafias, tráfico de mujeres." [The word Russian meant Soviet Union, the mother of all the workers in the world. . . . Nowadays, you say Russian and think the worst: extortion, mafia, women trafficking.][103] Like in *Crematorio,* the presence of Eastern European immigrants in *En la orilla* serves as a reminder that the Soviet alternative to capitalism has been discredited. If in the father's vocabulary the word "Russia" stood for an imaginary space for alternatives to capitalism, to Esteban this word has come to denote the worst excesses of the capitalist system that he witnesses every time he encounters prostitutes from the former Soviet Union who are lining the highway next to his village. Because of his father's dementia, however, Esteban has no opportunity to explain to him how different the emotional charge of the word "Russia" is to him. Father and son no longer have a shared vocabulary to conduct a conversation on the subjects that interest them. The muteness of Esteban's Republican father is symbolic of the absence of the voices of the intellectual and political heirs to Spanish Republicanism from today's political discourse in Spain. Like Liliana's dead ancestors, Republicans are often dismissed by their descendants because they cannot contribute anything that will lead to immediate economic gain.

There is a great abundance of novels about the Spanish Civil War that propose to recover the historical memory of the war's losers. Chirbes believes, however, that these works of literature often do little more than reinforce hegemonic ideology. In his 2010 collection of essays, the writer pointed out that these novels often offer a sentimentalized depiction of the Civil War that has no subversive potential.[104] These novels do not propose to address any of the problematic aspects of Spain's present. The civil conflict is exploited in such works of literature to reinforce the contrast with today's supposedly conflict-free existence. Civil War provides authors with a plethora of opportunities to construct attractive plots that will help to sell more copies of their books.[105] Most of the novels about the Spanish Civil War are sympathetic toward the Republicans. This sympathy, however, is entirely apolitical: "Victimhood has also been absorbed by an all-encompassing consumer society that is eager to experience safely controlled aseptic 'emotions' but that does not have the taste to analyze the implications and contradictions behind them."[106] The facile sentimentality of this approach to the war obscures from view the ideological dimensions of the conflict and its implications for today's Spain. Depictions of the war and the dictatorship that avoid mentioning the Nationalists' dedication "to implement[ing] capitalist modernization to the maximum benefit of the dominant classes through the use of slave labor (political prisoners) and state-controlled unions"[107] fail to bring to light the ways in which *franquismo* laid the foundations of the economic order that is collapsing in Spain today.

The way Chirbes writes about the country's past is entirely different from this apolitical approach to Spain's greatest political conflict of the twentieth century. The years of the Civil War and the decades of the Franco dictatorship have always been present in Chirbes's writing, and *En la orilla* is no exception. The writer believes, however, that a discussion of the country's past should have at its center a desire to understand Spain's present.[108] In Chirbes's novels, the echoes of the Civil War can still be heard clearly, and there is no Manichaean division of the war's participants into sainted victims and sadistic victimizers. In *Por cuenta propia*,[109] Chirbes rejects the easy mawkishness of presenting the Spanish Republicans as figures of a distant past who are in need of nothing but pity from the readers of today.[110] In one of his interviews, the author pointed out that, since the death of the dictator, the Spanish society did not change as much as it is usually believed and that his goal in writing *En la orilla* was to demonstrate that the past is very much alive today.[111] Chirbes is convinced that it is crucial to remember the foundations of the economic system that was created in the postwar Spain and that is going through a crisis today. In the words of Andreas Huyssen, the very nature of memory discourse creates a possibility that commercialization of memory will empty it of meaning:

> Memory discourses . . . partake in the detemporalizing processes that characterize a culture of consumption and obsolescence. Memory as representation, as making present, is always in danger of collapsing the constitutive tension between past and present, especially when the imagined past is sucked into the timeless present of the all-pervasive space of consumer culture.[112]

Chirbes is well aware of the capacity of the Civil War genre to slip into escapism that allows consumers to maintain an illusion of engaging with the past while limiting themselves to accessing only a superficial, sanitized version of history that is incapable of disturbing the economic inequities that exist today.

Esteban's failed life is, to a great degree, a result of his family's experiences in the war. The protagonist of *En la orilla* realizes that, like his father, he is also one of those who lost the Civil War. The father crushed his son's will to live in the same way the war's winners destroyed their Republican prisoners.[113] Esteban's apolitical stance stems from his rejection of the father who is a dark and menacing presence in his life. At the height of Spain's housing boom, Esteban takes advantage of the older man's senility to appropriate his savings and invest them into a company belonging to the local construction magnate, Tomás Pedrós. When the housing market collapses, Esteban is left without means and sees no other solution but to kill himself and his father. Esteban knows that the decision to invest his father's money goes against the elderly man's anti-capitalist principles.[114] Still, neither the son's awareness of the persecution that his father suffered after the war nor his sympathy toward his father's suffering at the hands of the war's victors prevents him from disrespecting the elderly man's principles. Esteban is not alone in this approach. The society of consumers is eager to weep over the fates of the Republican characters on a page or a screen, but, like Esteban, it has rejected the principles for which Spanish Republicans fought. In Esteban's words, his father is part of "esa legión de sombras, tan cargadas de dignidad como carentes de importancia" [this legion of shadows that are as filled with dignity as they are lacking in importance].[115] The country's problems will not be solved, however, until their historical roots are disinterred and analyzed.

The collapse of the housing market wipes out Esteban's modest fortune, and he decides to withdraw to the swamp to end his own life and that of his father. According to Chirbes, the metaphor of the swamp lies at the core of the novel.[116] The illusion of modernization, political consensus, and shared economic well-being could be maintained only while there existed a space where those who do not manage to inscribe themselves into the society of consumers could be displaced. Without the swamp, the image of Spain as a model member of the European Union that prospered because of wholeheartedly embracing neoliberal dogma could not be maintained:

> El pantano de que habla Chirbes es el protagonista mudo de esta historia, el lugar al que durante años han ido a parar los escombros y los residuos y también la basura humana, todo aquello que se pudre bajo el fango espeso de la tierra y la desilusión. [The swamp Chirbes talks about is the silent protagonist of this story, the place where for years the debris and the waste and also the human detritus would end up, everything that rots under the thick mud layer of earth and disappointment.][117]

It is becoming less and less possible to keep the swamp at bay or pretend that it is not there. Fluid capital is transforming a growing number of people into flotsam that has no value on the global market. The "surplus people" of neoliberalism can no longer be hidden from the view of those who are lucky to find employment in the liquid economy.

There was a time, however, when the swamp had a different meaning for the inhabitants of the region. After the end of the Civil War, the residents of the area who are sympathetic to the Republican cause imagine the swamp as the last remaining locus of resistance to Franco's regime. Esteban's father blames himself for not joining the *maquis*, who, as he believes, are hiding in the swamp and continuing the struggle against the Nationals.[118] The myth of the *maquis* resisting the dictatorship from their place of concealment in the swamp comes useful to the war's winners who rely upon it to lay the foundations of the new economic order. Under the pretense of searching for Republican guerrilla fighters, the new authorities drain the land and offer it as a reward to those who were loyal to the Falange.[119] The great fortunes of the Franco era were made by entwining political persecution with a search for profits, and Esteban believes that it is important to remember that the Civil War had economic, as well as political, consequences. Even though the heirs of the Falangists who became rich after appropriating the swamp distanced themselves from their fathers' fascist rhetoric[120] and participated enthusiastically in the Transition,[121] their prosperity was gained because of the Nationalist victory in the war. From the earliest stages of the civil conflict the Nationalist forces accompanied political violence in the occupied territories with extortionate activities aimed at appropriating the wealth of those who were suspected of opposing the new authorities.[122] The fines levied by the Law of Political Responsibility on everybody considered "hostile to the regime" allowed the war's winners to enrich themselves while excluding the Republican families not only from the political but also from the economic life of the country.[123] Chirbes's novel reminds the readers that many of the social and economic inequalities in today's Spain can be traced back to the Civil War.

Esteban realizes that the concepts upon which his father and his comrades relied in their political efforts are of no use in today's Spain:

> La lucha de clases se difuminó, se disolvió, la democracia ha sido un disolvente social: todo el mundo vive, compra y acude al hipermercado y a la barra del bar. [The class struggle evaporated, dissolved. Democracy has been a social solvent: everybody lives, buys and shows up at a hypermarket or a bar.][124]

The acknowledgment that the vocabulary of class struggle has lost its potency also appears in *Crematorio*. Rubén Bertomeu realizes that it makes no sense any longer to appeal to the working class: "La clase obrera ya no es protagonista de nada, ni sujeto de la historia. Ni siquiera es. Ha muerto." [The working class no longer protagonizes anything nor represents the subject of history. It doesn't even exist. It expired.][125] Rubén's wife, Mónica, uses the word "class" in relation to the expensive products and services she buys[126] and refers as "Communist" to those who come from a modest socioeconomic background.[127] The menacing potential of the term "Communist" has been reduced to alluding to the worries of the *nouveau riches* who fear that their newly acquired wealth might not suffice to purchase the social standing that they find desirable. In *En la orilla*, as well as in *Crematorio*, class struggle has been substituted with tensions between different immigrant groups and the nonimmigrant populations.

En la orilla begins with a short chapter titled "El hallazgo" [The Find] that narrates the events taking place on December 26, 2010, twelve days after Esteban and his father disappear in the marshes. The chapter is narrated from the perspective of Ahmed Ouallahi, a Moroccan immigrant who worked for Esteban and is the first one to find the bodies of his former employer and his father. As an immigrant, Ahmed is more sensitive than other characters to the complex structure of the immigrant communities in Spain and the tensions within them. Ahmed disapproves of the efforts on the part of his acquaintance, Abdeljaq, and other members of the Moroccan diaspora[128] to use religion as a way of marking their difference.[129] The crisis is creating even starker divisions between immigrant groups, and Ahmed is afraid that Moroccans are standing out too much and are likely to fall victims to an anti-immigrant backlash that will unavoidably accompany economic deterioration.[130] According to the 2012 study by Checa Olmos and Arjona Garrido, even though Spaniards have been, until recently, less likely to exhibit anti-immigrant feelings than their Western European counterparts, there is a disturbing trend showing that hostility to immigrants has been rising steadily in Spain since the late 1990s.[131]

Ahmed, Liliana, and Susana still find the concept of class consciousness at least somewhat relevant. Ahmed realizes that his exploitation as a worker is less a matter of religious allegiance than of his poverty.[132] Susana and Liliana are aware of class inequalities and, on an even more profound level, of how their gender exacerbates the exploitation they experience.[133] The words that open the novel, "El primero en ver la carroña es Ahmed Ouallahi" [The first to see the carrion is Ahmed Ouallahi],[134] lend an eerie aftertaste to the chapter protagonized by Ahmed after the readers discover that the carrion he finds in the marshes represents the bodies of Esteban and his father.[135] Still, Ahmed's lucid analysis of the complex reality he inhabits and the quiet courage of his life as an immigrant offer a degree of narrative respite from the undiluted darkness of the pages that follow. Chirbes steers clear of producing a simplified image of an immigrant as somebody who is deserving of either pity or condemnation. In *En la orilla,* immigrants are complex human beings who exist within a network of competing and overlapping allegiances. Esteban's incapacity to understand the concerns of Liliana and Ahmed deprives him of an opportunity to establish an enriching human connection that he so misses. The novel suggests that immigrants have more to offer to their new country than the cheap labor they currently provide. The intellectual and cultural charge that they bring from their countries of origin enables them potentially to make a valuable contribution to reinvigorating Spain's political space.

The last image Esteban sees as he stands in the marshes a few moments before ending his life is that of the detritus of civilization—rusted tubes, garbage, old rafts, etc.—rotting away in the swamp. Esteban wants to believe that, as he and his father recede into nothingness, creation can begin anew and the shoots of fresh reality can spring from their remains. The novel, however, does not end here. A short chapter titled "Éxodo" [Exodus] follows the story of Esteban's suicide. It is narrated by Tomás Pedrós, the crook who swindled Esteban out of his savings and who cannot stop consuming and devouring the reality around him even after his machinations have been exposed and he is forced to flee the country. Rubén Bertomeu appears in this part of the novel as "el cabrón Bertomeu" [that bastard Bertomeu][136] who works in the same industry as Pedrós and his friends. While Esteban expires in the march created by people like Pedrós and Bertomeu, the man who caused his ruin uses his position as a member of transnational elites to abandon the country and continue to enjoy his riches. The only note of hope in the novel that culminates in such a devastating way resides in its structure. *En la orilla* begins with a chapter that depicts the people who are coming to Spain and ends with a chapter that gives the readers a glimpse into the mindset of some of those who leave. The contrast between the sincerity and courage of a Muslim immigrant and the cynicism of a rich crook invites the readers to consider the possibility that the renewal of the country might come through its growing immigrant population.

In his review of *En la orilla,* Moisés Mori points out that the novel brings together elements from the entirety of the novelist's preceding novelistic production.[137] As we have seen, there are echoes of *Los disparos del cazador* (1994), *La caída de Madrid* (2000), and *Crematorio* (2007) in Chirbes's novel. In the author's opinion, the devastation depicted in *En la orilla* is a logical conclusion to the journey Spain traveled since the Civil War. In an interview granted to *Mundo Obrero* (a monthly periodical of the Communist Party of Spain), Chirbes pointed out that the Law of Historical Memory did not go far enough in its quest for historical truth and that it was crucial to dispel the mythology of the Transition to understand the manner in which the past informed the present.[138] *En la orilla* represents Chirbes's attempt to excavate the causes of Spain's current troubles by digging all the way into the past when the foundations of today's economic order were laid.

The writer's belief that the collapse of the Spanish economy in the second decade of the twenty-first century cannot be understood without turning to the past has not been to the liking of everyone among the novel's critics. In an otherwise glowing review of the novel, Iñaki Ezkerra,[139] a writer and a political activist, points out that he is discomfited by the echoes of the Civil War in *En la orilla.*[140] This is not the first time that Chirbes has been accused of paying too much attention to the war to the detriment of the artistic quality of his novelistic production and his relevance to the readers. Aniorte, for instance, believes that, before 2008, Chirbes enjoyed greater popularity in Germany than in Spain, in part, because Spain's literary market had been oversaturated with novels on the Spanish Civil War, while the German audience still had not tired of the subject.[141] Still, the readers' enthusiasm for *Crematorio* and *En la orilla* demonstrate that Chirbes's vision of the crisis resonates with the public.

LUIS GARCÍA MONTERO'S *NO ME CUENTES TU VIDA* (2012): A CRISIS OF INTERGENERATIONAL DIALOGUE

In the acknowledgments section of *Crematorio,* Chirbes lists Luis García Montero as one of the authors who inspired him (or, in Chirbes's words, one of the authors who was "plundered" by him in search for ideas) as he worked on the novel.[142] García Montero is equally interested in Chirbes's work, even if his enthusiasm for the writer's most recent novel might have been somewhat dampened by what García Montero perceives as Chirbes's unrelieved pessimism.[143] In his own novel of the crisis, titled *No me cuentes tu vida* [*Don't Tell Me Your Life*], however, García Montero creates an equally disturbing reflection on the consequences of the havoc that the crisis has wrought on Spain. García Montero's novel does not have as devastating an impact as *En la orilla,* yet the writer's vision of the crisis is in no way more optimistic than Chirbes's. The economic aspects of the crisis receive less attention in *No me cuentes* than ways in which the economic collapse casts doubt on the achievements of the Transition, creating a profound rift between those who, like García Montero himself, remember the closing years of the Franco dictatorship and the younger generation that is the most affected by the crisis. The novel warns its readers that there is a growing danger that the memory of resistance to the dictatorship will be lost and the young people of today and tomorrow will not have a tradition of political activism to mine for ideas that can be used in political struggle.

No me cuentes tu vida is the writer's second novel. García Montero's novelistic production began in 2009 with *Mañana no será lo que Dios quiera,*[144] which was awarded the Prize of the Union of Library Workers. Before its publication, the reading public knew García Montero as a poet "a quien el azar, el talento y, sobre todo, un puñado de apasionados detractores, han convertido en el emblema de la poesía de los 80" [whom luck, talent, and more than anything, a group of passionate detractors transformed into the symbol of the 1980 poetry].[145] The writer's poetic oeuvre of the 1980s was marked by the belief "in the historical construction of the individual" and rejected conformism and lack of political commitment that often defined the literary response to the Transition.[146] In 1995, García Montero was awarded Premio Nacional de Poesía for his collection of poetry *Habitaciones separadas,* and in 2003 the poet was honored with Premio Nacional de la Crítica for his *La intimidad de la serpiente.* García Montero brings to *No me cuentes tu vida* his refined poetic sensibility that is attentive to the profound emotional impact of the crisis. In her analysis of the writer's collection of short lyrical observations in prose, titled *Una forma de resistencia* (2012), María Escobedo points out that "es como si García Montero nos ofreciese entrar en la narrativa pero con la condición de no salir de la poesía" [it is as if García Montero offered us an entry into narrative but on the condition of not leaving poetry].[147] The same can be said about *No me cuentes tu vida* that was published in the same year. The novel's first-person narrator, Juan Montenegro, is a poet and the novel constitutes a narrative that Montenegro addresses, in a powerfully lyrical voice, to his son, Ramón, in hopes of bridging the generational divide that has emerged between father and son and is manifesting itself in the two men's responses to the crisis.

The economic situation of the Montenegro family does not suffer greatly because of the crisis, yet the emotional and psychological toll of the economic collapse is still felt by Juan and Ramón, straining the relationship between them and forcing father and son to ponder issues that used to leave them indifferent. Juan finds it hard to understand his son's mentality, formed in the environment of the precariousness of labor and generalized economic insecurity. When Ramón refuses to follow his parents' path into academia, it becomes obvious to Montenegro and his wife that the young people of Ramón's generation have lost confidence in the possibility of fashioning a lifelong career in an environment that is hostile to such ambitions:

> Mamá, no es así—le había explicado Ramón—. Los trabajos seguros han pasado de moda. Las cosas ya no son como cuando vosotros estudiasteis. Prácticas sin sueldo, becas miserables y con pocas posibilidades de que se conviertan en un puesto de trabajo, eso es lo que hay. [Mom, it isn't like that—Ramón had explained to her—. Permanent jobs are out of fashion. Things are not the way they were when you were students. Unpaid internships, miserly scholarships with few opportunities of transforming into a job, that's what there is.][148]

In an optimistic theoretical framing of postwork society published in 1998, the authors of "The Post-Work Manifesto" pointed out that, positive as the demise of the concept of full-time work might reveal itself to be at some future point in time, accepting the possibility of a life that is not organized around the concept of a career provokes great pain: "The very premise of a nonwork future evokes a split second, gut-wrenching shock of the inconceivable."[149] Since the publication of "The Post-Work Manifesto," it has become clear that the "unfettered free time"[150] of a postwork society does not lead to personal growth and enhanced civic engagement. *No me cuentes* points to the debilitating effects that being denied an opportunity to explore full-time employment has had on the younger generations of Spaniards. Throughout 2010 and 2011, the years when the novel is set, Juan observes his son's efforts to escape from the reality that is being devoured by the crisis, taking refuge in the hyperreal world of the Internet and video games.[151] Even in the absence of the need to worry about paying for his necessities, Ramón fails to find anything liberating in the situation of permanent joblessness that has come to define his generation.

Juan Montenegro grew up in Granada, "la ciudad borrada por la guerra y por la muerte de García Lorca" [a city erased by the war and the death of García Lorca],[152] and he does not conceive of a possibility that he could exist outside of political engagement motivated by the desire to recover everything that was destroyed by the Civil War and the Franco dictatorship.[153] Montenegro feels deeply wounded by his son's insistence that he has no interest in "las batallitas de la guerra civil [o] vuestras hazañas antifranquistas" [the petty little battles of the Civil War or your anti-francoist feats].[154] Juan is convinced that the young people of his son's generation could find inspiration in the resistance to the dictatorship that guided the political activism of their grandparents during the postwar years.[155] In an interview he granted while working on *No me cuentes*, García Montero makes it clear that his own vision of the way in which the historical memory of those who lost the Civil War can inspire the political struggles of today coincides with that of his protagonist.[156] Juan Montenegro dedicates himself to studying the life of poet Pedro Alfonso, who went into exile after the war because of his Communist beliefs and nostalgically remembers the clandestine activities of his wife's parents, Ana and Ramón, who worked for the famous Radio Pirenaica.[157] He hopes that their legacy of nonconformism will be of use to the young people of today.

Montenegro believes that his own generation is largely to blame for Spain's crumbling economy. The Spaniards who came of age in the last years of the dictatorship and experienced the Transition as their own political project made the mistakes that led to the inevitability of the country's eventual economic collapse. As he remembers the Transition era, Montenegro laments the failure to preserve the links between Spain's newly democratic system and the legacy of the Second Republic and the Republican resistance to the dictatorship:

> Con un pasado tan digno, con el pasado más digno de todos los pasados, había sido una barbaridad permitir una Transición basada en negar el pasado, en borrar como una vergüenza la historia. [With such a noble past, with a past that is more noble than any other, it was a barbarity to allow for a Transition based on denying the past, on erasing history as if it were shameful.][158]

According to the poet, the ideologues of the Transition adopted the belief that change is always good and any kind of transformation should be accepted as a necessary rupture with the uniformly disappointing past. This veneration of change and mobility destroys links between individuals to facilitate the unfettered mobility of capital.[159] Montenegro points out that alienation has been imposed as the only norm of behavior and this is precisely the kind of distancing that he is experiencing in his relationship with his son.[160] At stake here is not only the difficulty of establishing a dialogue between father and son but also the capacity of the writers of Montenegro's (and García Montero's) generation to remain relevant to those who have every right to consider themselves betrayed by the economic and political setup of the democratic Spain.

Montenegro's ability to reach out to the young people of his son's generation depends on his capacity to disinter the roots of the problems that Spain is experiencing today. As he returns to the places where he spent his childhood and early youth, Montenegro notices the vestiges of "the now discarded past sensory landscape"[161] that has been wiped out by the triumphant march of globalization. A profound rift has been created between the experiences of the preceding generations and the way the young people of today see the world around them. The reason Ramón fails to recognize the relevance to his own life of his parents' and grandparents' memories of the Civil War and the dictatorship of Franco is, partly, the impossibility of seeing the Spain of the past in the sanitized landscape of prefabricated buildings, mass-produced objects, and brand-name stores that can be found in many places around the world. The enthusiasm for change that Montenegro associates with the Transition has erased, indiscriminately, everything that could constitute a visual reminder of the times when Spain was marginalized in Europe because of the dictatorship.[162] The desire to shed, as swiftly as possible, the drab reality of life under the dictatorship left no space for a recognition that historical memory is enmeshed with the sensory landscape and that its recovery is contingent on feeling emotionally connected to the past. Ramón fails to relate to the experiences of his grandparents who militated against the dictatorship because he cannot access the Spain they remember through the sensory impressions that could have the potential of making it more tangible for him.

Montenegro believes that the only possibility of accessing the memory of the sensory landscape that has been erased from the map of the twenty-first-century Spain resides in making an effort to "recordar los olores, los sabores, el tacto de ropa, las canciones, los libros, las citas, los nombres, la necesidad, el miedo y algunos sentimientos" [remember the scents, the tastes, the feel of clothes, the songs, the books, the quotes, the names, the need, the fear and other feelings].[163] Montenegro wants to place his skill as a writer at the service of this goal, filling two notebooks with remembrances that trace his personal development throughout the closing years of the dictatorship, the Transition, and the evolution of the democratic Spain until the crisis that has put into question the transformations the country underwent since the 1970s. The recovery of historical memory is crucial precisely now because, in Montenegro's opinion, the only way of finding a form of political resistance to the injustices of today that will not remain "reducida a la pura insignificancia" [reduced to pure insignificance][164] lies in drawing inspiration from the struggle of those who resisted *franquismo*. The poet hopes that the narrative he creates for his son will serve as a bridge that will connect the generations separated by the profound changes that the country experienced in the recent decades. The crisis can be addressed only if the young people realize that they can draw upon the experience of political activism of the dissidents who fought against the dictatorship within Spain and in exile.

Like the characters of Chirbes's *Crematorio*, Montenegro is disappointed with the kind of democracy that has been constructed in Spain. The belief that democracy will be a panacea for all the ills of the Franco regime was based on an unrealistic vision of the functioning of democratic societies. In today's Spain, Montenegro observes the same fear of dissidence that he remembers from the closing years of the dictatorship.[165] Andrés, the poet's closest friend, agrees with Juan that the democratic institutions of Spain have been undermined by the all-powerful needs of capital.[166] From the very beginning of the Transition era, there existed a tacit agreement that no challenges to the capitalist system of property relations would be posed by any of the political forces in the country.[167] The Moncloa pacts of 1977 "were conservative and left property rights virtually intact. They thus served to protect the socioeconomic status quo inherited from Franco's authoritarian regime."[168] The 1982 electoral victory of the PSOE did nothing to facilitate a discussion of the problematic aspects of capitalism.[169] Today, the failings of the system of economic relations accepted as the only possible one during the Transition are creating a need to question the legacy of the Transition and to discuss whether it is possible to consider the Franco dictatorship fully defeated if the economic system it put in place remains uncontested.

The disillusionment with neoliberal democracy experienced by Montenegro and his friends is rendered even more powerful by the absence of a visible alternative. The poet had an opportunity to observe, in the years of the Cold War, the functioning of the Soviet bloc countries during his visits to Romania. As a result, he is disenchanted with socialism's capacity to offer an alternative to neoliberalism.[170] Montenegro withdraws from political activism, a decision that is reinforced by the realization that yesterday's fighters against the regime of Franco are using the skills gained in their revolutionary struggle to achieve economic success within the neoliberal system of property relations.[171] Juan's mother-in-law, Ana, for instance, returns from exile and channels her transformative energies into a business venture. Juan is respectful yet ironic in his description of the resounding economic success of the former revolutionary who moves seamlessly from fighting for social justice to espousing an entirely new struggle, the one for the profitability of her store. In the democratic Spain, the only "causa" [cause] and "verdadera revolución" [true revolution][172] available to Ana are those that consist in her assuming the role of the manager of a department store. Spain's transition to democracy was characterized by "fe en el progreso, [el] consumismo extrovertido y . . . una euro-euforia sin precedentes" [a belief in progress, extraverted consumerism and . . . an unprecedented euro-euphoria],[173] and this joyful embrace of European neoliberalism left no space for any other kind of revolution. Becoming part of Europe was seen as a victory over Francoism,[174] and it was easy to reach a conclusion that once Spain was integrated into the European Economic Community (and later into the EU), there was no longer any need for the political movements that came into existence to fight the dictatorship.

The fluidity of Ana's allegiances is not out of place in a world in flux where nothing remains immutable and no certainty can be trusted. The return to Spain of former political exiles like Ana constitutes one of many migratory flows that are reshaping the country and posing a new set of challenges to those who, like Juan Montenegro, are struggling to envision a path out of the crisis. If during the dictatorship many Spaniards emigrated to "ser europeos, parecerse a los jóvenes de Alemania" [be European, become alike to young Germans],[175] as a result of the establishment of a stable democracy in Spain the flow of migrants started moving in the opposite direction.[176] A growing number of immigrants come to Spain in search of "una precaria felicidad, una felicidad modesta, pero con buenos televisores, y con móviles, y con tarjetas de crédito" [a happiness that is precarious and modest but that has good TVs, and cell phones, and credit cards].[177] Mariana, the Montenegros' housekeeper, is an immigrant from Romania, a fact that the poet sees as quite significant in view of his own connection to that country.[178] The time when Spanish dissidents looked for refuge in Romania and other countries willing to offer them a space where they would be safe from the dictatorship of Franco is over, and today Romanians come to Spain trying to escape from their country's poverty.

When he discovers that Ramón is involved in a romantic relationship with Mariana, Juan experiences an instinctive rejection of this development. This harms his capacity to maintain a dialogue with his son and forces him to begin to analyze the reasons for his discomfort with the affair between Mariana and Ramón. Montenegro dislikes the idea of finding himself among those who assign blame for the economic collapse to immigrants. The panic that Europeans experience when confronted with the growing presence of immigrants in their midst is, in Juan's view, one of the more negative aspects of the European identity that Spain is adopting.[179] Still, Montenegro cannot help noticing that his relationship with Mariana erodes Ramón's resolve to resist full integration into the neoliberal economic system in the capacity of a perennially indebted consumer.

Before he begins a romantic relationship with Mariana, Ramón attempts to position himself vis-à-vis the increasingly volatile job market in a manner that will allow him to mimic the fluidity of the concept of work that characterizes the societies of advanced neoliberalism. Ramón realizes that, for the young people of his generation, the possibility of adapting to the transformations in work is contingent on shedding the encumbrances that might impede the workers' capacity to follow the unpredictable demands of the job market. To avoid being cast away by the rapidly moving flows of capital, today's workers have to be "as light and volatile as the new capitalist economy."[180] Those who fail to imitate the lightning-speed movements of capital find themselves "exposed, armless, to the inscrutable whims of mysterious 'investors' and 'shareholders,' and even more bewildering 'market forces.'"[181] The only possibility of keeping pace with the unconstrained mobility of capital lies in a worker's readiness to sever links with a specific physical space or a concrete social or familial milieu and enhance his or her capacity to travel light. For Ramón, the freedom from the vagaries of the job market consists of a descent into the hyperreal world of the Internet that exists outside any national borders.[182]

Mariana, however, comes from a poorer country and emigrates to Spain in search of "la vida que [le] prometían los anuncios de televisión" [the life promised to her by TV ads].[183] Together with many other migrants, she seeks an opportunity to inscribe herself into the neoliberal economic model that has disillusioned those who, like the Montenegros, have a greater familiarity with it. The welfare state that is being eroded in Spain is still attractive enough to newcomers who compare it not to the way it used to be pre-austerity but to the much weaker social safety nets in their countries of origin. Immigration flows are indissolubly linked to a specific economic model and its connection to certain geographic areas:

> Las raíces de los movimientos migratorios europeos coinciden significativamente con la implantación de un modelo económico concreto. En el caso de Europa se trata de un modelo de mercado único de base neoliberal que alimenta en el sujeto . . . el deseo nostálgico de acceso a un paraíso metamorfoseado, en este momento concreto, en lo que se conoce como sociedad del *bien-estar.* [The roots of European migratory movements coincide significantly with the implantation of a specific economic model. In Europe's case, this is about a single market model on a neoliberal basis that feeds in a subject . . . the nostalgic desire of access to a paradise that, at this particular moment, metamorphosed into what is known as a *welfare* state.][184]

Today, the Western European welfare state is crumbling, and Mariana wants to enjoy the remaining vestiges of this societal model that never had the opportunity fully to reach Romania. The immigrants' yearning to benefit from the remnants of the welfare state is useful to the political forces that prefer to engage with a vulnerable and acquiescent populace.[185] García Montero's novel abstains from blaming immigrants for their vulnerability to coercion and intimidation, yet at the same time, suggests that it is necessary to analyze the ways in which the political landscape of Spain changes because of the country's demographic transformations.

The novel's protagonist is disturbed by his son's reluctance to join the protest movements that are challenging the unwavering dedication to austerity measures on the part of Spain's government. Because of his involvement with Mariana, Ramón grows increasingly attracted to her value system and joins Mariana in the pursuit of economic well-being within the consumerist model that is nourished by long-term indebtedness. As much as Ramón's grandmother tries to convince herself that her grandson and Mariana are active participants in the 15-M movement, the reality is different. Ramón and Mariana approach the protesters out of curiosity but almost immediately retreat into their private dream of achieving a comfortable bourgeois existence.[186] Juan is discomfited by the realization that the person he blames for his son's withdrawal from political activism is an immigrant woman who works as hired help in his house. As a lifelong progressive Liberal, he wants to abstain from a facile condemnation of immigrants and searches for ways to glean a greater insight into the realities of immigrant existence that inform the life philosophy of Mariana and her circle of immigrant friends.

In a way reminiscent of the protagonist of Luis Martín-Santos's *Tiempo de silencio* (1962), Montenegro visits the slums of Cañada Real.[187] The trajectory of the shanty town's development reflects the direction of movement of migratory flows in the country. If in the 1950s and 1960s Cañada Real housed the people who had been displaced from rural areas by Franco's modernization efforts, starting from the decade of the 1990s, it attracted Romanian and Moroccan immigrants.[188] When he arrives in Cañada Real, Montenegro discovers that there is no personal memory or experience upon which he can draw to process the misery and marginalization that he is witnessing. The poverty of the shanty town is the only reality of today's Spain to which the poet cannot relate through his memories and analysis of the past. He feels as if the very existence of the slum denied his right both to a past and a future.[189] A society's capacity to preserve its historical memory is contingent on the existence of "affective communities" that share a collective identity and possess an emotional attachment to past events that are to be remembered.[190] Montenegro's belief that the crisis can be addressed only through accessing and engaging with the historical memory of the Civil War leads him to fear that the growing presence of immigrants might be used by the political forces that are hostile to the idea of recovering this history. At the same time, given that "people's experiences and understanding of their community thus reside in their orientation to its symbolism,"[191] if no efforts are made to render the symbols of Spain's historic identity legible to immigrants, preventing their marginalization will become even harder.

Montenegro's short visit to Cañada Real places him in disturbing proximity to the spaces inhabited by those whom Agamben sought to define with his concept of *homo sacer*.[192] The poet's efforts to analyze the damage that the crisis is doing to Spain are rendered futile by an encounter with a space of abjection that he cannot explain or even name. The slum belongs to what Bauman terms "nowherevilles," or places that are "conceived and planned as a hole in time as much as in space, a temporary suspension of the time sequence of identity building and territorial ascription."[193] The presence of the *homines sacri* of the Cañada Real proves intolerable to Montenegro because they serve as a reminder that "the state of exception comes more and more to the foreground as the fundamental political structure and ultimately begins to become the rule."[194] The "planeta olvidado" [forgotten planet] of the slum[195] only seems to be located at an enormous distance from the still prosperous consumerist society that surrounds it. The possibility of joining the growing ranks of "*superfluous* (displaced) *humanity*"[196] always lurks behind the consumerist *jouissance* of those who, like the Montenegros, do not yet feel the economic impact of the crisis. An encounter with "what disturbs identity, system, order. What does not respect borders, positions, rules"[197] in Cañada Real forces Montenegro to face the realization that a real understanding of the kind of breakdown that the crisis augurs cannot be gained without immersing oneself in the spaces where the societal order has already collapsed. The poet, however, is not prepared for more than a momentary glimpse of the abject and distances himself from Cañada Real both geographically and emotionally as soon as he can.

The presence of the slum so close to the administrative and financial center of the country can be explained by the many uses to which Cañada Real can be put by those who want to ensure that the dismantling of the welfare state does not meet with significant resistance. The existence of a subgroup of immigrants who are placed in the exterritorial enclaves like those of Cañada Real creates a rift within the immigrant community and prevents the formation of links of solidarity between newcomers to the country. Immigrants who, like Mariana, find it easier to inscribe themselves into the host society reject the inhabitants of the slums, refusing to see the similarity between their own desire to integrate into consumer culture and the dreams of the slum dwellers who name their children Armani, Messi, Frenadol, and Aznar.[198] The readiness of the more successful immigrants to distance themselves from their former compatriots living in Cañada Real does not, however, make it easier for them to find acceptance among those who view all immigrants with suspicion. The growing presence of immigrant populations in Spain is not changing the way immigrants are depicted in the media:

> How do immigrants become newsworthy in Spain? The study has shown that they become newsworthy when they are illegal or irregular members of society, or criminals. The regularized immigrants who live and work in Spain are definitely not newsworthy and hardly ever do

> they become part of the news. It is clear that only the more deviant immigrants are included in the media.[199]

García Montero refuses to rely upon a sensationalized vision of immigrants and offers a more nuanced approach to the negative and the positive effects of the growing immigrant presence in the country. The fragmentation of the immigrant community strengthens the structures of exploitation within the society of austerity, yet this issue cannot be resolved through a wholesale condemnation of immigrants.

The very concept of immigration is both a product of and a challenge to the nation-state model: "As much as modern states have been actively involved in producing immigration, they are also dependent on containing immigration. Sedentariness, not mobility, is their constitutive principle."[200] As the increasing fluidity of capital and information flows erodes the nation-state and strains the capacity of the social safety net to provide the resources needed to integrate immigrants, cultivation of historical memory can be relied upon as a way of generating greater acceptance toward immigrants. The marginalization of immigrants can be overcome through a collective engagement with Spain's historical memory that will create a feeling of belonging and commonality of purpose. The imaginary community of a nation-state cannot exist without a belief in the importance of the nation's past and consistent efforts to maintain the memory of the past alive.[201] This is not to say that members of immigrant communities are to be encouraged to substitute their own history with that of the host country. García Montero's novel suggests that the Spanish Civil War and the dictatorship of Franco can be discussed in a way that opens these subjects up to immigrants and allows the country's new residents to see this history as relevant to their own experiences. For this to happen, it is crucial to remember that the Civil War led to the creation of a sizable community of exiles from Spain, as well as to the formation of significant migratory flows from poorer to richer regions of the country. The image of an immigrant as an inscrutable, menacing Other can be undermined through accessing the memories of Spanish migrants of the pre-Transition era.

In her recent study of the legacy of the Spanish Civil War, historian Helen Graham warns about the danger of extreme nationalism gaining ground in the Spain ravaged by the high levels of unemployment and a growing uncertainty about the future. In Graham's opinion, efforts to analyze the legacy of the Civil War and the dictatorship of Franco "representan la mejor acción de resistencia contra un fascismo que parece renacer" [represent the best act of resistance against a fascism that seems to be reborn].[202] The protagonist of García Montero's novel finds that his immersion in the memories of the postwar era gives him a clearer understanding of Spain's crisis. He is better equipped to relate the experiences of the refugees from the Franco dictatorship to those of the immigrants who come to Spain today and can trace the country's economic woes to the peculiar nature of Spain's transition to democracy. *No me cuentes tu vida* invites readers to engage in their own analysis of the past as it relates to their familiar histories and to adopt a more nuanced stance vis-à-vis the growing immigrant community in Spain.

The title of García Montero's novel was inspired by the poem "No me cuentes tu vida" penned by the writer's close friend Benjamín Prado.[203] Two verses from the poem appear as one of the novel's epigraphs: "No me cuentes tu vida. / No me des la mitad de lo que ya no quieres." [Don't tell me your life. Don't give me half of what you no longer want.][204] In 2013, Prado published his own novel of the crisis, titled *Ajuste de cuentas* [*Settling the Scores*]. The personal, artistic, and ideological affinities between the two writers led them to create novels that can be seen as part of an ongoing creative dialogue. García Montero and Prado share the disillusionment with the societal structures created because of the Transition and believe that a return to the memory of the Civil War and the dictatorship is crucial for an understanding of what caused the current economic struggles. While García Montero infuses his writing with nostalgia for the landscapes that have been erased by the neoliberal economy, Prado's novel reflects the rage that many Spaniards feel in response to the austerity measures presented by the government of Mariano Rajoy as the only solution to the crisis.

BENJAMÍN PRADO'S *AJUSTE DE CUENTAS*: WRITING THE RAGE

Before 1999, Benjamín Prado's novelistic production was characterized by "actitud de huida del mundo y de sí mismos por parte de casi todos sus personajes" [an attitude of escapism from the world and themselves on the part of almost all of his characters].[205] Together with Ray Loriga, Prado is considered one of the most important representatives of the Peninsular Generation X movement characterized by the apolitical nature of its literary production, which is, for the most part, divorced from the specifically Spanish realities.[206] In his 1996 discussion of Prado's writing, Manuel Vázquez Montalbán pointed out that the writer's characters "parecen venir de una galaxia cultural en la que no existe la literatura ni la cultura española" [seem to have come from a cultural galaxy where neither Spanish literature nor Spanish culture exist].[207] The main criticism leveled against the writers of this artistic generation was their incapacity to connect with the historical legacy of Spain that led to attempts to fill the resulting vacuum with pop culture references suggested by the global music and film industry.[208] Generation X writers responded to the readers' desire to overcome the Franco-era isolation and position themselves as full-fledged citizens of the global cultural community. As a result, these writers' work was imbued with a "self-conscious insistence on their association with a global (i.e. primarily Anglophone) culture [that] often carried with it an adamant rejection of an autochthonous tradition."[209] The Civil War and the dictatorship of Franco were of no interest to the writers of this generation and were not present in their novelistic output.[210]

With the publication of *No sólo el fuego* (1999), however, Benjamín Prado effectuated a turn away from writing imbued by feelings of alienation from and indifference toward Spain's historical memory. The novel brings together the experiences of the Republicans who were forced to exile themselves from Spain in the aftermath of the war, the representatives of the postwar generation who participated in the anti-Franco resistance movements of the dictatorship's closing years, and the members of the younger generation who are finding it hard to relate to the issues that are of importance to their parents and grandparents. In his 2006 novel *Mala gente que camina* [Bad People Walking], Prado continued to explore the legacy of the Civil War. This novel addresses the postwar practice of removing the children of the Republican prisoners from their families with the goal of reeducating them in a way consistent with the ideology of the Nationalist Movement. *Mala gente* is based on a meticulous reading of testimonial accounts that are seamlessly integrated into the narrative.[211]

It is impossible to determine to what extent the writer's interest in the Spanish Civil War stemmed from the commercial success enjoyed by the novels that were part of the "memory boom" of the first decade of the twenty-first century.[212] What is clear, however, is that Prado's engagement with historical memory has had a profound effect on the writer's authorial voice. Gone are the "imported and often occult references to music, literature, and film" that were so central to Prado's *Raro* (1995) and *Nunca le des la mano a un pistolero zurdo* (1996).[213] Today, the writer's novelistic output reflects Prado's belief that it is only through an active engagement with historical memory that the most pressing issues of the moment can be resolved. In the words of De Fina, "narrators use stories as stages for the enactment, reflection or negation of social relationships and concretely contribute to perpetrate or modify them,"[214] and Prado is dedicated to the goal of challenging the system of social relations that arose from the postwar legacy. The writer believes that the possibility of meaningful social change depends on the Spaniards' readiness to reject the point of view expressed by one of the characters of *Mala gente que camina* who is convinced that "es mejor no resucitar esas viejas historias" [it is best not to resuscitate these old stories].[215]

Ajuste de cuentas, the writer's most recent novel, expresses the same disillusionment with the economy that was constructed in Spain because of the Transition, which lies at the center of Chirbes's *Crematorio* and *En la orilla* and García Montero's *No me cuentes tu vida*.

> Malditos bancos, malditas hipotecas subprime, malditos neoliberales, malditos mercados, malditos ejecutivos con sueldos de dieciocho millones de euros y jubilaciones de quince, maldito Ibex 35, malditas primas de riesgo, maldito Fondo Monetario Internacional, [Damn banks, damn subprime mortgages, damn neoliberals, damn markets, damn CEOs with the salaries of eighteen million euro and pensions of fifteen million, damn Ibex 35, damn risk premiums, damn International Monetary Fund,][216]

exclaims Juan Urbano, the novel's protagonist, who appeared in the writer's earlier novels, *Mala gente que camina* (2006) and *Operación Gladio* (2011). At the beginning of *Ajuste de cuentas*, Juan finds himself in the street, both literally and metaphorically, after being let go from both the radio station and the newspaper where he works. Having joined the legion of the newly unemployed, Juan has to shed his attachment to the middle-class luxuries that he can no longer afford.[217] Like many others, he sees no alternative to searching for what Ulrich Beck has famously referred to as "biographical solutions to systemic contradictions."[218] Wherever he goes, Juan encounters people who are attempting to make ends meet with the help of self-imposed domestic austerity measures.[219] These survival strategies that many of Prado's readers in Spain will recognize as their own are symbolic of the process that the country at large is undergoing: spending cuts can be felt everywhere, yet they do not manage to improve the general situation.

The economic collapse results, for Urbano and many people who find themselves in a similar situation, in an identity crisis that makes him feel lost and unable to decide on the direction in which he should now take his life.[220] Juan realizes that the economic crisis has robbed him of the small luxuries of daily life that used to support his vision of the self. Without them, he finds that "ser yo mismo estaba fuera de mi alcance en aquellos momentos" [being myself was not within my reach in these moments].[221] Even more pressing than encountering a new source of income is, for Juan, the need to fashion a new identity for himself that will shore him up against the ceaseless battering of the market forces. In the words of Zygmunt Bauman, "the search for identity is the ongoing struggle to arrest or slow down the flow, to solidify the fluid, to give form to the formless."[222] In a society of consumers that Juan inhabits, the writer's temporary incapacity to outfit his search for a new identity with visible trappings of economic success places him among the growing ranks of losers in the game of an unstoppable accumulation of goods.

Every day, newspapers tell of thousands of people who, like Urbano, are displaced from their lives and identities by the crisis. The terror of becoming one of the excluded, an agambian *homo sacer*, forces Juan to accept an offer of employment from Martín Duque, a man he despises. Duque is a millionaire who enriched himself in the real estate market and achieved the kind of social standing that allowed him to establish friendships with members of the royal family and Spain's financial and political elites.[223] After spending a few years in jail for economic crimes, Duque hires Juan Urbano to write a laudatory biography that would improve the millionaire's public image. The repugnance that Urbano feels toward Duque is less powerful than the writer's fear to remain without any sources of income, and Urbano accepts the offer to put his creative talent at the service of a man who has contributed to engineering the situation where representatives of the creative classes will find their chances of making a living dramatically reduced. Urbano has no recourse but to turn himself into a commodity and engage in a constant repositioning of himself as a product to be offered on the consumer market in hopes that he will remain attractive to potential purchasers: "In the society of consumers no one can become a subject without first turning himself into a commodity and no one can keep his or her subjectness secure without perpetually resuscitating, resurrecting and replenishing the capacities expected and required of a sellable commodity."[224] If the market has no demand for Urbano's services as a journalist, he is forced to refashion himself as a biographer to the rich.

As he plunges deeper into the vicissitudes of Duque's life, Urbano begins to realize that Spain is "un país construido sobre cimientos insostenibles" [a country built on unsustainable foundations].[225] Like Chirbes's Esteban, Prado's protagonist arrives at a conclusion that the crisis can be addressed only by analyzing the history that led to it. Duque's trajectory does not represent an isolated case but, rather, symbolizes

> las aspiraciones de un país que después de treinta y ocho años de dictadura y subdesarrollo quería huir de su pasado sombrío e instalarse en la prosperidad [the aspirations of a country that after thirty-eight years of a dictatorship and underdevelopment wanted to escape from its grim past and install itself in prosperity].[226]

This flight from the past, however, could create the kind of prosperity that was based on only a shaky foundation prone to collapse at the slightest sign of trouble. The admiration that accompanied Duque's every step during the years when he was accumulating his vast fortune transformed into public condemnation once the criminal activities that nourished his riches became too egregious to be ignored. In the same way, Spaniards' status as "model Europeans" acquired because of the country's eagerness to integrate into European institutions[227] is substituted with an offensive PIGS appellation after the global economic crisis begins. Just like nobody is willing to notice the societal structures that conditioned Duque's rise and fall, there is little interest in tracing the origins of the PIGS' marginalization in the European Union. Urbano's analysis of Duque's trajectory allows the writer to acquire a clearer vision of the consequences of Spain's rushed integration into the European economy.

Between late 1994 and early 2008, Spain's economy experienced an explosive growth whose nature nobody was willing to analyze at the time.[228] As he ponders the Spaniards' attitude toward this economic *boom*, Urbano realizes that it was characterized by a collective delusion of enormous proportions: "Era igual como si todos fuésemos, de forma consciente o inconsciente, miembros de una de esas sectas de fanáticos cuyo único fin posible es el suicidio colectivo" [It is as if all of us were, either consciously or not, members of one of those sects of fanatics whose only possible goal is collective suicide].[229] The dogma that nourished this fanaticism is the belief in the nearly supernatural powers of "free markets," which were considered indispensable for the construction of a lasting democracy. The foundations of the economic system that produced the dramatic economic growth of the late twentieth and the early twenty-first centuries were laid during the latter stage of the Franco dictatorship and strengthened, after the dictator's death, through "una cruzada informativa que pugnaba por la defensa y el reconocimiento de la economía de mercado" [an information crusade that fought for a defense and a recognition of market economy].[230] In 1977, Carlos Ferrer Salat, president of Spain's Confederation of Entrepreneurial Organizations, insisted that establishment of a functioning democracy was contingent upon an adoption of market economy.[231] Ferrer Salat's ideas were placed, virtually without any attempt at questioning them, at the center of the economic program of the Transition. For as long as the speed of economic growth could be maintained, there was little interest in questioning whether neoliberal economic practices were, indeed, an inescapable companion to representative democracy. Only after the economy collapsed with unexpectedly harsh consequences did the possibility of questioning the nature of Spain's democracy enter the mainstream discourse.[232] During the Transition, Spain's political Left embraced neoliberalism and severed all but the strictly symbolic links to its Republican past, choosing to ignore the continuities between the economic mechanisms put in place during the later stage of the Franco era and the economy of the newly democratic Spain.[233] The interest in the Civil War was limited to exploring its sentimental potential.

In Prado's preceding novel, titled *Mala gente que camina*, Urbano discovers that immersing himself in research on the subject of the Civil War brings him the peace of mind and the contentment that were absent from his life before he decided to emerge from his indifference toward the country's past.[234] In *Ajuste de cuentas*, Urbano continues his analysis of Spain's history and discovers that it can be of great use not only on a personal but also on a collective level. In the Spain ravaged by the crisis, Urbano sees traces of the Spanish Civil War and Franco's dictatorship. The legacy of *franquismo* has never been fully overcome, and its presence can still be glimpsed behind the daily reality of a country wrecked by the global economic crisis. In "la sociedad amedrentada" [the terrified society][235] of today's Spain, there is more fear than indignation, and the question that Urbano and his circle of friends cannot avoid asking is whether

> los treinta y ocho años de represión nos volvieron sumisos o es que ya lo éramos y por eso pudo durar tanto en El Pardo un pobre imbécil como el caudillo [the thirty-eight years of oppression made us submissive or whether we had already been that way and that is why a poor idiot like the *caudillo* managed to stay for such a long time in El Pardo].[236]

The continuity between the dictatorship and democracy was not solely economic. No significant effort was made to create a distance between the educational and cultural practices of the Franco era and those of the democratic Spain. In the words of novelist Juan Goytisolo, a fear of new ideas that was inherited from the dictatorship was preserved during the Transition.[237] *Ajuste de cuentas* points toward the many ways in which the legacy of Francoism makes it difficult to resist, both economically and psychologically, the austerity measures introduced in response to the crisis.

During a visit to his mother's neighborhood, Urbano observes a disturbing continuity between the manner in which the area was destroyed by bombings during the war and the ravages inflicted on the landscape by the neoliberal economic practices several decades later.[238] The buildings erected after the war by the Nationalist authorities experienced a dramatic growth in value during the years of the early twenty-first century housing boom.[239] The temptation of easy money convinces the residents of the neighborhood to sell their houses.[240] The area is transformed into "una engreída ciudad-dormitorio" [a conceited bedroom community] and is gradually conquered by "hipermercados, franquicias y multinacionales" [hypermarkets, franchises and multinational companies].[241] Not only do the changes visited on the landscape facilitate the ease with which multinational corporations extract profit from it, but they also complicate the task of accessing the historical and cultural memory associated with this landscape. The destruction of the sensory and material landscapes of regional cultures by the economy of globalization puts these cultures in danger of being wiped out:

> Sensory premises, memories and histories are being pulled out from under entire regional cultures and the capacity to reproduce social identities may be altered as a result. Such economic processes reveal the extent to which the ability to replicate cultural identity is a material practice embedded in the reciprocities, aesthetics, and sensory strata of material objects.[242]

During the visits to the neighborhood where he grew up, Urbano searches for the remnants of the world that was sacrificed to the dream of modernization. This act of cultural self-immolation was committed in the belief that it was going to allow Spain finally to join the ranks of countries whose right to belong to Europe was never in question.[243] Now that the crisis has revealed the tenuous nature of Spain's position as a member of the EU, the sacrifices made in the name of this illusion of belonging have become easier to question. Storefronts owned by international conglomerates have substituted the small businesses of the former residents of the neighborhood. To Urbano, the brand names that appear in their windows look like headstones in a cemetery where the lifestyle he associates with his childhood was buried.[244] Now that the people who inhabited the area have relocated to more affordable places or, possibly, emigrated because of the crisis, their store of memories has become inaccessible to Urbano. The triumphant march of capitalism has dispersed the communities that could draw on shared knowledge about the past to conceive of an alternative way of life.

The linear and progress-oriented vision of history that inspired the Transition led to the formation of a public mood that was reluctant to dwell on the painful aspects of the shared past.[245] The devastation of the crisis changed the mood in Spain and allowed the specter of the issues that had been expelled from the public sphere because of their negativity to return to the forefront. The success of the Transition was predicated on the capacity of the country's political elites to foster confidence in the transformations visited on Spain's political system:

> Without trials to stir up the resentment of the outgoing military, or truth commissions to reveal the role of civil society in the repressive apparatus, and only marginal efforts towards reparations, Spain's political elites could focus on constructing fair and resilient democratic institutions, and the Spanish public on learning to trust these institutions to channel their political energies and demands.[246]

The severity of the crisis eroded this trust and has made it possible to reevaluate the entire legacy of the Transition. Spain can now reconnect with its Republican past on an intellectual and a political level, as opposed to the purely sentimental engagement that characterized much of the Spanish Civil War boom of the precrisis years. It is no accident that participants of the 15-M mobilization for political and economic change often evoke the Second Republic and insist that its ideals merit being recovered today.[247] Like many of the characters in the novels of the crisis, Urbano questions the manner in which Western democracies function and wonders whether their excessive entanglement with corporate interests allows them to remain viable.[248] A return to the ideas that inspired the democratic movements of the Second Republic could allow for an expansion or, possibly, a radical transformation of the concept of democracy.

Urbano perceives what is happening in Spain as "un golpe de Estado invisible" [an invisible coup d'état].[249] The democratically elected government officials actively promote the interests of the large financial institutions to the detriment of the voters whom they are supposed to represent.[250] The destruction of the democratic system that constituted one of the goals of those who rebelled against the democratically elected government of the Second Republic on July 18, 1936, is being achieved in today's Spain without any need to use arms.[251] Urbano is tortured by a terrifying suspicion that the most salient result of the Transition was not to put an end to the dictatorship of Franco but to ensure that the foundational principles of the Franco rule remain in place for decades to come. One of the goals of the Nationalist uprising of 1936 and the repression visited by the dictatorship on anybody suspected of Republican sympathies was to ensure the permanence of social and economic hierarchies that existed in the prewar Spain.[252] The social stratification that Urbano observes in Spain today can only lead him to conclude that the functioning of the global economy in the twenty-first century produces the effects that would have been much more pleasing to the followers of Franco than to their opponents in Spain's civil conflict.[253]

The memory of the war and the dictatorship becomes especially relevant today, given that the demographic transformations experienced by the country parallel, to a significant degree, those that occurred in the years following the war. "Aquí eso pasó después de la Guerra Civil y esta a punto de ocurrir de nuevo: volvemos a ser un país de emigrantes" [Around here this happened after the Civil War and is about to happen again: we are once again becoming a country of emigrants], says Urbano in response to his mother's concern about the growing presence of immigrants in Spain.[254] The possibility of an active resistance to the dictatorship was diluted during the 1950s and 1960s by the migratory waves that displaced workers within the country and took many of them outside of Spain.[255]

There are, of course, crucial differences in the migration processes that marked the Spain of Franco and those that are transforming the country today. Still, Juan Urbano believes that there is reason to fear that the arrival in Spain of a great number of immigrants might be used by certain political and economic interests to extinguish the political awareness that is necessary to oppose the transfer of the state's authority and resources into the hands of exterritorial financial elites.

In a conversation he has with his mother on the subject of the growing Chinese community in Spain, Urbano rejects the vision offered by those who praise immigrants for supposedly being self-sacrificing and tireless workers who are eager to be exploited.[256] There is little difference, in the writer's opinion, between these comments and the fears that the immigrants "os invadan, que lo compren todo poco a poco, que llenen las ciudades de letreros en mandarín" [would invade you, would buy up everything little by little, and would fill the cities with signs in Chinese].[257] The otherness of immigrants is often exploited to channel the anxieties generated by the contradictions of the capitalist economy into a direction that will pose no danger to the preservation of this system of economic relations. An immigrant is imagined as a tireless worker bee who, instead of feeling disconcerted by the liquid flows of capital, interacts, gladly and easily, with the fluidity and exploits it for his or her own advantage. In the words of Richard Sennett, "the specter of uselessness" that haunts the denizens of post-nation societies "intersects with the fear of foreigners,"[258] producing a deep-seated sense of anxiety. Instead of questioning the economic system that expects workers to renounce any sort of rootedness and connectedness in favor of a constant displacement in search of employment, members of the growing precariat aim their anger at immigrants. The desperation that forces immigrants to accept subpar working conditions is easy to mistake for complicity with the system that insists on a constant increase in productivity amidst the erosion of the last vestiges of stability. At the core of the fear of an unknowable stranger lies the terror of an opaque and incomprehensible future in a rapidly changing world. Urbano's attempt to make a living as a biographer of Martín Duque forces him to experiment with geographic mobility both inside and outside the country, and the writer acquires a greater sensitivity to the plight of immigrants who traverse significant distances not out of any particular love for the fluidity of capital but, rather, because of the lack of an alternative way to survive.

As he approaches the closing chapters of the millionaire's biography, Urbano realizes that his decision to accept the position of Duque's apologist to maintain the trappings of middle-class existence was a mistake. The act of writing the biography offers Urbano an opportunity to reflect on his personal complicity in making it possible for people like Duque to enrich themselves at the expense of the suffering of others. Instead of a laudatory biographical account he was hired to produce, Urbano publishes an article that lists the crimes committed by Duque after his release from jail. The price that the writer is forced to pay for defying one of those who engineered Spain's real estate bubble could not be more symbolic: Urbano is forced to sell his apartment, which, to him, represents the greatest economic success of his life.[259] Even though the writer finds a way to balance his personal budget, he is conscious that many of his compatriots lack the opportunity to escape from their financial troubles.[260] The closing sentences of the novel suggest that the future awaiting Urbano is likely to be as dark as the vision that the writer has of the fortunes of the country at large. Urbano leaves the readers with a suspicion that Martín Duque hired assassins who will attempt to kill the writer to prevent him from writing a book about the years of Spain's economic boom when Duque and his cronies laid the foundations of today's crisis.[261] The uncertainty of Urbano's future mimics the mood of his Spanish readers and intensifies the complicity between the novel's protagonist and its audience. Prado leaves open the question of whether the final reckoning augured by the novel's title is the one between Duque and Urbano or those who are suffering because of the crisis and those who have enriched themselves as a result.

Prado believes that many more novels of the crisis will appear in the coming years because, as the writer pointed out in an interview on the subject of *Ajuste de cuentas*, the crisis "no es lo que parecía, y eso implica que hay que contárselo todo otra vez desde el principio" [is not what it seemed, and that means we have to tell everything once again from the start].[262] In Prado's opinion, current problems can be traced back to the dictatorship and to the many ways in which the ideology that nourished it remained present in the Spain of the Transition.[263] The author is convinced that an active engagement with Spain's history will allow Spain to create a future that will not be poisoned by the legacy of the dictatorship. Prado's novel manages to bring together, in an elegant fashion, the rage against the devastation of Spain by global capital that inspired the 15-M movement and the feeling of urgency to continue the work of rescuing Spain's historical memory from erasure. *Ajuste de cuentas* demonstrates that thinking about the past does not imperil the future-oriented project of resisting the destruction of the welfare state. To the contrary, the novel shows the necessity of putting the search for knowledge about the past in the service of addressing the most pressing issues of today. Still, Urbano's rebellion against the tyranny of liquid capital is a lonely endeavor. Like Chirbes's Esteban and García Montero's Juan Montenegro, Urbano is a denizen of a world filled with isolated individuals whose capacity to connect with others has been eroded by forces of fluidity. He hopes that his book will serve as a way for him to connect with like-minded individuals, yet he forgets that an experience of a reader who is alone with a printed page is as lonely as that of a writer who has created that page. Among the novelists of the crisis, only Belén Gopegui explores the possibility of collective action as a way of resisting the erosion of the welfare protections by the increasing liquidity of capital.

BELÉN GOPEGUI'S *EL COMITÉ DE LA NOCHE* (2014): RECOVERING FAITH IN POLITICAL ACTIVISM

Critics disagree as to whether Belén Gopegui belongs to the Generation X or stands out too greatly from the writers associated with this literary phenomenon.[264] Still, the writer's novelistic response to the global economic collapse shares important similarities with Prado's novel of the crisis. *El comité de la noche* [*The Committee of the Night*] points to writing as the most effective way to resist the tyranny of liquid capital and aims to involve the readers in a shared project of seeking ways to engage in political resistance. Like Urbano, Gopegui's protagonists find in the act of recording their experiences a possibility of articulating an alternative vision of reality in the world where the capitalist system of property relations positions itself as the only available one. For Gopegui, literature has the power of questioning and even changing the status quo. The characters of *El comité de la noche* believe that a flow of words has the power to arrest the flow of capital. They practice writing as a form of political activism and refuse to relinquish the hope that a world without the tyranny of capital can be built. Of all the novels analyzed in this chapter, *El comité de la noche* is the only one that envisions the possibility of collective action aimed at resisting the destruction of the welfare state. Prado's solitary writer who wages a lonely battle against the henchmen of capitalistic domination is substituted, in Gopegui's work, with activists who work together to create networks of resistance to capitalist exploitation. The novel's short introduction makes use of Schopenhauer's "hedgehog's dilemma" to posit the need to overcome alienation and reach out to others to engage in political activism.[265] Members of the clandestine resistance movement that takes responsibility for putting forth the documents constituting the text of the novel explain what motivates them to overcome inertia and alienation:

> A diferencia de los erizos, nos acercamos no sólo a otros erizos sino a la causa de estos días helados. El peligro y la moderación nos mantienen a una distancia adecuada para subsistir. Pero, a veces, nos seguimos acercando. [Unlike hedgehogs, we approach not only other hedgehogs but also the cause of these frozen days. Danger and caution keep us at a distance that is enough to survive. But at times we keep approaching.][266]

Readers are left with the choice of following the example of the novel's characters and seeking closeness with other human beings or accepting that disengagement is the norm in late capitalist societies.

Gopegui's novelistic output has always been political in nature. After becoming disillusioned with PSOE's willingness to resist Western European neoliberalism, Gopegui transferred her support to the PCE.[267] In the words of Martín Cabrera, Gopegui differs from other writers in Spain in her belief that a novel is not only "un objeto de consumo y entretenimiento, sino . . . un vehículo para indagar y transformar la realidad" [an object of consumption and entertainment but a vehicle of analyzing and transforming reality].[268] Gopegui's goal is to create works of fiction that will offer the readers a conduit to challenging the ideology that presents neoliberalism as the only alternative to dictatorship. *El comité de la noche* invites the readers to join the novel's characters in a rebellion against the structures of oppression that have been bared by the crisis. In fact, the very engagement with the events narrated in the novel in the capacity of a reader makes it inevitable, according to its protagonists, that one shall identify with the transformational goals articulated by these characters. "Describir es prescribir" [to describe is to prescribe], says Carla, one of the novel's protagonists, in an attempt to let her interlocutor know that, after hearing and recording her story of political activism, he has no choice but to join her struggle.[269]

The transcriber, the character who records Carla's memories of her political struggle, discovers that an active engagement with the written word makes it impossible for him to remain detached from the fight against the destruction of the welfare state by liquid capital. The text that the transcriber produces becomes a weapon he can use in this struggle, and this is precisely the role that Gopegui expects her novel to play for the readers:

> El compromiso de Gopegui es el de renunciar a que su obra literaria sea un mundo cerrado, hermoso, radical, inquietante o dócil pero, por encima de todo, inútil. Un objeto sin otra función que entretener, gustar y gustarse, conciliar a autor y lector con la idea de animal pasivo de ambos. [Gopegui is committed to preventing her work from being a world in itself, beautiful, radical, disquieting, docile, but above all, useless. An object without any other purpose but entertaining, pleasing, and reconciling the author and the reader with the idea of being passive animals.][270]

This is not, of course, to say that the novel lacks artistic value. To the contrary, Gopegui ensures that *El comité de la noche* never turns into a political manifesto and always retains its power as a work of art. From the beginning of her career as a novelist, Gopegiu has asserted the importance of creating novels that tell an engaging and accessible story while constantly "renovating her language with startlingly fresh, original metaphors and similes, rhetorical figures both personal and unmistakably feminine."[271] In *El comité de la noche,* Gopegui explores more adventurous narrative techniques than the ones she used in her previous novels. As the writer pointed out in a 2004 interview with Marta Rivera de la Cruz, "no creo que haya mucha diferencia entre la forma y el contenido" [I do not believe there is much difference between form and content].[272] The disruption of a linear chronological structure and the multiplicity of narrative voices in *El Comité* reinforce the novel's message that different ways of conceiving reality are possible.

Gopegui differs from the writers analyzed in this chapter in her refusal to look for the causes of the crisis solely inside Spain. The writer rejects the discourse that blames Spain for the severity of its experience of the crisis and that places it among the contemptuously nicknamed PIGS, or the nations that supposedly caused their own suffering by their out-of-control public spending and corruption. Álex and Carla, the two female protagonists of the novel, move between Spain and Slovakia, countries that have historically been marginalized in Europe. Their existence on the periphery of the European experience allows the women to gain a clearer perspective on the transformations that begin at the economic and symbolic center of Europe and radiate toward the European margins that are especially negatively affected by these changes. Álex belongs to a clandestine activist organization that attempts to place obstacles in the path of liquid capital that is sweeping away the tattered social safety net in the countries of the European Union. Carla, on the other hand, refuses to engage in political activism at first, yet soon discovers that it is not possible to find refuge from the mortiferous hegemony of capital. In a subversion of patriarchal gender norms that is central to the narrative universe of *El comité de la noche*,[273] the two female protagonists are the novel's active agents who lay down their lives for a political cause, while the male character acts as the custodian of their memory, who, unlike the geographically mobile Álex and Carla, moves only between the enclosed spaces of his house and office. As the transcriber discovers during his work of putting into writing Carla's oral testimony of her fight against a multinational corporation, however, an author who creates a text is, in turn, transformed by it.

Like Prado's Urbano and García Montero's Juan Montenegro, Álex experiences an identity crisis that coincides with the economic collapse of 2008–2009. She does not, however, believe that the feeling of not knowing what her role in life is should be attributed to the economic crisis. Rather, Álex suspects that the disruption of the global economic processes has allowed her to catch a glimpse of the crucial societal transformations that are marginalizing people like her and that have become easier to see as a result of the crisis.[274] After joining the growing ranks of the surplus workers who have been rejected by the increasingly volatile job market, Álex realizes that the existence of an expanding army of the unemployed is crucial to the functioning of the new liquid economy where social control is exercised through fostering the feelings of terror among those who can at any time be pushed out of productive employment and, consequently, deprived of any sense of self-worth.[275] The soaring unemployment is creating an environment of anxiety and insecurity where nobody is immune from experiencing Álex's fate of being cast aside by the fickle demands of the market. The concept of social classes has been rendered irrelevant, and, as a result, generating feelings of solidarity in a society of isolated individuals is next to impossible: "Pero centenares de historias de perdedores o fracasados nos han ido encerrando, aislando. . . . Ahora cada uno se la juega solo" [Hundreds of stories of losers and failures have been shutting us in, isolating us. . . . Nowadays everyone plays alone].[276] Economic exploitation is nothing new, yet the isolating feeling of shame attached to being one of the losers in the game of capitalist economic relations has made it that much harder for the exploited to unite and create a resistance movement.

An exploration of possibilities for generating solidarity among workers has always been central for Gopegui's novelistic output,[277] and *El comité de la noche* depicts the difficulties posed by the current economic crisis for establishing links of solidarity. The use of multiple narrative voices in the novel underscores the complex, yet not hopeless, nature of efforts aimed at establishing enriching human connections among individuals:

> The decentralization and fragmentation of the systemic narratives resulting from the use of many narrators or constant adjustments in focalization do not indicate isolation and the impossibility of communication among individuals . . . but rather they show the intense and unavoidable multileveled connections among diegetic selves in a network society.[278]

Both Álex and the transcriber begin their journey from a position of alienation that is marked in *El comité* through their voices being relegated to different sections of the novel where they exist in isolation from each other. The story of Álex's and Carla's resistance, however, manages to break through the alienation, and even the realization that the transcriber's dialogue with Carla was, in reality, a monologue prompted by the man's memory of his dead friend does not detract from the message that connectedness is possible.

Álex overcomes the debilitating effects of protracted unemployment when she discovers that putting down in writing her ideas about what is happening offers her a space of freedom to reflect and formulate a strategy of resistance. The members of Álex's small, clandestine organization have to rely on books and historical accounts to construct a genealogy of activism that will shore up the group against its current political and intellectual rootlessness.[279] The bridge that the group tries to tend to the past reminds the readers that, to a great extent, the possibility of organizing political resistance is linked to the capacity to access the memory of those who engaged in similar activism previously. The novel's powerful ending emphasizes the centrality of the past to the transformative efforts of the present and the future. The transcriber is forced to acknowledge the painful truth that he has been keeping at bay throughout his imagined dialogue with Carla: Álex and Carla were killed by a powerful corporation whose financial interests they attempted to thwart. The transcriber's conversations with Carla are a reconstruction of his dead comrade's beliefs. What the readers perceive, until the closing pages of the novel, as actions occurring in the diegetic present reveals itself to be a nostalgic invocation of the past:

> *El comité de la noche* es la historia de dos muertes y del hombre que las invoca para no olvidarse de quien puede ser todavía. En ese sentido, éste es un cuento de fantasmas. Un cuento de fantasmas que recorren toda Europa. [*El comité de la noche* is a story of two deaths and of a man who recollects them in order not to forget what he can still become. In this sense, this is a story about ghosts. The story about ghosts that are haunting all of Europe.][280]

The specters of Álex and Carla that haunt the transcriber bring to mind the famous opening words of Marx's and Engels's Communist Manifesto: "A spectre haunts Europe—the spectre of communism."[281] In Carla's words, "escribir es traer de vuelta a los expulsados del presente" [to write is to bring back those who have been expelled from the present].[282] The record of the women's struggle created by the transcriber rescues from oblivion the possibility of a different way of being and leads him to experience his own identity crisis.

Like Álex and the transcriber, Carla becomes unemployed because of the crisis. She is forced to leave Spain and accept a position with a company in Slovakia that manufactures medication based on human blood. As a result of her work with flows of blood, Carla becomes sensitized to the concept of fluidity.[283] She is aware of the destructive potential of liquid capital that is eroding the economic and social structures of the welfare state but does not believe that political activism can have a transformative potential and prefers to dedicate her energies to preventing her own existence from being swept up by unstoppable currents.[284] Carla discovers, however, that liquid capital will not rest until it subsumes all other flows, including the currents of human blood. The corporation that employs Carla attempts to sabotage the state-controlled blood drive in Bratislava to manufacture a crisis that will allow it to privatize the blood that is donated for medical purposes. "¿Por qué estúpida cuestión simbólica excluir la sangre cuando compramos y vendemos todo?" [For what stupid symbolic reason should we exclude blood when we buy and sell everything?] exclaims Gustav, Carla's supervisor, in an attempt to convince the woman that monetization of human bodies should not be resisted.[285] The realization that Gustav's employers will go to any lengths to penetrate human bodies to extract surplus value from their internal organs horrifies Carla and impels her to join the fight against the privatization of blood. Exploitation of labor no longer looks innocuous to her once she sees it as a precursor to the financial exploitation of the blood that courses through human bodies.

The efforts of private companies to privatize blood donations bring to light an increased weakening of the European welfare state. The unemployed are encouraged to donate blood to supplement the diminishing welfare benefits, which makes the very existence of growing unemployment profitable for the companies that need to secure uninterrupted flows of blood.[286] If the value that could be extracted from exploiting the labor of the unemployed is smaller than the profit that can be gained by keeping them jobless and forcing them to sell their blood, there is no reason to expect that the weakened national governments will be motivated to diminish unemployment. An excerpt from a 2012 article in *Europa Press* that serves as the novel's epigraph tends a bridge between the novelistic universe of *El comité de la noche* and the reality of Spain battered by the crisis: "Una multinacional farmacéutica plantea pagar setenta euros semanales a los parados que donen sangre" [A multinational pharmaceutical company offers to pay seventy euro per week to the unemployed who donate blood].[287] The article is one of the texts that Álex and her comrades discuss during a meeting, paying special attention to the suggestion of the company's CEO that supplementing welfare benefits with money earned selling blood can constitute "una forma de vivir" [a way to live][288] for the unemployed.[289] The casual admission by the CEO that welfare programs do not allow the jobless to maintain life unless they allow private companies to invade their bodies to extract profit from them propels the members of the clandestine organization into action.

Many of the novel's characters look for safe ways of addressing liquidity and creating the kind of borders that liquidity will not be able to sweep away. Uno, one of the members of Álex's clandestine organization, describes the fall of the Berlin Wall and the collapse of the USSR as an erosion of one of the barriers that kept the global capitalist expansion at bay.[290] It falls to the activists like Uno and his comrades to stop the flood of change. The transcriber, on the other hand, looks for strictly personal solutions to the threat of growing fluidity and believes that dancing might be a way to "disolver lo sólido no para que se desvanezca sino para que fluya" [dissolve the solid in a way that doesn't make it disappear but so that it flows].[291] Carla agrees that it is impossible to deny the liquid nature of existence in today's reality and suggests that joining forces with like-minded comrades is a way to make the fluidity of the self serve a useful purpose.[292] In one of his conversations with Carla, the transcriber expresses an apprehension that experiencing liquidity together with others might prove destructive, but Carla points out that a refusal to commingle with the like-minded will result in something even worse, which is living a useless life.[293] As they reach the closing pages of the novel, readers discover that both characters were right. Carla's decision to dissolve her self in the collective struggle of the clandestine group does result in her and Álex's death. At the same time, the flow of her words and ideas does penetrate the defenses of the transcriber, involving him in a reevaluation of his decision to retreat into the private sphere where echoes of the political activism of others will not reach him. In the risk society of late modernity, "handling fear and insecurity becomes an essential cultural qualification,"[294] and the transcriber realizes that there is no possibility that one might hide from liquid capital, which batters all individual existences.

At the end of *El comité de la noche*, the transcriber addresses the novel's readers with an impassioned plea to prevent the memory of Carla's struggle from being washed away by the liquid flows that have taken her life.[295] The readers' awareness of Carla's activism can form a dam that will prevent the stream of her words from flowing away and dissipating into nothingness. The identification between the transcriber and the readers makes his slippage into the inclusive first person plural feel natural.

The readers become part of the "nosotros" [we] that can make the choice to prevent Carla and Álex from slipping into oblivion. The need to preserve the memory of the struggle against exploitation that has led Chirbes, García Montero, and Prado to remind the readers of the history of anti-Franco resistance is echoed, in Gopegui's novel, by a suggestion that those who fight for justice today are part of a long-standing genealogy of activists. The transcriber leaves the readers with the hope that the threatening liquidity can be harnessed into the service of collective interests of the exploited.[296] The transcriber echoes the writer's own vision of the purpose of literature that, in Gopegui's words, has the capacity to address readers not only as individuals but as collectivities.[297]

There is in Spain, without a doubt, a feeling of nostalgia for the time—be it imagined or real—when political idealism was still possible and a future free of capitalist exploitation could be imagined. To a significant extent, the fascination of the reading public with the seemingly inexhaustible subject of the Spanish Civil War is owed to the need for exploring a more hopeful time in history:

> Si el presente es representado como una realidad posutópica y posrevolucionaria en la que las principales meta-narrativas transformadoras de la izquierda han entrado en una fase de impasse, el pasado emerge como un escenario casi mítico de grandes esperanzas, ambiciones y virtudes político-biográficas. [If the present is represented as a post-utopic and postrevolutionary reality where the principal transformational meta-narratives of the left are at an impasse, the past emerges as an almost mythical space of great hopes, ambitions and politico-biographical virtues.][298]

Gopegui wants to recover the possibility that a heroic revolutionary struggle need not be associated exclusively with the past. *El comité de la noche* suggests that the profound societal transformations we know as "the crisis" do not have to be accepted passively. The past should not be treated as a site for escapist fantasies but as a source of knowledge about the strategies of resistance that were employed by the revolutionary movements of the preceding generations. Since the structures of power and oppression have transformed, however, so should the activism that aims to counterbalance them. In the words of Touraine, "power used to be in the hands of princes, oligarchies, and ruling elites. . . . This image of power does not fit our reality any longer. Power is everywhere and nowhere."[299] The structure of the clandestine organization to which Álex belongs mimics the ubiquity of agents of power and refuses to recognize the limitations imposed by national borders. The past informs the efforts of activists in *El comité* yet does not serve as an obstacle on the way to transformations required by the specifics of the moment.

Chronology has always been important for Gopegui, and references to the exact date and time when the action is set often appear in her novels.[300] Unlike the writer's preceding novels that are "almost always rigorously contemporaneous," however, *El comité de la noche* is set in the future that is not distant enough to allow the readers to feel detachment from it.[301] A short introduction that precedes the two parts of the novel makes it clear that the diegetic present of *El comité de la noche* is located a few years after the novel's date of publication. The writings by Álex and the transcriber are presented as part of the records that have been kept in a secret digital archive but can now finally be opened for those who care to read them. The introduction addresses the readers with a familiar "tú," which includes them among those who might benefit from accessing the archives of Álex's clandestine organization. A letter written by Uno that is included among the records of the transcriber's sessions with Carla traces Uno's trajectory as a clandestine fighter against capitalist oppression. The letter makes it clear that Uno's encounters with Carla occur in 2018,[302] placing the transcriber's imaginary conversations with the woman some time shortly after that and suggesting that the opening of the archive is posterior to that date. *El comité de la noche* has the most complex timeline of all Gopegui's novels, which mirrors its greater audacity in what concerns the novel's ideological content and narrative strategies. For the readers who have been following Gopegui's work since the publication of her *La escala de los mapas* in 1993, the writer's willingness to explore different ways of writing might serve to emphasize the novel's message regarding the importance of seeking out alternative ways of being.[303]

At the core of the novel lies the protagonists' confidence in the possibility of political activism that will offer a viable alternative to the tyranny of liquid capital. This hope was lacking in the novels by Chirbes and García Montero but appears in Gopegui's *El comité de la noche*. In an article she wrote in 2005, Gopegui pointed out that the works of literature that do not question exploitation contribute to injustice.[304] The writer hopes that her work will penetrate the limits of individual alienation and contribute to the creation of a shared space where readers will consider the possibilities of departing from the capitalist status quo.[305] In what sounds like a direct response to the assertion of a character in García Montero's *No me cuentes tu vida* that nothing can be changed, or "eso es lo que hay" [this is all there is],[306] Gopegui's transcriber insists that this viewpoint helps to perpetuate injustice: "'Lo que hay' es la mayor ficción que se ha inventado. Lo que hay no existe sino que está siendo construido ahora mientras escribo." ['All there is' is the greatest lie ever invented. What there is does not exist but is being constructed as I write.][307]

Ten years before the publication of *El comité de la noche,* Biruté Ciplijauskaité observed that each of Gopegui's novels was inspired by a growing desire to "rebelarse contra el poder en cualquier nivel que sea" [rebel against power at any level].[308] A docile acquiescence to the assault of capital on the welfare state is alien to both the writer and the characters she creates, and this is more obvious than ever in her novel of the crisis. At the same time, the novel offers a space for the characters and the readers to come together in a shared labor of imagining radical departures from the status quo. As Lilley points out, this is precisely what is often missing from the current progressive discourse:

> The neoliberal period of the past three decades, with its all-encompassing ideology of self-advancement through the alchemy of the market, appears to have impeded severely the subversive imagination. . . . It is ironic that the most radical alternative to the current order that many leftists can envisage is a return to the Keynesian welfare state system.[309]

Gopegui's novel argues for the need to imagine scenarios of resistance that might be condemned as impractical or idealistic in regular political discourse. The belief, advanced by crisis essayists, that all one can hope to achieve is preserving a few welfare protections is too timid for Gopegui's characters. Instead, they are convinced that the crisis represents an opening for a radical questioning of the entire system of economic and social relations that has made this crisis inevitable.

CONCLUSION

The crisis has inspired some of Spain's leading writers to engage with the global transformations wrought by liquid capital. Since 2007, the year when Chirbes's *Crematorio* appeared in print, the genre of crisis novel has traveled from the utter confusion and hopelessness depicted in *Crematorio* and *En la orilla* to Gopegui's discussion of transformational activism that can arise from the crisis. In the seven years that passed between the publication dates of Chirbes's first crisis novel and *El comité de la noche,* Spain witnessed the birth of a mass protest movement that served as an inspiration to other resistance movements around the world. The alienation experienced by the characters created by Chirbes, García Montero, and Prado does not have to haunt those who are being marginalized by unemployment and existential insecurity. Amid "the explosion of collaborative practices developed by the 'experts in what happens to them' during the Spanish neoliberal crisis,"[310] there are opportunities to break through the isolating feelings of shame stemming from the belief that being rejected by the neoliberal system of economic relations is a result of one's own professional and personal insufficiency. Crisis novels are populated by characters who fail to reach out to others and discover that the troubles they experience cannot be addressed in isolation.

All the novels analyzed in this chapter talk about the displacement of a growing number of people from productive employment and the ways in which migratory currents directed both inside and outside of Spain impact the postwork reality of many Europeans. As an increasing number of professions are being automated out of existence, more people realize that a constant refashioning of one's professional self is the price one has to pay for maintaining a hope of finding work. The characters of crisis novels explore the changing definition of work and look for strategies of resisting the political forces that aim to channel the frustrations of joblessness and economic insecurity into an animosity toward migrants. The crisis novel genre posits the need to include immigrants in a conversation about the country's past and the ways in which the intensity of the current problems are an inevitable result of Spain's history. Chirbes's Esteban fails to connect with Ahmed and Liliana in any but the most superficial while García Montero's Montenegro never fully vanquishes the need to judge his immigrant daughter-in-law. It is only through the experience of having to cross national borders in search of work that the characters of Prado's and Gopegui's novels acquire insight into the relationship between migration and liquid capital.

The belief that the current situation is "una lamentable aberración que hay que solucionar por medio de la misma lógica que llevó a la crisis" [a lamentable aberration that has to be resolved through the same logic that caused the crisis][311] will inevitably preclude a search for radically new ways of constituting the political and the economic space. Crisis novels reject the approach adopted by the authors of the essays of the crisis and point to the need for the kind of solutions that do not recycle the old stereotypes of uniquely Spanish sloth and dishonesty that supposedly are to blame for the current situation. Crisis poetry, however, takes the discussion of the crisis even further and directly challenges the institutional narratives of Spain's place in the postnational global economy. While the essays by Muñoz Molina and Etxebarria are fully complicit with the ideology of the Culture of Transition, crisis novels begin to effectuate a departure from it and poetry of the crisis arrives at a radical break with the Transition-era mythology.

NOTES

1. Sanz Villanueva points out, for instance, that novels dedicated to the devastation wrought by ETA terrorism began to appear quite late, while no significant works of literature have yet been published about the 2004 Madrid train bombings inspired by al-Qaeda. Santos Sanz Villanueva, "Relatos del postfranquismo: un apunte y diez fichas," *El relato de la Transición / La Transición como relato*, eds. José Luis Calvo Carilla, Carmen Peña Ardid, et al. (Zaragoza: Prensas de la Universidad de Zaragoza, 2013), 29.

2. This is how the group introduces itself in the opening pages of the novel: "El Colectivo Todoazen es un grupo plural y multidisciplinar que centra su trabajo en el campo de las investigaciones narrativas. Han participado en la tarea de escribir este libro J.G. economista (que declara unos ingresos brutos anuales de 26.000 euros), I.E., sociólogo (que declara unos ingresos brutos anuales de 14.000 euros) y B.C., escritor (que declara unos ingresos brutos anuales de 9.500 euros)" [The Todoazen Collective is a pluralistic and multidisciplinary group whose work concentrates on the field of

narrative research. Those who participated in writing this book are the economist J.G. (who declares a gross annual income of 26,000 euros), the sociologist I.E. (who declares a gross annual income of 14,000 euros), and the writer B.C. (who declares a gross annual income of 9,500 euros).] Colectivo Todoazen, *El año que tampoco hicimos la revolución* (Barcelona: DeBolsillo, 2005, repr., 2007), 4. The novel's authors substitute their full names with the numbers denoting their annual income in a gesture that points to the reality where capital erases the value of individuality.

3. Colectivo Todoazen, *El año que tampoco hicimos la revolución*, 11.

4. Jordi Casanovas's stated goal in creating his play *Ruz/Bárcenas* (2014) was identical. Artists of different genres position the works of art they create as attempts to ground their audiences in islets of stability amidst torrents of information flows that make it next to impossible to observe the changes that are transforming our lives.

5. Luis Martín Cabrera, "Contra la suspensión de la mirada crítica: reflexiones sobre la persistencia del conflicto capital / trabajo en la cultura contemporánea española," *Arizona Journal of Hispanic Cultural Studies* 14 (2010): 125.

6. Luis Moreno-Caballud, *Cultures of Anyone: Studies on Cultural Democratization in the Spanish Neoliberal Crisis*, trans. Linda Grabner (Liverpool: Liverpool University Press, 2015), 55.

7. Luis Moreno-Caballud, "La imaginación sostenible: culturas y crisis económica en la España actual," *Hispanic Review* 80, no. 4 (Autumn 2012): 541.

8. José Belmonte Serrano and Celia Ruiz García, "*París-Austerlitz*: la escritura como salvación," *Monteagudo* 21 (2016): 357.

9. In his interview with Elena Hevia, Chirbes made a facetious reference to his popularity in Germany, saying that when Angela Merkel reads *En la orilla*, she will be moved to help Spain: "En esta novela damos mucha pena. Quizá por eso debería inundarnos de euros, más que nada para sanear el pantano." [This novel evokes a lot of pity. Maybe that's why she should drown us in euros, more than anything to clean up the marsh.] Elena Hevia, "España es un pantano que todo lo va pudriendo," *El Periódico de Catalunya*, March 20, 2013: 59.

10. See Jorge Herralde, "Rafael Chirbes: la voz de la verdad," *La constancia de un testigo. Ensayos sobre Rafael Chirbes*, ed. Augusta López Bernasocchi and José Manuel López de Abiada (Madrid: Verbum: 2011), 138–39; María-Teresa Ibáñez Ehrlich, *Ensayos sobre Rafael Chirbes* (Madrid: Iberoamericana, 2006), 7; Javier Rodríguez Marcos, "Material de derribo," *Babelia* 1, no. 110, March 2, 2015: 5.

11. Lorraine Ryan, " The Economic Degeneration of Masculinity in Rafael Chirbes's *En la orilla*," *Romance Quarterly* 62, no. 2 (2015): 84.

12. Matías Néspolo, "Vivimos en un callejón sin salida," *El Mundo*, March 20, 2013: 45.

13. Winston Manrique Sabogal, " Rafael Chirbes gana el Nacional de Narrativa por *En la orilla*," *El País*, October 7, 2014, http://cultura.elpais.com/cultura/2014/10/07/actualidad/1412667248_803360.html (accessed December 6, 2014).

14. Ibid., n.p.

15. José Luis Calvo Carilla, "Lecturas críticas sobre la Transición: el caso de Rafael Chirbes," *El relato de la Transición / La Transición como relato*, ed. José Luis Calvo Carilla, Carmen Peña Ardid, et al. (Zaragoza: Prensas de la Universidad de Zaragoza, 2013), 124.

16. Jean-François Carcelén, "En la orilla de Rafael Chirbes: paisaje después de la canalla," *Ínsula* 803 (November 2013): 11.

17. Rodríguez Marcos, "Material de derribo," 4.

18. "La Sexta ofrece el desenlace de *Crematorio* con la emisión de sus últimos dos capítulos," *FormulaTV*, February 19, 2012, www.formulatv.com/noticias/23672/lasexta-ofrece-desenlace-crematorio-emision-ultimos-dos-capitulos/2/ (accessed July 11, 2014).

19. In his interview with Borja Hermoso on the day before the first episode of the show aired, Chirbes expressed his reservations with the way the creators of the series rewrote his text, sensationalizing his message to attract viewers. Borja Hermoso, "Fue-

go real en el 'crematorio' de Chirbes," *El País*, March 7, 2011, http://elpais.com/diario/2011/03/07/cultura/1299452402_850215.html (accessed July 11, 2014).

20. The play is directed by Adolfo Fernández, who started working on *En la orilla* after finishing the production of Miguel Ángel Sánchez's *Ejecución hipotecaria.*

21. Prado Campos, "Chirbes sube al escenario," *El Confidencial*, November 23, 2014, www.elconfidencial.com/cultura/2014-11-23/chirbes-sube-al-escenario_483207 (accessed December 6, 2014).

22. Ignacio Sánchez-Cuenca, *La desfachatez intelectual: escritores e intelectuales ante la política* (Madrid: Catarata, 2016), 65.

23. Rafael Chirbes, *Por cuenta propia* (Barcelona: Anagrama, 2010), 18.

24. Calvo Carilla, "Lecturas críticas sobre la Transición: el caso de Rafael Chirbes," 124.

25. The writer died before being able to deliver his speech, and the award was accepted on his behalf by Chirbes's niece on June 1, 2016.

26. Rafael Chirbes, "Un parlamento que nunca pronuncié. Texto del discurso póstumo de Chirbes para la entrega del Premio Nacional de Narrativa," *Cuarto Poder*, June 1, 2016, www.cuartopoder.es/tribuna/2016/06/01/parlamento-no-pronuncie/8663 (accessed November 23, 2016).

27. Ibid., n.p.

28. Since then, Chirbes published *En la orilla*, a novel that offers an even more desperate vision of reality.

29. Augusta López Bernasocchi and José Manuel López de Abiada, "Hacia *Crematorio*, de Rafael Chirbes. Guía de lectura," *La constancia de un testigo. Ensayos sobre Rafael Chirbes*, ed. Augusta López Bernasocchi y José Manuel López de Abiada (Madrid: Verbum: 2011), 295.

30. Rafael Chirbes, *Crematorio* (Barcelona: Anagrama, 2007), 277.

31. In his interview with William J. Nichols, Chirbes explains the title of the novel as follows: "Nichols: ¿Y cree que hoy en día sigue el fantasma de la revolución? Chirbes: No. De hecho, la última novela se titula *Crematorio*. No quedan más que cenizas frías y nada más." [Nichols: And do you believe that the ghost of the revolution is present today? Chirbes: No. In fact, my last novel is titled *Crematorio*. All that is left is cold ash and nothing else.] William J. Nichols, "Sifting through the Ashes. An Interview with Rafael Chirbes," *Arizona Journal of Hispanic Cultural Studies* 12 (2008): 232.

32. Chirbes, *Crematorio*, 225–26.

33. López Bernasocchi and López de Abiada, "Hacia *Crematorio*, de Rafael Chirbes. Guía de lectura," 339.

34. Chirbes, *Crematorio*, 177.

35. It is still a matter of debate what exactly precipitated the collapse of the global financial markets in 2007–2008. At the same time, there is a widespread consensus that the belief in the power of the market to regulate itself championed by Friedman and his followers was at the root of the crisis. See Christian A. Conrad, *Morality and Economic Crisis: Enron, Subprime & Co.* (Hamburg: Disserta Verlag, 2010), 64–65; John Ryan, "The Greenspan and Bernanke Federal Reserve Roles in the Financial Crisis," *Lessons from the Financial Crisis: Causes, Consequences, and Our Economic Future*, ed. Robert W. Kolb (Hoboken, NJ: Wiley, 2010), 463; Alessandro Vercelli, "Economy and Economics: The Twin Crises," *The Global Economic Crisis: New Perspectives on the Critique of Economic Theory and Policy*, ed. Emiliano Brancaccio and Giuseppe Fontana (Oxon: Routledge, 201), 32–35.

36. For instance, Báez-Ramos states in her review of the novel that Silvia is Mónica's daughter, even though Mónica is not only twenty years Silvia's junior but also dedicates a significant portion of her narrative to detailing her grievances against her stepdaughter. See Josefa Báez-Ramos, "*Crematorio* by Rafael Chirbes," *Hispania* 91, no. 3 (September 2008): 627. Ayala-Dip, in his review of the novel, does not include Juan Mullor in the list of characters to whom Chirbes gives a voice of their own despite Mullor's being the only character aside from Rubén Bertomeu who speaks in the first

person. See J. Ernesto Ayala-Dip, "Retrato de los impostores. Reseña de *Crematorio* de Rafael Chirbes," *El Pa ís*, October 27, 2007, http://elpais.com/diario/2007/10/27/babelia/1193442618_850215.html (accessed July 19, 2014). Ródenas de Moya mistakes Yuri for Traian, a telling error that will be analyzed later in this chapter. See Domingo Ródenas de Moya, "El espejo hecho pedazos," *El Periódico*, July 24, 2014, www.anagrama-ed.es/view/10803/crematorio-ElPeriodico.pdf (accessed April 11, 2015). The same mistake appears in the review of the French translation of the novel published in *Le Monde*. See Xavier Houssin, "'Crémation,' de Rafael Chirbes: au plus court vers l'Apocalypse," *Le Monde*, April 9, 2009, www.anagrama-ed.es/view/10801/Crematorio -Le Monde.pdf (accessed July 24, 2014).

37. Carmen de Eusebio, "Rafael Chirbes: 'La tensión en el lenguaje debe entenderse como tensión en el proceso de aprendizaje al que se somete al lector,'" *Cuadernos hispanoamericanos* 757–58 (2013): 249.

38. Pierre Nora, "Between Memory and History: *Les Lieux de Mémoire*," *Representations* 26 (Spring 1989): 7.

39. Alfonso Fernández Carbajal, "La política de vivienda en España durante el franquismo," *Ciudad y Territorio. Estudios Territoriales* 35, no. 138 (2003): 652.

40. Louis E. Bueler, *The Tested Woman Plot: Women's Choices, Men's Judgments, and the Shaping of Stories* (Columbus: Ohio State University Press, 2001), 196.

41. Ibid., 196.

42. Chirbes, *Crematorio*, 22.

43. Antonio Sánchez Cazorla, *Fear and Progress: Ordinary Lives in Franco's Spain, 1939–1975* (Wiley-Blackwell: Chichester, 2009), 9.

44. Chirbes, *Crematorio*, 170.

45. Ibid., 67–68.

46. Ibid., 50.

47. Ibid., 409.

48. Ibid., 222.

49. Ibid., 400.

50. Ibid., 158.

51. Óscar Carreño, "El dorado descanso de los cambiadores de un mundo sin cambiar," *Quimera* 291 (2008): 70.

52. See, for instance, Fernando Valls's article "¡Sombras . . . , nada más! Primera lectura de *Los viejos amigos* y *Crematorio* de Rafael Chirbes," *La constancia de un testigo. Ensayos sobre Rafael Chirbes*, ed. Augusta López Bernasocchi and José Manuel López de Abiada. Madrid: Verbum: 2011), 482, where Yuri is omitted from the list of the novel's protagonists.

53. Chirbes, *Crematorio*, 160.

54. Ibid., 58.

55. Ibid., 58–59.

56. Ibid., 123.

57. Ibid., 59.

58. Ibid., 367.

59. Zygmunt Bauman, *Liquid Modernity* (Cambridge: Polity, 2000), 154.

60. Chirbes, *Crematorio*, 370.

61. An article in *El País* published in March 2013 sums up the damage done to the construction industry in Spain by the crisis, pointing out that immediately before the collapse 13 percent of all paid workers in Spain had been employed in construction. After the onset of the crisis, this number dropped to 6.3 percent. See Manuel V. Gómez and Cristina Galindo, "El ladrillo acelera su caída libre," *El País*, March 11, 2013, http://economia.elpais.com/economia/2013/03/10/actualidad/1362934741_926777.html (accessed October 11, 2014).

62. The creators of the TV show *Crematorio*, based on Chirbes's novel, are well aware of how central this idea of constant fluidity is to the novel. The memorable opening song of the series, "Cruzando el paraíso," [Traversing Paradise] by Loquillo (José María Sanz Beltrán) was edited to begin with the words "Nada permanece, todo

se desvanece" [Nothing remains, everything melts away] that belong to the second stanza of the song.

63. Chirbes, *Crematorio*, 271.
64. Ibid., 110.
65. Ibid., 50.
66. Ibid., 409.
67. In Chirbes's narrative universe, Mullor's last name carries negative associations. In the author's 1992 novel *La buena letra*, Raimundo Mullor of the Misent area is a Falangist who brutalizes the Republican soldiers after the war and comes to symbolize the shameless enrichment of the war's winners at the expense of those who lost the war.
68. Chirbes, *Crematorio*, 344.
69. Ibid., 368.
70. Ibid., 371.
71. Ibid., 370.
72. Ibid., 372.
73. Ibid., 372.
74. Ibid., 320.
75. Francis Fukuyama, *The End of History and the Last Man* (New York: The Free Press, 1992), xi.
76. Chirbes, *Crematorio*, 346.
77. Catherine Orsini-Saillet, "Ejemplaridad y ambigüedad en la obra novelesca de Rafael Chirbes," *La ejemplaridad en la narrativa española contemporánea (1950–2010)*, ed. Amélie Florenchie and Isabelle Touton (Madrid-Frankfurt am Main: Iberoamericana-Vervuert, 2011), 87.
78. William J. Nichols, "Sifting through the Ashes. An Interview with Rafael Chirbes," *Arizona Journal of Hispanic Cultural Studies* 12 (2008): 227.
79. Chirbes, *Crematorio*, 414.
80. Ibid., 415.
81. Daniel Leuenberger, "'Una imagen de mí mismo que no he querido romper': Perspectivas del pasado en *Los disparos del cazador*," *La constancia de un testigo: Ensayos sobre Rafael Chirbes*, ed. Augusta López Bernasocchi and José Manuel López de Abiada (Madrid: Verbum: 2011), 163.
82. Rodríguez Marcos, "Material de derribo," 4.
83. Chirbes is a lifelong admirer of Benito Pérez Galdós and creates, in his novels, a complex narrative universe that informs the entirety of his work. In one of his interviews, the writer pointed out that all his novels could be read as a single long one. See Nichols, "Sifting through the Ashes," 225. Analyzing *En la orilla* as part of a whole formed by Chirbes's entire novelistic output can enhance the understanding of the novel.
84. Rafael Chirbes, *En la orilla* (Barcelona: Anagrama, 2013), 19.
85. Ibid., 19.
86. Chirbes, *Crematorio*, 331.
87. Ibid., 337.
88. Radio España Independiente, known as "la Radio Pirenaica," was established in 1941 by the Communist Party of Spain in exile as the only remaining link between the exiled members of the party and their supporters who remained in Spain.
89. Chirbes, *En la orilla*, 161.
90. Ibid., 182–83.
91. Ibid., 229.
92. Ibid., 351.
93. Ibid., 350.
94. Ibid., 357.
95. Ibid., 161–65.
96. Ibid., 417–20.
97. Ibid., 400.

98. Luis García Montero, "Páginas en presente," *El País*, December 28, 2013, http://cultura.elpais.com/cultura/2013/12/19/actualidad/1387467794_395351.html (accessed February 14, 2015).
99. Chirbes, *En la orilla*, 108–109.
100. Bauman, *Liquid Modernity*, 164.
101. Zygmunt Bauman, *Liquid Love* (Cambridge: Polity, 2003), 69.
102. Chirbes, *En la orilla*, 396.
103. Ibid., 49.
104. Chirbes, *Por cuenta propia*, 16.
105. David Becerra Mayor, "*Episodios de una guerra interminable* de Almudena Grandes: ¿novelas de la memoria histórica?" *Kamchatka: revista de análisis cultural* 2 (December 2013): 243–44.
106. Antonio Cazorla-Sánchez, "From Anti-Fascism to Humanism: The Spanish Civil War as a Crisis of Memory," *Memory and Cultural History of the Spanish Civil War: Realms of Oblivion*, ed. Aurora G. Morcillo (Leiden/Boston: Brill, 2014), 45.
107. Jo Labanyi, "Memory and Modernity in Democratic Spain: The Difficulty of Coming to Terms with the Spanish Civil War," *Poetics Today* 28, no. 1 (Spring 2007): 92.
108. Chirbes, *Por cuenta propia*, 17.
109. This collection of essays was published when the writer was working on *En la orilla* and putting his artistic principles into practice in the novel.
110. Chirbes, *Por cuenta propia*, 18.
111. Blanca Berasátegui, "Rafael Chirbes, '*Crematorio* era el esplendor y *En la orilla* es la caída,'" *El Cultural*, March 1, 2013: 9.
112. Andreas Huyssen, *Present Pasts: Urban Palimpsests and the Politics of Memory* (Stanford: Stanford University Press, 2003),10.
113. Chirbes, *En la orilla*, 134.
114. Ibid., 49.
115. Ibid., 158.
116. Berasátegui, "Rafael Chirbes, '*Crematorio* era el esplendor y *En la orilla* es la caída,'" 9.
117. Javier García Recio, "Mirar sin adornos," *La Opinión de Málaga*, March 23, 2013: 46.
118. Chirbes, *En la orilla*, 96–97.
119. Ibid., 97.
120. Ibid., 98.
121. Ibid., 160.
122. Ángela Cenarro, "Beneficencia y asistencia social en la España franquista: el Auxilio Social y las políticas del régimen," *Pobreza, marginación, delincuencia y políticas sociales bajo el franquismo*, ed. Conxita Mir, Carme Agustí, and Josep Gelonch (Lleida: Edicions de la Universitat de Lleida, 2005), 94.
123. Ibid., 94.
124. Chirbes, *En la orilla*, 246.
125. Chirbes, *Crematorio*, 30.
126. Ibid., 37.
127. Ibid., 43.
128. Ahmed and Abdeljaq are, of course, fictional characters created by a Spanish author who is writing about the Moroccan immigrants in Spain as an outsider to their community. However, the existing divisions within the Muslim diaspora in Spain mirror those we see in Chirbes's novel. To give an example, anthropologist Mikaela Rogozen-Soltar observes in her 2012 study, "Managing Muslim Visibility: Conversion, Immigration, and Spanish Imaginaries of Islam," *American Anthropologist* 114, no. 4 (December 2012): 611–12, "Muslims in Granada consistently answered my questions about their relationships with non-Muslims by broaching the issue of differences within the Muslim community. . . . Muslims in Granada experience their efforts to represent Islam to wider Spanish publics as hinging on their ability to manage tensions within the city's diverse Muslim population."

129. Chirbes, *En la orilla*, 15.
130. Ibid., 17.
131. Juan Carlos Checa Olmos and Ángeles Arjona Garrido, "Anti-Immigrant Feeling in Spain," *Polish Sociological Review* 177 (2012): 48.
132. Chirbes, *En la orilla*, 18.
133. Ibid., 398–99.
134. Ibid., 11.
135. Javier Rodríguez Marcos observes on page 3 of "Material de derribo," *Babelia* 1, no. 110 (March 2, 2015) that the word "carroña" [carrion] offers yet another link between *Crematorio* and *En la orilla* since it appears in the last sentence of *Crematorio* and in the first sentence of *En la orilla*.
136. Chirbes, *En la orilla*, 429.
137. Moisés Mori, "De estatura humana. Voces de un realismo radical," Página Abierta 226 (May–June 2013): 58.
138. Antonio José Domínguez, "Entrevista al autor de la novela *En la orilla*," *Mundo Obrero*, June 21, 2013, www.mundoobrero.es/pl.php?id=2860 (accessed July 10, 2014).
139. In a 2013 article, published one month before his review of Chirbes's novel, Ezkerra attributed some responsibility for the crisis to the political forces that actively promoted the recovery of Spain's historical memory. See Iñaki Ezkerra, "¡Maldita sea!" *ABC*, Diario ABC, S.L., 17. In this, Ezkerra echoes the ideas expressed in his crisis essay by Muñoz Molina.
140. Iñaki Ezkerra, "Rafael Chirbes o después del ladrillo," *El Correo* (Bilbao, España), March 23, 2013: 7.
141. Javier Aniorte, "Rafael Chirbes, traducción y reconocimiento en Alemania: Los paisajes del alma," *Las letras valencianas en la literatura universal. Problemas de recepción y traducción: el paisaje y el tiempo*, ed. Juan Antonio Albaladejo Martínez (Sevilla: Bienza, 2012), 149–56.
142. Chirbes, *Crematorio*, 417.
143. In 2013, García Montero published a review of *En la orilla* that recognizes the artistic merits of the novel while questioning what the writer perceives as Chirbes's nihilism. See García Montero, "Páginas en presente," n.p.
144. Before the publication of this novel, García Montero experimented with writing prose, which culminated in his *Luna del Sur* (1992), which brought together a collection of musings in prose and three of the writer's poems, and *Impares, fila 13*, a novel written together with Felipe Benítez Reyes in 1996.
145. Luis García Martín, "*La intimidad de la serpiente*," *El Cultural*, February 27, 2003, El Cultural Electrónico, www.elcultural.com/revista/letras/La-intimidad-de-la-serpiente/6510 (accessed August 6, 2015).
146. Luis Bagué Quílez, "A Journey through the Desert: Trends of Commitment in Contemporary Spanish Poetry," *Post-Authoritarian Cultures: Spain and Latin America's Southern Cone*, ed. Luis Martín-Estudillo and Roberto Ampuero (Nashville: Vanderbilt University Press, 2008), 60.
147. María Escobedo, "Luis García Montero: 'La necesidad de cuidar y ser cuidado es el mejor antídoto contra la cultura del usar y tirar,'" *Cuadernos hispanoamericanos* 743 (May 2012): 124.
148. Luis García Montero, *No me cuentes tu vida* (Barcelona: Planeta, 2012), 82.
149. Stanley Aronowitz, Dawn Esposito, William DiFazio, and Margaret Yard, "The Post-Work Manifesto," *Post-Work*, ed. Stanley Aronowitz and Jonathan Cutler (New York: Routledge, 1998), 71.
150. Ibid.
151. García Montero, *No me cuentes tu vida*, 251–52.
152. Ibid., 58.
153. Ibid., 59.
154. Ibid., 190.
155. Ibid., 270.

156. Escobedo, "Luis García Montero: 'La necesidad de cuidar y ser cuidado es el mejor antídoto contra la cultura del usar y tirar,'" 128.

157. Pedro Alonso is the name that, in the novel, García Montero gives to his favorite poet, Rafael Alberti. García Montero wrote his doctoral dissertation about Alberti's poetry and later taught a course titled "The Living Words of Rafael Alberti" at the International University of Andalucía. See Ginés Donaire, "García Montero analiza la influencia del exilio como 'condición vital' en la obra de Alberti," *El País*, September 12, 2000, http://elpais.com/diario/2000/09/12/andalucia/968710942_850215.html (accessed September 23, 2015).

158. García Montero, *No me cuentes tu vida*, 165.

159. Bauman, *Liquid Modernity*, 4.

160. García Montero, *No me cuentes tu vida*, 280.

161. Nadia C. Seremetakis, "The Memory of the Senses, Part I: Marks of the Transitory," *The Senses Still: Perception and Memory as Material Culture in Modernity*, ed. Nadia C. Seremetakis (Chicago and London: University of Chicago Press, 1996), 8.

162. García Montero, *No me cuentes tu vida*, 136.

163. Ibid., 47–48.

164. Ibid., 390.

165. Ibid., 160–61.

166. Ibid., 161.

167. In the words of Paul Preston, the Moncloa agreements were "the culmination of the policies of moderation and self-sacrifice pursued by both the Socialists and Communists throughout the transition period." See Preston's *The Triumph of Democracy in Spain* (London: Methuen, 1986), 102. These ideological sacrifices had a profoundly negative impact on the working classes' capacity to withstand the global economic crisis of the late 1970s. Ibid., 102.

168. Omar G. Encarnación, "Labor and Pacted Democracy: Post-Franco Spain in Comparative Perspective," *Comparative Politics* 33, no. 2 (April 2001): 345.

169. Carmen Urioste, "The Hispanic and Luso-Brazilian World: La cultura española en el marco europeo: Entre lo global y lo local," *Hispania* 89, no. 3 (September 2006): 645–46.

170. García Montero, *No me cuentes tu vida*, 160.

171. Unlike his protagonist with whom he shares many biographical details, García Montero has not abandoned political activism. The poet was a member of the Communist Party of Spain between 1976 and 1986, the year when he joined Izquierda Unida. In the summer of 2015, the poet made a failed attempt to get elected as a representative for Madrid. According to the poet, political activism is his way of resisting the growing fluidity of all societal structures. See Juan Cruz, "Garzón ha hundido IU de Madrid por estrategia," *El País*, June 1, 2015. http://ccaa.elpais.com/ccaa/2015/05/30/madrid/1433009380_693704.html (accessed September 2, 2015).

172. García Montero, *No me cuentes tu vida*, 121.

173. Walther L. Bernecker, "El debate sobre las memorias históricas en la vida política española," *Escribir después de la dictadura: La producción literaria y cultural en las posdictaduras de Europa e Hispanoamérica*, ed. Janett Reinstädler (Madrid/Frankfurt am Main: Iberoamericana/Vervuert, 2011), 76.

174. Urioste, "The Hispanic and Luso-Brazilian World: La cultura española en el marco europeo: Entre lo global y lo local," 643.

175. García Montero, *No me cuentes tu vida*, 44.

176. The reversal of the direction of the migratory flow from an outward to an inward one has accompanied the transition from dictatorship to democracy: "It has become a topic to say that Spain has only recently turned from a country of emigration to one of immigration. The fact is that it is only in the 1990s that the net migratory balance for the Spanish population begins to show negative signs (i.e. there are more returnees than immigrants). The decade of the 1960s experienced the largest outward flows when 2.5% of the Spanish population emigrated to foreign lands. The rate decreased to 1.3% in the 70s, reaching a low of 0.5% in the 80s." See Rosa Aparicio and

Andrés Tornos, "Towards an Analysis of Spanish Integration Policy," *The Integration of Immigrants in European Societies: National Differences and Trends of Convergence*, ed. Friedrich Heckmann and Dominique Schnapper (Stuttgart: Lucius & Lucius, 2003), 213 The years of Spain's economic boom saw the number of migrants into Spain rising by 318 percent in the first decade of the twenty-first century. See Francisco Checa Olmos et al., "Immigration and Political Discourse in Spain: The Example of Party Platforms," *Discourses on Immigration in Times of Economic Crisis: A Critical Perspective*, ed. María Martínez Lirola (Newcastle upon Tyne: Cambridge Scholars 2013), 167. Because of the economic crisis, many Spaniards have left the country in search of employment, recreating the emigration patterns of the 1960s and early 1970s. See Nicolás Lorite García, "How the Media Affect Intercultural Relationships in Times of Change," *Discourses on Immigration in Times of Economic Crisis: A Critical Perspective*, ed. María Martínez Lirola (Newcastle upon Tyne: Cambridge Scholars, 2013), 216.

177. García Montero, *No me cuentes tu vida*, 29.

178. In 2012, the year when the novel was published, Romanians represented, on a par with Moroccans, one of the two largest immigrant groups in Spain. See Cristina E. Bradatan and Dumitru Sandu, "Before Crisis: Gender and Economic Outcomes of the Two Largest Immigrant Communities in Spain," *International Migration Review* 46, no. 1 (Spring 2012): 224.

179. García Montero, *No me cuentes tu vida*, 169.

180. Bauman, *Liquid Modernity*, 153.

181. Ibid., 166.

182. García Montero, *No me cuentes tu vida*, 259.

183. Ibid., 419.

184. Palmar Álvarez-Blanco, "De etnomanías y otros terrores. Literatura e inmigración en la España del siglo XXI," *Contornos de la narrativa española actual (2000–2010). Un diálogo entre creadores y críticos*, ed. Palmar Álvarez-Blanco and Toni Dorca (Madrid/Frankfurt am Main: Iberoamericana/Vervuert, 2011), 56.

185. Kitty Calavita, "Immigration, Law, and Marginalization in a Global Economy: Notes from Spain," *Law & Society Review* 32, no. 3 (1998): 538.

186. García Montero, *No me cuentes tu vida*, 456.

187. At the height of the crisis, European media started turning their attention to the existence of this slum on the outskirts of Madrid. UK's *The Independent*, for instance, reported in 2011: "Cañada Real Galiana is a 16km-long, 75m-wide strip of economic and social misery. Believed to be Europe's largest shanty town, it is a mere 15-minute drive from Madrid city centre. 'This place reminds me of one of the most run-down slums in Guatemala I used to work in,' says Susana Camacho, who works for Fundación Secretariado Gitano (FSG), a local NGO." Alasdair Fotheringham, "In Spain's heart, a slum to shame Europe. The continent's largest shanty town – just a 15-minute drive from the affluent centre of Madrid," *The Independent*, Independent Print Ltd., November 27, 2011, www.independent.co.uk/news/world/europe/in-spains-heart-a-slum-to-shame-europe-6268652.html (accessed October 1, 2015).

188. José Marcos and Bruno G. Gallo, "La Cañada Real ya tiene su plan," *El País: Madrid*, January 13, 2014, http://ccaa.elpais.com/ccaa/2014/01/13/madrid/1389644669_801094.html(accessed February 27, 2014).

189. García Montero, *No me cuentes tu vida*, 393.

190. Paloma Aguilar Fernández, "Los debates sobre la memoria histórica," *Claves de Razón Práctica* 172 (2007): 64–65.

191. Anthony P. Cohen, *The Symbolic Construction of Community* (London: Tavistock Publications, 1985), 16.

192. García Montero, *No me cuentes tu vida*, 393.

193. Bauman, *Liquid Love*, 142.

194. Giorgio Agamben, *Homo Sacer: Sovereign Power and Bare Life*, trans. Daniel Heller-Roazen (1995; repr. Stanford: Stanford University Press, 1998), 20.

195. Garcia Montero, *No me cuentes tu vida*, 393.

196. Enrique Dussel, "Beyond Eurocentrism: The World-System and the Limits of Modernity," trans. Eduardo Mendieta, *The Cultures of Globalization*, ed. Fredric Jameson and Masao Miyoshi (Durham and London: Duke University Press, 1998), 20.
197. Julia Kristeva, *Powers of Horror: An Essay on Abjection*, trans. Leon S. Roudiez (New York: Columbia University Press, 1982), 4.
198. Garcia Montero, *No me cuentes tu vida*, 397.
199. Isabel Álvarez, "Immigration and the Written Press: What Is It Actually Being Portrayed?" *The International Journal of Diversity in Organisations, Communities and Nations* 7, no. 5 (2007): 128.
200. Christian Joppke, "Immigration Challenges the Nation-State," *Challenge to the Nation-State: Immigration in Western Europe and the United States*, ed. Christian Joppke (Oxford: Oxford University Press, 1998), 6.
201. Aguilar Fernández, "Los debates sobre la memoria histórica," 65.
202. Helen Graham, *La guerra y su sombra: Una visión de la tragedia española en el largo siglo XX europeo*, trans. Sandra Souto Kustrin (Barcelona: Crítica, 2013), 265.
203. The poem appears in Prado's collection *No me cuentes tu vida (Antología, 1986–2011)* that was published in 2011.
204. García Montero, *No me cuentes tu vida*, 7.
205. Eva Navarro Martínez, "La novela de Benjamín Prado: Cómo construirse un mundo y una realidad propios," *Letras peninsulares* 14, no. 3 (Winter 2001–2002): 405.
206. Paul D. Begin, "The Pistols Strike Again! On the Function of Punk in the Peninsular 'Generation X' Fiction of Ray Loriga and Benjamín Prado," *Generation X Rocks: Contemporary Peninsular Fiction, Film, and Rock Culture*, ed. Christine Henseler and Randolph D. Pope (Nashville: Vanderbilt University Press, 2007), 16.
207. Manuel Vázquez Montalbán, *Un polaco en la corte del Rey Juan Carlos* (Madrid: Alfaguara, 1996), 382.
208. José F. Colmeiro, *Memoria histórica e identidad cultural: De la postguerra a la postmodernidad* (Barcelona: Anthropos, 2005), 232.
209. Cintia Santana, "What We Talk About When We Talk About Dirty Realism in Spain," *Generation X Rocks: Contemporary Peninsular Fiction, Film, and Rock Culture*, ed. Christine Henseler and Randolph D. Pope (Nashville: Vanderbilt University Press, 2007), 34.
210. Begin, "The Pistols Strike Again!" 30, note 5.
211. *Mala gente* relies on a variety of documentary sources. Some of the most important among them are *Los niños perdidos del franquismo* [*The Lost Children of Francoism*] by Ricard Vinyes, Montse Armengou, and Ricard Belis (Barcelona: Plaza & Janes, 2002), *Testimonios de mujeres en las cárceles franquistas* [*Testimony of Women in Francoist Jails*] by Tomasa Cuevas (Huesca: Instituto de Estudios Altoaragoneses, 2004), and *Desde la noche y la niebla: las* mujeres en las cárceles franquistas [From the Night and the Fog: Women in Francoist Jails] by Juana Doña (Madrid: Ediciones de la Torre, 1977) .
212. Prado never shied away from recognizing the impact that financial considerations have had on the way he organizes his career as a writer. In an interview granted to Stacey Dolgin Casado, for instance, the writer shared that his first novel was written because of an offer he received from an editor to pay him a significant amount of money to explore a genre that was new to him. See Stacey Dolgin Casado, "Benjamín Prado: La literatura es lo contrario del olvido," *Ojáncano* 33 (April 2008): 107–108.
213. Begin, "The Pistols Strike Again!" 27.
214. Anna De Fina, *Identity in Narrative: A Study of Immigrant Discourse* (Amsterdam and Philadelphia: John Benjamins, 2003), 19.
215. Benjamín Prado, *Mala gente que camina* (Madrid: Santillana, 2006), 314.
216. Benjamín Prado, *Ajuste de cuentas* (Madrid: Alfaguara, 2013), 96.
217. Ibid., 11.
218. Ulrich Beck, *Risk Society: Towards a New Modernity*, trans. Mark Ritter (London: Sage, 1992), 137.
219. Prado, *Ajuste de cuentas*, 113.
220. Ibid., 15.

221. Ibid., 82.
222. Bauman, *Liquid Modernity*, 82.
223. Prado, *Ajuste de cuentas*, 33.
224. Zygmunt Bauman, *Consuming Life* (Cambridge: Polity, 2007), 12.
225. Prado, *Ajuste de cuentas*, 185.
226. Ibid., 83.
227. Walther L. Bernecker, "España y la unión europea: una relación cambiante," *España: del consenso a la polarización. Cambios en la democracia española*, ed. Walther L. Bernecker and Günther Maihold (Madrid/Frankfurt am Main: Iberoamericana/Vervuert, 2007), 66.
228. Isidro López and Emmanuel Rodríguez, *Fin de ciclo. Financiarización, territorio y sociedad de propietarios en la onda larga del capitalismo hispano (1959–2010)* (Madrid: Traficantes de Sueños, 2010), 20.
229. Prado, *Ajuste de cuentas*, 167.
230. Anselmo Flores Andrade, "Los empresarios y la transición a la democracia en España," *Estudios Sociológicos* 18, no. 54 (2000): 716.
231. Ibid., 718–19.
232. Óscar J. Martín García, "A Country on a Tightrope: The Economic Crisis and the End of an Era in Spanish Politics," *Insight Turkey* 15, no. 3 (Summer 2013): 95.
233. Urioste, "The Hispanic and Luso-Brazilian World: La cultura española en el marco europeo: Entre lo global y lo local," 645–46.
234. Prado, *Mala gente que camina*, 254.
235. Prado, *Ajuste de cuentas*, 117.
236. Ibid., 117.
237. Juan Goytisolo, "Hemos vivido un sueño," *El País*, July 22, 2012, http://elpais.com/elpais/2012/07/19/opinion/1342710838_352755.html (accessed October 22, 2015).
238. Prado, *Ajuste de cuentas*, 53.
239. El Servicio Nacional de Regiones Devastadas [The National Service of Devastated Regions] was created in 1938 and renamed Dirección General de Regiones Devastadas y Reparaciones [The General Direction of Devastated Regions and Reparations]. Las Rozas, the suburb of Madrid where Urbano's mother lives, was one of the areas that was "adopted" by Franco with the goal of creating affordable housing for those who had been left homeless by the war. See Pedro Montoliú, *Madrid en la posguerra, 1939–1946: los años de la represión* (Madrid: Silex, 2005), 101–102.
240. Prado, *Ajuste de cuentas*, 97–99.
241. Ibid., 55.
242. Seremetakis, "The Memory of the Senses, Part I: Marks of the Transitory," 3.
243. Prado, *Ajuste de cuentas*, 53–55, 96–99.
244. Ibid., 142.
245. Bernecker, "El debate," 77.
246. Stephanie R. Golob, "Volver: The Return of/to Transitional Justice Politics in Spain," *Journal of Spanish Cultural Studies* 9, no. 2 (July 2008): 127.
247. For instance, Carlos Martínez García, president of ATTAC España (Association for Taxation of Financial Transactions and Citizen Activism), published an article in July 2011 titled "The Republic Is Not Only History but Also the Future," arguing that the 15-M protests were inspired by the same ideas that served as a foundation of the transformational agenda of the Second Republic. See Carlos Martínez García, "La República no solo es historia, es futuro," *ATTAC España*, July 22, 2011, www.attac.es/2011/07/22/la-republica-no-solo-es-historia-es-futuro/ (accessed November 27, 2016).
248. Prado, *Ajuste de cuentas*, 200.
249. Ibid., 274.
250. Ibid., 274–75.
251. Ibid., 186.
252. Graham, *La guerra*, 49.
253. Manolo Monereo, member of United Left, makes it clear in his book *De la crisis a la revolución democrática* [*From the Crisis to a Democratic Revolution*] that the vision of the

crisis as a *coup d'état* conducted through economic, instead of military, means does not solely belong to Prado's carácter. See Manolo Monereo, *De la crisis a la revolución democrática* (Madrid: El Viejo Topo, 2013), 143. The same idea was expressed by Rafael Chirbes in an interview granted to López de Abiada: "Algunos definen la nueva situación como un golpe de estado desde las finanzas: están imponiendo un estado de excepción que lleva visos de convertirse en norma si la gente no planta cara." [The new situation has been defined as a financial *coup d'état*: a state of exception is being imposed, and it looks like it will become the norm if people don't face it.] José Manuel López de Abiada, "Entrevista a Rafael Chirbes," *La constancia de un testigo. Ensayos sobre Rafael Chirbes*, ed. Augusta López Bernasocchi and José Manuel López de Abiada (Madrid: Verbum: 2011), 17.

254. Prado, *Ajuste de cuentas*, 140–41.

255. Graham, *La guerra*, 216–17.

256. Prado, *Ajuste de cuentas*, 140.

257. Ibid., 140.

258. Richard Sennett, *The Culture of the New Capitalism* (New Haven & London: Yale University Press, 2006), 90.

259. Prado, *Ajuste de cuentas*, 274.

260. Ibid., 274.

261. Ibid., 275.

262. Santiago Velázquez, "Benjamín Prado, un ajuste de cuentas," *Huffington Post.es*, October 24, 2013, www.huffingtonpost.es/santiago-velazquez/benjamin-prado-un-ajuste-_b_4129537.html (accessed January 21, 2014).

263. Ibid., n.p.

264. Song, for instance, includes Gopegui among the literary Generation X, while Henseler believes that Gopegui is out of place, stylistically and ideologically, among this group of writers. See H. Rosi Song, "Anti-conformist Fiction: The Spanish 'Generation X,'" in *A Companion to the Twentieth-Century Spanish Novel*, ed. Marta E. Altisent (Woodbridge and Rochester, NY: Tamesis, 2008, p. 197; and Christine Henseler, *Spanish Fiction in the Digital Age: Generation X Remixed* (New York: Palgrave Macmillan, 2011), p. 6. Odartey-Wellington points out that even though Gopegui has distanced herself from the work of such Generation X novelists as Ray Loriga and José Ángel Mañas, the writer's novels "reflect the same generational ontological concerns" as these authors' work. Dorothy Odartey-Wellington, *Contemporary Spanish Fiction: Generation X* (Newark: University of Delaware Press, 2008), p. 71.

265. "A number of porcupines huddled together for warmth on a cold day in winter; but, as they began to prick one another with their quills, they were obliged to disperse. However the cold drove them together again, when just the same thing happened. At last, after many turns of huddling and dispersing, they discovered that they would be best off by remaining at a little distance from one another. In the same way the need of society drives the human porcupines together, only to be mutually repelled by the many prickly and disagreeable qualities of their nature. . . . By this arrangement the mutual need of warmth is only very moderately satisfied; but then people do not get pricked." Arthur Schopenhauer, *Parerga and Paralipomena: Short Philosophical Essays*, Vol. 2, trans. E. F. J. Payne (Oxford: Clarendon Press, 1974), p. 651.

266. Belén Gopegui, *El comité de la noche* (Barcelona: Penguin Random House, 2014), 11.

267. Hayley Rabanal, *Belén Gopegui: The Pursuit of Solidarity in Post-Transition Spain* (Woodbridge, NY: Tamesis, 2011), 10–11.

268. Martín Cabrera, "Contra la suspensión de la mirada crítica: reflexiones sobre la persistencia del conflicto capital / trabajo en la cultura contemporánea española," 119.

269. Gopegui, *El comité de la noche*, 247.

270. Carlos Zanón, "Sangre joven, vampiros nuevos," *El País*, November 20, 2014, http://cultura.elpais.com/cultura/2014/11/13/babelia/1415875244_683644.html (accessed October 22, 2015).

271. Janet Pérez, "Tradition, Renovation, Innovation: The Novels of Belén Gopegui," *Anales de la literatura española contemporánea* 28, no. 1 (2003): 117.

272. Quoted in Biruté Ciplijauskaité, "Belén Gopegui entre la búsqueda y la denuncia de la realidad," in *La pluralidad narrativa. Escritores españoles contemporáneos (1984–2004)*, ed. Ángeles Encinar and Kathleen M. Glenn (Madrid: Biblioteca Nueva, 2005), 122.

273. Álex, for instance, begins her narrative with questioning the patriarchal linguistic norm that requires a mother and a father to be referred to with the masculine "los padres" and chooses, instead, to use the words "mis madres" to refer to her parents (28–29). Carla takes upon herself the role of the protector of little Elenka, the sister of her boyfriend, Michal, which leaves Michal to observe her struggle passively.

274. Gopegui, *El comité de la noche*, 24.

275. Ibid., 51.

276. Ibid., 33.

277. Rabanal, *Belén Gopegui*, 6–7.

278. Luis I. Prádanos, "Writing an Engaged Novel in the Network Society: Belén Gopegui, Systemic Narratives and Globalization," in *Global Issues in Contemporary Hispanic Women's Writing: Shaping Gender, the Environment, and Politics*, ed. Estrella Cibreiro and Francisca López (New York and London: Routledge, 2013), 209–10.

279. Gopegui, *El comité de la noche*, 40.

280. Pablo Muñoz, "Acerca del *Comité de la noche* de Belén Gopegui," *Diagonal* Diagonalperiódico.net, August 9, 2015, www.diagonalperiodico.net/culturas/27464-acerca-del-comite-la-noche-belen-gopegui.html (accessed October 22, 2015).

281. Karl Marx and Friedrich Engels, *The Communist Manifesto*, ed. D. Ryazanoff (1848; repr., New York: Russell & Russell, 1963), 25.

282. Gopegui, *El comité de la noche*, 78.

283. Prádanos points out that Gopegui's novelistic output demonstrates the writer's awareness of the work of Slavoj Žižek, Terry Eagleton, Richard Sennett, Ulrich Beck, Gilles Lipovetsky, and Vicente Verdú. See Prádanos, "Writing an Engaged Novel in the Network Society," 210. The attention given in *El comité de la noche* to the concept of fluidity makes it clear that Zygmunt Bauman can be added to the list.

284. Gopegui, *El comité de la noche*, 74.

285. Ibid., 114.

286. Ibid., 156.

287. Ibid., 9; see also, "Grifols apuesta por pagar las donaciones de plasma como complemento de ingresos para los parados," *Europa Press*, April 17, 2012.

288. Gopegui, *El comité de la noche*, 56.

289. The text of the article can be found online, and the full version of the sentence that makes a deep impression on Álex is as follows: "De volverse a aprobar en España la venta de plasma, Grifols pagaría por las donaciones unos 70 euros semanales, lo que sumado a la prestación de paro es 'una forma de vivir'" [If selling plasma becomes legal again in Spain, Grifols would pay 70 euro per week for donations, which, coupled with unemployment benefits, is 'a way to live'] ("Grifols apuesta," n.p.).

290. Gopegui, *El comité de la noche*, 219.

291. Ibid., 254.

292. Ibid., 74.

293. Ibid., 127.

294. Beck, *Risk Society*, 96.

295. Gopegui, *El comité de la noche*, 255.

296. Ibid., 257.

297. Belén Gopegui, "Tres condiciones necesarias, aunque no suficientes, para una literatura de izquierdas," in *Contornos de la narrativa española actual (2000–2010). Un diálogo entre creadores y críticos*, ed. Palmar Álvarez-Blanco and Toni Dorca (Madrid, Frankfurt am Main: Iberoamericana/Vervuert, 2011), 283.

298. Antonio Gómez López-Quiñones, "La misma guerra para un nuevo siglo: Textos y contextos de la novela sobre la Guerra Civil," in *Contornos de la narrativa española*

actual (2000–2010): Un diálogo entre creadores y críticos, ed. Palmar Álvarez-Blanco and Toni Dorca (Madrid and Frankfurt: Iberoamericana-Vervuert, 2011), 115.

299. Quoted in Manuel Castells, *The Power of Identity. The Information Age: Economy, Society, and Culture*, Vol. II (Oxford: Blackwell, 1998), 309.

300. Pérez, "Tradition, Renovation, Innovation," 128.

301. Ibid., 128.

302. Gopegui, *El comité de la noche*, 226.

303. Gopegui's first novel *La escala de los mapas* enjoyed great success and propelled the writer toward the ranks of Spain's most promising young writers. In the three years after its publication, the novel went through five editions and received praise from writers and critics, including Carmen Martín Gaite and Rafael Conte. See Pérez, "Tradition, Renovation, Innovation," 137, note 1.

304. Belén Gopegui, "Literatura y política bajo el capitalismo," *Guaraguao*. Asociación Centro de Estudio y Cooperación para América Latina. 9, no. 21 (Winter 2005): 12.

305. Ibid., 16.

306. García Montero, *No me cuentes tu vida*, 82.

307. Gopegui, *El comité de la noche*, 137.

308. Ciplijauskaité, "Belén Gopegui entre la búsqueda y la denuncia de la realidad," 121.

309. Sasha Lilley, "Introduction," in *Capital and Its Discontents: Conversations with Radical Thinkers in a Time of Tumult* (Oakland, CA: PM Press, 2011) 17.

310. Moreno-Caballud, *Cultures*, 284.

311. Luisa Elena Delgado, *La nación singular: fantasías de la normalidad democrática española (1996–2011)* (Madrid, España: Siglo XXI de España, 2014), 44.

THREE

Poetry

In Search of Solidarity

The electoral victory of the Partido Popular in 2000 contributed to creating the kind of political polarization in Spain that inspired many of the country's poets to return to political commitment in their artistic endeavors.[1] The crisis of 2008 deepened the interest on the part of Spanish poets in contributing to a discussion of Spain's political and economic structures. Poetry can be very effective in the production of structures of meaning that in Manuel Castells's words, are central to engaging in political resistance: "Few institutional systems can last long if they are based just on coercion. Torturing bodies is less effective than shaping minds. . . . This is why the fundamental power struggle is the battle for the construction of meaning in the minds of the people."[2] Poets of the crisis look for new ways of framing the crisis that will integrate the voices of the protesters and the collective movements of the crisis era. They believe that poetry cannot be allowed to become a luxury product that will be subjected to austerity measures in the service of the needs of fluid capital. In this chapter, I analyze two poetic anthologies, *En legítima defensa. Poetas en tiempos de crisis* [*In Self-Defense. Poets in Times of Crisis*] (2014) with an introduction by Antonio Gamoneda and *Marca(da) España. Retrato poético de una sociedad en crisis* [*Branding Spain. A Poetic Depiction of Society in Crisis.*] (2014) with a prologue by Santiago Alba Rico. These collections of poetry rely on different organizing principles, yet both advocate for poets' political engagement in response to the crisis and point to the importance of subverting hierarchies and overcoming the atomization that characterizes the neoliberal order.

The neoliberal economic philosophy "requires workers to identify the subjectivity of labor with the subjectivity of capital, to make belonging to the company the only subjectivity possible."[3] Authors of crisis poetry attempt to bare the mechanisms at play in this appropriation of subjectivity for the purposes of capitalist accumulation. Neoliberal societies are atomized by competitiveness and hierarchies that pit workers against each other, destroying links of solidarity among the exploited and making it easier for liquid capital to sweep away the remaining protections of the battered welfare state: "Alienation tends to invade all spheres of life under neoliberalism [contributing to] a process of isolation and estrangement among workers that renders impossible the construction of a working class front in opposition to capital."[4] Poetry of the crisis points to the atomization of neoliberal societies as a crucial issue that has been highlighted by the economic collapse. To overcome this alienation, the poetic volumes *En legítima defensa* and *Marca(da) España* reject the competitive hierarchies of professional achievement and put side by side poetry by the authors who have been recognized by the cultural establishment and those who are lacking such recognition. These collections of poetry belong to what Moreno-Caballud terms "cultures of anyone" that have arisen in response to the crisis and that possess an "ability not only to suggest answers to specific political and social problems, but also to question the authoritarian, competitive cultural lenses that condition our way of understanding those very problems, and to replace them with other, more democratic filters."[5]

Like the authors of novels and essays analyzed earlier, Spanish poets often turn to the Civil War to discuss both the roots and the emotional impact of the crisis. They reject the idea that historical memory is an unaffordable luxury in times of crisis and are dedicated to tracing the genealogy of the structures of exploitation inherited from the Franco dictatorship. Poets of the crisis believe that traces of the dictatorship can still be felt in the attempts to silence the protesters and trivialize the impact of their activism. These artists are skeptical of the Transition and believe that the current crisis offers an opportunity to challenge a monolithic vision of the Transition era as a time of great achievement that is not to be questioned. Poetry is unlikely to bring great profits to publishers and authors and, as a result, poets can enjoy, in their artistic labor, a degree of critical distance from the demands of capital. Many, if not most, of the contributors to these collections of poetry have to rely on other sources of income and have seen their capacity to make a living curtailed by the economic collapse. Several of these artists have been forced to leave Spain in search of work opportunities elsewhere. Their experience of the crisis is, thus, more personal than that of affluent best-selling novelists like Muñoz Molina. Poets of the crisis ally themselves with the 15-M movement and give voice to the rage felt by many as liquid capital sweeps away the remaining illusions as to the capacity of Spain's institutions to provide a line of defense against the depredation of global finance.

One of the strengths of these anthologies resides in bringing together the voices of the representatives of different generations, each of which offers its own poetic vision of the crisis. The anthologies experiment with fluidity not only through the inclusion of poets belonging to different generations but also by refusing to limit the contribution to the volumes based on the artists' countries of origins and residence. Permanent and temporary migration does not exclude the contributing poets from adding their voices to the discussion of Spain's predicament. To the contrary, their immigrant experience helps create a more nuanced vision of the crisis. *Marca(da) España*, the second of the anthologies analyzed here, also explores the fluid nature of the genres of artistic expressions. The poetic collection brings together photography and poetry, underscoring the erosion of boundaries that characterizes our times and posing the possibility of harnessing some of the aspects of fluidity to the goals of political resistance. The photographs by Reiner Wandler that the contributing poets used to inspire their poetic expression serve as a window into the experiences of the protesters and of those who have been impacted by the crisis in the most poignant ways.

EN LEGÍTIMA DEFENSA. POETAS EN TIEMPOS DE CRISIS (2014): POETS WHO REBEL

In 2014, Bartleby Editores released a collection of poems by 229 poets titled *En legítima defensa. Poetas en tiempos de crisis*. Bartleby was created in 1998 and is known today as one of the leading publishers of poetry in Spain. The anthology begins with a short prologue by Antonio Gamoneda that explains the reasons the collection of poetry was created. Gamoneda, the winner of the Premio Cervantes in 2006, is one of the most respected Spanish poets of our times. In the prologue, Gamoneda points out that "crisis" is a misnomer for what is really happening. By referring to the situation as a crisis we are releasing from responsibility those who made a conscious decision to allow economy to become dependent on financial speculation instead of production.[6] Gamoneda, who was eight years old when the Civil War ended, believes that democracy is not that different from a dictatorship in its relationship with capitalism. He refers to democracy as a "máscara sonriente" [a smiling mask] of capitalism since all it does is conceal that capital is the only true power today, irrespective of whether the political system of a specific society is democratic.[7] This idea contains an implicit criticism of the Transition since in what concerns the economy, every effort was made after the dictator's demise to preserve the economic structure inherited from the dictatorship.

From the very beginning of the Transition process, the Spanish Confederation of the Organizations of Entrepreneurs, or CEOE,[8] strove to ensure that no alternatives to capitalism were discussed as Spain moved toward democracy. With the legalization of the Communist Party of Spain (PCE) and the Spanish Socialist Workers' Party (PSOE) in 1977, there seemed to have appeared a possibility of competing discourses on the economy entering the country's public space. This prospect was not welcomed by Spain's moneyed classes, and they proceeded to ensure that there was no significant departure from the economic model ushered in during the dictatorship. The CEOE's president, Ferrer Salat, stated in 1977 that democracy could exist only in conjunction with a market economy,[9] and this soon became an undisputed maxim of the Transition. By the time the IXth Congress of the PCE was celebrated in 1978, it became clear that even the Communist Party of Spain was unwilling to offer a challenge to the capitalist status quo.[10] Spain's Transition to democracy coincided with the global economic crisis of the 1970s, the time when the global economy was reoriented toward financialization and the seeds of the current collapse were planted. Gamoneda's terse prologue to *En legítima defensa* points to this complex legacy that must be remembered if we are to understand the dimensions of the crisis.

Gamoneda shares Muñoz Molina's and Etxebarria's preoccupation with the erosion of the welfare state but does not stop at merely stating that it is taking place. Instead, the poet proposes an explanation for the destruction of the social safety net. Gamoneda believes that capitalism is finally tottering under the weight of its contradictions and is trying to protect itself from collapse by deepening social inequalities to prevent the formation of feelings of solidarity among workers.[11] *En legítima defensa* is a poetic contribution to the task of putting into words the suffering that the crisis is causing in a way that will repair the broken links of solidarity among those affected by globalization. In Gamoneda's opinion, the creation of this poetic anthology in itself constitutes a significant political act.[12] Gamoneda echoes Sartre's belief that the subjective nature of poetry precludes it from modifying objective reality, yet points out that poetry's capacity to make a strong impact on our subjectivity might play a crucial role in creating new ways of thinking about the crisis.[13] The impressive number of poets who agreed to contribute to the collection testifies to the urgency of the situation and the importance of this project. The colophon lists the three editions and the two reprints that *En legítima defensa* underwent in 2014, which demonstrates that the interest of readers toward the volume has not been insignificant.

The artists who contributed to the anthology belong to several generations and offer a vision of the crisis that is informed by their personal relationship with Spain's history. Three of the contributing poets were born before the Civil War and have retained memories of the war and even of the Second Republic. Julia Uceda, the 2003 winner of the National Poetry Prize, was born in 1925. Angelina Gatell, a writer who remembers the proclamation of the Second Republic,[14] and José Manuel Caballero

Bonald, one of the most celebrated poets in Spain and the recipient of the Cervantes Prize in 2012, as well as of the National Poetry Prize in 2006, were born in 1926. Francisca Aguirre, the daughter of the Republican painter Lorenzo Aguirre Sánchez who was executed by the dictatorship after the war, was born in 1930. These writers experienced the destruction brought by the war, witnessed the dictatorship from beginning to end, and participated in the country's journey toward democracy after Franco's death. Their engagement with this fraught history informs their response to the crisis.

The youngest among the contributors to *En legítima defensa* were born during the decade of the 1990s. Sesi García, a master's student at the Universidad Autónoma de Madrid, was born in 1992, and Cristian Alcaraz, a young poet from Málaga, is two years older. Both poets use blogs, Twitter, and other social media to promote their poetry and make themselves known.[15] García and Alcaraz came of age after the crisis began and belong to Spain's most recent "lost generation," constituted by young people whose life prospects are severely curtailed by the collapse of the country's economy. This generation of Spaniards feels betrayed by a society that offers the young no opportunities for professional and economic advancement and is sharing its experiences of the crisis in the art it creates. The number of young people who have found themselves out of the workplace and the classroom is so great that a term has been coined to refer to them, "generación nini" [the neither-nor generation]. In 2013, 22.5 percent of Spaniards between the ages of fifteen and twenty-nine belonged to the group of young people who neither study nor work. In 2014, this number diminished slightly, standing at 20.7 percent.[16] The young people who did not graduate from high school run the greatest risk of becoming a "nini." Thirty-one percent of high school dropouts in Spain are unemployed. Still, even a bachelor's degree is no guarantee of employment. Twenty-three percent of college graduates have not been able to find a job in Spain, and quite a few of them are considering emigration.[17]

There is no indication that the situation is likely to dramatically change soon, so these young people will have to find a way to adapt to the reality created by the crisis. María Cabrera González, the winner in 2012 of VII Premio de Poesía Emilio Alfaro Hardisson[18] awarded to young writers, transmits in her poem "Vaivén, lunes" the feelings to which many Spaniards of her generation have had to accustom themselves. After offering a lyrical description of Mondays that for somebody who does not have to go to work, might look "hechos de colores, / de peces con alma" [made out of colors, / of fishes with souls],[19] the poet reveals that her seemingly optimistic vision of unemployment masks a desire to return to work because the freedom to do whatever one likes as an unemployed person conceals the sadness of marginalization.[20] Joblessness is becoming so widespread that a new way of artistic engagement with it has arisen and could be termed "poetics of unemployment." The title of Cabrera's poem can be translated as "Monday Fluctuation," pointing to an existence in a state of flux that generates confusion and alienation.

Several of the poems included in the collection were written before the crisis yet were considered by their authors to be relevant to a discussion of today's state of affairs. Miguel Veyrat, a journalist who militated against the Franco dictatorship as a member of PCE, brought to *En legítima defensa* a poem titled "Canción para ensanchar el grito" ["A Song to Swell a Scream"] that was published in 1993 as part of the collection *Elogio del incendiario* [*Praise for the Arsonist*]. Veyrat's short poem is a call for a creation of a new language of activism, which is even more necessary today than it was in the 1990s.[21] José Manuel Caballero Bonald also submitted a poem written before the crisis to *En legítima defensa*. "Terror preventivo" ["Preventative Terror"] had first appeared in the poet's 2005 collection *Manual de infractores* [*Offenders' Manual*]. Caballero Bonald's vision of "atroz historia venidera" [an atrocious approaching history] that can be glimpsed from a "ventana borrascosa abierta al borde / de las ruinas" [a tempestuous window opened at the edge / of ruins][22] sounds eerily prophetic from the vantage point of today's knowledge of what awaited Spain soon. Antonio Crespo Massieu's "También la historia" ["History as Well"] first appeared in 2004 in the collection titled *En este lugar* [*In This Place*]. Like the poems by Veyrat and Caballero Bonald, "También la historia" ["History as Well"] demonstrates the continuity between the tragedies and the hopes of the past and the current crisis. The presence of these poems in the collection is crucial to positioning *En legítima defensa* within a poetic exchange that is not circumscribed by the specific events of the collapse of the financial markets of 2008–2009.

Neither the poets' country of origin nor their current place of residence limited the authors' participation in the volume. Poets who have responded artistically to the crisis in Spain were welcomed to contribute irrespective of their nationality or geographic location. For instance, Zhivka Baltadzhieva, a poet from Bulgaria who moved to Spain in 1990 and writes in both Spanish and Bulgarian, brought a poem titled "Berlín. Gógol" to *En legítima defensa*. Martín Rodríguez-Gaona is a writer from Lima, Perú, who contributed a poem titled "Apuntes para especies en vías de extinción" ["Notes for Endangered Species"]. Alongside the authors who moved to Spain from elsewhere, the volume contains works by artists who emigrated from Spain and currently reside in different countries. To give an example, Jorge Díaz Martínez, a writer from Córdoba and the author of "Un poema comercial" ["A Commercial Poem"], works at the Department of Romance Languages of the Palacky University in the Czech Republic. The structure of *En legítima defensa* reflects the fluid nature of the globalized world where national borders are losing relevance. For instance, in his poem "Carta de un emigrante desde Tokio o reflexión sobre la materia oscura" ["An Immigrant's Letter from Tokyo or a Reflection on an Obscure Matter"], Juan Pardo Vidal points to the similarity of experience in different parts of the world. Globalization is erasing differences, and the big cities of developed capitalist countries are becoming identical to one another:

> Solo hay una ciudad en el mundo,
> puede llamarse Tokio, o no,
> el nombre es siempre lo de menos.
> [There is only one city in the world
> call it Tokyo or not,
> the name never matters.][23]

Pardo Vidal's poem strives to awaken the readers to the possibility of a solidarity that will transcend linguistic and geographic distances among alienated urban inhabitants of different countries. This kind of solidarity is precisely what the structure of the collection aims to promote among the poets and the readers through the inclusion of poetry by and about immigrants.

The poems in *En legítima defensa* are arranged in alphabetical order based on the last names of their authors. This manner of organizing the poems overrides the hierarchies of fame that might otherwise dominate a collection containing work by writers who are in such different stages of their literary careers as, say, Felipe Benítez Reyes, who received Premio Nacional de Poesía and Premio de la Crítica in 1996, as well as a Premio Nadal in 2007, and authors who are beginning their journey as writers. The pieces that were included in the collection range widely in terms of their literary quality, yet the number of outstanding poems in *En legítima defensa* is too great to allow for an analysis of each of them in this chapter. I have selected four poems written by poets who belong to different generations and, in my view, are the most representative of the varying approaches to the crisis offered by the collection.

ABEL SANTOS, "CUENTAS LA SUERTE A PULSO" ["YOU TELL THE FORTUNE ON YOUR OWN"]

Abel Santos, a poet from Barcelona, contributed to *En legítima defensa* a poem titled "Cuentas la suerte a pulso" from his 2013 collection *Todo descansa en la superficie* [*Everything Rests on the Surface*]. In an interview granted to his fellow poet Fernando López Guisado, Santos shared his belief that poetry has a role to play in addressing the crisis. The poet believes that he can make a greater impact not as "un agitador de masas" [an agitator of the masses] but, rather, as a solitary observer who places himself at a certain distance from the reality that inspires his work.[24] Santos was born in 1976 and belongs to a generation of writers who are about the same age as Spain's post-Franco democracy. They have seen

PSOE get mired in a series of unending corruption scandals after adopting the slogan "cien años de honradez" [a hundred years of integrity] that was supposed to highlight the party's stellar reputation throughout its long existence.[25] Partido Popular has not fared any better than PSOE in avoiding charges of corruption. In the 1990s, the revelations of corruption in which both parties engaged "contributed to an atmosphere of generalized mistrust in the entire political class."[26] The democratic Spain is not any more corrupt than the dictatorship of Franco, of course. From the very first year of Franco's rule, a system where nepotism and bribery flourished was created,[27] and that system was never dismantled, serving as a foundation for the "economic miracle" of the 1960s.[28] Still, the relaxation of censorship and the proliferation of information outlets made the corruption scandals of the democratic era more resounding. The result has been a growing disillusionment of the younger generations of Spaniards with the effectiveness of political engagement.

Santos, however, is not suggesting that a poet should retire to an ivory tower to avoid any contact with problematic political and social phenomena. He believes that the task of a poet consists in seeing past the images of success offered by mass media and observing the reality that these images conceal.[29] Santos's "Cuentas la suerte a pulso" reaches past the superficial vision of professional achievement in the fluid world of late capitalism and offers a poignant depiction of the crisis as experienced by Spain's "lost generation." The poem's opening verses, "Madrid de 2009 / es una ciudad de medio millón de parados / según las últimas estadísticas" [Madrid of 2009 / is a city of half a million unemployed / according to the recent statistics],[30] offer a play on Dámaso Alonso's famous poem "Insomnio" ["Insomnia"] that begins with "Madrid es una ciudad de más de un millón de cadáveres (según las últimas estadísticas)" [Madrid is a city of over half a million cadavers (according to the recent statistics)].[31] Written in 1940, "Insomnio" points to the tragic reality of the postwar Spain where even those who survived the carnage lead the kind of existence that is not much better than death. This is Dámaso Alonso's most recognizable verse, and by placing it at the beginning of his poem Santos connects the devastation of the crisis with that of the Civil War. Unemployment is today's form of social control, and it is also an integral part of the economic system that was created during Franco's rule. Like every writer analyzed in this book,[32] Abel Santos believes that understanding the crisis is impossible without looking back at the Civil War and the dictatorship that followed it. Treating the crisis as a chance occurrence that bears no relation to anything that transpired before can only ensure that the circumstances that produced the collapse will remain unaddressed.

Santos transforms the second verse of Alonso's "Insomnio" into "a veces, en la noche de mi cuarto alquilado, / yo me revuelvo y me incorporo" [at times, in the night of my rented room, / I turn and sit up].[33] The addition of "de mi cuarto alquilado" [my rented room] introduces the reality of a generation that moves from one rented apartment to another in search of a patchwork of part-time jobs that will keep their holders afloat. While Dámaso Alonso responds to the desperation experienced in the aftermath of the war by turning to God,[34] Santos writes in an era when religion has lost much of its relevance for the representatives of the poet's generation.[35] A search for God has been substituted, in Santos's poem, by a search for an equally elusive specter of full-time employment:

> Y voy de trabajo en trabajo por días sueltos,
> porque 190 pulsaciones
> no son bastantes para las 200 que requería
> el puesto de grabador de datos.
> [And I go from a job to a job on odd days,
> because 190 keystrokes
> are not enough for the 200 required
> by the data entry position.][36]

Santos replaces Alonso's "más de un millón de cadáveres" [over half a million cadavers][37] with the much more prosaic number that is the typing speed required to obtain a job. There is no collective dimension to the way that the crisis is experienced in the poem. The concepts of community and collectivity have been eroded by uncontrollable market flows. There is no hint that isolated job seekers and contingent part-time workers whose number has soared because of the crisis will be able to come together in solidarity to search for a way to address their troubles collectively.

The job seeker in Santos's poem never mentions the millions of those who are in the same predicament. Instead, he concentrates on the numbers that define his individual productivity. These numbers are the only anchor he can use to avoid being swept away by the inexorable flows of the market economy, and they dominate every attempt he makes to find employment. Poetry, which tends to stand outside the logic of the market economy, is identified as the reason the poet has to make his living moving furniture at a private school.[38] The abundance of numbers in the poem points to a reality where calculations possess a greater importance than words. A poet's ability to explore the creative dimension of language is valued less by the market than anything that can be easily quantified. The seepage of the numbers into the poem stands for the colonization of every sphere of human activity by the logic of the market.

Dámaso Alonso is not the only poet whose presence can be felt in Santos's poem. Santos also integrates two verses from "Venticuatro años" ["Twenty-four"] by the Argentinean writer Raúl Núñez. Núñez, a poet and a novelist who moved to Spain in 1971, is not as well known as Alonso, which might be the reason he is mentioned by name in Santos's poem: "Desde que tenía 16, he tendido los ojos para siempre / a este hermano imbécil o santo del poema, / que dijo Raúl Núñez" [Since the age of 16, I have turned my eyes forever / to the imbecilic or sainted brother from the poem / told by Raúl Núñez].[39] In his prologue to the 2008 collection of Núñez's poems titled *Marihuana para los pájaros* [*Marijuana for Birds*], writer Alfons Cervera bemoaned the poet's absence from the "atiborrado universo *google* " [overcrowded universe of Google],[40] and Santos must be aware of the paucity of references to Núñez. Those of Santos's readers who seek out Núñez's poem will discover that "Venticuatro años" is the poet's manifesto that exalts poetic creation. Núñez ends his poem with proclaiming his belief that poetry will continue to exist even when nothing else does.[41] The reference to Núñez's poem with its insistence on the perdurability of poetry brings the only note of optimism to Santos's dark poetic vision of the world in crisis. Santos's integration of several verses from "Venticuatro años" into his poem stresses the centrality of generational divides to the poet's experience of the crisis. Núñez's "he vuelto / hoy me vuelvo a ir" [I have returned / today I'm leaving again] has led him to the same experience of rootlessness and economic uncertainty as the kind that Santos addresses in his poem.[42] In Núñez's poem, these experiences lead to an eruption of love for every aspect of the world that the poet has observed in his travels. Santos, however, makes it very clear that his capacity for love and acceptance does not reach across generational divides. He feels isolated by the way the crisis has affected people of his age and refuses to see any similarities between his experience of the crisis and that of the twenty-year-old students who work alongside him.[43]

The feelings of shame experienced by those who have been prevented by the crisis from developing professionally in the way that they believe would be more appropriate to their age have informed much of the literature of the crisis.[44] The number of precariously employed part-time workers has grown dramatically in Spain since the beginning of the economic crisis, and the greatest growth has been observed among those who were forced to accept part-time employment because of being unable to find full-time work. According to the data provided by the National Institute of Statistics in March 2015, the number of such workers grew from 750,000 to 1.75 million over the eight years of the crisis.[45] Still, the generational divides observed by writers of crisis literature often prevent these workers from developing a feeling of solidarity that is necessary for concerted political action. In the last verses of Santos's poem, love offers the only refuge from alienation. This is not, however, the inclusive feeling of love and acceptance directed toward the world at large that informs Núñez's poem. In "Cuentas la suerte a pulso" Santos retreats from the threatening complexity of human relations to the intimacy of his lover's embrace.[46] The vision of the crisis presented in the poem is that of an incomprehensible calamity, and there is nothing but patience to protect one from its effects. The only battle that the poet can still wage is the struggle with time: "Mi corazón es ahora un guerrero distinto / que se está ganando a pulso la eternidad contigo / en este contrato basura con el tiempo" [My heart is now a different fighter / that is struggling to win an eternity with you / in this rubbish contract with time].[47] Since the links of solidarity among those affected by the crisis are broken by the isolating logic of late capitalist society, the possibility of political activism is absent from Santos's vision of the world.

Santos is one of several contributors to *En legítima defensa* whose poem centers on the difficulty of breaking through alienation and establishing the kind of dialogue with others that might lead to meaningful political activism. Carlos Álvarez, author of the poem "En la taberna" ["At the Tavern"] belongs to a different generation than Santos, yet his poem shares the motifs of loneliness and isolation. Álvarez's father, a Republican, was executed by the Nationalists in 1936, and Álvarez dedicated himself to fighting against Franco's regime. He was jailed several times and was, together with Alfonso Sastre, one of the last prisoners of the dictatorship held in the Carabanchel prison between March 1974 and December 1975.[48] Álvarez's poem begins *in medias res*, with "Pero a veces las cosas no resultan tan claras" [But sometimes things are not that simple].[49] From the beginning, readers are invited into a dialogue about the crisis that the poet fails to establish outside of his poetic universe. The comrades the poet encounters in the tavern he frequents express agreement with his ideas, yet that moment of communion among friends is not enough to stave off the devastation of the crisis:

> Porque si bien es cierto que es muy fácil
> encontrar la palabra donde estamos de acuerdo,
> el hambre no se cansa de andar por nuestras calles
> y continúa el barro, el hastío y el miedo.
> [Because although it is true that it is very easy
> to find a word we agree on,
> hunger still roams our streets
> and mud, weariness and fear are still here.][50]

Álvarez's poetic persona finds it easier to break through isolation and reach out to others than Santos's, yet the reality of hunger and fear empties the dialogue he tries to establish of any true political content. The poem warns the readers to abstain from facile acquiescence that has no potential to produce change. If the readers of the collection treat the poems it contains as "la palabra donde estamos de acuerdo" [a word we agree on], which is easy to come by but hard to transform into anything greater than a momentary respite from alienation, *En legítima defensa* will fail to reach the purpose for which it was created.

FRANCISCA AGUIRRE, "LA SORPRENDENTE VIDA" [AMAZING LIFE]

Like Carlos Álvarez, Francisca Aguirre belongs to the generation that experienced the Civil War and its aftermath and retained vivid memories of the postwar persecution of Republicans and their family members.[51] Until quite recently, Aguirre's poetry was not as well known as that of other poets of her generation. In the words of Payeras Grau, for a lengthy period, Aguirre wrote "desde una posición marginal en el contexto de la poesía de su tiempo" [from a marginalized position in the context of the poetry of her times].[52] The reasons for Aguirre's marginalization within Spain's literary landscape are complex. Keefe Ugalde, for instance, points to the conjunction of the poet's gender, her difficult economic circumstances, and her fraught position as a daughter of an executed Republican as obstacles on Aguirre's way to publishing her poetry.[53] As the wife of the noted poet Félix Grande, Aguirre was always close to Spain's literary circles, yet her own poetry, which Aguirre had started to write in adolescence,[54] saw light for the first time when the poet was well into her forties. According to poet Olvido García Valdés, Aguirre belongs to the generation of women who suffered more than any other in the twentieth century because of Spain's peculiar historical path.[55] These women had to struggle to define their role as professionals, artists, and individuals outside of the patriarchal expectations imposed by the dictatorship.

Aguirre's first collection of poems, titled *Ítaca*, came out in 1976, a year after the dictator's demise. A slow and patient work of elaborating her poetic vision occupied the next three decades of the poet's life. In the recent years, Aguirre started gaining greater recognition for her artistic production. In 2010, she was awarded Premio Miguel Hernández, which had both a professional and a great personal significance for the poet:

> Por ser un homenaje a Miguel Hernández. Y porque el hermano mayor de mi madre estuvo encarcelado con él, y mi padre también fue condenado y sentenciado a muerte por el franquismo por republicano. [Because it's a tribute to Miguel Hernández. And because my mother's older brother was jailed next to him, and my father, too, was convicted and sentenced to death by Franco for being a Republican.][56]

In 2011, the poet received Premio Nacional de Poesía for her collection *Historia de una anatomía*.[57] In one of the few critical studies of Aguirre's poetry, John Wilcox points out that Aguirre's first collections published in the 1970s were "concerned not with Spain's immediate social and political ills but with suffering of a more recondite nature: the anguished idealism of the self."[58] "La sorprendente vida," the poem that Aguirre contributed to *En legítima defensa*, combines the existential anguish of the poet's earlier work with a greater awareness of the painful social and economic consequences of the crisis.

Aguirre brings to *En legítima defensa* an understanding of the crisis that is informed by the poet's personal, and often tragic, experiences of the country's history. This creates a sense of continuity between the poet's earlier artistic production and "La sorprendente vida." The poem is structured as a monologue addressed to those who might lack awareness of how similar Spain's current situation is, in existential terms, to what the country experienced in the past. The repetition of "es decir" [that is to say],[59] "creedme, os lo ruego" [believe me, I beg you], "creedme, os lo aseguro, sé muy bien lo que digo" [believe me, I assure you I know very well what I'm saying], "creedme" [believe me], "hacedme caso" [pay attention][60] infuses the poet's pleas to be heard with a sense of urgency. Time is running out for those who were born before the Civil War to transmit the memory of the war and the dictatorship to the younger generations. Aguirre believes that no fruitful analysis of the current economic crisis can be undertaken without a recognition that "este miserable presente, esta penosa realidad, / es copia de un tiempo ya vivido" [this miserable present, this painful reality / is a copy of a time already lived].[61] The poet rejects a linear vision of time and presents history as a vicious circle of suffering that can be broken only once her compatriots realize that what they are experiencing at the moment happened before.

The memory of the Civil War has always haunted Aguirre's poetry,[62] and "La sorprendente vida" is no exception. As the poet observes the reality of today's Spain, she recognizes the misery and the helplessness of "la buena gente" [the good people] in the face of those who imposed their rule on what the poet terms "the garden of life" in the postwar era.[63] The fear that silenced Aguirre's poetic voice throughout the decades of Franco's dictatorship reaches far beyond that specific moment in history. The repression to which those who considered themselves to be the masters of existence subjected "the good people"[64] had as its goal an eradication of life itself. In her autobiographical writing, Aguirre points out that the terror experienced by those who lost the war and their descendants has left indelible scars.[65] Like Prado's Juan Urbano, Aguirre believes that the fear that informed the experiences of those who grew up in the postwar era did not disappear after the end of Franco's dictatorship and informed the ways in which Spain's political space was constituted after 1975. Today, the devastation that Spain is experiencing represents, yet again, a war against life. Like many of the authors who have addressed the current crisis in their work, Aguirre warns against trivializing it as nothing greater than a temporary failure of the economy to function any better. Such an ahistorical approach is entirely alien to the poet's worldview.

Aguirre presents the history of Spain as a symbolic space where agents of evil strive to destroy everything in existence. The poet believes that forces of oppression, powerful as they may be, will fail at annihilating what she terms "the amazing life." No repressive regime or political force can wipe out the memory of the past that will nurture the rebellion of the amazing life against the "miserables amos" [miserable masters] who want to enslave it. Traces of historical memory are forever preserved in the face of even the greatest oppression, and the poet insists that "la ira de los hijos muertos" [the rage of the dead children] and "el grito de los muertos" [the scream of the dead][66] will always manage to break through forgetfulness and restore the dominion of life. This vision of memory is not new to Aguirre's poetry. In "Memoria arrodillada" ["Kneeling Memory"], a poem that was part of Aguirre's 1999 collection *Pavana del desasosiego* [*The Pavane of Unease*], the poet reminds her readers that traces of memory always lurk behind the sanitized official accounts of history.[67] The entirety of Aguirre's poetic oeuvre is dedicated to rescuing the forgotten stories of history's victims from the shadows and bringing the echoes of their voices to her readers. "Memoria arrodillada" aims to serve as a reminder that memory might have been brought to its knees, yet it is still possible to access it, and "La sorprendente vida" echoes this belief.

In "La sorprendente vida," Aguirre posits the existence of a universal law of life that imposes a severe penalty on a society that refuses to remember its history.[68] This implacable law can be trampled into the ground by the forces of evil but "the return of the repressed memories"[69] will always occur, bringing with it the kind of consequences that the "miserables amos" [miserable masters][70] of life do not anticipate. In their war against life, they forget that "esa señora es una enemiga muy mala" [this lady is a very cruel enemy][71] and that life will wreak vengeance on those who attempt to destroy it. Ultimately, suggests the poet, "los que creen ser amos de la vida" [those who believe they own life][72] will be defeated. The image of "miserable masters" whose greed is ravaging the garden of life and putting life itself on the verge of extinction is central to the poem. Aguirre is not alone in attributing the devastation that Spain is experiencing today to "el tesoro podrido de algunos miserables, / su ambición desmedida frente a tanta desdicha" [the rotten treasure of some misers, / their excessive ambition in the face of so much pain].[73] These verses of "La sorprendente vida" could be used to describe Chirbes's Rubén Bertomeu and Tomás Pedrós, as well as Prado's Martín Duque. Their relentless drive toward the accumulation of possessions and their indifference in the face of the suffering they cause make them incapable of appreciating what Aguirre terms "amazing life." This concept exists outside monetary exchange and can never be fully subdued to the logic of the market. The rebellion of life against the forces of evil that wish to destroy it will come at a great price, however, and Aguirre pleads with her readers to recognize that the civil conflicts of the past can repeat themselves in the future.[74] Unlike Muñoz Molina, Aguirre does not want the specter of the Civil War to be used to encourage complicity with the current distribution of political powers in Spain. The realization that an armed civil conflict can occur if the social and economic divisions continue deepening should serve as a deterrent for the uncontrollable greed of "los amos de la vida" [life's masters][75] and not to silence the war's memory.

There is no difference between the "life's masters" who propagated terror in the postwar years and those whose greed is destroying the democratic Spain of today. In her autobiographical account *Espejito, espejito* [*Mirror, Mirror*] (1995) that combines poetry and prose, Aguirre describes the hunger and the humiliation she experienced as a little girl during the postwar years. In spite of her family's insistence that she avoid accepting charity from the hands of the people who incarcerated her father, Aguirre does not manage to overcome the pangs of hunger and presents herself at the Auxilio Social, where "life's masters" offer her some food.[76] This becomes one of the defining experiences of the poet's life, and as she writes her poetry today, Aguirre wants to make sure that her readers remember the events of history that made it necessary for the children of the vanquished to beg for scraps of food from those who orphaned them.

After placing the current economic crisis within the larger context of Spain's recent history, Aguirre reminds her readers that the struggle between the dispossessed and their victimizers has existed throughout the history of humanity. The poet assures her audience that she has access to hidden knowledge that points to the possible consequences of such a battle within a deeply divided society:

> Creedme, os lo aseguro, sé muy bien lo que digo:
> hay datos desde mucho antes de Cristo,
> hay libros escondidos donde se cuenta
> la venganza terrible de la vida ante sus destructores.
> [Believe me, I assure you I know very well what I'm saying:
> there is information from long before the times of Christ,
> there are hidden books that narrate
> life's terrible vengeance against its destroyers.][77]

A poet's role, according to Aguirre, is to serve as a conduit for the hidden wisdom that augurs eventual defeat to those who try to destroy life in the service of their ambition and greed. By her poetic gift, a poet has an obligation to make heard the voices of the dispossessed who have been silenced throughout history. "La sorprendente vida" echoes the conviction expressed by Antonio Gamoneda in the prologue to *En legítima defensa* that a poet's task consists in "escribir desde el sufrimiento o ser solidarios con el sufrimiento" [writing from a place of suffering or in solidarity with suffering][78] and links the pain caused by the current crisis to that experienced throughout the history of humanity. Aguirre's suggestion for overcoming the existential loneliness that dominates the societies where liquid capital has broken links of understanding and comradeship among individuals is to look to history for an understanding of how systems of oppression perpetuate themselves over time. Ignorance about the past contributes to feelings of isolation since the current moment slips into being perceived as so exceptional that no patterns of resistance inherited from one's predecessors can be of use any longer. Aguirre's vision of history echoes that of Chirbes and Gopegui, who believe that it is crucial to preserve the memory of resistance if we are to confront the enduring structures of oppression.

LOLA BORGES BLÁZQUEZ, "EXPAÑA"

Born in 1984, Lola Borges Blázquez belongs to the generation of Spaniards who have seen their chances at achieving professional success destroyed by the crisis. Like many of her contemporaries, Borges Blázquez has had to leave Spain in search of professional fulfillment. The poet established herself in Montreal, and *La Cultural de Montreal,* a digital magazine dedicated to promoting the Spanish-language culture in Canada, introduced the young poet as follows:

> Lola Borges Blázquez dejó las playas de Valencia y un doctorado en derechos humanos para emigrar a Montreal, no precisamente por amor al invierno. Actualmente trabaja como redactora y traductora, da clases particulares de español y baila blues siempre que puede. [Lola Borges Blázquez left the beaches of Valencia and a doctoral program in human rights in order to emigrate to Montreal, but not because she loves winter. Currently, she works as an editor and translator, gives private classes of Spanish and dances the blues whenever she can.][79]

The trajectory of a young scholar who leaves a doctoral program at the Universitat de València to become an immigrant resigned to making a living from several part-time jobs in a foreign country is symptomatic of a brain drain that, according to the Bank of Spain, is exacerbating the effects of the crisis.[80] The number of Spaniards who are leaving the country because of the economic collapse has soared,[81] and there is a growing community of Spanish artists who are observing the crisis in Spain from overseas. If the Civil War and the dictatorship forced many of the country's thinkers and artists into exile for political reasons, the current cohort of émigrés is leaving Spain because of the collapse of the economy that has laid bare the problematic nature of the democratic system constructed in Spain after the dictator's death. In 2015, Borges Blázquez decided to return to Spain, in hopes that a changing political climate in the country would be more propitious for the creative efforts of young artists like herself.[82] However, the larger trend of workers emigrating from Spain has not been reversed. A report published by the National Institute of Statistics demonstrates that the growth of Spain's GDP has neither stemmed the flow of people leaving the country nor managed to bring back a significant number of émigrés.[83] The subject of exile is poised to remain relevant to Spaniards for quite some time to come.

Borges Blázquez contributed to *En legítima defensa* a poem titled "Expaña" that speaks to the experiences of the Spaniards who have had to exile themselves from the country because of the crisis. Borges Blázquez describes the writing of the poem in a language like that used by Etxebarria's and Muñoz Molina's descriptions of how they produced their crisis essays. In the poet's words, "Expaña" was "escrito de un tirón" [written all at once] with the goal of transmitting the impression that Spain no longer exists as a fully viable nation-state.[84] The poet transforms the name of her country in a way that integrates the prefix "ex" and points to the word "exilio" [exile] that reappears several times throughout the poem and serves as its closing verse. The word "exile" in the poem is accompanied by "¡auxilio!" [help!] and "¡al rescate!" [to the rescue!] that are repeated several times.[85] Spain needs help, yet the only assistance it gets is "el rescate bancario" [the bank bailout] that the government of Mariano Rajoy requested from the European Union and that has to be returned at a grave cost to Spain's economy. "Mi país se hunde entre cataratas de dinero extranjero" [My country is drowning in the waterfalls of foreign money], writes Borges Blázquez in "Expaña,"[86] echoing the feelings of many of her compatriots who fail to see any improvement to their standard of living because of the EU bailout.

The money flows that move in and out of Spain bring no discernible relief to those who are suffering because of the crisis, and the erosion of the social safety net by a far-reaching set of austerity measures provoked a wave of popular protests beginning in May 2011. The 15-M Movement was inspired, to a significant extent, by Stéphane Hessel's best-selling *Indignez-vous!* (*Become Indignant!*) that was published in France in 2010 and sold over 400,000 copies in its Spanish and Catalan translations.[87] Hessel, a ninety-three-year-old veteran of the French Resistance movement, who survived Nazi concentration camps and contributed to the creation of the UN's Universal Declaration of Human Rights, drew a parallel, in his slim volume, between the sense of outrage that inspired the French *résistants* to fight the German occupation and the indignation that should nourish the anti-austerity protests in today's Western Europe: "We, the veterans of the Resistance movements and fighting forces of Free France, call on the younger generations to revive and carry forward the tradition of the Resistance and its ideas. We say to you: Take over, keep going, get angry!"[88] Hessel's message is so potent that it resonates even with those in Spain who occupy the opposite end of the political spectrum. For instance, the ultra-conservative thinker Pedro J. de la Peña agrees that there is ample cause for indignation in a country that is as devastated by corruption scandals as Spain is.[89] Peña does not agree with many of the slogans that the Indignados use in their protests, yet he is convinced that the representatives of the younger generations would be better at managing the country than any of the older politicians today.[90]

Borges Blázquez's poem speaks to those who share Hessel's and Peña's feelings of outrage over the aggressive dismantling of the welfare state that is conducted using the economic crisis as a pretext. "Expaña" is structured in a way that helps the poet transmit the pain caused by the crisis. The frequency of the exclamations "¡auxilio! ¡exilio!" [help! exile!] intensifies toward the closing part of the poem, creating a sensation of growing desperation and mimicking the emotions that bring people to the "plazas llenas de protestas" [squares filled with protests].[91] As an expatriate, Borges Blázquez is in a position of having to describe and interpret her place of origin to the people she meets outside of the country, and as a result, "Expaña" is addressed not only to her audience in Spain but also to the poet's new compatriots. Eight of the poem's verses begin with the words "mi país" [my country] that point to an attempt to provide a definition for the country that the poet observes from a geographic and emotional distance: "Mi país es un 50% de población activa inactiva / de parados desesperados e inquietos" [My country is 50% of active population inactive, / of desperate and troubled unemployed],[92] "mi país cabe dentro de una televisión: / tortura programada" [my country fits inside a TV: / programmed torture],[93] "mi país teme educar la ciudadanía" [my country is afraid of educating the citizenry].[94] For those who watch news reports about Spain from overseas, the country has, indeed, been reduced to the alarming statistics of unemployment, reports on low educational achievements of younger Spaniards, and images of protesters in Madrid's Plaza Mayor. Borges Blázquez's poetic voice attempts to reach past the televised images of Spain and rescue a more nuanced vision of a country struggling with the legacy of the past that is compounding the problems of the present. It will be possible to ensure that the future of Spain is not defined by mass exile only if the taboos inherited from the past are finally broken. In the meanwhile, "continúan las masacres por tradición" [traditional massacres continue],[95] and the country is caught in the cycle of repeating its past mistakes.

"Expaña" is structured around repetitions that help to keep in place an elusive sense of identity. In the words of Judith Butler, "signification is not a founding act, but rather a regulated process of repetition."[96] Borges Blázquez's poem demonstrates the process by which an expatriate recreates the feeling of identity with the country of origin by repeating the words, the phrases, and the stories that serve as a conduit toward a sense of belonging. At the same time, as pointed out by Gayatri Spivak, repetition that serves as a basis of any identity always introduces change into the identity it is called upon to uphold: "One of the corollaries of the structure of alterity, which is the revised version of the structure of identity, is that every repetition is an alteration. . . . Repetition is the basis of identification. Thus, if repetition alters, it has to be faced that alteration identifies and identity is always impure."[97] The exiles from Spain, who, like Borges Blázquez, recreate the collective identity of Spaniards by repeating the tropes they associate with their country, engage in a recasting of this identity by the very act of repetition. They bring to this identity-building process the experience of observing Spain from a distance that is both geographic and emotional. The growing number of emigrés makes it impossible to discard their impact on the way Spanish identity is articulated. As national borders become more fluid and informational flows sweep away the remnants of the symbolic meaning of state boundaries, the task of constructing and maintaining collective identities falls to globally dispersed participants who can lay a claim to belonging to a community by sharing the affective and intellectual preoccupations of its members. Today, the concept of a national literature is associated less with a territory located within the boundaries of a specific nation-state than with a dispersed community of writers and readers who are geographically unmoored to various extents yet feel a sense of allegiance to the cultural production in a shared language.

The language of Borges Blázquez's poem mimics the colonization of today's reality by the vocabulary of business and finance while introducing the readers to the possibility of questioning the centrality of this terminology to their experience of life: "Tanto cotizas, tanto vales. / ¿Vales?—¡Exilio! ¡Exilio!" [You are worth what you pay. / Worth?—Exile! Exile!].[98] It might seem that, in these verses, the poet presents exile as a way out of the painful experience of the crisis in Spain. However, Borges Blázquez makes sure that her readers realize that the crisis she addresses in her poem reaches past the state of the economy and is not circumscribed by Spain's borders. Not only is the logic of global capitalism devastating the financial sector and the construction industry, but it is also damaging the environment.[99] There is no escape from the environmental consequences of unbridled consumption, and leaving Spain will not place one beyond the reach of the devastation caused by unconstrained accumulation of capital.

In a prologue to the volume that accompanied Borges Blázquez's reception of the 2008 Youth Institute Prize for Young Writers, poet and journalist Amalia Iglesias Serna had the following to say about Borges Blázquez's poetry: "Esta poesía tiene todos los componentes de palabra-vacuna para los males de nuestro tiempo, como si al pronunciarlos pudieran ser exorcizados." [This poetry has everything to function as word-vaccine for the ills of our times, as if the act of speaking could exorcize them.][100] "Expaña" is like the poems discussed by Iglesias Serna in its passionate dedication to naming the issues that are impacting the Spain of the crisis and trapping the country in the reality of being an ex-state that is pushing many of its children toward exile. The younger generation of Spaniards is prevented from shaping life within the country by productive work, but writers like Borges Blázquez still manage to make their voices heard in a cultural space that is currently quite inhospitable to those who suffer the most as a consequence of the crisis.

MARCA(DA) ESPAÑA. RETRATO POÉTICO DE UNA SOCIEDAD EN CRISIS (2014): A REJECTION OF BRANDING

In an interview granted to *Nueva Tribuna* in 2013, José María de la Quintana, the founder of the publishing house Amargord, pointed out that the crisis was creating "dificultades inconcebibles" [inconceivable difficulties] for those of his colleagues who wanted to continue publishing poetry.[101] Quintana, who is a poet and a novelist at the same time as a lifelong entrepreneur in the field of artistic production, is convinced, however, that it is crucial to find a way to let poets bring their work to the attention of the reading public. The act of writing and publishing poetry is, in Quintana's opinion, "un ejercicio de resistencia civil continuada ante la desaparición de un mercado que quieren ocupar los tecnólogos y el pensamiento único" [an exercise in continued civil disobedience in the face of the disappearance of a market that techies and groupthink want to occupy].[102] The collection of poetry *Marca(da) España. Retrato poético de una sociedad en crisis* released by Amargord in 2014 brings together the voices of fifty-two artists who have written poems in response to the crisis. The very existence of the collection undermines the validity of any single, unified vision of the crisis and reinforces the idea that the only productive way to address it is to bring together a multitude of voices belonging to those who have been affected by the country's economic collapse.

Even though publication of poetry has been rendered even more financially risky than usual by the crisis, Amargord has resisted the temptation to obviate the costs of traditional publishing by moving toward the production of digital books. Quintana believes in the value of a book as a physical object that stands outside the inevitably fluid space of digital flows.[103] A physical copy of a book acts as an anchor that can ground the readers in the tangible aspects of their reality and help resist the illusion that any search for certainty in a constantly mutable world is futile. One of the distinctive characteristics of the collections of poetry published by Amargord has always been the care with which the design of each book is tailored to match the poetic voices that appear in it.[104] The word "retrato" [portrait] in the title of the collection refers to the interplay between the poems that appear in the volume and the photographs by Reiner Wandler, a German reporter who has been covering Spain's crisis, that accompany each poem. For instance, the poem "Hambre, Hambre, Hambre" ["Hunger, Hunger, Hunger"] by Ana Rosetti appears next to a photograph featuring a man who is hunched over a garbage can. Antonio Orihuela's "España" ["Spain"] that begins with "Te sorprendería hasta dónde puede llegar la vulgaridad de los ricos" [You would be surprised by how vulgar the rich are][105] accompanies a photo of restaurant patrons who are looking at a group of protesters marching down the street. The transparent glass of the restaurant window acts as an invisible frontier between the two groups of people who are looking at each other in a way that denotes incomprehension and even animosity. The impenetrable barriers between social classes that are the subject of Orihuela's poem are illustrated in a poignant manner by Wandler's photograph.

In a radio interview with Fernando Berlín on the popular radio show *La Cafetera,* Wandler pointed out that his photographs had served as a foundation for the book. The reporter was contacted with a request to provide photographs that were to be used by poets either as an inspiration for the creation of new poems for *Marca(da) España* or as a guide in selecting a poem to contribute to the collection (*La Cafetera*). According to the "Nota final" [Afterword] that closes the book, most of the poems were written because of the poets' interaction with the photos they were given.[106] In many instances, this strategy produced a creative dialogue between artists working with different artistic media or even between an artist and an anonymous subject featured in a photo. The most powerful example of such a dialogue is a poem in prose titled "Así, no (en efecto): paralizados en el tiempo" ["Not Like This (Indeed); Paralyzed in Time"] by Matías Escalera Cordero. The poem appears next to a photo of a middle-aged man who is looking directly at the camera. Attached to his hat there is a yellow slip of paper with the words, "Así, no!" [Not Like This!].[107] Escalera Cordero addresses his poem to the man in the photo, pointing out the many similarities between the writer and the subject of the photograph: "Sí, mi querido anónimo compañero, ese gesto, tu seriedad reconcentrada, y esa mirada podrían ser los míos" [Yes, my dear anonymous friend, this gesture, your concentrated gravity, and this look could be mine].[108] The short statement of "Así, no!" [Not Like This!] that appeared in many of the popular protests of the 15-M movement prompts Escalera Cordero to ponder all the ways in which today's Spain differs from the country envisioned by those who, like the poet himself, fought against the dictatorship in the closing years of Franco's life. Escalera Cordero believes that the legacy of the dictatorship frustrates any attempt to revise the relations of power that have remained unchanged in Spain throughout generations.[109] The intense gaze of the man in the photograph underscores the urgency of breaking through "un tiempo histórico congelado, literalmente paralizado" [a frozen historical time, literally paralyzed][110] that, in the opinion of Escalera Cordero, has prevented any meaningful change from taking place in Spain. The poem acts as a bridge between the solemn protester and the readers who look in his eyes and find in them a reflection of their own desperation and rage.

In the prologue to *Marca(da) España,* Santiago Alba Rico, a Marxist writer and thinker, echoes the ideas expressed in Escalera Cordero's poem. Contrary to the belief that the crisis is a state of exception, Alba Rico argues that there is a continuity between the systems of oppression that existed in Spain throughout its history and those that are in place today and questions the idea of "marca España" [Spain as a brand].[111]

The concept of "marca España" that has enjoyed great popularity in the neoliberal Spain is rooted in the belief that an enmeshment between a national identity and corporate identities of business enterprises that originate in the country is not only inevitable but also so positive as to be in need of active support on the governmental level.[112] Within the philosophy of countries as brands, companies are expected to define the values that a country's citizens will adopt as part of their national identity. In this way, the maintenance of national identities is outsourced to private companies, and the government's role is reduced to ensuring that nothing stands in the way of a business's capacity to extract financial gain from its management of national identity. The name of the country itself becomes a type of asset that can either benefit a business or prove detrimental to its capacity to make a profit.[113] Spaniards who participated in the 15-M protest movement were warned about the damage their actions were causing "para la proyección internacional de la 'marca España'" [to the international visibility of 'Spain as a brand'].[114] As a consequence, the questioning of the very concept of "Spain as a brand" has become part of civil resistance in times of the crisis.

Within the framework of the "country as a brand" philosophy, the very existence of a nation-state has to be justified by its capacity to assist private companies in their task of selling goods and services under the assumption that the profitability of these companies will ultimately benefit the country's citizens. The goods that the country's brand name will help to sell are to displace the nation as the object of primary emotional identification for citizen consumers.[115] At the same time, the state's greatest obligations are no longer to its citizens but to the community of unmoored stakeholders with few, if any, connections to the state: "The multinational corporation used to be intertwined with the politics of the nation-state. Today . . . the global corporation has investors and shareholders throughout the world and a structure of ownership too complex to serve single national interests."[116] Unlike the country's citizens, the shareholders of major corporations are invested with the right to demand that the state guarantee the fulfillment of "la promesa que una empresa, o un país, hace a sus *stakeholders*" [the promise that a company, or a country, makes to its *stakeholders*].[117] A country's brand is "la promesa de unas formas de hacer y de pensar acordes con lo que sus principales *stakeholders* esperan de [el país]" [the promise of certain forms of doing and thinking that are in agreement with what the principal *stakeholders* expect from a country].[118] The principal stakeholders, or the companies that expect to benefit from their identification with the word "Spain" have the right to demand that everybody who carries a Spanish passport not only acts in a way that will be beneficial to these private enterprises but also conform their way of thinking to that prescribed by the requirements of Marca España.

The global economic crisis offered the perfect opportunity for large business entities to displace national governments from exercising control over national identities. In 2012, at the height of the crisis, a royal decree founded a committee titled the High Governmental Commission for Spain as a Brand[119] and charged it with the task of improving Spain's image within the concept of "country as a brand."[120] The committee is chaired by Carlos Espinosa de los Monteros y Bernaldo de Quirós, the IV Marquis of Valtierra. He is son to Francisco Javier Espinosa de los Monteros and nephew to General Eugenio Espinosa de los Monteros, who were present during Franco's meeting with Hitler in Hendaye in 1940 and advocated for Spain's increasing involvement with Nazi Germany.[121] The chair of the Marca España committee drew on his family's closeness to Franco to fashion a career that took him from a position in the dictator's Ministry of Commerce to the vice presidency of Inditex[122] and the presidency of Mercedes-Benz España in the democratic Spain.

The belief of Espinosa de los Monteros in the virtues of capitalism remained unshaken throughout the crisis. In a 2008 interview that the future leader of the Marca España project granted to *Diario de Navarra*, Espinosa de los Monteros advanced the belief that the crisis should not inspire a desire to place capitalism under critical scrutiny.[123] Espinosa de los Monteros has every reason to confide in a system that allowed the representatives of his social class to thrive even amid economic devastation. In 2013, one of his sons, Beltrán Espinosa de los Monteros, was promoted to the position of chief financial officer of a company belonging to the clothing conglomerate Inditex. Throughout the crisis, Inditex has been posting record profits, and the compensation of its corporate leadership has been reliably robust.[124] The Marca España committee makes it no secret that its central goal consists in ensuring that the word "Spain" bolsters sales when it comes attached to a product. This process of privatizing national identity makes the nation subservient to the needs of business entities that happen to establish their headquarters in the nation.

In view of a growing deterritorialization of financial elites[125] and the tenuous nature of the allegiance that a business might have to a specific nation at any given point in time, the substitution of the concept of national identity with the idea of a nation as a brand leads to a further erosion of the nation-state model. Given that the nation-state, weakened as it might be, offers the last remaining obstacle in the way of an uncontrollable movement of capital flows, it becomes clear that Marca España aids powerful business interests in removing this obstacle from their way. At the same time, the companies' risks of doing business are shared among all the citizens when the low quality of products sold by private companies transform into "la baja percepción de calidad asociada a España" [a perception of low quality associated with Spain].[126] The country itself becomes "low quality," and it becomes necessary for all Spaniards to disprove this negative appellation through an increased support for the governmental initiatives that will be beneficial to business conglomerates.

The creators of *Marca(da) España* point to the dangers implicit in conflating the needs of business conglomerates like Inditex with those of the country's citizens. The fluidity of identities that allows for no distance between the concept of a brand and that of a nation can be counteracted, to a degree, by an introduction of specific powerful images that will serve as anchors in the world of inexorable flows.[127] Alberto García Teresa, the author of *Poesía de la conciencia crítica: 1987–2011* [*Poetry of Critical Conscience: 1987–2011*] and a contributor to *Marca(da) España,* illustrates this point with his "Alto Comisionado para la Marca España" ["High Commission for Spain as a Brand"], the poem that opens the collection. The poem lists, in a powerful torrent that is unbroken with punctuation, the concepts that everybody who follows the news in Spain will recognize:

> Abaratamiento del despido libre identificaciones reforma constitucional artículo 135 amnistía fiscal porras de 60 a 107 centímetros encadenamiento de contratos temporales artificios lacrimógenos. [Cheaper firing free identifications constitutional reform article 135 fiscal amnesty batons from 60 to 107 centimeters series of temporary contracts tear gas methods].[128]

García Teresa's poem makes it clear that the violent repression experienced by the protesters in 2011–2012 is a direct result of neoliberal economic policies.[129] The professional jargon used by those who, like Espinosa de los Monteros, defend the system that benefits them, obscures the degree to which the coercive power of the government has been coopted by business interests. The poets who contributed to the collection look past the clichés that nourish the official discourse on the crisis and strive to analyze the current state of affairs in Spain as a logical development of the country's history. Like their colleagues who contributed to *En legítima defensa,* the poets whose work appears in *Marca(da) España* rely on a deeply historical vision of the crisis and refuse to accept the belief that it constitutes a state of exception that is likely to end.

The shadow of Francoism is present in Alba Rico's prologue as well as in many of the poems in the collection. Alba Rico believes that a privatization of Spain's national identity and a push to reimagine the word "Spain" as a brand name will put an end to the efforts to recover the memory of the victims of the war, many of whom are still buried in mass graves and remain nameless. Transforming "Spain" into "Spain™," or, in Alba Rico's words, into "una finca privada" [a private estate] will preclude everybody but the owners of the brand name from contesting the set of meanings attached to the word "Spain."[130] Alba Rico is conscious of the paradoxical nature of the ease with which the intellectual and the factual heirs of the Nationalist Spain are now agreeing to dismantle the nation-state. The ideological retreat from national allegiance effectuated by the political right can be used to contest the rhetoric of Spain's national identity from the vantage point of progressive ideology:

> Puede parecer extraño que haya sido precisamente la derecha la que ha convertido la España 'ideológica', imperial, católica y nacionalista, en una marca comercial. Esta desideologización económica quizás abre una posibilidad inesperada para revisar la historia y recuperar una parte de su contenido desde la democracia. [It might seem strange that it's precisely the Right that has transformed the "ideological," imperial, Catholic, and nationalist Spain into a commercial brand. This economical de-ideologization might open an unexpected opportunity to revise history and recuperate part of its content for democracy.][131]

There is little use in passively lamenting the assault on the nation-state model that has been inspired by the financial interests of large corporations. Instead, the contributors to *Marca(da) España* use the cracks that have appeared, because of the crisis, in the monolithic narrative of Spain's national identity created during the Transition to advance their own vision of what Spain should be like.

The structure of *Marca(da) España* eschews hierarchies and places the poems in the alphabetic order dictated by the first letters of the authors' first names. The poems by the recipients of the National Poetry Prize (Francisca Aguirre, Olvido García Valdés, Chantal Maillard, Juan Carlos Mestre, and Antonio Gamoneda) appear alongside the work of poets who have not yet received this degree of recognition. The photographs by Reiner Wandler tend to explore one of two themes: the visible signs of poverty brought about by the crisis and the protest movements of the recent years. The placards used by protesters are featured prominently in many of the photos and are often echoed in the poems that accompany them. For instance, the photograph of a hand holding a poster with a portrait of Franco and the words "¿Impunidad para el franquismo? No, gracias" [Impunity for Francoism? No, thanks] is followed by a poem by Ana Vega that begins with, "Impunidad o dejar vencerse" [Impunity or allow yourself to be beaten].[132] In this way, the poet and her readers participate in the protest even though they might not have been present when it took place. The enthusiasm generated by the public protests of 2011–2012 is preserved and augmented by the collection, continuing the discussions opened by the protests within the space of literary creation.

JESÚS URCELOY

A finalist of the National Poetry Prize in 2006, Jesús Urceloy contributed to *Marca(da) España* an untitled poem that traces today's hostility of many in Spain toward political dissent back to the legacy of the Franco era. The poem echoes the belief voiced by Escalera Cordero in his poem that "ese miedo y esa sumisión de los siervos que nuestros padres interiorizaron no ha desaparecido nunca de nuestras almas" [this fear and this servile submission interiorized by our parents never disappeared from our souls].[133] Urceloy's poem establishes a creative dialogue not only with the photograph of a lone protester behind a cordon of metal fences that accompanies his poem but also with the work of another poet who contributed to the volume. This contributes to positioning *Marca(da) España* not as a collection of isolated voices but as a shared response of a group of artists to Spain's crisis. Urceloy's poem offers a glimpse into Spain's recent history as seen by somebody who has preserved, throughout the years, a sense of profound animosity toward those who contest the existing social order. In the first stanza, a nameless man remembers the persecution of Juan, a neighbor suspected of Communist leanings during the Franco era. The mundane details of Juan's existence are offered in a low-key tone that brings together snippets of conversations between the neighbors who are gossiping about Juan's arrest: "La madre no / pobre viuda / el hijo / viven juntos" [The mother no / poor widow / the son / they live together].[134] The stanza ends in a sudden eruption of hatred coming from one of Juan's neighbors. As the poem progresses, it becomes clear that the speaker of the poem observes this scene in his childhood and remains forever infected with his neighbors' callousness toward the dissident.

The last stanza of the poem shows that, in adulthood, the poem's narrator has fully adopted the attitude of hatred toward political dissents. The sounds made by protesters occupying the central areas of Madrid during the protests of 2011 anger him, and his own affluence blinds him to the possibility that others might be struggling in the neoliberal Spain of the twenty-first century.[135] This indifference to the poverty of others is also part of the narrator's familial and historical legacy. On par with the memory of Juan's arrest, he preserves the remembrance of an incident involving a beggar who entered the building in search of food and was violently expelled by the neighbors. In the 1960s, when the incident occurs, discussions of poverty were not welcomed by the Franco regime that preferred to concentrate on the celebration of the so-called Spanish economic miracle.[136] As a small boy, the poem's narrator interiorizes the Franco-era contempt for the poor and is not prepared to modify his stance decades after the dictator's death.

The first four stanzas of Urceloy's poem open with the dates that allow the readers to situate the events described in the poem in their historical context. Three of the dates (1964, 1969, and 1974) belong to the years of the Franco dictatorship. The last date given, 1980, points to Spain's transition to democracy. The penultimate stanza lacks a specific date, yet clearly it is set during the first years of the twenty-first century characterized by a rapid enrichment of those who were willing to exploit the country's economic boom. The last stanza makes a reference to the popular protests that erupted in Spain in 2011. The chronologic structure of the poem underscores the lack of any true progress between 1964 and today. The changes that have occurred—the new roads, the subway, a clinic that opened in the neighborhood—remained cosmetic and did not manage to eradicate the fear of the authorities that are seen as the all-powerful, invisible dispensers of economic bounty who should not be questioned or opposed in any way. The speaker of the poem does not belong to the financial elites who are benefiting from the crisis.[137] Still, the modest gains in the economic and social status that his family has been able to make since the first years of democracy (an expensive car, an opportunity to live in a building with a porter) render him incapable of exercising solidarity with the protesters.

The poem is organized as a collage of photographic images that transmit the spirit of the time when each vignette is set. With great mastery, Urceloy strings together the images that will bring alive the sensory memories of the past for those who experienced life in the last two decades of the Franco dictatorship. Reiner Wandler's photograph that appears to the left of the poem is one of only seven (out of fifty-two in total) black and white images that have been used in the collection. This gives the photograph a documentary quality that makes it easier to inscribe into the collage of vignettes from Spain's past that appear in the poem. The poem reminds us that, like the events of the Franco era, the protests of 2011–2012 will eventually become part of historical memory. There is no divorce between the past and the present in the poem. Urceloy refuses to fetishize history as a way of turning it into a product ready for consumption. Instead, he proposes an active engagement with the past that will lead the readers to consider the ways in which the past can inspire them to make changes in the present.

Urceloy's readers are prompted to consider the current events as a logical development of everything that the country underwent in the second half of the twentieth century and abandon the vision of the crisis as an inexplicable calamity that is bound to end as suddenly and unpredictably as it began. The past is alive in the present and will continue to inform the future for as long as its power to cast a shadow over today's events is not acknowledged. The value of exploring the past, for Urceloy, lies precisely in its capacity to disrupt the existing structures of power and suggest scenarios of transformative political activism. In the photograph that accompanies the poem, the protester is positioned with his back turned toward the viewers/readers. This creates an illusion that everybody who reads the poem is placed directly behind the protester, supporting him in his confrontation with the agents of the police force. The power of poetry to produce social change by fostering an active engagement with the past is made clear in Urceloy's powerful piece.

ISABEL PÉREZ MONTALBÁN, "DICTADURA FINANCIERA"

In 2007, a collection of poetry was published under the title of *Once poetas críticos en la poesía española reciente* [*Eleven Critical Poets in the Recent Spanish Poetry*]. This was the first time when the term "poetas críticos" [critical poets] was used, and Isabel Pérez Montalbán was named as one of the writers who belong to this group.[138] The group's goal consisted in creating poetry that would point towards the possibilities of transforming reality through a marriage of artistic creation and political engagement.[139] Pérez Montalbán's poetry is nourished by the poet's conviction that a passionate engagement with reality is necessary to produce works of art that will be able to contribute to producing meaningful change. The poet contributed to *Marca(da) España* a poem titled "Dictadura financiera" ["Financial Dictatorship"]. The poem is accompanied by a photo of an older man standing under a "Do not enter" traffic sign with a placard "Dictadura de Bancos, NO" [NO to the Dictatorship of Banks] in his hand. The word "dictatorship" in the photograph and the poem's title suggests that the power of the banking industry in Spain is so oppressive that it is not entirely unreasonable to compare it with the rule of dictator Franco. Like many of the writers who have addressed the crisis in their work, Pérez Montalbán is questioning the value of a supposedly democratic society that is not managing to defend the interests of the country's citizens in the face of the depredations of transnational financial concerns.[140] Free-market policies that accompanied Spain's transition to democracy failed to translate into an increase in Spaniards' freedom. The crisis laid bare the extent to which governmental institutions are in thrall to banking interests. This resulted in a questioning of the extent to which the existing economic structures were inherited from the dictatorship.

The memory of Franco's dictatorship has always been present in Pérez Montalbán's poetry, informing the poet's efforts to elaborate a critical vision of today's Spain.[141] In "Dictadura financiera," the poet asks her readers to recognize that the dictatorship of financial institutions masks itself in a way that makes its insidious power harder to recognize.[142] The knowledge we have of the Franco dictatorship relies most often on the works of literature and cinema that have addressed this tragic period in Spain's history. Readers can relate to the complex characters who populate these works of art and understand the dimensions of the horror inflicted by the dictatorship on the individuals who found themselves on the losing side of the war. At the same time, the larger social dimensions of the conflict have often been lost in the "desplazamiento de lo político a favor de lo individual" [displacement of the political in favor of the individual] that tends to characterize these works of art.[143] The structures of economic oppression that arose from the war are often overshadowed, in novels and films about the Civil War, by the personal experiences of their characters. This is precisely the colonization of the public space by the uncontainable deluge of the private that Bauman warns about as one of the greatest dangers to the capacity of the denizens of modern societies to engage in transformative political action.[144] An author cannot avoid engaging in a creative selection of the situations and characters that will appear in her or his work of art. When Pérez Montalbán reminds her readers that there is a form of dictating people's actions that does not involve direct physical coercion, she is engaging in a political act that calls attention to the coercive power of the existing economic structures and the likelihood that their foundations were laid during the Franco era. The poet assumes the task of rescuing from oblivion the possibility of addressing the crisis in its historical dimension and not as an event that exists solely within the realm of the private.

The vision of the Civil War as collective madness that was promoted by the Franco dictatorship in the 1960s and later informed the conciliatory efforts of the Transition era[145] often occludes the profitability that defeating the Republicans and persecuting them after the end of the war had for the war's winners. The political goals of the Nationalist rebellion against the Republic were never divorced from the pursuit of economic gains: "Since the beginning of the war and long after the conflict ended, the rebel authorities carried out a policy that massively transferred property from the defeated Republicans to both the 'New State' and to its supporters."[146] The emergence of Spain from its international isolation during the 1950s brought a possibility of thwarting any possible opposition to the regime by accompanying the narrative of Franco as the guarantor of a lasting peace with that of the regime as a dispenser of economic bounty. The economic reforms introduced in 1959 as part of the "Stabilization Plan" resulted in a dramatic growth of per capita income and the GDP.[147] For many, the dictatorship has become associated with this improvement in the standard of living.

Novels and films about the Civil War and the Franco dictatorship have been experiencing a boom in recent years. According to the study conducted by Becerra Mayor, beginning in 1999, the number of Civil War novels published in Spain began to soar, reaching a peak in 2010.[148] For the most part, however, these novels are set either during the war on in the first years of the dictatorship because the tragic nature of the civil conflict and the postwar repression allows for a more powerful novelistic setting than the events of the dictatorship's latter years. As a result, the Franco dictatorship that novels and films link to torture, personal tragedy, separation of families, and the suffering of the victims has become divorced, in the popular consciousness, from the economic structures that underpinned it:

> Because of its emphasis on victimhood—on the most gruesome aspects of the war and early Francoism—the construction of historical memory fails to acknowledge that memory of the decades closer to 1975 argu-

> ably had much more weight in shaping the transition than did the civil war and the first decades of the dictatorship. In this regard, the economic improvements of the 1960s, the increased access to higher education for the lower classes and the arrival on the scene of generations that had not endured Francoism's hardest years were crucial.[149]

The resulting rift in the popular imagination between the dictatorship that tortured political prisoners during the Hunger Years and the *franquismo* that witnessed a dramatic improvement in the Spaniards' standard of living still informs a resistance to questioning many of the aspects of the dictatorship's legacy.

Pérez Montalbán's poem represents a space where the memory of the war can be reestablished in its ideological and economic significance. Only after asserting the importance of historical awareness does Pérez Montalbán bring the private back into the poem to point to the impossibility of protecting it from the encroachment of the structures of oppression: "La tiranía financiera / interrumpe los labios de un beso" [Financial tyranny / breaks apart kissing lips].[150] The belief that individual emotive experiences are free from the danger of being colonized by the tyranny of financial relations can no longer be sustained. Images of families spilled out into the streets from the houses they considered to be their private space are a potent symbol of the way the crisis has erased the boundary between the private and the public.[151] The house the poet talks about in the poem is not only a specific living space but also a metaphor of a refuge from the financial flows battering individual lives that is no longer accessible.

In the words of Zygmunt Bauman, the denizens of the liquid world of unstoppable financial flows learn to look to themselves for solutions to the problems they encounter: "Told repeatedly that he or she is the master of his or her own fate, the individual has little reason to accord 'topical relevance'. . . to anything which resists being engulfed within the self and dealt with by the self's facilities."[152] Pérez Montalbán questions this approach by placing the issue of dispossession at the heart of her poem and using the words "no tengo" [I don't have] as a leitmotif to "Dictadura financiera." The responsibility for the dispossession is shifted from those who suffer because of the evictions and the bankruptcies and onto "la Bolsa de valores / que juega a las casitas con sus clientes" [the stock exchange / that plays houses with its clients].[153] The poet calls for solidarity with the many victims of the system of economic relations that, by its very nature, is prone to being shaken by crises on a regular basis. The photograph of a protester that accompanies the poem links "Dictadura financiera" with the lived reality of those who are impacted by the crisis.

The poet appropriates the language of finance to point to the reserves of rage accumulated by the victims of the economic collapse: "Son mis venas depósito creciente / de la ira y del hambre, capital / sin comisiones y préstamo a débito / personal, sin aval inmueble" [My veins are a growing deposit / of rage and hunger, capital / without commission and a personal debit loan, / without a real estate guarantee].[154] The memory of dispossession constitutes their only inalienable possession that can be used to question and subvert the oppression to which they are subjected. Pérez Montalbán advocates for an active engagement with reality and a search for alternatives to the oppressive system of social and economic relations currently in existence. In her belief that poetry has a crucial role to play in tracing the crisis back to its roots, Pérez Montalbán is representative of the poets who agreed to contribute to this poetic volume.

CONCLUSION

The poetic output of recent years that does not position itself explicitly as crisis poetry nevertheless offers a valuable contribution to our understanding of the crisis. In his long-awaited collection *Canción errónea* [*Erroneous Song*] (2012) that was published after a lapse of eight years, Antonio Gamoneda, for instance, offers a series of musings on the nature of caducity that the poet confronts increasingly often now that he is in his eighties and that he also observes in the transformations occurring around him. The sense that not only the term of his physical life but also an entire era is ending pervades the collection. Gamoneda's status as one of Spain's leading poets was consolidated in the years when the country experienced explosive economic growth and enjoyed unprecedented integration into European political and economic structures:

> Gamoneda's emergence onto the national scene in the period between 1987 and 2006 . . . is quite dramatic, given the circumscribed nature of [his] earlier reception. . . . Gamoneda is considered, by some at least, to be the most significant living Spanish poet, and consequently as one of the most important writers in the Spanish language of the last thirty years.[155]

In the poet's most recent collection, death, forgetfulness, and fear are the axes around which the poems revolve, pointing to the disintegration of the certainties that nourished the consciousness of Spaniards during the post-Transition era.

The poet faces his own approaching death and strives to glean a better understanding of the concepts of memory and forgetting. A journey into his memory brings the poet back to the subject of the Civil War that has been central to the entirety to his poetic oeuvre. Gamoneda's attention to the possibility of recovering historical memory has been one of the defining characteristics of his poetic corpus that has set the poet apart from many of his contemporaries.[156] There was resistance to awarding Gamoneda the Cervantes Prize in 2006 because of the poet's support for the controversial Law of Historical Memory.[157] In *Canción errónea,* Gamoneda returns, repeatedly, to the idea of forgetfulness as the greatest threat to everything that he holds dear. The unburied dead of the country's past are absent from the tombs that should house them, and that makes the legacy of the country's violent past determine its present.[158] "Olvido" [forgetfulness] is the last word of the collection, and it refers to the poet's uncertainty as to whether he will be remembered after his death and serves as a reminder that Spain's history should not be forgotten.

Gamoneda's interest in history is intimately linked with the pain he experiences as he observes the tragedies of the present. The poet ventures into "el territorio dibujado por la pobreza" [the territory drawn by poverty] that keeps expanding and acting as an ever-growing source of fear.[159] In an interview about the collection's release in 2012, the poet indicated that he agreed with the sentiments that motivated the protests of the Indignados but did not believe that the format of the protests was likely to be productive:

> Yo soy un indignado, pero un indignado que piensa que los indignados no son realmente, digamos, *performativos.*[160] Las manifestaciones no sirven para nada. [I am one of the indignant but I'm an indignant person who thinks that the indignant are not really, so to say, *performative*. The manifestations don't serve any purpose.][161]

In the poet's opinion, only the creation of alternative economies at the level of neighborhoods and communities will provide an effective response to the crisis.[162] The poet's alienation from his indignant compatriots, however, does not prevent him from creating poetry that speaks to the experience of the shared trauma of the economic collapse. In *Canción errónea,* Gamoneda often expresses the rage he feels when observing the effects of the crisis. In the poem "En las redes violentas" ["In the Violent Networks"], for instance, rage is the emotion that the protesters share, even if they dissent as to what can be done to escape from the trap of the crisis.[163] The degradation of everything sacred stems from the primacy of high finance that has corrupted every area of human existence: "Simultáneamente, / pienso en mi madre y en convulsivas cifras financieras" [Simultaneously, / I think of my mother and the convulsive financial numbers].[164] The image of the mother that brings together the ideas of the origin of life and of "madre patria" [motherland] has been tarnished by the profit-seeking interests of high finance. The anger that infuses *Canción errónea* aims to destroy the primacy of "las finanzas financieras" [financial finance][165] and suggests a possibility of a human connection that rests on words and not numbers.

References to the crisis appear also in many of the poems that were included in the collection of politically engaged poetry titled *Disidentes. Antología de poetas críticos españoles (1990–2014)* [*Dissidents. Anthology of Spanish Critical Poets (1990–2014)*]. Edited by Alberto García-Teresa, a philologist and a literary critic, the collection brings together the work of artists who consider themselves "poetas críticos" [critical poets]. In the prologue to the collection, García-Teresa states that the poetry included in the volume constitutes "una expresión de disidencia y de antagonismo; una crítica a la estructura socioeconómica actual, a su ideología y a los valores que la sustentan" [an expression of dissidence and antagonism; a critique of the existing socioeconomic structure, its ideology and the values that nourish it].[166] *Disidentes* includes poetry that was written since 1990, the year that has a profound symbolic significance to the Western political Left, given that it falls between the demolition of the Berlin Wall and the dissolution of the USSR. Many of the poems in the collection were created during the years of the crisis and share the interest in the recovery of the memory of the Civil War, the questioning of the post-Transition status quo, and the tendency toward fluidity in both form and content that characterize most of crisis literature. Like *En legítima defensa* and *Marca(da) España, Disidentes* eschews professional hierarchies and organizes the poems in the order of their authors' date of birth. Jesús Lizano, a poet from Barcelona born in 1931, opens the collection with three of his poems written in the 1990s.[167] The collection closes with the work by Enrique Martín Corrales, born in 1992. In his 2011 poem "Objeción de conciencia" ["Conscious Objection"], Martín Corrales reflects upon the legacy of violence that nourishes the crisis and eradicates any trace of compassion from public spaces. The last verse in the poem, "nadie aprendió a llorar en wall street" [nobody learned to weep in wall street],[168] evokes the inhumanity of the financial institutions that have contributed, more than anything else, to the crisis. The economic structures that are arising as a result of the crisis and creating an inescapable cycle of poetry have to be maintained through a threat of violence: "Cuentan con los dedos las costillas, / la espuma de los contratos a tiempo parcial, los rifles" [They count ribs with their finger, / the foam of part-time contracts, the rifles].[169] Behind the foamy fluidity of precarious existences there stands an unbending strength of military and financial institutions that are ensuring that the crisis never really ends.

The leitmotif of Gsús Bonilla's 2014 poem "Ágora" [Agora], "hoy, ha podido llover" [today it could rain],[170] echoes the genre's interest in liquid flows that are eroding the capacity of public spaces to produce certainties that will arrest liquidity. The poem's rejection of a period as a punctuation mark reinforces the impression that the images brought together in the poem flow into each other in an unconstrained manner. The poet believes that his artistic task consists in bringing the growing liquidity to the attention of his readers. Bonilla's poetic voice points to the difficulty of withstanding the flows' power to destroy everything in their way as he effectuates a symbolic journey to the agora where a possibility of creating a space of public discussion can still be salvaged. The poet insists that "la asamblea escribe este poema" [the assembly writes this poem],[171] suggesting that the artistic production of the crisis can serve as a shared space where readers and artists participate in a dialogue about everything that is happening because of the crisis. The agora that gives its name to Bonilla's poem is being recreated as a space of debate and dissidence in the multitude of community organizations that were born in the protests of the 15-M movement. Unlike the authors of the crisis essays who suggest that their role consists in dispensing the wisdom they believe they possess to these communities, poets of the crisis refuse to stand outside of spaces of collective action and recreate a hierarchy of expert authority in their relationship with their audience. Collective memory and solidarity are the concepts that structure the collections of poetry that have been published in response to the crisis.

NOTES

1. Luis Bagué Quílez, "A Journey through the Desert: Trends of Commitment in Contemporary Spanish Poetry," in *Post-Authoritarian Cultures: Spain and Latin America's Southern Cone,* ed. Luis Martín-Estudillo and Roberto Ampuero (Nashville: Vanderbilt University Press, 2008), 69–70.
2. Manuel Castells, *Networks of Outrage and Hope: Social Movements in the Internet Age* (Cambridge: Polity, 2012), 5.
3. José Manuel Sánchez Bermúdez, *The Neoliberal Pattern of Domination: Capital's Reign in Decline* (Leiden and Boston: Brill, 2012), 220.
4. Ibid., 220, note 19.
5. Luis Moreno-Caballud, *Cultures of Anyone: Studies on Cultural Democratization in the Spanish Neoliberal Crisis,* trans. Linda Grabner (Liverpool: Liverpool University Press, 2015), 13.
6. Antonio Gamoneda, Prologue to *En legítima defensa (Antología). Poetas en tiempos de crisis* (Madrid: Bartleby Editores, 2014), 9.
7. Ibid., 9.
8. In Spanish, the organization is called Confederación Española de Organizaciones Empresariales.
9. Anselmo Flores Andrade, "Los empresarios y la transición a la democracia en España," *Estudios Sociológicos* 18, no. 54 (2000): 718–19.
10. Juan Luis Paniagua and Luis J. Ramiro, *Voz, conflicto y salida. Un estudio sobre faccionalismo: Nueva Izquierda, 1992–2001* (Madrid: Editorial Complutense, 2003), 62–63.
11. Gamoneda, Prologue to *En legítima defensa,* 9.
12. Ibid., 10.
13. Ibid.
14. Miguel A. Ortega Lucas, "Angelina Gatell: 'Los últimos testigos de la guerra no podemos callar sobre aquello,'" *Eldiario.es,* June 28, 2014, www.eldiario.es/andalucia/Angelina-Gatell-ultimos-testigos-podemos_0_275772479.html (accessed May 29, 2015).
15. Alcaraz blogs at http://enlosbolsillosdelpantalon.blogspot.com/, and García's blog is located at http://yoaquiiahora.blogspot.com/.
16. Alejandra Torres Reyes, "El número de 'ninis' baja por primera vez en España desde 2008," *El País,* May 15, 2015, http://politica.elpais.com/politica/2015/05/15/actualidad/1431706801_248114.html (accessed May 30, 2015).
17. Carmen Pérez-Lanzac, "La apatía de un 'nini.'" *El País,* November 2, 2014, http://politica.elpais.com/politica/2014/10/22/actualidad/1413974500_362946.html (accessed May 30, 2015).
18. "María Cabrera, ganadora del VII Premio de Poesía Joven Emilio Alfaro Hardisson 2012," *Ateneo de La Laguna.* Ateneo de La Laguna, July 2, 2015, www.ateneodelalaguna.es/content/view/495/4/ (accessed July 2, 2015).

19. María Cabrera González, "Vaivén, lunes" in *En legítima defensa (Antología). Poetas en tiempos de crisis* (Madrid: Bartleby Editores, 2014), 66.
20. Ibid., 67.
21. Miguel Veyrat, "Canción para ensanchar el grito," in *En legítima defensa*, 341.
22. José Manuel Caballero Bonald, "Terror preventivo," in *En legítima defensa*, 63.
23. Juan Pardo Vidal, "Carta de un emigrante desde Tokio o reflexión sobre la materia oscura," in *En legítima defensa*, 250.
24. Fernando López Guisado, "Abel Santos, poeta," *Elpulso.es*. El Pulso Digital, S.L., January 14, 2014, www.elpulso.es/abel-santos-poeta/ (accessed June 3, 2015).
25. Paul Heywood, "From Dictatorship to Democracy: Changing Forms of Corruption in Spain," in *Democracy and Corruption in Europe*, ed. Donatella Della Porta and Yves Mény (London: Pinter, 1997), 66–67.
26. Ibid., 67.
27. Richard Barker, *Skeletons in the Closet, Skeletons in the Ground: Repression, Victimization and Humiliation in a Small Andalusian Town* (Eastbourne: Sussex Academic Press, 2012), 180–81.
28. W. J. M. Kickert, "Public Governance: The Context of Administrative Innovations in Southern Europe," in *Organizing Innovation*, ed. M. Veenswijk (Amsterdam: IOS Press, 2005), 180.
29. López Guisado, "Abel Santos, poeta," n.p.
30. Abel Santos, "Cuentas la suerte a pulso," in *En legítima defensa*, 298.
31. Dámaso Alonso, "Insomnio," in *Poesía de la generación del 27: Antología crítica recomendada*, ed. Víctor de Lama (Madrid: EDAF, 1997), 261.
32. Except for Muñoz Molina, who, as we have seen, belies his declared disillusionment with history by constant references to the country's past.
33. Santos, "Cuentas la suerte a pulso," in *En legítima defensa*, 298.
34. Alonso, "Insomnio," in *Poesía de la generación del 27*, 261.
35. Alfonso Pérez-Agote, *Cambio religioso en España: los avatares de la secularización* (Madrid: Centro de investigaciones sociológicas, 2012), 119–20.
36. Santos, "Cuentas la suerte a pulso," in *En legítima defensa*, 298.
37. Alonso, "Insomnio," *Poesía de la generación del 27*, 261.
38. Santos, "Cuentas la suerte a pulso," in *En legítima defensa*, 298.
39. Ibid., 298.
40. Alfons Cervera, Prologue to *Marihuana para los pájaros* (Tenerife: Ediciones Baile del Sol, 2008), 9.
41. Núñez, "Venticuatro años" *Marihuana para los pájaros*, 38.
42. Ibid., 38.
43. Santos, "Cuentas la suerte a pulso," in *En legítima defensa*, 298.
44. López Menacho's biographical novel *Yo, precario* [*Precarious*], for instance, offers an account of a part-time worker who is ashamed of being the oldest among the employees in the string of low-paid temporary jobs he has to accept to stay afloat during the crisis. See Javier López Menacho, *Yo, precario* (Barcelona: Los libros del lince, 2013).
45. Manuel V. Gómez, "España y Grecia lideran el empleo a tiempo parcial por falta de otra opción." *El País*, July 13, 2015, http://economia.elpais.com/economia/2015/07/12/actualidad/1436725432_048159.html (accessed July 22, 2015).
46. Santos, "Cuentas la suerte a pulso," in *En legítima defensa*, 299.
47. Ibid., 299.
48. Aurore Ducellier, "Los últimos poetas de las cárceles franquistas: Carlos Álvarez y Alfonso Sastre en Carabanchel (1974–1975)," in *La prisión y las instituciones punitivas en la investigación histórica*, ed. Pedro Oliver Olmo and Jesús Carlos Urda Lozano (Cuenca: Ediciones de la Universidad Castilla—La Mancha, 2014), 778.
49. Carlos Álvarez, "En la taberna," in *En legítima defensa*, 29.
50. Ibid., 29.
51. When the future poet was twelve, her father was executed in Madrid's Porlier prison. See Margarita Almela Boix, "'Para que la vida no yazga envuelta en alto

olvido.' Imágenes de la memoria en la obra de Francisca Aguirre," in *Ecos de la memoria*, ed. Margarita Almela, María García Lorenzo, Helena Guzmán, and Marina Sanfilippo (Madrid: UNED, 2011), 16.

52. María Payeras Grau, "Francisca Aguirre ante la mar de Homero," in *Lo vivo lejano: poéticas españolas en diálogo con la tradición*, ed. Marcela Romano (Mar del Plata: EUDEM, 2009), 83.

53. Sharon Keefe Ugalde, "Traumatic Memories in Poetry of Francisca Aguirre," *Ojáncano* 40 (2011): 7.

54. Marta Caballero, "Francisca Aguirre: '*Historia de una anatomía* es mi esqueleto.'" *El Cultural*, November 17, 2011, El Cultural Electrónico, www.elcultural.com/noticias/letras/Francisca-Aguirre-Historia-de-una-anatomia-es-mi-esqueleto/2386 (accessed July 23, 2015).

55. Quoted in Javier Rodríguez Marcos, "La alicantina Francisca Aguirre, Premio Nacional de Poesía," *El País*, November 17, 2011, http://cultura.elpais.com/cultura/2011/11/17/actualidad/1321484405_850215.html (accessed July 23, 2015).

56. Ezequiel Moltó, "Versos para contar toda una vida," *Cultura El País*, March 22, 2010, http://cultura.elpais.com/cultura/2010/03/22/actualidad/1269212412_850215.html (accessed July 24, 2015).

57. Rodríguez Marcos, "La alicantina," n.p.

58. John C. Wilcox, "A Reconsideration of Two Spanish Women Poets: Ángela Figuera Aymerich and Francisca Aguirre," *Studies in 20th and 21st Century Literature* 16, no. 1 (Winter 1992): 77.

59. Francisca Aguirre, "La sorprendente vida," in *En legítima defensa*, 17.

60. Ibid., 18.

61. Ibid., 17.

62. Keefe Ugalde, "Traumatic Memories," 9.

63. Aguirre, "La sorprendente vida," in *En legítima defensa*, 17.

64. Ibid., 17.

65. Francisca Aguirre, *Espejito, espejito* (San Sebastián de los Reyes: Universidad Popular, 1995), 33.

66. Aguirre, "La sorprendente vida," in *En legítima defensa*, 18.

67. Francisca Aguirre, *Pavana del desasosiego* (Madrid: Ediciones Torremozas, 1999), 15.

68. Aguirre, "La sorprendente vida," in *En legítima defensa*, 18.

69. Sigmund Freud, "Further remarks on the neuro-psychoses of defence," in *The Standard Edition of the Complete Psychological Works of Sigmund Freud*, ed. J. Strachey, Volume 3 (1896; repr. London: Hogarth Press, 1962), 169.

70. Aguirre, "La sorprendente vida," in *En legítima defensa*, 17.

71. Ibid., 19.

72. Ibid., 19.

73. Ibid., 18.

74. Ibid., 18.

75. Ibid., 19.

76. Aguirre, *Espejito, espejito*, 18–19.

77. Aguirre, "La sorprendente vida," in *En legítima defensa*, 18.

78. Gamoneda, Prologue to *En legítima defensa*, 10.

79. "Contribuciones de Lola Borges," *La Cultural de Montreal*, La Cultural de Montreal, July 28, 2015, www.laculturaldemontreal.com/author/lola-borges/ (accessed July 28, 2015).

80. Antonio M. Vélez, "El Banco de España advierte de que la fuga de cerebros puede 'exacerbar los efectos de la crisis,'" *Eldiario.es*, Diario de Prensa Digital S.L., February 19, 2015, www.eldiario.es/economia/Banco-Espana-cerebros-exacerbar-economica_0_358364950.html (accessed July 30, 2015).

81. "In the years previous to the Great Recession, Spain received massive migration inflows: an average of 1.4% of its total domestic population each year between 2000 and 2007. In fact, these inflows continued during the first phase of the crisis, at a rate

of around 1.2% of the total domestic population per year in the period 2008–2010. By contrast, migration outflows were negligible in the period 2000–2007, and only increased to 0.4% of the total domestic population as an annual average in the period 2008–2010. More recently, there have been remarkable changes: in 2012 inflows fell to 0.8% and outflows rose to 1.2% of the domestic population." See Mario Izquierdo, Juan F. Jimeno, and Aitor Lacuesta, "Spain: From Immigration to Emigration?" *Documentos de trabajo* 1503 (Madrid: Banco de España, 2015), 7, www.bde.es/f/webbde/SES/Secciones/Publicaciones/PublicacionesSeriadas/DocumentosTrabajo/15/Fich/dt1503e.pdf (accessed July 30, 2015).

82. Lola Borges Blázquez, Personal interview, August 7, 2015.

83. Álvaro Sánchez, "La emigración de españoles bate el récord desde el inicio de la crisis." *El País*, December 4, 2015, http://politica.elpais.com/politica/2015/12/04/actualidad/1449220349_507822.html (December 4, 2015).

84. Borges Blázquez, Personal interview.

85. Lola Borges Blázquez, "Expaña," in *En legítima defensa*, 56–57.

86. Ibid., 56.

87. Carles Geli, "Un filón editorial," *El País*, February 27, 2013, http://cultura.elpais.com/cultura/2013/02/27/actualidad/1361969898_376895.html (accessed August 4, 2015).

88. Stéphane Hessel, *Time for Outrage! (Indignez-vous!)*, trans. Damion Searls and Alba Arrikha (London: Quartet Books, 2011), 22–23.

89. Pedro J. de la Peña, *Otro 98 es necesario* (Madrid: Huerga y Fierro, 2012), 64.

90. Ibid., 72.

91. Lola Borges Blázquez, "Expaña," in *En legítima defensa*, 57.

92. Ibid., 56.

93. Ibid., 57.

94. Ibid., 57.

95. Ibid., 57.

96. Judith Butler, *Gender Trouble: Feminism and the Subversion of Identity* (New York: Routledge, 1990), 145.

97. Gayatri Spivak, "Revolutions That as Yet Have No Model: Derrida's Limited Inc.," in *The Spivak Reader: Selected Works of Gayati Chakravorty Spivak*, ed. Donna Landry and Gerald MacLean (New York: Routledge, 1996), 86–87.

98. Borges Blázquez, "Expaña," in *En legítima defensa*, 57.

99. Ibid., 57.

100. Amalia Iglesias Serna, "Dos voces nuevas," *Poesía Injuve 2008* (Madrid: Instituto de la Juventud, 2008), 12, www.injuve.es/sites/default/files/Poesía.pdf (accessed December 20, 2015).

101. Juan Sala, " De la Quintana, editor de Amargord: La edición, un ejercicio de resistencia civil continuada," *NuevaTribuna.es* Página 7 Comunicación S.L., Madrid, February 27, 2013, www.nuevatribuna.es/articulo/cultura---ocio/de-la-quintana-editor-de-amargord-la-edicion-un-ejercicio-de-resistencia-civil-continuada/20130227104638088933.html (accessed September 1, 2015).

102. Ibid., n.p.

103. Ibid., n.p.

104. Indhira Suero, "Amargord, el reino de los rebeldes," in *Listín Diario. El periódico de los Dominicanos*, ed. Listín Diario, May 10, 2015. www.listindiario.com/ventana/2015/5/9/366511/Amargord-el-reino-de-los-rebeldes (accessed September 1, 2015).

105. Antonio Orihuela, "España," in *Marca(da) España. Retrato poético de una sociedad en crisis* (Madrid: Amargord, 2014), 35.

106. "Nota final" [Afterword] of *Marca(da) España*, 163.

107. Matías Escalera Cordero, "Así, no (en efecto); paralizados en el tiempo," in *Marca(da) España*, 130.

108. Ibid., 131.

109. Ibid., 133.

110. Ibid., 133.

111. Santiago Alba Rico, Prologue to *Marca(da) España*, 9.
112. Eugenio García Pérez, "Estudio comparativo de la percepción de la realidad española entre los estudiantes Erasmus que visitan Madrid y los estudiantes universitarios de la Universidad de Tirana, Albania," in *Elementos identitarios de la imagen de España, América Latina y de su historia en Albania*, ed. José Manuel Azcona and Anastasi Prodani (Madrid: Dykinson, 2013), 275.
113. Alfredo Martínez Expósito, *Cuestión de imagen: cine y Marca España* (Vigo: Academia del Hispanismo, 2015), 43.
114. Luisa Elena Delgado, *La nación singular: fantasías de la normalidad democrática española (1996–2011)* (Madrid, España: Siglo XXI de España, 2014), 16.
115. Martínez Expósito, *Cuestión de imagen*, 65.
116. Richard Sennett, *The Culture of the New Capitalism* (New Haven & London: Yale University Press, 2006), 18.
117. Justo Villafañe, "La Marca España desde la teoría de la reputación," in *La comunicación empresarial y la gestión de los intangibles en España y Latinoamérica. Informe anual 2014*, ed. Justo Villafañe (Barcelona: Gedisa, 2014), 114.
118. Ibid., 117.
119. Or "Alto Comisionado del Gobierno para la Marca España" in Spanish.
120. "Real Decreto 998/2012, de 28 de junio, por el que se crea el Alto Comisionado del Gobierno para la Marca España y se modifica el Real Decreto 1412/2000, de 21 de julio, de creación del Consejo de Política Exterior," *Boletín Oficial del Estado* 155.1 (29 junio 2012): 46129. www.boe.es/boe/dias/2012/06/29/pdfs/BOE-A-2012-8672.pdf (accessed September 3, 2015).
121. Wayne H. Bowen, *Spaniards and Nazi Germany: Collaboration in the New Order* (Columbia, MO: University of Missouri Press, 2000), 88–89; and Julio Fernández, "Muchos aristócratas se sumaron al Régimen en busca de beneficios personales," *Extraconfidencial*. Extraconfidencial.com, September 19, 2008, 3. http://extraconfidencial.com/noticias/muchos-aristocratas-se-sumaron-al-regimen-en-busca-de-beneficios-personales/ (accessed September 4, 2015).
122. Inditex, or Industria de Diseño Textil, is the largest fashion group in the world and is headquartered in Spain.
123. Marialuz Vicondoa, "La intervención en los mercados debe ser algo excepcional," *Diario de Navarra*, September 28, 2008, 45. www.ifuturo.org/sites/default/files/docs/2124_2008_09_28_DDN_Entrevista Espinosa Monteros.pdf (accessed September 7, 2015).
124. "Inditex sigue inmune a la crisis y gana un 28% más en el primer trimestre," *infoLibre.es*, Ediciones Prensa Libre S.L., June 10, 2015. www.infolibre.es/noticias/economia/2015/06/10/inditex_gana_521millones_primer_trimestre_33847_1011.html (accessed September 7, 2015).
125. Zygmunt Bauman, *Liquid Modernity* (Cambridge: Polity, 2000), 13.
126. Villafañe, "La Marca España," 101.
127. *Marca(da) España*, 10.
128. Alberto García Teresa, "Alto Comisionado para la Marca España," in *Marca(da) España*, 15.
129. In 2014, Amnesty International published a report titled *España: el derecho a protestar, amenazado* [*Spain: The Right to Protest Under Threat*] that listed the instances of an excessive use of force by the agents of police present at the protests. See Amnistía Internacional. *España: El derecho a protestar, amenazado* (Madrid: Amnesty International Publications, 2014), 2, http://amnistiainternacional.org/publicaciones/211-espana-el-derecho-a-protestar-amenazado.html (accessed September 7, 2015).
130. Alba Rico, Prologue to *Marca(da) España*, 9.
131. Ibid., 9.
132. *Marca(da) España*, 18–19.
133. Escalera Cordero, "Así, no (en efecto)," in *Marca(da) España*, 133.
134. Jesús Urceloy, Untitled poem, in *Marca(da) España*, 89.
135. Ibid., 89.

136. Jordi Estivill, "Los prolegómenos de las rentas mínimas en España y en Euskadi." *Intercambio social y desarrollo del bienestar*, ed. Luis Moreno (Madrid: Consejo Superior de Investigaciones Científicas, 1993), 298–99.

137. Spain's largest companies came out of the harshest years of the crisis with record profits. See "Las empresas del Ibex no conocen la crisis: ganaron un 63% más en 2014." *info Libre.es*. Ediciones Prensa Libre S.L., March 18, 2015. www.infolibre.es/noticias/economia/2015/03/18/las_empresas_del_ibex_conocen_crisis_ganaron_mas_2014_29985_1011.html (accessed September 11, 2015).

138. Marina Llorente, "Poemas críticos en la España contemporánea," *Hispania* 91, no. 3 (September 2008): 587, note 2.

139. Marina Llorente, "La *memoria histórica* en la poesía de Isabel Pérez Montalbán y David González," *Hispanic Review* 81, no. 2 (Spring 2013): 186.

140. Even those who are calling to moderation in the evaluation of the crisis are wondering if the word "democracy" can still be applied to the political system of Spain after the concessions made by the government of Mariano Rajoy to the transnational banking concerns. See Víctor Alonso Rocafort, "La crisis política, una representación oligárquica." *Lo llamaban democracia. De la crisis económica al cuestionamiento de un régimen político*, ed. Colectivo Novecento (Barcelona: Icaria, 2013), 51.

141. Llorente, "Poemas críticos," 583.

142. Isabel Pérez Montalbán, "Dictadura financiera," in *Marca(da) España*, 86.

143. David Becerra Mayor, *La Guerra Civil como moda literaria* (Madrid: Clave intelectual, 2015), 256.

144. Bauman, *Liquid Modernity*, 51.

145. Michael Richards, "Grand Narratives, Collective Memory, and Social History: Public Uses of the Past in Postwar Spain," in *Unearthing Franco's Legacy: Mass Graves and the Recovery of Historical Memory in Spain*, ed. Carlos Jerez-Ferrán and Samuel Amago (Notre Dame: University of Notre Dame Press, 2010), 135.

146. Fernando Martínez López and Miguel Gómez Oliver, "Political Responsibilities in Franco's Spain: Recovering the Memory of Economic Repression and Social Control in Andalusia, 1936-45," in *Memory and Cultural History of the Spanish Civil War: Realms of Oblivion*, ed. Aurora G. Morcillo (Leiden and Boston: Brill, 2014), 111.

147. Sima Lieberman, *The Contemporary Spanish Economy: A Historical Perspective* (1982; repr. Oxon: Routledge, 2006), 213–15.

148. Becerra Mayor, *La Guerra Civil*, 421–42.

149. Ángel Loureiro, "Pathetic Arguments," *Journal of Spanish Cultural Studies* 9, no. 2 (July 2008): 229.

150. Pérez Montalbán, "Dictadura financiera," in *Marca(da) España*, 87.

151. Evictions have become a daily reality in Spain, reaching the peak of 517 evictions per day in the first three months of 2012. See Rafael Carmona, "Se disparan los desahucios en España y alcanzan los 517 diarios," *ABC*. Diario Abc, S.L., July 23, 2012. www.abc.es/20120723/economia/abci-desahucios-espaa-201207231723.html (accessed September 20, 2015).

152. Bauman, *Liquid Modernity*, 39.

153. Pérez Montalbán, "Dictadura financiera," in *Marca(da) España*, 85.

154. Ibid., 86.

155. Jonathan Mayhew, "The Persistence of Memory: Antonio Gamoneda and the Literary Institutions of Late Modernity," *New Spain, New Literatures*, ed. Luis Martín-Escudillo and Nicholas Spadaccini (Nashville: Vanderbilt University Press, 2010), 149–50.

156. Ibid., 154.

157. Daniel Aguirre-Oteiza, "The Song of Disappearance: Memory, History, and Testimony in the Poetry of Antonio Gamoneda," *Studies in 20th & 21st Century Literature* 36, no. 2 (2012): 376–77, http://newprairiepress.org/cgi/viewcontent.cgi?article=1790&context=sttcl (accessed May 21, 2015).

158. Antonio Gamoneda, *Canción errónea* (Barcelona: Tusquets Editores, 2012), 45–46.

159. Ibid., 41.

160. Emphasis in the original.
161. Javier Rodríguez Marcos, "Antonio Gamoneda: 'Soy un indignado que disiente,'" *El País*, November 3, 2012. http://cultura.elpais.com/cultura/2012/10/31/actualidad/1351685094_698963.html (accessed December 23, 2015).
162. Ibid., n.p.
163. Gamoneda, *Canción errónea*, 85.
164. Ibid., 110.
165. Ibid., 73.
166. Alberto García-Teresa, Prologue to *Disidentes. Antología de poetas críticos españoles (1990–2014)*, ed. Alberto García-Teresa (Madrid: La Oveja Roja, 2015), 9.
167. The poet died in May 2015, after the collection was released.
168. Enrique Martín Corrales, "Objeción de conciencia," in *Disidentes. Antología de poetas críticos españoles (1990–2014)*, 418.
169. Ibid., 417.
170. Gsús Bonilla, "Ágora," in *Disidentes. Antología de poetas críticos españoles (1990–2014)*, 296–98.
171. Ibid., 298.

Conclusion

The Discussion Needs to Continue

In August 2016, the *Wall Street Journal* celebrated the lack of impact that the Spaniards' incapacity to elect a government had on the functioning of the economy: "Spain's robust economic expansion is defying concerns that a political impasse, now in its ninth month with no end in sight, would tarnish one of Europe's economic bright spots."[1] *Financial Times* was so enthusiastic about Spain's economic prospects throughout the second half of 2016 that its headlines acquired uncharacteristically lyrical undertones. "Spain's Recovery Story Shines Through the Global Gloom," proclaimed the November 26, 2016, article by Tobias Buck.[2] The vocabulary used by the journalist to describe the state of the country's economy—"buoyant consumption and rising exports," "more innovative," "increasingly lively"—leaves no doubt as to how far Spain has traveled in terms of improving its global image since the harshest years of the crisis that had placed it among the despised PIGS.[3] The journalists' optimism was echoed by the officials of the International Monetary Fund. The concluding statement of the annual assessment for the year 2016 conducted by the IMF offered glowing praise for Spain's economic progress and made no mention of the fraught electoral process that occupied almost the entirety of the year under review: "The Spanish economy has continued its impressive recovery and strong job creation. Earlier reforms and confidence-enhancing measures have paid off, and combined with external tailwinds and fiscal loosening fueled the strong economic rebound of the past two years."[4] Liquid capital has liberated itself from the strictures that the nation-state could impose on it, and as a result, the greatest political crisis Spain has experienced in its history as a democratic state has had no noticeable effect on the economy.

Mariano Rajoy seems to have taken his 2016 reappointment to the position of head of the Spanish government as a mandate to change nothing about the way his party has functioned since its electoral victory in 2011. In his investiture speech, Rajoy insisted that a discussion of the EU-mandated austerity measures or of the Catalan push for independence was out of the question:

> A mí no me está permitido negociar la unidad de España, o la igualdad de los españoles. Tampoco incumplir nuestros compromisos con la UE;

> lo mismo que no me está permitido quebrar la estabilidad presupuestaria. Sería inútil pretender que estas materias se sometan a negociación. Ni lo puedo hacer yo, ni lo puede hacer nadie. Digo más: es responsabilidad de todos que no se sometan a discusión. [I am not allowed to negotiate the unity of Spain or the equality of Spaniards. Nor to fail to meet our obligations to the EU, just like I'm not allowed to damage the budgetary stability. It would be useless to expect these matters to be negotiated. Neither I nor anybody else can do that. I'll say more: it is everybody's responsibility not to open them to discussion.][5]

Of course, Rajoy's efforts to erase the transformative experiences of the crisis years will not be successful. The mass protests and the discussion spaces they opened, the rise of Podemos, the multitude of activist groups and collectives, and the "cultures of anyone" that are "opening the construction of knowledge and of values to participation by anyone"[6] cannot be undone by the shaky electoral success of Partido Popular that took over ten months to translate into an ascension to power. By refusing to participate in these discussions, Rajoy is further delegitimizing an already tenuous mandate and precluding an exploration of the changing role of national governments in the globalized world.

Spain is not alone in experiencing unprecedented tensions in its most recent electoral cycle. The rise of right-wing populism on both sides of the Atlantic Ocean is a result of growing confusion in the face of the collapse of the industrial model and a displacement from productive employment of large segments of the population. For now, Spain has not produced a strong nationalist movement in the image of France's National Front, Austria's Freedom Party, or Hungary's Jobbik. Spain's response to the explosion of economic precariousness has not been a xenophobic, anti-immigrant movement but a leftist Podemos that calls for inclusion of marginalized groups and acceptance of immigrants. There is, of course, no guarantee that Spain will remain immune to the lure of right-wing populism that is proving so attractive to its neighbors. Still, for the moment, the expression "Spain is different" can finally acquire positive undertones in what concerns the lack of appeal that xenophobic populism currently has for Spaniards. In the words of philosopher José Luis Abellán, now is the time for the Spanish-speaking world to occupy a leading role in the creation of alternative forms of coexistence on a rapidly shrinking planet:

> El hecho de que el estado-nación haya entrado en un proceso de decadencia, con vistas a su superación, dentro de un impulso que hemos dado en llamar «globalización», vuelve a dar alas a la tendencia universalista que impulsó a la cultura española desde sus orígenes. . . . La cultura en lengua española puede volver a tomar un protagonismo de primer orden dentro del proceso de globalización que estamos viviendo, convirtiéndose en una cultura de la intermediación global. [The fact that the nation-state has begun to decay and is in the process of being

> left behind, within the impulse that has been termed "globalization," revives the universal trend that inspired the Spanish culture since its origins. . . . The Spanish-language culture can take a leading role within the process of globalization that we are experiencing, transforming into a culture of global dialogue.][7]

Abellán's vision might seem too optimistic, yet aside from a somewhat essentialist definition of the cultural production in the Spanish language, the philosopher's observations as to the value of the transformational processes and discussions taking place in the Spanish-speaking world merit attention. As I have attempted to demonstrate in this book, Spanish crisis writers exist in a vibrant cultural space where solidarity prevails and xenophobia is rejected.

The incapacity of national governments to constrain the movement of liquid capital has led to a crisis of legitimation of the constitutional order of the nation-state.[8] As we have seen, writers of the crisis are almost unanimous in their questioning of the value of a supposedly democratic system of government that leaves many people disenfranchised as a result of austerity measures that erode welfare protections and favor supranational banking concerns. The crisis has finished the work of stripping the Transition of its hallowed status that had already begun at the end of the twentieth and the beginning of the twenty-first centuries. Among the authors analyzed in this book, Muñoz Molina stands alone in his efforts to use the Transition-era rhetoric to silence the discussions about the legacy of the dictatorship and its impact on today's political and economic structures of Spain. The recovery of the historical memory of the civil war and the dictatorship will continue because, as the authors of crisis literature have convincingly demonstrated, the collapse of the country's economy in the aftermath of the global economic crisis cannot be fully understood without an analysis of how the foundations of this faulty economic order were laid down during the Franco era and never questioned during the Transition.

As borders grow increasingly porous to the flows of capital and the migratory currents that accompany the unconstrained flight of capital, new forms of coexistence will have to arise. In his exploration of the rising role of cities in the globalized world, Benjamin Barber points out that the new reality of interconnectedness requires new approaches to organizing our political space: "Today, after a long history of regional success, the nation-state is failing us on the global scale. It was the perfect political recipe for the liberty and independence of autonomous peoples and nations. It is utterly unsuited to interdependence."[9] Crisis writers place an emphasis on the need to build links of solidarity if we are to avoid explosions of xenophobia and anti-immigrant sentiment in increasingly heterogeneous societies. At the same time, the only effective response to the destruction of welfare protections by liquid capital can come from collective action. The act of reading itself presupposes certain isolation, yet novelists and poets of the crisis warn against abandoning efforts to reach out to others in favor of solitary reflection on the transformations we are witnessing. These writers offer no recipes for overcoming the effects of the crisis because, as they keep reminding us, the transition to the liquid model of economy creates issues that are too immense to be addressed by a single individual.

The triumphalist narratives as to the victory that has supposedly been gained over the crisis that are advanced by the Spanish government and enthusiastically supported by the supranational financial authorities like the IMF should not be allowed to blind us to the continued dismantling of welfare protections in the service of the needs of liquid capital. The precarization of employment that we are witnessing is only the first step in the constitution of postwork societies where productive employment will be out of reach for a great number of people. The small daily changes that are taking us in this direction often go unnoticed in the maelstrom of exaggeratedly scandalous news stories. The unabating media spectacle of politics leads to "the obliteration of the real and the substitution of an ersatz, contrived, and manufactured pseudo-reality for the ordinary experiences of everyday life."[10] The postcrisis recovery that Spain is experiencing does not cancel out the suffering of those who were evicted from their apartments, like Charly in Miguel Ángel Sánchez's *Ejecución hipotecaria,* those who had to leave the country in search of employment like Carla in Gopegui's *El comité de la noche* or several of the contributors to *Marca(da) España* and *En legítima defensa,* or those who can expect to make a living only from a patchwork of precarious part-time jobs like Prado's Juan Urbano and García Montero's Ramón Montenegro. The "haunting spectre of insecurity"[11] that is present in the lives of all but the very rich is not going to disappear because it is an unavoidable side effect of the liquid economy. Crisis literature will remain relevant for a long time to come because the liquefaction of existence that it discusses is only beginning.

NOTES

1. Jeannette Neumann, "Why Is Spain's Economy Expanding So Robustly Without a Government?," *Wall Street Journal,* August 25, 2016, www.wsj.com/articles/why-is-spains-economy-expanding-so-robustly-without-a-government-1472136858 (accessed November 7, 2016).

2. Tobias Buck, "Spain's Recovery Story Shines Through the Global Gloom," *Financial Times.* The Financial Times Ltd., November 29, 2016, www.ft.com/content/549d7f08-9a09-11e6-8f9b-70e3cabccfae (accessed December 18, 2016).

3. Ibid., n.p.

4. "Spain: Staff Concluding Statement of the 2016 Article IV Mission," *International Monetary Fund,* International Monetary Fund, December 13, 2016, www.imf.org/en/News/Articles/2016/12/13/MS121316-Spain-Staff-Concluding-Statement-of-Article-IV-Mission (accessed December 18, 2016).

5. "Discurso de Mariano Rajoy. Sesión de Investidura," Partido Popular, Oficina de Información, *El Mundo*, October 29, 2016, http://estaticos.elmundo.es/documentos/2016/10/29/discurso_investidura_rajoy.pdf, 4 (accessed November 8, 2016).

6. Luis Moreno-Caballud, *Cultures of Anyone: Studies on Cultural Democratization in the Spanish Neoliberal Crisis*, trans. Linda Grabner (Liverpool: Liverpool University Press, 2015), 4.

7. Quoted in Luisa Elena Delgado, *La nación singular: fantasías de la normalidad democrática española (1996–2011)* (Madrid, España: Siglo XXI de España, 2014), 156.

8. Philip Bobbitt, *The Shield of Achilles: War, Piece, and the Course of History* (New York: Anchor Books, 2003), 213.

9. Benjamin R. Barber, *If Mayors Ruled the World: Dysfunctional Nations, Rising Cities* (New Haven: Yale University Press, 2013), 3.

10. Douglas Kellner, *Media Spectacle* (London & New York: Routledge, 2003), 16.

11. Zygmunt Bauman, *Strangers at Our Door* (Cambridge: Polity, 2016), 33.

Bibliography

Abellán, José Luis. "España en el siglo XXI: Hacia una cultura de la intermediación global." Conference paper presented at *Global Crossroads 2012: Redefining Spain in the 21st Century*. April 11–14, 2012. University of Auckland, New Zealand.

Afinoguénova, Eugenia and Jaume Martí-Olivella. "A Nation under Tourists' Eyes: Tourism and Identity Discourses in Spain." In *Spain Is (Still) Different: Tourism and Discourse in Spanish Identity*. Edited by Eugenia Afinoguénova and Jaume Martí-Olivella, xi–xxxviii. Plymouth, MA: Lexington Books, 2008.

Agamben, Giorgio. *Homo Sacer: Sovereign Power and Bare Life*. Translated by Daniel Heller-Roazen. 1995. Reprint, Stanford: Stanford University Press, 1998.

Aguilar Fernández, Paloma. "Justice, Politics, and Memory in the Spanish Transition." In *The Politics of Memory: Transitional Justice in Democratizing Societies*. Edited by Alexandra Barahona de Brito, Carmen González-Enríquez, and Paloma Aguilar, 92–118. Oxford: Oxford University Press, 2001.

———. "La presencia de la guerra civil y del franquismo en la democracia española." *Pasajes* 11 (Spring 2003): 12–23.

———." Los debates sobre la memoria histórica." *Claves de Razón Práctica* 172 (2007): 64–68. www.academia.edu/9740546/LOS_DEBATES_SOBRE_LA_MEMORIA_HISTÓRICA.

Aguirre, Francisca. *Espejito, espejito*. San Sebastián de los Reyes: Universidad Popular, 1995.

———. "La sorprendente vida." In *En legítima defensa (Antología). Poetas en tiempos de crisis*. Edited by Manuel Rico, 17–19. Madrid: Bartleby Editores, 2014.

———. *Pavana del desasosiego*. Madrid: Ediciones Torremozas, 1999.

Aguirre-Oteiza, Daniel. "The Song of Disappearance: Memory, History, and Testimony in the Poetry of Antonio Gamoneda." *Studies in 20th & 21st Century Literature* 36, no. 2 (2012): 373-–90. http://newprairiepress.org/cgi/viewcontent.cgi?article=1790&context=sttcl.

Alba Rico, Santiago. Prologue to *Marca(da) España. Retrato poético de una sociedad en crisis*. 8–11. Madrid: Amargord, 2014.

Alcaraz, Christian. "Christian Alcaraz." http://enlosbolsillosdelpantalon.blogspot.com/.

Alonso, Dámaso. "Insomnio." In *Poesía de la generación del 27: Antología crítica recomendada*. Edited by Víctor de Lama, 261–62. Madrid: EDAF, 1997.

Álvarez, Carlos. "En la taberna." In *En legítima defensa (Antología). Poetas en tiempos de crisis*. Edited by Manuel Rico, 29. Madrid: Bartleby Editores, 2014.

Álvarez, Isabel. "Immigration and the Written Press: What Is It Actually Being Portrayed?" *The International Journal of Diversity in Organizations, Communities and Nations* 7, no. 5 (2007): 121–29. http://ijd.cgpublisher.com/product/pub.29/prod.576.

Álvarez-Blanco, Palmar. "De etnomanías y otros terrores. Literatura e inmigración en la España del siglo XXI." In *Contornos de la narrativa española actual (2000–2010). Un diálogo entre creadores y críticos*. Edited by Palmar Álvarez-Blanco and Toni Dorca, 56–65. Madrid/Frankfurt am Main: Iberoamericana/Vervuert, 2011.

Álvarez-Blanco, Palmar and Toni Dorca, eds. *Contornos de la narrativa española actual (2000–2010). Un diálogo entre creadores y críticos*. Madrid and Frankfurt am Main: Iberoamericana/Vervuert, 2011.

Álvarez Fernández, José Ignacio. *Memoria y trauma en los testimonios de la represión franquista*. Barcelona: Anthropos, 2007.

Álvarez Junco, José. *Mater dolorosa. La idea de España en el siglo XIX*. Madrid: Taurus, 2001.

Amin, Ash. "Post-Fordism: Models, Fantasies and Phantoms of Transition." In *Post-Fordism: A Reader*. Edited by Ash Amin. Oxford: Blackwell, 1994.

Amnistía Internacional. *España: El derecho a protestar, amenazado*. Madrid: Amnesty International Publications, 2014. http://amnistiainternacional.org/publicaciones/211-espana-el-derecho-a-protestar-amenazado.html.

Andalucía: Golpe a la crisis. (Doce narradores en clave del cuento). Madrid: Ediciones Atlantis, 2012.

Aniorte, Javier. "Rafael Chirbes, traducción y reconocimiento en Alemania: Los paisajes del alma." In *Las letras valencianas en la literatura universal. Problemas de recepción y traducción: el paisaje y el tiempo*. Edited by Juan Antonio Albaladejo Martínez, 149–56. Sevilla: Bienza: 2012.

Aparicio, Rosa, and Andrés Tornos. "Towards an Analysis of Spanish Integration Policy." In *The Integration of Immigrants in European Societies: National Differences and Trends of Convergence*. Edited by Friedrich Heckmann and Dominique Schnapper, 213–52. Stuttgart: Lucius & Lucius, 2003.

Aronowitz, Stanley, Dawn Esposito, William DiFazio, and Margaret Yard. "The Post-Work Manifesto." In *Post-Work*. Edited by Stanley Aronowitz and Jonathan Cutler, 31–80. New York: Routledge, 1998.

Ayala-Dip, J. Ernesto. "Retrato de los impostores. Reseña de *Crematorio* de Rafael Chirbes." *El País*, October 27, 2007. http://elpais.com/diario/2007/10/27/babelia/1193442618_850215.html.

Azancot, Nuria. "Rafael Chirbes: '*Crematorio* me ha llenado de dudas y me ha tenido en un pozo oscuro durante muchos meses.'" *El Cultural*, December 27, 2007: 12–15.

Azurmendi, Mikel. "Diez tesis sobre el multiculturalismo." *Cuadernos de Pensamiento Político* 8 (October–December 2005): 97–111.

Báez-Ramos, Josefa. "*Crematorio* by Rafael Chirbes." *Hispania* 91, no. 3 (September 2008): 627–28.

Bagué Quílez, Luis. "A Journey through the Desert: Trends of Commitment in Contemporary Spanish Poetry." In *Post-Authoritarian Cultures: Spain and Latin America's Southern Cone*. Edited by Luis Martín-Estudillo and Roberto Ampuero, 58–74. Nashville: Vanderbilt University Press, 2008.

Bañón Hernández, Antonio, Samantha Requena Romero, and Ma Eugenia González Cortés. "Health, Immigration and the Welfare State in Times of Crisis: A Critical Discourse Analysis." In *Discourses on Immigration in Times of Economic Crisis: A Critical Perspective*. Edited by María Martínez Lirola, 113–41. Newcastle upon Tyne: Cambridge Scholars, 2013.

Barber, Benjamin R. *If Mayors Ruled the World: Dysfunctional Nations, Rising Cities*. New Haven: Yale University Press, 2013.

Barker, Richard. *Skeletons in the Closet, Skeletons in the Ground: Repression, Victimization and Humiliation in a Small Andalusian Town*. Eastbourne: Sussex Academic Press, 2012.

Bassets, Marc. "Una nueva primavera en Estados Unidos." *El País*, March 15, 2015. http://economia.elpais.com/economia/2015/03/13/actualidad/1426278977_656369.html.

Bauman, Zygmunt. *Liquid Modernity*. Cambridge: Polity, 2000.

———. *Liquid Love*. Cambridge: Polity, 2003.

———. *Consuming Life*. Cambridge: Polity, 2007.

———. *Strangers at Our Door*. Cambridge: Polity, 2016.

Bauman, Zygmunt, and Carlo Bordoni. *State of Crisis*. Cambridge: Polity, 2014.

Becerra Mayor, David. "*Episodios de una g uerra interminable* de Almudena Grandes: ¿novelas de la memoria histórica?" *Kamchatka: revista de análisis cultural* 2 (December 2013): 241–70. https://ojs.uv.es/index.php/kamchatka/article/view/3162.

———. *La Guerra Civil como moda literaria*. Madrid: Clave intelectual, 2015.

Beck, Ulrich. *Risk Society: Towards a New Modernity*. Translated by Mark Ritter. London: Sage, 1992.

———. *German Europe*. Translated by Rodney Livingstone. 2012. Reprint, Cambridge: Polity Press, 2013.

———. *The Metamorphosis of the World*. Cambridge: Polity Press, 2016.

Begin, Paul D. "The Pistols Strike Again! On the Function of Punk in the Peninsular 'Generation X' Fiction of Ray Loriga and Benjamín Prado." In *Generation X Rocks: Contemporary Peninsular Fiction, Film, and Rock Culture*. Edited by Christine Henseler and Randolph D. Pope, 15–32. Nashville: Vanderbilt University Press, 2007.

Belmonte Serrano, José, and Celia Ruiz García. "*París-Austerlitz*: la escritura como salvación." *Monteagudo* 21 (2016): 357–62. http://revistas.um.es/monteagudo/article/view/258421/194591.

Berasátegui, Blanca. "Rafael Chirbes. '*Crematorio* era el esplendor y *En la orilla* es la caída.'" *El Cultural*, March 1, 2013: 8–11. El Cultural Electrónico. www.elcultural.com/revista/letras/Rafael-Chirbes/32403.

Berdyaev, Nicholas. *The Meaning of the Creative Act*. Translated by Donald A. Lowrie. London: Gollanz, 1955.

Bermúdez, Silvia. "Let's Talk About Sex?: From Almudena Grandes to Lucía Etxebarria, the Volatile Values of the Spanish Literary Market." In *Women's Narrative and Film in Twentieth-Century Spain: A World of Difference(s)*. Edited by Ofelia Ferrán and Kathleen Mary Glenn, 223–37. New York: Routledge, 2002.

Bernal, Antonio-Miguel. *España, proyecto inacabado: costes / beneficios del imperio*. Madrid: Marcial Pons, 2005.

Bernecker, Walther L. "España y la unión europea: una relación cambiante." In *España: del consenso a la polarización. Cambios en la democracia española*. Edited by Walther L. Bernecker and Günther Maihold, 45–69. Madrid/Frankfurt am Main: Iberoamericana/Vervuert, 2007.

———. "El debate sobre las memorias históricas en la vida política española." In *Escribir después de la dictadura: La producción literaria y cultural en las posdictaduras de Europa e Hispanoamérica*. Edited by Janett Reinstädler, 64–96. Madrid/Frankfurt am Main: Iberoamericana/Vervuert, 2011.

Bobbitt, Philip. *The Shield of Achilles: War, Peace, and the Course of History*. New York: Anchor Books, 2003.

Boix, Margarita Almela. "'Para que la vida no yazga envuelta en alto olvido.' Imágenes de la memoria en la obra de Francisca Aguirre." In *Ecos de la memoria*. Edited by Margarita Almela Boix, María García Lorenzo, Helena Guzmán, and Marina Sanfilippo, 11–37. Madrid: UNED, 2011.

Bolaños, Alejandro. "Las grandes empresas solo crean trabajo temporal en 2015." *El País*, November 24, 2015. http://economia.elpais.com/economia/2015/11/24/actualidad/1448368671_571076.html.

Bonilla, Gsús. "Ágora." In *Disidentes. Antología de poetas críticos españoles (1990–2014)*. Edited by Alberto García-Teresa, 289–91. Madrid: La Oveja Roja, 2015.

Borges Blázquez, Lola. "Expaña." In *En legítima defensa (Antología). Poetas en tiempos de crisis*. Edited by Manuel Rico, 56–57. Madrid: Bartleby Editores, 2014.

———. Personal interview. August 7, 2015.

Bowen, Wayne H. *Spaniards and Nazi Germany: Collaboration in the New Order*. Columbia, MO: University of Missouri Press, 2000.

Bradatan, Cristina E., and Dumitru Sandu. "Before Crisis: Gender and Economic Outcomes of the Two Largest Immigrant Communities in Spain." *International Migration Review* 46, no. 1 (Spring 2012): 221–43.

Bueler, Louis E. *The Tested Woman Plot: Women's Choices, Men's Judgments, and the Shaping of Stories*. Columbus: Ohio State University Press, 2001.

Buck, Tobias. "Spain's Recovery Story Shines Through the Global Gloom." *Financial Times*, November 29, 2016. www.ft.com/content/549d7f08-9a09-11e6-8f9b-70e3cabccfae.

Busqueta, Josep Manel, et al. *Desentrañando la Unión Europea. Informes de economía crítica* 10. Seminari d'Economia Crítica: TAIFA, 2014. http://seminaritaifa.org/pdf/Informe_10_ES.pdf.

Butler, Judith. *Gender Trouble: Feminism and the Subversion of Identity*. New York: Routledge, 1990.

Caballero, Marta. "Francisca Aguirre: ' *Historia de una anatomía* es mi esqueleto.'" *El Cultural*, November 17, 2011. El Cultural Electrónico. www.elcultural.com/noticias/letras/Francisca-Aguirre-Historia-de-una-anatomia-es-mi-esqueleto/2386.

Caballero Bonald, José Manuel. "Terror preventivo." In *En legítima defensa (Antología). Poetas en tiempos de crisis*. Edited by Manuel Rico, 63. Madrid: Bartleby Editores, 2014.

Cabrera González, María. "Vaivén, lunes." In *En legítima defensa (Antología). Poetas en tiempos de crisis*. Edited by Manuel Rico, 66–67. Madrid: Bartleby Editores, 2014.

Calavita, Kitty. "Immigration, Law, and Marginalization in a Global Economy: Notes from Spain." *Law & Society Review* 32, no. 3 (1998): 529–66.

Calvo Carilla, José Luis. "Lecturas críticas sobre la Transición: el caso de Rafael Chirbes." In *El relato de la Transición / La Transición como relato*. Edited by José Luis Calvo Carilla, Carmen Peña Ardid, et al., 119–46. Zaragoza: Prensas de la Universidad de Zaragoza, 2013.

Calvo Serer, Rafael. *España, sin problema*. Third ed. 1949. Reprint, Madrid: Ediciones Rialp, 1957.

Campos, Prado. "Chirbes sube al escenario." *El Confidencial*, November 23, 2014. www.elconfidencial.com/cultura/2014-11-23/chirbes-sube-al-escenario_483207/.

Carcelén, Jean-François. "En la orilla de Rafael Chirbes: paisaje después de la canalla." *Ínsula* 803 (November 2013): 11–13.

Carmona, Rafael. "Se disparan los desahucios en España y alcanzan los 517 diarios." *ABC*. Diario Abc, S.L., July 23, 2012. www.abc.es/20120723/economia/abci-desahucios-espaa-201207231723.html.

Carreño, Óscar. "El dorado descanso de los cambiadores de un mundo sin cambiar." *Quimera* 291 (2008): 70.

Casanovas, Jordi. *Ruz/Bárcenas*. Teatre Lliure y Teatro del Barrio: 2014. www.scribd.com/document/285590025/RUZ-BARCENAS.

Castellani, Jean-Pierre. "Antonio Muñoz Molina entre literatura y periodismo: las columnas." *Olivar* 2, no. 2 (2001): 123–34. www.olivar.fahce.unlp.edu.ar/article/view/OLIv02n02n02/pdf.

Castells, Manuel. *The Power of Identity. The Information Age: Economy, Society, and Culture*. Vol. II. Oxford: Blackwell, 1998.

———. *Networks of Outrage and Hope: Social Movements in the Internet Age*. Cambridge: Polity, 2012.

Castles, Stephen, Hein de Haas, and Mark J. Miller. *The Age of Migration: International Population Movements in the Modern World*. 5th ed. London: Palgrave Macmillan, 2014.

Castilla-León: Golpe a la crisis. (Cinco narradores en clave del cuento). Madrid: Ediciones Atlantis, 2012.

Cazorla-Sánchez, Antonio. "From Anti-Fascism to Humanism: The Spanish Civil War as a Crisis of Memory." In *Memory and Cultural History of the Spanish Civil War: Realms of Oblivion*. Edited by Aurora G. Morcillo, 21–50. Leiden/Boston: Brill, 2014.

Cenarro, Ángela. "Beneficencia y asistencia social en la España franquista: el Auxilio Social ylas políticas del régimen." In *Pobreza, marginación, delincuencia y políticas sociales bajo el franquismo*. Edited by Conxita Mir, Carme Agustí, and Josep Gelonch, 93–111. Lleida: Edicions de la Universitat de Lleida, 2005.

Checa Olmos, Francisco, Juan Carlos Checa Olmos, and Ángeles Arjona Garrido. "Immigration and Political Discourse in Spain: The Example of Party Platforms." In *Discourses on Immigration in Times of Economic Crisis: A Critical Perspective*. Edited by María Martínez Lirola, 167–93. Newcastle upon Tyne: Cambridge Scholars, 2013.

Checa Olmos, Juan Carlos, and Ángeles Arjona Garrido. "Anti-Immigrant Feeling in Spain." *Polish Sociological Review* 177 (2012): 39–53.
Chirbes, Rafael. *Crematorio*. Barcelona: Anagrama, 2007.
———. *En la orilla*. Barcelona: Anagrama, 2013.
———. *La caída de Madrid*. Barcelona: Anagrama, 2000.
———. *Pecados originales. La buena letra y Los disparos del cazador*. Barcelona: Anagrama, 2013.
———. *Por cuenta propia*. Barcelona: Anagrama, 2010.
———. "Un parlamento que nunca pronuncié. Texto del discurso póstumo de Chirbes para laentrega del Premio Nacional de Narrativa." *Cuarto Poder*, June 1, 2016. www.cuartopoder.es/tribuna/2016/06/01/parlamento-no-pronuncie/8663.
Ciplijauskaité, Biruté. "Belén Gopegui entre la búsqueda y la denuncia de la realidad." In *La pluralidad narrativa. Escritores españoles contemporáneos (1984–2004)*. Edited by Ángeles Encinar and Kathleen M. Glenn, 119–31. Madrid: Biblioteca Nueva, 2005.
Clavel, André. "Danse avec le diable. Rafael Chirbes explore l'Espagne et ses ombres." *Lire*, April 1, 2009. www.lexpress.fr/culture/livre/cremation_815709.html.
Cohen, Anthony P. *The Symbolic Construction of Community*. London: Tavistock Publications, 1985.
Colectivo Todoazen. *El año que tampoco hicimos la revolución*. 2005. Reprint, Barcelona: DeBolsillo, 2007.
Colmeiro, José F. *Memoria histórica e identidad cultural: De la postguerra a la postmodernidad*. Barcelona: Anthropos, 2005.
Conrad, Christian A. *Morality and Economic Crisis: Enron, Subprime & Co*. Hamburg: Disserta Verlag, 2010.
"Contribuciones de Lola Borges." *La Cultural de Montreal*. La Cultural de Montreal. July 28, 2015. www.laculturaldemontreal.com/author/lola-borges/.
Cortés, Rebeca. "Lucía Etxebarría entra en 'Campamento de Verano' para pagar una deuda con Hacienda." *ABC*. Diario Abc, S.L., July 17, 2013. www.abc.es/estilo/gente/20130717/abci-deuda-hacienda-lleva-lucia-201307170942.html.
Covarrubias, Sebastián de. *Tesoro de la lengua castellana o española*. Edited by Martín de Riquer. 1611. Reprint, Barcelona: Horta, 1943.
Cruz, Jacqueline. "Of Good Torturers and Evil Workers: Antonio Muñoz Molina's *Plenilunio*." In *Traces of Contamination: Unearthing the Francoist Legacy in Contemporary Spanish Discourse*. Edited by Eloy E. Merino and H. Rosi Song, 199—220. Lewisburg: Bucknell University Press, 2005.
Cruz, Juan. "Garzón ha hundido IU de Madrid por estrategia." *El País*, June 1, 2015. http://ccaa.elpais.com/ccaa/2015/05/30/madrid/1433009380_693704.html.
Cué, Carlos E. "Rajoy: 'La crisis ya es historia.'" *El País*, December 11, 2014. http://politica.elpais.com/politica/2014/12/11/actualidad/1418305803_331591.html.
Cuñado, Isabel. "Despertar tras la amnesia: guerra civil y postmemoria en la novela española del siglo XXI." *Dissidences* 3, no. 1 (2007): 1–11. http://digitalcommons.bowdoin.edu/cgi/viewcontent.cgi?article=1058&context=dissidences.
Curry, Alice. *Environmental Crisis in Young Adult Fiction: A Poetics of Earth*. New York: Palgrave Macmillan, 2013.
Davis, Madeleine. "Is Spain Recovering Its Memory? Breaking the 'Pacto del Olvido.'" *Human Rights Quarterly* 27, no. 3 (August 2005): 858–80.
De Fina, Anna. *Identity in Narrative: A Study of Immigrant Discourse*. Amsterdam & Philadelphia: John Benjamins, 2003.
Delgado, Luisa Elena. *La nación singular: fantasías de la normalidad democrática española (1996–2011)*. Madrid, España: Siglo XXI de España, 2014.
Diccionario manual e ilustrado de la lengua española. Madrid: Espasa Calpe, 1950.
"Discurso de Mariano Rajoy. Sesión de Investidura." Partido Popular. Oficina de Información. *El Mundo*, October 29, 2016. http://estaticos.elmundo.es/documentos/2016/10/29/discurso_investidura_rajoy.pdf.
Dolgin Casado, Stacey. "Benjamín Prado: La literatura es lo contrario del olvido." *Ojáncano* 33 (April 2008): 103–13.

Domínguez, Antonio José. "Entrevista al autor de la novela *En la orilla.*" *Mundo Obrero,* June 21, 2013. www.mundoobrero.es/pl.php?id=2860.

Donaire, Ginés. "García Montero analiza la influencia del exilio como 'condición vital' en la obra de Alberti." *El País,* September 12, 2000. http://elpais.com/diario/2000/09/12/andalucia/968710942_850215.html.

———. "Antonio Muñoz Molina viaja al centro de su imaginario." *El País,* January 8, 2015. http://ccaa.elpais.com/ccaa/2015/01/08/andalucia/1420712798_259802.html.

Ducellier, Aurore. "Los últimos poetas de las cárceles franquistas: Carlos Álvarez y Alfonso Sastre en Carabanchel (1974–1975)." In *La prisión y las instituciones punitivas en lainvestigación histórica.* Edited by Pedro Oliver Olmo y Jesús Carlos Urda Lozano, 777–95. Cuenca: Ediciones de la Universidad Castilla—La Mancha, 2014.

Dussel, Enrique. "Beyond Eurocentrism: The World-System and the Limits of Modernity." In *The Cultures of Globalization.* Edited by Fredric Jameson and Masao Miyoshi, 3–31. Translated by Eduardo Mendieta. Durham and London: Duke University Press, 1998.

Edicionesatlantis.com: Catálogo. Ediciones Atlantis. December 1, 2015. www.edicionesatlantis.com/catalogo/12/andalucia-golpe-a-la-crisis/680/.

Encarnación, Omar G. "Labor and Pacted Democracy: Post-Franco Spain in Comparative Perspective." *Comparative Politics* 33, no. 2 (April 2001): 337–55.

En legítima defensa (Antología). Poetas en tiempos de crisis. Madrid: Bartleby Editores, 2014.

Enric, Juliana, *Modesta España. Paisaje después de la austeridad.* Barcelona: RBA Libros, 2012.

Escalera Cordero, Matías. "Así, no (en efecto)." In *Marca(da) España. Retrato poético de una sociedad en crisis.* 131–35. Madrid: Amargord, 2014.

Escobedo, María. "Luis cía Montero: 'La necesidad de cuidar y ser cuidado es el mejor antídoto contra la cultura del usar y tirar.'" *Cuadernos hispanoamericanos* 743 (May 2012): 123–35.

Escudero, Rafael, Patricia Campelo, Carmen Pérez González, and Emilio Silva. *Qué hacemos por la memoria histórica.* Madrid: Ediciones Akal, 2013.

Espinosa Maestre, Francisco. "De saturaciones y olvidos. Reflexiones en torno a un pasado queno puede pasar." *Hispania Nova* 7 (2007): n.p. http://hispanianova.rediris.es/7/dossier/07d013.pdf.

Estivill, Jordi. "Los prolegómenos de las rentas mínimas en España y en Euskadi." In *Intercambio social y desarrollo del bienestar.* Edited by Luis Moreno, 289–319. Madrid: Consejo Superior de Investigaciones Científicas, 1993.

Etxebarria, Lucía. "Por qué está corriendo un desnudo mío por la red." *Vanity Fair Blogs. Vanity Fair.* January 24, 2012. http://blogs.revistavanityfair.es/vanityshow/2012/01/24/lucia-etxebarria.

———. "Acabo de quedarme." *Facebook.* Facebook. 30 March 2015. https://www.facebook.com/lucia.etxebarria.3.

———. "Carta abierta al diario Público y a Podemos de Lucía Etxebarría." *Público,* March 12, 2016. www.publico.es/culturas/carta-abierta-al-diario-publico.html.

———. *Liquidación por derribo.* Barcelona: Planeta, 2013.

Eusebio, Carmen de. "Rafael Chirbes: 'La tensión en el lenguaje debe entenderse como tensiónen el proceso de aprendizaje al que se somete al lector.'" *Cuadernos hispanoamericanos* 757–58 (2013): 247–57.

Ezkerra, Iñaki. "¡Maldita sea!" *ABC.* Diario ABC, S.L., February 22, 2013: 17. http://hemeroteca.abc.es/nav/Navigate.exe/hemeroteca/madrid/abc/2013/02/22/017.html.

———. "Rafael Chirbes o después del ladrillo." *El Correo* [Bilbao, España], March 23, 2013: 7. www.anagrama-ed.es/view/11766/Chirbes NH 512 -El Correo.pdf.

Faber, Sebastián. "Review of Antonio Muñoz Molina, *Todo lo que era sólido*" (Barcelona: Seix Barral, 2012). *ALCES XXI* 1 (2013): 733–47. http://alcesxxi.org/revista1/revista1/pdfs/Faber2.pdf.

Fernández, Julio. "Muchos aristócratas se sumaron al Régimen en busca de beneficios personales." *Extraconfidencial.* Extraconfidencial.com. September 19, 2008: 1–4. http:/

/extraconfidencial.com/noticias/muchos-aristocratas-se-sumaron-al-regimen-en-busca-de-beneficios-personales/.
Fernández Carbajal, Alfonso. "La política de vivienda en España durante el franquismo." *Ciudad y Territorio. Estudios Territoriales* 35, no. 138 (2003): 639–54.
Fernández Cubas, Cristina. "Hablar con viejas." In *La habitación de Nona*, 45–56. Barcelona: Tusquets Editores, 2015.
Fernández-Savater, Amador. "Emborronar la CT (del «No a la guerra» al 15-M)." In *CT o la Cultura de la Transición. Crítica a 35 años de cultura española*. Edited by Guillem Martínez, 37–51. Barcelona: Random House Mondadori, 2012.
Ferrer, Jesús. "Chirbes no está en crisis." *La Razón*, March 7, 2013: 65. www.anagrama-ed.es/view/11771/Chirbes NH 512 -La Razon.pdf.
Flores Andrade, Anselmo. "Los empresarios y la transición a la democracia en España." *Estudios Sociológicos* 18, no. 54 (2000): 695–726.
Forner, Juan Pablo. *Oración apologética por la España y su mérito literario*. 1786. Reprint, Madrid: Publicaciones Españolas, 1956.
Fotheringham, Alasdair. "In Spain's heart, a slum to shame Europe. The continent's largest shanty town – just a 15-minute drive from the affluent center of Madrid." *The Independent*. Independent Print Ltd., November 27, 2011. www.independent.co.uk/news/world/europe/in-spains-heart-a-slum-to-shame-europe-6268652.html.
Freud, Sigmund. "Further remarks on the neuro-psychoses of defense." In *The Standard Edition of the Complete Psychological Works of Sigmund Freud*. Edited by J. Strachey, 159–85. Vol. 3. 1896. Reprint, London: Hogarth Press, 1962.
Fukuyama, Francis. *The End of History and the Last Man*. New York: The Free Press, 1992.
Fusi, Juan Pablo, and Jordi Palafox. *España: 1808–1996. El desafío de la modernidad*. Madrid: Espasa Calpe, 1997.
Gamoneda, Antonio. *Canción errónea*. Barcelona: Tusquets Editores, 2012.
———. Prologue to *En legítima defensa (Antología). Poetas en tiempos de crisis*. Edited by Manuel Rico, 9–10. Madrid: Bartleby Editores, 2014.
Garcia Garcia, Sergio. *Yo, aquí y ahora*. http://yoaquiiahora.blogspot.com/.
García Martín, Luis. "*La intimidad de la serpiente*." *El Cultural*, February 27, 2003. El Cultural Electrónico. www.elcultural.com/revista/letras/La-intimidad-de-la-serpiente/6510.
García Montero, Luis. *No me cuentes tu vida*. Barcelona: Planeta, 2012.
———. "Páginas en presente." *El País*, December 28, 2013. http://cultura.elpais.com/cultura/2013/12/19/actualidad/1387467794_395351.html.
García Pérez, Eugenio. "Estudio comparativo de la percepción de la realidad española entre los estudiantes Erasmus que visitan Madrid y los estudiantes universitarios de la Universidad de Tirana, Albania." In *Elementos identitarios de la imagen de España, América Latina y desu historia en Albania*. Edited by José Manuel Azcona and Anastasi Prodani, 275–88. Madrid: Dykinson, 2013.
García Recio, Javier. "Mirar sin adornos." *La Opinión de Málaga*, March 23, 2013: 46. www.opinionmalaga.com/especiales/libros/2013/10/04/mirar-sin-adornos/.
García-Teresa, Alberto. Prologue to *Disidentes. Antología de poetas críticos españoles (1990–2014)*. Edited by Alberto García-Teresa, 9–11. Madrid: La Oveja Roja, 2015.
Geli, Carles. "Un filón editorial." *El País*, February 27, 2013. http://cultura.elpais.com/cultura/2013/02/27/actualidad/1361969898_376895.html.
Gills, Barry K. "Going South: Capitalist Crisis, Systemic Crisis, Civilisational Crisis." *Third World Quarterly* 31, no. 2 (2010): 169–84.
Golob, Stephanie R. "Volver: The Return of/to Transitional Justice Politics in Spain." *Journal of Spanish Cultural Studies* 9, no. 2 (July 2008): 127–41. http://www.tandfonline.com/doi/abs/10.1080/14636200802283647.
Gómez, Manuel V. "España y Grecia lideran el empleo a tiempo parcial por falta de otra opción." *El País*, July 13, 2015. http://economia.elpais.com/economia/2015/07/12/actualidad/1436725432_048159.html.

Gómez, Manuel V., and Cristina Galindo. "El ladrillo acelera su caída libre." *El País*, March 11, 2013. http://economia.elpais.com/economia/2013/03/10/actualidad/1362934741_926777.html.

Gómez, Manuel V., and Carmen Sánchez-Silva. "La precariedad laboral va para largo." *El País*, March 8, 2014. http://economia.elpais.com/economia/2014/03/07/actualidad/1394227355_704422.html.

Gómez López-Quiñones, Antonio. *La guerra persistente. Memoria, violencia y utopía: representaciones contemporáneas de la Guerra Civil española*. Madrid: Iberoamericana, 2006.

———. "La misma guerra para un nuevo siglo: Textos y contextos de la novela sobre la Guerra Civil." In *Contornos de la narrativa española actual (2000–2010): Un diálogo entre creadores y críticos*. Edited by Palmar Álvarez-Blanco and Toni Dorca, 111–19. Madrid and Frankfurt: Iberoamericana-Vervuert, 2011.

Gopegui, Belén. *El comité de la noche*. Barcelona: Penguin Random House, 2014.

———. "Tres condiciones necesarias, aunque no suficientes, para una literatura de izquierdas." In *Contornos de la narrativa española actual (2000–2010). Un diálogo entre creadores y críticos*. Edited by Palmar Álvarez-Blanco and Toni Dorca, 281–83. Madrid/Frankfurt am Main: Iberoamericana/Vervuert, 2011.

———. "Literatura y política bajo el capitalismo." *Guaraguao*. Asociación Centro de Estudio y Cooperación para América Latina. 9, no. 21 (Winter 2005): 9–20. www.jstor.org/stable/25596474.

Goytisolo, Juan. "Hemos vivido un sueño." *El País*, July 22, 2012. http://elpais.com/elpais/2012/07/19/opinion/1342710838_352755.html.

Graham, Helen. "Coming to Terms with the Past: Spain's Memory Wars." *History Today* 54, no. 5 (May 2004): 29–31.

———. *La guerra y su sombra: Una visión de la tragedia española en el largo siglo XX europeo*. Translated by Sandra Souto Kustrin. Barcelona: Crítica, 2013.

Gramsci, Antonio. *Prison Notebooks*. Edited and translated by Joseph A. Buttigieg. Vol. II. New York: Columbia University Press, 1996.

Grandes, Almudena. *Los besos en el pan*. Barcelona: Tusquets, 2015.

"Grifols apuesta por pagar las donaciones de plasma como complemento de ingresos para los parados." *Europa Press*, April 17, 2012. www.europapress.es/economia/noticia-economia-empresas-grifols-apuesta-pagar-donaciones-plasma-complemento-ingresos-parados-20120417153907.html.

Guillén, Arturo. "Europe: A Crisis Within a Crisis." *International Journal of Political Economy* 41, no. 3 (Fall 2012): 41–68.

Gutiérrez, Pablo. *Democracia*. Barcelona: Seix Barral, 2012.

Habermas, Jürgen. *The Postnational Constellation: Political Essays*. Edited and translated by Max Pensky. Cambridge, MA: MIT Press, 2001.

Hall, Stuart. "Brave New World." *Marxism Today* (Oct 1988): 24–29. Unz.org. www.unz.org/Pub/MarxismToday-1988oct-00024.

Harrison, Ewan, and Sara McLaughlin Mitchell. *The Triumph of Democracy and the Eclipse of the West*. New York: Palgrave Macmillan, 2014.

Henseler, Christine. *Spanish Fiction in the Digital Age: Generation X Remixed*. New York: Palgrave Macmillan, 2011.

Henseler Christine and Randolph D. Pope, eds. *Generation X Rocks: Contemporary Peninsular Fiction, Film, and Rock Culture*. Nashville: Vanderbilt University Press, 2007.

Hermoso, Borja. "Fuego real en el 'crematorio' de Chirbes." *El País*, March 7, 2011. http://elpais.com/diario/2011/03/07/cultura/1299452402_850215.html.

Herralde, Jorge. "Rafael Chirbes: la voz de la verdad." *La constancia de un testigo. Ensayossobre Rafael Chirbes*. Edited by Augusta López Bernasocchi and José Manuel López de Abiada, 135–41. Madrid: Verbum: 2011.

Hessel, Stéphane. *Time for Outrage! (Indignez-vous!)*. Translated by Damion Searls and Alba Arrikha. London: Quartet Books, 2011.

Hevia, Elena. "España es un pantano que todo lo va pudriendo." *El Periódico de Catalunya*, March 20, 2013: 58–59. www.elperiodico.com/es/noticias/ocio-y-cultura/rafael-chirbes-espana-pantano-que-todo-pudriendo-2345048.

Heywood, Paul. "From Dictatorship to Democracy: Changing Forms of Corruption in Spain." In *Democracy and Corruption in Europe*. Edited by Donatella Della Porta and Yves Mény, 65–84. London: Pinter, 1997.

"Historias de Usera." *Historias de Usera*. Kubik Fabrik 2016. www.historiasdeusera.com/las-historias.

Houssin, Xavier. "'Crémation,' de Rafael Chirbes: au plus court vers l'Apocalypse." *Le Monde*, April 9, 2009. www.anagrama-ed.es/view/10801/Crematorio -Le Monde.pdf.

Humlebæk, Carsten. "Creating a New Cohesive National Discourse in Spain after Franco." In *Post-Authoritarian Cultures: Spain and Latin America's Southern Cone*. Edited by Luis Martín-Estudillo and Roberto Ampuero, 196–217. Nashville: Vanderbilt University Press, 2008.

———. *Spain: Inventing the Nation*. London: Bloomsbury Academic, 2015.

Huyssen, Andreas. *Present Pasts: Urban Palimpsests and the Politics of Memory*. Stanford: Stanford University Press, 2003.

Iarocci, Michael. *Properties of Modernity: Romantic Spain, Modern Europe, and the Legacies of Empire*. Nashville: Vanderbilt University Press, 2006.

Ibáñez Ehrlich, María-Teresa. *Ensayos sobre Rafael Chirbes*. Madrid: Iberoamericana, 2006.

Iglesias, Eduardo. *Los elegidos*. Barcelona: Los libros del lince, 2014.

Iglesias Serna, Amalia. "Dos voces nuevas." *Poesía Injuve 2008*. Madrid: Instituto de la Juventud, 2008. 11–14. www.injuve.es/sites/default/files/Poesía.pdf.

"Inditex sigue inmune a la crisis y gana un 28% más en el primer trimestre." *infoLibre.es*. Ediciones Prensa Libre S.L., June 10, 2015. www.infolibre.es/noticias/economia/2015/06/10/inditex_gana_521millones_primer_trimestre_33847_1011.html.

Izquierdo, Mario, Juan F. Jimeno, and Aitor Lacuesta. "Spain: From Immigration to Emigration?" *Documentos de trabajo* 1503. Madrid: Banco de España, 2015. www.bde.es/f/webbde/SES/Secciones/Publicaciones/PublicacionesSeriadas/DocumentosTrabajo/15/Fich/dt1503e.pdf.

Joppke, Christian. "Immigration Challenges the Nation-State." In *Challenge to the Nation-State: Immigration in Western Europe and the United States*. Edited by Christian Joppke, 5–46. Oxford: Oxford University Press, 1998.

Keefe Ugalde, Sharon. "Traumatic Memories in Poetry of Francisca Aguirre." *Ojáncano* 40 (2011): 7–20.

Kellner, Douglas. *Media Spectacle*. London & New York: Routledge, 2003.

Kickert, W. J. M. "Public Governance: The Context of Administrative Innovations in Southern Europe." In *Organizing Innovation*. Edited by M. Veenswijk, 173–91. Amsterdam: IOS Press, 2005.

Koch, Tommaso. "Las tensas relaciones de Lucía Etxebarria en la Red." *Cultura. El País*, December 20, 2011. http://cultura.elpais.com/cultura/2011/12/20/actualidad/1324335603_850215.html.

Kristeva, Julia. *Powers of Horror: An Essay on Abjection*. Translated by Leon S. Roudiez. New York: Columbia University Press, 1982.

"La Audiencia Nacional investigará a las cúpulas de Caja España y Caja Duero." *El País*, October 29, 2014. www.elmundo.es/economia/2014/07/29/53d7cc4c22601d15558b459d.html.

Labanyi, Jo. "Memory and Modernity in Democratic Spain: The Difficulty of Coming to Terms with the Spanish Civil War." *Poetics Today* 28, no. 1 (Spring 2007): 89–116.

———. *Spanish Literature: A Very Short Introduction*. Oxford: Oxford University Press, 2010.

Labrador Méndez, Germán. "Las vidas *subprime*: la circulación de *historias de vida* como tecnología de imaginación política en la crisis española (2007–2012)." *Hispanic Review* 80, no. 4 (Autumn 2012): 557–81.

Lafuente, Gumersindo and Silvia Bravo. "El paro y la desigualdad no dejan ver la recuperación." *El País*, August 1, 2015. http://politica.elpais.com/politica/2015/08/01/actualidad/1438444946_541840.html.

Laín Entralgo, Pedro. *España como problema*. Madrid: Seminario de Problemas Hispanoamericanos, 1948.

Lama, Víctor de, ed. *Poesía de la generación del 27: Antología crítica recomendada*. Madrid: EDAF, 1997.

"Las empresas del Ibex no conocen la crisis: ganaron un 63% más en 2014." *info Libre.es*. Ediciones Prensa Libre S.L., March 18, 2015. www.infolibre.es/noticias/economia/2015/03/18/las_empresas_del_ibex_conocen_crisis_ganaron_mas_2014_29985_1011.html.

"La Sexta ofrece el desenlace de *Crematorio* con la emisión de sus últimos dos capítulos." *FormulaTV*, February 19, 2012. www.formulatv.com/noticias/23672/lasexta-ofrece-desenlace-crematorio-emision-ultimos-dos-capitulos/2/.

Leuenberger, Daniel. "'Una imagen de mí mismo que no he querido romper.' Perspectivas delpasado en *Los disparos del cazador*." In *La constancia de un testigo. Ensayos sobre Rafael Chirbes*. Edited by Augusta López Bernasocchi and José Manuel López de Abiada, 163–78. Madrid: Verbum: 2011.

"Ley 52/2007, de 26 de diciembre, por la que se reconocen y amplían derechos y se establecen medidas en favor de quienes padecieron persecución o violencia durante la guerra civil yla dictadura." *Boletín Oficial del Estado* 310 (December 27, 2007): 53410–16. www.boe.es/buscar/pdf/2007/BOE-A-2007-22296-consolidado.pdf.

Liddell, Henry George, and Robert Scott. *A Greek-English Lexicon*. Oxford: Clarendon Press, 1996.

Lieberman, Sima. *The Contemporary Spanish Economy: A Historical Perspective*. 1982. Reprint, Oxon: Routledge, 2006.

"*Liquidación por derribo*. Planeta de Libros." *Planeta de Libros*. Grupo Planeta, n.d. www.planetadelibros.com/liquidacion-por-derribo-libro-116567.html.

Lilley, Sasha. "Introduction," in *Capital and Its Discontents: Conversations with Radical Thinkers in a Time of Tumult*, 1–23. Oakland, CA: PM Press, 2011.

Lizcano, Emmánuel. "Sin los cuentos sobre la crisis, a los de arriba no les salen las cuentas." In *Fuera de lugar: conversaciones entre crisis y transformación*. Edited by Amador Fernández-Savater, 141–50. Madrid: Machado Libros, 2013.

Lladó, Xavier. "España incluye el franquismo dentro de los '70 años de paz.'" *elMón*. Totmedia. September 8, 2015. http://elmon.cat/noticia/107092/index.html.

Llorente, Marina. "Poemas críticos en la España contemporánea." *Hispania* 91, no. 3 (September 2008): 579–89.

———. "La *memoria histórica* en la poesía de Isabel Pérez Montalbán y David González." *Hispanic Review* 81, no. 2 (Spring 2013): 181–200.

———. "Exile and Erasure: A Poetic Reconstruction of the Spanish Past in Antonio Crespo Massieu's *Elegía en Portbou*." In *Sites of Memory in Spain and Latin America: Trauma, Politics, and Resistance*. Edited by Aída Díaz de León, Marina Llorente, and Marcella Salvi, 63–76. Lanham, MD: Lexington Books, 2015.

López, Isidro. "Consensonomics: la ideología económica en la CT." In *CT o la Cultura de la Transición. Crítica a 35 años de cultura española*. Edited by Guillem Martínez, 77–88. Barcelona: Random House Mondadori, 2012.

López, Isidro, and Emmanuel Rodríguez. *Fin de ciclo. Financiarización, territorio y sociedad de propietarios en la onda larga del capitalismo hispano (1959–2010)*. Madrid: Traficantesde Sueños, 2010. www.traficantes.net/sites/default/files/pdfs/Fin de ciclo-Traficantes de Sueños_0.pdf.

López Bernasocchi, Augusta, and José Manuel López de Abiada, eds. *La constancia de un testigo. Ensayos sobre Rafael Chirbes*. Madrid: Verbum: 2011.

López de Abiada, José Manuel. "Entrevista a Rafael Chirbes." In *La constancia de un testigo. Ensayos sobre Rafael Chirbes*. Edited by Augusta López Bernasocchi and José Manuel López de Abiada, 12–20. Madrid: Verbum: 2011.

López Bernasocchi, Augusta, and José Manuel López de Abiada. "Hacia *Crematorio*, de Rafael Chirbes. Guía de lectura." In *La constancia de un testigo. Ensayos sobre Rafael Chirbes*. Edited by Augusta López Bernasocchi and José Manuel López de Abiada, 279–369. Madrid: Verbum, 2011.

López Guisado, Fernando. "Abel Santos, poeta." *Elpulso.es*. El Pulso Digital, S.L., January 14, 2014. www.elpulso.es/abel-santos-poeta/.

López Menacho, Javier. *Yo, precario*. Barcelona: Los libros del lince, 2013.

López-Valero Colbert, Olga. *The Gaze on the Past: Popular Culture and History in Antonio Muñoz Molina's Novels*. Lewisburg: Bucknell University Press, 2007.

Lorite García, Nicolás. "How the Media Affect Intercultural Relationships in Times of Change." In *Discourses on Immigration in Times of Economic Crisis: A Critical Perspective*. Edited by María Martínez Lirola, 216–37. Newcastle upon Tyne: Cambridge Scholars, 2013.

Loureiro, Ángel. "Pathetic Arguments." *Journal of Spanish Cultural Studies* 9, no. 2 (July 2008): 225–37.

Lucas, Antonio. "Fallece Rafael Chirbes, la letra y la rabia de la crisis." *El Mundo*, August 16, 2015. www.elmundo.es/cultura/2015/08/15/55cf71bd46163f45298b4577.html.

"Lucía Etxeberría denuncia a integrantes de 'Sálvame' y de 'Campamento de Verano' por acoso y maltrato." *La voz de Galicia*, August 1, 2013. www.lavozdegalicia.es/noticia/television/2013/08/01/etxeberria-denuncia-integrantes-salvame-campamento-verano-acoso-maltrato/00031375346977884762705.htm.

"Lucía Etxebarria la lía en Twitter con el teléfono de información sobre el accidente aéreo."*ABC*. Diario Abc, S.L., n.p. March 24, 2015. www.abc.es/estilo/gente/20150324/abci-lucia-etxebarria-twitter-telefono-201503241835.html.

Manetto, Francesco. "Iglesias renuncia a una reforma integral de la Constitución." *El País*, November 20, 2015. http://politica.elpais.com/politica/2015/11/20/actualidad/1448052762_141488.html.

Manrique Sabogal, Winston. " Rafael Chirbes gana el Nacional de Narrativa por *En la orilla*." *El País*, October 7, 2014. http://cultura.elpais.com/cultura/2014/10/07/actualidad/1412667248_803360.html.

Marca(da) España. Retrato poético de una sociedad en crisis. Madrid: Amargord, 2014.

Marcos, José, and Bruno G. Gallo. "La Cañada Real ya tiene su plan." *El País: Madrid*, January 13, 2014. http://ccaa.elpais.com/ccaa/2014/01/13/madrid/1389644669_801094.html.

"María Cabrera, ganadora del VII Premio de Poesía Joven Emilio Alfaro Hardisson 2012." *Ateneo de La Laguna*. www.ateneodelalaguna.es/content/view/495/4/.

Martín Cabrera, Luis. "Contra la suspensión de la mirada crítica: reflexiones sobre la persistencia del conflicto capital / trabajo en la cultura contemporánea española." *Arizona Journal of Hispanic Cultural Studies* 14 (2010): 117–38.

Martín Corrales, Enrique. "Objeción de conciencia." In *Disidentes. Antología de poetas críticos españoles (1990–2014)*. Edited by Alberto García-Teresa, 417–18. Madrid: La Oveja Roja, 2015.

Martín-Estudillo, Luis, and Roberto Ampuero, eds. *Post-Authoritarian Cultures: Spain and Latin America's Southern Cone*. Nashville: Vanderbilt University Press, 2008.

Martín García, Óscar J. "A Country on a Tightrope: The Economic Crisis and the End of an Era in Spanish Politics." *Insight Turkey* 15, no. 3 (Summer 2013): 95–105.

Martínez, Guillem, ed. *CT o la Cultura de la Transición. Crítica a 35 años de cultura española*. Barcelona: Random House Mondadori, 2012.

Martínez-Alier, J. and Jordi Roca. "Spain after Franco: From Corporatist Ideology to Corporatist Reality." *International Journal of Political Economy* 17, no. 4 (Winter 1987/1988): 56–87.

Martínez Expósito, Alfredo. *Cuestión de imagen: cine y Marca España*. Vigo: Academia del Hispanismo, 2015.

Martínez García, Carlos. "La República no solo es historia, es futuro." *ATTAC España*, July 22, 2011. www.attac.es/2011/07/22/la-republica-no-solo-es-historia-es-futuro/.

Martínez Lirola, María, ed. *Discourses on Immigration in Times of Economic Crisis: A Critical Perspective*. Newcastle upon Tyne: Cambridge Scholars, 2013.

Martínez López, Fernando, and Miguel Gómez Oliver. "Political Responsibilities in Franco's Spain: Recovering the Memory of Economic Repression and Social Control in Andalusia, 1936-45." *Memory and Cultural History of the Spanish Civil War: Realms of Oblivion*. Edited by Aurora G. Morcillo, 111–44. Leiden and Boston: Brill, 2014.

Marx, Karl, and Friedrich Engels. *The Communist Manifesto*. Edited by D. Ryazanoff. 1848. Reprint, New York: Russell & Russell, 1963.

Mateo, Juan José. "Rivera se compromete a apoyar las exhumaciones de la Guerra Civil." *El País*, November 18, 2015 http://politica.elpais.com/politica/2015/11/17/actualidad/1447796568_381704.html.

Mayhew, Jonathan. "The Persistence of Memory: Antonio Gamoneda and the Literary Institutions of Late Modernity." In *New Spain, New Literatures*. Edited by Luis Martín-Escudillo and Nicholas Spadaccini, 149–62. Nashville: Vanderbilt University Press, 2010.

Mermall, Thomas. "Culture and the Essay in Modern Spain." *The Cambridge Companion to Modern Spanish Culture*. Edited by David T. Gies, 163–72. Cambridge: Cambridge University Press, 1999.

Molinas, César (Cesar_Molinas). "Prueba también 'Todo lo que era sólido' de Muñoz Molina. Son dos maneras de escribir el mismo libro." September 24, 2013, 10:41 p.m. Tweet.

———. *Qué hacer con España: del capitalismo castizo a la refundación de un país*. Barcelona: Destino, 2013.

Moltó, Ezequiel. "Versos para contar toda una vida." *Cultura El País*, March 22, 2010. http://cultura.elpais.com/cultura/2010/03/22/actualidad/1269212412_850215.html.

Monereo, Manolo. *De la crisis a la revolución democrática*. Madrid: El Viejo Topo, 2013.

Montoliú, Pedro. *Madrid en la posguerra, 1939–1946: los años de la represión*. Madrid: Silex, 2005.

Morcillo, Aurora G., ed. *Memory and Cultural History of the Spanish Civil War: Realms of Oblivion*. Leiden and Boston: Brill, 2014.

Moreno-Caballud, Luis. "La imaginación sostenible: culturas y crisis económica en la España actual." *Hispanic Review* 80, no. 4 (Autumn 2012): 535–55.

———. *Cultures of Anyone: Studies on Cultural Democratization in the Spanish Neoliberal Crisis*. Translated by Linda Grabner. Liverpool: Liverpool University Press, 2015.

Mori, Moisés. "De estatura humana. Voces de un realismo radical." Página Abierta 226 (May–June 2013): 58. Pensamiento crítico. www.pensamientocritico.org/moimor0713.htm.

Muñoz, Pablo. "Acerca del *Comité de la noche* de Belén Gopegui." *Diagonal*. Diagonalperiódico.net. August 9, 2015. www.diagonalperiodico.net/culturas/27464-acerca-del-comite-la-noche-belen-gopegui.html.

Muñoz Molina, Antonio. *Como la sombra que se va*. Barcelona: Seix Barral, 2014.

———. *Todo lo que era sólido*. Barcelona: Seix Barral, 2013.

Navarro, Elvira. *La trabajadora*. Barcelona: Literatura Random House, 2014.

Navarro, Vicente. "The Social Crisis of the Eurozone: The Case of Spain." *International Journal of Health Services* 43, no. 2 (2013): 189–92.

Navarro Martínez, Eva. "La novela de Benjamín Prado: Cómo construirse un mundo y unarealidad propios." *Letras peninsulares* 14, no. 3 (Winter 2001–2002): 405–26.

Néspolo, Matías. "Vivimos en un callejón sin salida." *El Mundo*, March 20, 2013: 45. Editorial Anagrama. www.anagrama-ed.es/view/11777/Chirbes NH 512 -El Mundo E.pdf.

Neumann, Jeannette. "Why Is Spain's Economy Expanding So Robustly Without a Government?" *Wall Street Journal*, August 25, 2016. www.wsj.com/articles/why-is-spains-economy-expanding-so-robustly-without-a-government-1472136858.

Nichols, William J. "Sifting through the Ashes. An Interview with Rafael Chirbes." *Arizona Journal of Hispanic Cultural Studies* 12 (2008): 219–35.

Nora, Pierre. "Between Memory and History: *Les Lieux de Mémoire*." *Representations* 26 (Spring 1989): 7–24.

"Nota final." In *Marca(da) España. Retrato poético de una sociedad en crisis*. 163. Madrid: Amargord, 2014.

Núñez, Raúl. *Marihuana para los pájaros*. Tenerife: Ediciones Baile del Sol, 2008.

Odartey-Wellington, Dorothy. *Contemporary Spanish Fiction: Generation X*. Newark: University of Delaware Press, 2008.

Oñoro Otero, Cristina. "Otras maneras de habitar el espacio urbano: los Nuevos Espacios y Formatos teatrales de Madrid (2008–2014)." In *Espacios urbanos en el teatro español de lossiglos XX y XXI*. Edited by Cerstin Bauer-Funke, 377–94. Hildesheim: Georg Olms Verlag, 2016.

Orihuela, Antonio. "España." In *Marca(da) España. Retrato poético de una sociedad en crisis*. 35–37. Madrid: Amargord, 2014.

Orsini-Saillet, Catherine. "Ejemplaridad y ambigüedad en la obra novelesca de Rafael Chirbes." In *La ejemplaridad en la narrativa española contemporánea (1950–2010)*. Edited by Amélie Florenchie and Isabelle Touton, 77–94. Madrid-Frankfurt am Main: Iberoamericana-Vervuert: 2011.

Ortega Lucas, Miguel A. "Angelina Gatell: 'Los últimos testigos de la guerra no podemos callar sobre aquello.'" *Eldiario.es*, June 28, 2014. www.eldiario.es/andalucia/Angelina-Gatell-ultimos-testigos-podemos_0_275772479.html.

Ortega y Gasset, José. *España invertebrada. Bosquejo de algunos pensamientos históricos*. 8th ed. 1921. Reprint, Madrid: Revista de Occidente, 1952.

Paniagua, Juan Luis, and Luis J. Ramiro. *Voz, conflicto y salida. Un estudio sobre faccionalismo: Nueva Izquierda, 1992–2001*. Madrid: Editorial Complutense, 2003.

Pardo Vidal, Juan. "Carta de un emigrante desde Tokio o reflexión sobre la materia oscura." In *En legítima defensa (Antología). Poetas en tiempos de crisis*. Edited by Manuel Rico, 249–50. Madrid: Bartleby Editores, 2014.

Payeras Grau, María. "Francisca Aguirre ante la mar de Homero." In *Lo vivo lejano: poéticas españolas en diálogo con la tradición*. Edited by Marcela Romano, 83–102. Mar del Plata: EUDEM, 2009.

Peña, Pedro J. de la. *Otro 98 es necesario*. Madrid: Huerga y Fierro, 2012.

Pérez, Janet. "Tradition, Renovation, Innovation: The Novels of Belén Gopegui." *Anales de la literatura española contemporánea* 28, no. 1 (2003): 115–38.

Pérez-Agote, Alfonso. *Cambio religioso en España: los avatares de la secularización*. Madrid: Centro de investigaciones sociológicas, 2012.

Pérez-Lanzac, Carmen. "La apatía de un 'nini.'" *El País*, November 2, 2014. http://politica.elpais.com/politica/2014/10/22/actualidad/1413974500_362946.html.

Pérez Montalbán, Isabel. "Dictadura financiera." In *Marca(da) España. Retrato poético de una sociedad en crisis*. 85–87. Madrid: Amargord, 2014.

Ploetz, Dagmar. "Novelista y viajero. Aspectos literarios, etnológicos, existenciales: un viaje deida y vuelta de lo sensorial al conocimiento." In *La constancia de un testigo. Ensayos sobreRafael Chirbes*. Edited by Augusta López Bernasocchi and José Manuel López de Abiada, 448–64. Madrid: Verbum: 2011.

Podemos, https://participa.podemos.info/es.

Prádanos, Luis I. "Writing an Engaged Novel in the Network Society: Belén Gopegui, Systemic Narratives and Globalization." In *Global Issues in Contemporary Hispanic Women's Writing: Shaping Gender, the Environment, and Politics*. Edited by Estrella Cibreiro and Francisca López, 208–23. New York and London: Routledge, 2013.

Prado, Benjamín. *Ajuste de cuentas*. Madrid: Alfaguara, 2013.

———. *Mala gente que camina*. Madrid: Santillana, 2006.

Preston, Paul. *The Triumph of Democracy in Spain*. London: Methuen, 1986.

"Proyecto Barrio." *Teatro del Barrio*. www.teatrodelbarrio.com/full-width/.

"¿Qué es LaZonaKubik?" *La Zona Kubik*. Kubik Fabrik, 2016, http://lazonakubik.com/que-es-lzk/.

"¿Quiénes somos?" *Economistas Frente a la Crisis*, 2011, http://economistasfrenteala crisis.com/.

Rabanal, Hayley. *Belén Gopegui: The Pursuit of Solidarity in Post-Transition Spain*. Woodbridge, NY: Tamesis, 2011.
"Rajoy, ante los líderes iberoamericanos: 'España está saliendo ya de la crisis.'" *El Mundo,* October 19, 2013. www.elmundo.es/elmundo/2013/10/19/espana/1382201074.html.
"Rajoy cierra la Oficina de Víctimas como prometió en el 2008: 'Ni un solo euro para recuperarel pasado.'" *Elplural.com,* March 2, 2012. www.elplural.com/2012/03/02/rajoy-cierra-la-oficina-de-victimas-de-la-guerra-civil-y-la-dictadura-como-prometio-en-el-2008-%25e2%2580%259cni-un-solo-euro-para-recuperar-el-pasado%25e2%2580%259d.
"Rajoy, sobre la subvención a la Fundación Francisco Franco: 'No lo sabía.'" *El Periódico,* October 28, 2015. www.elperiodico.com/es/noticias/politica/rajoy-desconoce-subvencion-fundacion-francisco-franco-4624649.
Ramírez Baeza, Fernando. *Subprime*. Alicante: Ayuntamiento de Alicante, 2010.
"Real Decreto 998/2012, de 28 de junio, por el que se crea el Alto Comisionado del Gobierno para la Marca España y se modifica el Real Decreto 1412/2000, de 21 de julio, decreación del Consejo de Política Exterior." *Boletín Oficial del Estado* 155, no. 1 (June 29, 2012): 46129–32. www.boe.es/boe/dias/2012/06/29/pdfs/BOE-A-2012-8672.pdf.
"Recession." Definition 4. *Oxford English Dictionary*. 2nd ed. Vol. IV. Oxford: Clarendon Press, 1989.
"Reiner Wandler en La Cafetera." *La Cafetera*. Radiocable. December 15, 2014. Radio.
Richards, Michael. "Grand Narratives, Collective Memory, and Social History: Public Uses of the Past in Postwar Spain." In *Unearthing Franco's Legacy: Mass Graves and the Recovery of Historical Memory in Spain.* Edited by Carlos Jerez-Ferrán and Samuel Amago, 121–45. Notre Dame: University of Notre Dame Press, 2010.
Richardson, Nathan. "'No pensar,' or Does the Contemporary Spanish Novel of Memory Really Want to Know?: *Tiempo de silencio, Corazón tan blanco, Soldados de Salamina* and Beyond." Letras Hispanas 7, no. 1 (2010): 2–16.
Rocafort, Víctor Alonso. "La crisis política, una representación oligárquica." In *Lo llamaban democracia. De la crisis económica al cuestionamiento de un régimen político.* Edited by Colectivo Novecento. Barcelona: Icaria, 2013.
Ródenas de Moya, Domingo. "El espejo hecho pedazos." *El Periódico,* July 24, 2014. www.anagrama-ed.es/PDF/Crematorio-ElPeriodico.pdf.
Rodríguez Fischer, Ana. "Una mezcla mareante." *Revista de libros* 119 (November 2006): 49. www.revistadelibros.com/articulo_imprimible.php?art=1483&t=articulos.
Rodríguez Marcos, Javier. "La alicantina Francisca Aguirre, Premio Nacional de Poesía." *El País,* November 17, 2011. http://cultura.elpais.com/cultura/2011/11/17/actualidad/1321484405_850215.html.
———. "Antonio Gamoneda: 'Soy un indignado que disiente.'" *El País,* November 3, 2012. http://cultura.elpais.com/cultura/2012/10/31/actualidad/1351685094_698963.html.
———. "La gran novela de la crisis en España." *El País,* March 2, 2013. http://cultura.elpais.com/cultura/2013/02/28/actualidad/1362067884_779080.html.
———. "Una crisis de novela." *El País,* March 16, 2013. http://sociedad.elpais.com/sociedad/2013/03/16/actualidad/1363470608_130051.html
———. "Material de derribo." *Babelia* 1, no. 110 (March 2, 2015): 3–6.
Rodríguez Rivera, Francisco Enrique. *La constitución española de 1978*. Sevilla: Editorial Mad, 2005.
Rogozen-Soltar, Mikaela. "Managing Muslim Visibility: Conversion, Immigration, and Spanish Imaginaries of Islam." *American Anthropologist* 114, no. 4 (December 2012): 611–23.
Romo, José Luis. "La escena 'off' se desinfla." *El Mundo,* January 9, 2016. www.elmundo.es/madrid/2016/01/09/569164de268e3e4f238b4624.html.
Royo, Sebastián. *Lessons from the Economic Crisis in Spain.* New York: Palgrave Macmillan, 2013.

———. "Reforms Betrayed? Zapatero and Continuities in Economic Policy." In *Spain's "Second Transition"? The Socialist Government of José Luis Rodríguez Zapatero*. Edited by Bonnie N. Field, 57–74. Oxon: Routledge, 2011.

Ruiz Torres, Pedro. "Los discursos de la memoria histórica en España." *Hispania Nova* 7 (2007): n.p. http://hispanianova.rediris.es/7/dossier/07d001.pdf.

Ryan, John. "The Greenspan and Bernanke Federal Reserve Roles in the Financial Crisis." In *Lessons from the Financial Crisis: Causes, Consequences, and Our Economic Future*. Edited by Robert W. Kolb, 461–66. Hoboken, NJ: Wiley, 2010.

Ryan, Lorraine. " The Economic Degeneration of Masculinity in Rafael Chirbes's *En la orilla*." *Romance Quarterly* 62, no. 2 (2015): 83–96.

Sala, Juan. "De la Quintana, editor de Amargord: 'La edición, un ejercicio de resistencia civil continuada.'" *NuevaTribuna.es*. Página 7 Comunicación S.L., Madrid. February 27, 2013.www.nuevatribuna.es/articulo/cultura---ocio/de-la-quintana-editor-de-amargord-la-edicion-un-ejercicio-de-resistencia-civil-continuada/20130227104638088933.html.

Sánchez, Álvaro. "La emigración de españoles bate el récord desde el inicio de la crisis." *El País*, December 4, 2015. http://politica.elpais.com/politica/2015/12/04/actualidad/1449220349_507822.html.

Sánchez, Francisco J. "From Neo-Francoist Memory to Political Feeling in Narratives of Unearthing: Sánchez Dragó's *Muertes Paralelas* (2006) and Andrés Trapiello's *Ayer no más* (2012)." *Romance Quarterly* 62, no. 1 (2014): 13–27.

Sánchez, Miguel Ángel. *Ejecución hipotecaria*. Madrid: Fundación SGAE, 2014.

Sánchez-Albornoz, Claudio. *España, un enigma histórico*. Vol. I. Second ed. 1956. Reprint, Buenos Aires: Editorial Sudamericana, 1962.

Sánchez Bermúdez, José Manuel. *The Neoliberal Pattern of Domination: Capital's Reign in Decline*. Leiden and Boston: Brill, 2012.

Sánchez Cazorla, Antonio. *Fear and Progress: Ordinary Lives in Franco's Spain, 1939–1975*. Wiley-Blackwell: Chichester, 2009.

Sánchez-Cuenca, Ignacio. *La desfachatez intelectual: escritores e intelectuales ante la política*. Madrid: Catarata, 2016.

Santamaría Colmenero, Sara. "El peso de la nación en Antonio Muñoz Molina: patriotismo constitucional y el consenso de la Transición." *Journal of Spanish Cultural Studies* 17, no. 2 (2016): 177–95.

Santana, Cintia. "What We Talk About When We Talk About Dirty Realism in Spain." In *Generation X Rocks: Contemporary Peninsular Fiction, Film, and Rock Culture*. Edited by Christine Henseler and Randolph D. Pope, 33–56. Nashville: Vanderbilt University Press, 2007.

Santos, Abel. "Cuentas la suerte a pulso." In *En legítima defensa (Antología). Poetas en tiempos de crisis*. Edited by Manuel Rico, 298–99. Madrid: Bartleby Editores, 2014.

Sanz Villanueva, Santos. "Relatos del postfranquismo: un apunte y diez fichas." In *El relatode la Transición / La Transición como relato*. Edited by José Luis Calvo Carilla, Carmen Peña Ardid, et al., 13–41. Zaragoza: Prensas de la Universidad de Zaragoza, 2013.

Schopenhauer, Arthur. *Parerga and Paralipomena: Short Philosophical Essays*. Vol. 2. Translated by E. F. J. Payne. Oxford: Clarendon Press, 1974.

Segovia Bernabé, José Luis. "La realización del orden justo en la sociedad: responsabilidades." *Corintios XIII: Revista de teología y pastoral de la caridad* 134 (2010): 39–78

Sennett, Richard. *The Culture of the New Capitalism*. New Haven & London: Yale University Press, 2006.

Seremetakis, Nadia C. "The Memory of the Senses, Part I: Marks of the Transitory." In *The Senses Still: Perception and Memory as Material Culture in Modernity*. Edited by Nadia C. Seremetakis, 1–18. Chicago and London: University of Chicago Press, 1996.

Silió, Elisa. "Las batas de los hospitales públicos tienen hasta 80 tipos de bacterias." *El País*, November 19, 2015. http://ccaa.elpais.com/ccaa/2015/11/19/madrid/1447954475_929623.html.

———. "El PSOE y Podemos rechazan los presupuestos del PP por antisociales." *El País*, December 3, 2015. http://ccaa.elpais.com/ccaa/2015/12/03/madrid/1449157351_631072.html.

Song, H. Rosi. "Anti-conformist Fiction: The Spanish 'Generation X.'" In *A Companion to the Twentieth-Century Spanish Novel*. Edited by Marta E. Altisent, 197–207. Woodbridge and Rochester, NY: Tamesis, 2008.

"Spain: Staff Concluding Statement of the 2016 Article IV Mission." *International Monetary Fund*. International Monetary Fund. December 13, 2016. www.imf.org/en/News/Articles/2016/12/13/MS121316-Spain-Staff-Concluding-Statement-of-Article-IV-Mission.

Spivak, Gayatri. "Revolutions That as Yet Have No Model: Derrida's Limited Inc." In *The Spivak Reader: Selected Works of Gayati Chakravorty Spivak*. Edited by Donna Landry and Gerald MacLean, 75–106. New York: Routledge, 1996.

Suero, Indhira. "Amargord, el reino de los rebeldes." In *Listín Diario. El periódico de los Dominicanos*. Edited by Listín Diario. May 10, 2015. www.listindiario.com/ventana/2015/5/9/366511/Amargord-el-reino-de-los-rebeldes.

"Tejerina: 'En el Gobierno hemos trabajado como mulas contra la crisis.'" *El Norte de Castilla*, October 15, 2015. www.elnortedecastilla.es/castillayleon/201510/15/tejerina-gobierno-hemos-trabajado-20151015103610.html.

The Holy Bible, New King James Version. Nashville: T. Nelson, 1982.

"*Todo lo que era sólido*. Planeta de Libros." In *Planeta de Libros*. Grupo Planeta, n.d. www.planetadelibros.com/todo-lo-que-era-solido-libro-90928.html.

Torres Reyes, Alejandra. "El número de 'ninis' baja por primera vez en España desde 2008." *El País*, May 15, 2015. http://politica.elpais.com/politica/2015/05/15/actualidad/1431706801_248114.html.

Touraine, Alain. *After the Crisis*. Translated by Helen Morrison. 2010. Reprint, Cambridge: Polity Press, 2014.

Tovias, Alfred. "Spain in the European Community." In *Democratic Spain: Reshaping External Relations in a Changing World*. Edited by Richard Gillespie, Fernando Rodrigo, and Jonathan Story, 85–105. London & New York: Routledge, 1995.

Urceloy, Jesús. Untitled poem. In *Marca(da) España. Retrato poético de una sociedad en crisis*, 89. Madrid: Amargord, 2014.

Urioste, Carmen. "The Hispanic and Luso-Brazilian World: La cultura española en el marco europeo: Entre lo global y lo local." *Hispania* 89, no. 3 (September 2006): 641–50.

Vallejo-Nágera, Antonio. "Neurosis y problemas médicos del paro obrero." *Anales de la academia nacional de medicina* LV, no. 1 (1935): 199–216.

Valls, Fernando. "¡Sombras . . . , nada más! Primera lectura de *Los viejos amigos* y *Crematorio*de Rafael Chirbes." In *La constancia de un testigo. Ensayos sobre Rafael Chirbes*. Edited by Augusta López Bernasocchi and José Manuel López de Abiada, 478–88. Madrid: Verbum: 2011.

———. "Podredumbre." *Babelia* 1, no. 110 (March 2, 2015): 6.

Vázquez Montalbán, Manuel. *Un polaco en la corte del Rey Juan Carlos*. Madrid: Alfaguara, 1996.

Velázquez, Santiago. "Benjamín Prado, un ajuste de cuentas." *Huffington Post.es*. October 24, 2013. www.huffingtonpost.es/santiago-velazquez/benjamin-prado-un-ajuste-_b_4129537.html.

Vélez, Antonio M. "El Banco de España advierte de que la fuga de cerebros puede 'exacerbar los efectos de la crisis.'" *Eldiario.es*. Diario de Prensa Digital S.L., February 19, 2015. www.eldiario.es/economia/Banco-Espana-cerebros-exacerbar-economica_0_358364950.html.

Vercelli, Alessandro. "Economy and Economics: The Twin Crises." In *The Global Economic Crisis: New Perspectives on the Critique of Economic Theory and Policy*. Edited by Emiliano Brancaccio and Giuseppe Fontana, 27–41. Oxon: Routledge, 2011.

Verdú, Vicente. *El capitalismo funeral. La crisis o la Tercera Guerra Mundial*. Barcelona: Anagrama, 2009.

Veyrat, Miguel. "Canción para ensanchar el grito." In *En legítima defensa (Antología) Poetas en tiempos de crisis*. Edited by Manuel Rico, 341. Madrid: Bartleby Editores, 2014.

Vicondoa, Marialuz. "La intervención en los mercados debe ser algo excepcional." *Diario de Navarra*, September 28, 2008, 45. www.ifuturo.org/sites/default/files/docs/2124_2008_09_28_DDN_Entrevista Espinosa Monteros.pdf.

Villafañe, Justo. "La Marca España desde la teoría de la reputación." In *La comunicación empresarial y la gestión de los intangibles en España y Latinoamérica. Informe anual 2014*. Edited by Justo Villafañe, 97–149. Barcelona: Gedisa, 2014.

Vinyes, Ricard, Montse Armengou, and Ricard Belis. *Los niños perdidos del franquismo*. Translated by Daniel Royo. Barcelona: Plaza & Janés, 2002.

Wilcox, John C. "A Reconsideration of Two Spanish Women Poets: Ángela Figuera Aymerich and Francisca Aguirre." *Studies in 20th and 21st Century Literature* 16, no. 1 (Winter 1992): 65–92.

Zambrano, María. *Delirium and Destiny: A Spaniard in Her Twenties*. Translated by Carol Maier. 1952. Reprint, Albany: State University of New York Press, 1999.

Zanón, Carlos. "Sangre joven, vampiros nuevos." *El País*, November 20, 2014. http://cultura.elpais.com/cultura/2014/11/13/babelia/1415875244_683644.html.

Zovko, Maja. "Algunas peculiaridades de la narrativa actual sobre la inmigración extranjera en España." *Grup de Recerca sobre Migracions*. Galería de Investigacion sobre Migraciones. 3 (2014): 1–13.http://geografia.uab.es/migracions/eng/workingpapers.htm.

Index

About the Author

Dr. Olga Bezhanova received her PhD in Spanish literature from Yale University in 2008. She worked as a visiting professor at Cornell University before accepting a permanent position at Southern Illinois University, Edwardsville. Dr. Bezhanova has published articles in *Anales galdosianos, Revista Canadiense de Estudios Hispánicos, Romance Quarterly, Hispanófila, Revista de literatura, Letras hispanas, Bulletin of Spanish Studies,* and others. Her 2014 book, *Growing Up in an Inhospitable World: Female* Bildungsroman *in Spain,* was awarded the Victoria Urbano Prize for the Best Critical Monograph by the Asociación Internacional de Literatura y Cultura Femenina Hispánica.

www.ingramcontent.com/pod-product-compliance
Ingram Content Group UK Ltd.
Pitfield, Milton Keynes, MK11 3LW, UK
UKHW041629031026
15587UKWH00001B/176